A BOOK OF HOMAGE TO SHAKESPEARE

TO COMMEMORATE THE THREE HUNDREDTH
ANNIVERSARY OF SHAKESPEARE'S DEATH MCMXVI

*Reissued with a new introduction by Gordon McMullan
to commemorate the Four Hundredth Anniversary
of Shakespeare's death*

OXFORD

UNIVERSITY PRESS

Great Clarendon Street, Oxford, OX2 6DP,
United Kingdom

Oxford University Press is a department of the University of Oxford.
It furthers the University's objective of excellence in research, scholarship,
and education by publishing worldwide. Oxford is a registered trade mark of
Oxford University Press in the UK and in certain other countries

Published in the United States of America by Oxford University Press
198 Madison Avenue, New York, NY 10016, United States of America

British Library Cataloguing in Publication Data

Data available

ISBN 978–0–19–876969–9

Printed and bound by
CPI Group (UK) Ltd, Croydon CR0 4YY

A Book of Homage to Shakespeare, 1916

AN INTRODUCTION

I

ON 23 April 1916, Oxford University Press published a magnificent volume entitled *A Book of Homage to Shakespeare*, edited by Professor Israel Gollancz. Created to mark the Tercentenary of Shakespeare's death in the very midst of the First World War, it was a substantial folio-sized volume of 557 pages bound in white leather with Shakespeare's coat of arms embossed in gold, with nine leaves of plates, each protected by tissue: with textured pages laid out with a generous and elegant text design, it is a strikingly beautiful material object in its own right, quite apart from its contents, which include contributions by writers from Rudyard Kipling to Rabindranath Tagore, from John Galsworthy to Maurice Maeterlinck. One thousand two hundred and fifty copies were printed, a fifth designed as presentation copies, with the rest put on general sale. Within its pages, sandwiched between an opening poem by Thomas Hardy about Stratford-upon-Avon and the London-based editor's closing paean to the global community—'Shakespeare's own kindred, whatsoe'er their speech'—are 105 essays, dialogues, and fragments, and sixty-one poems, including twenty-six translations, from locations as far apart as India, Ireland, America, Armenia, Burma, South Africa, Russia, and Japan. *A Book of Homage to Shakespeare* is thus a celebration both local and global, and it marks a pivotal moment in literary history—a moment at which Shakespeare was the poet both of Empire and of a world emerging into a new, very different global order.

Looking back at the *Book of Homage* a hundred years later is a curious experience: some contributions seem so current, some so very much of their moment, yet all are expressive of a rapidly changing world, socially, politically, and culturally. A global war, a global Shakespeare: it is this unforeseen, unwelcome yet productive convergence that makes the *Book* so special and so fully deserving of the kind of readerly reassessment now made possible by Oxford University Press's timely reissue for the 2016 Shakespeare Quatercentenary. Not only is it extremely handsome as a material object, a testament to the printer's craft in the early twentieth century, it is also a document of its time *par excellence*. It expresses the time and place—the many places—of the First World War both in what it includes and in what it excludes; it expresses too the time and place of Shakespeare in international culture three hundred years after the playwright's death; and it offers a vision of the Shakespearean future that is strikingly and intriguingly complex. It is what Coppélia Kahn has called a 'cultural performance'— that is, it 'enact[s] a kind of communal identity signified through myths of origin'—a valuable way of looking at the *Book of Homage* for several reasons, not least because it requires us to view it not as a blithe and arbitrary collection of 'stray thoughts' about Shakespeare but as a consciously shaped *performance* of a particular moment in national and global culture.[1]

For the *Book of Homage* is decidedly not what it has been assumed to be by commentators—a kind of caricature of itself, pompous, imperialistic, blind to a changing world. On the contrary, through the resilience, patience, and flexibility of its editor, Professor Israel Gollancz of King's College London, it gives us access to a vision of the world in 1916 that can only be seen from the unique place that Shakespeare held—and in certain ways continues to hold—in global culture. It is a fascinating blend of Newboltian earnestness and frank cosmopolitanism—in the cricketing terms so beloved of Newbolt's generation, it plays with a straight bat, yet it also spins the ball unexpectedly at times—and it offers both an unrestrained celebration of Shakespeare the National Poet and a demonstration of the extraordinary geographical reach of what we might call the 'Shakespeare effect'. Reading it a hundred years on, we can see very clearly the extent to which academic and public engagement with Shakespeare has changed since 1916 yet also the extent to which the same basic questions and problems nag at us, still by no means resolved. In this introduction to the reissue, I will

---

[1] Coppélia Kahn, 'Reading Shakespeare Imperially: The 1916 Tercentenary', *Shakespeare Quarterly* 52 (2001), 456–78 (457). Kahn cites in particular the work of Joseph Roach on 'cultural performance': see Roach, *Cities of the Dead: Circum-Atlantic Performance* (New York: Columbia University Press, 1996), 3.

outline the book's contents and the history of its inception and creation, focusing on its editor and guiding spirit, Israel Gollancz, and on certain key contributions that best express its internal logic and help to reveal it as a far more complex phenomenon than might be expected, balancing the celebration of empire with elements both of resistance to Shakespeare as the uncontested figurehead for empire and of self-fashioning, implicit and explicit, on the part of its contributors.

II

Easter was late in 1916, falling on 23 April, St George's Day. This coincidence of faith and patriotism was inevitably both heightened and tempered by the ongoing struggles of the First World War. April 1916 came amidst the protracted fighting of the Battle of Verdun, a long and bloody conflict yet one which was only a foretaste of the horrors to come at the Somme the summer following. For the many Australian and New Zealand troops in London, meanwhile, April 1916 saw the first anniversary of the *débacle* at Gallipoli, the first ANZAC Day, a moment that saw the emergence of a key myth of origin in the transformation of both former colonies into nations in their own right and which was marked by ANZAC troops marching through central London and attending a matinée variety performance. Easter 1916 also saw a very different, very direct response to colonial experience: the Easter Rising in Dublin, the date chosen for its resonances of rebirth and renewal and remembered with the most complex of emotions by W. B. Yeats in his poem 'Easter 1916': 'All changed, changed utterly: | A terrible beauty is born.' That Easter was in so many ways, then, a time of conflict, of tension, of change.

Easter 1916 happened also to mark the Tercentenary of the death of William Shakespeare. It had been agreed long before war broke out, however, that national commemorations of England's National Poet would be postponed until the May Day weekend (with the solemn explanation that the change of calendar from Julian to Gregorian in the late sixteenth century meant that 1 May 1916 was in fact four hundred years to the day from 23 April 1616) in order to avoid any unintended conflation of Shakespeare with Christ—a decision that underlines, even as it seeks to elide, the quasi-religious reverence in which Shakespeare and his writings were held at this time. This tendency is most apparent in the brief publication *Shakespeare Tercentenary Observance in the Schools and other Institutions* issued by the Tercentenary Committee for 'Shakespeare Day', 3 May 1916, which set out, in effect, a liturgy for the occasion: a Bible reading ('Let us now praise famous men' from Ecclesiasticus), three Shakespeare songs (eight are provided in an appendix), a 'Discourse on Shakespeare', some 'Scenes or passages from Shakespeare' and, finally, the National Anthem.[2] It is perhaps not surprising, in context, that the authorities were obliged to explain a week or two beforehand that, no, Westminster Abbey would not be holding a service in memory of Shakespeare on Easter Day itself.

On 2 May, *The Times* reported the Shakespeare Tercentenary celebrations that had taken place the day before at London's Mansion House, noting the reading-out of messages from the King and Queen and from US President Woodrow Wilson and the presence of a wide range of dignitaries from the Archbishop of Canterbury to the US and Spanish ambassadors (the neutrality of the United States and of Spain was, as Richard Foulkes has noted, 'an obvious subtext to the occasion'), the High Commissioners of Australia and South Africa, representatives of the governments of China, Belgium, Switzerland, and Greece, and a roll call of academics (including Israel Gollancz, editor of the *Book of Homage*), theatre practitioners, writers, and other intellectual, cultural, and creative celebrities.[3] The Lord Mayor opened proceedings, noting that whatever the attitude of his early modern predecessors to the business of acting, he could now, 'in the name of the City of London, heartily and reverently join in that universal tribute of homage which this great anniversary was eliciting throughout the civilized world'. The event continued with tributes from the various dignitaries, including the US ambassador (who reported that 'the people of that great English-speaking world beyond the sea were expressing their gratitude for their great inheritance—that

---

[2] *Shakespeare Tercentenary Observance in the Schools and other Institutions,* including 'Notes on Shakespeare the Patriot' by Professor I. Gollancz (London: Geo. W. Jones, 1916).

[3] See Richard Foulkes, 'The Theatre of War: The 1916 Tercentenary', chapter 8 of *Performing Shakespeare in the Age of Empire* (Cambridge: Cambridge University Press, 2002), 180–204 (199).

they were born into the language of Shakespeare and into the development of that civilization and into that racial trick of thought of which he gave the very highest expression'), the Australian High Commissioner ('if we could clear away the mist that surrounded our decision and indecision at this time and speak the language and the thoughts of Shakespeare's days we should make all well-meaning men and women happy and make tyrants afraid'), and the South African High Commissioner ('it was a splendid fact that in the throes of a convulsion which was causing the whole world to reel and totter the nation of Shakespeare stood firm and smiling'). As the *Liverpool Courier* put it, '[t]he Mansion House th[at] afternoon presented a scene of tranquility and intellectual refreshment, the very antithesis of the war and the Dublin rebellion'.[4] The occasion thus detached Shakespeare from global events which might, in another light, have suggested that the historical stability celebrated by so many Tercentenary celebrants was distinctly and uncomfortably illusory.

Other newspaper accounts of the day looked more locally, hinting at the organizational history that lay behind the event. One columnist wrote wryly that

[f]rom one point of view the War seems to have done real good in regard to the Shakespeare Tercentenary, for the celebration of which Lord Plymouth, as chairman of the Executive Committee; the Lord Mayor of London, as treasurer; and Dr. Israel Gollancz, as hon. Secretary, have already issued a formidable but inexpensive and otherwise satisfactory programme. At least, there is now withdrawn all temptation to waste any money on statues and marble shrines and things of that sort. We do not even hear anything of the 'Shakespeare Garden' scheme, which was brought out officially at the Mansion House a year or two ago, when the National Theatre enthusiasts were growing restive. Somehow, in that Shakespeare Garden I could not help detecting the thin end of the statue! As it is, 'the Executive Committee have convinced themselves that they are rightly interpreting their duties in arranging for the observance in a simple and dignified manner, consonant with the mood of the nation.' And so say all of us![5]

This offers an ironic glance at the protracted nature of the struggle to find an appropriate form of Shakespearean commemoration for 1916. As Gollancz notes in his preface to the *Book of Homage*, plans to mark the

---

[4] *Liverpool Courier*, 2 May 1916.
[5] Unknown newspaper, 6 February 1916.

Tercentenary had been afoot for more than a decade. 'For years past', he wrote,

—as far back as 1904—many of us had been looking forward to the Shakespeare Tercentenary as the occasion for some fitting memorial to symbolize the intellectual fraternity of mankind in the universal homage accorded to the genius of the greatest Englishman' (vii).

Those plans had, however, been curtailed by the war—'the dream of the world's brotherhood to be demonstrated by its common and united commemoration of Shakespeare, with many another fond illusion, was rudely shattered' (vii)—and they had, in any case, already been subject to a good deal of struggle and under-achievement even before the war began.

Initially, the plan had been for the creation of a memorial to Shakespeare to be located in London, and in 1908 a competition was announced for the creation of a statue that would be 'an all-world tribute', the proposals including a design, now in the National Theatre archive, for a kind of cross between the Albert Memorial and the Scott Monument with Shakespeare at its heart. Increasing dissent from theatrical circles began to be heard, however, arguing fiercely that the appropriate way to commemorate the great playwright would be to build not a statue but a theatre. Just a few months after the announcement of the competition for a statue, the Shakespeare Memorial National Theatre (SMNT) committee was formed from a merger of two separate groups: disgruntled members of the Shakespeare Memorial Committee and supporters of the movement for a National Theatre, which had begun in 1848 with support from Charles Dickens, Matthew Arnold, and others, and had received a substantial boost five years earlier when Harley Granville-Barker and William Archer privately circulated detailed plans for a theatre appropriate to 'national' status. Within a year, *The Sphere,* at the SMNT's behest, published a broadsheet page with images of all the national theatres of Europe, decrying the absence of such a building in London; in that same year, 1909, the movement for a Tercentenary celebration merged with the SMNT, and a promotional leaflet was published arguing for building the proposed theatre by 1916. The ball seemed to be rolling.

Two key fundraising events took place in 1910 and 1912: both were successful occasions but neither in the end was actually productive of funds for the project. The first of these was the Shakespeare Memorial Ball of 1911, held on 20 June 'in support of the Shakespeare Memorial Fund'. This was a shamelessly privileged establishment event, the Ball Committee made up solely of women aristocrats and led by Mrs George Cornwallis-West (the American-born former Lady Randolph Churchill, mother of Winston), and the event, which took place at the Royal Albert Hall, consisting of an extravagant themed dinner and a series of vignettes of royal and aristocratic parties, grouped and costumed as the cast of particular Shakespeare plays, dancing lengthy sets of waltzes and quadrilles. A lavish publication, the *Souvenir of the Shakespeare Memorial National Theatre Ball,* emerged in 1912, packed with images of the social eite in Shakespearean costume and listing scores of royal attendees, beginning with 'Their Imperial and Royal Highnesses the German Crown Prince and Crown Princess'—the last time the British royal family would parade their German origins in this way. Far from raising money for the SMNT, however, the Ball *Souvenir,* like the Ball itself, was a financial disaster, the cost significantly outweighing the funds received.

The second event, in 1912, was the 'Shakespeare's England' exhibition at Earl's Court. This was a large-scale, privately sponsored event lasting from May to October; it was designed by Edwin Lutyens, architect of empire, and its leading light was again Mrs George Cornwallis-West (which presumably explains the timing of the publication of the Ball *Souvenir*). Lutyens designed an entire 'Tudor village' based on actual locations around Britain, an 'historic grouping of old typical buildings'.[6] The exhibition was designed as an immersive experience to give Londoners the chance to 'walk straight into the sixteenth century and visualise the environment and atmosphere' and to give them 'an accurate representation of the life of England three hundred years ago'.[7] Buildings replicated included Shakespeare's birthplace and an Oxford college, the two most visually striking reconstructions being Francis Drake's ship the *Revenge,* floating in an artificial harbour, and a

---

[6] *Building News,* 26 April 1912, 596; quoted in Marion F. O'Connor, 'Theatre of the Empire: "Shakespeare's England" at Earl's Court, 1912', in Jean E. Howard and Marion F. O'Connor (eds.), *Shakespeare Reproduced: The Text in History and Ideology* (New York: Methuen, 1987), 68–98 (79).

[7] *The Graphic,* 11 May 1912, 674–5; exhibition official publicity, quoted in *The Sketch,* 15 May 1912, 188; see O'Connor, 'Theatre of the Empire', 79.

working replica of the Globe theatre, reportedly the most popular attraction for its cycle of half-hour excerpts from plays by Shakespeare and his contemporaries. It was derived from a design made by William Poel, a pioneer in the reconstruction of early theatres, back in 1897, though Poel was himself highly critical of the Earl's Court Globe, calling it a 'travesty'. That the 'historic buildings' other than the replica Globe contained cafés and shops selling distinctly modern merchandise from boot polish to chocolate underlines the level of divergence of the event from the aims of the SMNT. More to the point, like the Ball, 'Shakespeare's England' lost money. In both cases the hopes and interests of Gollancz and the SMNT were largely brushed aside and the events used as vehicles for quite different purposes, above all by Cornwallis-West, who used them to cement her connections with royalty and to entertain her society friends. Marion O'Connor cites a letter from Lutyens to his wife noting that Cornwallis-West was not operating in good faith and regretting his involvement: 'I feel rotten sorry that I had anything to do with it, as under the banner of good intentions and names of bona fide Endeavours she means to whip up the public & her society smarts—to her own benefit!'[8] Thus even before the onset of war, the protracted difficulties of the business of fundraising had doomed the project to build a theatre in time for the Tercentenary, a fact that Gollancz acknowledged at the opening of his preface to the *Book of Homage*:

We had hoped that, on a site that has already been acquired, a stately building, to be associated with that august name, equipped and adequately endowed for the furtherance of Shakespearian drama and dramatic art generally, would have made the year 1916 memorable in the annals of the English stage.

The failure of this hope must have been deeply frustrating for Gollancz and the other genuine believers on the SMNT committee.

Israel Gollancz was a remarkable figure: genial, persistent, omnipresent, never—it seems—daunted, even when plans went repeatedly awry. His energy and commitment to the Tercentenary are simply unmatched. Born in 1863 (though his memorial plaque at King's College London, in

---

[8] Edwin Lutyens, letter to Emily Lutyens, London, 9 August 1911; see O'Connor, 'Theatre of the Empire', 78.

a telltale commemorative conflation, states his birth year as 1864, the tercentenary of the birth of Shakespeare), Gollancz was the son of a rabbi who had emigrated to London from Poland, the younger brother of Sir Hermann Gollancz, who became Chief Rabbi, and uncle of the publisher Victor Gollancz. He became the first Jewish professor of English at the University of London—which changed its regulations in order to appoint him—and he was a respected academic, primarily a medievalist—editor of *Pearl* and *Gawain* and numerous other Old and Middle English texts—but also a Shakespearean, editor of the bestselling Temple Shakespeare edition. He was also a remarkably energetic cultural entrepreneur, a founder member of the British Academy (where an annual lecture in his memory was established at his death), Director of the Early English Text Society, creator of the Cervantes and Camões chairs of Spanish and Portuguese literature at King's (the first of which was announced by the Spanish ambassador at the 1916 Mansion House celebration), and the one consistent figure in the various Shakespeare memorial committees in the lead-up to 1916. He died in 1930, and the tributes paid to him make clear the genuine affection felt by his former students, friends, and acquaintances.

Not everyone was quite so happy about his role in the Tercentenary process, however. Geoffrey Whitworth, historian of the National Theatre, describes Gollancz's involvement as follows:

[B]ehind [the] kaleidoscopic maze of committees, flitting to and fro, one glimpses the mercurial figure of Israel Gollancz, [. . .] benign, discreet, master of innocent intrigue, [. . .] with every thread in his hands, and alone capable of unravelling the tangled skein when the right moment came.[9]

Gollancz was unquestionably active and energetic in the pursuit of the goals of the Tercentenary, but this description of him as a kind of consummate plotter seems a little insensitive given the quiet resistance with which Gollancz had to deal in some quarters, which in at least one instance manifested itself as outright anti-Semitism. The Folger Shakespeare Library holds a fragment entitled 'Shakespeare's Tercentenary: A Masque' by Lord Alfred Douglas, Oscar Wilde's former lover 'Bosie', in which Douglas, a

---

[9] Geoffrey Whitworth, *The Making of a National Theatre* (London: Faber, 1951), 44.

notorious Jew-hater, makes fun of the Tercentenary committee and in particular of Gollancz. The 'masque' opens sarcastically with the lines

> This is great Shakespeare's tercentenary,
> And consequently lo! The German Jew
> (As is most meet) supported by a few
> Distinguished gentlemen.

The 'German Jew' here appears to be Gollancz—Douglas in his bigotry failing to distinguish between Polish and German—but the attitude is obvious enough and is especially uncomfortable in the context of the language of race that pervades the *Book of Homage* (in, for instance, the US ambassador's phrase 'the racial trick of thought of which [Shakespeare] gave the very highest expression', and in 'Heart of the Race', the American critic Charles Mills Gayley's poem in the *Book*). What is this man with a distinctly un-English, un-Christian name doing leading the celebrations for England's National Poet? Happily, his admirers outweighed the backbiters, and certainly Gollancz, who was knighted in 1919 for his role in the Tercentenary process, seems to have remained undaunted: he would again play a major role in the 1923 tercentenary of the publication of Shakespeare's First Folio. But it is important to remember that his endless supply of energy and commitment to the cause was not appreciated—for reasons not at all edifying—by everyone.

By 1916, the SMNT committee had acquired a plot of land for the Memorial Theatre they hoped to build—in Bloomsbury, at the corner of Keppel and Gower Streets, opposite the site where the University of London's Senate House would soon be built—and the committee had to decide what could be done with it in wartime conditions. Attempts to raise money for the building of a theatre would be considered inappropriate—unpatriotic, even—and it seems to have been Gollancz who found the solution. He brokered an arrangement with the YMCA for the creation of temporary accommodation for Commonwealth troops—mainly New Zealanders, but also Australians—on the theatre site, to be known as the 'Shakespeare Hut'. The word 'hut', the standard term at the time for the YMCA's temporary buildings both at the front and back home, does not, however, begin to do the building justice. Temporary it may have been, but it included substantial accommodation (scores of thousands of beds were let to ANZAC troops between 1916 and the war's end), dining facilities, a shop, and even a concert hall in which Shakespearean performances took place—strictly for the ANZAC soldiers—featuring some of the finest actors of the day, including Ellen Terry and Johnston Forbes-Robertson, whose wife Gertrude Elliott combined women's suffrage activism with management of the Hut's theatrical programme.[10] It was hardly the theatre the SMNT committee had imagined, but it did at least mean that Shakespearean performances of a kind took place in a commemorative space on the chosen site.[11] More to the point, protracted though the process was, there was, eventually, despite all the setbacks, a long-lasting performance legacy from the Tercentenary activities, since the SMNT's plans did finally culminate in the establishment of the National Theatre—initially, from 1963, at the Old Vic, and then in 1976 at last moving into its own purpose-built space on the South Bank, its foundation stone beginning with the words 'In Memory of William Shakespeare'.

III

In May 1916, however, the National Theatre was at best a distant dream. The Mansion House event, for all its grandeur, was a drastically scaled-down celebration, as judged appropriate to wartime conditions. No statue, no new theatre, was announced. The Keppel Street site was yet to be occupied. A different kind of memorial, however, both less and more permanent, did emerge. At the beginning of its account of the Mansion House celebrations, *The Times* records a message from the King and Queen acknowledging receipt of their copy of *A Book of Homage to Shakespeare*: 'Their Majesties have graciously commanded that their thanks be sent

---

[10] See Ailsa Grant Ferguson, 'Lady Forbes-Robertson's War Work: Gertrude Elliott and the Shakespeare Hut Performances, 1916–1919', in Gordon McMullan, Lena Cowen Orlin, and Virginia Mason Vaughan (eds.), *Woman Making Shakespeare: Text, Reception, Performance* (London: Bloomsbury Arden Shakespeare, 2014), 233–42.

[11] See Ailsa Grant Ferguson, '"When Wasteful War Shall Statues Overturn": Forgetting the Shakespeare Hut', *Shakespeare* 10 (2014), 276–92.

to you for this illustrious record of reverence for him to whose memory the whole civilised world is now doing honour.' And alongside is a column describing the publication of this 'sumptuous volume' which, in the words of the columnist, 'may be said to record, in a peculiarly catholic way, what after 300 years the best literary representatives of British and allied culture are saying about Shakespeare'. Presumably the writer means by 'peculiarly' the *Oxford English Dictionary*'s primary definition—'special, remarkable, distinctive'—rather than its secondary meaning of 'unusual, strange, odd', but in truth each of these possibilities resonates when we reflect on the remarkably wide-ranging contents of the *Book of Homage*.

A global publication created at the height of the First World War, the *Book of Homage* underlines the hegemonic status of Shakespeare in the early twentieth century as an icon of Englishness and empire, yet it also serves as a precursor of the contemporary role of Shakespeare as a figure of global culture. At first sight, it looks as if the *Book of Homage* and Oxford University Press's other Shakespeare-related publication for 1916, a two-volume academic reference work called *Shakespeare's England* (no relation to the 1912 exhibition of the same name), serve the same function, both invoking a certain nostalgia for a purer English hour. A closer inspection of the *Book of Homage,* however, suggests that things are not quite so simple. For one thing, the volume has an astonishingly ambitious sweep, with 166 contributions in verse and prose in languages from Sanskrit to Setswana, from Urdu to Icelandic, celebrating an extraordinary range of versions of, and meanings for, 'Shakespeare'. The volume represents both the British Empire and the world beyond the empire, though with the inevitable omission in wartime of Germany, Austria-Hungary, and Turkey—an omission, at least in respect of Germany, that Gollancz deeply regretted—and many of the choices of contributor seem on closer inspection not to have been entirely straightforward, politically or culturally. Of the 166 contributions, there are only six by women, but these included figures a little outside the mainstream such as Charlotte Stopes, early feminist writer (and mother of the birth-control pioneer Marie Stopes), whose poem begins somewhat tongue-in-cheek with the couplet 'Dame Nature on a Holiday bethought her of a plan, | To mix new elements and clay, and make a proper man'.[12] The *Book of Homage* is, in other words, in a number of unexpected ways rather more than it seems: its forms of 'homage' are complex and contradictory, and it fully repays reflective re-reading.

Quite apart from its literary and cultural significance, the *Book of Homage* is, as I have noted, a beautiful book: elegantly printed and laid out, with the name of Humphrey Milford, publisher to Oxford University, on the title page. Milford had taken over Oxford University Press three years earlier and set out to turn it from a local to a global concern: its first *General Catalogue* appeared in 1916, and only a year later Milford took on the vast project of the *Dictionary of National Biography*. The *Book of Homage* was an ideal opportunity to market the Press across the world, and it is clear that he pulled out all the stops, both in the book's physical form and in its contents. The contributors range from novelists John Galsworthy (on Shakespeare the 'great tree', 'a refuge and home for the spirits of men') and Edmund Gosse ('a technical adroitness which had never been dreamed of before and was never rivalled after') to poets Wilfred Campbell ('Immortal searcher of the hearts of men, | Who knewest, as none else, this human life') and René de Clercq ('Let thy glory burst forth, like sunshine, through these clouds of world-woe, | So that e'en Goethe's folk may to thy pure might yield homage'), from the Nobel Laureate Rabindranath Tagore ('the palm groves by the Indian sea raise their tremulous branches to the sky murmuring your praise') to the Nobel-Prize-winning human biologist Sir Ronald Ross—whose sonnet has particular poignancy, given that his son had been killed at Le Cateau in 1914: 'in the darkness men die where they stood, | . . . cease in a flash where mad-eyed cherubim | Of Death destroy them in the night and mud: | . . . We dying . . . | Behold the silver star serene on high, | That is thy spirit there, O Master Mind sublime'.[13] Each contributor offers a perspective appropriate to their context—'Dante e Shakespeare'

---

[12] On Stopes, see Kathleen E. McLuskie, 'Remembering Charlotte Stopes', in McMullan, Orlin, and Vaughan, *Women Making Shakespeare*, 195–205.

[13] Gollancz's choice of Ross as a contributor was, it turns out, prescient, since Ross's Institute and Hospital for Tropical Diseases became part of the London School of Hygiene and Tropical Medicine, built after the war on the Keppel Street site acquired by the Shakespeare Memorial National Theatre committee for the Shakespeare theatre they planned and which was instead occupied during the war by the 'Shakespeare Hut'.

by Italian senator Isidoro del Lungo, 'Comment Faire Connaître Shakespeare aux Petits Français' by the French inspector-general of schools, 'An Eddic Homage to William Shakespeare' by Icelandic scholar Jón Stefánsson, 'Denmark and Shakespeare' by Danish actor Karl Mantzius, and so forth—and most either praise Shakespeare's genius or choose a particular element in Shakespeare's *oeuvre* on which to focus, from his inventiveness with language to his 'unworldliness', from his sense of humour to his alleged Catholicism. It is, to say the least, an eclectic mix.

It seems that the contributors were given instructions not to be overly formal. Viscount Bryce, president of the British Academy, notes that Gollancz had explained to him that what was sought was 'stray thoughts jotted down without the formality of an essay, even if they do no more than suggest some points or lines of thought on which readers may agree with or differ from the writer' (22). Generally speaking, those who responded to this request did best; the more earnestly serious essays—M. H. Spielmann's account, early in the volume, of the various Shakespeare portraits, say, or Sidney Colvin's essay on the sack of Troy—are not always the most effective, reading suspiciously like materials that were to hand when the invitation came, not items penned especially for the volume. Some of the most technically accomplished essays come from the professional Shakespeareans of the day, including essays on Shakespeare's language by Sidney Lee and others and on specific aspects of the plays and poems by A. C. Bradley, A. W. Pollard, E. K. Chambers, and others. Amongst these, the stand-out contribution is perhaps W. W. Greg's 'A Critical Mousetrap', only two pages in length but brimful of insight into the baffling moment in *Hamlet* when Claudius 'rushes terror-stricken from the hall' during the play-within-a-play, despite the fact that he has seen without response the same action in the dumb show preceding, a problem that continues to provoke ingenious, if not always convincing, solutions by theatre directors.

This academic recognition of Shakespeare 'the man of the theatre, the actor, the manager' rather than the poet *per se* is reinforced by two of the leading theatre professionals of the day, Frank Benson and Henry Irving. For Benson, who would star in a gala Tercentenary performance of *Julius Caesar* at Drury Lane Theatre the day after the Mansion House celebration, '[i]f we can interpret the poet's meaning, we shall have told our audiences something of the touch of Nature that makes the whole world kin' (39). For Irving, similarly, Shakespeare 'was a master-craftsman in his day, [...] a genius not of the closet but of the stage; ... to understand truly Shakespeare and his work it is necessary to understand something of, and to have some sympathy with, the theatre' (41–2). It is perhaps surprising that other key theatre professionals of the period are absent from the volume, but by this stage of the war two of the most prominent were in the United States: Sir Herbert Beerbohm Tree, actor-manager at His Majesty's Theatre, had taken his *Henry VIII* to New York and became involved in that city's own Tercentenary celebrations, and Sir Johnston Forbes-Robertson, who would in due course perform at the Shakespeare Hut, was in the States when war broke out and returned only just in time for 'Shakespeare Day'.[14]

Some of the essays are more aware than others of the specifics of the moment. A. W. Ward looks at the historical circumstances of the year of Shakespeare's death and the subsequent centenaries of 1716 and 1816, situating the history of Shakespearean reception within a broad European framework; while W. J. Courthope, in his poem, cites wartime locales: 'Mighty is the power | Of Freedom, Britain's heirloom, sacred dower, | By Flanders' blood secured, and Suvla's grave!' Others, by contrast, suggest a sense of temporal or cultural dislocation, of frank puzzlement, especially of the impossibility of *knowing* Shakespeare in the way that modernity wishes to know its chosen figures from the past. Austin Dobson, in his poem 'The Riddle', suggests that physical memorials may not be the point: 'Men may explore thy Secret still, yet thou, | Serene, unsearchable, above them all, | Look'st down, as from some lofty mountain-brow, | And art thyself thine own Memorial' (13). Thomas Hardy's opening poem—in keeping both with his late poetry in general and with his responses to the war in particular— is curiously plangent, beginning with the line 'Bright baffling soul, least

[14] On Tercentenary celebrations in the USA, see Coppélia Kahn, 'Caliban at the Stadium: Shakespeare and the Making of Americans', *Massachusetts Review* 41 (2000), 256–84; Monika Smialkowska, 'Shakespeare in History, History through Shakespeare: *Caliban by The Yellow Sands*', *Multicultural Shakespeare: Translation, Appropriation and Performance*, 4 (2007), 17–27; Smialkowska, '"A Democratic Art at a Democratic Price": The American Celebrations of the Shakespeare Tercentenary, 1916', *Transatlantica* 1 (2010), 1–24; and Smialkowska, 'Shakespeare and "Native Americans": Forging Identities through the 1916 Shakespeare Tercentenary', *Critical Survey* 22 (2010), 76–90.

capturable of themes' and expressing frustration that Shakespeare should have left so little evidence of his personal life beyond his creative writing—'Thou, who displayed'st a life of commonplace, | Leaving no intimate word or personal trace | Of high design outside the artistry | Of thy penned dreams' (1)—and then wry humour about the Stratford townspeople who did not recognize the prophet in their midst: '"Ah, one of the tradesmen's sons, I now recall . . . | Witty, I've heard . . . | We did not know him . . . Well, good day. Death comes to all."'

Others work hard to resist this sense of dislocation by placing Shakespeare within his personal, geographical, and cultural context. There is, unsurprisingly, a good deal of metropolitanism. H. B. Wheatley addresses Shakespeare's love affair with London—

As a true son he loved his native town of Stratford, but his character was formed in London by the great men with whom he associated. London was his University, and teachers at that University were the wonderful men that abounded in 'the spacious days' of Eliza's reign. . . . [H]e did not forget what he owed to London, and London will never forget what she owes to him (249)

—and Gordon Bottomley defends the proposed London location for the memorial theatre: 'In devising a National Memorial to keep Shakespeare's achievement more vividly and constantly in the minds of his countrymen', he claims, 'it is inevitable that a metropolitan theatre . . . should seem most worth working for' (45), while Mabel E. Wotton, one of the New Woman writers who first emerged in the 1880s and 1890s, tracks down the location of the Mermaid Inn that Shakespeare is said to have frequented. Other contributors foreground localities both beyond the capital—Arthur Gray on Cambridge, Frederick Boas on Oxford, M. Dormer Harris on Warwickshire—and beyond England: H. J. C. Grierson writes on Shakespeare and Scotland, D. H. Madden and Douglas Hyde on Shakespeare and Ireland, John Edward Lloyd on 'Shakespeare's Welshmen', and there are poems in Welsh by Morris Jones and J. O. Williams, which are partially translated by way of marginal glosses.[15]

[15] On the Scottish response to the 1916 Tercentenary, see Emily Anderson, 'The Shakespeare Death Tercentenary Celebrations in England and Scotland: How British was Shakespeare in 1916?' *Forum* 19 (2014), 1–14; on Douglas Hyde, see below xxvi–xxviii.

All told, there are sixty-one poems and twenty-six translations, the latter representing contemporary assumptions about the languages the volume's recipients and purchasers could be presumed to be able to read. Latin is untranslated, as are fifteen contributions in French (in addition to translations from Russian into not English but French), five in Italian, four in Spanish, and one in Portuguese. Those for which translations are provided, on the other hand, include Hebrew, Sanskrit, Greek, Dutch, Icelandic, Danish, Swedish, Russian, Serbian, Finnish, Japanese, Chinese, Persian, and Armenian. Ancient languages are included with modern: J. E. Sandys provides an epigram and A. W. Mair a dialogue in ancient Greek, Herbert Warren a poetic commemoration in Latin, and Gollancz's brother Sir Hermann a poem in Hebrew blending Shakespearean quotations with Biblical passages. Gollancz set out to treat languages other than English with equal deference, providing parallel translation for Irish Gaelic as for Finnish, for Welsh as for Burmese, underlining the *Book*'s global ethos. And because both of this global perspective and of the war, the publication history of *A Book of Homage* does not cease with the appearance of the book itself. Due to the challenges of international mail in wartime, not all contributions turned up in time for publication. There was, for instance, a further item in Icelandic by Matthias Jochumsson, which Gollancz published later in the year in pamphlet form, printed by Oxford University Press to the same standard and on the same quality paper as the *Book of Homage*, entitled *On the Tercentenary Commemoration of Shakespeare Ultima Thule Sendeth Greeting*.[16] For Gollancz, then, the celebrations of Easter 1916 continued for a considerable time—to the wry amusement of his friends, one of whom, on receipt of the additional poem, wrote in a private letter that 'I expect you are pretty sick of Tercentenaries by this time—and perhaps you may even hail the day when Shakespeare changed his name to Bacon.'[17]

---

[16] Matthias Jochumsson, *1616–1916 On the Tercentenary Commemoration of Shakespeare Ultima Thule Sendeth Greeting,* with translation into English by Israel Gollancz (London: Oxford University Press, 1916).

[17] Letter from Sir Edward Maunde Thompson to Israel Gollancz, Mayfield, Sussex, 10 Jan. 1917, Princeton Gollancz Archive.

III

In his inaugural professorial lecture at the University of Liverpool, Jonathan Bate placed Israel Gollancz alongside Sir Walter Raleigh—not the Elizabethan courtier, explorer, and spy, but the early twentieth-century academic of the same name who became the first Professor of English Literature at Oxford University—as an unashamed and slightly risible patriot, one whom Bate, writing in 1993, connected with the then Secretary of State for Education Kenneth Baker, who in addition to his political duties edited the *Faber Book of English History in Verse,* as a right-wing propagandist with 'an exalted sense of duty'.[18] For Bate, Gollancz's outlook is summarized neatly in the 'Notes on Shakespeare the Patriot' he included in the *Tercentenary Observance* pamphlet:

While all the world acclaims him, those who are privileged to be his fellow-country-men owe to themselves the high duty of gratefully recalling, on this occasion of the Tercentenary of his death, some of the lessons he has left us, and, especially at the present time, how it behoves us as patriots to strive to play our part in war as in peace, and how best to maintain our faith in the ultimate triumph of a noble humanity. (*Tercentenary Observance,* 11)

Bate's argument in his lecture requires a Gollancz who is straightforwardly and uncomplicatedly patriotic, and critics have generally treated him in much the same way, as an earnest English propagandist—and certainly several contributors to the *Book of Homage* (not surprisingly, given the war-time circumstances) either directly address the war or emphasise patriotism above all else in a way that was echoed by the journalists reviewing the Tercentenary events. The *Daily Chronicle* for 2 May, for instance, argued that

[w]e, who are Shakespeare's countrymen, shall do well to make the Tercentenary an occasion for once more tempering and renewing our spirit at the great fountain-head of thought, feeling and imagination, which has done more than any book except the English Bible to form the character of the English nation.

The *Book of Homage* includes several contributors who write in similar vein. G. C. Moore Smith's poem '1916', for instance, sees Shakespeare's text as

---

[18] Jonathan Bate, 'Shakespeare Nationalised, Shakespeare Privatised', *English* 42 (1993), 1–18 (5).

a beacon of patriotism in hard times: 'When to dark doubts our England would resign, | Thy patriot-voice recalls her from her fears; | Shakespeare of England . . .' (237); Gordon Bottomley argues that '[i]n time of war it is well to do homage to the first Englishman who has subjugated the enemy. The characteristic thoroughness of the Teutonic appreciation of Shakespeare is the best proof of the completeness of his triumph' (43); and Lionel Cust concludes a brief discussion of Tudor portraiture with a patriotic peroration:

No man was more thoroughly English than Shakespeare, English in the place and circumstances of his birth, English in the smattering of education which he got in the local grammar school, . . . English the spirit of adventure which took him to live by his wits in London; . . . English also is Shakespeare's own reticence about the circumstances of his own life. (101)

Patriotism, contempt for the Germans and repeated assertions of Shakespeare's essential Englishness—Englishness, not Britishness—seem to have been the order of the day.[19]

Yet the story is not quite so clear-cut. A glance at another publication from the same year, Francis Colmer's anthology *Shakespeare in Time of War*, serves to underline this.[20] Colmer begins by noting that '[i]t is a dark hour that has fallen to us in which to celebrate the tercentenary of the death of William Shakespeare', and he moves quickly to the subject of Germany:

[O]f all nations the Germans seem to have aroused his dislike most. He has not a good word to say for them, except in irony. To him they were for the most part cozeners, thieves, and drunkards. Nothing good came out of Germany. (Colmer, xxvi)

He proceeds to organize a series of extracts from Shakespeare under topical headings. He cites from *The Merchant of Venice*: 'How like you the young German. . . . | When he is best, he is a little worse than a man, | And when he is worst, he is little better than a beast'. Under the heading '*Landstürm* and *Landwehr*' he quotes Falstaff—'I did never see such pitiful rascals. Tut, tut, good enough to toss: food for powder, food for

---

[19] See e.g. Balz Engler, 'Shakespeare in the Trenches', *Shakespeare Survey* 44 (1992), 105–111.
[20] Francis Colmer, *Shakespeare in Time of War: Excerpts from the Plays Arranged with Topical Allusion* (London: Smith, Elder, 1916).

powder'—while under 'German Airmen' he turns to *Macbeth*—'Infected be the air whereon they ride | And damn'd all those that trust them'—and under 'The Kaiser Wilhelm II' he cites *The Tempest*: 'A devil, a born devil, on whose nature | Nurture can never stick'. The entire book continues in this vein.

The *Book of Homage* is very different, echoing its editor's fundamentally cosmopolitan outlook. The most obvious way in which Gollancz parts from Colmer is in his attitude to Germany, which is apparent in one of his more unexpected inclusions in the *Book of Homage*, an essay by C. H. Herford on 'The German Contribution of Shakespeare Criticism'—a distinctly brave inclusion in the context of the war and alongside contributions from the bereaved such as Ronald Ross. Herford notes that '[t]he War has made impracticable the co-operation of any German Shakespeare scholar in this collective tribute to his memory', yet he insists that 'no estrangement, however bitter and profound—still less the occasional extravagance of German claims—can affect the history of the services rendered by Germany to the study and interpretation of Shakespeare' (231). And he concludes that

Germany's contribution to Shakespeare study may [. . .] be summed up as of two kinds: first, rigorous and exhaustive sifting of the literary material; second, a wealth of ideas,—hypotheses, generalizations, *aperçus*—often fanciful, sometimes in the highest degree extravagant, even laughable, but put forward with an intellectual seriousness, and applied with a passion for truth, which have made them often more fruitful than the soberer speculations of more temperate minds. (235)

This unexpectedly open attitude to Germany is one that Gollancz shared. His social connections beyond the UK were principally German: his wife, Alide Goldschmidt, was German-Jewish, as was his great friend and patron Frida Mond, and he sustained a strong connection with the *Deutsche Shakespeare-Gesellschaft*, the first national Shakespeare society in the world, speaking at the society's annual conference in Weimar both prior to the war and then again, with remarkable speed, in 1919, receiving effusive thanks from its president Alois Brandl who, giving the British Academy's Annual Shakespeare Lecture back in 1913, had spoken about Germany's love of

Shakespeare and, poignantly in retrospect, bade his audience '*Au revoir* till Shakespeare Day, in 1916'.[21]

It is not, however, only to Germany that Gollancz lifted his eyes; he had a vision for Shakespeare that was genuinely global in scope. As far back as 1906, announcing the competition for the design of the Shakespeare Memorial, he had argued for a 'movement' that 'will be truly international', adding that by 1916 'there is good reason to believe that the various municipalities will readily join in what should ultimately prove to be world-wide commemoration'—'an endeavour to link the world by the one common enthusiasm, ever-increasing, for the great World-Poet of modern times'.[22] Summing up, he claimed that 'it may reasonably be expected that organisations will be formed throughout the world, "from China to Peru", to help the carrying out of the idea of a World Monument to Shakespeare', and he expressed the fervent hope that this 'should be an accomplished fact by the year 1916, the Tercentenary of the Poet's death, when there will assuredly be a universal Festival, commemorating the world's debt to the greatest of Englishmen' (3). A little later, in his 'Epilogue' to the Shakespeare Memorial Ball *Souvenir* of 1912, he stressed the same theme: 'Transcending all divisions of race, nationality, and speech', he argued, 'Shakespeare [. . .] links together all peoples of the world as the world-poet'. And these aims inform his choice, as editor, of contributions to the *Book of Homage*. It is a document of empire, certainly, but it also imagines a global culture going far beyond the confines of the British Empire, effectively heralding the era of 'global Shakespeare'.

The *Book* thus has a complex relationship to its cultural moment and to global politics, and three contributions in particular stand out in this regard, none of which is what it might initially seem. The first of these is the lengthy poem in Irish Gaelic—the first of the non-English languages

---

[21] Alois Brandl, *Shakespeare and Germany*, Third Annual British Academy Shakespeare Lecture (London: British Academy, 1913), 14.

[22] Statement by 'Professor I. Gollancz, Hon. Sec. of the Memorial Committee, Mansion House, May 9th. 1906', 2, Princeton Gollancz Archive. The emphatic 'truly' and 'good reason to' are added to the typescript in Gollancz's hand.

in the *Book of Homage* to be accompanied by a parallel translation—by Douglas Hyde, who would become the first President of the Irish Republic, entitled 'An Rud Thárla do Ghaedheal ag Stratford ar an Abhainn' ('How it Fared with a Gael at Stratford-on-Avon'). It is in a number of ways extraordinary, this contribution, and a number of critics have offered accounts of the particular tensions in the build-up to its inclusion.[23] Gollancz's sense of humour is apparent in his placing of Hyde's contribution directly after the essay by D. H. Madden, also an Irishman but with a very different political outlook, as his final sentence makes clear:

> To-day an earnest and active Dublin branch of the Empire Shakespeare Society celebrates the Tercentenary of the Master's death; with maimed rites, by reason of the war, but with love of the man, and gratitude for the priceless gift that the civilized world has received at his hands. (274)

Neither Gollancz nor Madden could have known, obviously enough, that publication of these words would coincide with the Easter Rising, but Madden's enthusiasm for a society with the words 'Empire' and 'Shakespeare' together in its title contrasts sharply with the known opinions of the other Irish contributor.

Douglas Hyde appears, as Andrew Murphy notes, 'rather an odd person for Gollancz to have approached in connection with the book' (52): he was founder and president of the Gaelic League, created for the promotion of the Irish language and Irish culture, a process that made clear, in the words of a speech Hyde had given in 1892, 'The Necessity of De-Anglicising Ireland'. Gollancz nonetheless asked him for a contribution, and he happily obliged with a poem that, again in Murphy's words, 'must surely have [...] surprised' (54) Gollancz, since its premise is the journey of an Irishman who acknowledges early on that 'England was not liked of me' (*Homage* 276) and observes in a head note that he had 'sorely suffered, he and his

---

[23] Werner Habicht, 'Shakespeare Celebrations in Time of War', *Shakespeare Quarterly* 52:4 (2001): 441–55; Andrew Murphy, 'Bhíos ag Stratfordar an abhainn: Shakespeare, Douglas Hyde, 1916', in Janet Clare and Stephen O'Neill (eds.), *Shakespeare and the Irish Writer* (Dublin: University College Dublin Press, 2010), 51–63. On Shakespeare and the Easter Rising, see also Murphy's chapter, 'Shakespeare's Rising: Ireland and the Tercentenary', in Coppélia Kahn and Clara Calvo (eds.), *Celebrating Shakespeare: Commemoration and Cultural Memory* (Cambridge: Cambridge University Press, 2015), 161–181.

folk; hatred was in his heart' (*Homage* 275) but whose distaste for England is calmed by a visit to Stratford. To Gollancz's request for a translation—in keeping with other contributions in languages Gollancz could not expect his readers to be able to read—he replied a little warily: 'I shd not like to give a translation unless all the other tributes in non-English tongues are translated also. It would look very disparaging to Irish!' He sent a translation nonetheless, and the poem is typeset in the elegant manner of many of the translations in the *Book of Homage*, with the English in a narrow column in the right margin.

It is only when you look closely at the parallel stanzas, Gaelic and English, that certain visual discrepancies arise. Most of the four-line stanzas are matched by either four or at least three full lines of English, but the antepenultimate stanza, number 25, is accompanied by a translation noticeably briefer than any other. The Gaelic reads as follows:

> A Albion do sgrios mo shinnsir,
> A Albion na bhfocal sleamhain,
> Má bhuaileann námhaid ar do dhorus
> Tóg é chum Stratford ar an abhainn.

The English alongside it, however, is very clearly reduced:

> O Albion,
> If an enemy knock at thy door,
> Take him to Stratford on the Avon!

This seems curious, but to Gaelic speakers it would have been highly amusing, since a full translation reads as follows:

> O Albion, deceitful sinful guileful
> Hypocritical destructive lying slippery,
> If an enemy knock at thy door,
> —Take him to Stratford on the Avon.

As you would expect, there was a certain amount of correspondence between Gollancz and Hyde about this. Gollancz inquired politely if it would be acceptable to Hyde if the translation could be toned down in a few places, and Hyde graciously replied: 'You have been so kind and have taken such an awful lot of trouble over the Homage book that of course no one could find it in their heart to hold out against anything you desire'—though he could not resist a little further mischief, adding: 'Would this do you. "O Albion who destroyedst my ancestors, O Albion of the smooth words"—and goodness knows that's letting "la perfide" down easily!' Gollancz's diplomatic skills were clearly at a premium here.

In the end, Gollancz's censored translation appeared in the printed volume, but there is no question that a great deal remained, even in the English version, that had the potential to upset readers of the *Book of Homage* at the moment of Easter 1916. More to the point, the Gaelic version remained as it was submitted, with no cuts or tonings-down, enabling any reader of the language to appreciate a poem of considerable subversion in the heart of the volume. There is a tendency for critics to view Gollancz as a weak-willed patriot, censoring in a mealy-mouthed sort of way, but there is another way to view his role and that is to ask why he requested a contribution from Hyde in the first place, knowing that the product was unlikely to sit comfortably alongside, say, William Pember Reeves's poem 'The Dream Imperial'. And there is a further contribution to the *Book of Homage*—perhaps the most fascinating of all—which raises questions about what exactly Gollancz was doing as editor. It is the one entitled 'A South African's Homage', and it has been addressed eloquently by a number of critics. Located as it is just after Gayley's poem 'Heart of the Race', it stands out for a number of reasons, not least because it is the only essay in the collection with an unnamed author. Anonymous he may be, but the entry in the table of contents has an element of *trompe l'oeil*, since there is a name listed—William Tsikinya-Chaka—which it takes a moment for the reader to realize is not the name of the contributor but a transliteration into Setswana of 'William Shakespeare', a visual interchangeability it is hard not to see as wilful.

The writer was Solomon Tsekisho Plaatje (1876–1932), newspaper editor, activist, and first general secretary of the South African Native National Congress (later the African National Congress), a major figure in the history of South African liberation. That he is not named is not so surprising, given his politics. We do not know how Gollancz met him, but we do know that he was in London from 1914 to 1917 as part of a delegation of SANNC activists seeking the repeal of the 1913 Land Act, a law that drastically curtailed the right of black Africans to own or occupy land. The appeal eventually failed; meanwhile, Plaatje lectured and worked as a language assistant at the University of London, and in 1916 he published three books: *Native Life in South Africa, Before and Since the European War and the Boer Rebellion*; a book of Setswana proverbs; and *A Sechuana Reader*, the latter co-written with Daniel Jones of University College London. As this suggests, he was a highly productive writer, translating four of Shakespeare's plays into Setswana and publishing the first novel in English by a black African. At some stage, perhaps through university connections, he seems to have met Gollancz, and the invitation to contribute to the *Book of Homage* emerged.

His contribution is fascinating, and not only because of the unexpected language in which it is written—which, considering Plaatje's accomplishments as a writer in English, marks a deliberate choice. Certainly the partial translation in the right margin seems at times mischievous. Thus Plaatje begins by noting that, having gone to see *Hamlet* at the theatre in Kimberley, he 'became curious to know more about Shakespeare and his works' and found social value in so doing: 'Intelligence in Africa is still carried from mouth to mouth by means of conversations after working hours, and, reading a number of Shakespeare's works, I always had a fresh story to tell' (336). The next translation is one sentence, 'I first read *The Merchant of Venice*', and then there is a longer sentence: 'The characters were so realistic that I was asked more than once to which of certain speculators, then operating round Kimberley, Shakespeare referred as Shylock' (336). Tongue is, by this point, firmly in cheek; at the same time, Plaatje's politics are becoming clear. And he proceeds to develop a personal, political, and linguistic story by way of Shakespeare.

He notes that '[w]hile reading *Cymbeline*' he met his future wife and explains that, marrying as he was across tribal and linguistic borderlines, the pair used English to communicate their feelings:

I was not then as well acquainted with her language—the Xosa—as I am now; and although she had a better grip of mine—the Sechuana—I was doubtful whether I could make her understand my innermost feelings in it, so in coming to an understanding we both used the language of educated people—the language which Shakespeare wrote—which happened to be the only official language of our country at that time. (337)

He develops this Shakespearean linguistic romance by noting, deadpan, that '[i]t may be depended upon that we both read *Romeo and Juliet*' (337). 'My people', he continues,

resented the idea of my marrying a girl who spoke a language which [...] had clicks in it; while her people likewise abominated the idea of giving their daughter in marriage to a fellow who spoke with a language so imperfect as to be without any clicks. But the civilized laws of Cape Colony saved us from a double tragedy in a cemetery. (337)

The last sentence offers a complex perspective, social and political, that interpellates the reader as complicit both in his or her knowledge of the Shakespeare canon and in the humour with which the politics of colonial rule is lightly implied, and it is to politics that Plaatje directs his irony from here onwards. He notes that in 1910, when Halley's Comet appeared, three rulers—'King Edward VII and two great Bechuana chiefs—Sebele and Bathoeng—died', and he reports that in writing newspaper obituaries for all three rulers he included the same Shakespeare quotation at the head of each—'When beggars die there are no comets seen; | The heavens themselves blaze forth the death of princes'—thus neatly aligning the British king with the South African chiefs (338). And he does similar work in his final section, praising Shakespeare for his 'keen grasp of human character' and addressing the emergence of African literature:

It is to be hoped that with the maturity of African literature, now still in its infancy, writers and translators will consider the matter of giving to Africans the benefit of some at least of Shakespeare's works. That this could be done is suggested by the probability that some of the stories on which his dramas are based find equivalents in African folklore.

Plaatje thus enacts a cultural performance by way of a life story set out as a journey into appreciation of Shakespeare. It is tempting to read this as symptomatic of what postcolonial theory would call a 'subaltern' subject position, the 'educated native' finding his self-construction by way of a symbol of colonial power. But the word 'equivalent' is key here: Shakespeare is placed alongside, not above, African literature. As Kahn observes, '[i]n paying tribute to him in the *Homage*, Plaatje doesn't concede to Shakespeare some originary authority' (Kahn, 'Reading Shakespeare Imperially', 474); rather, he renegotiates that authority in relation to his own language and to the language of his wife, and he finds a form of postcolonial self-fashioning by way of one of the most revered figureheads of colonial rule. In a manner very akin to that of Hyde, Plaatje thus deploys an engaging mix of resistance, playfulness, and wry humour to fashion a new identity through, not in spite of, Shakespeare.

The contributors to the *Book of Homage* may be celebrating Shakespeare, then, but they all, in their quite different ways, fashion their own versions of selfhood in response to Gollancz's invitation to be involved. And not the least of these self-fashioners, unexpectedly, is Gollancz himself. The final contribution on which I will focus is not—ostensibly, at least—by one of the volume's self-conscious outsider figures but by the individual you might consider the most obvious insider of all, the volume's editor. At first sight, it is not very promising. It has the unprepossessing title 'Bits of Timber: Some Observations on Shakespearian Names—"Shylock", "Polonius", "Malvolio"', and it appears to be little more than a few pages of philological ramblings with little in the way of a driving premise—disappointing, perhaps, in the context of some of Gollancz's earlier flights of global rhetoric. Yet his contribution has a quiet edge that speaks both to his particular context and to some of the resistance he encountered as a Jewish professor of English leading the Tercentenary charge.[24]

He begins with an account of names in *The Merchant of Venice*, tracing the origins of the names Shylock and Antonio to a particular early modern book, Peter Morwyng's translation of the pseudo-Josephus *A compendious and most marveylous History of the latter Times of the Jewes Commune Weale*, which he describes as '[t]he book which was read by Elizabethans for everything relating to the later Jewish history'. At the beginning of the book, he notes, there is a passage about a battle between Jews and Romans in which a leader called '*Schiloch the Babylonian*' is sent to fight the Romans and encounters 'a Roman captaine called *Antonius*, a valiant man, and a good warrior' (171). Gollancz suggests that '[t]his passage may well account for' Shakespeare's juxtaposition of the names 'Shylock' and 'Antonio'. He then offers a further gloss on the name Shylock: 'I am strongly inclined', he notes, 'to explain the use of the name as due to the quite erroneous association of "Shiloch" with "Shallach", the Biblical Hebrew for "cormorant", the bird that "swoops", or dives after its prey', adding that '[i]n Elizabethan England "cormorant" was

[24] See Gordon McMullan, 'Goblin's Market: Anti-Semitism, Commemorative Entrepreneurship, and the Invention of "Global" Shakespeare in 1916', in Kahn and Calvo, *Celebrating Shakespeare*, 182–201.

an expressive synonym for "usurer"' (172). So Shakespeare 'created almost a special English idiom for Shylock', aware of what Gollancz calls 'the peculiar force of the words "to bait fish withal", uttered by his Cormorant Usurer' Shylock, whom he described as 'a legendary monstrosity fraught with all the greater possibilities inasmuch as at that time Jews were not yet permitted to reside in England, and there was still the popular prejudice' (172). Gollancz insists that Shakespeare, in depicting Shylock, was not succumbing to that 'popular prejudice' but presenting him as a new kind of tragic hero: 'Shakespeare's humanity and understanding saved Shylock from being the mere Cormorant-monster'. At this point he moves rather abruptly to his second play, *Hamlet*, to reflect on the origin of the name 'Polonius'—so different from the name 'Corambis' given to the character with the same function in the First (or 'Bad') Quarto of the play—and he suggests a source in a recent Polish translation of Grimaldus's *De Optimo Senatore* ('The Counsellor') by Wawrzyniec Goslicki ('Laurentius Goslicius'), Bishop of Posen (Poznan), thus underlining the awareness of Poland and Polish culture in Elizabethan and early Jacobean England.

Why might Gollancz pair these apparently unconnected instances of philological curiosity in this way? The answer lies in his own origins and identity. The city of Poznan is located in the disputed territory between Germany and Poland from which Gollancz's father had emigrated to England and, as we have seen, as a Jew organizing the Shakespeare Tercentenary, Gollancz had been reminded of the persistence of anti-Semitism in Britain four centuries on from the writing of *The Merchant of Venice*. In addressing Shylock's identity, in reflecting on the prejudice to which he is subject in the play and in emphasizing his family's origins in Poland, Gollancz is in effect *signing* his work, locating himself within the global culture of the *Book of Homage* and implying the complexity of his own identity as a patriotic Jewish Briton of Polish origins—Kahn calls him 'a hybrid in spades, and at the very core of the British intellectual establishment'—in a context bound by, on the one hand, the imperialism of William Pember Reeves and, on the other, the questioning of that world view by Hyde, Plaatje, and other contributors to the *Book*. There is a hint of Gollancz's characteristic sense of humour in the way in which he does this, not least in the context of the poem contributed to the *Book of Homage* by his namesake Israel Zangwill, who in describing Shakespeare as 'Impartial bard of Briton, Roman, Gaul, | Jew, Gentile, white or black' raises as much as resolves the question of the contemporary possibility of identifying as both British and Jewish.[25] He is, in other words, well aware of his own particular form of hybridity, and his editing of *A Book of Homage to Shakespeare* is—unexpectedly, counterintuitively—one way in which he was able both to address it and use it to advantage.

Gollancz was a commemorative entrepreneur of extraordinary energy, openness, and flexibility, and his editing of the *Book of Homage* reflects his personality and his perspective. The *Book* is inclusive, wide-reaching, and unexpectedly subtle. It performs a cultural moment with great care, enabling the reader to find within its pages the Shakespeare with which he or she is most familiar and uncomfortable, making the most of its very eclecticism to allow the reader a wide choice of pathways through the contributions. The enthusiast for empire can read it untroubled, yet the incipient nationalist, Irish or South African, could also find within its pages expressions of hope in a changing world. Its apparent arbitrariness turns out to be nothing of the sort, its lightly shaped contents, on closer inspection, grouped with precision and juxtaposed at times with evident humour. As an expression of the condition of Shakespeare studies in its moment the *Book of Homage* is unparalleled, but it is far more than that: it makes very apparent how pivotal the year 1916 was in the negotiation between the fading imperial Shakespeare and the emerging global Shakespeare, and it invites the reader to recognize and absorb a range of perspectives, by no means all compatible, on the National Poet. More to the point, it demonstrates through its extraordinarily varied and multivalent voices the ongoing role of Shakespeare as currency for cultural, political, and social debate, for the conserving of ideas on the wane and the encouragement of ideas in their infancy. The *Book of Homage* offers a fascinating snapshot of its moment in literary and cultural history, one that richly repays revisiting.

Gordon McMullan
King's College London

---

[25] See *Book of Homage*, 248. On Zangwill, see Bryan Cheyette, 'Englishness and Extraterritoriality: British-Jewish Writing and Diaspora Culture', *Studies in Contemporary Jewry* 12 (1996), 21–39.

Martin Droeshout sculpsit London.   F.W.imp.   Shakespeare Tercentenary 1916

1916

A BOOK OF HOMAGE TO
SHAKESPEARE

EDITED BY ISRAEL GOLLANCZ, LITT.D., F.B.A.

HONORARY SECRETARY OF THE SHAKESPEARE TERCENTENARY COMMITTEE

HUMPHREY MILFORD
OXFORD UNIVERSITY PRESS

PREFACE

FOR years past—as far back as 1904—many of us had been looking forward to the Shakespeare Tercentenary as the occasion for some fitting memorial to symbolize the intellectual fraternity of mankind in the universal homage accorded to the genius of the greatest Englishman. We had hoped that, on a site which has already been acquired, a stately building, to be associated with his august name, equipped and adequately endowed for the furtherance of Shakespearian drama and dramatic art generally, would have made the year 1916 memorable in the annals of the English stage.

At a noteworthy meeting held in July 1914 of delegates nominated by many institutions, universities, societies, and other bodies, to consider the question of the observance of the Shakespeare Tercentenary, Lord Bryce as President of the British Academy presiding, it was unanimously resolved, on the motion of the American Ambassador, His Excellency W. H. Page, 'That the Tercentenary of the death of Shakespeare should be commemorated in a manner worthy of the veneration in which the memory of Shakespeare is held by the English-speaking peoples and by the world at large'. The delegates, representing the British Empire, the United States, and foreign countries, were constituted as a General Committee, and an Executive Committee was appointed, with Lord Plymouth as Chairman, and myself as Honorary Secretary.

Then came the War; and the dream of the world's brotherhood to be demonstrated by its common and united commemoration of Shakespeare, with many another fond illusion, was rudely shattered. In face of sterner duties all such projects fell necessarily into abeyance. Some months ago, however, it was recognized (and the call came to us from many quarters at home and abroad) that not even under present conditions should the Shakespeare Tercentenary be allowed to pass unobserved, though the scope of our original programme would of necessity be modified,—though we could not hope to witness even the foundation of the proposed Shakespeare Theatre, nor to welcome, as we had anticipated, the many devotees of the poet who would have wished to participate in our Commemoration.

We knew we should have our friends with us in spirit on the great occasion ; and it seemed to me, in one way at least, possible to link their homage with ours, and to hand down to posterity a worthy Record of the widespread reverence for Shakespeare as shared with the English-speaking world by our Allies and Neutral States, namely, by the publication, in honour of the Tercentenary, of a Book of Homage to Shakespeare, with contributions in prose and verse, representing the ubiquity of the poet's mighty influence. Accordingly, encouraged by those whom I ventured to consult, and subsequently with the approval of the Tercentenary Committee, I took upon myself the responsible and onerous task, complicated by present conditions ; and the ready and generous co-operation of one hundred and sixty-six Homagers finds expression in the present volume. Time and space necessitated certain limitations ; and it has not been possible to include many who would have been willing to join in our Homage, and whose tributes to the poet would have been valued by all Shakespearians. The original plan of the book fixed the maximum number of contributors at one hundred. It soon became clear that this would have to be increased, and that the British Empire alone could not well be represented by less than one hundred contributors, with some seventy more representing America, France, Italy, Greece, Spain and Spanish-speaking countries, Portugal, Roumania, Switzerland, Belgium, Holland, Iceland, Denmark, Sweden, Norway, Russia, Serbia, Poland, ' Jugoslavia ', Finland, Japan, China, Persia, Armenia—to follow the arrangement of the book, where the nations are grouped by languages, namely, English, Romance, Dutch, Scandinavian, Slavonic, &c. These languages, however, do not exhaust the list, for from British subjects we have tributes, not only in the classic dead languages of antiquity, Greek, Latin, Hebrew, Sanskrit, but also in the living languages of Ireland, Wales, India (Bengalee, Urdu, and Burmese), Egypt (Arabic), and South Africa (the Bechuana dialect).

It is indeed a long-drawn procession that is here presented ; and before it is graciously ushered in by our honoured chieftain Mr. Thomas Hardy, it is my pleasant duty to record my profound thanks to him and to all those who have made it possible for the Book of Homage to come forth amid the throes of this world-travail. I am grateful to many of my contributors for much kind indulgence in difficult and delicate questions; and I owe a special debt of gratitude to the trusty advisers who have given me the benefit of their valued counsel. I regret that, for various reasons, it has not been possible to give translations in all cases where a full English rendering would have been desirable; the marginal paraphrases will, I trust, prove helpful, as indicating the general purport of certain contributions in languages not generally known. A few contributions have unfortunately not reached me in time for inclusion in the volume.

While the work has been in progress, we have had to mourn the loss of some whose names would have added lustre to the Roll of our Homagers—the late Mr. Henry James, so noble a link between the English-speaking peoples; my ever revered and kind friend Mr. Stopford Brooke, to whom, for his Primer of English Literature and its inspiring force, the teaching of English literature, in my opinion, owes more than to any other man of our time; Canon Ellacombe, the nonagenarian, whose *Plant-Lore and Garden-Craft of Shakespeare* made Shakespeare's Garden of Flowers burgeon forth anew; Count Ugo Balzani, endeared to many Englishmen, who had been nominated by the Lincei, of Rome, to represent that learned Academy at the Tercentenary Commemoration, who was present at the meeting constituting the General Committee in 1914, and who was preparing his Homage to Shakespeare at the time of his lamented death; and, lastly, Her Majesty Queen Elizabeth of Roumania, whose memory, as Carmen Sylva, is enshrined in the hearts of those who cherish the tender blossoms of sweet poesy. All these and others should be gratefully remembered, for they are with us in our Homage.

I desire to express my sincerest thanks to many who have helped me in various ways—Mr. Nevill Forbes, Reader in Russian in the University of Oxford (for his excellent translations of the Russian and other Slavonic contributions); Professor Margoliouth, Laudian Professor of

Arabic in the University of Oxford (for reading the proofs of the Arabic poems, and for summarizing their contents) ; Professor Paul Hamelius, of the University of Liège (for valued assistance with Dutch and Flemish); Sir Charles Eliot, Principal of the University of Hong-kong, and the Rev. S. B. Drake, King's College, London, in respect of Chinese ; Professor Longford (for advice on Japanese) ; Mrs. Rhys Davids (for her good offices in helping me to secure adequate representation of Burmese); Miss Laurence Alma-Tadema ; Mr. Mikhail, an Egyptian student of King's College ; Miss Alice Werner, Miss Winifred Stephens, and Miss Mabel Day.

I would add my best thanks to Mr. J. F. Blumhardt, Professor of Hindustani, University College, London, for generously preparing for me a comprehensive catalogue of all the versions of Shakespeare in the Aryan languages and dialects of India, for a survey I had contemplated of the renderings of Shakespeare into foreign languages.

Finally, I wish to place on record my profound appreciation of the manner in which Mr. F. J. Hall, Controller of the Oxford University Press, and his staff, have carried this work through, under exceptional difficulties. But for Mr. Hall's zeal, and the marvellous organization of the Oxford University Press, the Book could not possibly have been published in time for the Tercentenary. The workmanship speaks for itself. I desire also to express my thanks to Mr. Emery Walker for his share in the artistic side of the volume.

It is my hope that this Shakespeare Tercentenary Book may inaugurate the annual issue of a volume of Shakespeare studies, or, at all events, that it may help forward some Shakespearian work ; and to this purpose I propose to devote the profits, if any, accruing from this labour of loyal homage and dutiful reverence, from this Book of Homage to Shakespeare—and to Shakespeare's England.

I. G.

KING'S COLLEGE,
LONDON, W.C.
April 20, 1916.

CONTENTS

PAGE

THOMAS HARDY, O.M.

    To Shakespeare after 300 Years 1

M. H. SPIELMANN, F.S.A.

    'This Figure, that thou here seest put' . . . 3

AUSTIN DOBSON

    The Riddle 13

FREDERIC HARRISON, D.C.L., Litt.D., LL.D.

    A Dream of Parnassus 14

LAURENCE BINYON, author of *London Visions*, &c.

    England's Poet 21

THE RT. HON. VISCOUNT BRYCE, O.M., President of the British
    Academy

    Some Stray Thoughts 22

HIS EMINENCE CARDINAL GASQUET, author of *Henry VIII and
    the English Monasteries*, &c.

    Shakespeare 25

JOHN DRINKWATER, author of *Poems of Men and Hours*, &c.

    For April 23, 1616–1916 30

REV. WILLIAM BARRY, D.D. (Rome), author of *The New Antigone*

    The Catholic Strain in Shakespeare 31

MRS. ALICE MEYNELL

    Heroines 35

PAGE

JOHN GALSWORTHY, author of *The Silver Box*, &c.

    THE GREAT TREE 37

F. R. BENSON, LL.D.

    A STRATFORDIAN'S HOMAGE 39

H. B. IRVING, M.A. (Oxford)

    THE HOMAGE OF THE ACTORS 41

GORDON BOTTOMLEY

    ON PEACEFUL PENETRATION 43

ALFRED PERCEVAL GRAVES, author of *Songs of Killarney*, &c.

    THE FAIRIES' HOMAGE 47

PROFESSOR W. P. KER, LL.D., F.B.A., University Professor of English Language and Literature, University College, London; author of *Epic and Romance*, &c.

    CERVANTES, SHAKESPEARE, AND THE PASTORAL IDEA . . 49

EDMUND GOSSE, C.B., LL.D.

    THE SONGS OF SHAKESPEARE 52

EVELYN UNDERHILL (MRS. STUART MOORE), author of *Mysticism, a Study in the Nature and Development of Man's Spiritual Consciousness, Practical Mysticism*, &c.

    WILLIAM SHAKESPEARE 56

JOHN BURNET, LL.D., Professor of Greek in the University of St. Andrews

    SHAKESPEARE AND GREEK PHILOSOPHY 58

W. MACNEILE DIXON, Litt.D., Professor of English Literature in the University of Glasgow; author of *English Poetry from Blake to Browning*

    IN REMEMBRANCE OF OUR WORTHY MASTER SHAKESPEARE . 62

W. H. HADOW, D.Mus., Principal, Armstrong College, Newcastle

    SHAKESPEARE AND MUSIC 64

PAGE

J. A. FULLER-MAITLAND, editor of *Grove's Dictionary of Music*, &c.

    BIANCA'S MUSIC-LESSON 70

WILLIAM BARCLAY SQUIRE, Assistant-Keeper, British Museum; author of *Catalogue of old Printed Music in the British Museum*, &c.

    SHAKESPEARIAN OPERAS 75

REGINALD BLOMFIELD, R.A., author of *History of Renaissance Architecture in England*, &c.

    WILLIAM SHAKESPEARE 84

SIR SIDNEY COLVIN, Hon. D.Litt., Oxford, Member of the Royal Academy of Belgium, late Keeper of Prints and Drawings, British Museum

    THE SACK OF TROY IN SHAKESPEARE'S 'LUCRECE' AND IN SOME FIFTEENTH-CENTURY DRAWINGS AND TAPESTRIES . 88

LIONEL CUST, C.V.O., Litt.D., F.S.A., formerly Director of the National Portrait Gallery

    SHAKESPEARE 100

LIEUT.-COL. SIR RONALD ROSS, K.C.B., F.R.S., Nobel Laureate; author of *Malarial Fever: its Cause, Prevention, and Treatment*

    SHAKESPEARE, 1916 104

W. H. DAVIES, author of *The Autobiography of a Super-Tramp*

    SHAKESPEARE WORKS 105

HENRY BRADLEY, Hon. D.Litt., Oxford, F.B.A., editor of *The New English Dictionary*

    SHAKESPEARE AND THE ENGLISH LANGUAGE 106

SIR SIDNEY LEE, Litt.D., F.B.A., University Professor of English Language and Literature, East London College; author of *A Life of Shakespeare*, &c.

    SHAKESPEARE INVENTOR OF LANGUAGE 110

PAGE

HERBERT TRENCH, formerly Fellow of All Souls College, Oxford ;
    author of *Deirdre Wedded*, &c.

    SHAKESPEARE   115

ALFRED NOYES, Hon. Litt.D. (Yale), author of *Drake, Forty Singing
    Seamen*, &c.

    THE SHADOW OF THE MASTER   116

MRS. C. C. STOPES, author of *Shakespeare's Environment*, &c.

    THE MAKING OF SHAKESPEARE   118

THE VERY REV. H. C. BEECHING, D.D., Dean of Norwich

    THE BENEFIT OF THE DOUBT   120

A. CLUTTON-BROCK, author of *Shelley, the Man and the Poet*, &c.

    THE UNWORLDLINESS OF SHAKESPEARE   126

MORTON LUCE, author of *Shakespeare, the Man and his Work*, &c.

    THE CHARACTER OF SHAKESPEARE   129

W. F. TRENCH, M.A. (Cantab.), Litt.D. (Dublin), Professor of English
    Literature in the University of Dublin ; author of *Shake-
    speare's Hamlet*, &c.

    SHAKESPEARE : THE NEED FOR MEDITATION .   .   .   135

GEORGE SAINTSBURY, D.Litt., F.B.A., late Professor of English
    Literature in the University of Edinburgh ; author of *History
    of English Prosody*, &c.

    SHAKESPEARE AS TOUCHSTONE   137

THE RT. HON. J. M. ROBERTSON, M.P., author of *Montaigne and
    Shakespeare*, &c.

    THE PARADOX OF SHAKESPEARE   141

W. J. COURTHOPE, C.B., Litt.D., F.B.A., formerly Professor of Poetry
    in the University of Oxford; author of *History of English
    Poetry*, &c.

    THE TERCENTENARY OF SHAKESPEARE'S DEATH—1916 .   .   146

PAGE

THE RT. HON. SIR J. RENNELL RODD, G.C.M.G., G.C.V.O., British Ambassador at Rome; author of *Ballads of the Fleet*, &c.

A THOUGHT FROM ITALY 148

JOHN BAILEY, author of *Dr. Johnson and his Circle*, &c.

A NOTE ON FALSTAFF 149

E. K. CHAMBERS, C.B., author of *The Mediæval Stage*, &c.

THE OCCASION OF 'A MIDSUMMER-NIGHT'S DREAM' . . 154

OLIVER ELTON, Professor of English Literature in the University of Liverpool; author of *Survey of English Literature, 1780–1830*, &c.

HELENA 161

W. L. COURTNEY, LL.D., Fellow of New College, Oxford

ORSINO TO OLIVIA 162

A. C. BRADLEY, LL.D., F.B.A., formerly Professor of Poetry in the University of Oxford; author of *Shakespearean Tragedy*, &c.

FESTE THE JESTER 164

ISRAEL GOLLANCZ, Litt.D., F.B.A., University Professor of English Language and Literature, King's College, London; Secretary of the British Academy; Honorary Secretary of the Shakespeare Tercentenary Committee; editor of *The Temple Shakespeare*, &c.

BITS OF TIMBER: SOME OBSERVATIONS ON SHAKESPEARIAN NAMES—'SHYLOCK', 'POLONIUS', 'MALVOLIO' . . 170

W. W. GREG, Litt.D., author of *Pastoral Poetry and Pastoral Drama*, &c.

A CRITICAL MOUSETRAP 179

R. WARWICK BOND, Professor of English Literature, University College, Nottingham; editor of *The Complete Works of John Lyly*

1600 181

PAGE

SIR HENRY NEWBOLT, Professor of Poetry in the Royal Society of
    Literature; author of *Admirals all*, &c.
    A NOTE ON 'ANTONY AND CLEOPATRA'   183

M. W. MacCALLUM, Professor of Modern Literature, University of
    Sydney; author of *Shakespeare's Roman Plays and their*
    Background, &c.
    THE CAWDOR PROBLEM   186

HUGH WALKER, LL.D., Professor of English Literature, St. David's
    College, Lampeter; author of *Literature of the Victorian*
    Era, &c.
    THE KNOCKING AT THE GATE ONCE MORE   .   .   .   190

J. W. MACKAIL, LL.D., F.B.A., formerly Professor of Poetry in the
    University of Oxford; author of *The Springs of Helicon*, &c.
    MOTHER AND SON IN 'CYMBELINE'   193

A. C. BENSON, C.V.O., LL.D., President of Magdalene College, Cam-
    bridge; author of *The Upton Letters*, &c.
    ARIEL   197

RUDYARD KIPLING
    THE VISION OF THE ENCHANTED ISLAND   .   .   .   200

J. LE GAY BRERETON, author of *Elizabethan Drama : Notes and*
    Studies, &c.
    DE WITT AT THE SWAN   204

W. J. LAWRENCE (Dublin), author of *The Elizabethan Playhouse*, &c.
    A FORGOTTEN PLAYHOUSE CUSTOM OF SHAKESPEARE'S DAY   .   207

THE RT. HON. W. J. M. STARKIE, LL.D., Litt.D., editor of
    Aristophanes
    WIT AND HUMOUR IN SHAKESPEARE   212

A. R. SKEMP, Professor of English in the University of Bristol
    SHAKESPEARE   227

PAGE

R. G. MOULTON, M.A. (Cantab.), Professor of Literary Theory and Interpretation in the University of Chicago; author of *Shakespeare as a Dramatic Artist*, &c.

SHAKESPEARE AS THE CENTRAL POINT IN WORLD LITERATURE . 228

C. H. HERFORD, Litt.D., Professor of English Literature, University of Manchester; author of *The Literary Relations of England and Germany in the Sixteenth Century*, &c.

THE GERMAN CONTRIBUTION TO SHAKESPEARE CRITICISM . 231

G. C. MOORE SMITH, Litt.D., Hon. Ph.D. (Louvain), Professor of English Language and Literature, University of Sheffield; editor of *Club Law*, &c.

SONNETS, 1616 : 1916 236

A. W. POLLARD, Assistant Keeper, British Museum; author of *Shakespeare's Folios and Quartos*, &c.

A BIBLIOGRAPHER'S PRAISE 238

SIR A. W. WARD, Litt.D., F.B.A., Master of Peterhouse, Cambridge; author of *History of English Dramatic Literature*, &c.

1616 AND ITS CENTENARIES 241

ISRAEL ZANGWILL, author of *Children of the Ghetto*, &c.

THE TWO EMPIRES 248

H. B. WHEATLEY, D.C.L., late President of the Bibliographical Society; author of *Mediæval London*, &c.

LONDON'S HOMAGE TO SHAKESPEARE 249

MISS MABEL E. WOTTON

A MEETING-PLACE FOR SHAKESPEARE AND DRAYTON IN THE CITY OF LONDON 252

FREDERICK S. BOAS, LL.D., author of *University Drama in the Tudor Age*, &c.

OXFORD AND SHAKESPEARE 254

b

PAGE

ARTHUR GRAY, Master of Jesus College, Cambridge

    SHAKESPEARE AND CAMBRIDGE   260

MISS M. DORMER HARRIS, editor of *The Coventry Leet Book*, &c.

    SHAKESPEARE AND WARWICKSHIRE   264

H. J. C. GRIERSON, LL.D., Professor of English Literature in the University of Edinburgh; editor of the *Poems of John Donne*

    SHAKESPEARE AND SCOTLAND   266

THE RT. HON. MR. JUSTICE MADDEN, LL.D., Litt.D., Vice-Chancellor of Dublin University; author of *The Diary of Master Silence*, &c.

    SHAKESPEARE AND IRELAND   270

DOUGLAS HYDE, (An Craoibhin Aoibhinn), Litt.D., LL.D., author of *A Literary History of Ireland, Love Songs of Connacht*, &c.

    AN RUD THÁRLA DO GHAEDHEAL AG STRATFORD AR AN ABHAINN (HOW IT FARED WITH A GAEL AT STRATFORD-ON-AVON) . 275

JOHN EDWARD LLOYD, Professor of History, University College of North Wales, Bangor; author of *A History of Wales*, &c.

    SHAKESPEARE'S WELSHMEN   280

J. MORRIS JONES, Professor of Welsh, University College of North Wales

    I GOF BARDD AVON (TO THE MEMORY OF THE BARD OF AVON). 284

REV. J. O. WILLIAMS, PEDROG (Liverpool)

    Y BARDD A GANODD I'R BYD   286

J. W. H. ATKINS, Professor of English Language and Literature, University College of Wales, Aberystwyth; late Fellow of St. John's College, Cambridge

    SHAKESPEARE AND KING ARTHUR   288

SIR JOHN SANDYS, Litt.D., F.B.A., Public Orator in the University of Cambridge

    A GREEK EPIGRAM ON THE TOMB OF SHAKESPEARE .   . 291

PAGE

ALEXANDER W. MAIR, Litt.D., Professor of Greek in the University of Edinburgh; editor of *Hesiod*, &c.

GREEK DIALOGUE IN PRAISE OF SHAKESPEARE . . . 292

SIR HERBERT WARREN, K.C.V.O., President of Magdalen College, Oxford; late Professor of Poetry, University of Oxford

COMMEMORATIO DORYSSOI 306

THE REV. H. GOLLANCZ, D.Litt., Goldsmid Professor of Hebrew, University College, London; editor of *The Ethical Treatises of Berachya*, &c.

HEBREW ODE 307

A. A. MACDONELL, Ph.D., F.B.A., Boden Professor of Sanskrit in the University of Oxford, author of *A History of Sanskrit Literature*, &c.

A SANSKRIT PANEGYRIC 310

THE HON. WILLIAM PEMBER REEVES, Ph.D. (Athens); Director of London School of Economics; formerly High Commissioner for New Zealand; author of *The Long White Cloud, a History of New Zealand*, &c.

THE DREAM IMPERIAL 312

WILFRED CAMPBELL, LL.D., Canadian poet, author of *Lake Lyrics*, &c.

SHAKESPEARE 314

CAPTAIN CHARLES G. D. ROBERTS, LL.D., Canadian poet, author of *The Book of the Native*, &c.

TO SHAKESPEARE, 1916 315

CANON F. G. SCOTT, C.M.G., D.C.L.; Senior Chaplain, 1st Canadian Division, B.E.F.; author of *The Hymn of Empire, and Other Poems*, &c.

'SHAKESPEARE' 316

ANANDA COOMARASWAMY, author of *The Arts and Crafts of India and Ceylon*, &c.

INTELLECTUAL FRATERNITY 317

PAGE

SIR RABINDRANATH TAGORE, D.Litt.; Nobel Laureate for
    Literature; author of *Gitanjali; The Crescent Moon*, &c.

    SHAKESPEARE 320

MOHAMMED IGVAL, scholar and advocate (Lahore), and
SARDAR JOGUNDRA SINGH, Indian novelist

    TO SHAKESPEARE: A TRIBUTE FROM THE EAST . . . 322

S. Z. AUNG, Burmese Buddhist scholar and philosopher

    FROM THE BURMESE BUDDHISTS 324

MAUNG TIN, M.A., of Rangoon College; editor of *Khuddaka pātha*

    SHAKESPEARE: A BURMAN'S APPRECIATION 329

HIS EXCELLENCY MOHAMMED ḤĀFIZ IBRĀHIM, famous Arabic
    poet

    TO THE MEMORY OF SHAKESPEARE 331

HIS EXCELLENCY WALIY AD-DIN YEYEN BEY, Egyptian poet

    SHAKESPEARE 333

A SOUTH AFRICAN'S HOMAGE

    WILLIAM TSIKINYA-CHAKA 336

CHARLES MILLS GAYLEY, Litt.D., LL.D., Professor of English
    Literature in the University of California; editor of *Repre-
    sentative English Comedies*, &c.

    HEART OF THE RACE 340

HORACE HOWARD FURNESS, JUNR., editor of the *Variorum
    Shakespeare*

    THE HOMAGE OF THE SHAKSPERE SOCIETY OF PHILADELPHIA . 342

CLAYTON HAMILTON, dramatic critic, author of *Stagecraft*, &c.

    THE PARADOX OF SHAKESPEARE 347

JOHN GRIER HIBBEN, Ph.D., LL.D., President of Princeton
    University

    SHAKESPEARE 350

PAGE

ROBERT UNDERWOOD JOHNSON, Litt.D., LL.D., Secretary of the
American Academy of Arts and Letters; author of *Songs of Liberty*, &c.

SHAKESPEARE 351

JOHN MATTHEWS MANLY, LL.D., Professor of English Literature
in the University of Chicago ; editor of *Specimens of the Pre-Shakespearean Drama*

TWO NEGLECTED TASKS 353

BRANDER MATTHEWS, Litt.D., Professor of Dramatic Literature,
Columbia University ; author of *Shakspere as a Playwright*

IF SHAKSPERE SHOULD COME BACK ? 356

FREDERICK MORGAN PADELFORD, Ph.D., Professor of the English
Language and Literature in the University of Washington ;
editor of *Early Sixteenth Century Lyrics*, &c.

SONNETS : I. SHAKESPEARE. II. THE FOREST OF ARDEN . 360

WILLIAM LYON PHELPS, Professor of English Literature at Yale
University

A PLEA FOR CHARLES THE WRESTLER 362

FELIX E. SCHELLING, Professor of English Literature in the University of Pennsylvania ; author of *Elizabethan Drama*, &c.

THE COMMON FOLK OF SHAKESPEARE 364

OWEN WISTER, M.A. (Harvard), author of *The Virginian*, &c.

FROM A LOVER OF SHAKESPEARE AND OF ENGLAND . . 373

GEORGE SANTAYANA, Litt.D., Ph.D., author of *The Life of Reason*, &c.

SONNET 377

HENRI CHANTAVOINE

A SHAKESPEARE 378

PAGE

HENRI BERGSON, de l'Académie française ; Corresponding Fellow
of the British Academy

HOMMAGE A SHAKESPEARE 379

MAURICE BOUCHOR, author of *Les Chansons de Shakespeare mises
en vers français*

SHAKESPEARE 381

ÉMILE BOUTROUX, de l'Académie française ; Corresponding Fellow
of the British Academy

L'ART ET LA NATURE, DANS SHAKESPEARE ET DANS BACON . 383

ALBERT FEUILLERAT, Professor of English Language and Literature
in the University of Rennes ; author of *John Lyly ; Black-
friar Records*, &c.

SIMPLES NOTES 387

ÉMILE HOVELAQUE, Inspecteur Général de l'Instruction Publique

COMMENT FAIRE CONNAÎTRE SHAKESPEARE AUX PETITS FRANÇAIS 392

HIS EXCELLENCY J.-J. JUSSERAND, French Ambassador at
Washington ; Corresponding Fellow of the British Academy ;
author of *Histoire littéraire du peuple anglais*

FRAGMENTS SUR SHAKESPEARE 399

ÉMILE LEGOUIS, Professor of English Language and Literature at
the Sorbonne ; author of *The Early Life of Wordsworth*

ÇÀ ET LÀ 405

ROMAIN ROLLAND, author of *Jean-Christophe*, &c.

A MON MEILLEUR AMI—SHAKESPEARE 411

PIERRE VILLEY, Professor of French Literature, University of Caen

MONTAIGNE ET SHAKESPEARE 417

HENRI DE RÉGNIER, de l'Académie française

A SHAKESPEARE 421

PAGE

HIS EXCELLENCY JOANNES GENNADIUS, D.C.L., Litt.D., LL.D.,
Greek Minister

ΤΗΙ ΜΝΗΜΗΙ ΤΟΥ ΚΛΕΙΝΟΥ ΚΑΙ ΕΡΑΤΕΙΝΟΥ ΣΑΚΕΣΠΗΡΟΥ (To the
Memory of the Renowned and Gentle Shakespeare) . 422

ISIDORO DEL LUNGO, Senator ; author of *Women of Florence*

Dante e Shakespeare 427

LUIGI LUZZATTI, Italian Minister

Pro Shakespeare ! 428

CAVALIERE ADOLFO DE BOSIS

Shakespeare 429

CINO CHIARINI, Professor of English Literature, Florence

Shakespeare 430

PAOLO ORANO, man of letters, Rome

'Hamlet è Giordano Bruno ?' 432

JOSÉ DE ARMAS, Member of the Royal Spanish Academy ; author of
El Quijote y su Época

Conversación de dos almas 434

HIS EXCELLENCY SEÑOR DON ALFONSO MERRY DEL VAL,
Spanish Ambassador

To Shakespeare, from a Spaniard 435

A. MAURA, President of the Royal Spanish Academy

Shakespeare 437

ARMANDO PALACIO VALDÉS, Member of the Royal Spanish
Academy

El Cielo de Shakspeare 439

C. SILVA VILDÓSOLA, South American publicist

Shakespeare y las Literaturas Hispano-Americanas. . 441

PAGE

HIS EXCELLENCY M. TEXEIRA-GOMES, Portuguese Minister
    PORTUGUESE TRIBUTE 447

GEORGE YOUNG, M.V.O., late of the British Legation, Lisbon ;
    author of *Portugal through its Poetry*, &c.
    PORTUGAL AND THE SHAKESPEARE TERCENTENARY . . 449

HIS EXCELLENCY NICOLAS MIŞU, Envoy Extraordinary and
    Roumanian Minister
    ROUMANIA's HOMAGE 452

LOUIS FRÉDÉRIC CHOISY, Professor of Comparative Literature in
    the University of Geneva
    L'IMPERSONNALITÉ DE SHAKESPEARE 454

RENÉ MORAX, Swiss poet and dramatist
    SHAKESPEARE 457

ÉMILE VERHAEREN
    SHAKESPEARE VU DE PROFIL 460

MAURICE MAETERLINCK
    SHAKESPEARE 461

PAUL HAMELIUS, Professor of English Language and Literature in
    the University of Liège
    SHAKESPEARE AND BELGIUM 462

RENÉ DE CLERCQ, Flemish poet
    ALS DEEZ TIJDEN GROOT (GREAT LIKE THESE TIMES) . . 464

CYRIEL BUYSSE, Flemish writer
    IN GEDACHTE MET SHAKESPEARE 466

ALBERT VERWEY, Dutch poet
    GRATO M' È 'L SONNO 467

W. G. C. BYVANCK, Librarian of the Royal Library, The Hague
    READING SHAKESPEARE'S SONNETS 468

PAGE

B. A. P. VAN DAM, M.D., author of *William Shakespeare's Prosody and Text*

    ARE THERE INTERPOLATIONS IN THE TEXT OF 'HAMLET'? . 473

OTTO JESPERSEN, Professor of English Philology at the University of Copenhagen ; author of *Growth and Structure of the English Language,* &c.

    A MARGINAL NOTE ON SHAKESPEARE'S LANGUAGE AND A TEXTUAL CRUX IN 'KING LEAR' 481

JÓN STEFÁNSSON, Ph.D., Icelandic scholar

    AN EDDIC HOMAGE TO WILLIAM SHAKESPEARE .   .   . 484

NIELS MØLLER, Danish poet

    PAA VEJ TIL SHAKESPEARE (ON THE WAY TO SHAKESPEARE) . 486

GEORGE BRANDES, LL.D., Professor ; Commander of the Orders of Danebrog and St. Olaf, &c. ; author of *William Shakespeare*

    SHAKESPEARE 490

KARL MANTZIUS, Danish actor and scholar ; author of *A History of Theatrical Art in Ancient and Modern Times*

    DENMARK AND SHAKESPEARE   491

VALD. VEDEL, Professor of Literary History, Copenhagen

    'PERSONALITY' ELLER 'IMPERSONALITY'   .   .   . 492

KARL WARBURG, Professor of Literary History in the University of Stockholm

    HAMLET I SVERIGE   495

C. COLLIN, Professor of English Literature in the University of Christiania

    SHAKESPEARE AND THE NORWEGIAN DRAMA .   .   . 499

PAGE

K. BALMONT, Russian poet and scholar (with translations by NEVILL FORBES)

    I. THE GENIUS OF THE SEEING HEART 506

    II. ON THE SHOAL OF TIME 512

    III. THE ALL-EMBRACING 514

MAXIMILIAN VOLOSHIN, Russian poet (with translation by NEVILL FORBES)

    PORTIA 516

'AMARI', Russian poet

    ANOTHER RUSSIAN HOMAGE 518

FATHER NICHOLAS VELIMIROVIC, of Belgrade

    SHAKESPEARE—THE PANANTHROPOS 520

PAVLE POPOVIČ, Professor of Southern Slav Literature in the University of Belgrade; author of *A History of Serbian Literature*, &c.

    SHAKESPEARE IN SERBIA 524

SRGJAN TUSIĆ, Jugoslav dramatist

    THE HOMAGE OF THE JUGOSLAVS 528

HENRYK SIENKIEWICZ, Polish novelist; author of *Quo Vadis*, &c. (with translation by Miss LAURENCE ALMA-TADEMA)

    DLACZEGO MOGŁEM CZYTAČ SZEKSPIRA (WHY I WAS ABLE TO READ SHAKESPEARE) 530

EINO LEINO, Finnish poet

    SHAKESPEARE-TUNNELMA (with English translation) . . 534

YRJO HIRN, Professor of Aesthetics and Modern Literature in the University of Helsingfors

    SHAKESPEARE IN FINLAND 536

JUHANI AHO, Finnish man of letters

    ENSIMÄINEN SUOMALAINEN SHAKESPEAREN ENSI-ILTA SUOMESSA 538

CONTENTS

PAGE

YUZO TSUBOUCHI, Emeritus Professor of English Literature, Waseda University, Tokyo; translator of Shakespeare into Japanese

SHAKESPEARE AND CHIKAMATSU 543

GONNOSKÉ KOMAI, Japanese War Correspondent and poet

TO SHAKESPEARE, THE GREATEST CONQUEROR OF ALL . . 547

LIU PO TUAN, Chinese poet (Hong-kong)

CHINESE HOMAGE 548

AHMAD KHAN, Persian scholar

PERSIAN HOMAGE 550

K. H. FUNDUKLIAN, translator of *Antony and Cleopatra*, &c., into Armenian

ARMENIAN TRIBUTE 551

MISS ZABELLE C. BOYAJIAN, author of *Yesterc*, a novel dealing with Armenian life, &c.

ARMENIA'S LOVE TO SHAKESPEARE 552

EPILOGUE 553

LIST OF CONTRIBUTORS IN ALPHABETICAL ORDER . . 555

LIST OF ILLUSTRATIONS

I. 'This Figure, that thou here seest put'

1. WILLIAM SHAKESPEARE. Print engraved by Martin Droeshout. Probably executed 1622/3. Elaborated from the Proof. From the plate in the First Folio . . . . *Frontispiece*

2. WILLIAM SHAKESPEARE. From the (coloured) effigy, carved by Garret Johnson the Younger, in Holy Trinity Church, Stratford-on-Avon . . . . . . *To face p.* 4

3. WILLIAM SHAKESPEARE. (Head only.) From the earliest Proof (known as 'the Unique Proof') of the engraving by Martin Droeshout, discovered by J. O. Halliwell[-Phillipps] in 1864, before elaboration for the First Folio. In the possession of Mr. H. C. Folger, of New York. By consent of the Trustees of the Shakespeare Birthplace. (Copyright) . . *To face p.* 6

4. WILLIAM SHAKESPEARE. The Chandos Portrait. In the National Portrait Gallery . . . . . *To face p.* 8

5. WILLIAM SHAKESPEARE. (Head only.) Painted by Sir Godfrey Kneller in 1693, from the Chandos Portrait, for presentation to John Dryden. In the possession of the Earl Fitzwilliam, through whose courtesy it is here, for the first time, reproduced . . . . *To face p.* 10

II. The Siege of Troy in Shakespeare's ' Lucrece ' and in some Fifteenth-Century Drawings and Tapestries

6. PLATE I (A). Hector dissuaded from going to battle by his womenkind and by Priam. From a fragment of one of a series of sketches in the Louvre for tapestries representing the Siege of Troy.

   PLATE I (B). A battle of Greeks and Trojans, with Trojan women looking on from the walls. From an engraving after one of a series of tapestries representing the Siege of Troy . *To face p.* 96

7. PLATE II. The sack of Troy, with the murder of Priam, the sacrifice of Polyxena, &c. From one of a series of sketches in the Louvre for tapestries representing the Siege of Troy . *To face p.* 98

---

8. Bodleian Aubrey MS. 8, fol. 45ᵛ . . . . . *To face p.* 120

9. The Platt of Frederick and Basilea . . . . *To face p.* 208

A BOOK OF HOMAGE TO
SHAKESPEARE

A BOOK OF
HOMAGE TO SHAKESPEARE

TO SHAKESPEARE AFTER 300 YEARS

BRIGHT baffling Soul, least capturable of themes,
Thou, who display'dst a life of commonplace,
Leaving no intimate word or personal trace
Of high design outside the artistry
      Of thy penned dreams,
Still shalt remain at heart unread eternally.

Through human orbits thy discourse to-day,
Despite thy formal pilgrimage, throbs on
In harmonies that cow Oblivion,
And, like the wind, with all-uncared effect
      Maintain a sway
Not fore-desired, in tracks unchosen and unchecked.

And yet, at thy last breath, with mindless note
The borough clocks as usual tongued the hour,
The Avon idled past the garth and tower,
Thy age was published on thy passing-bell
      But in due rote
With other men's that year accorded a like knell.

B

And at the strokes some townsman (met, maybe,
And thereon queried by some squire's good dame
Driving in shopward) may have given thy name,
With, ' Yes, a worthy man and well-to-do ;
      Though, as for me,
I knew him but by just a neighbour's nod, 'tis true.

' I' faith, few knew him much here, save by word,
He having elsewhere led his busier life ;
Though to be sure he left with us his wife.'
—' Ah, one of the tradesmen's sons, I now recall . . .
      Witty, I've heard . . .
We did not know him . . . Well, good-day.   Death comes to all.'

So—like a strange bright-pinioned bird we find
To mingle with the barn-door brood awhile,
Then vanish from their homely domicile—
Into man's poesy, we weet not whence,
      Flew thy strange mind,
Lodged there a radiant guest, and sped for ever thence.

THOMAS HARDY.

February 14, 1916.

'THIS FIGURE, THAT THOU HERE SEEST PUT'

' It is a great comfort, to my thinking,' wrote Charles Dickens to William Sandys the antiquary, seventy years ago, ' that so little is known concerning the poet.   It is a fine mystery; and I tremble every day lest something should come out.   If he had had a Boswell, society wouldn't have respected his grave, but would calmly have had his skull in the phrenological shop-windows.'

It is doubtless true enough.   The curiosity of the ordinary man, intensified in the hero-worshipper, has little respect for mystery and still less patience with it.   The desire of every thinker, the ambition of every reasoning and contemplative mind, is to draw aside the curtain that shrouds the unknown.   The more elusive the solution the more ardent the quest : the theologist of every age has sought to probe the nature and mystery of the Godhead Itself.

To the biographer, as Carlyle declared, an authentic portrait of his subject is an urgent necessity : he needs the facial testimony to examine and cross-examine, to ponder, to analyse, to compare.   The greatest of those of whom no genuine portraits exist have frequently been a temptation which the intellectual artist has not sought to resist.   Shakespeare, however, is relatively of our own day.   The art of portraiture had reached its zenith at about the time when he was moving upon the world's stage, and its practice, *tant bien que mal*, was already common in England.   The two known portraits of the actor-poet which were brought into existence near the time of his death were the work of craftsmen unhappily but indifferently equipped, and not of poet-artists. Whatever their skill in accurate draughtsmanship and modelling, they lacked the power of rendering life, and the sense of beauty was not theirs.

It is therefore not surprising that, in course of time, people should become dissatisfied with these matter-of-fact and banal representations, so poorly executed by chisel and graver, despite the fact that Shakespeare's image had been by them authoritatively recorded.   Dissatisfaction bred doubt; in some, repudiation; and in the desire to eliminate all grounds for scepticism and to establish or refute the authenticity of the accepted portraits, a small phalanx of noisy, over-articulate devotees clamoured for the opening of Shakespeare's grave in order that the poet's features might be gazed upon and . . . photographed—if, as was believed to be likely, the Stratford soil had stayed the decomposing hand of Death. Alternatively, the skull might be studied, measurements might be taken, diagrams and drawings made, whereby the portraits could be tested, and—had the cold objectivity of the calm proposal found favour and the request been granted—within a few weeks, we may be sure, ' society would have had his skull in the phrenological shop-windows '.

But the finer feeling of the nation declared itself against so revolting an experiment which had been so strenuously contended for on both sides of the Atlantic. The argument that similar inquiries had been carried into effect at the hands of the charnel-house explorer in the case of Robert the Bruce, Burns, and a score of others not less celebrated, fell upon ears either deaf or shocked ; and Dickens's fear lest ' something should come out ' was set at rest, likely enough, for ever. The additional proof that was to silence cavillers and confirm still further the confidence of the world in the only two portraits that have any real claim to truth and genuine likeness had to be forgone ; and the effigy in Holy Trinity Church in Stratford and the print by Martin Droeshout were left to stand unassisted, as they easily may, without corroboration dug up out of the desecrated tomb. Without any outrage of sentiment they must justify themselves and vindicate one another. Many persons unfamiliar with the study of iconography and unversed in comparative portraiture may still find difficulty in reconciling some of the more superficial characteristics of the two likenesses : that is to say, the youthfulness as rendered in Droeshout's print, with the maturity presented by the Bust.

But how many know these two works as they really are, or were intended to be ? How many have had the opportunity of judging of Shakespeare's face as sculptor and engraver, each in his turn, represented it ? Few—very few indeed. For the bust cannot now be seen, much less judged, behind its coat of colour-decoration which in several important respects contradicts the glyptic forms ; and the print as it appears in the First Folio, and as it is known to the world, is almost a travesty of the plate as Droeshout originally left it.

Let us consider these two portraits, and see how far we should recognize in them the actual lineaments of the man Shakespeare as he lived. First as to the Bust.

William Shakespeare

From the Bust by Garret Johnson the Younger. Stratford-on-Avon

In the first place we must dismiss from our recollection nearly all the so-called ' plaster casts from the original bust ' from which most people derive their knowledge and receive their strongest impression, and on which they form their opinion concerning Shakespeare's head and features—because the vast majority of these objects are taken, not from the bust itself, but from mere copies of it very inaccurately modelled. We must look at the bust itself, which the younger Garret Johnson cut.

When we examine closely and with attention the sculptor's naïve work, we realize to our surprise that this effigy (which, although it gazes with such rapt ineptitude from its niche, appealed with curious force to Chantrey, Landor, Washington Irving, and many others) has been fundamentally modified both as to forms and expression by the polychrome (technically called ' beautifying ') applied by a painter who wilfully defied the intention of the sculptor. The painted eyebrows with their strongly arched sweep correspond ill with the carved indications of them. The wellnigh formless lips frame a mouth little understood, it would seem, by the colourist. The full staring pupils, crudely painted in, are barely natural in their doll-like gaze. In all these points and more the painter's misrendering conceals the Shakespeare of the sculptor's chisel, roughly but honestly carved.

Thus with its forms varied and expression changed, features are thrown into inharmonious relief, and true dimensions and actual modelling are gravely prejudiced. If this we owe to the original colouring, supposing it to be unjustified, hardly could we withhold our sympathy from the much-reviled Malone who in 1793 caused the ' beautifying ' to be over-painted with stone-colour ; for even those who fulminated against his vandalism enjoyed, thanks to his so-called ' daubing ', a sight denied to our generation. Not then did Shakespeare's open mouth resolve itself into what has been called ' a grin of death ' ; it revealed the parted, speaking lips of one who declaimed, as an actor-poet might, the words he had just set down on the paper at his hand : a conception as simply and naturally imagined as it was clumsily and frankly realized.

If we assume that the present colours faithfully reproduce those which were from the first employed, in order to impart an effect of life, it may be deduced that the chromatic scheme was introduced with the view of securing a truer resemblance than the sculptor had achieved. What if the family and friends of the departed poet, dissatisfied with young Garret Johnson's performance, had acted on his advice that a ' face-painter ' should be called in—as was a common practice—to give the final touch of life which he himself had missed ? The colourist's duty would be to bring the head into truer relation with the facts as these were explained to him. But, even then, it must be remembered that the present colouring is a relatively modern reconstitution of that of 1748-9, before which time the painting was more perfect, according to Halliwell-Phillipps, or contrarily, according to Malone, had not ever defaced the plain stone of the bust. An element of uncertainty on this point and on the value of the chromatic elements of the portrait must necessarily exist ; yet as to the truth of the main essentials of the sculptured image no doubt can be entertained. For when all is said we must recognize here, as in the Droeshout print, the particularity of paramount importance, the outstanding characteristic which is the unquestionable test and touchstone of every portrait of the poet—the upright forehead, the dome-like skull, which Professor Arthur Keith has shown to be the ' round head ' of the Bronze Age—identified as the physical mark of the true Celt (as Europe understands the term) and the cranial symbol of the world's finest artists and most inspired among the poets and men of imagination.

Nor, in similar fashion, can the full significance of Martin Droeshout's print be wholly understood, even by those who study it in the First Folio, because it is only in the earliest proof state that the head of Shakespeare can be rightly and fully judged. For there the poet is revealed, it may safely be inferred, as he was in early manhood. It is a face we can accept—the visage of one little more than a youth, with a slight downy moustache, a small lip-beard, a strong chin devoid of growth, and fair eyebrows set low on the orbital ridges of the frontal bone. The forehead is bald, perhaps prematurely, perhaps deliberately shaved, either to conform to the sometime fashion which Hentzner's Elizabethan records tell of, or else for greater ease in playing venerable characters such as old Adam, Kno'well, and the like—such parts, indeed, as young players of the period were commonly entrusted with : when even boy-actors, such as the famous Pavy, might achieve a great reputation by their rendering of them. In any case, it is ' a noble front', the full and lofty dome which the Bronze Age had brought here from the Continent, the form that housed brains of poetic genius, capable of the most exalted beauty of conception. So much, indeed, has modern anthropology established. As for the frank young English face—the calm placidity of its observant gaze, the delicate firmness of features and expression, the characteristic aspect of large sympathy held

Copyright
MHS

William Shakespeare
From Martin Droeshout's Earliest "Unique" Proof
before elaboration for the First Folio
See Frontispiece

in control by critical judgement, the strong reserve of individuality—these have survived, in spite of all, the deficiencies of the young Droeshout's art, of his stiffness of rendering, and his still inexperienced hand. We have here, then, Shakespeare of the Sonnets and of *Love's Labour's Lost* rather than Shakespeare of the Tragedies.

Not elsewhere, it may be believed, do we come so close to the living Man of Stratford as in the earliest proof of the print, which once belonged to Halliwell-Phillipps but which years ago, alas, was acquired in the United States. Not even in the early proof in the Bodleian Library do we see him with anything like such vivid appearance of truth, because not only is that a darker, heavier impression, but because it is besides a later ' state ' of the plate. In this retouched condition we recognize in the worked-up forehead the beginnings of that ' horrible hydrocephalous development ', as Mr. Arthur Benson called it, which in the ordinary print as seen in the First Folio (and grossly exaggerated in the Fourth) has struck a chill sentiment of revolt into the hearts of generations of Shakespeare-lovers. In the manifest effort to add an appearance of advancing years to what had been a picture of ripe adolescence, the inexperienced engraver impaired his plate and produced a portrait almost as wooden as the painted bust. The broad, massive forehead, with the hair growing naturally from the scalp, has here developed a defiant bulbousness and a shape tending towards the conical, with locks sprouting with strange suddenness, wig-like and artificial, from its side. The re-formed and altered eyebrows, the darkened pupils which formerly were fair, the distressing bagginess accentuated under the eyes, the enlarged moustache smudging the upper lip to the confines of the cheeks, the two-days' stubble added to the chin, the over-emphasized line marking the division of jaw and neck, the forced lights and shadows with consequent destruction of harmony and breadth of illumination—these are further defects in the portrait by which Droeshout has made Shakespeare known to all the world. They divest the portrait most grievously of the appearance of life and of the largeness of nature which are such striking qualities in the plate as the engraver first completed and 'proved' it. Nevertheless, and in spite of all, the eye of ordinary discernment can penetrate this screen of errors, and through the shortcomings of the artist recognize the life and nature which, with but indifferent success it is true, he has sought to realize and interpret.

Nevertheless, to the unprejudiced beholder, this uncouth print, with all its imperfections—'lamentable ', as Walpole pronounced it, as a work of art—bears in its delineation the unmistakable stamp of truth. Ver Huell,[1] the enthusiastic biographer and critic of Houbraken and the extoller of his freely-rendered engraving—the most popular of all the renderings—of the Chandos portrait of Shakespeare, admits that he was carried away by Droeshout's plate and was left cold by Houbraken's masterpiece of the burin. 'The head is fine,' says he, in his estimate of the Dutchman's prodigious performance, 'I might almost say too fine, and I greatly prefer to this idealized bust-piece Martin Droeshout's plate. There, indeed, we see the lineaments which so well realize the author of Romeo not less than of Julius Caesar. What nobility in the forehead !—with what feeling has the artist rendered the pensive and penetrating expression of the eyes and the gentle irony of a smile that is softened by the sweetness of his soul !'

Can we doubt that it was for its general truth that the portrait was selected and published in the great Folio in spite of the artlessness of the art, the stiffness of the pose, and the hardness of the execution ? After all, there was no absolute necessity for the inclusion of a portrait at all. There was even available (if the claims made on its behalf could be accepted) the infinitely more romantic, more artistic, Italianate portrait which we call the Chandos. What merit other than that of invaluable authenticity could have constrained Shakespeare's associates and friends to preface his immortal works, which they were about to give to the world in so impressive a form, with an image so indifferently rendered—an image clearly based on an original of the Hilliard or early Zuccaro type, almost 'primitive' in manner ? Surely the only motive and the sole justification for the adoption of such a plate was the recognized genuineness and authority of the record.

Moreover, if we look critically at the two portraits—the one put forth by the poet's admiring friends and fellow workers, and the other by his mourning family and fellow townsmen—we find that in their main essentials they are in substantial agreement and therefore they corroborate one another. We must, of course, bear in mind the widely different circumstances attendant on the production of these portraits and the varied details characteristic of them :—the difference of period—how the one portrait represents the sitter in his early prime, and the other at the time of his death ; the difference of material—how the one is sculptured roughly with the chisel in stone and intended to be viewed at a distance, the other cut in metal by the graver, to be printed on paper and scrutinized from a few inches away ; the difference of personality and outlook of the artists—men of different craft, of

---

[1] *Jacobus Houbraken et son œuvre, par A. Ver Huell*, 1875.

William Shakespeare
The Chandos Portrait (In the National Portrait Gallery)

different individuality, and of difference in artistic conception which they brought to their different tasks. Their sole personal points of contact were that they shared weakness in technique and accomplishment and that they were called to their work without having the inestimable advantage of sittings from the living model. We see in these two works, notwithstanding undoubted imperfections, the inter-confirmation of the great upright cranium, the straight nose, the large wide-open eyes, even the mode, retained by the poet throughout his life, of the moustache brushed upward and the mass of hair curling heavily over the ears. These two representations, then, support one another in their main essentials, in much the same manner and degree as Chantrey's bust and Raeburn's painted portrait of Sir Walter Scott confirm without exactly resembling one another, or, say, Nollekens's bust and Reynolds's painting of Laurence Sterne.

However great, therefore, the talent of artists may be, a painter's portrait and a sculptor's bust are rarely in exact agreement save in the salient items of resemblance, especially when years have elapsed between the production of the two likenesses. This is the more marked when unskilled hands have been at work—most marked of all when the portraitists have been called upon to bring into existence a posthumous likeness. When, in the same art, we find two painters such as Nasmyth and Raeburn producing portraits of Robert Burns, at different ages, it is true, but so dissimilar that few persons at the first glance, or even at the second, would assert that the two pictures are supposed to represent one and the same man—we cannot be surprised that the Stratford bust and the Droeshout plate confirm one another mainly on points of major importance and seem to differ only in superficial details and unessentials.

There is a touch of absurdity, or at least of oddness, in the well-nigh universal predilection displayed in favour of the Chandos portrait. That the majority should select for special adulation this rather swarthy face of foreign aspect, mainly in virtue of its relatively picturesque and romantic guise, is perhaps not wholly surprising in a majority. Moreover, it has the advantage over the two authentic portraits in that it represents an obviously living man humanly and naturally represented upon canvas. Even Burger was impressed by its 'refinement and melancholy' in spite of its lack of expression, and as a portrait he held it to be a pearl beyond price. But he, like the majority (who have called for at least a dozen reproductions of this portrait for each of those of truer value), took it blindly for granted that this placid, sombre, and rather weak-willed, amiable personage really pictures our English Shakespeare of pure midland stock.

It is nothing to them, or very little, that the early history of this painting is more than suspect, and that the traditions woven round it as to origin and early ownership cannot withstand the test of strict investigation. The fact that demonstrably false witness has been borne as to the picture's source, and that fiction mars the tracing of its early passage from hand to hand—that the chain of evidence comprises links which are not merely lamentably weak but which are sometimes found to be not really links at all—has affected little, or scarcely at all, the popularity of the portrait. Too often the subject of grotesque perversions at the hands of engravers reckless and indifferent to truth and character, it has conquered the world, spreading in every land the queerest notion of the type of English manhood.

This is not the occasion on which to enter any more closely than has here been done into the validity of the claims on public confidence of the Chandos portrait ; but the picture cannot be ignored, if only for the reason that the Chandos Shakespeare is undeniably the Shakespeare recognized by all men. It was even published in the form of engraving by the Shakespeare Society itself. The story that it belonged to D'Avenant (who, we are told, for the sake of his personal aggrandizement and self-conceit, claimed blood-kinship with his poet-godfather), has gone for much. The knowledge that Sir Godfrey Kneller made an impressive copy of it at the time when it was Betterton's, has gone for a good deal more. For it may well be assumed that Kneller, quintessence of vanity as he was, would scarcely have demeaned his genius, of which he entertained so fantastic an opinion, by copying a mere fanciful picture which, without authenticity to justify it, could but dishonour his brush. Nor presumably would Dryden have prized it as he did—prized it as Jonson loved Shakespeare, ' on this side idolatry ' —nor would he have apostrophized it with such an emphasis of rapture and admiration, had he known it for a copy of doubtful value. There is here, at least, sufficient evidence to show that not more than five-and-seventy years after Shakespeare's death the Chandos portrait was already held in high esteem and was respected as a record of presumably unchallenged truth.

The reproduction in this *Book of Homage* of Kneller's famous picture, now for the first time set before the public since it was painted

William Shakespeare
Head from Sir Godfrey Kneller's copy of the
Chandos Portrait painted for Dryden

two hundred and twenty-three years ago (in 1693), will certainly be welcomed as a matter of singular interest by all who unite to-day in offering tribute to Shakespeare's genius. To the owner of it, the Earl Fitzwilliam, who some years ago courteously permitted me to have the picture photographed, are due our thanks for the gratification with which the publication will be received.

The portrait is much larger than the Chandos ; it is, indeed, a full half-length. The head seems, by its undoubted nobility, to justify Dryden's paean of praise and veneration in that Fourteenth Epistle of 1694 with which he acknowledged and rewarded the painter's offering, in a masterpiece of super-flattery nicely adjusted to Kneller's vast powers of consumption. Who does not remember his lines ?—

> ' Shakespear, thy Gift, I place before my sight ;
> With awe, I ask his Blessing ere I write ;
> With Reverence look on his Majestick Face ;
> Proud to be less, tho' of his Godlike Race.
> His Soul Inspires me, while thy Praise I write,
> And I, like Teucer, under Ajax fight.'

The face, which so far departs from that of the Chandos portrait as to add a dignity, almost a majesty (as Dryden truly says), quite unknown to the parent-picture, is surely a conception not unworthy to represent the creator of the Plays and Poems. It is not surprising that it should have fired John Dryden's imagination, still less that it should appeal with equal force to ours, seeing that the painter has plainly sought to improve the forms and to modify the Latin character of the original, in the light of Droeshout's print.

It is true that the skull is not the skull figured by the Stratford bust and in the Folio print. Yet the forehead is now much more upright than in the Chandos picture, even though it is not yet perpendicular enough ; the high cheek-bones have been lowered and brought inwards, whereby the face is become narrower and the corresponding projection of the contour reduced ; the nose is thinner and less aquiline, and the nostrils more refined in modelling, so that the whole feature approximates far more to that in the print. On the other hand, the cheeks have been hollowed and the mouth straightened, while the falling moustache belies the usual mode affected by the Poet and thus defies the tradition of the three portraits which could have served for guidance. Kneller then asserts himself ; he imparts to the eyes a look of intelligence and elevated thought, and invests the whole with a general air of authority lamentably absent from the original. The result, in spite of all discrepancies, is a brave and skilful attempt, felicitously realized, the success made possible by consummate art, to render the Chandos portrait acceptable to the adherents of the more authoritative likeness of the Folio, and to conciliate, as well as art could do it, the objections of the critical. It is clearly a copy from this picture which Ranelagh Barret made for Edward Capell—the portrait which generations of men have seen in the Library of Trinity College, Cambridge, and have criticized for its heavy-handed divarications from the Chandos original.

Here, then, was expressed in the sincerest and most reverential manner possible to them, the homage paid severally by English Poetry and foreign Art of the seventeenth century to Shakespeare's memory in Shakespeare's person. In the spirit of the superlative admiration and esteem thus conveyed in Shakespeare's own century, we of the present, on the three hundredth anniversary of the day when the poet of all time lay down and slept, approach the altar of the world's gratitude and bring our offering of thanks and praise. We may muse upon his personality and picture to ourselves what manner of man was he in outward physical aspect. We can no longer hope to discover a new true portrait of him such as will confirm or correct the true authoritative likenesses we already have. With these we may rest content, for we recognize in their main indications the lineaments of the face which met the gaze of his own day, and the form of the massive head that gave lodging to the sovereign brain, mightiest in powers of humanity and art, that has enriched and ennobled the modern world.

M. H. SPIELMANN.

THE RIDDLE

W. S. 1564–1616

WHAT like wert thou, O Riddle of our race,
  Whose steadfast eye the mind of man could see,
And, by excess of intuition, trace
  In the rude germ its full maturity?

Thou, ' of imagination all compact ',
  Alone among thy fellows, could'st ally
The thought and word, the impulse and the act,
  Cause and effect, unerringly. But why?

Who shall make answer?   To our ken a shade,
  Thou—for whom souls lay open—art as dark
As shapeless phantoms of the night that fade
  With daybreak and the singing of the lark.

Men may explore thy Secret still, yet thou,
  Serene, unsearchable, above them all,
Look'st down, as from some lofty mountain-brow,
  And art thyself thine own Memorial.

AUSTIN DOBSON.

A DREAM OF PARNASSUS

Fresh from letters of Shakespearian friends, and sadly wondering how in this War of Nations our immortal Poet would come to his meed of honour, after three hundred years of mission over the globe, I chanced to raise my eyes to my library wall, whereon there hangs the Arundel copy of Raphael's fresco of Parnassus in the Stanza of the Vatican. There Apollo with his lyre holds a conclave of the Muses, round whom are gathered the poets of all ages, whilst blind old Homer chants the Wrath of Achilles and the Burial of Hector, his brother Bards standing wrapt in admiration and awe.

So musing and wandering in thought, I fell asleep in my easy chair and dreamed. And this was my Dream.

THE DREAM

THE Muse Melpomene, with a crown of vine-leaves holding a tragic mask, seemed enthroned on the sacred Mount of Inspiration. Beside her was Thaleia, having a comic mask and a wreath of ivy : both presided at the altar on which I saw a tripod of gold inscribed τῷ ὑψίστῳ.

Around and below the Muses was gathered a throng, whose noble countenances seemed to be those of familiar friends, and their stately robes denoted various races, manners, and ages. All seemed to be leading towards the altar, that he might receive the tripod, one whom I recognized at once by his lofty forehead, trim beard, flowing locks, and his air of serene thought. He seemed to shrink from their attentions, bewildered almost by their praises, as one hardly worthy of such a prize.

The Muse with a gesture was inviting those around her to express their suffrages in order that by general consent she might award the honour to the most fit. She pointed first to a noble old man with bald head and venerable beard, deep sad eyes, and the shrunken limbs of a mighty veteran in arms. The aged warrior stood forth, and I heard his solemn voice that rang through the assembly as if he had been Isaiah the son of Amoz calling out to the people of Zion.

'Fair Goddess,' he said, ' the golden tripod is his of right, in these latter days of wildly-whirring poesy. The old order changeth. In very truth and no longer in fable, the whole earth reels and quakes. In old times a tragedy was an act of public worship. We gave the people Hymns of Valour and Psalms of contrition for sin. But the ancient Gods and Heroes of seven-foot stature whom we knew are no more. To-day the new generations have thoughts and pleasures, knowledge and interests, that we old soldiers could not share and are ready to cast aside. I have learnt that ours was but a petty corner of the earth : our fears, our hopes, our joys, our loves never roamed over the vast world they tell me is now open to men—a world of which I had but some dim vision, but enough to revolt my very soul. I am too old to learn this new way. I had no heart to mingle Beauty and Mirth with the catastrophes of Fate and the agonies of the Soul which swept through my brain. Let me go back to my lonely seat, where I rest musing on the glories and the faith of Hellas. The prizes of life are for those who are happy and who are young.'

Then there stepped up to him the most beautiful and the most graceful of elders, having the sweetest voice ever uttered by man.

'We too ', he said, ' yield willingly the prize of tragedy to this youth. Our ancient world is past. We love to recall how beautiful it was. We hope they now enjoy a world as beautiful and as sunlit as was our rare City of the violet crown. As our glorious Chief has said, we who lived to celebrate our radiant Athene could ill bear the tumultuous trumpetings, of which we catch faint echoes in our Islands of the Blessed. If we ever sought to touch the deepest nerves of sympathetic hearts by tales of agony and guilt, we would ever relieve the tension at intervals with soft melodies and ethereal raptures. We are told now of generations of men built of sterner mould, who have no need of the rest given by choral visions of pure delight. They say they have other kinds of rest and of relief ; nor do they mind if Pindaric rhapsodies are thrust into the midst of hot action and visible horrors. To us Beauty, Dignity, and Grace were Divine gifts too precious to be forborne for an hour, even in the midst of the most tragic *peripeteia*. Let us trust these will never be forgotten in the multitudinous blare of Modern Art.'

'Why !' called out aloud a nobly bearded Chief who thrust himself boldly before the elder pair, ' Did I not tell you that the " grand air " and obsolete sublimities would weary any public really up-to-date ?

I was myself a prophet of "modernity", of the "new woman", of the "real man". That youth from the Island of the West only followed my lead of realism and of romance. I vote for him, for he quite freed the world of your Marathonian conventions and superstitious mysteries.'

'Ah! my old anarchist friend,' cried out a jovial reveller who had been making mouths at the last speaker behind a comic mask, 'Yes! you opened new ways indeed ; but you have yet to prove that it was opened in the right way. To make the Gods chop logic and to turn heroes into street beggars would vulgarize, not modernize, Art. I too vote for the young one, who still seems unaware how close he is to some old friends. His virago Queen might kill her Sovereign but not her own babies, nor did she mount up off the stage to heaven in a dragon car. And when he brought on a veteran King in rags, the poor old man was not a disguised Hero but stark mad, and yet withal he felt himself to be— and he looked it—every inch a King. There was nothing sordid in his rags.

'Again, gracious Ladies, let me add that our friend here wears his comic wreath just as well as his tragic wreath. None of us old fellows ever pretended to wear both. He alone has mingled both : he made Mirth and Terror—Fantasy and Reality—join in one irresistible dance of glorious life. I never tried my hand at Terror or Pity, just as old Marathon there never touched the lyre of Mirth or the scourge of Satire. Our candidate for the supreme prize joined Awe and Loveliness, Mirth and Horror, Fun and Fantasy ; making both embrace to the begetting of a radiant progeny of immortal sons and daughters that shall outlive Time. Him, O ye divine mistresses of the Mount of Inspiration, O ye bards of fame and name—him I proclaim to be in truth— ὕψιστος.'

'Euge! Optime!'—called out an Imperial Roman in his toga marked with a broad purple band, looking for all the world like a Nero in melodrama ; 'surely, the gentle youth only adopted and developed my scheme of Art. They often tell me that I was too fond of violence, of blood, of stage surprises ; that I relied too much on oratory, machinery, and ghosts. Ah! sweet Goddesses of a gentler race, you, I trust, never saw a Roman tribunal nor an amphitheatre, nor ever heard a Roman mob yell over a hecatomb of gladiators. I only gave them what they loved. Our young friend's "general" public would have blood too—enjoyed a stage heaped with corpses, and I dare say forced him to show them tortures, monsters, and ghosts enough. He had to do what I did to please them rather than myself. And he used, as so many other later poets did, not a few of the inventions they all borrowed from me.'

Now here I noticed a group of poets standing together and quite apart, whose elaborate costumes and air of superior refinement seemed to mark them out as masters of some special culture. Two of them had a mien of almost religious solemnity, whilst two others seemed to beam with keen wit and native humour. With the measured cadences of a speech of subtle modulation and an air of studious courtesy, the younger of the foremost pair stood forth and spoke thus.

'Our humble obeisance to the August Ladies who so graciously preside over us to-day ! In our time we sought to maintain in all things the superb manner of the Grand Monarch we served and of the elegant society whose favour we enjoyed. Even in the hour of deepest passion, we felt that *deportment* must not be forgotten. High Art means tone, a harmony of colour, just balance of values, imperturbable self-restraint. We hear that in the new age these essentials have been too little prized. Alas ! we know that our ancient dynasty is no more. Republicans and heretics have it all their own way. A new world, they cry, demands a new Art. Be it so ! We shall not dispute their claim. Culture has its own world still : and there it has more crowns than it can wear with grace and ease in an age of tumult and change.'

'There is no need to retire,' called out a rasping voice behind the last speaker, and I saw one thrust himself forward, one whose curled wig, lace frill and ruffles, eye of hawk and biting lips seem the embodiment of an entire age. 'The ancients can never be dethroned,' he cried; 'good manners, sense, truth, realities can never be displaced by extravagance, brutalities, and the ravings of genius run mad.'

Then I saw the last speaker roughly pulled back by a passionate orator with the voice of a sea-captain on his quarter-deck in a gale. He shouted out : 'Romance, Nature, Passion rule this age : the fetters of old times are broken : Democracy has triumphed : and the life of democrats is cast in a world of variety, tumult, and spasm. All hail to our immortal master, who shows us humanity freed from the bonds of antique superstition !'

I saw too a venerable poet in a Spanish cloak of the Renascence, whose towering front, pointed beard, and flowing locks might recall to us our own poet had he lived to reach some eighty years. He stood apart, spoke low, but he beamed a look of agreement and welcome. When appealed to by others for his vote, he said simply : 'I too accept your verdict, though I belong to a different world of thought, of manners,

C

and of faith. Those whom I knew, they who knew me, had ways of their own, their own ideals to worship, their own honour to guard. It was to glorify these that I laboured. There is room for us all, if each of us in truth holds fast to himself, his people, and his saints.'

Little too was said by another whose Roman features I could not forget, having seen them carved in marble on his tomb in Santa Croce. ' The world has passed on far beyond me and the heroes and demigods with whom I held converse in spirit. Republican as I am by my reason, I stand fast by all that is heroic, noble, and proud. There is no field for us of the Old Guard now. We leave to you the field of the new world of which we know so little, to whose favours we so rarely aspire.' And he wrapped around his noble head the martial cloak he wore, and he withdrew as if he had been Julius as he fell at the base of the Statue of Pompeius.

And now the Muse, beaming on our poet, seemed to be inviting him to come forward to receive the prize, so clearly awarded by the general voice of his brother bards. Then there stepped forth a truly magnificent personage, whose grand countenance might serve for the Olympian Zeus of Pheidias, albeit he wore the civilian dress of a modern Teuton.

' Gracious Ladies and brother Spirits,' he said, ' our friend here is still so much overcome by the welcome he has received that he shrinks from attempting to express his thanks in person, and he begs me to speak in his name. As we two sate apart communing together on the boundless range of our Art, he assures me that he was hardly conscious of intending all the profound ideas that his friends of the later times have discovered for him. He vows that he never put himself personally to his audience at all, and yet they now try to make him out a dozen different men rolled into one. He says that he never enjoyed such training, nor pretended to such learning, as have those who have spoken in his honour. His life had given him little leisure for study, nor was he free to work out in ease all his thoughts, as he would have desired. He was a servant of his Sovereign, a humble member of a working guild, and the simple minister to the enjoyments of the gallants and good fellows of his time. How many a page, he almost moaned out to me in our private talks, he would have torn up, blotted out, or re-written, if he ever had any sort of idea that his too hurried words would be remembered by any but those who first heard them in public. Once or twice in his life, he says, he did deliberately revise and publish to the world some pieces of his work to which his whole soul was given. Too often, he now learns, his compositions have been impudently plundered, grossly misread, and carelessly printed. His short life has been one of storm and stress, of jollity and good fellowship, of lightning work to meet peremptory calls which his official duties would not suffer him to neglect. Too often, he assures me, his name had been used to cover that which was none of his. So conscious is he of this, and that even some of his own was far from his best, that he wishes me to speak in his name.

'Let me add one word more. All of those who have spoken to-day lived long lives of ease and devotion to their art : all but one of them lived to an honoured old age. Such was not the lot of our friend, who ended his bodily life, after years of trouble and of labour, much earlier than they. And when he gave up his daily task of supplying incessant new matter for his colleagues, and had withdrawn in the maturity of his powers to his native town, where he might recast all that he cared to leave to the future—then by a sudden stroke he came to an unexpected end. It was for this reason that his work has needed such generations of interpreters and commentators—of which my own countrymen, we are proud to believe, have been the most generous and the most industrious. We all hail him—but for the negligible accident of his birth—to be one of our own most cherished glories.'

'Sir !' called out a burly figure in a short wig, surrounded by a group of admiring friends—and the big man spoke with the voice of one who never suffered contradiction—'Sir ! you are quite right to admit that our poet was not always at his best vein, and did sometimes forget common-sense, nature, and plain speech. We have quite cleared up these occasional slips at home, whilst our foreign friends have made mountains out of molehills. And as to the " accident of birth ",' he said to a short man, with a singularly speaking countenance, whose arm he held, ' why ! Davy, we of the West Midlands think it no " accident " at all. Sir ! it is the hub of this world, and our man is its King.'

Here I noticed a somewhat hectic youth with a big head and a shock of red hair, call out in a thin shrill voice—' No ! I will not allow a word of his to be wrong. It was all so sublime, ineffable, ecstatic !' But his passionate utterance was lost in the tide of applause from the throng that pressed on behind him. They came on in their thousands, bearing the standards of their nations. I could see the Tricolour in many bands and of many colours, some upright, some crosswise, the Stars and

Stripes, Black Eagles, Lions, Strange Beasts—even the Dragon and the Chrysanthemum flag. Long serried ranks of the Poets of all ages, races, and speech, poured on in troops that seemed unending. All by voice and gesture invited the Muse to confer on him the Golden Tripod.

But here my Dream ended—as Dreams do end—just as the great award was about to be made.

FREDERIC HARRISON.

ENGLAND'S POET

To other voices, other majesties,
Removed this while, Peace shall resort again.
But he was with us in our darkest pain
And stormiest hour : his faith royally dyes
The colours of our cause ; his voice replies
To all our doubt, dear spirit ! heart and vein
Of England's old adventure ! his proud strain
Rose from our earth to the sea-breathing skies.

Even over chaos and the murdering roar
Comes that world-winning music, whose full stops
Sounded all man, the bestial and divine ;
Terrible as thunder, fresh as April drops !
He stands, he speaks, the soul-transfigured sign
Of all our story, on the English shore.

LAURENCE BINYON.

SOME STRAY THOUGHTS

As the editor of this volume tells me it is desired to include in it stray thoughts jotted down without the formality of an essay, even if they do no more than suggest some points or lines of thought on which readers may agree with or differ from the writer, I have put down a few such points. One of them has often been noted, but it may be noted again, because it comes more and more back to whoever, in reading other great poets, cannot help comparing them to Shakespeare. He is the one among them all who least bears the imprint of a particular time or a particular local environment. Many critics have proved to their own satisfaction that he could only have been an Englishman of the sixteenth century. Heinrich Heine's famous dictum notwithstanding, we can all bring plenty of arguments to show that Shakespeare's genius was an English genius, in the legitimate line of English poetical development, with Chaucer before him, with Milton and Dryden and many another after him, however much he surpassed them all. Nevertheless, the fact remains that we can quite well think of him as detached from any age or country in a sense in which we cannot so think of Dante or Ariosto, Milton or Molière or Goethe. And with this goes the fact that there is no great writer whose personal character and tastes and likings we can so little determine from his writings. We cannot even tell whether he had any, and what, political opinions. There is nothing to indicate, or even to furnish material for conjecturing, what religious doctrines he held—a thing more remarkable in his time than it would be in ours. Many ingenious attempts have been made to fix upon particular passages as conveying views that were distinctively his own, but when all is said and done how little positive result remains. We do not even know what places he had visited nor what he had read, nor what poets had influenced him. He knew some Latin, but in the Roman plays there is no trace of Virgil or Lucan. There is but little trace in *Troilus and Cressida* of Homer, except in the character of Thersites, probably inspired by Chapman's translation of the *Iliad*.

The story is of course post-classical, but the action is laid in Troy. Was he ever at Dover, where men gathered samphire on the cliffs? Had he ever seen the misty mountain tops at dawn? The Malvern hills, not visible from Stratford, were the nearest hills one could call mountains, though by no means lofty. (So one may ask whether Bunyan's Delectable Mountains in the *Pilgrim's Progress* were the chalk downs of Bedfordshire.) Or did his imagination vivify what he had heard of as readily as what he had seen? His mind seems to mirror everything alike, as the surface of his gently flowing Avon mirrors whirling clouds and blue sky, the noonday rays and the dying glow of sunset.

This detachment, this habit of presenting all types of character, all phases of life and forms of passion, with the same impartial insight, may perhaps be said to belong to every great dramatist. It is the dramatist's business. Molière is an example. Yet each of the other great dramatists has provided us with better data for guessing at what he was himself than Shakespeare has done. In him the intellect is strikingly individual in its way of thinking and its way of expressing thought, but it is all developed from within, having caught up very little from time or place, and it seems somehow distinct from the man, as others saw him moving about in the daily life of London or Warwickshire. We recognize now and then in other poets something that we call Shakespearian because it reminds us of Shakespeare's peculiar forms of expression. But this distinctive quality in his thought and style, marked though it is, does not reveal the man; perhaps not even in the Sonnets, which seem, if one may venture an opinion on so controversial a subject, to be rather dramatic than personal.

Dante has an amazing range of thought and power of making his characters live, but how intensely personal he is! So also—not to speak of men like Horace or Pope, who weave themselves into the texture of their verse—so is Lucretius, so are Petrarch, Milton, Wordsworth, Goethe, Shelley, Byron, Leopardi, and in less measure Pindar and Virgil. We feel as if we could get near them and imagine them as they were in life. Of all the great imaginative works, those which are likest to Shakespeare's in this impersonality of the author, this supreme gift of seeing all phases of life and presenting them all with the same fidelity to the infinite variety of nature, are the Homeric poems and especially the *Iliad*. (Think of Nestor and Achilles, Priam and Andromache.) There is in those poems something of what one may call (if the apparent contradiction be permissible) the sympathetic aloofness of Shakespeare. His aloofness is neither cold nor cynical: it is the detachment needed for an observation which sees calmly, and therefore can mete out equal justice to all that it sees.

One is tempted to connect with this detached attitude in Shakespeare his apparent indifference to fame. A poet's want of interest in the fate of his own work is so rare that it might lead us to fancy that he did not know how good that work was. (Read and consider what Robert Browning says about him in *Bishop Blougram's Apology*.) Is there any parallel in the great masters of literature to this indifference? Can it be explained by the spontaneity and seeming absence of effort with which he composed, as if this made him feel that there could be nothing wonderful in what came to him so easily? Did he enjoy the process of creation so much as not to care what happened to the product when the process was over? Or are we to think that that sense of the insignificance and transitoriness of all human things, which is every now and then discerned as an undercurrent of his thought, extended itself to his own work? When the time came when he had no longer occasion to write, did he, like Prospero, break his wand, with no sigh of regret?

We shall never exhaust the Shakespearian problems. A time may come when scholars will be much more nearly agreed than they are now as to which of the plays, or which parts of the doubtful plays, are really from his hand, just as scholars are more agreed now than they were seventy years ago as to the date and authorship of most of the books of the New Testament. But the questions we ask about the relation of the genius to the man will remain, and may be no nearer solution when the next centenary arrives.

BRYCE.

SHAKESPEARE

THERE are few, probably, who have not derived from Shakespeare's writings at least some part of the inspiration of their lives, and have not found in his wise words practical encouragement in times of difficulty and distress. In these anxious days, when the whole power of England and its Allies is engaged in the defence of liberty and justice, no words of any modern writer could light the fires of national pride and devotion as do Shakespeare's lofty expressions of patriotism and affection for his country,—

> This royal throne of kings, this sceptred isle.

The thought of the great and ever-watchful fleet, to which we owe to-day so much, recalls the lines,—

> O, do but think,
> You stand upon the rivage, and behold
> A city on the inconstant billows dancing,
> For so appears this fleet majestical.

Whilst to those who are able and yet hesitate to take up the burden of the struggle the poet seems to say,—

> Who is he, whose chin is but enriched
> With one appearing hair, that will not follow
> Those call'd and choice-drawn cavaliers to France?

But probably it is the personal debt that we owe to the inspiring words of the ' immortal bard ' that draws us to him and demands our individual homage. Speaking for myself, I confess that I owe to the penetrating fire of his verse more than I can say. I was fortunate enough in my early days to have my lot cast in a school where by long tradition a play of Shakespeare was acted each year, and I well remember the effect of the atmosphere we breathed during the weeks of preparation, when the rhythm of the Poet's incomparable language was always ringing in our ears. Alas !—at least in my opinion—modern requirements have caused this annual feast of Shakespearian poetry to be discontinued, and in its place is possibly substituted some play, studied like the classic of a past age.

In reality Shakespeare should never be regarded as the poet of past times. His position in the world of letters is similar to that of Dante. What must strike any observer who lives in Italy is the influence exerted by the latter over the people, even in these days. His verses seem to come to their lips on every occasion as the truest expression of their inmost feelings. It should be the same with us in regard to Shakespeare, for his words aptly give form to almost every lofty thought, even in our days. Why this is so is clear. His poems do not merely express the peculiar sentiments of the age in which they were written ; nor describe only characters with which we are no longer familiar. They are for every age : and for this reason, because they represent nature as it is at all times. 'Nothing', wrote Dr. Johnson, 'can please many, and please long, but just representations of general nature.' And in applying this truth to Shakespeare he says that he ' is above all writers, at least above all modern writers, the poet of nature ; the poet that holds up to his readers a faithful mirror of manners and of life. His characters are not modified by the customs of particular places, unpractised by the rest of the world. . . . They are the genuine progeny of common humanity, such as the world will always supply, and observation will always find. His persons act and speak by the influence of those general passions and principles by which all minds are agitated and the whole system of life is continued in motion. In the writings of other poets a character is too often an individual ; in those of Shakespeare, it is commonly a species.'

This explains the attraction which the immortal works of our great national poet has for us to-day, and it is the fundamental reason for the willing homage we pay to his genius.

My special admiration for his plays and poems is based, too, on other considerations. I am astonished at the accurate knowledge he displays of the moral teachings and doctrines of the Church. His ethics are irreproachable. Conscience, according to Shakespeare's philosophy, is man's supreme guide ; God's law should be the rule of his life. Man's free will, strengthened by prayer and God's grace, can master his lower nature and enable him to rise to better things and gain for him an ever-lasting reward. His whole conception of the dignity and position of man is lofty and true. Indeed, one of the most beautiful and accurate expressions of the Christian life to be found in any lay writer occurs in Sonnet CXLVI.

To Shakespeare man's nature is complex. If his soul can reach into the unseen world, his body is but of the earth and has appetites in common with the beasts. How clearly, for example, *Hamlet* puts this teaching : ' What a piece of work is a man ! How noble in reason ! how infinite in faculty ! in form, in moving, how express and admirable ! in action how like an angel ! in apprehension how like a god ! the beauty of the world ! the paragon of animals ! '

Or again : how clearly the poet states his belief in the existence of the immortal soul that man holds from God, and in the responsibility he incurs on this account :

> What is man,
> If his chief good and market of his time
> Be but to sleep and feed ? a beast, no more.

Then as to morality in general : however coarse the poet may appear to us at times, in words, jests, or insinuations, according to the manner of his age, no professed moralist could be more severe on vice than he shows himself in his poetry. To him God is no mere abstract force or principle, but the Almighty Creator of all things, who has a personal care of all who have come from His hands. He is the ' high all-seer ' and has countless eyes to view men's acts. He is omniscient ; knows when we are falsely accused ; never slumbers nor sleeps ; reads the hearts of men, and in Heaven ' sits a Judge, that no king can corrupt '. He is our Father, cares for the aged, feeds the ravens and caters for the sparrow. He is the widow's ' champion and defence ' ; is the ' upright, just, and true disposing God ' ; is the one supreme appeal—' God above deal between thee and me '. He is the guardian of the night, ' when the searching eye of heaven is hid ', &c. He

> To believing souls
> Gives light in darkness, comfort in despair.

Mercy is His attribute : ' 'Tis mightiest in the mightiest ', and His mercy constrains us to be merciful to our brethren. All human duties and obligations are founded on our duty to Him. Kings and all in authority are His deputies and ministers. Man and wife are united in Him, and therefore marriage is indissoluble. This great God, too, is the Lord of armies.

> O ! thou, whose captain I account myself,
> Look on my forces with a gracious eye ;
> Put in their hands thy bruising irons of wrath,
> That they may crush down with a heavy fall

The usurping helmets of our adversaries.
Make us thy ministers of chastisement,
That we may praise thee in thy victory!
To thee I do commend my watchful soul,
Ere I let fall the windows of mine eyes;
Sleeping and waking! O defend me still!

Instances might be multiplied almost indefinitely of the true, solid teaching on Christian faith and morals which is to be found in Shakespeare's plays and poems. If only for this reason I gladly bow in homage to him for his imperishable work.

But my admiration and reverence for his name are strengthened by his very reticence, for what he might have said under the peculiar circumstances of the times in which he lived and did not say. In the 'spacious days' of Queen Elizabeth, and at the beginning of the seventeenth century, the clergy as a class, with the monks and nuns of the old religion, were not popular. The friar, the monk, and the priest were at this time considered to be fair game for the coarse jest and ribald witticism of poet and playwright. To attack their fair name would have been to tickle the ears of the crowd. Yet we may search the plays of Shakespeare through and through, and not find any such trait. On the contrary, the liberality of his treatment of the clergy is apparent everywhere, and even his sympathy is evidenced in more than one instance. A striking example of this is to be seen in his play of *King John*, not so much by what he wrote as by what he omitted to write. It is certain that in this play he revised the old play of *The Troublesome Reign of King John*, which contains a ribald scene describing the ransacking of an abbey. Shakespeare deliberately omitted this scene in re-casting the play. That it must have been deliberate we can hardly doubt, since he makes few such omissions. Here, then, the poet had an opportunity of appealing to the coarse tastes of his age and of ingratiating himself with all who desired to blacken the reputations of those who belonged to the 'old order', and refused to take it. We can see in the works of some of his contemporaries, such as Greene in his *Friar Bacon*, or Marlowe in his *Jew of Malta*, what excellent capital for popularity he set aside as unworthy of his muse.

In the same way, in dealing with English history, it is remarkable that he left on one side subjects which might have purchased popularity. The overthrow of the Papal authority, as it was treated in the anonymous play of *The Troublesome Reign of King John*, or in *The Faerie Queene*; the gunpowder plot, as used by Ben Jonson in his *Catiline*; the destruction of the Armada, as treated by Dekker; the glorification of Elizabeth, as added by Fletcher to *Henry VIII*, were all subjects which would certainly lend themselves to catching the popular sentiment, and which we can have no doubt were of set purpose left on one side by Shakespeare. This deliberate silence, therefore, and this refusal to bid for popularity by joining in the chorus of defamation of the past so freely indulged in by other writers of his day, in my opinion raises Shakespeare to a pedestal high above, not merely his contemporaries, but above even such illustrious men as Spenser and Milton. If we grant that it was aesthetics and high art rather than ethics which counselled him to take this course, even this does not detract from the largeness of mind which preserved him from the temptation to pander to the prejudices of the time.

For this reason, too, I honour and reverence the memory of this great poet, and am pleased to respond to this call for homage.

F. A. CARD. GASQUET.

ROME,
PALAZZO DI S. CALISTO
IN TRASTEVERE.

FOR APRIL 23RD

1616–1916

ONE thing to-day
For England let us pray—
That, when this bitterness of blood is spent,
Out of the darkness of the discontent
Perplexing man with man, poor pride with pride,
Shall come to her, and loverly abide,
Sure knowledge that these lamentable days
Were given to death and the bewildered praise
Of dear young limbs and eager eyes forestilled,
That in her home, where Shakespeare's passion grew
From song to song, should thrive the happy-willed
Free life that Shakespeare drew.

JOHN DRINKWATER.

BIRMINGHAM.

THE CATHOLIC STRAIN IN SHAKESPEARE

'To one that knew nothing of Christian beliefs', said Lafcadio Hearn, 'the plays of Shakespeare must remain incomprehensible.' For religion lays bare the heart of a nation, even as it shapes its law and custom. Carlyle has anticipated the interpreter of Japan. 'In some sense', he allows, 'this glorious Elizabethan era with its Shakespeare, as the outcome and flowerage of all which had preceded it, is itself attributable to the Catholicism of the Middle Ages. The Christian Faith, which was the theme of Dante's song, had produced this Practical Life which Shakespeare was to sing.' Hence the supreme poet could never be a Puritan. The question is not so much personal to the man of Stratford-on-Avon, whether he conformed to the Church by law established or stood out as a recusant. We pay homage to something larger and deeper than the individual who has become its mouthpiece during all future days ; we recognize the genius, rightly so termed, that sums up and for ever crystallizes an otherwise extinct world by means of him. Therefore, to quote Carlyle once more, he is 'the noblest product' of Catholicism ; but, I hasten to add, he appears amid the splendours kindled by a new morning, by the Renaissance, of a literature no longer mediaeval. There is, then, a Catholic strain in Shakespeare, crossing and entangling the modern, with remarkable consequences.

Elizabethan drama rose out of the mystery and morality plays of which the origin must be sought in the Roman Mass. Their aim was distinctly religious, while Scripture and the legends of the Saints furnished their matter. Shakespeare, taking a wider scope and setting history on the stage, did, nevertheless, contrive in *Macbeth* an instance of the 'morality' made perfect ; for, with a depth and directness never surpassed, it reveals the law of conscience avenging itself on guilt by an inward working. The witches and their shows are but a phantasm ;

the chief agent of doom is the sinner, sicklied or driven mad under stress of self-accusation. *Richard III*, not so profound, discovers conscience in the persons and events that visibly at last bear down on the culprit and smite him before battle. So far, the colouring is Christian rather than simply Catholic. But what I may term the atmosphere of *Romeo and Juliet*, of the *Merchant of Venice*, and the Comedies, their warmth, ease, and grace of movement, so unmistakably Italian, would vanish away if we took from them the religious background; and this must be mediaeval, since it was neither Pagan nor Puritan. Not many years later its glow was gone. If we reflect upon the secret of living art, which is as little antiquarian as it is prophetic afar off, we shall feel that the Catholic past in England, its continuation in Italy, afforded just the perspective in time and space that Shakespeare needed to hold the mirror up to nature. Even his Roman plays strike home by virtue of this ever fresh quality. It comes out in *Henry VIII*, if we grant that Shakespeare is the author of Queen Katharine's speeches; to my mind, *A Winter's Tale*, *As You Like It*, and *Twelfth Night*, bear each a character derived from long Catholic usage now passing into Renaissance forms. Henry V is a crusader in spirit; in *Henry VI*, spiteful as it is against Joan of Arc, we light upon the prophecy, now fulfilled, that the Maid shall take the place of St. Denis and inspire the armies of France. In *King John*, which reads fiercely anti-Papal, the poet has omitted from his revised copy a scene that dishonoured monasticism. He chants, too, with a pathos not untouched by reminiscence of its fall, the 'bare ruined choirs, where late the sweet birds sang'. His Friar Lawrence lingers in our thoughts of Verona's lovers, as a purely human, even all too human, figure. But the grandest of his Catholic creations lives in *Measure for Measure*. The 'votarist of Saint Clare', Isabella, remains 'a thing enskied and sainted' among the heavy shadows of vice, hypocrisy, or scepticism, hanging over this difficult drama. Was her name a family tradition? Isabella Shakespeare, to whom the Stratford house claimed kinship, had once been Prioress of the Benedictine cloister at Wroxall. *Measure for Measure*, as a story of the 'Virgin-Martyr', is painfully impressive by its insistence on law which cannot be broken. Its theme, from the earliest ages familiar to Catholic ears, holds in it a transcendent Puritanism.

I was once asked whether in Shakespeare's plays any reference could be found in praise of the Madonna, our Lady St. Mary. There is one, I think, in *All's Well that Ends Well*, which Dante himself

might have signed. The Countess, grieving over Bertram, her wayward **son, cries out,**

> What angel shall
> Bless this unworthy husband? He cannot thrive,
> Unless *her* prayers, whom Heaven delights to hear,
> And loves to grant, reprieve him from the wrath
> Of greatest justice.—Act III, Sc. iv.

None but the Queen of Angels, as the Litany of Loreto invokes her, can be thought of under such high language as able by prayer to 'reprieve' a sinful soul. Surely it is not Helena, though a pilgrim to St. James of Compostella, whom these words fit. Or, if so, they are significant of a loftier faith where the full scope and grandeur of them had been long acclaimed by Christendom. But other lines bearing the mystic seal occur to me; as, for instance, when we read in *Macbeth* of 'the Lord's anointed temple', and how sacrilege has stolen thence 'the life of the building'. Catholic dogma will turn imagery like this to its profit, to the hidden life of Christ in the tabernacle, and to the sanctuaries which were violated in a day of rebuke and blasphemy. It does not follow that Shakespeare had these outrages in mind, but they darkened the history of a time only just gone by. Like Virgilian currents of suggestion, the pensive sayings in which our dramatist abounds bear us to many shores. At length we come with Shakespeare into the open sea where all the winds are struggling; we reach the incoherence of Hamlet and Lear's pessimism, on which from Prospero's fairy island the pale sunshine falls as in a dream.

The 'incoherence of Hamlet' is the play itself. No Puritan halfway house can be seen anywhere; but the Catholic faith in Purgatory, penance, sacraments, judgement, is here at death-grips with a sceptical doubt, the very heart of the prince who knows not how to flee from his own question. It is Kant's *Dream of a Ghost-seer*, flung into drama with unheard-of magnificence and equal melancholy ages before the philosopher, but a forecast which was beginning to be realized even while Shakespeare wrote. Faith has become a point of interrogation; nothing stands sure; love and life take us in if we trust them; and 'the rest is silence'. Acute critics have detected in what I will call the pessimist dramas, *Hamlet, Measure for Measure, Othello, Lear*, and even *The Tempest*, an influence which they charge to Montaigne, the French 'captain of the band'. It may be thus; but 'der Geist, der stets verneint', the Everlasting No, walked about London streets, when he was not haunting a Gascon squire at home. The fall of a universal

D

religion in many lands must have brought forth a doubt such as attends on earthquake. Europe has been asking of its wisest ever since, ' Canst thou minister to a mind diseased ? ' Hamlet is ' Everyman '. And King Lear outdoes the meditative Dane, with his frenzied shriek, the last word of anarchism :

> As flies to wanton boys are we to the gods,
> They kill us for their sport.

But I will make my bow to Prospero, sometime Duke of Milan, Catholic and Italian, a beautiful old man, magician and father of Miranda, whom I have known since I was a lad of six, and now I revere him as the master of dreams which the crowd calls science, but I glimpses of God's angels moving the wide universe. Hamlet will not always be incoherent. The all-embracing Catholic Faith, out from whence our Shakespeare came, looks upon him as its child of genius, with starry eyes and a heart deep as man's deepest sorrow—which is not to have found his God. He will find, for he has suffered. And, by the miracle that yet is to be wrought, Hamlet's incoherence will turn in that day to the ' marriage of true minds ', when Faith weds with Life, and Love with Knowledge.

WILLIAM BARRY.

ST. PETER'S, LEAMINGTON.

HEROINES

THOUGHTS about Shakespeare cannot pretend to be new. Therefore it is enough that the thoughts of us all should be practised rather than spoken. It might, for example, be insolent for any man to say that Shakespeare is a magnificent humourist for every age, yet to the thinking of our age a very tedious wit; but the man who would not venture to say this aloud knows his *Second Part of Henry IV*, for its humour, through and through, and has not read *Love's Labour's Lost*, for its wit, more than perhaps once. We all know Shakespeare as it were privately, and thus a demand for words about him touches our autobiography. What we think about Shakespeare is part of the public's privacy as well as of our own. For we are all more than content to be like Poins, to whom Prince Henry says, ' Thou art a blessed fellow to think as every man thinks; never a man's thought keeps in the roadway better than thine.' We are safe in the middle of the roadway in our thoughts of Shakespeare. Very few men have tried to be original in regard to Shakespeare, and their dreary experiment had best be forgotten. It will probably not be imitated. Shakespeare's greater readers have done no more than multiply one affection, one praise. Ruskin and Emerson are only more articulate than the rest of their respective nations. It is true that Ruskin seemed to make a kind of discovery when he showed this fact in the dramas—that Shakespeare has no heroes, but only heroines. The ' discovery' only *seems*; Ruskin states the matter, but every simple reader knows that Juliet was steadfast and wise in stratagem and Romeo rash, Juliet single-hearted and Romeo changeable; that Imogen was true and that Posthumus Leonatus was by her magnanimity awarded a kind of triumph when all he should have hoped from her mercy was pardon; that Hermione forgives her lord his suspicion, and the theft of her child, and sixteen years of innocent exile, without a word of forgiveness. Every reader knows the indomitable will of Helena, who condescends to pursue and win a paltry boy, and sweetly thinks herself rewarded by the possession of that poor quarry ; the lovely simplicity of Desdemona, which lies as that of a frightened child lies, to save herself from the violence of the noble savage whom she loves ; the inarticulate and modest devotion of Virgilia to a great man not too great for insane self-love ; Cordelia's integrity and self-possession among raving men ; Isabella's courage in face of a coward brother ; Viola's valour and her single love in search of the *contre-coup* of her Duke's affections ; Julia, true to a juggling lover ; Queen Katharine betrayed by a hypocrite ; nay, the maid called Barbara who was forsaken. Barbara, Desdemona, Juliet, Imogen, Virgilia, Miranda, Viola, Hermione, Perdita, Julia, Helena, the other Helena, Mariana, Rosalind, were all enamoured, all impassioned, and all constant.

Why did Shakespeare make heroines and not heroes ? It was assuredly because Shakespeare had a master passion for chastity, and because this quality was most credible, in a world not governed by theology, there where he attributed it, lodged it, and adored it—in this *candidatus exercitus* of women.

There is one thing that additionally and adventitiously proves this passion of Shakespeare's spirit, and that is his abstention from the brilliancy and beauty wherewith he knows how to invest the wanton : his vitality in Cressida, his incomparable splendour in Cleopatra. Yet stay—is not Cressida alone in inconstancy ? and is it not a senseless action to name Cressida in Cleopatra's glorious company ? Shakespeare, able to make unparalleled Cressidas, made only one. Cleopatra is clean, not by water but by her 'integrity of fire'. She too is constant, she too is 'for the dark', for eternity. She entrusts her passion to another world. Let her stand close to the majestic side of Hermione, even though Hermione might not permit Perdita to kiss her.

Does this recognition of Shakespeare's master passion look like the claim to a discovery ? Heaven forbid, for it should not.

ALICE MEYNELL.

THE GREAT TREE

WHEN the human spirit, joyful or disconsolate, seeks perch for its happy feet, or stay for flagging wings, it comes back again and again to the great tree of Shakespeare's genius, whose evergreen no heat withers, no cold blights, whose security no wind can loosen.

Rooted in the good brown soil, sunlight or the starshine on its leaves, this great tree stands, a refuge and home for the spirits of men.

Why are the writings of Shakespeare such an everlasting solace and inspiration ?

Because, in an incomprehensible world, full of the savage and the stupid and the suffering, stocked with monstrous contrasts and the most queer happenings, they do not fly to another world for compensation. They are of Earth and not of Heaven. They blink nothing, dare everything, but even in tragedy never lose their sane unconscious rapture, their prepossession with that entrancing occupation which we call ' life '. Firm in reality, they embody the faith that sufficient unto this Earth is the beauty and the meaning thereof. Theirs is, as it were, the proud exuberance of Nature, and no eye turned on the hereafter ; and so they fill us with gladness to be alive—though ' the rain it raineth every day '.

Truth condescended for a moment when Shakespeare lived, withdrew her bandage and looked out ; and good and evil, beauty and distortion, laughter and gloom for once were mirrored as they are, under this sun and moon.

What a wide, free, careless spirit was this man Shakespeare's—incarnate lesson to all narrow-headed mortals, with strait moralities, and pedantic hearts ! And what a Song he sang ; clothing Beauty for all time in actuality, in strangeness, and variety !

' He wanted arte,' Ben Jonson said ; ' I would he had blotted a thousand lines ! ' No doubt ! And yet, Ben Jonson : What is art ?

In every tree, even the greatest, dead wood and leaves shrivelled from birth, abound ; but never was a tree where the rich sap ran up more freely, never a tree whose height and circumference were greater, whose leaves so glistened ; where astonished Spring fluttered such green buds ; breezes made happier sound in Summer, whispering ; the Autumn gales a deeper roaring ; nor, in Winter, reigned so rare a silent beauty of snow.

In this Great Tree, I think there shall never be, in the time of man,

‘ Bare ruin'd choirs, where late the sweet birds sang.’

JOHN GALSWORTHY.

March, 1916.

A STRATFORDIAN'S HOMAGE

'OH, I see,' said a friend one day, at the end of a performance of *Hamlet*, 'you Stratfordians are trying to Shakespearize England.' 'The world, too, if we can,' I replied.

But primarily we are only wandering actors, not philanthropists, and as artists it is not ours to say this is right or this is wrong, only this is life as it has been, as it is, and as it may be if you will have it thus ; and as artists our desire is to take part in some of the most perfect dramas that the world has ever seen or will see.

The size and shape of the theatres alter, the patterns of scenery and conventions of art-expression change, but the eternal truths of existence remain the same for all ages.

It is such truths that the poet embodies in his work ; truths that deal with the strong things of life ; the sigh of the sea, the trumpet-note of the thunder, the song of the bird, the sunlight and the dark, the fall of a leaf from the tree, of a star from Heaven, the nightingale's lament, the buzzing of a gnat—all blend in the magician's melody.   Love pleads, Life struggles, Death flings wide the gates of understanding, all created things are busy—the song of Drama, doing and being.

If we can interpret the poet's meaning, we shall have told our audience something of the touch of Nature that makes the whole world kin, something of the realization of brotherhood through patriotism and the intensification of national life.   We shall have shown them something of the pride, pomp, and circumstance of glorious war ; something of the great peace enthroned in the human heart.   We shall have given them glimpses of the pendulum of human progress, swinging between free development for the individual and the preservation of the racial type— liberty under the law.

Hither come pilgrims from the ends of the earth to enrich themselves and their fellows with those ideas for which Shakespeare stands as the representative genius of our race, as the master-poet of the world.

'I have found the heart of England', preached the sage from

Bengal, ' in Stratford-on-Avon, and it was as the heart of Shakespeare ; faithful, yet tolerant, and gentle as it was strong.'

With the rhythmic balance of Hellenic movement, and with all the fervour of Hebraism, Shakespeare touches the secret springs of character, reveals the wisdom and tenderness of Mother Earth, interprets the language of bird and beast and flower, and manifests a Catholic Christianity that acknowledges, in all charity, its debt to and dependence upon a noble paganism.

' And I will lead you forth to play in the sunshine, close to the waterfall, in a land of vines and sunshine, yea, and of men that sing far, far away for ever.'

F. R. BENSON.

STRATFORD-ON-AVON.

THE HOMAGE OF THE ACTORS

To Shakespeare—the man of the theatre, the actor, the manager—we of the theatre pay peculiar homage. To the men of letters, the critics and commentators, we leave Shakespeare the poet, but with this reservation, that to understand truly Shakespeare and his work it is necessary to understand something of, and to have some sympathy with, the theatre; to recognize more fully than some writers are willing to allow, the considerable part which Shakespeare's sense of the theatre and experience of its art played in the development of his genius. The art of the theatre is as individual a thing as the art of painting or sculpture, and entirely separate and distinct from the art of the poet or novelist. Its conditions are circumscribed and peculiar, the talent or genius for it a thing apart. No play can live in the theatre by purely literary merit; poetic genius alone cannot make an actable play. The theatre has, at times, incurred undeserved reprobation at the hands of those who have thought that success as poets or story-tellers must imply success in the theatre; that, if they condescended to bring their work on to the stage, they would have no difficulty in achieving the same success which had attended them in their own particular art. They have forgotten that the favours of the Dramatic Muse are as difficult to secure, and must be as artfully won, as those of any other of the Muses. The poor lady has sometimes suffered rudely at their hands because she has preferred the persistent and laborious suitor to one too confident and condescending in his approach. We of the theatre know that Shakespeare as a playwright lives on the stage to-day apart from his contemporary dramatists because he, alone of them all, was not only the greatest poet but the one great dramatist among them. He knew from inside and respected the medium through which he worked, the temper of an audience, those secrets of dramatic effect which, to the playwright, represent the mechanism of the well-told story or the well-ordered poem. In short, Shakespeare knew his business as a man of the theatre; he was a master-craftsman in his day, a journeyman at times, a genius not of the closet but of the stage ; and for that very reason, and that alone, his plays hold their own in the theatre to-day, in all languages and among all civilized peoples.

As actors we owe our homage to Shakespeare. Never more than in this hour of our country's fate has he been an inspiration to the men of his calling to acquit themselves well, ' to make mouths at the invisible event, exposing what is mortal and unsure to all that fortune, death and danger dare '. And when some would seek to strip from this actor's brows, because he was an actor, the laurels of his genius, we reply that those who know something of the world of the theatre, its rivalry, never more keen than in Shakespeare's day, who can picture the surroundings in which he worked and strove for success, are convinced beyond any reasonable doubt that it would have been impossible, by all the laws of sense and probability, for a dramatist in Shakespeare's position to have foisted on to his colleagues and the public the work of another brain. So sensational and vital a secret of authorship could never have been kept in the small world of the theatre of that day, a world of active competition and, we know in Shakespeare's case, bitter jealousy. We of the theatre realize this, and to us such a consideration is answer enough to the utmost efforts of perverse ingenuity. Strong in our faith we pay our homage to this actor who has given to our English theatre an heritage of which we, by our own unaided efforts, have striven in the past—and are striving to-day—to be the worthy repositories. Our greatest desire must be ever to follow faithfully the example of those two loyal players who preserved for posterity the work ' of so worthy a friend and fellow as was our Shakespeare '.

H. B. IRVING.

ON PEACEFUL PENETRATION

In time of war it is well to do homage to the first Englishman who has subjugated the enemy. The characteristic thoroughness of the Teutonic appreciation of Shakespeare is the best proof of the completeness of his triumph.

But an infinitely harder task still awaits him : the subjugation of England is yet unachieved, and it is only when that age-long conflict is complete that we shall be able to celebrate any Shakespearian anniversary appropriately, and render him the only homage which would convince him, if he could return among us, that his countrymen believe in his glory and value his achievement at its surpassing worth.

Not marble nor a gilded monument can accomplish what Shakespeare asks from us ; a service in Stratford Church may commemorate the enclosing of his dust ; but only in that newer temple on the banks of Avon can the fitting rite be held, and while it stands solitary in the English shires it would be impossible to persuade his spirit, if we knew how to invoke it, that the tribute of our commemoration is sincere or anything more than a detachable ornament perfunctorily pinned on to the fabric of our modern life for occasions of display.

Shakespeare's infinite variety would turn that of Cleopatra into a monotony if they could be set in comparison ; yet age would appear to have withered it, custom to have staled it, if his position in his own country were the only standard of judgement. For several generations it has seemed a noble thought, a piece of profound wisdom, to say that he is too great for the theatre and that he can only yield his innermost riches to the student in his closet. This may well be true when the student in his closet is the actor busied in identifying himself with his part ; but in its larger application this doctrine that Shakespeare can best be worshipped in a temple built without hands has been held long enough for us to ask what its results are, and to note that during its currency the English theatre has descended from level to level of debasement and cheapness.

It is certainly not too soon to urge that it might be well to try worshipping him in temples built with hands again. Most of the great poetry in the world was written for the sake of its sound in men's mouths; it should be apparent that this was especially so in the case of dramatic poetry, yet a mischievous by-product of the invention of printing has been the gradual production of the idea, now almost become an instinct, that poetry is half a visual art, a pleasure of the eye to be gained by the look of words on printed pages. Yet Milton, sounding his lines in darkness, thought as little of testing poetry by such a standard as Shakespeare did when he supplied his theatre with manuscripts and left them there. Messieurs Mouth and Company are as truly the real publishers for poetry as they were in the days of Aeschylus, and England will never know the wonder and delight and awe-stirring powers of Shakespeare until his words are heard ten thousand times oftener than they are printed, until his plays become again part of the daily routine of English theatres rather than the *hors-d'œuvre* of festivals, and the total seating accommodation of English theatres has become at least as great and as well distributed as the total seating accommodation of English churches and chapels.

If he had been born before the Reformation this first essential would have been his from the beginning, for he would have worked for the universal employer that gave complete and endless opportunities to those great Italian dramatists Giotto and Giovanni Bellini and Tintoretto. The church was then the theatre; and sometimes it seems as if the theatre will never be universal again, or realize its opportunities adequately, until it returns to the church—or, indeed, until the church realizes the dramaturgic nature of its ceremonies and teaching, and becomes a theatre.

In the Middle Ages Shakespeare thus would have been sure of an auditorium and an instructed audience in every parish, and he would have been a national possession to Englishmen in a way that he never has been yet. In the beginning of the nineteenth century such an opportunity, though in a lesser degree, began to seem possible; modest theatres with stock companies sprang up in most of the comfortable country towns in every shire, and energy and resource showed itself everywhere in the number of great plays taken in hand, the sustained interest of provincial audiences in serious drama, and the number of competent actors which the system produced. But the commercial development of England came and altered the balance of importance of the provincial towns, and was followed by the railways, which centralized the satisfaction of the community's needs at a few nodal points ; and the whole organization disappeared.

The loss was very real. I have in mind the district with which I am most familiar, a rocky, thinly populated stretch of country on the north-west coast of England. A hundred years ago its life and activities centred about two market-towns at its borders : to-day those towns persist little changed, perhaps rather larger and more prosperous under modern conditions. Their amusements are administered in a couple of picture-palaces and a modest concert-hall at which a musical comedy touring company occasionally pauses for three nights : no one would think it worth his while to build a theatre in either of them, no one in his senses would think it possible to maintain a stock company in such a theatre even if it were built ; yet in each of them there exists intact the physical structure of what was a well-appointed theatre in the days of Mrs. Siddons and Kean, and in one of those theatres—now a cheap dancing academy—Kean once acted, the townsfolk still proudly record. Kean once acted, and perhaps Wordsworth and De Quincey applauded ; for there De Quincey edited the local paper, and thither Wordsworth must come when he would take coach for the outer world. But neither Irving nor Forbes-Robertson ever acted there, and it is safe to assume that the bicentenary of Shakespeare's death had interest and reality in many mountain villages and fell-side farms where its tercentenary will pass unrevered or unknown.

In devising a National Memorial to keep Shakespeare's achievement more vividly and constantly in the minds of his countrymen, it is inevitable that a metropolitan theatre, where all great plays may find performance regardless of dividends, and where the passage of time may create a school of great acting and severe technique, should seem most worth working for. The need for such a theatre is paramount and even peremptory, if only to provide a standard and an authority from which young poets may revolt, and upon which youth in general may spend its passion for contradiction, in the profitable and well-trained fashion which the Royal Academy of Arts has taught to six generations of brilliant painters. In passing it may be urged that, when such a theatre is consummated, it might well profit by the modern discoveries in theatre construction and scenic management which have not yet reached London, and indeed make every experiment which has no attraction for syndicates or shareholders.

But when such a theatre is finished, the task of building Shakespeare's memorial in a nation's mind will only be begun. Perhaps it will not be thought irrelevant that a rustic and provincial writer should insist, even tediously, that decentralization and universal penetration alone can complete the work. Such touring companies as those of Mr. F. R. Benson do something, and something considerable : the isolated enterprise of Mr. Barry Jackson and Mr. John Drinkwater has raised in Birmingham the most modern theatre in England, and practises in it, with a stock company, the performance of Shakespeare's plays and those of his great companions, not on red-letter days alone, but as part of a daily duty. If such a theatre as the Birmingham Repertory Theatre were to be built in every prosperous town in England, Shakespeare would have come into his own before the arrival of his quatercentenary ; but the inertia and indifference and dislike of innovation, the demand for the minor gaieties and the baser sentimentalities now prevalent, can only be overcome by a public effort. If the Memorial Committee could enlarge its scheme to include provincial memorial theatres, and companies to carry the seldom-seen plays to every part of England, Shakespeare might soon be the popular dramatist in his own country that he is in the rest of Europe.

I yield my homage earnestly and eagerly to the creative force that worked instinctively and easily in Nature's way, and with results that were Nature's own ; to the mastery of the deep springs of mirth, of a superb sense of design working with human bodies as its integers, and of life's supreme illumination by tragic splendour, which can still make the world seem for a little while as vivid and august to lesser men as it was continually to the miracle-worker himself ; but I cannot help regretting that the corporate homage of Shakespeare's countrymen should still be so imperfectly at Shakespeare's service.

GORDON BOTTOMLEY.

THE FAIRIES' HOMAGE

EACH bough hung quiet in its place
  O'er Stratford's starry lea,
Yet round and round with giddy race
  I saw the dead leaves flee,
      In and out
      In eerie rout—
A sight most strange to see.
And then I heard with quick heart-beat
  Multitudinous fairy feet
      Marching come
      With elfin hum
And music faint and sweet.

Within a beech's hollow trunk,
  Whose bursting buds had strowed
Those red, dead eddying leaves, I shrunk
  And breathless there abode,
      While those fine
      Fays in line
Past me flowed and flowed.
'Twas Shakespeare's Fairy Host indeed.
  Oberon and Titania lead;
      Then, good Troth!
      Puck, Cobweb, Moth,
Pease-blossom, Mustard Seed.

Thereat, the climate, changing quite,
  Yields Athens to the view,
Beneath whose bright Midsummer Night
  Puck plays his pranks anew—
      Works Bottom's strange
      And monstrous change ;
Befools four lovers true :
And in requital for her harms
  To Oberon, Titania charms
      From sleep to wake
      Bewitched and take
An Ass-head to her arms !

That marvellous Dream on English Air
  Dissolves,—the Host moves on,
I follow them from out my lair
  O'er moonlit meadows wan ;
      Till round the porch
      Of Stratford Church
Like bees they swarm anon ;
While ' Hail, all Hail ! ' their homage-cry
  Swells sweetly up into the sky,
      ' For, Master Will,
      Thy magic skill
Has made us live for aye.'

ALFRED PERCEVAL GRAVES.

CERVANTES, SHAKESPEARE, AND THE PASTORAL IDEA

ENGLAND and Spain in the great age seem to have had a common understanding of many things ; they agreed in many points of art without debate or discussion, or any overt communication, as far as one can make out.   No form of verse in French or Italian resembles English verse in its rules and licences as does the Spanish measure called *arte mayor*.   Even the trick of the heroic couplet used as a tag at the end of a blank-verse tirade is common to Lope de Vega and Shakespeare.

In several passages Cervantes might almost be translating Sir Philip Sidney.   The great dialogue on romance and the drama at the end of the first part of *Don Quixote* (1605) is more like the *Apologie for Poetrie* than many things that have been quoted by ' parallelists ' as evidence of plagiarism :

What greater absurdity can there be in drama (says the Curate) than to bring in a child in swaddling clothes at the beginning of the first act and to find him in the second a grown man and bearded ? . . . As for the observance of place what can I say except that I have seen a play where the first act began in Europe, the second in Asia, the third ended in Africa, and if there had been a fourth it would have passed in America, and so the play would have comprehended the four quarters of the world.

In the previous chapter the Canon of Toledo, speaking undoubtedly the opinions of Cervantes, had described an ideal of romance with all that devotion to classical ideals which is so strong in Sidney.   The author of *Don Quixote*, writing the first great modern novel and talking about the art of romance, gives as his ideal of prose fiction a work in which all the characters are noble classical types—' the wit of Ulysses, the piety of Aeneas, the valour of Achilles, the sorrows of Hector ; treating of which the author with the freedom of the prose form may vary his style, and be epic, lyric, tragical, comical, or what you will '— ending with the weighty sentence : ' For Epic can be written not only in verse but in prose.'

It might be a description of Sidney's *Arcadia* ; it is a prophecy of the last work of Cervantes, *Persiles y Sigismunda*, the serious and classical

E

romance in which he imitated Heliodorus. Heliodorus, thirty years before, had been saluted by Sidney as an author of prose epic (which is the same thing as heroical romance) :

> For Xenophon who did imitate so excellently as to give us *effigiem justi imperii*, the portraiture of a just empire, under the name of *Cyrus* (as Cicero saith of him) made therein an absolute heroical poem. So did Heliodorus in his sugred invention of that picture of love in *Theagenes and Chariclea*. And yet both these write in prose, &c.

Cervantes is somewhere between Sidney and Shakespeare in his respect for the classical idols. Sidney and Cervantes are subdued, as Shakespeare is not, in presence of the great authorities. The imposture of the Renaissance, the superstitious worship of literary ideas, is shown most clearly in reference to Heliodorus. There must be something in prose corresponding to epic poetry. So Heliodorus is made into the pattern of heroic romance, almost equal to Homer. He satisfies the conditions of an abstract critical theory. Sidney and Cervantes— occasionally—revel in terms of literary species. So does Shakespeare, as we know; this is the sort of intellect that Shakespeare names Polonius.

Cervantes spent a great deal of time in the service of conventional literary ideals ; but if he wrote the *Galatea*, he also wrote *Don Quixote*, and he belonged to a country that was fond of fresh life in its stories. Shakespeare kept out of the danger of Arcadia, and paid respect to no literary ideas (such as heroic poem or heroic romance), however much they might be preached about by the critics. But Shakespeare had few prejudices ; that 'great but irregular genius' did not scruple to use the tricks of classical tragedy (e. g. stichomythia), if it suited his purpose to do so, and he was not going to renounce Arcadia because Polonius and his friends were eloquent about the pastoral idea. Shakespeare and Cervantes agree in certain places with regard to pastoral. They agree in playing a double game about it. Pastoral is ridiculed in the penance of Don Quixote ; yet the story of Don Quixote is full of the most beautiful pastoral episodes—Marcela the best of them, it may be. *As You Like It* is of course the play where Shakespeare criticises pastoral, and shows the vanity of it, and how different from the golden world are the briers of the forest of Arden and the biting of the northern wind. We are not seriously taken in by this hypocrisy ; we know that in spite of Touchstone we too are in Arcadia, in the rich landscape along with youth and fair speech. Touchstone leaves Arcadia much as it was, and the appeal to the dead shepherd proves how harmless is his negative attitude.

In the story of Preciosa, the Spanish gipsy, the first of the *Novelas exemplares*, Cervantes plays for an effect like that of Shakespeare's green wood in *As You Like It*. The scene is not Arcadia, but Madrid and the country about Toledo, Estremadura and Murcia. The gipsies of the story are rogues and vagabonds. But the story is a pastoral romance none the less; the free life of the gipsies is praised in such terms as turn the hardships into pleasant fancies. Preciosa has just enough of the gipsy character to save the author from instant detection; she is good at begging, and she has the professional lisp.[1] But her world is Arcadia, the pure pastoral beauty where Florizel and Perdita also have their home. And here, to end, it may be observed that Cervantes and Shakespeare with Preciosa and Perdita have been glad to repeat the old device of the classical comedy. They might perhaps have done without it, but for the sake of Preciosa and the other long-lost child we spectators will always applaud loudly when the box of baby-things—$\pi\eta\rho\iota\delta\iota\text{o}\nu\ \gamma\nu\omega\rho\iota\sigma\mu\acute{\alpha}\tau\omega\nu$—is produced in the last scene, to bring back the heroine to her own again.

W. P. KER.

---

[1] '¿Quiérenme dar barato? ceñores, dijo Preciosa, que como gitana hablaba ceceoso, y esto es artificio en ellos, que no naturaleza.'—CERVANTES, *La Gitanilla de Madrid*.

THE SONGS OF SHAKESPEARE

AMONG the 'co-supremes and stars of love' which form the constellated glory of our greatest poet there is one small splendour which we are apt to overlook in our general survey.   But, if we isolate it from other considerations, it is surely no small thing that Shakespeare created and introduced into our literature the Dramatic Song.   If with statistical finger we turn the pages of all his plays, we shall discover, not perhaps without surprise, that these contain not fewer than fifty strains of lyrical measure.   Some of the fifty, to be sure, are mere star-dust, but others include some of the very jewels of our tongue.   They range in form from the sophisticated quatorzains of *The Two Gentlemen of Verona* (where, however, comes ' Who is Silvia ? ') to the reckless snatches of melody in *Hamlet*.   But all have a character which is Shakespearean, and this regardless of the question so often raised, and so incapable of reply, as to whether some of the wilder ones are Shakespeare's composition or no.   Whoever originally may have written such scraps as ' They bore him bare-faced on the bier ' and ' Come o'er the bourne, Bessy, to me ', the spirit of Shakespeare now pervades and possesses them.

Our poet was a prodigious innovator in this as in so many other matters.   Of course, the idea and practice of musical interludes in plays was not quite novel.   In Shakespeare's early youth that remarkable artist in language, John Lyly, had presented songs in several of his plays, and these were notable for what his contemporary, Henry Upchear, called ' their labouring beauty '.   We may notice that Lyly's songs were not printed till long after Shakespeare's death, but doubtless he had listened to them.   Peele and Greene had brilliant lyrical gifts, but they did not exercise them in their dramas, nor did Lodge, whose novel of *Rosalynde* (1590) contains the only two precedent songs which we could willingly add to Shakespeare's juvenile repertory.   But while I think it would be rash to deny that the lyrics of Lodge and Lyly had their direct influence on the style of Shakespeare, neither of those admirable precursors conceived the possibility of making the Song an integral part of the development of the Drama. This was Shakespeare's invention, and he applied it with a technical adroitness which had never been dreamed of before and was never rivalled after.

This was not apprehended by the early critics of our divine poet, and has never yet, perhaps, received all the attention it deserves. We may find ourselves bewildered if we glance at what the eighteenth-century commentators said, for instance, about the songs in *Twelfth Night*. They called the adorable rhapsodies of the Clown ' absurd ' and ' unintelligible '; ' O Mistress mine ' was in their ears ' meaningless '; ' When that I was ' appeared to them ' degraded buffoonery '. They did not perceive the close and indispensable connexion between the Clown's song and the action of the piece, although the poet had been careful to point out that it was a moral song ' dulcet in contagion ', and too good, except for sarcasm, to be wasted on Sir Andrew and Sir Toby. The critics neglected to note what the Duke says about ' Come away, come away, Death ', and they prattled in their blindness as to whether this must not really have been sung by Viola, all the while insensible to the poignant dramatic value of it as warbled by the ironic Clown in the presence of the blinded pair. But indeed the whole of *Twelfth Night* is burdened with melody ; behind every garden-door a lute is tinkling, and at each change of scene some unseen hand is overheard touching a harp-string. The lovely, infatuated lyrics arrive, dramatically, to relieve this musical tension at its height.

Rather different, and perhaps still more subtle, is the case of *A Winter's Tale*, where the musical obsession is less prominent, and where the songs are all delivered from the fantastic lips of Autolycus. Here again the old critics were very wonderful. Dr. Burney puts ' When daffodils begin to peer ' and ' Lawn as white as driven snow ' into one bag, and flings it upon the dust-heap, as ' two nonsensical songs ' sung by ' a pickpocket '. Dr. Warburton blushed to think that such ' nonsense ' could be foisted on Shakespeare's text. Strange that those learned men were unable to see, not merely that the rogue-songs are intensely human and pointedly Shakespearean, but that they are an integral part of the drama. They complete the revelation of the complex temperament of Autolycus, with his passion for flowers and millinery, his hysterical balancing between laughter and tears, his impish mendacity, his sudden sentimentality, like the Clown's

> Not a friend, not a friend greet
> My poor corpse, where my bones shall be thrown !

It is in these subtle lyrical amalgams of humour and tenderness that the firm hand of the creator of character reveals itself.

But it is in *The Tempest* that Shakespeare's supremacy as a writer of songs is most brilliantly developed. Here are seven or eight lyrics, and among them are some of the loveliest things that any man has written. What was ever composed more liquid, more elastic, more delicately fairy-like than Ariel's First Song?

> Come unto these yellow sands,
>   And then take hands:
> Curtsied when you have, and kiss'd,—
>   The wild waves whist.

That is, not ' kissed the wild waves ', as ingenious punctuators pretend, but, parenthetically, ' kissed one another,—the wild waves being silent the while.' Even fairies do not kiss waves, than which no embrace could be conceived less rewarding. Has any one remarked the echo of Marlowe here, from *Hero and Leander*,

> when all is whist and still,
> Save that the sea playing on yellow sand
> Sends forth a rattling murmur to the land?

But Marlowe, with all his gifts, could never have written the lyrical parts of *The Tempest*. This song is in emotional sympathy with Ferdinand, and in the truest sense dramatic, not a piece of pretty verse foisted in to add to the entertainment.

Ariel's Second Song has been compared with Webster's ' Call for the robin redbreast' in *The White Devil*, but, solemn as Webster's dirge is, it tolls, it does not sing to us. Shakespeare's ' ditty,' as Ferdinand calls it, is like a breath of the west wind over an Aeolian harp. Where, in any language, has ease of metre triumphed more adorably than in Ariel's Fourth Song,—'Where the bee sucks '? Dowden saw in Ariel the imaginative genius of English poetry, recently delivered from Sycorax. If we glance at Dryden's recension of *The Tempest* we may be inclined to think that the 'wicked dam' soon won back her mastery. With all respect to Dryden, what are we to think of his discretion in eking out Shakespeare's insufficiencies with such staves as this :

> Upon the floods will sing and play
> And celebrate a halcyon day ;
> Great Nephew Aeolus make no noise,
> Muzzle your roaring boys.

and so forth ? What had happened to the ear of England in seventy years ?

As a matter of fact the perfection of dramatic song scarcely survived Shakespeare himself. The early Jacobeans, Heywood, Ford, and Dekker in particular, broke out occasionally in delicate ditties. But most playwrights, like Massinger, were persistently pedestrian. The only man who came at all close to Shakespeare as a lyrist was John Fletcher, whose 'Lay a garland on my hearse' nobody could challenge if it were found printed first in a Shakespeare quarto. The three great songs in *Valentinian* have almost more splendour than any of Shakespeare's, though never quite the intimate beauty, the singing spontaneity of 'Under the greenwood tree' or 'Hark, hark, the lark'. It has grown to be the habit of anthologists to assert Shakespeare's right to 'Roses, their sharp spikes being gone'. The mere fact of its loveliness and perfection gives them no authority to do so; and to my ear the rather stately procession of syllables is reminiscent of Fletcher. We shall never be certain, and who would not swear that 'Hear, ye ladies that are coy' was by the same hand that wrote 'Sigh no more, ladies', if we were not sure of the contrary? But the most effective test, even in the case of Fletcher, is to see whether the trill of song is, or is not, an inherent portion of the dramatic structure of the play. This is the hall-mark of Shakespeare, and perhaps of him alone.

EDMUND GOSSE.

WILLIAM SHAKESPEARE

DIED APRIL 23, 1616

AND then—the rest ?
What did he find
In the unfettered universe of mind,
To whom one star revealed
Complete and unconcealed
The maze of various man, in coloured music wrought—
God's rich creative thought
Of ardour, grief, and laughter all compact—
And more, beyond the patch of fencèd fact,
Where at the edge of dream the air 's alive with wings,
Showed him the hidden world of delicate fair things ?

With what new zest,
His inward vision healed
Of rheumy Time, and from the clipping zone
Of Space set free,
He roamed those meadows of Eternity
Where the storm blows that comes from the unknown
To shake the crazy windows of the soul
With gusts of strange desire !
Thrust by that favouring gale
Did he set out, as Prospero, to sail
The lonely splendours of the Nameless Sea ?
Where did he make the land ?
Upon what coasts, what sudden magic isles ?

And what quick spirits met he on the strand ?
What new mysterious loves swifter than fire
Streaming from out the love that ever smiles,
What musical sweet shapes, what things grotesque and dear
      We know not here,
What starry songs of what exultant quire
      Now fill the span
Of his wide-open thought, who grasped the heart of man ?

      Saints have confest
That by deep gazing they achieve to know
The hiddenness of God, His rich delight ;
      And so
There 's a keen love some poets have possest,
      Sharper than sight
To prick the dark that wraps our spirits round
And, beyond Time, see men in its own light.
      Those look upon His face,
      These in a glass have found
The moving pageant of His eager will :
All the nobility and naughtiness,
      Simplicity and skill
Of living souls, that do our dusk redeem
With flaming deed and strangely-smouldering dream.
Great contemplator of humanity !
'Twas thus you saw, and showed to us again
The one divine immortal comedy :
Horror and tears, laughter and loveliness,
      All rapture and all pain
Held in one unity's immense embrace,
      Set in one narrow place.
Now, in the unwalled playhouse of the True,
You know the life from which that drama drew.

EVELYN UNDERHILL.

SHAKESPEARE AND GREEK PHILOSOPHY

SHAKESPEARE has given us the finest interpretation in any language of one of the central doctrines of Greek philosophy. That does not mean, of course, that he was a student of the subject in the ordinary sense. Though I am convinced that his classical attainments were far more considerable than is sometimes supposed, I do not suggest that he had read Plato's *Timaeus*. What I claim for him is something more than that, namely, that he was able to disentangle the essential meaning of the Pythagorean doctrines preserved in that dialogue, though these were only known to him through a very distorted tradition. Milton knew them well in their original form ; but his Platonism, nobly as it is expressed, yet lacks a touch which is present in Lorenzo's brief discourse on Music in Act V of the *Merchant of Venice*. It may be worth while to add that such sympathetic interpretation of Greek thought was quite ' out of the welkin ' of Francis Bacon.

The commentators fail to throw much light on Lorenzo's theory. They do not appear to have heard of Plato's *Timaeus*, though that dialogue has had more influence on European literature than almost any work that could be named, and though it is the ultimate source of so much that is best in English literature in particular. Above all, they do not possess the clue to the whole discourse, namely, the Pythagorean doctrine of Music as the ' purgation ' ($\kappa\acute{a}\theta\alpha\rho\sigma\iota\varsigma$) of the soul. Let us see whether, with that clue in our hands, we can follow Lorenzo's argument more closely, and state his theory rather more fully than the exigencies of dramatic art have allowed him to state it himself.

Let us start from the words ' Such harmony is in immortal souls ', and note at once that the term ' harmony ' in this connexion does not bear its modern meaning. Greek music had no harmony in our sense, and $\acute{a}\rho\mu\nu\nu\acute{i}\alpha$ meant ' scale ' or ' octave '. Now the sun, the moon, and the five planets, along with the heaven of the fixed stars, were believed to form a harmony in this sense, an octave scale, the intervals of which were determined by the distances between the planetary orbits. That octave has its counterpart in the immortal soul of each one of us; for the circular motions of the soul of man only reproduce on a smaller scale the mightier revolutions in the soul of the world, which are just the paths of the heavenly orbs. Were it not for the earthly and perishable nature of the body, our souls would therefore sound in perfect unison with the grander music of the Cosmos. As it is, there is a corporeal barrier between the Soul of Man and the Soul of the World. The function of Music is to overcome this barrier, and it can do so because it is able to reach the soul, while its scales reproduce the intervals of the celestial diapason. It is thus an intermediary between the universe and ourselves. So, when we hear music, our nature is changed for the time, the motions of our ' spirits ' are brought into accord with those of the heavenly bodies, and we are at one with what is highest. We see rudimentary traces of this even in some of the animals. On the other hand, a human soul from which music can elicit no response is altogether out of tune with the Soul of the World. It is not only the body in this case that bars the way; the soul itself rings untrue. All that is Pythagorean doctrine, and in the light of it Lorenzo's speech becomes quite clear.

It is curious that Lorenzo says nothing about the ' crystal spheres '. As a matter of fact, these are a later addition to the doctrine, and are not to be found in the *Timaeus*. It almost looks as if Shakespeare saw them to be irrelevant, as in fact they are. He does, however, introduce one modification of the imagery, which gives us a valuable hint as to the channels through which it reached him. In the Myth of Er in Plato's *Republic* we read that there is a Siren on each of the planetary rings who sings in monotone her proper note in the octave. Lorenzo substitutes angels and cherubim, and that goes back in the long run to ' Dionysius the Areopagite '. We may fairly infer that the theory of the celestial ' harmony ' reached Shakespeare, as it reached Dante, in a mediaeval dress, and it is not hard to see how that may have come about.

Plato's *Timaeus* was never wholly lost to western Europe, as his other dialogues were; for the greater part of it was accessible in the Latin version of Chalcidius (fourth century A. D.), with an elaborate commentary based mainly on Posidonius. In that commentary the doctrine is to be found, Sirens and all. It is, says Chalcidius, the *consortium corporis* which causes the *ratio harmonica* in the human soul to fade away into oblivion, so that the souls of the many are ' unmodulated '. Music is the cure (*medela*) for this; for it alone can recall the motions of our soul when they deviate from their orbits (*exorbitantes*) to the original concord (*ad veterem symphoniam*). In general, we may say that Posidonius, who was specially interested in early Pythagoreanism, made use of his knowledge to illuminate the obscurities of the *Timaeus*, and that Chalcidius handed on the torch to the Middle Ages.

The School of Chartres was the legitimate successor of Plato's Academy, and its teaching was based on the work of Chalcidius. In the twelfth century Bernard Silvester of Tours sought to rival the *Timaeus* itself in his *De mundi universitate*, and it was he that made the terms Macrocosm and Microcosm familiar. They are not to be found in Greek, though Philo and others speak of man as a μικρός or βραχὺς κόσμος, the *brevis mundus* of Chalcidius. It is here too that personified Nature makes her appearance, practically for the first time. Then comes the *De planctu naturae* of Alan of Lille, to whom Chaucer refers his readers for a description of the goddess Nature, and from whom he borrows her designation as ' God's vicar general '. The Platonism of Chartres was popularized by Jean de Meung's continuation of the *Roman de la Rose*, and by the fifteenth century the leading doctrines of the *Timaeus* were common property, especially in England. There was an eager desire to know more of Plato, and Humphrey, Duke of Gloucester, procured a translation of the *Phaedo* and the *Meno* from Sicily. Inevitably this interest in Platonism was reflected in the Moralities of the next age, which betray their affiliation to the school of Chartres by the leading part they often assign to Nature, a personification practically unknown in continental literature till a later date, but of the highest importance for English poetry and English science. Obvious examples are the *Interlude of the Four Elements* (though that is Aristotelian, not Platonic), and *The Marriage of Wit and Science*, the very title of which is pure Plato. It is a probable conjecture that Shakespeare's Platonism first came to him from sources of this kind, which would account for the angels and the cherubim, though we must not exclude other possibilities. It is certain, at any rate, that there was a vast mass of floating traditional lore, of Pythagorean and Platonic origin, in the England of Shakespeare's youth, and that he was just the man to be influenced by it.

The ' muddy vesture of decay ' deserves a few words to itself. The Pythagoreans generally spoke of the body as the tomb or prison of the soul, but there was also an old Orphic doctrine that the body was the soul's garment (χιτών). At a later date this was revived in Gnostic circles and the ' vesture ' was identified with the coats of skins (χιτῶνες δερμάτινοι) made by God for Adam and Eve. The image was adopted by Porphyry and his successors, and so passed into mediaeval Platonism. The epithets 'muddy' (χοϊκός) and 'of decay' (φθαρτός) reveal the origin of the phrase, however it may have reached Shakespeare. He can hardly have got it from St. Paul; for 'muddy' is a more accurate rendering of χοϊκός than the *terrenus* of the Vulgate or the 'earthy' of the English version.

The result of all this is that Shakespeare has picked out the pure gold from the dross with an unerring instinct. The Aristotelian and Scholastic accretions which disfigured the doctrine have all dropped away, and the thought of Pythagoras stands revealed in its original simplicity. We need not wonder at that. The sympathetic insight into another soul, which is the gift of the interpreter, is at bottom the same thing as dramatic genius. It is, after all, no great marvel that the creator of Hamlet and Falstaff could also recreate Pythagoras from the stray hints tradition had preserved.

JOHN BURNET.

ST. ANDREWS.

IN REMEMBRANCE OF
OUR WORTHY MASTER SHAKESPEARE

A Quatorzain in the commendation of Master William Shakespeare and his Country, wherein the Author hath imitated, albeit imperfectly, the manner of our Elizabethan poets.

OUR own Thou art, and England's self in Thee,
Drest in the rare perfections of thy book,
As some fair queen may in her mirror look
To learn where lies her beauty's mystery.
Thyself art England, all the world may see,
Her tongue, her pen ; so has thy Muse outgone
The quire of Castaly and Helicon
And quite o'erpassed their starry Italy.
Thus hast thou conquered Time who conquers men,
And writ alone her virtue's argument ;
Here is our England's wealth : what wonder then
That this thy page breeds more astonishment
Than that famed garden set i' the ocean seas
Or fabled fruit of the Hesperides.

The chief ground and matter of this sonnet resteth upon a tale set forth by the philosopher and mythologian Plato, in the tenth book of his ΠΟΛΙΤΕΙΑ.

As on the spindle of Necessity
Roll the bright orbs of being, ring on ring,
To the unwearied song the Sirens sing,
Nor age nor falter on the eternal way ;
So in thy Heavens, child of destiny,
On music's wide imperishable wing,
All years above or season's reckoning,
Star follows star in crystalline array.
There too the Fates enthron'd may each one see,
Calm memorable goddesses, and mark
How the lot falls to that man or to this,
And ponder in his heart each firm decree,
Ere on the ultimate ocean he embark
Himself to hear the doom of Lachesis.

W. MACNEILE DIXON.

THE UNIVERSITY,
GLASGOW.

SHAKESPEARE AND MUSIC

THERE is no English poet to whom music has been a more intimate and vital source of inspiration than it was to Shakespeare. His lyrics are the purest melodies in our language : his plays are instinct with the impulse and delight of song : it is music that soothes the love sickness of Orsino, that fills the starry night when Lorenzo and Jessica exchange their vows, that sets the fairies circling round the couch of Titania, that pours new enchantment over the magic of Prospero's isle. The whole air is filled with the concourse of sweet sounds : under Sylvia's window, in Katherine's chamber, before the porch of Mariana's moated grange : Cleopatra cannot go a-fishing without her minstrels, the jolly hunters in Arden Forest celebrate their quarry with a rousing chorus. Even in the darkest hours of tragedy music comes as a relief and a consolation : Desdemona sings of her forebodings ; Ophelia of her broken heart ; Edgar, on the storm-swept heath, breaks into half-forgotten fragments of wild melody. And behind all these grave matters of character and incident, of suspended fortunes and final issue, stretches the broad country-side which Shakespeare loved ; the dancers on the village-green keeping time to the pipe and tabor ; the reapers ' three-man song-men all and very good ones, but they are most of them means and basses ' ; Autolycus with his pack of ballads singing along the footpath way ; roisterers joining in a catch at the ale-house door : a coppice of wood-notes, artless and untaught, carolling for very joy and fullness of life.

It is therefore notable that the age of Shakespeare was also the greatest and most fertile in the history of our national music. The first English madrigal was printed in 1588 : for a generation before that we had held honourable rivalry with the Flemish and Italian church composers ; during the generation which followed we may claim to have won our way to pre-eminence. Tallis, who died in 1585, summed up in his own work all the strength and skill, all the vigour and learning which the music of his time could attain : William Byrd, his younger colleague—perhaps his pupil—added a new sweetness of melody, a new grace of style, and, what is of far greater moment, a sense of the depth and mystery of music which is comparable to that of Shakespeare himself. And close upon Byrd follows a noble procession of madrigal composers : Weelkes and Wilbye, Bennet and Bateson, Morley who calls Byrd ' my loving master ', and Gibbons who was honoured by his collaboration : to the *Triumphs of Oriana* twenty-five Englishmen contributed, and every work is a masterpiece. Nor were the performers less conspicuous. Dowland was the most famous lutenist in Europe : Bull and Philips were among the most famous organ-players : the pieces in the Fitzwilliam Virginal Book testify to an astonishing degree of skill and proficiency. And all this garden of delights grew from a soil ready prepared for it. Music, in Elizabeth's reign, was taken for granted as a part of every one's education. ' Supper being ended,' says Philomathes,[1] ' and Musicke bookes (according to the custome) being brought to the table : the mistresse of the house presented me with a part earnestly requesting me to sing. But when after many excuses, I protested unfainedly that I could not, every one began to wonder. Yea, some whispered to others demanding how I was brought up.' Queen Elizabeth was a skilful performer on the virginals, and readily forgave the indiscreet ambassador who had overheard her, on his assurance that she played better than Mary Queen of Scots. Many of the instrumental pieces which still survive are severally dedicated to lords and ladies of the court : some are marked with special instructions for the patrons who were to play them : some are by amateur composers, Robert Hales, for instance, and ' Mr. Daniells ', and Captain Tobias Hume whose ' profession hath been that of arms ' and whose music ' hath been always generous because never mercenarie '. It is true that the society of Shakespeare's time anticipated our own in the hospitable welcome which it offered to the artists of foreign countries. ' Some there be ', says Campion in 1613, ' who admit only French and Italian aires, as if every country had not its proper aire which the people thereof naturally usurp in their music.' But, apart from passing fashion, such generosity was the intercourse of nations which could meet on terms of comradeship, and was repaid, at least in part, by the respect that was shown to our musicians abroad.

The wealthier houses in Shakespeare's time had at disposal a large variety of musical instruments. The organ was rarely to be found among them, though Chappington and Dalham were famous organ-

---

[1] Morley, *A plaine and easie introduction to Practicall Musicke*, p. 1.

F

builders, but the regal, a small portative organ, was not uncommon, and the virginal [1] stood in high favour among the ladies of the household. It is the more noteworthy that Shakespeare never mentions either of these by name (he uses ' virginalling ' as a metaphor in *The Winter's Tale*), and that his only description of a virginal player has been censured by careful critics for a technical mistake. The recorders [2], which provide Hamlet with a text, were fipple-flutes of special construction, bored with not less than eight holes and usually kept in a quartet of differing compass that they might harmonize together into a consort. The same practice obtained with the viols—treble, alto, tenor, and bass—the last of these being the viol da gamba which Sir Andrew Aguecheek ' played better than any man in Illyria '. The ' leero ' viol—the Italian *lira da braccio*—is occasionally mentioned as an understudy : the ' scoulding violins ', as Mace calls them, though sometimes used in ensembles, were still harsh and untuneful ; fitter for the country fair than for the ears of civilized society. But by far the most popular of all instruments was the lute. As a manly accomplishment it ranked but little below the sword—indeed Richard Crookback morosely complains that grim-visaged War had given it place : it formed an essential part of every song accompaniment from Dowland to Campion : in the very barbers' shops, where now we have newspapers and comic prints, a lute hung ready to solace the waiting customer. Three or four kinds of guitar are also mentioned in the compositions of the time— the cittern, flat-backed and wire-stringed, to the carved head of which Holofernes the schoolmaster is disrespectfully compared ; the pandora which, in spite of its outlandish name, seems to have been invented by a Londoner ; the orphereon, dainty in shape but rather awkward to handle ; yet though all these had their votaries—the Imperial Votaress among them—they never challenged the pre-eminence of the lute proper. The accusation that it was expensive in strings is indignantly denied by its champion Thomas Mace, and if true marks its only fault : it was graceful in shape and sweet in tone, effective but not exacting, and the music for it was written in a tablature which is one of the easiest forms of notation ever invented. A few other instruments might be added—the transverse flute, the harp, the various kinds of flageolet— but even without these there is enough to show that the virtuoso of the time had an abundance of choice.

[1] The name virginal was then commonly applied to all keyed instruments in which the string was plucked with a quill.
[2] See Christopher Welch's *Six Lectures on the Recorder*.

Combinations of instruments, so ordered as to produce a harmonious scheme of colour, were as yet somewhat crude and primitive. The four viols often doubled and sometimes replaced the singers in a madrigal : the bass viol supported the lute in the accompaniments of ' aires ' : more elaborate were the consort lessons of Morley and Rosseter, written for treble and bass viols, pandora, cittern, and recorder, and larger bands of what was commonly called ' broken music ' were employed for masques and at wedding-feasts.[1] The louder instruments —hautbois, shawms, trumpets, cornets, sackbuts, and drums—were usually reserved for occasions of special state and pageantry, and their choice seems to have aimed more at volume than at balance of sound.[2] Indeed one of the oddities of nomenclature is the current adoption of the word ' noise ', without any malicious intent, for a band of musicians and more distinctively of string-players. When the drawer at the Boar's Head bids his fellow ' see if thou cannot find out Sneak's noise ' he is merely making use of an accepted technical term. It is the more remarkable because the ' chamber ' music of the time, and especially that played upon strings, would seem to our ears soft in tone, and— except for a few dance measures—grave in character. A valuable piece of evidence on the whole subject may be found in the third Century of Bacon's *Sylva Sylvarum* :

All concords and discords of music are (no doubt) sympathies and antipathies of sounds. And so likewise in that music which we call broken music, or consort music, some consorts of instruments are sweeter than others (a thing not sufficiently yet observed) as the Irish harp and base viol agree well ; the recorder and stringed music agree well ; organs and the voice agree well, &c. : but the virginals and the lute, or the Welsh harp and Irish harp, or the voice and pipes alone, agree not so well. But for the melioration of music there is yet much left (in this point of exquisite consorts) to try and inquire.

For some reason, not yet sufficiently explained, the stream of ecclesiastical music which had been since the days of Henry VII one of the chief glories of English art began at the close of the century to run for a while with thinner and shallower volume. Byrd published nothing between 1591 and 1607 : Morley wrote some pieces for the church service, but his heart was in ballet and madrigal : Dering, Tomkins, Gibbons, belong to the later period. It would, perhaps, be indiscreet to attribute to this the fact that Shakespeare makes hardly

---

[1] See Galpin's *Old English Instruments of Music,* ch. xv, ' The Consort.'
[2] The band which played at Queen Elizabeth's funeral comprised seven each of violins, recorders, and flutes, six hautbois and sackbuts, six ' lutes and others ', four ' drums and fifes ', and no less than twenty-two trumpets. See *The King's Music*, by H. C. de Lafontaine, p. 45.

any mention of church music, except of the unorthodox sort illustrated by the dirge in *Much Ado About Nothing*. Falstaff incredibly maintains that he lost his voice 'singing of anthems', but even he admits that he has 'forgotten what the inside of a church is made of', and of his fellow choristers there are few or none. At the same time Shakespeare good-humouredly banters an abuse from which our church music has often suffered—the forcible adaptation to sacred words of incongruous secular melodies. The 'puritan' in *The Winter's Tale*, who 'sang psalms to hornpipes', is hardly a caricature : Greensleeves, in spite of Mistress Page's protest, was actually 'moralized to the Scriptures' and used as a hymn. Among the secular vocal forms the madrigal held pride of place : next came the aires and ballets, of lighter character and, as a rule, of more recurrent rhythm. The aires add an interesting chapter to the history of the solo song. Dowland writes them in four parts, 'so made that all the parts together or either of them severally may be sung to the lute orpherion or viol de gambo'. Campion, a few years later, writes in the first instance for the solo voice, but adds that 'upon occasion they have been filled in with more parts which whoso pleases may use, who likes not may leave'. It is possible that the difference marks a definite advance in the skill and proficiency of the singer. Most of Shakespeare's soloists are boys or women, and of the two most notable exceptions one is, for a vocalist, unusually profuse in apologies.[1]

There were four chief types of instrumental music : descriptive pieces, like Mundy's 'Weather' and the 'Stag hunt' of Tobias Hume ; airs with variations ; fantasies or fancies, not the artless ditties of Justice Shallow but elaborate contrapuntal pieces which developed during this period into the organized structure of the fugue ; and, most widely beloved of all, the dance-measures. The first English collection of dances appears to be that which Anthony Holborne published in 1599, but before this there were many examples in common use : the pavan, called *par excellence* 'the measure', and described by Beatrice as 'full of state and ancientry' ; the galliard or sink-a-pace, which followed it as the humorous servant follows the hero in a Spanish comedy ; the almain, with its strong rhythm and its texture of crotchets ; the jig, as 'hot and hasty' as courtship, 'and full as fantastical'. The choice is narrower than that of contemporary French music, narrower even than that of our own seventeenth century, but it bears full witness to the joy and delight of dancing, and it spreads through the plays from

---

[1] *Much Ado About Nothing,* II. iii.

the pageantry of Capulet or Leonato to the Hay of honest Dull, and the bergomask of the Athenian clowns.

When music entered so deeply into the life of the people it is natural that it should occupy a considerable place in dramatic representation.[1] The performance usually began with a flourish of trumpets, their cue given, as Dekker said, by ' the quaking prologue '; trumpets and drums were used for the entry of great personages, or for the martial music of battles; the banquet in *Timon* has its consort of hautbois, *As You Like It* ends with a dance, *Twelfth Night* with a song. The dumb-shows were accompanied by instruments often specially chosen for dramatic effect : dance-music whiled away the time between the acts of Comedy, and not improbably between the acts of Tragedy as well. Private theatres, influenced no doubt by Italian usage, employed highly skilled bands of performers and installed them in a music-room at the side of the stage : public theatres, where the accommodation was narrower and the musicians of humbler rank, sent them to the tiring-room or the balcony, or some other place of makeshift, where the audience criticized them unmercifully and often interrupted them to call for a favourite tune. It was all very simple and unsophisticated, but it had far more vitality than the self-conscious and Alexandrine art of a later day.

For the central characteristic of all our Elizabethan music is its spontaneity. Not that it was unlearned—the madrigal composers were men of immense learning—but from highest to lowest it was infused with the large elemental feelings of our common humanity. The same spirit of adventure which animated explorers and seamen ran through every pulse of the national life : the vigour and manhood which could do everything because it dared everything, conquered the provinces of art as it overran the Indies or circumnavigated the globe. There is no truth in the saying that the arts have prospered best amid a decadent people : they are the natural expression of chivalry and fearlessness and high enterprise. Shakespeare consummated the greatest age in our history : it is no coincidence that he found among his contemporaries a music which we have never surpassed.

[1] See, on this subject, Mr. Cowling's excellent monograph *Music on the Shakespearean Stage*.

W. H. HADOW.

BIANCA'S MUSIC-LESSON

VERY few of Shakespeare's plays deal with music as minutely as is done in *The Taming of the Shrew*. The lover's disguise as a music-master, that situation which Beaumarchais and Rossini turned to such good account in later years, amply justifies a freer use of technical terms than Shakespeare allows himself elsewhere. And it is curious that even apart from the character of Hortensio, another musical allusion is made, in the scene where Petruchio wrings Grumio by the ears, and says ' I'll try how you can *sol-fa* and sing it ! ' It would almost seem as though, in view of the very technical passage that was to come in Act III, Shakespeare felt at liberty to make a joke that only the more musical people in the audience would understand. Besides the use of the syllables *sol-fa* in musical notation, these two were used, of course by derivation from the other meaning, to denote the stick or roll of paper for beating time. It is at least possible that the order to Grumio to knock at Hortensio's door implies that the servant had a stick in his hand.

In the scene where Hortensio has the lute broken over his head appears the pun on the word ' fret ' which was afterwards repeated in *Hamlet*. There the joke is a little forced, for a recorder, being a wind instrument, has no frets. Frets are an essential feature of instruments of the lute family ; they are the fixed or movable bars across the fingerboard which make it easier for the player to keep in tune, and the absence of which gives the violin and its kindred the great power of slight gradations in pitch, as well as making them the hardest of all to play. The epithet ' twangling Jack ', later in Hortensio's tale of Katharine's behaviour, is of course the common allusion to the little pieces of wood that hold the quill or leather plectra in the early keyboard instruments, such as the virginal and harpsichord. To call a lutenist a ' fiddler ' or to allude to the virginal would no doubt be as much of an insult in

Shakespeare's time as it was, down to the end of last century, to call any musical person a 'fiddler'; there must be many living who remember the term being applied to musical people generally as a sneer.

Coming now to the longest of the musical passages in the play, the lesson in the gamut in which Hortensio declares himself as Bianca's lover, it is clear that the music-lesson is a parallel, more or less close, to the Latin lesson given by Lucentio, and as that is pure nonsense—that is to say, as the Latin words have no sort of connexion with the conversation of the lovers—it is possible to assume that the musical terms are equally removed from the phrases used by Hortensio. But I think that the music-lesson has a little more method than the Latin one, or at least there are in it more suggestions taken from the musical terms used. As I fear that very few musicians in the present day could honestly say with Bianca, that they are 'past the gamut long ago' (at least, in the sense of having learnt it in their youth), perhaps a short explanation of its nature may not be out of place, since it served a very real purpose in the music of its time, and without some knowledge of what that purpose was, we shall be, like many of the older editors of the plays, at a loss to explain some of Hortensio's love-making.

As soon as the art of music was freed from the dominion of the old modes (usually called 'ecclesiastical' for no reason except that the plain-song of the Church preserved them in written music), and found it possible to pass from one key to another nearly related to it, they saw that there was a key on each side, as it were, of the central or 'natural' key of C, to which modulation could readily be effected. That of G, the scale of which was called the *hexachordum durum*, had all the notes of its hexachord inside the scale of C, since the differential note, F, on which the modulation chiefly depended, lay outside the *hexachordum durum*. On the other side of the *hexachordum naturale* (the first six notes of the scale of C), there lay the *hexachordum molle* (the scale of F), so-called because its characteristic fourth note must be flattened in order to conform to the pattern of the others, in which the first semitone must always occur between the third note and the fourth. The old syllables, derived from the initial syllables of a hymn 'Ut queant laxis', to St. John Baptist, were useful as showing the place of the semitones, whatever the pitch. So the names *ut, re, mi, fa, sol,* and *la* always stood for the first notes of the major scale, with a semitone always between *mi* and *fa*. In order that the starting-points of these three scales should

be remembered, a table was constructed in which the scales were given with their 'sol-fa' equivalents :

THE GAMUT

F						
E					la	
D				la	sol	
C				sol	fa	
B				♭fa	♮mi	
A			la	mi	re	
G			sol	re	ut	
F			fa	ut		
E			la	mi		
D		la	sol	re		
C		sol	fa	ut	— — — — — —
B		♭fa	♮mi			
A	la	mi	re			
G	sol	re	ut			
F	fa	ut				
E	la	mi				
D	sol	re				
C	fa	ut				
B	mi					
A	re					
Γ	ut					

At the same time the table showed the great stave of eleven lines, on which, using also the spaces between them, all the notes of the seven hexachords were included, there being one line above the gamut, called now the treble F. Here we have the usual two staves of pianoforte music, with the line for middle C shown as dotted. On this line was placed the C clef, that stumbling-block to the readers of to-day. The names by which the individual notes were known were made up by reading across the table. Thus the highest note was called ' E la ', the next ' D la sol ', and so on. As the gamut was always taught from the bottom, the first note, from which the table took its name, was called ' Gamma ut ' or ' Gamut ', because the Greek letter was used for the note that had been added below the limits of the old tetrachords (called προσλαμβανόμενος). As the second hexachord does not start until the note C, the two notes between it and the lowest have only one name each, ' A re ' and ' B mi '. The beginning of the second hexachord is indicated by the name ' C fa ut ', and the remaining two notes of the first hexachord are 'D sol re' and 'E la mi'. These names were used, down to the times of the old English Church composers, for the keys in which their anthems and services were composed. What we should now call the key of E minor, for example, was known as that of 'E la mi', and afterwards as 'the key of E with the lesser third'.

As I have already said, the first necessary alteration of note took place at the upper B, since it served not only as the third, or *mi* of the major scale, but as the fourth, or *fa* of the scale beginning on F. In this capacity it had to be flattened, to make it a semitone above the *mi*, the note A. The two forms of the note B were expressed by two forms of the written letter, one by the round b of the cursive alphabet, the other by the gothic letter ♭. These two are of course the origin of the modern signs for the flat (♭) and sharp (♯)[1] respectively.

Bearing in mind as much as may be of this dull explanation, let us consider the written gamut which Bianca reads aloud. The first line,

Gamut I am, the ground of all accord,

describes the lowest note of the scale, and sets forth Hortensio's conviction that he is an eligible suitor for Bianca. In the line

'A re,' to plead Hortensio's passion

is it too fanciful to suppose that the name of the note suggests the French *à* or Italian *a*, and the form of the phrase ' to ' plead, as though he would have given it in full, ' a rappresentare l'amore ' or some such words ? The note B naturally suggests Bianca's name, and on this note I shall have something more to say presently. One is reminded of the old joke in *Punch* about a song with the refrain ' Be mine ' being appropriately set to music in the key of B minor. So little knowledge had the printers of the Quarto and the Folios that in them the name of the note stands as 'Beeme'. The next line possibly derives its form of phrase from the word 'ut', although the relative use of the word 'that' does not of course represent the conjunction. Leaving for later consideration the next line, it may be pointed out that the key called 'E la mi' is elegiac in character, and might very well have such words as 'have pity' set to it. The preceding line, '"D sol re," one clef, two notes have I,' is the one puzzling thing in the verse, for there is no possible sense in which that step of the scale can be said to have two notes. The appro-

---

[1] It is perhaps hardly necessary to add that the sign for the natural (♮) is another modification of the same letter, introduced later than the other two signs. The sharp and flat were anciently used to restore the original pitch after an accidental, as we now use the natural.

priateness of the words to Hortensio's disguise is obvious, but how do they fit the gamut? The only note of which they can be true is the higher B, the octave above ' B mi '. For, as explained above, this note has to take on two forms, B flat and B natural, according to the different hexachords to which it belongs. Are we to suppose that Shakespeare did not know this, or that he made Hortensio ignorant of what he professed to teach? I think he wanted the quip about the ambiguity of the note B somewhere in his verse, yet to go regularly up the scale for five lines more till he got to the upper B would have lengthened out the scene unduly; besides, ' B mi ' was already appropriated to Bianca, so that he just transferred the ambiguous character of that note to one for which there was no special pun.

It will be noticed that in the table given above the place of the notes on the musical stave is taught side by side with the useful, if arbitrary, syllables which contain the germ of that well-known adaptation of the gamut by Miss Glover, known throughout the British dominions as the ' Tonic Sol-Fa Notation '. The principle that not merely the starting-points of the hexachords, but any and every note of the scale, can be viewed as the *ut* or *do* (as the tonic, or keynote, is now called) of its own scale, is of inestimable value, and the modern development of the gamut, the ' modulator ' which hangs in every elementary schoolroom at the present moment, contains many important truths, of some of which most Tonic Sol-Fa teachers seem unaware. It is a sad pity that the syllables have become divorced from the staff notation in too many cases, so that proficiency in their utterance is popularly supposed to be ' reading ' music at sight. If the two systems had always been kept together, with the syllables used as an introduction to the staff, as they are in the gamut, the diffusion of real musical skill throughout the country would be far greater than it is now. Those who find in the prevalence of the ' new ' notation the chief obstacle to real advance in the training of choirs in difficult music, will be inclined to say with Bianca :

> I like it not:
> Old fashions please me best; I am not so nice,
> To change true rules for odd inventions.

J. A. FULLER-MAITLAND.

SHAKESPEARIAN OPERAS

FROM time to time various attempts have been made to compile a complete bibliography of music connected with Shakespeare's plays and poems. The most elaborate, if not the most correct, was the *List of all the Songs and Passages in Shakspere which have been set to Music*, issued in 1884, as No. 3 of Series VIII of the publications of the New Shakspere Society. But this list was in many respects incomplete and inaccurate. The work, indeed, is one of very great difficulty and would require not only considerable research but also more musical knowledge than was possessed by the authors of the New Shakspere Society's list. To accomplish it properly some sort of classification would be absolutely necessary. In the first rank might be placed Incidental Music (vocal and instrumental) intended, like the Shakespearian settings of Arne, to accompany stage performances of the various plays ; another category should include vocal settings of words by Shakespeare, not primarily intended for stage performance ; a third class would be devoted to instrumental and vocal works inspired by, or intended to illustrate musically, works by Shakespeare ; while a final section could be devoted to operas founded on subjects derived from the plays. As a contribution to the last of these categories the present notes have been drawn up. They have no claim to completeness and are only to be looked upon as hints or suggestions for future workers. At the outset very great difficulties are encountered, for of all branches of theatrical literature that of operatic librettos has been most neglected by bibliographers. Usually printed for special occasions in very small editions, the librettos of operas have often appeared without complying with the registration formalities of the Copyright Acts, and, in England at least, have consequently seldom found their way into public libraries. Even when they have done so, they have generally been entered under the names of the authors, and who, among many, could say off-hand who are the authors of even such well-known works as Beethoven's *Fidelio*, Verdi's *Trovatore*, or Humperdinck's *Hänsel und Gretel* ? When, as in the case of the great mass of operas on Shakespearian subjects, we have to deal with a number of works which have only enjoyed an ephemeral existence, the difficulty is multiplied indefinitely, and we are forced to have recourse to the standard opera-dictionaries of Clément and Larousse and Riemann, where the works are entered under their titles. But here fresh difficulties are encountered, for it is often impossible to tell from their titles whether the operas are really based on Shakespeare, and even whether they are operas at all, or only productions of Shakespeare's plays interlarded with additional music, as in the case of the many so-called operas for which Sir Henry Bishop was responsible in London in the early part of the nineteenth century. Of late the neglected subject of opera-librettos seems to have attracted the attention of bibliographers. The Library of Congress (Washington) has acquired what is probably the richest collection of such works, and Mr. O. G. Sonneck, the librarian in charge of the musical department, has issued an admirably exhaustive catalogue of the earlier part of the collection. The British Museum has also turned its attention to librettos and has acquired some valuable collections, which have been incorporated in the printed general Catalogue. The whole of this has been recently read through and the librettos re-catalogued under the names of the operas, with a view to the publication of a libretto-catalogue somewhat on the lines of the Library of Congress Catalogue. This work is at present still in manuscript, but it has been made use of in drawing up the following notes. In their preparation it has been thought best to adopt an alphabetical arrangement under the names of the different plays : where a play is omitted it is to be understood that no opera on the subject has been discovered.

Antony and Cleopatra.

There is a long list (under ' Cléopâtre ') in the *Dictionnaire Lyrique* of Clément and Larousse, and another list (under ' Kleopatra ') in Riemann's *Opern-Handbuch* of operas in which Cleopatra is the heroine, but it is doubtful whether any of these can be said to be based on Shakespeare's play. Enna's *Cleopatra* (1894), Massé's *Nuit de Cléopâtre* (1885), Massenet's *Cléopâtre* (1914), and Collin de Blamont's ballet *Cléopâtre* (1748), have no connexion with the play. The *Antonius und Kleopatra* of J. C. Kaffka (1779) and of Count E. F. von Sayn-Wittgenstein (1883), and R. Kreutzer's ballet *Les Amours d'Antoine et de Cléopâtre* (1808) seem possibly, from their titles, to be founded on Shakespeare.

As You Like It.

The play was turned into an opera by P. A. Rolli for Francesco Maria Veracini and produced as *Rosalinda* during the composer's visit to London in 1744. There are other operas with the same name : *La Rosalinda*, by G. M. Capelli (Venice, 1692) and by M. A. Ziani (Venice, 1693), but these have no connexion with Shakespeare's comedy, nor has the *Rosalinda* of J. Lockman and J. C. Smith (London, 1740). There are also two operas called *Rosalinde* by N. A. Strungk (Leipzig, 1695) and F. van Duyse (Antwerp, 1864) as to which information is wanting. *As You Like It* was played in London in 1824, arranged as an opera by Bishop.

The Comedy of Errors.

A musical pasticcio by Bishop was concocted on the play and produced in London in 1819.

Coriolanus.

Numerous old Italian operas on *Coriolanus*, generally entitled *Caio Marzio Coriolano*, are recorded in the dictionaries, but it is uncertain whether any of them are founded on Shakespeare.

Hamlet.

The librettos of the earlier Italian works on *Hamlet* were generally by Apostolo Zeno and P. Pariati ; the French adaptation by Ducis was made use of later. Operas by the following composers are recorded (in chronological order) : C. F. Gasparini (Rome, 1705—played in London in 1712), Domenico Scarlatti (Rome, 1715), G. Carcano (Venice, 1742), Caruso (Florence, 1790), Foppa (Padua, 1792), Andreozzi (Genoa, 1793), Count von Gallenberg—a ' Pantomime tragique '—(Paris, 1816), Mercadante (Milan, 1823), Mareczek (Brünn, 1840), Buzzola (Venice, 1848), Moroni (Rome, 1860), Faccio—book by Boito—(Genoa, 1865), Ambroise Thomas (Paris, 1868), A. Stadtfeld (Bonn, 1881), and A. Hignard (Nantes, 1888). Of all these, only Ambroise Thomas's opera survived for a time. To judge by the few excerpts that have been published, Faccio's work was the most remarkable of the long series ; it had the advantage of an admirable libretto, in which Shakespeare's tragedy was closely followed.

Julius Caesar.

There are innumerable operas—mostly of the eighteenth century—on *Julius Caesar*, as to which Riemann and Clément and Larousse may be consulted. But it is very doubtful whether any of them are founded on Shakespeare.

King Henry IV.

The early career of Henry V has formed the subject of a certain number of operas, but most of these (e. g. Hérold's *La Gioventù di Enrico V* (Naples, 1817), and Pacini's work with the same title (Rome, 1821)) have nothing to do with Shakespeare. An exception is Mercadante's *Gioventù di Enrico V* (Milan, 1834), the libretto of which, by F. Romani, is founded on Shakespeare's *Henry IV*. Further information is desirable as to P. J. de Volder's *La Jeunesse de Henri Cinq* (Ghent, *c.* 1825) and other operas on the same subject recorded in the dictionaries. The Falstaff scenes may have been used in some of the operas of that name, but they are here entered under *The Merry Wives of Windsor*.

King Lear.

The earliest opera on this tragedy seems to be the *Cordelia* of C. Kreutzer (Donaueschingen, 1819); the same title is borne by works by Séméladis (Versailles, 1854) and Gobati (Bologna, 1881). A *Lear* by A. Reynaud saw the light at Toulouse in 1888. The *Cordelia* of the Russian composer N. T. Solowiew (1885) is founded on Sardou's *La Haine*; the subject is quite different from Shakespeare's tragedy. It is well known that Verdi at one time thought of taking *Lear* as the subject of an opera, but unfortunately the idea was never carried out.

King Richard III.

G. Salvayre's *Richard III* (Petrograd, 1883) is founded on Shakespeare's play, though much altered. The *Riccardo III* of G. B. Meiners (Milan, 1859), on the other hand, has no connexion with the English poet. As to the *Richardus Impius Angliae Rex* of J. Eberlin (Salzburg, 1750) and the *Riccardo III* of L. Canepa (Milan, 1879), information is lacking.

Macbeth.

Much incidental music has been written for *Macbeth*, but the subject has not escaped the attention of librettists. It was treated as a *Ballo tragico* by F. Clerico (Milan, 1802), and again as a *Ballo mimico* by C. Pugni (Milan, 1830)—a very curious work, in the sleep-walking scene of which Lady Macbeth kills her own son, thinking he is Duncan!

The earliest opera on the subject seems to be the *Macbeth* of H. Chélard (Paris, 1827), played in London in 1832, the libretto of which was by the composer of the *Marseillaise*, Rouget de l'Isle, who has given Duncan a daughter and introduced the sleep-walking scene before the discovery of the King's murder. Taubert's *Macbeth* (Berlin, 1857) follows the tragedy fairly closely. There is an early opera on *Macbeth* by Verdi, originally produced in Florence in 1847 and revised and partly rewritten for Paris in 1865. In spite of some fine passages there is little in the work to foreshadow the composer's great achievements in *Otello* and *Falstaff* : the opera is written in the conventional Italian idiom of the day and it has never survived. The most recent musical drama on Shakespeare's tragedy is the *Macbeth* of E. Bloch, played at the Paris Opéra Comique in 1910. It is interesting to note that in 1809 there was published the First Act of a libretto on *Macbeth* by J. von Collin : sketches by Beethoven for an overture and chorus in this were printed by G. Nottebohm in the *Musikalisches Wochenblatt* for 1879.

The Merchant of Venice.

The only opera on this play was composed by C. Pinsuti and produced at Milan in 1874. Clément and Larousse record a Dutch opera on the subject, by J. A. Just, performed at Amsterdam about 1787, but this work is the *Koopman van Smyrna*, first produced at Bonn in 1782.

The Merry Wives of Windsor.

An obscure violinist named Papavoine seems to have been the first to use this play as the foundation of an opera. His work, entitled *Le Vieux Coquet*, was produced in Paris in 1761, but was withdrawn after one performance. There are German operas on the play by P. Ritter (Mannheim, 1794) and Ditters von Dittersdorf (Oels, 1796) as to which little seems to be known. Salieri's *Falstaff, osia Le tre Burle* (Dresden, 1799) has a good libretto, printed in Italian and German. A musical version of the play, chiefly by Braham, Horn, and Parry, was produced in London in 1823. An Italian opera—*Falstaff* —by Balfe (London, 1838), Otto Nicolai's *Die Lustigen Weiber von Windsor* (Berlin, 1849), Adolphe Adam's *Falstaff* (Paris, 1856), and Verdi's *Falstaff* (Milan, 1893) complete the list. It is curious that the *Merry Wives* should have given rise to two operas like that of Nicolai—which has enjoyed longer popularity than any other Shakespearian opera—and the *Falstaff* of Verdi, a work of consummate genius which the public has never yet appreciated at its real value.

A Midsummer Night's Dream.

This is one of the earliest of Shakespeare's plays which was laid hands on for operatic purposes. It was turned by some anonymous adaptor into a (so-called) opera, with admirable music by Henry Purcell, produced in London in 1692. The adaptation is very curious, for Shakespeare's dialogue is partly retained, while the musical additions have the least possible relation to the play, with the result that not one word of Shakespeare's has been set by Purcell. Other operas on the play are *The Fairies*, by J. C. Smith (London, 1755), and (probably) Manusardi's *Un Sogno di Primavera* (Milan, 1842); Busby's *Fair Fugitives* (London, 1803), which is given in some dictionaries as founded on Shakespeare, has nothing to do with the play, nor have Ambroise Thomas's *Songe d'une Nuit d'Été* (Paris, 1850) and Offenbach's *Rêve d'une Nuit d'Été* (Paris, 1855). The Zarzuela *El Sueño de una Noche de Verano*, by Gaztambide (Madrid, 1852), probably belongs to the same category as the two last-named works. A musical version of Shakespeare's play was produced by Bishop in London in 1816 and the *Clowns' Masque* forms the foundation of the *Pyramus and Thisbe* of Leveridge (London, 1716) and of Lampe (London, 1745).

Much Ado About Nothing.

There are four operas founded on this play, viz. *Béatrice et Bénédict*, by Berlioz (Baden-Baden, 1862); *Beaucoup de Bruit pour rien*, by P. Puget (Paris, 1899); *Much Ado About Nothing*, by Stanford (London, 1900) and *Ero*, by C. Podestà (Cremona, 1900).

Othello.

Rossini's *Otello* (Naples, 1816) enjoyed a long run of popularity, but seems now to be defunct ; a *Ballo Tragico*, arranged by S. Vigano (composer not stated), was produced in Milan in 1818, and the same place saw in 1887 the first performance of Verdi's *Otello*, the composer's operatic masterpiece. A ' Juguete cómico lírico ' by M. Nieto, entitled *Otelo y Desdémona* (Madrid, 1883), has nothing to do with Shakespeare's tragedy.

Romeo and Juliet.

This play has formed the basis of a very large number of operas and ballets, with various titles. The earliest seems to be a *Dramma per musica* in two Acts, published at Berlin in 1773, without any composer's name. It was followed in quick succession by works on the same subject by G. Benda (Gotha, 1776), J. G. Schwanenberg (Leipzig, 1776), L. Marescalchi (Rome, 1789), S. von Rumling (Munich, 1790), Dalayrac (Paris, 1792), Steibelt (Paris, 1793), Zingarelli (Milan, 1796), Porta (Paris, 1806), I. Schuster (Vienna, 1808), P. C. Guglielmi (London, 1810), Vaccai (Milan, 1825), Bellini (Venice, 1830), a ballet without composer's name (Milan, 1830), F. Gioja—a ballet (Milan, 1833), Marchetti (Trieste, 1865), Gounod (Paris, 1867), A. Mercadal (Mahon, 1873), Marquis d'Ivry (Paris, 1878), and H. R. Shelley (published in New York, 1901). An operatic version of Berlioz's *Roméo et Juliette* symphony was published in Paris *c.* 1880.

The Taming of the Shrew.

A musical version, chiefly by Beaham and T. S. Cooke, saw the light in London in 1828, but the only real opera on the play is H. Goetz's *Der Widerspänstigen Zähmung* (Mannheim, 1874), an excellent work which seems to have fallen into undeserved neglect. The ballad farce *A Cure for a Scold* (London, 1735) is founded on Shakespeare's play, but considerably altered (by James Worsdale). V. Martin's *Capricciosa corretta* (Lisbon, 1797), mentioned in some of the dictionaries, has an entirely different plot.

The Tempest.

There is more difficulty in giving a correct list of operas on this play than in any other case, owing to the uncertainty as to dates and to the habit which musical lexicographers have of assuming that every work called *La Tempesta, Der Geisterinsel, Der Sturm*, &c., must be based on Shakespeare. The following list is therefore entirely tentative and subject to revision. The earliest opera on the play is the version of Thomas Shadwell, with music by Matthew Locke, played in London in 1673. This seems to have been revised in 1676 and again in 1690 or 1695 (the date has never been definitely ascertained) with the well-known and beautiful music of Henry Purcell. Other operas recorded as being on the same subject are as follows : J. C. Smith (London, 1756) ; Aspelmayr (Vienna, 1782) ; J. H. Rolle (Berlin, 1784) ; Fabrizi (Rome, 1788) ; Winter (Munich, 1793) ; Fleischmann (Ratisbon, 1796) ; Reichardt (Berlin, 1798) ; Wenzel Müller (Vienna, 1798) ; Zumsteeg (Stuttgart, 1798) ; P. Ritter (Aurich, 1799) ; Caruso (Naples, 1799) ; J. H. Hensel (Hirschberg, 1799) ; P. Wranitzky (*c.* 1800) ; A. J. Emmert (Salzburg, 1806) ; E. Raymond (*c.* 1840) ; Rung (Copenhagen, 1847) ; Halévy (London, 1850) ; Napravnik (Prague, *c.* 1860) ; Kaschperov (Petrograd, 1867) ; Urich (probably not on Shakespeare, Brussels, 1879) ; Chapi (a zarzuela, almost certainly not on Shakespeare, Madrid, 1883) ; E. Frank (Hanover, 1887) ; Urspruch (Frankfurt, 1888) ; Ambroise Thomas (a ballet, Paris, 1889) ; and Z. Fibich (Prague, 1895).

Timon of Athens.

The *Timone Misantropo* of the Emperor Leopold I (Vienna, 1696) was probably founded on Shakespeare's play.

Twelfth Night.

A musical version was produced by Bishop in London in 1820, but the only genuine opera from the play seems to be the *Cesario* of W. Taubert (Berlin, 1874).

The Two Gentlemen of Verona.

Bishop produced a musical version, played in London in 1821.

The Winter's Tale.

This play forms the basis of the *Hermione* of Max Bruch (Berlin, 1872).

Owing to the incomplete character of the above lists, it is not possible, without further research, to give definite statistics as to the operas that have been derived from Shakespeare's plays. But it is clearly evident that *The Tempest* and *Romeo and Juliet* have proved the most tempting subjects to librettists, followed closely by *Hamlet* and *longo intervallo* by *The Merry Wives of Windsor*. As to the nationality of the composers, probably we shall not be far wrong in giving them as about thirty-three per cent. Italian, thirty per cent. German, nineteen per cent. French, eleven per cent. English, and the remainder of other nationalities.

W. Barclay Squire.

WILLIAM SHAKESPEARE

AN artist may seem out of place in this procession of the initiated and his rustic pipe unworthy of its subject. ' *Tristis at ille, tamen cantabunt Arcades.*' Shakespeare is our common heritage. He exists for all, not only for the scholar and the critic, and however inadequate its expression, our gratitude for all that we owe to this surpassing genius is not less fervent and sincere than theirs. What that feeling is I will endeavour to define.

It has been suggested that this obligation may have some special bearing in the case of artists, that is, as I take it, that they may have found in Shakespeare direct technical motives in their several arts. Industrious students have collected references to the arts in his works, and have even sought to draw up a sort of aesthetic of Shakespeare.

To me this seems false criticism, and the wrong point of view from which to approach him. Literature and the arts have their own limits and conditions, and they are by no means interchangeable, and when Shakespeare turned to the arts, he used them as he used all nature, for the setting and environment of his humanity, to give the atmosphere he wanted, and without any ulterior intention. He drew on what he saw or had heard, without formulating to himself any theory of the arts, without any idea of providing in his word-paintings matter for direct translation into terms of graphic or plastic art. That his plays have provided inexhaustible subjects for illustration does not affect the point that Shakespeare's attitude to the arts was objective, and that when he refers to them he does so, not from the technical standpoint of an artist, but from that of a poet and a student and observer of universal nature. There is the famous word-picture in the *Rape of Lucrece*, where the poet gives a panorama of the siege of Troy—adding scene to scene and detail to detail with a profusion which would be simply impossible in an actual picture. The poet no doubt had some picture before him, and let his fancy play on it in order to convey to his reader a cumulative impression of all the turmoil and emotions of the siege of Troy, but it would be the first business of a painter to eliminate the greater part of the detail which came within the scope of the poet's imagination. One might as well attempt to design a house from Bacon's *Essay*, as attempt to convey in any one picture the impressions given by Shakespeare's verse. Poets do not exist to write specifications for architects and painters.

Yet this in no way affects our debt of gratitude to Shakespeare. The common basis of all imaginative art is our humanity, our likes and dislikes, our hopes and fears, our ideals and our scheme of values ; and the man who most of all extends the range of our outlook, quickens our imagination and teaches us to see beauty everywhere, and to discern the vital interests of life, is the man to whom we shall turn again and again, with ever-increasing gratitude. In Shakespeare, more than in any poet or playwright that has ever lived, we find this teacher. The wise old Latin prided himself on his interest in all humanity. Shakespeare had that interest in a transcendent degree, because he did not limit his interest to men and cities, but included in his outlook the whole range of nature with man as part of it. So it is, that he has provided an immense spiritual background for all imaginative artists. He has done the one supreme thing. He has given us not only visions but the power of seeing, and he has given us this power unreservedly and with the inexhaustible bounty of some great natural force. Other writers of genius have their own special conditions. The splendid verse of Milton, Swift's clean-cut prose, Keat's lyrics, require their own mood, their own particular temperament for their full appreciation. It is not so with Shakespeare. He appeals to us anywhere and under all conditions with the inexhaustible richness of his genius, with a certain universality that passes beyond the limits of time and local circumstance.

Literature alone survives in strenuous times, and not only survives but seems to burn with brighter and more ardent fires. Shakespeare's age was the age *par excellence* of great adventure, and then, as now, Englishmen were fighting for their lives and liberties, for their ideals and for all that makes life worth living for themselves and their posterity, and that age remains the period of the unrivalled flowering of English literature with no real counterpart in the arts of the time. The writer was ahead of the artist. He had grasped the spirit of the far-away Renaissance, its large humanity, its spacious outlook, when our sculptors and our painters had not yet recovered their heritage, and our builders still thought in terms of Gothic, however much they might try to catch the fashion with their travesties of the orders. The man of ideas, the man who had to realize his ideas clearly in order to make them articulate, was generations ahead of the artist who plodded humbly in his wake, a figure not without pathetic interest in its gropings after ideals ill-understood. John Shute might say of his treatise of the orders, ' That with it as with a klew or thread, or plaine pathway a man may most easily pearse and lightly pasover the most darke and unknown corners of the whole process ' of Architecture. The thread snapped in the hand of the user. Elizabethan architecture and Elizabethan art generally stand on a very different plane from that of Elizabethan literature. It is dear to us for its associations, not for its intrinsic value. We like to think of the low-browed, half-timbered hostelries in which Falstaff took his pleasures, of Justice Shallow's trim garden and orchard ' where in an arbour we will eat a last year's pippin of my own graffing ', of rare and curious jewellery because Elizabeth and her ladies wear it, of the quaint embroidery of their gowns, of all that kindly, homely art that we associate with the England of Elizabeth.

But if we turn on to it the cold dry light of historical criticism we have to admit that it is not first-rate, not very important in the history of art, a very humble companion of our sixteenth-century literature. We may love it for what it means to us, but we should be under no illusion as to its relative position in the history of art. In other ages the painter, the sculptor, and the architect, have as much to say to us as the writer. Michael Angelo dominates Italy of the sixteenth century, Wren speaks to us as clearly as Dryden, Turner's vision of nature impresses us more than the poetry of Wordsworth, but the England of Elizabeth will always be summed up for us in the plays and poetry of Shakespeare ; they are the real setting and background of that splendid age.

One would have thought that there could be no misconception as to a figure so typically English. The Germans have claimed him for their own, yet it is impossible to conceive anything more remote from Shakespeare's serene and happy genius than the modern German attitude to life, to nature, and to art, than the habit of mind that finds its pleasure in the dissonances of Strauss, that conceives of the masterpieces of Greek Tragedy in the terms of a blatant showman, that prefers the horrible and morbid to the beauty of the cloud in the sky, the wind in the reeds, beauty of movement, form, and colour. We turn to Shakespeare and find the clearest and cleanest mind, the sanest thinker that has ever written in ours or any other language. His splendid vision saw beauty everywhere ; in the sky, in the sea, in the city, in the solitary place—everything yielded its measure of beauty to his magic touch, and beyond and above all price is the large humanity of this extraordinary nature, so rich in sympathy, so intense in its sensitiveness to every sort of vital impression.

He has fixed for us the true type of Englishman. I do not mean any one special character, but rather a figure as it were that slowly enters into our consciousness, that disengages itself from the complexity of his creations as the standard and ideal of all Englishmen. Our race has its manifold weaknesses, but it has never yet wholly failed in its passionate love of freedom and justice, its hatred of oppression and sympathy with the weak and lowly, in dogged courage, in keen and ever-present humour, and not least of all in that rare capacity for ideals, little suspected by those who do not know us, yet so deep-seated and inveterate that it realizes itself not in speech but in action. This is the high ideal of character that is recognized by our race throughout the world, and it has been set for us for all time by the unique and incomparable genius of Shakespeare.

REGINALD BLOMFIELD.

FROGNAL, HAMPSTEAD,
February, 1916.

THE SACK OF TROY IN SHAKESPEARE'S 'LUCRECE' AND IN SOME FIFTEENTH-CENTURY DRAWINGS AND TAPESTRIES[1]

WHAT are the points of contact to be noticed between the art of Shakespeare as poet and dramatist and the graphic and plastic arts as they were known and practised in his time : in other words, where and to what extent do we find him showing familiarity with works of painting or sculpture or deriving suggestions from them ? In the great kingdom of Shakespeare study the province to which these questions point is a very small one, but has perhaps not yet been quite thoroughly explored. The only contribution I feel qualified to make to the present Memorial Volume—and a very humble contribution it will be—is an examination of a particular nook or corner of that province which happens long to have interested me.

I do not intend to discuss the character or conversation of the professional painter who plays a part in *Timon of Athens*; neither shall I dwell on the amatory pictures from Ovid with which the nobleman in *The Taming of the Shrew* (in what is supposed, be it remembered, to be the non-Shakespearian part of it) directs his servants to tickle the clownish senses of Christopher Sly. Nor shall I revive the old debate whether the two pictures between which Hamlet bids his mother make comparison in the closet scene were meant to be real pictures or merely pictures of the mind, and whether, in the former case, Shakespeare thought of them as full-sized portraits or as miniatures—as things that might have been done, let us say, to instance two among his contemporaries, by Mark Garrard or Nicolas Hilliard respectively. I will not

---

[1] The chief authorities on the works of art referred to are: A. Jubinal, *Les Anciennes Tapisseries historiées*, Paris, 1838-9; Paul Schumann, *Der Trojanische Krieg, französische Handzeichnungen zu Teppichen, u.s.w.*, Dresden, 1898; Jean Guiffrey, *Histoire de la tapisserie depuis le moyen âge*, 1886; id. 'La Guerre de Troie', &c., in *Revue de l'Art*, tom. v (1899); and the Catalogue of the Rheims Museum.

even let myself—though I should like to—linger on the question what kind of a picture, sacred or profane, an Annunciation to the Shepherds or a descent of Mercury on a mission from Jove (for a picture of some kind I am sure it was), suggested the enraptured lines in which Romeo cries to Juliet that she is

> As glorious to this night, being o'er my head,
> As is a winged messenger of heaven
> Unto the white-upturned wond'ring eyes
> Of mortals, that fall back to gaze on him
> When he bestrides the lazy-pacing clouds,
> And sails upon the bosom of the air.

Personally I can never help associating those lines with the shepherd who throws back his head to gaze up at the child angel riding on the cloud in that wonderful purple-blue mountain background of Titian's Virgin and Child with Saint Catherine in the National Gallery— a picture which Shakespeare is quite unlikely to have seen. Again, with reference to the famous speech of Jaques in *As You Like It* about the seven ages of man, seeing that the subject was a stock one alike in morality play and masque, in paintings and decorations of all kinds, in the head-pieces of illuminated and printed calendars and in the woodcuts of cheap popular broadsides, I will not ask from which among all the many and various current treatments of it, scenic or graphic, Shakespeare may have taken his cue : I will only allow myself to note in passing (I know not whether it has been noted before) a curious identity between the phrase of Jaques concerning the type of the fourth age, the soldier,

> Jealous in honour, sudden and quick in quarrel,
> Seeking the bubble reputation
> Even in the cannon's mouth,

and that used by the Italian painter-critic Carlo Ridolfi when he tells of a similar figure in a painting, now lost, of the same subject of the Ages of Man (or Symbol of Human Life) by Giorgione : 'Nel mezzo eravi un uomo di robusto aspetto tutto armato . . . *pronto di vendicare ogni piccola offesa* e preparato negli arringhi di Marte a versare il sangue per lo desio della gloria.'

The sole and special passage of Shakespeare on which for the present purpose I want the reader to fix his attention is the description in his early poem, *The Rape of Lucrece*, of the painting of the Sack of Troy which occupies the eyes and thoughts of the dishonoured matron while she waits till her husband Collatine shall come from the camp at her summons. It is far the longest account of a work of art in any part of Shakespeare's writings, filling a little over two hundred lines. For my purpose the first hundred or so must of necessity be quoted in full :

At last she calls to mind where hangs a piece
Of skilful painting, made for Priam's Troy ;
Before the which is drawn the power of Greece,
For Helen's rape the city to destroy,
Threatening cloud-kissing Ilion with annoy ;
   Which the conceited painter drew so proud,
   As heaven, it seem'd, to kiss the turrets bow'd.

A thousand lamentable objects there,
In scorn of nature, art gave lifeless life ;
Many a dry drop seem'd a weeping tear,
Shed for the slaughter'd husband by the wife :
The red blood reek'd, to show the painter's strife ;
   And dying eyes gleam'd forth their ashy lights,
   Like dying coals burnt out in tedious nights.

There might you see the labouring pioneer
Begrimed with sweat, and smeared all with dust ;
And from the towers of Troy there would appear
The very eyes of men through loop-holes thrust,
Gazing upon the Greeks with little lust :
   Such sweet observance in this work was had,
   That one might see those far-off eyes look sad.

In great commanders grace and majesty
You might behold, triumphing in their faces ;
In youth quick bearing and dexterity ;
And here and there the painter interlaces
Pale cowards, marching on with trembling paces ;
   Which heartless peasants did so well resemble,
   That one would swear he saw them quake and tremble.

In Ajax and Ulysses, O ! what art
Of physiognomy might one behold ;
The face of either cipher'd either's heart ;
Their face their manners most expressly told :
In Ajax' eyes blunt rage and rigour roll'd ;
   But the mild glance that sly Ulysses lent
   Show'd deep regard and smiling government.

There pleading might you see grave Nestor stand,
As 'twere encouraging the Greeks to fight ;
Making such sober action with his hand,
That it beguil'd attention, charm'd the sight.
In speech, it seem'd, his beard, all silver white,
   Wagg'd up and down, and from his lips did fly
   Thin winding breath, which purl'd up to the sky.

About him were a press of gaping faces,
Which seem'd to swallow up his sound advice;
All jointly listening, but with several graces,
As if some mermaid did their ears entice,
Some high, some low, the painter was so nice;
  The scalps of many, almost hid behind,
  To jump up higher seem'd, to mock the mind.

Here one man's hand lean'd on another's head,
His nose being shadow'd by his neighbour's ear;
Here one being throng'd bears back, all boll'n and red;
Another smother'd, seems to pelt and swear;
And in their rage such signs of rage they bear,
  As, but for loss of Nestor's golden words,
  It seem'd they would debate with angry swords.

For much imaginary work was there;
Conceit deceitful, so compact, so kind,
That for Achilles' image stood his spear,
Grip'd in an armed hand; himself behind,
Was left unseen, save to the eye of mind:
  A hand, a foot, a face, a leg, a head,
  Stood for the whole to be imagined.

And from the walls of strong-besieged Troy
When their brave hope, bold Hector, march'd to field,
Stood many Trojan mothers, sharing joy
To see their youthful sons bright weapons wield;
And to their hope they such odd action yield,
  That through their light joy seemed to appear,
  Like bright things stain'd, a kind of heavy fear.

And from the strand of Dardan, where they fought,
To Simois' reedy banks the red blood ran,
Whose waves to imitate the battle sought
With swelling ridges; and their ranks began
To break upon the galled shore, and than
  Retire again, till, meeting greater ranks,
  They join and shoot their foam at Simois' banks.

To this well-painted piece is Lucrece come,
To find a face where all distress is stell'd.
Many she sees where cares have carved some,
But none where all distress and dolour dwell'd,
Till she despairing Hecuba beheld,
  Staring on Priam's wounds with her old eyes,
  Which bleeding under Pyrrhus' proud foot lies.

When a poet describes a work of the manual arts at length, it is often hard to be sure whether he is working from imagination or from something he has really seen and noted with his eyes, or partly from one and partly from the other. But there are cases, and this is one, where the particularity of the description and the insistence on technical details make it certain that actual and interested observation has furnished the original material, however much imagination may have added to or vivified it. Of what kind, then, we have to ask ourselves, will the painting of the Siege of Troy have been which had thus caught and fixed Shakespeare's attention in the early years of his career as actor and poet in London ? Among the pictures on panel or canvas either executed in England by immigrants from Germany or the Low Countries or imported from abroad up to this date (1593), the vast majority, according to what has always been the chief English national demand, were portraits. Subjects of poetry or mythology were not wanting ; but it is difficult to conceive that there can have existed any such crowded and complicated history or battle piece, figuring many successive scenes within the four corners of a single frame, as would answer to the description above quoted. On the other hand, in the spacious figured tapestries that had been coming over since the later years of the fifteenth century from the looms of Flanders and northern France such compositions were the rule. The thousand objects to which art, in the painting described by the poet, 'gave lifeless life', their number and minuteness, the visible tears and blood, the gleam of dying eyes, the expressions in the eyes of the men looking out from the loopholes of the tower, the multitudinousness of the figures, the diversity and vividness of their gestures and expressions, and especially the manner, so precisely described, of their crowding and packing above and behind one another to the top of the composition—all these things, even when we have made full allowance for the dramatizing and intensifying effects introduced by the play of the poet's imagination, seem to point unmistakably to a work on the scale of a great tapestry-hanging, not of an ordinary framed picture on panel or canvas.

But would Shakespeare have called a tapestry a 'painting'? We have no clear instance of his doing so : but he certainly would have had no scruple in giving that name to the imitation tapestries or 'painted cloths' which in his day and earlier were so much in use as substitutes for or supplements to the costly products of the looms of Arras or Brussels. We have a difficulty in realizing all the part played by woven or painted hangings in those days, both in the fixed decoration of halls and chambers and for show on special occasions and representations. Of the cheaper, the painted variety, owing to their fragility and the tendency of the distemper colours to scale from the surface, few specimens remain in existence : the most important are four sets in illustration of mystery plays preserved until lately in the Museum at Rheims. But

Shakespeare, even taken by himself, has sufficient references to painted cloths to prove their general and familiar use in his day. Remember how Costard, in *Love's Labour's Lost*, tells Sir Nathaniel, when he has broken down in the part of Alexander in the masque, that for a punishment he shall be scraped out of the painted cloth of the Nine Worthies and Ajax put in his stead; and remember Falstaff's ragged regiment, ' as ragged as Lazarus in the painted cloth, where the glutton's dog licked his sores '.

But before assuming that the painting, ' made for Priam's Troy ', upon which Lucrece is represented poring in her despair, was such a painted hanging on the scale and in the manner of tapestry, let us see what kind of place the Siege of Troy took among the subjects commonly represented in the true works of that craft. In point of fact it is one of the subjects for which tapestry designers and weavers, doubtless following the taste of the great princes and nobles for whom they worked, had a special predilection. Next to series of Bible subjects, among fifteenth-century products of the loom, we have remains or records of series of Troy subjects in greater number than of any other. Among the comparatively recent acquisitions of the Louvre is a set of eight highly finished drawings on a small scale for just such a series : examples of the ' petits patrons ', as they were called, which artists of talent and repute were called on to supply and from which were afterwards prepared the full-sized cartoons actually used by the weavers at the loom. They date from 1480 or a little later; and among actual Troy tapestries of about the same date which are still preserved in fragments or entire, several correspond with these very designs and are founded on them.

One such, belonging to a series which formerly adorned the Château Bayard in Dauphiné, is now in the Victoria and Albert Museum : it represents the arrival of Penthesilea to the succour of Troy after the death of Hector, her victories, and her final overthrow at the hand of Pyrrhus. Another from the same or an exactly similar series, in the cathedral of Zamora in Spain, shows a scene of the Iliupersis or final destruction of the city. Some of the descriptive French verses found pinned in manuscript to the backs of the Louvre drawings are actually woven large along the upper margin of this picture. (Both in tapestries and their painted imitations it was customary to introduce such inscribed borders telling the story represented ; also to identify the persons by inscribing their names on their garments or weapons, and sometimes to put sayings and sentences on scrolls issuing from their mouths : this is what Orlando means in *As You Like It* when he says, ' I answer you right painted cloth '. Portions of another set of tapestries founded on the Louvre drawings, formerly in the Château d'Aulhac, are now in the Court of Justice at Issoire in the Puy-de-Dôme, and of yet another in the Château de Sully in the Loiret. There exist also fragments of other sets of somewhat later date and founded on different drawings.

Thus we have the means of testing by actual comparison how far the Troy picture so minutely described in Shakespeare's *Lucrece* corresponds or fails to correspond with the representations of the subject current in French and Flemish tapestries from a hundred years before his time. To make that comparison is the object of the present paper. It may be necessary to remind readers not specially conversant with the subject that the tale of Troy as known to the Middle Ages and the early Renaissance was a very different thing from the tale as we know it from Homer. To the Middle Ages Homer was only a name and was traditionally reputed a writer of no credit. Two late and spurious Latin writings, one current under the name of Dares of Phrygia, the other under that of Dictys of Crete, were the recognized and established authorities for the story of the wars of Troy, and were supposed to have been translated from Greek originals written by contemporary witnesses of the events. From these books, with additions from Virgil and Ovid, were compiled all the writings belonging to the Troy cycle which had currency in the Middle Ages, including the great monumental work of the cycle, the *Roman de Troie*, spun towards the close of the twelfth century by the French court poet Benoît de Sainte-Maure in some 40,000 lines of octosyllabic verse. A hundred years later the Sicilian Guido delle Colonne compiled from the romance poem of Sainte-Maure a Latin prose *Historia Destructionis Troiae*, which became much better known than the original, and on which the English poet Lydgate in his turn founded his *Troy Book*, and many other writers their summaries and allusions, till an elaborate French prose version in three books, finished in 1464 by one Raoul Le Fèvre, priest and chaplain to Philip Duke of Burgundy, gave the story a new lease of life, gaining great popularity in the circles which such reading reached and helping to fill men's minds with images of the Grecian and Trojan heroes doing battle in the guise of mediaeval knights, and so to stimulate the demand for their presentment in works of art. As is well known, William Caxton, then resident and working in Brussels, began rendering Le Fèvre's *Recueil* into English for his amusement and was encouraged by the English Duchess Margaret to complete it : and this translation, finished in 1471 and put in type some three years later, under the title *Recuyell of the Histories of*

Troy, was the first book ever printed in the English language. It was reprinted by Wynkyn de Worde in 1503 and again by Copland in 1553, and was familiar to Shakespeare and his contemporaries.

The tale of Troy, as thus transformed in the Middle Ages and popularized at the dawn of the Renaissance, included a vast amount of histories both antecedent and subsequent to the main matter of the siege and destruction of the city by the Greeks in revenge for the rape of Helen; as for instance the stories of Peleus and Thetis, the history of Jason and the Golden Fleece, the lives and achievements of Hercules and Theseus, with the first destruction of Troy in vengeance for the treachery of Laomedon, the return of the Greek heroes, including the murder of Agamemnon, the vengeance of Orestes, and the accidental killing of Ulysses by his son. Particularly Le Fèvre in his *Recueil* enormously amplifies the preliminaries : it is not until his third book that we get to the final siege under Agamemnon. This was the part of the story from which the tapestry designers chose their subjects, and even so, the matters which they had to illustrate took in much which we now think of as foreign to or outside the tale. They have to show how Priam dispatched Antenor and other Trojans to plead for the return of his sister Hesione, who had been carried off by Hercules to Greece, where she became the wife of Telamon ; how, this embassy being ill-received, he next sent his son Paris with a company to carry off some noble damsel of Greece for whom Hesione might be required in exchange ; how Paris, having been called upon by Mercury in a dream to adjudge the prize of beauty between the three goddesses, gave it to Venus ; how he won the love of Helen and carried her off from the temple of the goddess at Cythera ; then his return with Helen to Troy ; the war consequently made by the Greeks ; their expedition and landing ; the prophecies of Calchas and of Cassandra ; the subsequent series of battles before the walls of Troy ; the multifarious actions and debates in which the heroes, both Greek and Trojan, play sometimes the same parts with which we are familiar from Homer, but sometimes parts totally different ; the loves of Troilus and Briseida (or Creseida) ; the love of Achilles for Polixena, and his advice to the Greeks to give up the siege ; the successive deaths of Hector and of Achilles, the latter presently succeeded as foremost Grecian champion by his son Pyrrhus ; the succour brought to Troy by the Amazon queen Penthesilea until she is slain by Pyrrhus ; the treachery of Antenor, who by bribery betrays the sacred image of Pallas into the hands of the Greeks ; the offer of the Greeks, as a feigned condition of peace, to requite the loss and appease the goddess by the gift of a huge horse of brass (not, in the *Recueil* version, of wood) ; the breaking out of the Grecian heroes from their concealment within the horse and the ensuing sack and rapine, with the murder of Priam in the temple of Apollo ; the taking captive of Hecuba and Cassandra and Andromache ; the departure of the Greeks, and the sacrifice of Polixena by Pyrrhus on the tomb of his father before that departure could be accomplished.

All this multitude of incidents could not, of course, be told in a single tapestry picture, whatever its scale and however crowded its composition, but had to be distributed through a series of such pictures. The regular process, as documents of the time prove, was to employ some learned clerk to prescribe, to the artist employed to make the preliminary designs, the order and arrangement of the scenes to be represented in each picture—if order or arrangement it can be called, for the result was essentially a jumble, in which the several scenes were crowded in promiscuous contact over and under and beside one another, without boundary or separation. The Louvre series of such designs contains eight compositions, and the omission of certain subjects seems to prove that there were originally more. I here reproduce (Plate I, A) a fragment of one of the series showing, above, the scene of the parting of Hector and Andromache, Hector being armed for the battle by his squire while Andromache kneels holding up their babe and imploring him not to go, and his mother and sisters and Helen join in the prayer ; and below, the same hero, armed and mounted, encountering in the street his father Priam, who with lifted hand dissuades him (a non-Homeric incident of the mediaeval versions) from taking the field. Plate I, B shows a portion of one of the designs of the same series as actually executed in full size on a fragment of tapestry from the Château d'Aulhac, figuring a battle under the walls of Troy, with Troilus defending the wounded Hector against Achilles (' Here manly Hector faints '), and below, the death of Memnon, with the Trojan women above, looking on from the walls. Plate II reproduces the greater part of the Louvre drawing for the scene of the final sack, the same composition as we see actually carried out on a great scale in the tapestry in the cathedral of Zamora.

Now let us go back to the text of Shakespeare in *Lucrece* and compare it with the examples of tapestry design thus illustrated. It is clear that Shakespeare is thinking of a single picture, not of a series, but of a picture which included a number of different scenes and actions : Nestor haranguing the Greeks, Hector sallying out to battle, Ajax

Plate I

A

B

quarrelling with Ulysses; other Greek commanders playing parts undefined; a battle beside the Simois, and the final sack of the city, with the murder of Priam and the mourning of Hecuba. This means that the design and composition he has in his mind's eye are of the characteristic jumbled kind exemplified in our Plate II, where we see the turrets of 'cloud-kissing Ilion' (inscribed 'le chateau Ylion') closing the scene at the top, except where we get a glimpse of the Grecian ships to the extreme left; the gates of the city, also to the left, through which the Grecian warriors, after their pretended retreat to Tenedos, crowd in by the help of their comrades who pour out from the belly of the horse (in our reproduction a strip has had to be cut from this left-hand edge of the scene). In front of and beyond the horse a confused scene of battle and slaughter, with many single combats, is piled up without any diminishing effect of perspective to indicate distance. To the right of the centre we see, above, the city beginning to flame, Greeks battering down the houses with mace and pickaxe, Helen and the other women of Priam's household taken captive, and below, the temple of Apollo, with Priam slain by Pyrrhus as he clings to the altar, and Hecuba throwing up her hands in despair at the sight; to the extreme right, above, the Greeks departing to their ships, and below, as a prelude to their homeward voyage, the sacrifice of Polixena by Pyrrhus on the tomb of Achilles. This manner of densely crowding the figures above and among and behind one another is described in minute detail, and with apparently surprised interest, by Shakespeare, in relation, however, not to a warlike action but to a peaceful one, the discourse of Nestor to the Grecian host; see the seventh, eighth, and ninth stanzas above quoted, beginning

> About him were a press of gaping faces,

and ending

> A hand, a foot, a face, a leg, a head,
> Stood for the whole to be imagined.

This description definitely gives a fifteenth-century character to the design which Shakespeare is describing, seeing that in the sixteenth, with the growth of Italian influence and the knowledge of perspective, this primitive manner of filling the space with superposed and intertangled crowds was gradually abandoned, in tapestry as in other fields of design, for a system of clearer and more scientific distribution.

Of the other particular incidents mentioned by Shakespeare, some can and some cannot be strictly paralleled from the Louvre drawings or from tapestries executed after them. Nestor figures in one of the drawings, but fighting, not haranguing. The speaking gesture, however, which Shakespeare attributes to him ('Making such sober action with his hand') could well be illustrated from other scenes in the drawings, as for example that where Antenor and a group of Trojan chiefs plan their expedition to Greece, or that in which Achilles urges upon the other princes the abandonment of the siege.   Neither of these is here reproduced : but see the action of Priam as he pleads with Hector in our Plate I, A.   Plate I, B shows the Trojan women looking out from the walls as described by Shakespeare in the tenth stanza of our quotation, though what they are watching is not a scene of gallant setting forth but one of battle ferociously engaged.   This illustration shows, moreover, how the figures in tapestry of this date were habitually identified by inscriptions ([poly]damas, achilles, troillus, hector, le roy meño [for Memnon], and so forth).   Just so, we may be sure, were they identified in Shakespeare's ' well-painted piece '.

Another group on which Shakespeare dwells, as affording Lucrece the sight of a misery equal to her own, is that of Priam murdered by Pyrrhus, with Hecuba standing by lamenting.   A corresponding tapestry group is depicted in our Plate II (the figure of Hecuba partly intercepted by that of the sacker with his pickaxe raised), dramatically and expressively enough, although the action is not strictly the same as that which Shakespeare describes.   Representations of this scene in painting or tapestry were doubtless much in the mind's eye of Elizabethan writers, and served, along with such printed texts as they knew, to suggest those lines of Marlowe, in his play of *Dido, Queen of Carthage*, which Shakespeare parodies in the well-known scene of Hamlet with the players. It is to be noted that in *Lucrece*, as in the existing tapestries, the scene is treated according to the mediaeval version and not according to Virgil, who represents all the women of the palace as present at the murder.

Following the long passage quoted above from *Lucrece* comes another, not needed to be given at length, in which the heroine, accusing the picture itself, arraigns the lust of Paris and at the same time cries for vengeance on Pyrrhus and the Greeks who are Troy's enemies, and ends :

> Lo, here weeps Hecuba, here Priam dies,
> Here manly Hector faints, here Troilus swounds,
> Here friend by friend in bloody channel lies,
> And friend to friend gives unadvised wounds,
> And one man's lust these many lives confounds :
>   Had doting Priam check'd his son's desire,
>   Troy had been bright with fame and not with fire.

Then we have another and longer passage in which, looking round for objects of compassion, Lucrece perceives the figure of the traitor Sinon

Plate II

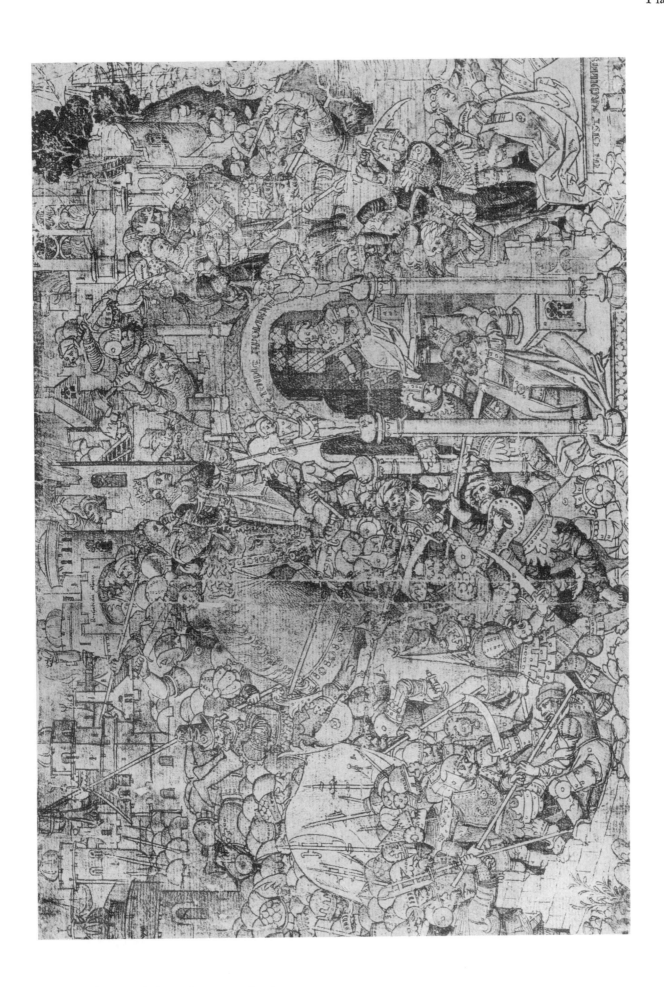

where he stands disguised, in pitiable garb and mien, and inveigles the Trojans with the false tale of the wooden horse. She turns upon this figure and likens the plausible wickedness of Sinon to that of her own betrayer, Tarquin. Now in the mediaeval versions of the Troy story Sinon plays a very small part. He is just mentioned as the inventor or co-inventor of the wooden (or brazen) horse, and as entering the city with it, and no more : probably the figure mounted on the horse in Plate II is he. But the story of his feigned tale to Priam, which fills so great a place in the second book of the *Aeneid*, fills none in the *Roman de Troie* or the *Recuyell*, and it is not from mediaeval tradition but direct from Virgil that Shakespeare, or the painter whose work he describes, has taken it.

To sum up, then, we have to conceive of the painting so minutely dwelt upon in Shakespeare's *Lucrece* as a painted cloth or hanging designed, in the main, according to the traditions of the French and Flemish tapestry-designers of 1480–1500, but already containing scenes —especially the Sinon scene—which did not occur in their accepted literary sources, and which accordingly they were not accustomed to include. As to the praises which Shakespeare lavishes on the execution, the 'sweet observance' in the faces of the women watching from the walls, the 'grace and majesty' of the commanders, the subtle 'art of physiognomy' in the respective countenances of Ajax and Ulysses, the moving representation of

Time's ruin, beauty's wrack, and grim care's reign

in Hecuba, the guile shown lurking beneath the tears of Sinon—as to these, we must attribute at least the chief part of them to the dramatizing power of the poet's imagination. Even in the finest works of tapestry play of facial expression is, from the nature of the craft, not a strong point, and in our existing Troy tapestries much is lost of the not inconsiderable share of that quality which appears in the Louvre preliminary sketches. Painting done with a brush has of course more freedom : but it is not likely that the painter of such a figured cloth as we conceive to have caught Shakespeare's eye and attention could have been of a rank to give his faces a tithe of the living character which the poet claims for them, and we must take him as describing, in this respect, not so much what he actually found in the picture as what his own genius would have prompted him to put there had he been an artist.

SIDNEY COLVIN.

H 2

SHAKESPEARE

FOR some years past I have been making a study of portraiture during the Tudor period, a period extending in this purview from the death of Holbein, in 1543, to the arrival of Van Dyck, in 1632; in short, a period of about one hundred years. One hundred years of English history! How much this means and has always meant. Think of the hundred years that have been spent since Napoleon Bonaparte lost his last stake on the field of Waterloo. Who will be bold enough to foretell what may have happened to England before another hundred years have elapsed. Three hundred years ago William Shakespeare was laid to rest in the church of the Holy Trinity at Stratford-upon-Avon, in which town, fifty-two years before, he had first seen the light. In the year that William Shakespeare was born Elizabeth had been but six years on the throne. All the great actors in the great world-drama of the Elizabethan era figured on the stage of history during the lifetime of William Shakespeare. Set a number of Elizabethan portraits in rows before the eye, men and women together; add, if you like, portraits of ten or twenty years earlier, and ten or twenty years of the reign of King James I. Study them well, for in these portraits you will see much of the making of England. You will see real men and real women beneath the rich and fantastic costumes, which seem so strange to our dullard comprehensions. Leicester, Essex, Raleigh, Drake, Frobisher, Hawkins, Burghley, Walsingham, Sidney, Queen Bess herself—how bright they shine in the empyrean of history. Truly this was a Period, perhaps the greatest Period in the history of England!

During this Period England was in the making. The Tudor sovereigns were interlopers, whose very nobility of birth was a matter of doubt. Sprung originally from a dubious union between a Welsh adventurer and a French queen, grafted on to royal stock by marriage with a princess, whose own claim to royal lineage was vitiated by more than doubtful legitimacy, the Tudors found themselves confronted with the great families who traced their royal or noble lineage to Plantagenet and Norman ancestors. The Tudors therefore, from Henry VII to Elizabeth, played the people of England against the old nobility, and by this encouragement raised the country folk out of the furrows of feudalism. Students of family history and genealogy are familiar with the rise under the Tudor dynasty of the yeoman farmer to the dignity of a gentleman. The spirit of adventure was encouraged, and younger sons of the yeoman and the squire sought and won their fortunes in commerce, at the law, or in adventures in foreign lands. Then they returned and settled back on the land of their birth, where they founded noble families of good English stock.

From such a stock came William Shakespeare, both on his father's and his mother's side, from a family of local yeomen fighting their way up to the ranks of gentility. No man was more thoroughly English than Shakespeare, English in the place and circumstances of his birth, English in the smattering of education which he got in the local grammar school, but which proved—as with most Englishmen—that ' small Latin and less Greek ' may be good foundations for success in after life. English were the haphazard adventures of his early life at Stratford-upon-Avon, and the marriage in which he became, perhaps unintentionally, involved; English the spirit of adventure which took him up to live by his wits in London; most English of all the way in which he returned, when prosperity shone on him, to his native town, with apparently no aspirations beyond those of land-ownership and an alderman's gown. English also is Shakespeare's own reticence about the circumstances of his own life. At no time does he seem to have been conscious of his greatness or of the part he was taking in the formation of the national character. Shakespeare was throughout life what is sometimes called middle-class, but is better described as *bourgeois*. He liked to be called a gentleman, entitled to bear a coat-of-arms, but he always recognized the social gulf which lay between him and such high-born magnates as the Earls of Pembroke, Southampton, or Leicester. The perils of high birth and position were familiar to Shakespeare. Literary gifts had not saved Surrey, Wyat, or Raleigh from the block, Philip Sidney from the fatal wound at Zutphen, or Francis Bacon from that sad fall from the highest post in the land. Shakespeare himself sums up the dangers of greatness in the fall of Cardinal Wolsey :

> How wretched
> Is that poor man that hangs on princes' favours!
> There is, betwixt the smile we would aspire to,
> That sweet aspect of princes, and their ruin,
> More pangs and fears than wars or women have.

So much the greater was the achievement of William Shakespeare. Sum up all the literature of the great Elizabethan Period and it will be found that out of the mass of precious literature, which this Period put forth, two creations emerge which have had a share in the shaping of the world : the plays of Shakespeare and the Authorized Version of the Bible. The English-speaking race has spread itself since Shakespeare's day over a great part of the inhabited world, and wherever the English race has penetrated and settled it has brought with it Shakespeare and the Bible. It was only inexorable fate which prevented Shakespeare from being alive when the *Mayflower* sailed from Southampton to the New World. The struggle for the New World was one of the dominating ideas of the Elizabethan Period, but it has been the peaceful influence of the Bible and Shakespeare which has bound the English-speaking races in one chain of family union. All the armaments in the world could not have done this.

Not many years after Shakespeare's death Van Dyck painted the Cavalier poet, Sir John Suckling, standing with a folio volume of Shakespeare in his hand. Shakespeare might have been alive at the time when this portrait was painted, so that this tribute from one poet to another may be regarded as contemporary, like that of Ben Jonson. Shakespeare was no advertiser of himself or his goods. He never obtrudes himself into his works, except perhaps in the Sonnets, which are charged with the exaggerated passion and romance of youth. Yet throughout the long series of Shakespeare's works, both poems and dramas, there is a note of individualism which makes a thought, a phrase, a scene, such as could only have been conceived and written by Shakespeare. With Shakespeare we move in no enchanted palace as with Spenser, in no solemn cathedral aisles as with Milton ; we do not tread the depths of hell as with Dante, or get merged in the empyrean ; we need no guide to scale a mountain height as with Goethe. Shakespeare is just ourselves, though he has been dead for three hundred years, our never-failing friend and counsellor, whose thoughts are as fresh and as bright, as sage and as suggestive, as they were three hundred years ago. Shakespeare is immortal because he can never grow old ; although he may be looked upon as the final consummation of the great Elizabethan Period, his work belongs to the twentieth century as much as to the seventeenth.

Again, let it be repeated that of no other writings can this be said, except the Authorized Version of the Bible. It may safely be said that the sun never sets on Shakespeare and the Bible. Three hundred years have elapsed since William Shakespeare was laid to rest at Stratford-upon-Avon, but in every part of the globe, wherever the English heart beats true, Shakespeare's words ring as loud and true to-day as they did when King Henry V first spoke them on the boards of the Globe Theatre:

> On, on, you noblest English,
> Whose blood is fetch'd from fathers of war-proof!
> Fathers, that like so many Alexanders,
> Have in these parts from morn till even fought,
> And sheath'd their swords for lack of argument:
> Dishonour not your mothers; now attest,
> That those whom you call'd fathers did beget you.
> Be copy now to men of grosser blood,
> And teach them how to war; and you, good yeomen,
> Whose limbs were made in England, show us here
> The mettle of your pasture; let us swear
> That you are worth your breeding, which I doubt not:
> For there is none of you so mean and base,
> That hath not noble lustre in your eyes;
> I see you stand like greyhounds on the slips,
> Straining upon the start. The game's a-foot:
> Follow your spirit; and, upon this charge,
> Cry, God for Harry, England, and Saint George.

Nobles and yeomen, officers and men, hand in hand, are facing the strongest enemy that England has ever known, stronger than the Spain which threatened England in the days of Elizabeth, stronger than the France of Joan of Arc or of Napoleon. The greatness of England is mirrored throughout the works of Shakespeare. It is fitting that at such a crisis in the history of England the nation should be called upon to remember the truest, the most complete Englishman, not only of the Elizabethan Period, but of our own England, our own Empire, and our relations in the United States of America; the England, not only of ourselves, but of our children and our children's children to the end of time.

LIONEL CUST.

SHAKESPEARE, 1916

Now when the sinking Sun reeketh with blood,
And the gore-gushing vapours rent by him
Rend him and bury him : now the World is dim
As when great thunders gather for the flood,
And in the darkness men die where they stood,
And dying slay, or scatter'd limb from limb
Cease in a flash where mad-eyed cherubim
Of Death destroy them in the night and mud :
When landmarks vanish—murder is become
A glory—cowardice, conscience—and to lie,
A law—to govern, but to serve a time :—
We dying, lifting bloodied eyes and dumb,
Behold the silver star serene on high,
That is thy spirit there, O Master Mind sublime.

RONALD ROSS.

March 22, 1916.

SHAKESPEARE WORKS

THINKING of my caged birds indoors,
    My books, whose music serves my will ;
Which, when I bid them sing, will sing,
    And when I sing myself are still ;

And that my scent is drops of ink,
    Which, were my song as great as I,
Would sweeten man till he was dust,
    And make the world one Araby ;

Thinking how my hot passions make
    Strong floods of shallows that run cold—
Oh how I burn to make my dreams
    Lighten and thunder through the world !

W. H. DAVIES.

SHAKESPEARE AND THE ENGLISH LANGUAGE

IT is commonly acknowledged that the two literary influences that have had the most to do with the development of the English language are Shakespeare and the Bible. Which of these influences has been the more powerful it would not be easy to determine. But even if it be true that the foremost place in this respect must be given to the Bible, this does not imply that the contribution of the whole body of the translators to the formation of the language has surpassed or equalled in amount or importance that of the one poet. The English language does indeed owe many felicitous innovations to the genius of these men—above all, to the sagaciously directed industry of Tindale and the poetic instinct of Coverdale ; yet the addition which the Bible has made to the resources of the language is only in very small part to be ascribed to them. Even if the translators had possessed no qualifications beyond a knowledge of Hebrew and Greek, and the most ordinary degree of skill in the use of their own language, their work would have none the less abounded in transplanted Oriental idioms and metaphors ; and these would still have found their way, enriched in meaning by their sacred associations, into the common speech of Englishmen. The indebtedness of the English language to the Bible is indeed enormous ; but by far the heavier part of the debt is owed, not to the translators, but to the Hebrew and Greek originals. Nor must we—though it is difficult to keep the two things apart—confound the influence of the Bible on our language with its influence on our literature. It has been a priceless advantage to English literature that our writers have usually known their Bible well, and were able to trust their readers to recognize an allusion to it. But while this allusive use of the Bible means a great enrichment of the resources of effective literary expression at the disposal of English writers, it is in the main the literature and not the language that has been the gainer ; except in so far as expressions that were originally allusive have gained a currency in which their source is no longer constantly recognized.

All this has to be borne in mind if we are to estimate correctly the share of Shakespeare in the making of the English language, as compared with that of the translators of the Bible. We must remember that what he gave to his native tongue he gave of his own. Setting aside, as we ought in this connexion, the multitude of Shakespearian allusions in daily proverbial use which owe all their effect to the suggestion of the context, there are not a few of the poet's turns of phrase that may fairly be said to have become idioms of the language, being continually used without even a thought that they must have had some definite literary origin. Even when we are familiar with the passages of the plays in which they occur, it often suddenly strikes us that we have overlooked some peculiar appropriateness in their place, which proves that they were there used for the first time. Such are 'a tower of strength[1]', 'coign of vantage', 'household words', 'in my heart's core', 'the head and front', 'yeoman service', 'curled darlings', 'to out-Herod Herod', 'metal more attractive', 'a palpable hit', 'to the manner born', 'pomp and circumstance', 'made of sterner stuff', 'the melting mood'. Many peculiar shades of meaning of ordinary words, which would otherwise be hard to account for, have been traced to reminiscences, not always accurate, of passages of Shakespeare in which the use of the word, if not quite normal, is at least well within the limits of poetic licence. In Shakespeare's hands the language is strangely ductile; he continually uses words in novel extended senses which, when defined with the pedantic rigour inevitable in a dictionary, seem strained or faulty, but which one feels to need no justification when they are read in their context. Some of his metaphorical uses, such as the application of the word *canopy* to the sky, have so taken root in the language that it is not easy to realize how audacious they must have seemed to the first readers.

It is needless to dwell on Shakespeare's well-known prodigality and felicity in the invention of compound words. What has not been so commonly observed is his fertility in the formation of new words by means of suffixes and prefixes, and by the conversion of verbs into nouns

---

[1] Shakespeare's sentence, 'The king's name is a tower of strength' (*Rich. III*, v. iii. 12), looks like a reminiscence of *Proverbs* xviii. 10, which if literally translated from the Hebrew would read, 'The name of the Lord is a tower of strength'. The curious thing is that no English translation has the literal rendering in this passage. The Douay version has it in *Psalm* lx[i]. 3, following the *turris fortitudinis* of the Vulgate; but the Douay Bible is much later than Shakespeare's use of the phrase. One is tempted to imagine that Shakespeare must somewhere have seen a literal translation of the passage in *Proverbs*, and have been struck with the felicity of the expression. The proverbial currency of the phrase certainly seems to be due to Shakespeare, not to the Bible.

or of nouns into verbs. It is true that many of these formations failed to be adopted by others, or have become obsolete ; but many still survive. So far as the evidence goes, he may have been the first user of the words *changeful, gloomy, courtship*. The list of words now familiar in literary use for which he is the earliest known authority would be of considerable length, and would for most people contain some startling surprises. One might expect to find in it such words as *cerements, illume*, but certainly not *denote, depositary, impartial, investment*. It can hardly be supposed that Shakespeare was the first writer to employ these words ; but the fact that no earlier examples can be quoted does show his eagerness to avail himself of any useful innovations in vocabulary. The same point may be illustrated by the large number of words for which the first known instance is only a few years older than the date of their occurrence in his works. His linguistic usage, one might say, always looks forward rather than backward. For archaism as such he had, to all appearance, no liking. Hardly anywhere in his writings (the ' Gower ' prologues in *Pericles* are probably not his) is there ground for suspecting any intention to revive obsolete words or forms. He seems to have been similarly uninterested in English rustic dialect, which is rather surprising when we consider the evident relish with which he reproduces the comicalities of the speech of Welshmen. Although it had long been an established custom on the stage that countrymen should be represented as speaking what was supposed to be their native dialect, Shakespeare puts this conventional jargon only into the mouth of the disguised noble ; the actual rustics in the plays speak ordinary English.

Popular manuals of English literature usually contain some statement as to the number of words composing the vocabulary of Shakespeare's plays and poems. The estimates vary between fifteen thousand and twenty-four thousand words. I have never met with any account of the methods by which any of these conflicting results have been arrived at, nor do I know who is responsible for any of them. The question of the numerical compass of the poet's vocabulary cannot from any point of view be said to be of great importance, but as a matter of curiosity there are probably many who would be glad to see it authoritatively settled. It is certainly quite capable of being settled ; no very extravagant expenditure of time would be required to count accurately the words registered in Bartlett's *Concordance to Shakespeare*. It is true that the task would demand some degree of trained skill and constant watchfulness, as Mr. Bartlett's method of arrangement is about as inconvenient as possible for the purpose of such an enumeration.

There would, besides, often be no little difficulty in deciding what ought to be considered as a ' word '. The verbal nouns in *-ing*, for instance, and the participial adjectives, could hardly be brought under a fixed rule. Some of these formations have an unmistakable claim to a separate place in the list, while others it would be absurd to count as distinct from their verbs ; but with regard to very many of them there would be room for doubt. A similar difficulty would arise in the treatment of the compound words of the poet's own invention. Still, if the counting were intelligently done, the margin of uncertainty in the result might, after all, not be very great. Probably sooner or later somebody will be found willing to take the trouble to make an exhaustive enumeration of Shakespeare's words. In the meantime, it may be pointed out that Onions's *Shakespeare Glossary* contains about ten thousand words ; and as that work deals only with such words as call for some kind of comment, it seems reasonable to infer that the complete vocabulary would extend to double that number. There appears to be no reason to doubt the correctness of the common belief that the English poet who surpasses all others in the skilful use of words also ranks first in the number of the words that he has pressed into his service.

HENRY BRADLEY.

SHAKESPEARE INVENTOR OF LANGUAGE

I

SHAKESPEARE excelled all predecessors, contemporaries, or successors in his rôle of inventor of language. A magical faculty of expression was habitual to him, whereby word and thought fitted one another to perfection. The imaginative splendour of his diction, and its stirring harmonies, are commonly as noticeable as the impressiveness of the ideas. Yet often we are magnetized by the luminous simplicity of the phrase, by the absence of ornament, by the presence of a graphic directness and force which draw from all readers or hearers an instinctive recognition. They realize that the thought or feeling could be rightly expressed in no other way, although they are conscious at the same time that it is a way that is beyond their power to reach unaided. It is because Shakespeare has said superlatively well what so many think and feel, but cannot say with his apposite vigour, that so many of his simpler phrases have become household words, the idioms of our daily speech. Indeed, there is some value in the comparison which has been drawn between the English language to-day and a modern city of Italy, into the walls of whose palaces and into the pavements of whose streets have been worked fragments of the marble grandeur of the old Roman Empire. The tessellated fragments of many-coloured stone suggest the opalescent relics of Shakespearian language mortised into our common speech.

II

Of Shakespeare's boldness in inventing new sonorous terms of foreign derivation, many instances could be given, but none more impressive than that familiar passage in *Macbeth*, when Macbeth, in his agony at the sight of Duncan's blood on his hand, cries out :

> Will all great Neptune's ocean wash this blood
> Clean from my hand? No, this my hand will rather
> The multitudinous seas incarnadine,
> Making the green one red.

No one before had thought of such expressions as the epithet *multitudinous* or the verb *incarnadine*. *Incarnadine* of course means to colour with red dye ; it is not perhaps a word that circumstances often require, and it did not find general admission to the language. But its companion *multitudinous* served a wider purpose, and is with us all still.

III

Shakespeare's gifts to our daily speech may be classified in three divisions : (1) sentences of his devising which now enjoy proverbial currency, (2) brief phrases of two or three words, and finally (3) common single words, including epithets compounded of more words than one. All the examples which I cite are undisputed coinage of the dramatist's brain and pen.

There are several speeches in great scenes, of which wellnigh every syllable has, in one or other of these three shapes, been absorbed by our daily utterance. Let me quote one such passage : Othello's last speech. Who is not familiar with wellnigh every sentence in a hundred connexions which involve issues of current life altogether detached from the original setting ?

> I have done the state some service,
> And they know it. No more of that . . .
> Speak of me as I am ; nothing extenuate,
> Nor set down aught in malice : then must you speak
> Of one who loved not wisely but too well.

Sentences of Shakespeare's which have passed into proverbs include many such as these :

' The better part of valour is discretion.'
' Brevity is the soul of wit.'
' Assume a virtue if you have it not.'
' The course of true love never did run smooth.'
' Every why hath a wherefore.'
' Though this be madness, there is method in it.'
' Thus conscience doth make cowards of us all.'

Perhaps the isolated phrases which our speech owes to Shakespeare bring home to us most emphatically the figurative picturesqueness with which he has endowed our lips in the casual business of life. Here are a few :

' In my mind's eye.'
' More in sorrow than in anger.'

' The primrose path.'
' A thing of shreds and patches.'
' The milk of human kindness.'
' A ministering angel.'
' A towering passion.'
' A man more sinned against than sinning.'
' Every inch a king.'
' A divided duty.'
' A foregone conclusion.'
' Pride, pomp and circumstance of glorious war.'
' Give us a taste of your quality ' and ' Pluck the heart out of my mystery ' are two of many sentences of which the main words are woven into the universal verbal web.

It is worthy of remark that all these arresting phrases which mingle with our daily breath come from Shakespeare's tragedies ; from *Hamlet*, *Lear*, *Othello*, or *Macbeth*. The public intelligence has thus instinctively recognized where Shakespeare's genius soared to its highest pitch.

All such phrases illustrate Shakespeare's peculiar power of infusing into words which hitherto only bore a literal sense, a new figurative significance which they have since retained. When the dramatist wrote ' cold comfort ', or ' hollow friendship ', he gave proof of this marvellous power of turning physical conceptions to imaginative or poetic account.

Single words which we owe to Shakespeare's verbal ingenuity are equally memorable. He had no narrow prejudices against foreign terms which served his purpose. At times he did not trouble to anglicize a foreign formation. He left it to the future to complete the naturalizing process. Such seems to be the history of the words bandit, barricade, renegade, and hurricane. These words Shakespeare introduced into the language in the foreign forms of bandetto, barricado, renegado, hurricano. Some of his verbal gifts to us which are framed on onomatopoeic principles perpetuate, it would seem, sudden flashes of verbal inspiration. Such seem to be dwindle, hurry, bump, gibber, whiz. More imposing inventions, which involve greater intellectual effort, are moral (of a fable), fallacy, libertine, and any number of illuminating epithets ; for example, ominous, jovial, inauspicious.

IV

One mode of forming new epithets was an invention of Shakespeare's contemporaries and no device of his own peculiar coinage. But Shakespeare adopted and developed it with such fertility that he may well claim the honour of having taught to future ages its picturesque efficacy. I refer to his constant employment of the double epithet, whereby he clad ideas of some complexity in an original verbal garb, uniting charm with clarity. Homer knew the practice, but after his time it disappeared from civilized speech; not to be revived till experiment was made again with it by the French poets of the sixteenth century. Sir Philip Sidney, first of Englishmen to employ the device, deliberately borrowed it from France, and Edmund Spenser made trial of it under Sidney's influence. But Shakespeare was the English poet to discover the full potentialities of such word-formation, and many of his composite inventions rank with our most important and most impressive verbal debts to him. None before Shakespeare employed such epithets as snow-white, milk-white, tear-stained, cold-blooded, crest-fallen, down-trodden, low-spirited, heart-burning, ill-favoured, hollow-eyed, hot-blooded, heart-whole, home-bred, well-proportioned, eventful.

Like combinations enjoy less colloquial currency and rank with the more select idioms which flourish in the narrower circles of literary culture. Such are fancy-free, trumpet-tongued, cloud-capped, silver-sweet, honey-heavy, sleek-headed, mouth-honour, heaven-kissing.

V

Many less dignified methods of forming compound words were in vogue in Shakespeare's time, and there was no current kind of verbal experiment to which he did not lend a hand. To his inventiveness on the duplicating principle which made at the moment so strong a popular appeal, we owe off-hand colloquialisms like handy-dandy, helter-skelter, hugger-mugger, skimble-skamble.

Shakespeare's contemporaries, not himself, can claim the parental honours in the cognate cases of higgledy-piggledy, and, I believe, riff-raff.

VI

So penetrating is the Shakespearian influence on our language, such a hold has his phraseology on the popular as well as on the cultivated ear, that much of his phraseology has been absorbed by our unwritten, our non-literary, talk of the street.

' Cudgel thy brains.'

' I know a trick worth two of that.'

' Very like a whale.'

' Too much of a good thing '—are among Shakespeare's contributions to the vernacular which are often characterized as illiterate. The popular use of ' bounce ', in the sense of boastful falsehood, is one of Shakespeare's numerous verbal innovations, which are generally reckoned more forcible than polite.

Thus I claim that Shakespeare ranks as national hero by virtue (among other achievements) of the vast expansion he effected in the scope of our national diction. Educated and uneducated alike have benefited by his genius for graphic neologisms. Territorial expansion scarcely fosters a nation's intellectual vigour more signally than a widening of its command of expressive speech, which ennobles the lips, and both clarifies and broadens thought.

SIDNEY LEE.

SHAKESPEARE

IF many a daring spirit must discover
The chartless world, why should they glory lack?
Because athwart the skyline they sank over,
Few, few, the shipmen be that have come back.

Yet one, wrecked oft, hath by a giddy cord
The rugged head of Destiny regain'd,
Who from the maelstrom's lap hath swum aboard—
Who from the polar sleep himself unchain'd.

And he, acquainted well with every tone
Of madness whining in his shroudage slender,
From storm and mutiny emerged alone,
Self-righted from the dreadful self-surrender:

Rich from the isles where sojourn long is death,
Won back to cool Thames and Elizabeth,
Sea-weary, yes, but human still, and whole—
A circumnavigator of the soul.

HERBERT TRENCH.

THE SHADOW OF THE MASTER

1916

CRIMSON was the twilight, under that crab-tree
Where—old tales tell us—all a midsummer's night,
A mad young poacher, drunk with mead of elfin-land,
Lodged with the fern-owl, and looked at the stars.

There, from the dusk, where the dream of Piers Plowman
Darkens on the sunrise, to this dusk of our own,
I read, in a history, the record of our world.

The hawk-moth, the currant-moth, the red-striped tiger-moth
Shimmered all around me, so white shone those pages ;
And, in among the blue boughs, the bats flew low.

I slumbered, the history slipped from my hand,
Then I saw a dead man, dreadful in the moon-dawn,
The ghost of the Master, bowed upon that book.

He muttered as he searched it,—*What vast convulsion
Mocks my sexton's curse now, shakes our English clay?*
Whereupon I told him, and asked him in turn
Whether he espied any light in those pages
Which painted an epoch later than his own.

I am a shadow, he said, *and I see none.*

I am a shadow, he said, *and I see none.*

Then, O then he murmured to himself (while the moon hung
Crimson as a lanthorn of Cathay in that crab-tree),
Laughing at his work and the world, as I thought,
Yet with some bitterness, yet with some beauty
Mocking his own music, these wraiths of his rhymes;

II

God, when I turn the leaves of that dark book
    Wherein our wisest teach us to recall
Those glorious flags which in old tempests shook
    And those proud thrones which held my youth in thrall;

When I see clear what seemed to childish eyes
    The glorious colouring of each pictured age;
And for their dominant tints now recognize
    How thumbed with innocent blood is every page;

O, then I know this world is fast asleep
    Bound in Time's womb, till some far morning break;
And, though light grows upon the dreadful deep,
    We are dungeoned in thick night.   We are not awake.

The world's unborn, for all our hopes and schemes;
And all its myriads only move in dreams.

III

It was a crimson twilight, under that crab-tree.
Moths beat about me, and bats flew low.
I read, in a history, the record of our world.

If there be light, said the Master,
I am a shadow, and I see none . . .

I am a shadow, and I see none.

ALFRED NOYES.

THE MAKING OF SHAKESPEARE

DAME NATURE on a Holiday bethought her of a plan,
To mix new elements and clay, and make a proper man.

She knew the fine rare dust to seek in England's central shire,
Brought dew from red Parnassus' peak on dawning cloud of fire :
With fingers deft she did them knead in young Adonis' form,
Of Saxon and of Norman breed, with British strain to warm.

His ears were shells from mystic beach, which taught him what to hear ;
She kept the lightning for his speech, to make foul airs grow clear ;
She for his eyes found sunbeams rare, to see by their own light ;
And hid some stars amid his hair, to guide his steps aright.

She took the West Wind from the main, for breath so soft and deep ;
She made the North Wind sweep his brain, it keen and clear to keep ;
She let the South Wind bathe his heart to make it warm and true ;
She would not use the East Wind's art, so shrewd and snell it blew,
But called a breeze down from the sky to purify his soul,
And left it to be guarded by a conscience firm and whole.

(St. George had come to earth that year the Dragon's brood to fight ;[1]
He struck upon his shield his spear, and waked the babe to light.)

She, like a kind godmother, cared to make his training sound ;
Found him a home where well he fared with relatives around ;
Gave him a mother wise and brave, and a right merry sire,
A learned pedagogue she gave, and then—*his Heart's Desire*.

[1] It was a Plague year.

II

Dame Fortune her misfortunes rained as jealous for her play,
And she his *Having* all distrained, and took his means away,
With iron chains she fettered him, loaded with heavy weight,
Plunged in strange tides to sink or swim, and left him to his fate.

He did not sink, but bravely fought 'gainst storm and wind and tide;
Impediments ashore he brought, and poverty defied.
When on the stony shore he stood he bore down Fortune's taint,
And fought again the Dragon's brood, like to his patron saint.

Dame Nature smiled again, content, her gifts so well bestowed,
And she her own *White Magic* lent, to lighten still his load.
He learned the speech of beast and bird, men, women, angels, stars;
The love-lore of the past he heard, and fought in ancient wars.
She gave him power to make them live, to teach men's eyes to see,
And beauty, goodness, truth, to give in Music's poesy.

Men recognized Dame Nature's cheer, seen in her darling's power;
They envied, blamed, praised, loved, and clear his stars shone on his hour.
Creator of full many a ' part ', and maker of his stage,
He thus became the soul and heart,—th' expresser of his age.

And what three hundred years ago was made, doth still endure,
Having a life within to glow and prove his genius sure.
If *then* he was so greatly graced, *now* his perennial pow'r
Hath on his brow new glory placed, ' the Present ' still *his Hour*.
Nothing so great hath risen between, to dwarf him to our eyes:
The grandest bard our race hath seen, so let our pæans rise,
And ' Hail to William Shakespeare! ' cry, our comfort, our delight,
' Our treasury, our armoury, our champion, and our knight! '

CHARLOTTE CARMICHAEL STOPES.

THE BENEFIT OF THE DOUBT

THERE are certain pieces of evidence bearing on the personal character of Shakespeare which I observe that my old friend Sir Sidney Lee, in the new edition of his monumental biography, does not put to the poet's account. A biographer who has to hold the scales between popular hero-worship and partisan detraction in the interest of some eccentric hypothesis, may be excused if he assume the port of Rhadamanthus. But the rank and file of us need not put so much constraint on our instincts. If the evidence in question is good enough, if it fits in with the mental picture we have formed of the dramatist from his plays, and is not inconsistent with contemporary testimony, we shall incline to accept it, giving the great man the benefit of any doubt.

There are two passages which I have chiefly in mind : of one I can speak quite shortly; the other will require a closer investigation. The first is the newly discovered scrap of information about Shakespeare's social habits which Aubrey apparently derived from the actor William Beeston, whose father was with Shakespeare in the Lord Chamberlain's company. An account of the page of rough notes on which this entry was found, together with a facsimile here reproduced, was contributed to *The Collections of the Malone Society* (i. 324) by Mr. E. K. Chambers. Mr. Madan, Bodley's Librarian, whom Sir Sidney Lee quotes as referring the entry to Fletcher, has since made a thorough investigation of the way in which this page of notes was put together, and has convinced himself that the entry refers to Shakespeare. As Sir George Warner also agrees, it is not necessary to argue this point further. It must also, I think, be allowed that Mr. Chambers gives the only possible transcription of the passage :

the more to be admired q. [i.e. *quod*, because] he was not a company keeper, | lived in Shoreditch, would not be debauched, and if invited to | writ : he was in paine.

Sir Sidney Lee reads ' if invited to write, he was in paine '; but the word is unmistakably ' writ ' followed by a colon, and the omission of the stop after ' invited to ' at the end of the line is paralleled by other

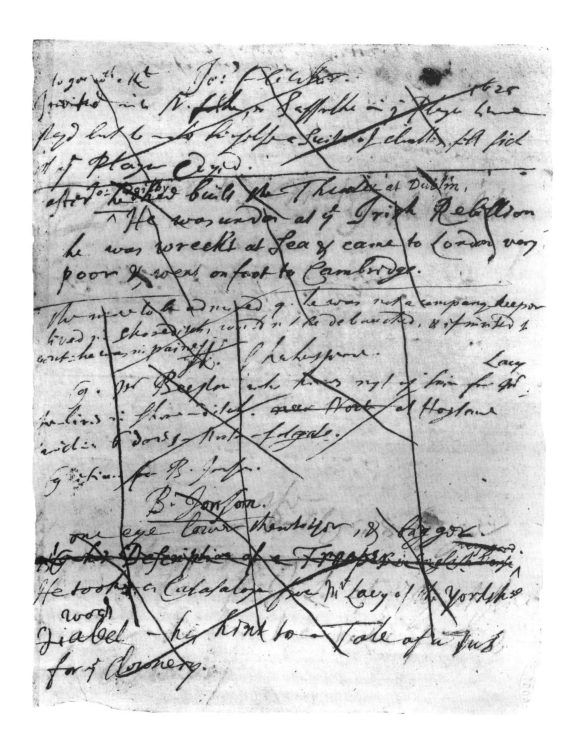

Bodleian Aubrey MS. 8, fol. 45^{v}

examples on the same page. The word ' debauched ' must be understood in its general Elizabethan use of excess in eating or drinking,
especially the latter ; as when Trinculo calls Caliban ' a deboshed fish '
because he had ' drowned his tongue in sack '.

Taking it then as certain that Aubrey's rough note refers to Shakespeare, and that it testifies to his disinclination to drinking parties, the
interesting question arises how it is to be reconciled with the other note
about his social habits which we also owe to Aubrey : ' He was very
good company, and of a very ready and pleasant smooth wit.' This
tradition we instinctively accept ; and support it by the passage in
Fuller's *Worthies*, which must be based on tradition also, about the
' wit-combats ' between Shakespeare and Ben Jonson ; which are
assumed, not unreasonably, to have taken place at the Mermaid. Shakespeare, then, was ' very good company ' and yet ' not a company-
keeper '. It may have been the superficial inconsistency between the
two traditions which led Aubrey not to add the latter note to the former
in his ' brief life ' of Shakespeare ; or of course the omission may have
been due to mere oversight. However this was, the inconsistency is
explained if we remember that the newly discovered tradition comes
from an actor. There must have been merry-makings of actors and
their patrons, where the wine would be more than the wit ; and we may
judge that it was from such parties as these that Shakespeare was in
the habit of excusing himself on the ground of indisposition. We
certainly get an impression from certain passages in the plays that their
writer felt a disgust for drunkenness : at least we may reasonably
doubt, if Ben Jonson had written *Hamlet* and had cast about for a topic of
conversation on the battlements of Elsinore while waiting for the ghost,
whether he would have stopped the gap with a temperance lecture.

A second point in which I would claim for Shakespeare the benefit
of the doubt is as to the part played by him in the attempted enclosure
of the common fields of Welcombe in 1614. Our information comes
from a rough diary kept by Shakespeare's cousin Thomas Greene, who
was at the time Town Clerk of Stratford. This diary was reproduced
in facsimile with a transcript in 1885, but as only fifty copies were
printed it is but little known. The story of the proposed enclosure
is told at greater or less length, and, I must add, with more or less in-
accuracy, by the various biographers ; with most detail by Mrs. Stopes
in *Shakespeare's Environment*, pp. 81–91, 336–42. It would seem that
two young gentlemen of the house of Combe, nephews of Shakespeare's
friend, John Combe, made up their minds to enclose part of the common

fields, and were supported in their scheme by a very influential person, Mr. Mannering, steward of the Lord Chancellor, who was officially lord of the royal manor of Stratford. A very general motive for enclosure in those days was better farming, because, as the land in these common fields was owned in strips of an acre, or half an acre, a good farmer might find himself next to a very bad one, and his land suffer in consequence. That the system has been discarded in England is some proof that it had great practical disadvantages. We may conjecture that, as the Chancellor was said to approve the scheme,[1] it was not without its recommendations ; and Greene, in his diary, notes a saying of Mr. Mannering that 'if he might not do it well, he cared not for enclosing, and cared not how little he did meddle therein '. A more particular motive for enclosure was generally the wish for some reason to lay down the arable land in pasture. We are told that the increase of arable through the reclamation of waste land in the north of Warwickshire had led to a demand for more pasture in the south ;[2] and it was the declared intention of the Combes to convert some 200 acres into pasture. Such enclosures were always unpopular, as they reduced the demand for labour. Seven years before, there had been disturbances at Hill Morton in the east of the county, where 3,000 persons assembled, and systematically laid open the enclosed lands. In the present case, the proposal to enclose was resisted by the Town Council of Stratford, on the special ground that the tithes upon the ' corn and grain ' had been assigned by Edward VI, in their charter of incorporation, for the maintenance of the vicar, the town bridge, grammar school, and almshouses ; and that the recent fire had so impoverished the town that they could not consent to such a diminution of the tithes as must accompany the proposed enclosure. There seems no doubt that the Combes at first intended to buy out the commoners and ignore the wishes of the Corporation. Their agent Replingham told Thomas Greene that ' he cared not for their consents '. But when the opposition grew, and the Corporation presented a petition both to the Privy Council in London and to the Chief Justice (who was the great lawyer Coke) at the local Assizes, William Combe sent them a letter[3] making various alternative

---

[1] Mr. Elton notes that Lord Chancellor Ellesmere in this very year had decreed enclosures to be for the public advantage (*William Shakespeare, his family and friends*, p. 148).

[2] *Common Land and Inclosure*, by E. C. K. Gonner, p. 147.

[3] The letter, dated 24 June, 1616, is printed in the Appendix to Ingleby's edition of Greene's Diary, and it is surprising that none of the biographers think it worth notice. One of Combe's proposals was to give the Corporation the amount of the tithe ' in yearly rent to be paid out of any land I have '.

offers of compensation for the tithe they would lose on the land enclosed ; proposals which, on paper, certainly appear equitable ; but the town, we must suppose for sufficient reason, declined them all.

The only question that matters to us to-day is the view Shakespeare took of the transaction. His own holding of about 120 acres, not being in the Welcombe field, was not affected by the proposal. But he was one of a syndicate which had bought a lease of the tithes ; and the throwing of the land out of tillage would mean a serious loss ; for his income from the tithes on the land converted to pasture would cease, unless an arrangement were made for tithing the stock. Meanwhile the bargain with the Corporation would have to be kept, and there were twenty-two years of the lease still to run. Accordingly the first thing we hear is that Shakespeare entered into an agreement with the Combes' agent Replingham to assure him, and also his cousin Thomas Greene, against loss 'thro' the decreasing of the yearly value of the tithes by reason of the decay of tillage'. Whether the other members of the syndicate made similar agreements, we do not know : Greene, from whom all our information comes, is not concerned with them. Can we see then what was Shakespeare's attitude to the proposed enclosure ? Both Halliwell-Phillips and Sir Sidney Lee are of opinion that he, at least tacitly, supported the Combes. In such a course there would have been nothing unworthy if he knew that they proposed to make good to the town the loss of the tithes when the lease fell in, as they would certainly have been compelled to do by the Privy Council ; but, since the Corporation definitely declared against the scheme, to support it would have been unpatriotic. The relevant passages from Greene's diary are the following :

17 No : My Cosen Shakespeare commyng yesterday to towne I went to see him howe he did, he told me that they assured him they meant to inclose noe further than to gospell bushe and so upp straight (leavying out part of the dyngles to the ffield) to the gate in Clopton hedge and take in Salisburyes peece : and that they mean in Aprill to servey the Land and then to gyve satisfaccion and not before and he and Mr. Hall say they think there will be nothying done at all.

This conversation occurred in November 1614, when Greene was in London about the business of the Corporation's petition to the Privy Council. At this stage Shakespeare and his son-in-law Dr. Hall give it as their opinion that the Combes will drop their proposal in face of the opposition it has aroused.

23 Dec. A Hall. Lettres wrytten one to Mr. Mannerying another to Mr. Shakspeare with almost all the companyes hands to eyther : I alsoe wrytte of myself to my Cosen Shakspeare the coppyes of all our oathes [?] made then, alsoe a not(e) of the Inconvenyences w old g(row) by the Inclosure.

The letter to Mannering alone has been preserved. It sets forth the 'good and godly uses and intents' to which the tithes were allotted in the charter of incorporation, and describes in pathetic terms the destitution which had fallen through recent fires on the town, 'where lyve above seaven hundred poore which receave Almes, whose curses and clamours Wilbee daylie poured out to god against the interprisors of such a thinge'. Whether either Mannering or Shakespeare replied, or, if they did, to what effect, Greene does not tell us; but we have no right to presume silence.

Sept. [1615] W. Shakespeares tellying J. Greene that I was not able to beare the encloseinge of Welcombe.

This is the darkest of all the dark sentences in Greene's hastily scribbled diary, as it is the most interesting. J. Greene was a brother. It seems unnecessary that Shakespeare should have told J. Greene a fact about his brother which, if it were a fact, he must have known better than 'cosen Shakespeare', and doubly unnecessary that Thomas Greene should have made a note of it. But the fact is highly questionable. All through the diary there are scattered evidences that, while Greene acted with perfect loyalty to his Council, he was not himself averse to the project of enclosure. On January 9, 1615, there is the report of a long conversation between Greene and somebody whose name he has forgotten to give, probably Combe himself, in which Greene is promised ten pounds to buy a gelding, if he would propound a peace; the course suggested being a friendly suit which Greene was to urge Sir Henry Raynsford to propose. Greene demurred on the ground that Sir Henry would say that the suggestion came from him, and such a motion would be taken as 'too favourable' to the scheme of enclosure, 'I knowing their fixed resolutions'. Clearly, therefore, Greene had no such 'fixed resolutions' himself. He continues: 'I told him yt was known that he was here, and that I thought I did nothing but both sydes heard of yt; and therefore I caryed myself as free from all offence as I could; I told him I would do yt before Wednesday night to some of the principall of them;' and he notes in the margin: 'I did yt the same night at their commyng downe to me anon after, viz. Mr. Bayly, Mr. Baker, Mr. Walford, Mr. Chandler.' As Mr. Bayly is the Bailiff, there was nothing underhand in Greene's conduct, but it is impossible to represent the most honourable of go-betweens as a strong anti-enclosure man. Sir Sidney Lee thinks that 'Shakespeare's new statement amounted to nothing more than a reassertion of the continued hostility of Thomas

Greene to William Combe's nefarious purpose'. I should reply first that the purpose was in no way 'nefarious', for the 'friendly suit' referred to above implied compensation to be fixed by the court; and secondly that Greene's 'hostility' is contradicted by his own very clear evidence. He adds : 'Those who wish to regard Shakespeare as a champion of popular rights have endeavoured to interpret the " I " in " I was not able " as " he ", but palaeographers only recognize the reading " I ".' But here it must be pointed out that the learned judge has not got all the facts on his notes. The palaeographer who edited the facsimile of Greene's diary, the late Dr. C. M. Ingleby, pointed out in his preface that Greene had a queer habit of writing ' I ' when he meant ' he '; and ' he ' when he meant ' I '; sometimes correcting his blunder, and sometimes not. He quotes an uncorrected example from the first page of the diary : ' I willed him to learn what *I* could, and I told him soe would I.' Rhadamanthus himself would be forced to admit that the second ' I ' here is a mistake for ' he '. It must also be admitted in the other case, unless we prefer to impute to Shakespeare a want of insight into his cousin's lawyer-like habit of mind, and to Greene himself a puerile satisfaction in chronicling such a misjudgement.

If Shakespeare backed the Combes, we should have to charge him with unneighbourliness. But that is precisely the charge which it is so hard to credit. Dr. Wallace's discovery of his good-natured interest in the affairs of the son-in-law of the Huguenot tire-maker with whom he lodged in 1604, points in the opposite direction; and so does an incident to which Mrs. Stopes first called attention, which is chronicled in the very next entry in Greene's diary to that under discussion.

> 5 Sept. his sendyng James for the executours of Mr. Barber to agre as ys sayd with them for Mr. Barbers interest.

Mrs. Stopes discovered that this Barber had been harried, possibly to death, by the Combes ' about a debt he stood surety for Mris Quyney '. Sir Sidney Lee here comments : ' Shakespeare would seem to have been benevolently desirous of relieving Barber's estate from the pressure which Combe was placing upon it.' I think then we have good reason to plead for the benefit of the doubt in the matter of the enclosure.

H. C. BEECHING.

THE UNWORLDLINESS OF SHAKESPEARE

HAMLET and *King Lear* have a peculiar quality of unworldliness not to be found in other plays of Shakespeare. This unworldliness is expressed not only in words, though they express it often enough, but in the very conduct of the play. It shows itself even in a curious in-difference to dramatic success, an indifference that is certainly not mere failure. In both plays Shakespeare is writing at the height of his powers, and writing, as usual, instinctively for the stage. But, except at the opening of each play, he is beyond aiming at dramatic effect. Rather he uses the dramatic form, with a skill that has become unconscious, to reveal states of the soul ; and, when he has attained to the revelation of these, he seems to forget the practical business of the drama. In both plays all his dramatic contrivance is used to reach a certain situation as swiftly as possible ; but when it is reached the rest of the play consists of variations upon it, in which the soul of Hamlet or Lear is laid bare. In most plays we watch to see what will happen next, but at the height of *Hamlet* and *King Lear* this anxiety about the course of events ceases ; the dramatic action seems to fade away and the material conflict to be stilled, so that we may see souls independent of time and place. Hamlet and Lear are terribly beset by circumstances ; but, when they are most beset, they escape into a solitude of their own minds where we are alone with them and overhear their innermost secrets. Then the dramatic action seems to have had no object except to lead them into this solitude, where speech becomes thought, and there are no longer any events except those of the soul.

There is a point in *King Lear* where the theme of the play seems to be released from the material conflict and to rise suddenly into music. It is where Lear enters with Cordelia as a prisoner and cries :

We two alone will sing like birds i' the cage.

To himself he is alone with Cordelia, and he has learnt at last in the innocence of his madness to enter into a heaven of intimacy with her, where he can laugh at the world like a blessed spirit—

> Laugh
> At gilded butterflies, and hear poor rogues
> Talk of court news; and we'll talk with them too,
> Who loses and who wins; who's in, who's out;
> And take upon 's the mystery of things,
> As if we were God's spies: and we'll wear out
> In a wall'd prison, packs and sets of great ones
> That ebb and flow by the moon.

That phrase—' Take upon 's the mystery of things '—expresses exactly what seems to happen to Lear and Hamlet when they pass into this sudden peace at the height of the storm ; and Hamlet himself speaks not only to Rosencrantz and Guildenstern, or of one particular incident, but to all worldly wisdom, when he says : ' You would play upon me ; you would seem to know my stops ; you would pluck out the heart of my mystery.' These moments of the soul are not, cannot be, explained even by the poet himself. This unworldliness, unearthliness even, attained to through the disaster of an earthly conflict, is something beyond all analysis, something that we can only parallel in the works of Dostoevsky, where there is the same use of the story to reveal states of the soul, the same indifference to dramatic effect and even to the difficulties of the reader. Hamlet is puzzling, like Dostoevsky's people, because Shakespeare draws his very soul and not his motives. He is the most vivid character in all drama, yet we know his motives no more than we know our own when we are deeply moved. What we do know is the peculiar quality of his mind, and above all that passionate un-worldliness which makes him so lonely at the court of Denmark that he cannot find a companion even in the man or the woman that he loves. He must be always misunderstood there, as he has been misunderstood ever since ; and this weighs on his mind even when he is dying. His tragedy is really the tragedy of loneliness, and his seeming madness is the exasperation of loneliness, which always becomes most intense when he is with worldly people and stung by some proof of their mis-understanding. We may be sure that in it Shakespeare expressed the exasperation of his own loneliness, which he must have felt as soon as success lost its freshness for him. He could not content himself, even, with the success of the artist, of brilliant plays like *Henry V* or *As You Like It*. So he turned from the world with a religious longing for escape, which, being a poet, he could find only in his art and, imaginatively, in the purged souls of Lear and Cordelia and Hamlet, which are all his own soul projected imaginatively into the purging of tragedy. These two plays tell us that he could not consent to a private happiness of this world, that he took upon himself the mystery of things and the suffering of infinite possibilities. They tell us, whatever his outward life may have been, of the far adventures of his soul, through which he reached these furthest heights of poetry.

A. CLUTTON-BROCK.

THE CHARACTER OF SHAKESPEARE

As far as I can judge, no greater service can be rendered to Shakespeare, and therefore also to literature, than by some vindication of the character of our great poet. In a recent book (*Shakespeare : the Man and his Work*) I first endeavoured to disprove the theories of those writers who represent him as long dominated by a degrading passion for a degraded woman—the 'Dark Lady' of the Sonnets. My critics kindly gave it as their opinion that I had proved my case—which was this : 'Whether as the lady of the intrigue, or as mere mistress, the woman has an impossible story, utterly untrustworthy as material for biography.'

Secondly, inasmuch as religion and ethics are often a twofold morality of sentiment and practice, I next endeavoured to ascertain Shakespeare's religious opinions, with the aid chiefly of his Sonnets. I found that (if I may again quote from *Shakespeare : the Man and his Work*) 'however much the phrase may startle our more enlightened atheism, he was " a God-fearing Christian "'. In this endeavour also my critics accounted me successful. On the present occasion I trust to reinforce my former arguments by a brief examination of the Poems of Shakespeare.

If nothing had been known about Spenser except that he was the author of the *Faerie Queene* (and the same might be said of Milton and his *Comus*), we should still have been able to form a reliable estimate of his ethics and his religious opinions. Now, as it seems to me, the two poems *Venus and Adonis* and the *Rape of Lucrece* will enable any unbiased reader to form a similar estimate with regard to Shakespeare ; in other words, that he was, like Spenser, 'a God-fearing Christian'. This I shall at least endeavour to demonstrate.

All criticism is ultimately comparative ; there is no such thing as inductive criticism. We read these poems, and we say : 'Marlowe among Elizabethans might emulate their beauty and poetic force, but the spirituality of their vision, the loftiness of their wisdom, he could not emulate ; under this head we must refer again to Spenser.' Then we note the description of *Lucrece* as a ' graver labour ' ; this phrase would hardly have been employed by Marlowe, though it might by the author of the *Foure Hymnes*. But even with the corroboration of contemporary opinion we need not extort from the phrase any undue significance ; it implies at least that the *Venus* was a lighter theme, chosen in some measure to please a patron, and that the later poem, if not a corrective, would express the poet's weightier convictions. And of course the poems are in some respects counterparts—the obverse and reverse of one poetic coin.

Turning now to the *Venus*, we first examine its motives, all of which, we may note, are to be found in the Sonnets. There is the central theme—' When a woman woos ' ; next, the two ' patron ' themes of youth and beauty in man, and

> Seeds spring from seeds, and beauty breedeth beauty ;
> Thou wast begot ; to get it is thy duty ;

and of the remaining reflections by far the most important are those that point to the contrast between love and lust.

This is treated something after the manner of *antitheta*. First, we have the arts and arguments of Venus—an ' idle over-handled theme ', the poet calls it—

> ' Love is a spirit all compact of fire . . .'
> ' Affection is a coal that must be cool'd . . .'
> ' Make use of time ; let not advantage slip . . .'
> ' What were thy lips the worse for one poor kiss ? . . .'

The seductive yet pernicious doctrine of ' natural ' love—

> Love, free as air, at sight of human ties,
> Spreads his light wings, and, in a moment, flies—

is more or less deliberately supported by many of our present-day writers, some of them being of great repute amongst us ; but a greater than these was Shakespeare. Greater also than these was that other large-browed Elizabethan, and him I will quote first—

> ' Being one, why should not a man be content with one ?'
> ' As soul and body are one, so man and wife.'
> ' Wanton love corrupteth and debaseth it (mankind).'

Now let us hear the kindred words of Shakespeare, who, as is most meet and intelligible, frequently produces or reproduces the wisdom of Francis Bacon, and as frequently refines it and adorns ; so here, in the reply of Adonis—

> I hate not love, but your device in love,
> That lends embracements unto every stranger.

And again—

> Call it not love, for Love to heaven is fled,
> Since sweating Lust on earth usurp'd his name.

There is more—much more—to the same purpose, but I must pass on to the other poem, the *Lucrece.* In this also by far the most important of the reflections insist upon the contrast between love and lust ; to quote under this head would be to repeat almost half the poem. Here again is no work of Marlowe ; to him it would be utterly impossible ; it is the refined spirit of Spenser, or again (though Spenser was less fettered by dogma) of Milton. As far as I am aware, the most striking feature of the poem has not hitherto been recognized ; it is this : even as the palace of Lucrece is strewn by the author with Elizabethan rushes, so the pagan theme is saturated with Elizabethan Christianity. With this Christianity the poet is profoundly imbued, and fearlessly and naturally he expounds it. In fact, whatever of Christian doctrine or dogma is wanting in the Sonnets will be found here, and found in an extraordinary overplus. Even in regard to demonology, wherein the poet would naturally be on his strictest guard, the Roman Jove is out-rivalled by the Christian Jehovah.

In this short essay, illustration of every point—indeed, of any but a very few points—is impossible. I will note here, however, that the 'high almighty Jove' (cf. Milton's 'all-judging Jove') invoked by Lucrece is not easily identified with 'him who gave' Tarquin his sword wherewith to 'kill iniquity' ; and that when Tarquin falls to reflecting on the futility of praying to the 'eternal power' for success in such an enterprise, and adds, 'The powers to whom I pray abhor this fact,' one can hardly believe that the reference is to any of 'the gods that Romans bow before' ; especially seeing that a line or two later the poet concludes with this fragment of Christian doctrine :

> The blackest sin is cleared with absolution.

In all this we are at least reminded of Bacon's 'taking Pluto for the Devil'.

This, however, shall be a matter of opinion ; but I should like to quote from one of the less equivocal passages (and there are hundreds such), chiefly because it throws strong light on one of the most important of the Sonnets, namely, the CXLVIth.   The following is a part of it :

> Besides, his soul's fair temple is defaced . . .

And the soul speaks for herself, as follows :

> She says, her subjects with foul insurrection
> Have batter'd down her consecrated wall,
> And by their mortal fault brought in subjection
> Her immortality, and made her thrall
> To living death and pain perpetual . . .'

Among the many points of comparison between the whole passage (ll. 712–28) and the Sonnet, perhaps the most interesting is the poet's employment of both the scriptural doctrines in regard to our human body ; in the Sonnet it is the 'vile body' that shall be 'destroyed by worms' ; for there the poet is speaking—and with a conscientious modesty—of himself ; but in the poem he gives us the other biblical doctrine (only adumbrated in the Sonnet) which speaks of the body as a 'temple', and 'holy', whether as the temple of the Deity or of the Holy Ghost or as the mansion of the divine-human spirit.   The figure occurs again in *Lucrece* (l. 1173) :

> Her sacred temple spotted, spoil'd, corrupted ;

and indeed the whole passage (ll. 1163–76) in which this line is found should be read by the side of the former.   Notable, for example, among so much that is noteworthy, is the expression (of the soul) 'the other made divine' (l. 1164).

Here, though incomplete, I must leave my textual investigation of the two poems, and turn to another important subject.

It might be urged that these Christian reflections, although they occur in such a remarkable excess, arise out of the subject ; that they belong to art, and have no relation to practical life.   But the fallacy may be met in a thousand ways.   'All beauty', we reply, ' is related to life, and therefore also to morality.   Next, a true artist is a man, not a machine, and as a man his speech bewrayeth him ; whether he will or will not, you shall know him by his deeds, his emotions, his very thoughts ; aye, and that intimately.   Nor do these reflections arise out of the subject ; on the contrary, they are foreign to it.   You will not find them in the pages of Ovid ; you would not have found them, we repeat, in the pages of Marlowe.   They are peculiar to Shakespeare, to Spenser, Sidney,

Raleigh—that is, to the spiritually-minded Elizabethan. Religious opinions, I may add, like political opinions, are an obsession that may even imperil the creations of the artist.'

But for a moment I will abandon whatever isolated evidence may be afforded by these two poems, and bring in a wider argument. It is the main argument of the book referred to above—*Shakespeare : the Man and his Work*—namely this, that we must judge Shakespeare only by what is habitual, only by prevailing tendencies. If I were asked to mention the most persistent of the various elements of Shakespeare's moral philosophy, I should reply unhesitatingly, ' this contrast between love and lust '. His doctrine may be thus stated : ' Unlawful passion is a vice, a torture, and loathsome, and it goes by the name of lust ; whereas lawful passion is a virtue, a delight, and beautiful, and it goes by the name of love.' This doctrine is traceable throughout his writings. We have begun with his early poems ; if we pass on to the Sonnets, there also we have it in abundance, sometimes with a tinge of convention and dejected admission, as in Sonnet CXXIX, but far more frequently as the expression of an emotion almost startling in its sincerity—

> I do betray
> My nobler part to my gross body's treason ;

this repentant cry, moreover, is nobly supported by the stern and spiritual resolve of the CXLVIth Sonnet above mentioned, which, likely enough, is an epilogue to the whole Sonnet series.

Next we follow the doctrine through the long series of plays till we reach *Measure for Measure*. Here we are aware of an astonishing culmination of *antitheta* due to long pondering on the subject. We see these *antitheta* thrown, as it were, into the scales of a vast weighing-machine. Awestruck we watch the slow successive balancings, but the scale that falls at last, and falls heavily, is on the side of the angels. From this point onward we have no more of convention (and we never had much), no more of dejected doubt, no more even of *antitheta* ; henceforth all is the plain speaking of a plain conviction.

Into the heaven-reflecting lake of *The Tempest* are poured the various streams of Shakespeare's noble and most spiritual philosophy. Therein are mingled the rarer action of virtue, the old piety that lived each day as if the last, the old simple faith in ' Providence divine ', and the newer faith in a human brotherhood. There also are the education that ennobles, the civilization that works only by uplifting, and, as I venture to believe, the finer knowledge that bears flower of reverence and fruit of wisdom.   Thither more certainly flow the vital streams of conscience, free will, repentance, forgiveness, charity, and almost every other moral faculty and aspiration.   But the stream whose course I have traced so imperfectly brings perhaps the most important tribute ; for the play of *The Tempest* appears to concern itself chiefly with the beauty, ecstasy, and sanctity of a pure love consummated by marriage.   Not alone to ' holy wedlock ' (as he styles it in *Lucrece*) does the poet pay this last tribute of his spiritual genius ; significantly he pleads the wholesome discipline of courtship, and the yet more imperative need of pre-nuptial purity ; and he concludes by uttering what is perhaps the plainest and sternest of all his moral denunciations, for on unmarried love, he tells us—

> No sweet aspersion shall the heavens let fall . . .
>   but barren hate,
> Sour-eyed disdain and discord shall bestrew
> The union of your bed with weeds so loathly
> That you shall hate it both.   (*The Tempest,* IV. i. 18–23.)

' Parts ', says Dr. Johnson, ' are not to be examined till the whole has been surveyed ' ; and the light I have endeavoured to throw on the two poems of Shakespeare is now seen to be a collective radiance, the radiance of a moral philosophy whose elements differ only as one star differeth from another star in glory.

MORTON LUCE.

SHAKESPEARE: THE NEED FOR MEDITATION

LET it be reasserted with fervency to-day that there is no limit to the possibilities of fresh interpretation of Shakespeare. Recent advance in psychology extends the horizon. But every subtle interpretation will be met by the facile retort that it would have surprised Shakespeare to hear of meanings attributed to him. For popular criticism has not time to comprehend the truth that the supreme poet remains unaware of the full significance of his utterance. An old truth even in the days of Plato, it is implicitly assented to, inasmuch as reference to poetic 'inspiration' is a commonplace. The perfect poem is felt to have, instead of the inchoateness or formlessness of everyday self-expression, the harmony, unity, life of Nature's works. She being the producer of life and perfect form—she, and not man's conscious will—the poetry is therefore felt to be inspired by her.

Indeed, if we grant the poet's right to the title of creator, what is it to declare, after Plato, that he does not know the full significance of his utterance, but to declare that he is not a God? But there is no other truth so rich in implication and consequence as this, that man was made in the image of God. Wherefore Shakespeare, moulding with creative energy the dust of chaotic experience, makes of it cosmos and breathes into it life. And because Life is infinite, there is no terminus to the Shakespeare student's voyage of research.

But every one is in too great a hurry; and we must train ourselves in meditation. In the words of Hamlet to the Ghost—

> Haste me to know it, that I with wings as swift
> As meditation . . . may sweep to my revenge—

there will be heard some day, by all who have understanding, the laughter of the supreme master of irony, causing the hero, in the very words with which he expresses the readiness of his will, to express unawares his impotence. Could Hamlet have thought of wings swifter than meditation, it might have better availed him. But if we be called, not to the swoop of revenge, as he was, but to the study of the deepest mind yet found among men, then the leisure of those brooding wings, and not the hawk's flight of journalism, is what we shall need.

Milton, feeling that there were unplumbed depths in Shakespeare, expressed in fantastic words of homage his sense of the need of unhurried meditation :

> Thou, our fancy of itself bereaving,
> Dost make us marble with too much conceiving.

If we have inherited Milton's feeling, then the real advance in psychology in our days may mean for us an increased measure of insight. Criticism remains rich in heart-stirring possibilities of romantic discovery.

WILBRAHAM FITZJOHN TRENCH.

SHAKESPEARE AS TOUCHSTONE

NOT indeed in the theatrical sense of ' as '—indeed one of the innumerable legends assigns him quite a different part in the play : nor referring to one of his own most delightful creations at all. But it was said once of a writer—great in his own way, though the word ' greatness ' can hardly be used in the same sense (even with change of degree) of him and of Shakespeare—that he ' was a touchstone : for he invariably displeased all fools '.

The difference of the greatness, however, appears in this very limitation. It is much in a man's favour that he should displease fools ; but merely arousing their displeasure does not necessarily imply any very wonderful or multifarious greatness in himself : certainly it does not imply any infinite quality. Nor is it perhaps true that Shakespeare displeases all fools, though it may be more arguable that all whom he does displease deserve the classification.

The way in which he shows his touchstoneship is much more subtle and has much more of that uncanny infinity which is not improperly ascribed to him. He may not displease all fools : some fools may indeed be—or may think themselves—very proud of him, and admire him—or think they admire him—highly. But he has a terrible and unerring power of disclosing folly in those who talk of him, be they admirers or decriers. It may be said, ' But is not this the case with every subject of long and varied discussion ? ' To some extent perhaps, and to a greater no doubt, the longer and the more varied the discussion has been. For in such cases there is an ever-growing temptation either to platitude simple or, still worse, to ' platitude reversed '—to paradox, laborious innovation, affected heresy and the like, all of which are among the worst forms of folly.

Yet it is difficult to remember any other subject, even among those that have, at one or more times, been absolutely fashionable—and where there is fashion there is nearly always folly—which has had quite this dread power. The Man in the Iron Mask, Junius, ' Was Pope a poet ? ', ' Was Queen Mary guilty ? '—great store of folly has no doubt been evolved by the application of all these tests to fit persons ; but they were not infallible as such.   Shakespeare is.

He is indeed not only infallible directly in discovering folly in the persons who talk about him ; he has the doubly uncanny faculty of exercising a sort of secondary assay.   Rymer in the early days, and Rümelin in later ones, succumb to his power in denouncing him ; and then other persons, defending or excusing Rümelin or Rymer, exhibit the fatal signs as a sort of contagion, though they may themselves be apparently sound on the main Shakespearian question.   Not the cups and mirrors of eastern and western Romance, which revealed a lady's weakness or a knight's treachery, had this daemonic power of transferred detection.   Yet, on the other hand, the equity of its operation can be illustrated by the example of Ernest Hello.   Nobody has abused Shakespeare more ; but nobody, even in praising him, has shown less folly.   The premisses were wrong ; the standpoint out of range or focus ; the glasses coloured and bevelled unduly ; so that the judgement must be reversed or disallowed.   But there has been no folly in this judge, and he need not be written down what so many judges have to be written down.

Still the case is parlous ; and it is said that some persons, pusillanimous it may be but not wholly foolish, have actually declined to write books about Shakespeare, and have made special intercession for themselves before committing smaller risks about him to paper.   As one looks over the three hundred years during which there has been possibility of Shakespeare discussion, the procession of ' touched ' and discovered folly is great and rather terrible, if sometimes also very amusing.   Dryden himself, emerging unstained and triumphant in the best of his utterances, fails, as is too well known, in at least one instance— bears a spot on the otherwise untarnished surface.   Of Rymer's abuse no more need be said ; indeed, it is almost too amusing to be really abusive, and it is rather surprising that no one has recently taken the line that it was ' only his fun '—a willing sacrifice at the altar of the Comic Spirit, as they would perhaps call it.   Poor Shadwell's patronage has something of the same quality of amusement, but remains, alas ! unparadoxable as an evidence of folly.   Except Johnson (from whom Folly fled invariably even when he was most prejudiced and most wrong-premissed) and Maurice Morgann (from whom Queen Whims drove her poor relation Folly off), almost all eighteenth-century critics, well deserving as they may be of the excuses or defences which have been recently made for them, betray the spot which the touchstone has made.   Since Coleridge (though not in him) the occasional foolish faces of praise have been mingled with the crowd of those of blame—though of course the latter have been the more numerous, while in a large number of cases it has not been necessary that the voluntary victim should take a side either in admiration or depreciation. On one of these sides there are the good folks who are sure that Shakespeare was disgusted by all his naughty characters ; those who try to make him out a partisan of their own views in politics, religion, and what not ; those who are quite sure that he not only ' could be ' but always was ' very serious '—who accordingly make elaborate apologetic explanations for things like the gallery-stuffing of the early plays, or even extenuate themselves in one sense at extenuating him in another, and trying to prove that passages, scenes, and even whole plays which they do not like are not his; with others of various amiably foolish kinds. On the opposite side—the side of repudiation—it is needless, and would indeed be impossible, to enumerate the various divisions and corps of the armies of Doubters and Bloodmen who attack our Mansoul. From the champions of the Unities to contemporaries who question whether Shakespeare has always attended properly to that ' conflict ' which, it seems, is as necessary to a drama as a brown tree once was to a picture— one knows them all. Of Baconians and other enemies of ' the Stratforder ' who need talk ?—do they not one and all bear on their arms the badge of Moria ? And so of the rest.

But it is of the middle division, glanced at above, that the writer of this modest contribution has been chiefly thinking. Although a man may be quite free from theories of what drama ought to be and not in the least convinced that Shakespeare was written by Taylor the Waterpoet—still there are innumerable instances showing that when he takes up the study of the bard, the hood of Chaucer's contemporaries and the nightcap of Pope's becomes, in some hideous fashion, metamorphosed into another kind of headgear. It does not apparently matter much what his special line of investigation may be. Forty years ago, as some may directly remember and as others must have learnt from history, the prevailing craze was that of cutting up the plays, or some of them, into little stars and attributing these to Shakespeare's predecessor-contemporaries who must, according to such theories, have composed on the principle prevailing in ' places where they sing '—the parts of speeches being parcelled out like the phrasing of an anthem. But this game has, to some extent, been played out as regards Shakespeare, and has passed to other dramatists. Beaumont and Fletcher have already suffered much from it ; and those who live long enough will probably see passages of Goff bestowed upon Nabbes, and unrecognized fragments of Robert Davenport discovered in the plays of Lodowick Carlell. For some time the exercises in which Wisdom no doubt sometimes displays more or less of herself, but where Folly is often visible at full length, have been for the most part transformed to the interpretation of plot and character—certainly a spacious field enough, and one on and about which one might hunt long and merrily on the chance of discovering Wisdom, and in the certainty of meeting with Folly. But this is no place for particular records of the various gems. Were such a survey undertaken it would certainly confirm the general theory advanced in this paper—that for a Touchstone of Folly there is nothing like Shakespeare—ignoble as may at first seem to be the use to which we put our greatest.

And yet, as has indeed been already hinted to the intelligent, though the use may be ignoble, the fact is very much the reverse. For it is only a function or special administration of that gift of universality which the first great critic of Shakespeare hit upon as his main characteristic, and which all great critics of him (except one or two who have been deflected from the true way by some malign obstacle or influence) have recognized since. For the universal, of its very nature and definition, cannot be limited even to the enormous range of Shakespeare's actual utterances. It must include, or, to use a more exact word, extend to, not merely everything that he touches but everything that touches him. He brings out the qualities of a foolish critic of his plays, just as he does those of a foolish personage in them—and poor Rymer, again, in the seventeenth century—let us not be so ill mannered as to specify anybody in the twentieth—has, like Shallow or Simple, to present himself as he is. Of course, the touchstone character is not limited to folly. It extends to wisdom as well, and we should not have known the full intellectual power of Coleridge, or the full appreciative power of Hazlitt, if it had not been for Shakespeare. Of course, likewise, as some clever one may say, this accounts for the foolish things that may have been said in this very paper. There is no possibility of denying it— supposing that there have been any. But the fact would establish the theory if it were not wholly complimentary to the theorizer. And base is the slave who would not prefer the establishment of his doctrine to the gratification of his personality.

GEORGE SAINTSBURY.

POLYGON HOUSE,
    SOUTHAMPTON,
        Lady Day, 1916.

THE PARADOX OF SHAKESPEARE

ONE of the finest of all the essays written upon Shakespeare, that of Charles Lamb on the Tragedies, is hardly ever cited or discussed, so far as I have observed, among Shakespearians. The reason, I think, is that men are unwilling either to accept its thesis or to deny it—a very good reason, perhaps, for leaving a question alone. 'It may seem a paradox,' writes Lamb, 'but I cannot help being of opinion that the plays of Shakespeare are less calculated for performance on a stage than those of almost any other dramatist whatever. Their distinguishing excellence is a reason that they should be so. There is so much in them which comes not under the province of acting, with which eye and tone and gesture have nothing to do.'

Lamb of course should not have said : ' It may *seem* a paradox, *but* ' —he was propounding a paradox in the proper sense of the word, as Shakespeare used it, that is to say, a proposition that seems false, but is true. And though the proposition is likely to be spontaneously resisted by many, as it naturally was by Irving, no one, so far as I know, has ever sought to confute it save by way of simple denial and contrary asseveration, a process from which Lamb's analysis escapes untouched.

There is indeed just enough of suggestion in Lamb's essay of ' paradox ' in the popular and perverted force of the term, enough of the mood that flouts a truism or a convention for the flouting's sake, to give it so much of that aspect and literary status as serves to keep it out of the arena of serious critical debate. The initial motive of indignation at the epitaph which ranked Garrick as kindred in mind with Shakespeare was of a kind which often enough served Lamb for ' para-doxing ' in the received sense ; and his handling of the old play of *George Barnwell*, with its ' trifling peccadillo, a murder of an uncle or so ', might very well keep up the confusion for readers not inclined to face the problem. And, lover as he was of the great art of acting, in which no man took more delight than he, he yet permitted himself to write as if he saw in it nothing but the personal demerits of its practitioners.

But he was perfectly serious about his main thesis ; and, so far as his broad statement goes, he was perfectly right. He truly stated what, on the analogy of the ' Paradox of Acting ', as put by Diderot, we may properly term the Paradox of Shakespeare.

A glimpse of its truth must instantly come to any one who muses thoughtfully on the significance of the fact that the whole intellectual world is to-day commemorating, in the midst of the most tremendous war in all history, a theatre-poet of three hundred years ago who made his living, and a modest competence, as an actor and a playwright, a ' public entertainer ' working on a commercial basis. What has availed to make him thus immortal, as immortality goes in the modern world ? Other men of that era, Luther and Copernicus, Rabelais and Montaigne, the great artists and poets of Italy, have had a still longer run of fame, with security for its continuance, on more or less obvious grounds. Protestants revere Luther ; all educated men salute Copernicus ; the writers, poets, and artists are esteemed as such. But Shakespeare, who of all writers wins the widest tribute, is not extolled primarily or essentially as a writer of plays. Most of us have never seen half his plays staged, and our posterity is probably likely to see still less of them. Manifestly, it is by his readers that Shakespeare is pedestalled : he who wrote for the stage finds immortality in the study, like classics in general.

Lamb's main thesis is that Shakespeare's work has a spiritual or intellectual content which of necessity eludes representation ; that the presentment obtrudes a multitude of details which positively shut out for us the greatest thought-impressions that the plays can make ; and that Hamlet or Othello on the stage is psychically for us a different being from the spirit revealed to us by the reading. ' This was sometimes a paradox, but now the time gives it proof.' It is the tacit testimony of all students, of all who have really lived with Shakespeare. Lamb, of course, should have added that the stage can never give us the continuous impalpable inner music of the verse, the thrill of rhythm which fuses with our sense of the words, the ideas, the character, the problem. A faithful rendering of the verse as verse, sometimes demanded by critics from actors, would probably hinder instead of furthering the mimetic effect, the air of reality necessarily sought by the player : Irving, who knew his business on that side, used to make his superior effect of actuality as against his colleagues by positively disregarding verse measure. Verse is an ' ideal ' medium for dramatic dialogue, representing not life, not *mimesis*, but verbal art : the ' nature ' to which it holds up the mirror is not ' practic ' but ' theoric ' : its world is subjective, not objective. The player in *Hamlet* might have suggested to the critic-Prince that it is 'from the purpose of playing'.

We seem to come, then, to what looks like a paradox in the popular meaning, a mere extravagance, flouting common-sense ; to wit, the verdict that the admittedly greatest of all dramatists was not rightly or essentially a dramatist but something else ; and that the end at which he certainly aimed throughout his life is not the end which he best achieves. Yet so it is : this is the true paradox.

The main fact is substantiated, for one thing, by the growing infrequency and the experimental character of the stage representations. Germans boast, and sometimes thereby disconcert the ingenuous Briton, that among them Shakespeare is much more played than among us. But that fact, so far from proving a higher appreciation of Shakespeare in Germany than here, is really a proof to the contrary. Germans run Shakespeare on the stage as they run their State ideal, in the spirit of idolatry or convention-worship, not as a matter of independent critical judgement. They have been drilled and told what to admire, as they have been drilled and told what to think, to say, and to do. People who suppose they can get Shakespeare on the stage, in translation, as they can get him in the book, in his own tongue, are bowing to a convention, not to the reality, which is subjective. The cultured Englishman knows this, with or without the help of Lamb : the average German does not. Shakespeare is to-day more widely read in his own tongue than ever, and this will continue while his plays are staged less and less.

Perhaps we shall better realize the truth of the paradox if we note some of the exceptions suggested by Lamb's 'almost'. Shakespeare's dramas, clearly, are not less 'calculated' for performance on a stage than those of Marlowe, who, though not properly an epic poet, as is suggested by Professor Schröer of Freiburg, is, especially in his earlier plays, much less of a stage poet than our master. *Tamburlaine*, as poetry and as primitive psychic creation, is to-day simply unplayable ; but Faustus and Barabas, in their different ways, are also irreducible to the plane of the theatre. Marlowe, in a word, had in his simpler 'elemental' fashion charged these creations with a conceptual content which eludes the stage, the poetry and the character-concept being alike extraneous to the mechanism of representation. And even when he devotes himself to quasi-realism, the law of the poetic drama holds good for his work. If Professor Schröer had perceived, as editors are now beginning to do, that Fleay was right in pronouncing *Richard the Third* a creation of

Marlowe, he would have altered his proposition: Richard is the result
of a steady progress towards dramatic as distinct from poetic construction. But, as Lamb expressly contends, Richard in his degree also
transcends drama proper. The intellectual monster, the poetic villain,
like the poetic hero, exists as an idea behind the enacted man.

Shakespeare, then, with his far more various and profounder gifts,
and with his far greater measure of practical judgement in combination
with these, did but fulfil in his far truer and greater ideal world
the destiny of the poet turned dramatist. Endowed with the most
consummate faculty of sympathy and comprehension, he was made a
dramatist by his vocation, to his and our unspeakable profit; for there
is nothing in his two long poems to suggest that, poet as he was, he could
ever have 'found himself' save in the dramatic form. And the evolution of the plays tells of an original bias to the poetic, the discursive,
which only the needs and pressures of the stage could reduce to dramatic
service. In *Love's Labour's Lost* and the *Midsummer Night's Dream*
we have poetic extravaganzas rather than plays: the early Comedies of
action are presumptively recasts of older work; and *King John*, written
after an old model, is poetic, discursive, eloquent, to the limit of the
theatre's acceptance. It is only after a dozen years of stage experience
that we get *Othello*, with its intense compression; and in *Othello*, with
all its lightning-like effects of action, the sheer idealism of the conception, as Lamb maintained, outgoes the process on the stage.

But there is another side to the problem. The tragedies of Jonson,
assuredly, are not 'calculated' for representation; and here we have
the express evidence of theatrical history, as it were in defiance of Lamb's
thesis, that in the Stuart days audiences delighted in Shakespeare who
turned away from 'tedious but well-laboured *Catiline*'. Jonson, in
tragedy, missed his end on the stage without attaining another in the
study; for in his case even great rhetoric has failed to attain that something more than drama which is the secret of the dominion of Shakespeare. With all his strength, he had neither the elemental creative
force of Marlowe nor the all-comprehending sympathy of Shakespeare:
he is but the doctrinaire of poetic tragedy. There has never been a
Jonson club, I think, since Jonson's generation, when his personality
'made a school' for him. For posterity, his work lacks magic.

But already we are faced by the qualification which must be placed
on Lamb's paradox. The stage vogue of Shakespeare tells that not only
was his sheer stage-craft the best of his age, but *something* in his work
conquered that age, even on the boards. It can hardly be that actors

then were subtler than now : it must have been that his vision of life, his high-poised sanity and his imaginative reach, forced themselves on a generation accustomed to poetic drama, though the later vogue of the hectic tragedy of Beaumont and Fletcher indicates the critical limits of the popular culture. And since that day, down to our own, something of the overtones and undertones of Shakespeare's incomparable speech, something of his larger message, must have touched the more impressible even of the audiences, for many of whom the sensations of the ghosts and the fencing in *Hamlet* and *Macbeth* were the capital items.

And in the comedies, too, though Lamb claimed that he could prove his case for these as for the tragedies if he would, the play of fun and feeling, the unserious poetry, so much nearer the plane of the actual, must have meant some seizure of Shakespeare's charm. *As You Like It* is not a world of ' cloudy companionship ' and hovering reverie ; and to witness it is to be in the poet's sunshine, though the stage lets slip through its fingers the music and the moonlit poetry of Belmont, to say nothing of the wonder-world of *The Tempest*. But thus still the paradox holds : the Shakespeare of the stage is in the main but the integument in which the greatest of dramatic poets infused his utmost art of rhythmic speech and of brooding sympathy with the fates of men. Wellnigh all his plots came to him as vehicles tested by theatrical success in other hands ; and to them he committed his invisible freight of poetry and thought, the infinite dream of his imagination. The paradox of Shakespeare, in short, is that of the master-poet led by economic destiny to the work in which alone, to an end he could not have foreseen, his poetic power could attain its supremest possibilities, that task which, if economically free, he would probably not have chosen, of being the poetic mouthpiece of a world of imagined men and women. Becoming a theatre-poet to make his livelihood, he builded better than he can possibly have known. And thus, perhaps, his paradox is finally just the paradox of all genius that reaches consummation.

J. M. ROBERTSON.

KNIGHT'S PLACE,
   PEMBURY, KENT.

L

THE TERCENTENARY OF SHAKESPEARE'S DEATH—1916

> Come the three corners of the world in arms,
> And we shall shock them. Nought shall make us rue,
> If England to itself do rest but true.
> *King John*, Act V, Sc. vii.

CALM at the height of Danger's darkest hour,
  With hearts enduring, hands outstretched to save
That civil world the foe would fain devour,
  The whelming rush of barbarous hosts we brave ;
And, trusting to the safe, well-guarded wave,
  Confront the battle. Mighty is the power
  Of Freedom, Britain's heirloom, sacred dower,
By Flanders' blood secured, and Suvla's grave !

But yet a stronger talisman we own,
  A nobler Unity our souls confess,
Felt in each Briton's heart ev'n while unsung,
  Alike in torrid air and frozen zone ;
A free-born Empire's patriot consciousness,
  Tuned to the music of our Shakespeare's tongue.

The same, loosely paraphrased in Italian.

Nel mezzo di periglio l'alma forte
   Rinforzo stende ed ospitalitate
   Dall' Anglia alle genti abbandonate,
Che vuol vorar di Prusia il crudel corte;
Dove, gl' eredi d'una degna sorte,
   Fidiamo noi all' onde ben guardate,
   E voi l' arca nostra sicurate,
Col sangue, Flandra, e, Suvla, colla morte.
Vi resta a noi più forte talismano,
   Dell' unità che splende al mondo intero,
Che quando pure senza rime vanta
   L' Inglese, ed il Dominio di lontano;
La conscienza libera d' Impero:
   Fra noi ella nacque, ed il Shakespeare la canta.

W. J. COURTHOPE.

A THOUGHT FROM ITALY

I SEE them peopled, as he weaves the spell,
Verona, Padua, Venice,—a new crown
Of honour added to their old renown :
But if his own eyes saw them none may tell.
No trivial spirit of his ampler days
Revealed the poet's secret, which is well.
He is exempt from question or dispraise,
And time has left us but the miracle.
We may not know if ever he came here,
Whose intuitions baffle and transcend
Our knowledge, and begin where we must end ;
But I would dream it, and such dreams are dear,
Since all the sun, the magic, and the mirth
Are in his words, ' that pleasant country's earth.'

J. RENNELL RODD.

ROME.

A NOTE ON FALSTAFF

To be invited to join in a tribute to the memory of Shakespeare is to receive an embarrassing and perilous honour. Let me try to escape some at least of its dangers by avoiding the impertinence of any direct words about his genius, and trying rather to give an indirect proof of its transcendent working as seen in a case in which it has, I think, as it were, over-reached itself.

Falstaff is admittedly Shakespeare's greatest humorous creation and perhaps the greatest purely humorous figure in the literature of the world. Now it is an invariable characteristic of humour that to a greater or less extent it dissolves morality. In so far as the humour of a humorous person takes possession of us we do not notice, or at least do not condemn, his vices. This is so in our view of actual historical characters. The drunkenness of Charles Lamb, the conjugal infidelities of La Fontaine, are not judged as they would be judged if we were not entirely preoccupied with our delight in their humour and with the affection which flows out to people who give us that delight. And the same thing is still more noticeable in the case of fictitious characters. We ought to think of Mrs. Gamp as an abominable old woman, dirty, drunken, heartless. But in fact we never think anything of the sort. Indeed we do not think at all : if we did we might be forced to think hard things of the old sinner, but she takes good care to keep us better occupied. Whenever she is present, we take our ease in our inn, drinking with greedy delight of her inexhaustible fountain, far too happy to remember anything graver than our happiness.

Falstaff is, of course, an incomparably greater figure than Mrs. Gamp, and naturally the effect he produces is still more remarkable. Nobody exactly likes Mrs. Gamp : we all love Falstaff. Why ? Not only because Falstaff is greater than Mrs. Gamp, but because she is a figure which we see in the street and he is a figure we find in the looking-glass. It is a magnifying glass, no doubt, but still what it shows us is ourselves. Ourselves, not as we are, but as we can fancy we might have been ;

expanded, exalted, extended in every direction of bodily life, all the breadth and depth and height of it. Not a man of us but is conscious in himself of some seed that might have grown into Falstaff's joyous and victorious pleasure in the life of the senses. There, we feel, but for the grace of God, and but for our own inherent weakness and stupidity, go we: just as in *Hamlet* we feel our own glorified selves in another way, dreaming, hesitating, self-questioning, only that it is all raised a thousandfold in quantity and quality, and that Hamlet, like Falstaff, can give free and glorious form and utterance to what in us is only incoherent and inarticulate chaos. So in both we love ourselves, as indeed it is always some kinship with ourselves that we love in others. That is the truth behind the *homo sum, humani nihil alienum* of Terence and behind greater sayings than Terence ever uttered. But in Falstaff we love a quality that has always been found peculiarly human and lovable. What delights us in him is not merely the sense of an infinite freedom that he gives us, the escape into a world in which the police and the Ten Commandments are not only impotent, but ridiculous, and in which the spirit, as it were, of the body is as free from the constraint of the soul, as in Shelley's poetry the spirit of the soul is free from the constraint of the body. All this exalts us and gives us joy. But what specially wins our love is something else. It is that Falstaff, at his most triumphant times, is triumphant at his own expense. If he did not know that he was a gross tun of flesh, a drunkard, a coward, and a liar we should know it much more and love him much less. Here, as in religion, the way of confession is the way of forgiveness. And forgiving is very near loving. So when we hear La Fontaine laughing at his own follies and confessing his own sins, we not only forgive him, we love him. Perhaps he is the only French poet for whom we have exactly that indulgent affection, because no other has anything like so much of what we think the supreme element of humour, that which induces a man to laugh freely at himself; a quality which has been much more English than French, as wit, which is akin to satire and mostly exercised at the expense of other people, has been more brilliant in France than in England.

Well, of course Falstaff is peculiarly rich in this crowning gift. 'Thou seest I have more flesh than another man; and therefore more frailty.' 'I do here walk before thee like a sow that hath overwhelmed all her litter but one.' 'A goodly portly man, i' faith, and a corpulent; of a cheerful look, a pleasing eye, and a most noble carriage . . . and now I remember me, his name is Falstaff: if that man should be lewdly given, he deceiveth me; for, Harry, I see virtue in his looks.' It is everywhere, of course, in both the plays. And probably it is this supreme quality that, added on to all the rest, has given Falstaff the unique distinction which Shakespeare never meant him to have.

It is the triumph of Mrs. Gamp and her like, as we were saying just now, to suspend the action of the moral judgement. And if of Mrs. Gamp, of course a hundred times more of Falstaff. But Falstaff has a glory which he shares with no one else. If other humorous creations suspend judgement, he can do much more. He can victoriously reverse it. His humorous confession of his sins so disarms and delights us, that he has positively persuaded more than one subtle person to deny their existence altogether. Maurice Morgann in the eighteenth century was his first conquest. Others have followed, the most significant being the finest of living Shakespearean critics, Mr. A. C. Bradley, who substantially agrees with Morgann that Falstaff was not a coward, and adds that he was not a liar either, in the ordinary sense of that word.

My object now is not to discuss this theory in detail, which would require far more space than I can ask for here. It is rather to draw attention to the proof it affords of Shakespeare's amazing power, even when exercised, as it were, to his own defeat. He has so flooded Falstaff with the dazzling light of his genius that some of those among his critics who are most able to bear and enjoy such light, have been blinded by it to the other and grosser elements in Falstaff which to duller eyes are plain and indubitable. For that the theory is a complete mistake is, I venture to think, certain, for two broad reasons which almost render unnecessary the detailed discussion of the evidence of the text. This last is admittedly not all on one side of the argument, though even here the preponderance seems to me considerable. But details discovered in the closet can never be an answer to the broad effect made upon the stage. No man ever understood the theatre better than Shakespeare. It is certain that all the large and general impressions his characters make upon the stage can only be the impressions which he intended them to make. Now what that impression has always been in the case of Falstaff is not doubtful. The audience has throughout regarded him as a coward and a liar, and Shakespeare must have known that it would and meant that it should. To attempt to reverse this impression on the strength of little-noticed inconsistencies, such as the surrender of Sir John Colevile, is as hopeless a business as the similar attempt to make of Shylock a sympathetic figure, because Shakespeare made him a human being instead of a stage Jew. Shakespeare wrote for the pit, not for the critics : and though the critics are always adding to our wonder and delight by discovering things which, unperceived by the pit, were consciously or unconsciously in the poet's mind, yet on these broad issues the continuous verdict of the pit is final.

There is another general consideration which seems to me equally fatal to the view taken by Morgann and his successors. Is there not—I suggest it with great hesitation—some lack of humour in suggesting that Falstaff was not a coward and a liar? What is left of the humour of the great scene at the Boar's Head if ' A plague of all cowards, I say ' is to come from a brave man's mouth? And where is the humour of ' Lord, Lord, how this world is given to lying ', if the speaker be as truthful as the Duke of Wellington? What is left of the humour of the Prince's chaff ' I lack some of thy instinct ' if all the audience does not know that Falstaff is what the Prince elsewhere calls him ' a natural coward without instinct ' ? And where is the fun of the whole refutation —' Mark now how a plain tale shall put you down '—if Falstaff had not intended and expected to pass himself off as the hero of the affair? That is not the language in which a man replies to a joke ; and if Falstaff did not intend to be believed why, I wonder, did he hack his sword to make it evidence? Mr. Bradley thinks it absurd to suppose that he would have made the mistake about declaring the men were ' in Kendal green ' just after asserting that it was so dark that he could not see his hand. Has Mr. Bradley never been in a police court? Every day there gives proof of how difficult it is to tell a lie without at the same time providing its refutation? Certainly no small part of the humour of the scene lies in Falstaff's glorious escape from the refutation of his story. But to suppose that the whole scene is a kind of make-believe, that he did not expect to be believed, and they did not intend to put him to shame, seems to me to destroy half the delight of his victorious escape, which we enjoy and admire precisely because it seemed so inevitable that he would be reduced to confusion by the Prince's exposure.

No, Mr. Bradley and those who agree with him are simply the strongest evidence of the amazing magic of Shakespeare's creation. The true explanation of their delusion is akin to that which Mr. Bradley himself so ingeniously and convincingly offers of the puzzling scene of the rejection of Falstaff. That scene is unpleasant, which is certainly not what Shakespeare meant it to be. He must have intended us to think Henry's conduct natural and to sympathize with it. But we do not. And the reason must be, in Mr. Bradley's words, that Shakespeare had ' created so extraordinary a being and fixed him so firmly on his intellectual throne that when he sought to dethrone him he could not '. So with those who are blind to Falstaff's lying and cowardice. Shakespeare has shown them such a light that they can see nothing else, not even what he meant them to see. He has given them such delight that they will not admit the reality of anything that might detract from it. He has created a being so overflowing with an inexhaustible fountain of life and humanity that they love him and enter into him and become themselves so much a part of him that they are ready to explain away his vices as we all explain away our own. So far Shakespeare has overshot his own mark. Not on the stage, nor with the plain man. There the liar and coward will always be as visible as the genius. But for men of more than ordinary susceptibility to intellectual pleasure Shakespeare has in Falstaff provided a too intoxicating banquet. They find in Falstaff a man to whom lying with genius was simply a natural and pleasurable activity of his nature, who lies with glorious delight and commonly with triumphant success, who is himself supremely happy when he lies and makes all who hear or read him supremely happy too. They find that when they are with him they are in Heaven, which is a place where acts are their own ends, and they will not admit that he runs away, except for the pleasure of it, or lies, except as an artist, delighting in doing what he knows he can do as no other man can, and without any ulterior object of profit or reward. So with such men, and so far, Shakespeare fails, with this glorious failure. Their judgements are drowned in a flood of intellectual delight.

JOHN BAILEY.

THE OCCASION OF 'A MIDSUMMER NIGHT'S DREAM'

IT has long been recognized that the epithalamic ending of *A Midsummer Night's Dream* points to performance at a wedding, and that the compliment to the 'fair vestal throned by the west' points to a wedding at which Queen Elizabeth was present. The most plausible date hitherto suggested is January 26, 1595, on which William Stanley, Earl of Derby, married the Lady Elizabeth Vere, daughter of the Earl of Oxford, granddaughter of William, Lord Burghley, and goddaughter and maid of honour to the queen. This would fit in well enough with the allusions in the play to the bad weather of 1594, and to the lion at the baptism of Prince Henry of Scotland on August 30 of the same year ; while the presence of Elizabeth has been inferred from the words of Stowe, who says that 'The 26 of January William Earl of Derby married the Earl of Oxford's daughter at the court then at Greenwich, which marriage feast was there most royally kept'. I have long been puzzled by the statement that the wedding was 'at the court' ; not so much because the Treasurer of the Chamber made no payment for a court play on January 26, 1595, since the performance might have been ordered, not by the queen, but by the friends of the bride or bridegroom, as because the wedding itself does not appear in the list of those solemnized in the royal chapel and closet which is preserved in the so-called 'Cheque-Book' of the Chapel (ed. E. F. Rimbault, 160), and I have now good reason to think that Stowe made a mistake on this point, for in the accounts of the churchwardens of St. Martin's, Westminster (ed. J. V. Kitto, 471), I find for the year 1595 the following entry :

Item paid the xxx[th] of January for ringinge At her Ma[ties] Comynge to y[e] Lord Threasurers to y[e] Earle of Darbies weddinge And at her Departure from thence y[e] fyrst of ffebruary ij[s].

The court appears, indeed, to have been established at Greenwich from the middle of December, 1594, to the middle of February 1595. But it was not uncommon for Elizabeth, especially in her somewhat restless old age, to leave the court for a day or two's sojourn with some favoured courtier in London or the neighbouring villages ; and it was evidently upon such an occasion that she did honour to the nuptials of Elizabeth Vere at Burghley House in the Strand.   There is no entry of the marriage in the registers of St. Martin's or of St. Clement Danes, in which parishes Burghley House stood, and I think it is probable that it took place in the chapel of the Savoy, hard by, the registers of which are lost, for a contemporary record of another wedding, a few years later, tells us (*H.M.C., Rutland MSS.* i. 379) :

> The feast was held here at Burghley howse.   M^{rs} bryde with her hayre hanging downe was led betwen two yong bachelors from Burghley Howse thorough the streete, strawed, to the Savoy gate against my lodging, and so to that church.

I do not think that it is necessary, on the strength of the St. Martin's entry, to reject Stowe's date as well as his locality.   The bell-ringings for Elizabeth's removals are often entered with only approximate accuracy, possibly because the churchwardens recorded the dates of the payments rather than those of the services rendered.   And Stowe's January 26 can in fact be confirmed from another source.   On January 27 Anthony Bacon wrote from London to Francis Bacon at Twickenham, telling him that Antonio Perez had highly commended the queen's grace and the royal magnificence of some court solemnity then on hand (T. Birch, *Elizabeth*, i. 199), and this crossed a letter of the same date from Francis to Anthony (Spedding, *Life and Letters*, i. 353), in which he said :

> I hope by this time Antonio Perez hath seen the Queen dance (that is not it, but her disposition of body to be fresh and good I pray God both subjects and strangers may long be witnesses of).   I would be sorry the bride and bridegroom should be as the weather hath fallen out, that is go to bed fair and rise lowring.

Spedding could not identify the bride and bridegroom, but there can be no doubt about them.   Elizabeth, of course, was ready to dance on the edge of her grave ; Burghley, the master of the feast, old and gouty, was for other than for dancing measures.   He had written to Robert Cecil on December 2 (T. Wright, *Elizabeth and her Times*, ii. 440) :

> For her hope to have me dance, I must have a longer tyme to learn to go, but I will be ready in mynd to dance with my hart, when I shall behold her favorable disposition to do such honor to her mayd, for the old man's sake.

And on January 2 he added :

> Though my hand is unable to fight, and my right eye unable to take a levell, yet they both do stoop to return my humble thankes for continuance of her favor at this tyme, when I am more fitter for an hospital, than to be a party for a marriage.

These notices of the wedding indicate a mask, rather than a play ; but the two would not be incompatible. The internal evidence of *A Midsummer Night's Dream* does not take us much farther. The much-travelled Theseus might have been thought appropriate to William Stanley, whose own travels are said to have taken him as far as the Holy Land and Russia, and in later Lancashire legends grew to quite mythical proportions. There is the famous passage in which occurs the compliment to Elizabeth. The attempts of the older commentators to turn the mermaid and the falling stars and the little western flower into an allegory of Mary Queen of Scots and the northern rebellion, or of the intrigue of Leicester with the Countess of Essex, may be summarily disregarded. Whatever else complimentary poetry is, it must be in the first place gratifying to the person complimented, and in the second place reasonably topical. The northern rebellion and Leicester's marriage were both forgotten far-off things in 1595, nor was either of them calculated to give Elizabeth much pleasure in the retrospect. The marriage in particular had caused her bitter mortification in its day, and if Edmund Tilney had allowed Shakespeare to allude to it before her, he would have signed his own warrant for the Tower, and Shakespeare's for the Marshalsea. What Shakespeare was describing was, as it professed to be, a water-pageant with fireworks. But again, it is only a want of historical perspective or a sentimental desire to find a reminiscence of Shakespeare's childhood in his plays, which can explain the common identification of this water-pageant with that given at Kenilworth as far back as 1575. The princely pleasures of Kenilworth loom large to us out of the fragmentary records of Elizabeth's progresses, because they were set down in a racy pamphlet at the time, and because Scott used them as material for a novel. But there were many such entertainments both before and after, and if Shakespeare had any particular one in mind, it is far more likely to have been that which had occurred comparatively recently, when Elizabeth visited the Earl of Hertford at Elvetham in September, 1591. As a matter of fact, there was not a mermaid on a dolphin's back either at Kenilworth or at Elvetham. At Kenilworth there was a Triton on a mermaid's back, which is not quite the same thing. There was the Lady of the Lake, who might perhaps be called a sea-maid. And there was Arion on a dolphin's back, who sang to the music of instruments in the dolphin's belly. There were fireworks also, but apparently not on the same day as the water-pageant. At Elvetham there was ' a pompous aray of sea-persons', including Nereus, five Tritons, Neptune, and Oceanus, with 'other sea-gods' and a train in 'ouglie marine suites'. They brought in Neaera, the 'sea-nymph,' who sang a ditty. Meanwhile a 'snail-mount' in the water resembled 'a monster, having hornes of wild-fire continuously burning'; but here also the principal display of fireworks was on another day. Obviously, so far as subject-matter goes, Elvetham might, just as well as Kenilworth, have furnished the motive for the extremely sketchy reminiscences of Oberon. It may be added that at Elvetham the queen of the fairies, not for the first time in the history of Elizabethan pageantry, had made her appearance. She is called Aureola, not Titania, but names the king as Auberon. It goes without saying that Cupid all armed is not mentioned in either account. He could only be seen by Oberon. But it is to Cupid and the wound inflicted by his bolt on the little western flower that the whole description leads up. The flower has a part in the action of the play, and possibly we ought not to seek for any further motive for its introduction. But if it points, as some think, at an enamoured woman, how can this possibly be Lady Essex, or anybody else but the bride in whose glorification, next only to that of Elizabeth, the play was written? I do not assert that William Stanley and Elizabeth Vere, then sixteen, met and loved at Elvetham in 1591. Indeed, as will be seen before the end of this article, I do not assert that William Stanley and Elizabeth Vere were the bridegroom and bride of the play at all. But Elizabeth Vere, as one of the queen's maids, is at least likely to have been there, and William Stanley, who was coming and going in 1589 and 1590 between London and his father's houses in the north (*Stanley Papers*, ii. 66, 78, 82), may quite well have been there too. Elizabeth Vere's marriage had been one of the preoccupations of Lord Burghley, who had evidently taken over the responsibilities of her fantastic father, the Earl of Oxford, for some years before 1595. Early in 1591 the Earl of Bedford was spoken of (*S. P. Dom. Eliz.* ccxxxviii. 69), but it came to nothing, and Bedford married 'the Muses' evening, as their morning, star,' Lucy Harrington. About 1592 Burghley had been making suit for the Earl of Northumberland, 'but my Lady Veare hath answered her grandfather that she can not fancye him' (*H. M. C., Rutland MSS.* i. 300). William Stanley was at this time only an undistinguished younger son, and Burghley, perhaps the greatest of our civil servants, had the civil servant's not uncommon foible for founding a dynasty. It was in 1594 that the deaths in rapid succession of his father and his elder brother left Stanley the most eligible match in England.

Philostrate offers as a wedding device the 'satire keen and critical', of—

> The thrice three Muses mourning for the death
> Of Learning, late deceased in beggary.

This has been regarded as support for the Stanley-Vere identification, on the ground that Spenser's *Tears of the Muses* was dedicated in 1591 to Lady Strange, the wife of Stanley's brother and predecessor in the title. I have used the argument myself, but I now doubt its validity. It is not at all clear that this lady would have been at the wedding. There was bitter feud in 1595 between her and her brother-in-law over the succession to the Derby estates, and already on May 9, 1594, she had written to Burghley (*H. M. C., Hatfield MSS.* iv. 527):

> I hear of a motion of marriage between the Earl, my brother, and my Lady Vere, your niece, but how true the news is I know not, only I wish her a better husband.

One wonders how far Lady Derby was cognisant of the rumours sedulously spread about the country by the Jesuits as to the death of the late Earl, which had been sudden, had suggested suspicions of poisoning or witchcraft, and had robbed the Catholic intriguers of a hoped-for pretender. One version (*H. M. C., Hatfield MSS.* v. 253) ascribed a crime to 'my lord that now is'; another (*S. P. Dom. Eliz.* ccxlix. 92) to Burghley, in order that he might marry the young Lady Vere to the Earl's brother. I now come to the rather curious fact that at the Stanley-Vere wedding there actually does appear to have been a show of the nine muses, although it was not in the least concerned with 'Learning, late deceased in beggary.' This emerges from a letter written by Arthur Throgmorton to Robert Cecil (*H. M. C., Hatfield MSS.* v. 99). It is a curious side-light, not merely upon the methods, but upon some of the underlying motives of Elizabethan pageantry.

> Matter of mirth from a good mind can minister no matter of malice, both being, as I believe, far from such sourness (and for myself I will answer for soundness.) I am bold to write my determination, grounded upon grief and true duty to the Queen, thankfulness to my lord of Derby, (whose honourable brother honoured my marriage) and to assure you I bear no spleen to yourself. If I may I mind to come in a masque, brought in by the nine muses, whose music, I hope, shall so modify the easy softened mind of her Majesty as both I and mine may find mercy. The song, the substance I have herewith sent you, myself, whilst the singing, to lie prostrate at her Majesty's feet till she says she will save me. Upon my resurrection the song shall be delivered by one of the muses, with a ring made for a wedding ring set round with diamonds, and with a ruby like a heart placed in a coronet, with this inscription, *Elizabetha potest.* I durst not do this before I had acquainted you herewith, understanding her Majesty had appointed the masquers, which

resolution hath made me the unreadier: yet, if this night I may know her Majesty's leave and your liking, I hope not to come too late, though the time be short for such a show and my preparations posted for such a presence. I desire to come in before the other masque, for I am sorrowful and solemn, and my stay shall not be long. I rest upon your resolution, which must be for this business to-night or not at all.

The letter is only endorsed ' Jan. 1594,' but the reference to Lord Derby serves to relate it. Arthur Throgmorton of Paulerspury was brother of Elizabeth Throgmorton, who married Sir Walter Raleigh. But he can hardly have been wishing in 1595 to purge the offence given by his sister in 1592, and of his own marriage I only know that it was to Anne, daughter of Sir John Lucas of Essex (Bridges, *Northamptonshire*, i. 312). Nor can one quite see why he should have intruded his private affairs upon Derby's festival.

This note is growing upon my hands into a dissertation. I must refrain from discussing the troubled early married life of the Stanleys, which justified Bacon's fear that they might ' go to bed fair and rise lowring ', rather than Oberon's benediction of ' the best bride-bed '; or the later connexion of the earl with a company of players, which led a quite competent archivist to the astounding discovery that he, another W. S., was the real author of Shakespeare's plays. But I am afraid I must add that I am by no means convinced that *A Midsummer Night's Dream* was given on January 26, 1595, at all, although the plausibilities are perhaps more in favour of that date than any other. I should like, however, to be able to explore more fully the circumstances of a wedding which has never yet been considered, that of Thomas, son of Henry Lord Berkeley, and Elizabeth, daughter of Sir George Carey, on February 19, 1596. This is stated in the latest edition of G. E. C.'s peerage, probably on the evidence of the unprinted registers of St. Anne's, to have taken place from the Blackfriars, which is extremely likely, as Sir George Carey had his town house there, next door to the building which became Burbage's Blackfriars theatre. But I do not know that the queen was present, although she may well have been, as Elizabeth Carey was another of her goddaughters, and granddaughter of her first cousin and Lord Chamberlain, Henry Lord Hunsdon. The attractiveness of the suggestion lies in the fact that Shakespeare's company were Lord Hunsdon's men, and subsequently passed under Sir George Carey's own patronage, when he in his turn became Lord Hunsdon on his father's death later in 1596. Lady Carey was a sister of the Lady Strange to whom *The Tears of the Muses* was dedicated. Sir George Carey is known to have been present at the Elvetham entertainment of 1591, but it would hardly be possible to put the origin of the Berkeley-Carey match there, for it was only in 1595 that this was arranged, after negotiations for Lord Herbert, afterwards Earl of Pembroke, had fallen through, and the Berkeley family chronicler definitely places the beginnings of affection between the young couple in the autumn of that year (Collins, *Sydney Papers*, i. 353, 372 ; T. Smyth, *Lives of the Berkeleys*, ii. 383, 395).

E. K. CHAMBERS.

HELENA

ALL'S WELL !—Nay, Spirit, was it well that she,
  Thy clear-eyed favourite, the wise, the rare,
  The ' rose of youth ', must her deep heart lay bare,
And Helen wait on Bertram's contumely ?

Must Love's own humble, dauntless devotee
  Make Night accomplice, and, a changeling, dare
  The loveless love-encounter, and prepare
To tread the brink of shame ? May all this be,

And all end well ?—That Spirit, from his seat
  Elysian, seems to murmur : ' Sometimes know,
    In Love's unreason hidden, Nature's voice ;
In Love's resolve, Her will ; and though his feet
  Walk by wild ways precipitous, yet, so
    Love's self be true, Love may at last rejoice.'

OLIVER ELTON.

UNIVERSITY OF LIVERPOOL.

M

ORSINO TO OLIVIA

'If music be the food of love, play on.'
Twelfth Night, ACT I, Scene i.

I

WHAT wilt thou give me? Thou canst give me naught;
  Thou hast denied the honey of thy lips,
Thou dared'st not offer what my sick heart sought,
  Love's full awakening and apocalypse.
If much thou gav'st, 'twas but a beggar's fee:
  Or if but little, 'twas a winter's smile,
A mockery of friendliness—the while
  Thy heart was set on dreams more worthy thee.

Half-given and half-withdrawn, thy kindness fell
  Athwart my aching and tempestuous need
Like the lone note of some forgotten bell,
  Which swings its message faint across the mead—
Sound heard in stillness through the vacant air,
  An echo of dead passion and despair.

II

Yet, for I love thee so, I needs must cling
  To the old haunts, albeit the trees are bare,
And in the ruined branches no birds sing
  Mid death and desolation everywhere.
The shadow of my presence at thy door
  Thou canst not banish to forgetfulness:
My footfall echoes ghost-like on thy floor,
  And scarce-heard voices whisper my distress.

Spurn if thou wilt—and still my patient heart
  Is humbler than the humblest to adore
Whate'er thy fancy scatters from its store
  Of happiness or grief, content or smart:
I only ask a momentary grace—
To see once more the wonder of thy face!

W. L. COURTNEY.

FESTE THE JESTER

LEAR's Fool stands in a place apart—a sacred place ; but, of Shakespeare's other Fools,[1] Feste, the so-called Clown in *Twelfth Night*, has always lain nearest to my heart. He is not, perhaps, more amusing than Touchstone, to whom I bow profoundly in passing ; but I love him more.

Whether Lear's Fool was not slightly touched in his wits is disputable. Though Touchstone is both sane and wise, we sometimes wonder what would happen if he had to shift for himself. Here and there he is ridiculous as well as humorous ; we laugh *at* him, and not only *with* him. We never laugh at Feste. He would not dream of marrying Audrey. Nobody would hint that he was a ' natural ' or propose to ' steal ' him (*A. Y. L. I.* i. ii. 52, 57 ; iii. 131). He is as sane as his mistress ; his position considered, he cannot be called even eccentric, scarcely even flighty ; and he possesses not only the ready wit required by his profession, and an intellectual agility greater than it requires, but also an insight into character and into practical situations so swift and sure that he seems to supply, in fuller measure than any of Shakespeare's other Fools, the poet's own comment on the story. He enters, and at once we know that Maria's secret is no secret to him. She warns him that he will be hanged for playing the truant. ' Many a good hanging ', he replies, ' prevents a bad marriage ' ; and if Maria wants

---

[1] I mean the Fools proper, i. e. professional jesters attached to a court or house. In effect they are but four, Touchstone, Feste, Lavache in *All 's Well*, and Lear's Fool ; for it is not clear that Trinculo is the court-jester, and the Clown in *Othello*, like the Fool (a brothel-fool) in *Timon*, has but a trivial part. Neither humorists like Launce and Launcelot Gobbo, nor ' low ' characters, unintentionally humorous, like the old peasant at the end of *Antony and Cleopatra* or the young shepherd called ' clown ' in *The Winter's Tale*, are Fools proper. The distinction is quite clear, but it tends to be obscured for readers because the wider designation ' clown ' is applied to persons of either class in the few lists of Dramatis Personae printed in the Folio, in the complete lists of our modern editions, and also, alike in these editions and in the Folio, in stage-directions and in the headings of speeches. Such directions and headings were meant for the actors, and the principal comic man of the company doubtless played both Launce and Feste. Feste, I may observe, is called ' Clown ' in the stage-directions and speech-headings, but in the text always ' Fool '. Lear's Fool is ' Fool ' even in the former.

an instance of a bad marriage, she soon gets it : ' Well, go thy way ; if Sir Toby would leave drinking, thou wert as witty a piece of Eve's flesh as any in Illyria.' (Gervinus, on the contrary, regarded this marriage as a judgement on Sir Toby ; but then Gervinus, though a most respectable critic, was no Fool.) Maria departs and Olivia enters. Her brother is dead, and she wears the deepest mourning and has announced her intention of going veiled and weeping her loss every day for seven years. But, in Feste's view, her state of mind would be rational only if she believed her brother's soul to be in hell ; and he does not conceal his opinion. The Duke comes next, and, as his manner ruffles Feste, the mirror of truth is held firmly before him too : ' Now, the melancholy god protect thee, and the tailor make thy doublet of changeable taffeta, for thy mind is a very opal.' In these encounters we admire the Fool's wisdom the more because it makes no impression on his antagonists, who regard it as mere foolery. And his occasional pregnant sayings and phrases meet the same fate. His assertion that he is the better for his foes and the worse for his friends the Duke takes for a mere absurdity or an inadvertence of expression, though he is tickled by Feste's proof of his affirmation through double negation.[1] The philosopher may speak to Sebastian of ' this great lubber the world ' ; he may tell Viola how ' foolery, sir, does walk about the orb like the sun ; it shines everywhere ' ; he may remark to the whole company how ' the whirligig of time brings in his revenges ' ; but nobody heeds him. Why should any one heed a man who gets his living by talking nonsense, and who may be whipped if he displeases his employer ?

All the agility of wit and fancy, all the penetration and wisdom, which Feste shows in his calling, would not by themselves explain our feeling for him. But his mind to him a kingdom is, and one full of such present joys that he finds contentment there. Outwardly he may be little better than a slave ; but Epictetus was a slave outright and yet absolutely free : and so is Feste. That world of quibbles which are pointless to his audience, of incongruities which nobody else can see,

---

[1] Feste's statement of his proof can hardly be called lucid, and his illustration (' conclusions to be as kisses, if your four negatives make your two affirmatives ') seems to have cost the commentators much fruitless labour. If anything definite was in the Fool's mind it may have been this. The gentleman asks for a kiss. The lady, denying it, exclaims ' No no no no.' But, as the first negative (an adjective) negates the second (a substantive), and the third in like manner the fourth, these four negatives yield two enthusiastic affirmatives, and the gentleman, thanks to the power of logic, gets twice what he asked for. This is not Feste's only gird at the wisdom of the schools. It has been gravely surmised that he was educated for the priesthood and, but for some escapade, would have played Sir Topas in earnest.

M 3

of flitting fancies which he only cares to pursue, is his sunny realm. He is alone when he invents that aphorism of Quinapalus and builds his hopes on it ; and it was not merely to get sixpence from Sir Andrew that he told of Pigrogromitus and the Vapians passing the equinoctial of Queubus. He had often passed it in that company himself. Maria and Sir Toby (who do enjoy his more obvious jests) are present when, clothed in the curate's gown and beard, he befools the imprisoned Malvolio so gloriously ; but the prisoner is his only witness when, for his own sole delight, himself as Sir Topas converses with himself the Fool. But for this inward gaiety he could never have joined with all his heart in the roaring revelry of Sir Toby ; but he does not need this revelry, and, unlike Sir Toby and Sir Toby's surgeon, he remains master of his senses. Having thus a world of his own, and being lord of himself, he cares little for Fortune. His mistress may turn him away ; but, ' to be turned away, let summer bear it out.' This ' sunshine of the breast ' is always with him and spreads its radiance over the whole scene in which he moves. And so we love him.

We have another reason. The Fool's voice is as melodious as the ' sweet content ' of his soul. To think of him is to remember ' Come away, come away, Death ', and ' O Mistress mine ', and ' When that I was ', and fragments of folk-song and ballad, and a catch that ' makes the welkin dance indeed '. To think of *Twelfth Night* is to think of music. It opens with instrumental music and ends with a song. All Shakespeare's best praise of music, except the famous passage in *The Merchant of Venice*, occurs in it. And almost all the music and the praise of music come from Feste or have to do with Feste. In this he stands alone among Shakespeare's Fools ; and that this, with the influence it has on our feeling for him, was intended by the poet, should be plain. It is no accident that, when the Duke pays him for his ' pains ' in singing, he answers, ' No pains, sir ; I take pleasure in singing, sir ' ; that the revelry for which he risks punishment is a revelry of song ; that, when he is left alone, he still sings. And, all this being so, I venture to construe in the light of it what has seemed strange to me in the passage that follows the singing of ' Come away '. Usually, when Feste receives his ' gratillity ', he promptly tries to get it doubled ; but here he not only abstains from any such effort but is short, if not disagreeably sharp, with the Duke. The fact is, he is offended, even disgusted ; and offended, not as Fool, but as music-lover and artist. We others know what the Duke said beforehand of the song, but Feste does not know it. Now he sings, and his soul is in the song. Yet, as the last note dies away, the comment he hears from this noble aesthete is, ' There 's for thy pains ' !

I have a last grace to notice in our wise, happy, melodious Fool. He was little injured by his calling. He speaks as he likes; but from first to last, whether he is revelling or chopping logic, or playing with words, and to whomsoever he speaks or sings, he keeps his tongue free from obscenity. The fact is in accord with the spirit of this ever-blessed play, which could not have endured the 'foul-mouthed' Fool of *All's Well*, and from which Aldis Wright in his school edition found, I think, but three lines (not the Fool's) to omit. But the trait is none the less characteristic of Feste, and we like him the better for it.

It remains to look at another side of the whole matter. One is scarcely sorry for Touchstone, but one is very sorry for Feste, and pity, though not a painful pity, heightens our admiration and deepens our sympathy. The position of the professional jester we must needs feel to be more or less hard, if not of necessity degrading. In Feste's case it is peculiarly hard. He is perfectly sane, and there is nothing to show that he is unfit for independence. In important respects he is, more than Shakespeare's other fools, superior in mind to his superiors in rank. And he has no Celia, no Countess, no Lear, to protect or love him. He had been Fool to Olivia's father, who 'took much delight in him'; but Olivia, though not unkind, cannot be said to love him. We find him, on his first appearance, in disgrace and (if Maria is right) in danger of being punished or even turned away. His mistress, entering, tells him that he is a dry fool, that she'll no more of him, and (later) that his fooling grows old and people dislike it. Her displeasure, doubtless, has a cause, and it is transient, but her words are none the less significant. Feste is a relic of the past. The steward, a person highly valued by his lady, is Feste's enemy. Though Maria likes him and, within limits, would stand his friend, there is no tone of affection in her words to him, and certainly none in those of any other person. We cannot but feel very sorry for him.

This peculiar position explains certain traits in Feste himself which might otherwise diminish our sympathy. One is that he himself, though he shows no serious malevolence even to his enemy, shows no affection for any one. His liking for Maria does not amount to fondness. He enjoys drinking and singing with Sir Toby, but despises his drunkenness and does not care for him. His attitude to strangers is decidedly cool, and he does not appear to be attracted even by Viola. The fact is, he recognizes very clearly that, as this world goes, a man whom nobody loves must look out for himself. Hence (this is the second trait) he is a shameless beggar, much the most so of Shakespeare's Fools. He is fully justified, and he begs so amusingly that we welcome his begging;

but shameless it is. But he is laying up treasures on earth against the day when some freak of his own, or some whim in his mistress, will bring his dismissal, and the short summer of his freedom will be followed by the wind and the rain. And so, finally, he is as careful as his love of fun will allow to keep clear of any really dangerous enterprise. He must join in the revel of the knights and the defiance of the steward ; but from the moment when Malvolio retires with a threat to Maria, and Maria begins to expound her plot against him, Feste keeps silence ; and, though she expressly assigns him a part in the conspiracy, he takes none. The plot succeeds magnificently, and Malvolio is shut up, chained as a lunatic, in a dark room ; and that comic genius Maria has a new scheme, which requires the active help of the Fool. But her words, ' Nay, I prithee, put on this gown and this beard,' show that he objects ; and if his hesitation is momentary, it is not merely because the temptation is strong. For, after all, he runs but little risk, since Malvolio cannot see him, and he is a master in the management of his voice. And so, agreeing with Sir Toby's view that their sport cannot with safety be pursued to the upshot, after a while, when he is left alone with the steward, he takes steps to end it and consents, in his own voice, to provide the lunatic with light, pen, ink, and paper for his letter to Olivia.

We are not offended by Feste's eagerness for sixpences and his avoidance of risks. By helping us to realize the hardness of his lot, they add to our sympathy and make us admire the more the serenity and gaiety of his spirit. And at the close of the play these feelings reach their height. He is left alone ; for Lady Belch, no doubt, is by her husband's bed-side, and the thin-faced gull Sir Andrew has vanished, and the rich and noble lovers with all their attendants have streamed away to dream of the golden time to come, without a thought of the poor jester. There is no one to hear him sing ; but what does that matter ? He takes pleasure in singing. And a song comes into his head ; an old rude song about the stages of man's life, in each of which the rain rains every day ; a song at once cheerful and rueful, stoical and humorous ; and this suits his mood and he sings it. But, since he is even more of a philosopher than the author of the song, and since, after all, he is not merely a Fool but the actor who is playing that part in a theatre, he adds at the end a stanza of his own :

> A great while ago the world begun,
>   With hey, ho, the wind and the rain ;
> But that's all one, our play is done,
>   And we'll strive to please you every day.[1]

[1] Those who witnessed, some years ago, Mr. Granville Barker's production of

Shakespeare himself, I feel sure, added that stanza to the old song ; and when he came to write *King Lear* he, I think, wrote yet another, which Feste might well have sung. To the immortal words,

> Poor Fool and knave, I have one part in my heart
> That's sorry yet for thee,

the Fool replies,

> He that has and a little tiny wit,
>   With hey, ho, the wind and the rain,
> Must make content with his fortunes fit,
>   Though the rain it raineth every day.

So Shakespeare brings the two Fools together ; and, whether or no he did this wittingly, I am equally grateful to him. But I cannot be grateful to those critics who see in Feste's song only an illustration of the bad custom by which sometimes, when a play was finished, the clown remained, or appeared, on the stage to talk nonsense or to sing some old ' trash ' ; nor yet to those who tell us that it was ' the players ' who tacked this particular ' trash ' to the end of *Twelfth Night*. They may conceivably be right in perceiving no difference between the first four stanzas and the last, but they cannot possibly be right in failing to perceive how appropriate the song is to the singer, and how in the line

> But that's all one, our play is done,

he repeats an expression used a minute before in his last speech.[1] We owe these things, not to the players, but to that player in Shakespeare's company who was also a poet, to Shakespeare himself—the same Shakespeare who perhaps had hummed the old song, half-ruefully and half-cheerfully, to its accordant air, as he walked home alone to his lodging from the theatre or even from some noble's mansion ; he who, looking down from an immeasurable height on the mind of the public and the noble, had yet to be their servant and jester, and to depend upon their favour ; not wholly uncorrupted by this dependence, but yet superior to it and, also, determined, like Feste, to lay by the sixpences it brought him, until at last he could say the words, ' Our revels now are ended,' and could break—was it a magician's staff or a Fool's bauble ?

Twelfth Night and Mr. Hayden Coffin's presentment of the Fool's part must always remember them with great pleasure, and not least the singing of this song.

[1] ' I was one, sir, in this interlude ; one Sir Topas, sir ; *but that's all one.*' No edition that I have consulted notices the repetition.

A. C. BRADLEY.

BITS OF TIMBER: SOME OBSERVATIONS ON SHAKESPEARIAN NAMES—'SHYLOCK'; 'POLONIUS'; 'MALVOLIO'

I

SHAKESPEARE in *The Merchant of Venice*, as elsewhere, unconsciously divined the germ of the myth on which his genius worked. Endless analogues are quoted for the two stories blended in the play; and we know Shakespeare's debt to the *Pecorone* of Ser Giovanni Fiorentino and the rest. The legend, I feel sure, represents an early homilist's attempt to exemplify the two texts: 'Greater love hath no man than this, that a man lay down his life for his friends,' and 'Christ also loved the church and gave himself for it'. The vivid exposition of these texts produced in due course the legend of 'the Pound of Flesh', and 'the Wooing of the Lady'. Under the cover of a similitude— a different allegory—the texts are well expounded in the early English book known as *The Nuns' Rule*; and the teacher there adds, in order to drive home the lesson, 'Do not men account him a good friend who layeth his pledge in Jewry to release his companion? God Almighty laid himself in Jewry for us,' &c.[1]

The older play on the subject, shown in London at the Bull before 1580, may well have contained some abstract characters, linking it to the Morality drama. Shakespeare's *Merchant of Venice*, starting as a study of usury, in its treatment of the theme gives glimpses of the suggested origin of the legend; and the play is rightly named after the *Merchant*, whose part is one of simple dignity, and not after Shylock, the predominant character of the play. Portia's great plea for mercy, epitomizing a whole Moral play, reveals, as it were, the inmost significance of the Lady of Belmont, as originally personifying the soul, or salvation, or the Church, and links her to the far-spread beautiful allegory of 'The Four Daughters of God'.[2]

[1] *Ancren Riwle,* ed. Morton (Camden Society), p. 394; the date of the book is about 1225.

[2] From this point of view it is interesting to recall such earlier plays as *The Three Ladies of London,* and *The Three Lords and Three Ladies of London,* by Robert Wilson.

A contemporary of Shakespeare, Joseph Fletcher, saw something of this aspect of the play, in his poem, *Christ's Bloodie Sweat*, 1613 :—

> He died indeed, not as an actor dies,
> To die today, and live again tomorrow,
> In shew to please the audience, or disguise
> The idle habit of inforcéd sorrow:
>   The cross his stage was, and he played the part
>   Of one that for his friend did pawn his heart.

Various speculations have been hazarded as to the origin of the name ' Shylock '. ' Caleb Shillocke, his prophecie,' often adduced, is later than the play ; and the suggested connexion with Scialac—' a Maronite of Mount Lebanon ' living in 1614, hardly commends itself to serious consideration, nor do the other theories propounded.

Whether Shakespeare or his predecessor gave the name to the character cannot be absolutely determined ; but in view of the poet's careful choice of names, and especially of other names in the play, the inference points to him.

The book which was read by Elizabethans for everything relating to the later Jewish history, and which went through edition after edition, was Peter Morwyng's translation of the pseudo-Josephus, ' A compendious and most marveylous History of the latter Times of the Jewes Commune Weale.' The influence of this book on Elizabethan literature would repay careful study. Malone already suggested that some lines in *King John* may well have been derived from Morwyng's ' History ' :—

> Do like the mutines of Jerusalem,
> Be friends awhile and both conjointly bend
> Your sharpest deeds of malice on this town. . . .
> That done, dissever your united strengths,
> And part your mingled colours once again.[1]

In Marlowe's *Jew of Malta*, and elsewhere in the plays of Elizabethan dramatists, the influence of the book can be detected.

Near the beginning of the ' History ' we read : ' About that time it was signified also to them of Jerusalem that the Askalonites had entered in friendship with the Romans. They sent therefore Neger the Edomite, and *Schiloch the Babylonian*, and Jehochanan, with a power of the common people ; these came to Askalon, and besieged it a great space. Within the town was a Roman captaine called *Antonius*,[2] a valiant man, and a good warrior.' This passage may well account for ' Shylock ' ; and possibly also for ' Antonio '.

[1] *King John*, II. i. 378.   [2] Elsewhere always ' Antonie '.

The name of Marlowe's Jew of Malta, ' Barabas,' is easily understood. But why should ' Shiloch ' be chosen for the Jew of Venice ?
I am strongly inclined to explain the use of the name as due to the quite
erroneous association of ' Shiloch ' with ' Shallach ', the Biblical Hebrew
for ' cormorant ', the bird that ' swoops ', or dives after its prey. It came
into the lists of biblical animals and into glossaries from Leviticus xi. 17
where it is mentioned among the forbidden fowls ' to be held in abomina-
tion '. In Elizabethan English ' cormorant ' was an expressive synonym
for ' usurer ' ; and perhaps the best commentary on the use of the word
may be drawn from John Taylor's Satires, entitled *The Water-Cor-
morant his complaint against a brood of Land-Cormorants*, published
in 1622. The same mind that chose ' Jessica ', ' Iscah the daughter
of Haran ', and so well emphasized the supposed significance of the name
as ' she that looketh out ', and that created almost a special English idiom
for Shylock, evidently knew the peculiar force of the words ' to bait
fish withal ', uttered by his Cormorant Usurer—the Cormorant of
a fictitious legend, having its starting-point in the attempt vividly
to exemplify the biblical texts already quoted—a legendary monstrosity fraught with all the greater possibilities inasmuch as at that
time Jews were not yet permitted to reside in England, and there
was still the traditional popular prejudice. From this point of view,
the play must be considered in connexion with the considerable
Elizabethan literature on Usury ; the question then at issue being
whether, from religious as well as from moral and economic standpoints,
Englishmen were justified in taking ' usances ', often exorbitant as
would appear from contemporary references.

Shakespeare's humanity and understanding saved Shylock from
being the mere Cormorant-monster. It is not enough to contrast him
—however favourably—with his prototype ' The Jew of Malta '. De-
spised, maddened by the sense of wrong, obsessed by the fixed idea of
claiming his due at all costs, he has kinship with the type of tragic
character best represented by Hieronimo, the wronged and demented
father, who in *The Spanish Tragedy* madly achieves, at the cost of
his very life, the vengeance on which he has set his whole jangled
mind.

Lorenzo is Shakespeare's mouthpiece for the lesson of the play ;
and it is enunciated by him to Shylock's daughter, who was lost to
her father more cruelly than was the slain Horatio to the distraught
Hieronimo. Jessica, ' she who looked out ' beyond her father's home,
by her heartless defection goaded him to Hieronimo-like distraction.

To her, the ' Juliet ' of the play, this lesser Romeo expounds the lofty doctrine of mystic harmony :—

> Such harmony is in immortal souls;
> But, whilst this muddy vesture of decay
> Doth grossly close it in, we cannot hear it.

II

The question of the name ' Polonius ' opens up a fascinating line of investigation, and it is many years ago since first my curiosity was whetted to discover why it was that Shakespeare deliberately changed the name of the character from ' Corambis ', as it appears in the First Quarto, to ' Polonius ' in the authorized version of *Hamlet*. Why the change, and what the origin and significance of the names ? The substitution of ' Falstaff ' for ' Oldcastle ' in *Henry IV* is abundant proof that such variations merit investigation. The name ' Corambis ', or more correctly ' Corambus ', the form found in the early German version of *Fratricide Punished*, and as a passing name in Shakespeare's *All's Well that Ends Well*, is, I feel sure, the creation of the author of the pre-Shakespearian *Hamlet*, who, if Kyd, made a characteristic use of his ' little Latin ' by cleverly re-Latinizing *crambe* (with its popular variant *Crambo*) used in contemporary English for twice-cooked cabbage, i.e. tedious and unpleasant iteration, with reference to the Latin phrase *Crambe repetita* (cp. *Occidit miseros crambe repetita magistros*). ' Corambe ' and variants are found in Latin-English dictionaries of the period. ' Corambis ' or ' Corambus ', therefore, was merely, as it were, ' old Crambo ', an excellent name for the inherent characteristic of the Counsellor, who in the original of the story, as told by Saxo Grammaticus in the Danish History, had exalted ideas of his own profound astuteness, for which he paid the heavy penalty. Evidently the possibilities of the character were effectively developed by the earlier dramatist ; and one may hazard the conjecture that the character was so set forth as to portray some marked characteristics of Elizabeth's aged Counsellor, the great statesman Burleigh, for whom contemporary men of letters had but scant reverence. Spenser's scorn of Burleigh in *The Ruins of Time* and *Mother Hubbard's Tale*, 1591, finds an echo in the writings of many a contemporary author :

> O griefe of griefes, ô gall of all good heartes,
> To see that vertue should dispised bee,
> Of him, that first was raisde for vertuous parts,

And now broad spreading like an aged tree,
Lets none shoot up, that nigh him planted bee:
O let the man, of whom the Muse is scorned,
Nor aliue, nor dead be of the Muse adorned.

We know that *The Ruins of Time* was ' called in ', and that, when in 1611 the First Folio of Spenser's Poems (minus *Mother Hubbard's Tale*, however) was published, the obnoxious passage was toned down, so as to be general and not specific in its application.

Burleigh died in 1598 ; and his son Robert Cecil became one of the foremost men of the State. We may certainly assume that the change of name from ' Corambis ' to ' Polonius ' was made by Shakespeare soon after 1598 when he was still transforming the older play ; and that he was anxious to make it clear that his Counsellor (Second Quarto oddly reads ' Counsel, as Polonius ') was not to be associated in the public mind with the earlier caricature of the great statesman who had gone to his rest. It is noteworthy that there are no very essential differences between the general utterances of Corambis in the First Quarto and those of Polonius in the Second Quarto ; and the inference would be either that Shakespeare in his early revision of the old play had taken over the name, or that the old popular name ' Corambis ' was attached to the character, instead of ' Polonius ', by the unauthorized purloiners answerable for the publication of the First Quarto.

It is to be noted that one of the most popular books of its kind in England at this time, and famous throughout Europe—a work somehow or other overlooked by previous investigators [1]—was an exhaustive manual for counsellors and diplomatists, entitled *De Optimo Senatore* (Venice, 1568 ; Basle, 1593, &c.) by perhaps the greatest Polish statesman of the age, Laurentius Grimalius Goslicius, Bishop of Posen. An English translation, entitled ' The Counsellor ', appeared in 1598, the very year that Burleigh died. Its long descriptive title sets forth the contents of the book :

A golden work replenished with the chief learning of the most excellent philosophers and lawgivers, and not only profitable but very necessary for all those that be admitted to the administration of a well-governed Commonweal; written in Latin by Laurentius Grimaldus (*sic*), and consecrated to the honour *of the Polonian Empire*.

Another English translation of a portion of the work is to be found in the British Museum.[2] But, apart from the English translation, the

[1] See summary of a paper read by me before the British Academy, April 27, 1904, *Proceedings of British Academy*, vol. i.
[2] Add. MSS. 18613.

original Latin was known in England ; as may be seen from a reference in Gabriel Harvey's *Pierces Supererogation* (1593). The translation must, however, have done much to make the work generally known. We may feel sure that it was this translation that Shakespeare looked into, and, to the honour of the ' Polonian ' name, dubbed the counsellor of the King of Denmark by a name which could only mean the Polonian, or the Pole. It is strange that this book, which was so famous, and which was re-issued and re-translated in different versions in the sixteenth, seventeenth, and eighteenth centuries, seems altogether to have escaped notice in modern times, until some years back, when I hazarded the conjecture that here was to be found the solution of the problem of ' Polonius '. At the time my critics asked for evidence (which I could not then adduce) of the alleged popularity of the work in question ; but since then I have been able from contemporary evidence to satisfy criticism on this point. A Polish historian of the time, secretary to King Stephen, addressing Goslicius in the preface to a work published in the year 1600, praises him for his literary achievements, and—writing of course in Latin—adds a special commendation in respect of his work *De Optimo Senatore* 'than which ', he says, ' according to report, no work *in England* is more delighted in, or more thumbed ' :—

Unus ille de optimo Senatore liber tuus, quantam non modo tibi sed et cunctae genti nostrae conciliaverit gloriam, arbitror dubitare neminem, quum sincere quidam mihi dixerit, nullius libentius, quam illum librum in Anglia teri in manibus hominum, de optimo senatore.[1]

There was a continued tradition in England concerning this work. In 1604, the year in which Grimalius died, a second edition appeared of the English translation, or, more likely, some copies of the old book with a new title-page. In 1660, there was published in English without the slightest indication of its being a translated work, the greater part of *The Sage Senator*, to which was ' annexed the new Models of Modern Policy, by J. G.' In 1733, Oldisworth, the political pamphleteer, issued an elaborate English translation, with a lengthy and enthusiastic, though inaccurate, introduction. In the Preface he states that in his work ' the Author has traced his Senator from the cradle to the School, and thence to the University, the Camp, the Bar, and the Bench of Justice. He has followed him in all his travels, and through every stage and period of

---

[1] I find the passage quoted in a small Latin dissertation on Goslicius, by Romanus Lopinski (Halle, 1872), p. 49. There is, of course, no idea on the part of the author that the quotation bore on this theory. In a lecture at the Royal Institution on February 26, 1914, the second of two lectures dealing with ' Hamlet in Legend and Drama ', I first called attention to this valuable corroboration, for which I had been long seeking.

his private and public life, to his last and highest attainment as a Minister of State'.

The Counsellor is in two Books; at the end of Book I the author admits the possibility 'of wearying the reader's mind and thereby becoming tedious'. 'This is too long'—as Polonius observed with reference to the Player's Speech.

A summary of the work is beyond the limits of a brief Note; but a few passages may be quoted by way of illustration :

'I do therefore think expedient that in the person of our Counsellor there should be such ripeness of age as might exercise the virtues beseeming so honourable a personage, and in his calling hold so great a gravity and reputation as all other citizens and subjects may hope at his hand to receive comfort, quiet, and counsel profitable to the whole commonwealth.'

'Our Counsellor then, instructed in the precepts of Philosophy, shall not from thenceforth be shut up, &c.'

'The Commonwealth therefore requireth the counsel of some notable and divine man, in whom it may repose the care of her happiness and well-doing. By his direction and government all perils, sedition, discords, mutations and inclinations may be suppressed, and thereby enjoy a happy peace and tranquility.'

'It behoveth him to be witty, docile, of good memory, of sound understanding, circumspect, provident, wary, and wily.'

'Let the Counsellor know his own wit.'

'Our Counsellor should be circumspect, not only in those things which do happen privately, but also in every other that may be hurtful to the Commonwealth.'

Many other passages may be adduced showing how Counsellors

> . . . Of wisdom and of reach,
> With windlasses and with assays of bias,
> By indirections find directions out.

But it is not merely to the words and character of Polonius that suggestive parallels may be found in this Manual. Some of the most striking chapters of the book are devoted to man as a creature endowed with reason, and some of the loftiest sentiments of *Hamlet* sound to me like echoes from passages in the work, notably the famous words :

'What a piece of work is man! how noble in reason! how infinite in faculty! in form and moving how express and admirable! in action how like an angel! in apprehension how like a god! the beauty of the world! the paragon of animals!'[1]

With this speech of Hamlet, compare the following :

'Among all creatures contained within the circle of the earth, that which we call man is the chiefest and of most reputation, for he alone of all other living things of what nature

---

[1] The First Quarto seems to give a garbled version of the lines as we have them in the Second Quarto.

soever is made not only an inhabitant and citizen of the world, but also a lord and prince therein.'

'Reason doth make men like unto God.'

'The wise man by his virtue resembleth the likeness of God.'

'But what is that which in man is most excellent? Surely Reason!'

'The chief duty of man is to know that his original proceedeth from God, and from Him to have received Reason, whereby he resembleth his Maker. But for that the Reason of man is shut up within the body as a prison whereby it knoweth not itself, it behoveth the mind to break forth from that place of restraint, and to win liberty.'

Measure for Measure was written about the same time as *Hamlet*. It should be noted that a section of Grimalius's work was on the responsibilities of the counsellor as judge, and some of the most striking passages in the book have reference to magistrates good and bad. 'The evil example of magistrates works more ill than their virtues work good,' wrote Goslicius, and he amplifies the theme. Shakespeare, who had already, with lighter touch, portrayed vain and testy magistrates, now in Hamletian mood portrayed 'Angelo'—the Counsellor 'most still, most secret, and most grave'—deputy of the Duke, *whom he supposed travelled to Poland.* The very spirit of Goslicius seems to speak through Shakespeare in the famous words:

> He who the sword of heaven will bear
> Should be as holy as severe.

III

It is generally admitted that the 'Befooling of Malvolio'—the comic interlude in *Twelfth Night, or, What You Will*—is Shakespeare's own invention, grafted upon a romantic Italian love-story. 'Malevolti' is the nearest form of the name discovered in the possible sources or analogies of the main plot; 'Malvolio' looks like a parallel to 'Benvolio'. The character is obviously topical, as are also Sir Toby and Aguecheek. In view of the fondness of the Elizabethans, and Shakespeare in particular, of playing upon 'Will', Malvolio may well stand for 'Ill Will'. Nothing has been adduced against the theory hazarded by me some years ago that finds the original of Malvolio in Sir Ambrose Willoughby, Queen Elizabeth's Chief Sewer and Squire of the Presence, whose quarrel with the Earl of Southampton is referred to in a letter (printed in the *Sydney Papers*) from Rowland White, dated January, 1598:

'The quarrel of my Lord Southampton to Ambrose Willoughby,' he wrote on January 21, 'grew upon this: that he with Sir Walter Raleigh and Mr. Parker being at primero in the Presence Chamber; the Queen was gone to bed, and he being there as Squire for the Body, desired them to give over. Soon after he spoke to them again, that if they would not leave he would call in the guard to pull down the board, which,

Sir Walter Raleigh seeing, put up his money and went his ways. But my Lord Southampton took exceptions at him, and told him he would remember it; and so finding him between the Tennis Court wall and the garden shook him, and Willoughby pulled out some of his locks. The Queen gave Willoughby thanks for what he did in his Presence, and told him he had done better if he had sent him to the Porter's Lodge to see who durst have fetched him out.'

The quarrel was evidently the occasion of much gossip. Southampton kept away from the court for a time, and found comfort in witnessing plays. What more likely than that his devotee Shakespeare should cleverly utilize the incident? It would have been a congenial task to hit off on the stage the pretentious Squire of the Presence. The Fourth Scene of the Second Act of the play (' Do ye make an alehouse of my lady's house,' &c.) may well illustrate Shakespeare's manner of transforming the incident, without losing the essential traits which might make the caricature recognizable.

If this theory of ' Malvolio ' is correct, the original performance of the play points to Twelfth Night, 1599. The date generally assigned, ' about 1600 ' to this and other comedies is, in my opinion, too late. *Twelfth Night* was evidently written before (not after) the tragic fall of Essex and Southampton.

Ambrose Willoughby was the second son of Charles, Baron Willoughby of Parham. As early as 1589 he is described in State Papers ' as one of the Sewers of her Majesty's own table '; but in 1593 he received the life-appointment as Sewer—an office previously held by Sir Henry Brooke *alias* Cobham, Sir Percival Hart, and Sir Edward Nevill. In June 1602 Willoughby had a violent quarrel with Grey Brydges (later Lord Chandos), and ' was hurt in the head and body, for abusing his father and himself at a conference of arbitrement 'twixt them and Mistress Brydges', i.e. Elizabeth, Grey's first cousin, who claimed part of the family estates. Willoughby seems to have borne ' ill-will ' towards Grey and his father, both of them friends of Essex, and to some extent implicated in the insurrection. The friends of Essex and Southampton would not regard with much favour Elizabeth's Squire of the Presence. On James's accession, when Southampton was set free, Willoughby was relieved of his office, surrendering it ' voluntarily ' to ' the King's beloved Servant Sir Thomas Penruddock'.

The cumulative evidence seems fully to justify the claim that the passage in Rowland White's letter gives us the needful clue to the personality of ' Malvolio ', and thus to the date of the composition of the play, as being before Twelfth Night, 1599, possibly with slight additions later.

I. GOLLANCZ.

A CRITICAL MOUSETRAP[1]

THERE is a point in connexion with the players' play in *Hamlet*, which, if significant at all, has certainly not received from commentators the attention it deserves. The orthodox and obvious interpretation of the action is, of course, familiar. King Claudius, who has disposed of his brother and predecessor by the very peculiar device of pouring poison into his ears, is witnessing the performance of a play which Hamlet facetiously calls the ' Mousetrap '. This reproduces in a remarkably complete manner the circumstances of his own crime, and when the critical moment arrives and he sees the most intimate details of his action represented before the assembled court, his nerve gives way and he rushes terror-stricken from the hall. It should be observed that his alarm must be ascribed solely to the action of the play, for the language is in no way significant.

Now, this interpretation is open to a most serious objection. For the play itself is preceded by a dumb-show in which the whole action of the piece is minutely set forth. So far as the action is concerned, and it is the action alone that is significant, the play proper adds nothing new whatever. Consequently, on the assumptions usually made, either the King must have betrayed himself over the dumb-show, or there is no conceivable reason why he should betray himself at all. Incidentally I must point out that there is no getting rid of the dumb-show, for not only is the textual tradition unassailable, but the spectators are actually made to comment upon this unusual feature of the performance.

So far as I can see there are only two possible lines for criticism to take. Either Shakespeare blundered badly in the crucial scene of the play, or else the orthodox interpretation is wrong. If the former, there

---

[1] Before the outbreak of war made unwonted claims on the activities of so many harmless students, I had drafted a somewhat elaborate study of the problem propounded in the present note. But the criticisms of various friends to whom I submitted it convinced me that my presentation of the case required considerable modification before it could be passed as even moderately satisfactory. Not having found time for the necessary revision, I take this opportunity for a bald statement of the problem, hoping in a happier future to return to the subject at greater length.

is no more to be said : but if logic goes for anything in dramatic criticism, then it follows from the action of the scene that it is not the stage poisoning that upsets the King, and consequently that Claudius did not poison his brother in the manner represented. But this immediately leads to a far more important conclusion. If the King did not murder his predecessor by pouring poison into his ears, then the account of the affair given by the Ghost to Hamlet is untrue, in other words the Ghost's narrative is not a revelation from the dead but a figment of Hamlet's brain.

It will be obvious how important are the implications of this view and what difficulties are involved in its acceptance. I have not yet satisfied myself as to the exact nature of the implications or as to the exact extent of the difficulties, and I therefore put forward this note rather as a suggestion than as a formal proposition. On two cardinal points, however, I think I can indicate the direction in which a solution may be found.

We have for one thing to account for the obvious fact that the King does actually interrupt the performance of the players at the very moment of the murder. To Hamlet this is, of course, proof positive of the truth of his suspicions ; but a careful examination of the scene will, I think, show that ample explanation of the King's action is afforded by the wild and menacing behaviour of Hamlet himself. Then there is the ghostly interview to be considered. Is this scene, upon the orthodox assumptions, so satisfactory as to make us reject any alternative ? Hardly : and to my mind an analysis of the Ghost's narrative supplies the very strongest and strangest confirmation of the theory here proposed. For it can, I believe, be shown that every point in the pretended revelation is but the reflection of something that we either know, or can reasonably infer, to be present in Hamlet's own mind including the minute and surprising details of the murder itself.

W. W. GREG.

1600

ANOTHER ripe and ready for the boards !
Methinks it laughs with graciousness ; and yet
Despite this ever-smiling Southwark face,
The laughter is not mine, the conquering vein
Still less ! albeit in both I please myself,
And both bring profit in a tide that swells
Above my wildest hopes.   How had I hailed
This flux of fortune in the distant days
When, staggering 'neath his load, the old man groaned
O'er vanishing repute and debts unpaid,
And I could bring no succour ! 'Tis all changed :
The wheel comes fair about ; but has not brought
Oblivion of bitterness : even now
He glooms and sickens, and my pen moves slow.
Yet Anne is settled safe—Anne and her girls—
Proud of her fine new house, the most perhaps
Such husband could require ; and for the boy,
He needs our care no longer.   Had I cared
While care might have availed—vain, vain ! no more !
Could a man bridle his necessities,
Tether and drive at will, there yet had been
One to inherit this quick-coming wealth,
And idle coat, whose getting spoiled a play,
Flattered the father, mother—son perchance !
But no ! while all men count me fortunate,
I cannot taste my havings, still adrought
'Mid flowing waters that assuage no thirst.

N

And these my discontents admonish me
That not the harvest but the husbandry
Is life for me—these taskmasters that urge
My doubtful steps on paths untrodden yet,
Perturbing thoughts, unanswered questionings,
That speak of life as no illuminate page,
Success, disaster, good and evil ways
Sharply divided—but a devious track
Through dark and clear, that baffles prophecy
And falsifies the forthright estimate ;
Strange scene where Fortune flings the wretch her prize,
And Good does acts that seem intolerable,
And suffers, to a purpose. Where 's the book
I fashioned, half from Kyd, and left for lack
Of leisure ? I am minded now to inscribe
Somewhat of these dim stirrings, or in that,
Or in the Roman ; they are not unlike,
Like with a difference.—Nay, 'tis almost night !
Well, I will enter Night, disdaining Day
With all her sunshine yields, and, wrestling there
With haunting shadows that beset my peace,
Find victory or defeat, and, after, rest,
If rest be granted. Haply that dim coast
Descried afar across this billowy waste
Where strong souls struggle and founder, holds some life
A man may grasp, more firm, more real than this ;
And I may reach it.
                              Boy, there ! hie thee quick
To the Mitre, where a company of friends
Expects me : say, I shall not come to-night.

R. WARWICK BOND.

NOTTINGHAM.

A NOTE ON ANTONY AND CLEOPATRA

To praise Shakespeare it is only necessary to take up any one of the authentic plays and read it, but to praise him worthily it is necessary to be strict with him and with ourselves. Indiscriminate adulation has not only dishonoured many of his admirers, it has concealed and debased Shakespeare himself as the fine lines of woodwork are concealed and debased by layers of paint. As to the play to be selected there will be many opinions. If I choose *Antony and Cleopatra* it is not because I find in it any character wholly sympathetic or admirable, but because in that play and in its persons I feel Shakespeare moving with most perfect mastery. In setting forth the story of a Hamlet, an Imogen, a Desdemona, or the life of some generation of historic England, he is certain of conquering us, because he has at least one point at which his force is overwhelming, his weapon heart-piercing : but in the alien life of the Imperial vices he must win at every turn or fail to carry us.

The difficulties appear to be immense. The story is a great story, with all the prestige of ancient Rome and of the gorgeous East ; with the whole known world for its stage, and the masters of the world for its dramatis personae. Their qualities, good and bad, are such as can be judged by any one who has watched human nature, yet they are on a scale beyond our experience and must be shown not merely with clearness and intensity but with the element of greatness added. To add this element of greatness, not only to one character, but to every character of importance in the play, and yet to keep the voices true throughout, would be hard for any writer, and perhaps especially hard, we might think, for Shakespeare. He was writing for a generation which loved poetry, eloquence, and sententiousness—loved even conceits, florid metaphors, and bombast. We cannot for a moment imagine that a great artist could have been tempted to use these as aids external to his own intuition, mechanical tricks to heighten an effect. But to a certain extent he shared the tastes of his generation, and the question for us is this : how far, in a play where greatness of manner was demanded of him by his subject, did he preserve a tone which was not only true to the ear of his own age, but remains true for us too and therefore probably for all time.

I believe that the more attentively *Antony and Cleopatra* is read, the better it will be found to bring Shakespeare through this severe test. It is a long play, but I have found not more than a dozen places in it where a phrase disturbs the attention as irrelevant to the matter or inconsistent with the tone given throughout to the character speaking. Antony once mixes three metaphors :

> The hearts
> That spaniel'd me at heels, to whom I gave
> Their wishes, do discandy, melt their sweets
> On blossoming Caesar; and this pine is bark'd,
> That overtopp'd them all.

But in a speech which is a torrent of energy this is hardly unnatural. Twice he is surprisingly elegant : ' he wears the rose of youth upon him ' is an odd poetical phrase in a challenge, and odder still from a bluff general to his troops is

> This morning, like the spirit of a youth
> That means to be of note, begins betimes.

The same inconsistency appears in the scene where Octavia weeps and Antony remarks—to Caesar too !—' The April 's in her eyes . . . ', ending much more characteristically with an abrupt ' Be cheerful '. Compared with the perfectly apt image of the ' swan's down-feather ' which follows it, this ' April ' shows as a mere conceit. But these are small cavils : if a serious charge were brought against the play it would be upon the use of magniloquence or bombast. It is undeniable that Antony, with all his splendid vitality and directness, is in several places irrelevantly given to words. When he exclaims in the supreme height of his impatience,

> Let Rome in Tiber melt, and the wide arch
> Of the rang'd empire fall! Here is my space.

he clogs the first phrase with the second and delays the flood of his anger. When he bids Eros unarm him, it is right enough that he should speak of the sevenfold shield of Ajax, and cry, ' Bruised pieces, go !', but ' O ! cleave, my sides ; Heart, once be stronger than thy continent, Crack thy frail case ! ' is unhappily thrust between. In each of these instances, as in others, an easy proof of the irrelevancy of the phrases complained of, is to read the passage as it would stand without them. It will, I think, be found to gain much by the omission.

Four cases would, if I am right, be proved against Cleopatra : at the end of Act III it is difficult not to be thrown off by the forced image of the poison'd hail to be engendered in her heart and thence dropped in her neck. The other three flaws all occur in the magnificent Scene xiii of Act IV. When her dying lord is carried in, Cleopatra's natural cry:

> O Antony,
> Antony, Antony! Help, Charmian!

is unfortunately preceded by two lines of gigantesque apostrophe to the sun. Twenty lines later her very telling cry of distress at being too weak to lift the dying man is interrupted by the sonorous bit of learning about Juno, Mercury, and Jove: and in the next speech ' the false housewife Fortune ' is still more false and unfortunate. To say this is to judge very strictly: but how can any standard be too high for a scene of such supreme word-magic—a scene which contains Antony's speeches ' I am dying, Egypt, dying . . . ', and ' The miserable change now at my end . . . ', and Cleopatra's

> We'll bury him; and then what's brave, what's noble,
> Let's do it after the high Roman fashion,
> And make death proud to take us.

It is very noteworthy that from this point to the end the play is by any standard faultless. In Act V there is one rhetorical passage, but it is a description of Antony, elaborated by the indignant queen to confound Dolabella, and it is entirely successful. In all the rest the vital energy of Cleopatra which has burned so irresistibly through the whole play, blazes out until it reaches the last splendour of her ' immortal longings ', and her final ' Peace, peace! ' with the baby at her breast, ' That sucks the nurse asleep '.

The almost flawless truth of this play is then the measure of Shakespeare's power. The story is not in itself beautiful: the characters are not beautiful nor even pitiful. Antony and Cleopatra are not young lovers: they have both been faithless in their time, they are each in sudden moments faithless to the other, and worse still, they wrongly judge each other by themselves. He is profligate and weak: she is cruel, vain, and full of guile. But they both have the quality which, for want of leisure to define it, I have called greatness: an elevation, an energy of the soul very rare among men, and to us very uplifting to contemplate. This greatness of theirs Shakespeare has been able to express for us, because he himself possessed it: by the mere outbreathing of it he created them.

HENRY NEWBOLT.

THE CAWDOR PROBLEM

THE notices of Cawdor's treason and punishment in *Macbeth* present some well-known difficulties.

The first reference to him occurs when Ross, who has just arrived in hot haste from Fife, where the battle took place, announces (I. ii. 50):

> Norway himself,
> With terrible numbers,
> Assisted by that most disloyal traitor,
> The Thane of Cawdor, began a dismal conflict.

Duncan presently proceeds (I. ii. 63):

> No more that Thane of Cawdor shall deceive
> Our bosom interest: go pronounce his present death,
> And with his former title greet Macbeth.

Accordingly, in the next scene (I. iii. 105) Ross and Angus meet Banquo and Macbeth on the heath, and tell the latter of his new dignity. He has already been perplexed at the witches' salutation (I. iii. 72):

> How of Cawdor? the Thane of Cawdor lives,
> A prosperous gentleman.

And now he bursts out with the same incredulity (I. iii. 108):

> The Thane of Cawdor lives: why do you dress me
> In borrow'd robes?

Angus answers (I. iii. 109):

> Who was the thane lives yet;
> But under heavy judgement bears that life
> Which he deserves to lose. Whether he was combined
> With those of Norway, or did line the rebel
> With hidden help and vantage, or that with both
> He laboured in his country's wreck, I know not:
> But treasons capital, confess'd and proved,
> Have overthrown him.

Finally we hear of the culprit's death. Duncan asks (I. iv. 1):

> Is execution done on Cawdor? Are not
> Those in commission yet return'd?

Malcolm replies (1. iv. 2) :

> My liege,
> They are not yet come back. But I have spoke
> With one that saw him die; who did report
> That very frankly he confess'd his treasons,
> Implored your highness' pardon, and set forth
> A deep repentance.

Now it is undoubtedly odd that if Cawdor helped Norway, Ross should know of it while Macbeth did not : it is also odd that after Ross's definite statement, Angus should be doubtful whether Cawdor had helped Macdonwald, Norway, or both ; and finally it is odd that Angus, who has accompanied Ross on his mission, should be able to speak of Cawdor's treasons as ' confess'd and proved ', when we are afterwards told that the traitor made his penitential confession immediately before his execution.

The different statements certainly do not at the first glance fit into each other ; still, a little consideration will show that they involve no radical contradiction, but only need to be expanded, and perhaps supplemented.

So much is evident, that Cawdor had kept his disloyalty secret. Even Angus speaks of the ' hidden help and vantage ' he afforded, and at the very moment when Ross, with haste looking through his eyes, tells of Cawdor's supporting Norway he is in close proximity to the king, who can order his immediate execution. He may have remained at court all the time, keeping up appearances as long as he could and conducting his plots through agents. At any rate, since he did not appear openly in the matter, it is not wonderful that Macbeth should be ignorant of his treachery ; it is only strange that Ross should know of it. But after all he might hear rumours during his ride from Fife to Forres. Whence could these rumours come ? Possibly from information leaking out about the proceedings taken against Cawdor at court, the admissions of the accused, and the incriminating evidence. For surely it is implied that he has been on trial before Duncan commands or sanctions his execution. The king's words seem to confirm a sentence that has come as the conclusion of a legal examination : ' Go pronounce his present death.' That would be gross tyranny if its sole ground were the unsupported statement of Ross, and if Cawdor's guilt had not previously been investigated : and such tyranny would be peculiarly incongruous with the character of the king, who afterwards receives Macbeth's testimony to his gentleness and justice (I. vii. 16),

> This Duncan
> Hath borne his faculties so meek, hath been
> So clear in his great office.

It is far more probable that the king at last resolves to act on the finding of the commission, that is presently referred to in connexion with the execution and that, we may suppose, has been inquiring into the case. That 'very frankly he confess'd his treasons' on the eve of death when solemnly setting forth his final penitence and regrets, need not mean that Cawdor had made no admissions before, when his offences were brought home to him at the trial, and that therefore Angus could not speak of his 'treasons capital, confess'd and proved'.

There remains only the difficulty that Ross definitely mentions Cawdor's help of Norway, while Angus is afterwards doubtful whether he was helping Norway, Macdonwald, or both ; but that may be due to a difference in the reports they have heard, or to a greater or less hastiness of belief in themselves. Certainly at a later date Ross shows himself rather credulous in regard to chance hearsay ; for after Duncan's murder, when Macduff tells him that the flight of Malcolm and Donalbain (II. iv. 26) :

> Suspicion of the deed.   puts upon them

he accepts the suspicion as proven fact without a moment's hesitation (II. iv. 27) :

> 'Gainst nature still!
> Thriftless ambition, that will ravin up
> Thine own life's means!

It is therefore not out of character at least that he should adopt without criticism the first version of Cawdor's practices that strikes him or comes to his ears, while Angus takes into account various possible alternatives.

If, then, we piece out the fragmentary story in the above or some such way, we find no absolute discrepancies in it, though a good deal that wants explanation. That being so, two of the hypotheses to account for the apparent difficulties lose their force. It is unnecessary to suppose with some that Shakespeare, having antedated the Cawdor episode, which in Holinshed follows considerably later, forgot the bearings of his own alteration. It is also unnecessary to assume with others the intervention of an editor who distorted the original plan of the play. The third hypothesis, that the existing version is an abridgement for stage purposes, and that the obscurity arises from the omission of explanatory passages or scenes, is to a certain extent confirmed. Even in regard to it, however, it should be remembered that the incident is a very subordinate one, and that Shakespeare, while having a complete and consistent picture of it in his own mind, may well have considered it sufficient to convey it only in isolated jottings.

M. W. MacCallum.

The University of Sydney.

THE KNOCKING AT THE GATE ONCE MORE

IN that piece of subtle psychology and eloquent English, *On the Knocking at the Gate in Macbeth*, De Quincey tells us that from his boyish days he had been puzzled to account for the fact that the knocking at the gates ' reflected back upon the murderer a peculiar awfulness and a depth of solemnity '. His understanding said positively that it could *not* produce any effect ; but in spite of his understanding he felt that it did. The Williams murders in 1812 gave him the key to the explanation ; for then the very same incident of a knocking occurred after the murder of the Marrs. De Quincey's explanation is that the marvellous effect of the terrific murder scene depends upon a contrast between the normal human nature, ' the divine nature of love and mercy ', and the fiendish nature of the two murderers. The dialogues and soliloquies convey the sense that the human nature has vanished and the fiendish nature has taken its place ; and the effect is finally consummated by the knocking at the gate ; for then ' the world of darkness passes away like a pageantry in the clouds ', and the human makes its reflux upon the fiendish. It is at the meeting-point of the two worlds that the contrast between them is sharpest.

The question whether Shakespeare took the hint of his great scene from some real incident such as that which occurred in the murder of the Marrs, or invented it himself, is unimportant as well as insoluble. He has made the incident and the principle upon which it rests for ever his own ; for if De Quincey afterwards found the explanation he was led to it by the light which Shakespeare supplied. My purpose is not to discuss whether Shakespeare was guided to his principle by some specific experience, or reached it through the exercise of his own faculties, but simply to illustrate by further examples the truth which was revealed to De Quincey by the crimes of Williams.

Since these illuminating crimes at least two very striking incidents have occurred to attest the keenness of Shakespeare's insight and the soundness of De Quincey's interpretation. In one case it fortunately happened that a poet, though a poet who was still only a small schoolboy, was present. In *A Lark's Flight*, perhaps the finest essay in that fine volume *Dreamthorp*, Alexander Smith relates the story of an execution at Glasgow for a murder which was committed about thirty years after the Williams murders. The essayist skilfully groups the incidents of his story—the heedless play of the happy little boys and girls on the evening preceding the execution, its sudden interruption by the arrival of the materials for the scaffold (it was, of course, the day of public executions), the marshalling of the little army of horse, foot, and artillery to overawe the disorderly, and the procession of the two doomed Irish navvies through the sunshine of a May morning. Around the scaffold the soldiers had kept clear a wide space on which the young wheat was springing, and just when the men appeared beneath the beam ' the incident, so simple, so natural, so much in the ordinary course of things, and yet so frightful in its tragic suggestions, took place '. The hush of awe had fallen upon the crowd. ' Just then, out of the grassy space at the foot of the scaffold, in the dead silence audible to all, a lark rose from the side of its nest, and went singing upward in its happy flight. O heaven ! how did that song translate itself into dying ears ? Did it bring in one wild burning moment father, and mother, and poor Irish cabin, and prayers said at bed-time, and the smell of turf fires, and innocent sweet-hearting, and rising and setting suns ? Did it—but the dragoon's horse has become restive, and his brass helmet bobs up and down and blots everything, and there is a sharp sound ; and I feel the great crowd heave and swing, and hear it torn by a sharp shiver of pity, and the men whom I saw so near but a moment ago are at immeasurable distance, and have solved the great enigma,—and the lark has not yet finished his flight ; you can see and hear him yonder in the fringe of a white May cloud.'

Simple, natural, in the ordinary course of things, yet frightful indeed in its tragic suggestions ! As simple as the knocking at the gate, and not so much inferior in its tragic suggestions ; for, in face of ' the great enigma ', what is the difference between the blood-stained King of Scotland and the blood-stained Irish navvy ? Here surely is independent evidence to the keenness of Shakespeare's insight and the soundness of De Quincey's interpretation. Yet the knocking at the gate never occurred to Smith. He goes on to give illustrations of the principle of contrast ; illustrations from history and from literature ; but not that which is the most remarkable of all.

A century has passed since the murders which so profoundly

impressed De Quincey ; a crime is being enacted whose crimson horror makes the Williams murders pale ; and once more we find that the simplest incident in nature suffices to throw into startling relief its horror and its guilt.   In letters from the trenches men betray their sense of it, never suspecting that they are under the sway of a principle which it took the greatest of poets to discover, and one of the greatest of critics to interpret.

'The weather for the last week has been gorgeous.   It seems such a waste of time trying to kill other people when the sun is so nice and friendly,' wrote one man last September.   He was making no effort to be literary, and the simplicity of his language makes him all the more impressive.   The sun is 'so nice and friendly'—and man, when the human nature is utterly withdrawn, is so devilish.   Last spring a group of men were found in a trench with tears running down their cheeks. There was no apparent cause, and when the discoverer asked an explanation he was told that it was because, in the intervals of the crash of artillery, the men could hear the birds singing in the bushes.   The note of spring joy, in contrast with the awful tragedy around, overcame them.   These men were not poets, like Alexander Smith, but they needed only to be human in order to feel, like him, the frightful tragic suggestions of the contrast between the sun 'so nice and friendly' and the song-bird on the one hand, and, on the other, the reign of murder and sudden death around them.   They were not, like Shakespeare, profound psychologists, but for that very reason their instinctive response to the stimulus which he knew would best bring home to the onlooker the nature of the deed is all the more instructive.   And there may be other criminals besides Macbeth sighing out from the sorely charged heart, in response to something just as simple, their

> Wake Duncan with thy knocking! I would thou couldst!

HUGH WALKER.

St. David's College,
    Lampeter.

MOTHER AND SON IN 'CYMBELINE'

IN the portraiture of Cloten in this play has been noted, at least as far back as Johnson, what seems a perplexing inconsistency. Represented as ' an arrogant piece of flesh ', ' a brutal and brainless fool ', he is yet spoken of by his step-father in terms of warm regard, and at the beginning of the scene with the Roman ambassador he appears to acquit himself not only with credit, but with ability. The high eloquence of

> There be many Caesars
> Ere such another Julius. Britain is
> A world by itself—

is not the language of ' an ass ', ' a thing too bad for bad report ', one who ' cannot take two from twenty, for his heart, and leave eighteen '.

It would be going too far to say of Shakespeare, as Shakespeare once incautiously said of Julius Caesar himself, that he ' did never wrong but with just cause '. But very often things in Shakespeare that we stumble at would be quite clear if we took more pains to realize them in their setting and context. We are too apt to read detachedly, and thus to miss the dramatic value of speeches, their relevance to the dramatic interplay of will and character. It is essential not to treat any single figure in the plays, or any single thing said, as isolated.

The queen, Cloten's mother, is ' a woman that bears all down with her brain '. She has won her position by no sensuous arts of allurement, but by sheer capacity and adroitness. Cymbeline has grown to lean on her. He turns habitually to her for good advice ; and he gets it from her, in no less measure than he gets from her attention, deference, and all the outward show of affection. She, on her side, does not care for him at all ; her mind is wholly fixed, not on personal ambition, but on the advancement of her son. Far too clever herself not to realize how coarse-fibred and stupid Cloten is, she sets herself with infinite skill and patience to cover his deficiencies and gloss over his want of manners as well as of sense and decency. She succeeds in imposing him on her husband, though not on the court generally : ' the sole son of my queen ', ' our dear son ', is honestly thought by Cymbeline, under her influence, to be a useful and even necessary adviser in matters of state. She is always close at hand to coach and prompt Cloten, to excuse or explain away his blunders and vicious habits, to represent her own ability and foresight as his. She is a perfect mother, much as Lady Macbeth is a perfect wife. To her, Cloten is not wholly un-amenable, and he has a sort of animal affection for her apart from the dominance of a strong and subtle over a weak and coarse mind. So long as she can keep beside or close behind him she can guide him fairly straight, though this requires perpetual and unrelaxing vigilance ; but the moment her hand is withdrawn, he shows himself the fool and brute that he is.

If we look at the scene with the Roman ambassador in this light, it ceases to be a perplexity. The queen has prepared a speech for her son with elaborate care, such as, though wholly beyond his capacity, is not too obviously out of keeping with his temperament. She has made him learn it by heart, and is ready to give him his cue. When the time comes, she gives it, in the words

> And, to kill the marvel,
> Shall be so ever.

Cloten takes it up :

> There be many Caesars
> Ere such another Julius. Britain is
> A world by itself.

But then, in his self-complacent folly, he strikes off into language of his own, such as we have already heard him use with the two lords :

> And we will nothing pay
> For wearing our own noses.

His mother, prepared for something of the kind, swiftly and adroitly breaks in before he has made a complete fool of himself in public. His own way (we see it throughout the scenes in which he appears) is to get some senseless phrase or childish misconception (like ' his meanest garment ' in the scene with Imogen) into his head, and go on fatuously repeating it. She picks up what she had told him to say, and goes on with it herself :

> That opportunity,
> Which then they had to take from 's, to resume
> We have again :

continuing with some twenty lines of real if slightly turgid eloquence. But Cloten is intoxicated with his own importance on so great an occasion, and will not be lightly silenced, especially as he has not yet made the most of Caesar's nose. At her first pause, he breaks in :

> Come, there's no more tribute to be paid. Our kingdom is stronger than it was at that time; and, as I said, there is no more such Caesars; other of them may have crooked noses, but to owe such straight arms, none.

This is all his own, and he is delighted with it. Cymbeline is affronted and shocked. ' Son, let your mother end,' he says sharply. But Cloten is in full cry, and plunges on :

> We have yet many among us can gripe as hard as Cassibelan; I do not say I am one, but I have a hand. Why tribute? why should we pay tribute? If Caesar can hide the sun from us with a blanket, or put the moon in his pocket, we will pay him tribute for light; else, sir, no more tribute, pray you now.

The queen is too much upset and mortified to intervene again; but Cymbeline now takes matters into his own hands. In the subsequent parting scene with the ambassador, Cloten has clearly had instructions to hold his tongue. His share in the conversation is confined to one short sentence, in which he does not discredit himself. With all his arrogance and folly, he is not without a certain rough good humour when things are going to his mind and he is not crossed. Not until, after Lucius has left, the news of Imogen's flight is brought, does he relapse into his customary brutality.

After this scene the queen does not appear again. In his supreme act of self-originated blundering, Cloten goes off on his fool's errand to Milford alone, without telling his mother, and there comes by his death. The next we hear of her is that she is dangerously ill;

> A fever with the absence of her son,
> A madness, of which her life's in danger.

Cloten's disappearance has shattered her spider's web of crime and cunning. For his sake she had staked everything. She had, as she thought, disposed of Pisanio by poison. She had made up her mind that Imogen, ' except she bend her humour ', shall taste of the drug too. According to her own hysterical death-bed confession—if it is to be believed—she was preparing a ' mortal mineral ' to make away with Cymbeline himself when once she had ' worked her son into the adoption of the crown '. Her son vanished; all this fabric of ingenious patient crime went to wreckage : and the tigress-mother

> Failing of her end by his strange absence,
> Grew shameless-desperate; open'd, in despite
> Of heaven and men, her purposes; repented
> The evils she hatch'd were not effected: so,
> Despairing, died.

'That irregulous devil', Imogen calls Cloten in her agony. 'O delicate fiend!' Cymbeline exclaims of the queen when the truth comes out. For Cloten's brainless devilry the end was certain; for 'it is the fools who are paid first'. It is poetical justice, but it is also true to life. But still more deeply true to life is the tragic irony of his mother's more miserable end. She perishes, not because of her many crimes, but because of her one virtue; not because her own craft and adroitness failed, but because the only creature whom she loved failed her. One can fancy, if they rejoined in the underworld, that her thoughts and plans would still be for him, and that they would still come to the same shipwreck. Her punishment for being a fiend was to have borne a fool.

J. W. MACKAIL.

ARIEL

THE character and figure of Ariel has always appeared to me one of the most strangely typical of Shakespeare's inventions, a creature at first carelessly and lightly conceived, a useful fairy, with all the virtues of an Orderly ! But Ariel takes shape and grows under the writer's hand, becoming more and more distinct, a separate problem, a perfect creation, gradually embodied and realized in the few score of lines devoted to the fantastic and sexless little being.

At first sight Ariel is a mere reflection of his master, with a taste for high-piled phrases, such as on Prospero's lips sound loftily enough ; but when Ariel indulges in them are like the bombastic parody of a child mimicking its elders.

> Jove's lightnings, the precursors
> O' the dreadful thunder-claps, more momentary
> And sight-outrunning were not; the fire, and cracks
> Of sulphurous roaring, the most mighty Neptune
> Seem'd to besiege, and make his bold waves tremble,
> Yea, his dread trident shake.

This is dull rhetoric at best !

But then it seems that Ariel emerges more clearly from the haze of the mind ; and is it not characteristic of Shakespeare that he does not return and revise, but lets the whole conception stand on the page, just as it was set down ? That is not unlike Shakespeare, to say a thing, to remould it better, and yet again better, and to leave it all written, exactly as it grew up.

There comes the scene when Ariel shows a childlike petulance, followed by a childlike repentance ; and at that point, I believe, the delicate-limbed beautiful creature sprang out in Shakespeare's mind. It is difficult to resist a movement of indignation when Prospero, like a cross-grained old schoolmaster, browbeats the pretty creature, who stands before him pouting, methinks, nibbling a rosy thumb, answering in monosyllables, and glad like a pet dog when the scolding is over.

> How now ? moody ?
> What is 't thou canst demand ?

O

To which menace says Ariel, looking up blue-eyed, with palms pressed together,

> My liberty!

And what could be more childlike, when he has promised to be good, than the pretty touch of eagerness?

> What shall I do? Say what. What shall I do?

When the scolding begins he is 'malignant thing', 'dull thing'. As Prospero's mood changes, he becomes 'quaint', and then, as the play goes on, he becomes 'my bird', 'my chick'; and even the little caged much-labouring, much-enduring spirit wants a tender word:

> Do you love me master? No?

Three of Shakespeare's loveliest lyrics, 'Come unto these yellow sands,' 'Full fathom five,' 'Where the bee sucks' (it is refreshing even to set down their titles!), are put into Ariel's mouth, to show how his maker loves the delicate spirit—three lyrics, of which I can only say that the more poetry I have read, and even written, the more wholly inconceivable to me is the process by which such strange and beautiful imagery is built up. Yet even so there is a touch of weakness in the sequel of the first:

> The strains of strutting chanticleer
> Cry Cock-a-diddle-dow.

But 'Full fathom five' is indeed no mortal business! Could an ugly thing be so transfigured into a beautiful mystery more speedily? While in 'Where the bee sucks', the whole heart of Ariel, the passionless joy of nature, asking nothing but a sweet continuance, is presented free of all stain of human emotion or regret!

Three other touches in the Ariel episode have a special interest. The curious touch of coarseness—which I confess seems to me a real blunder, if it were not Shakespeare's blunder, about the stench of the foul pool into which the roysterers had been led; then again the passage in which Ariel pleads for pity on the courtiers in their sorrow,

> That if you now beheld them, your affections
> Would become tender.

'Dost thou think so, spirit?' says Prospero, surprised.

'Mine would, sir, were I human,' says Ariel, and Prospero replies, 'And mine shall.'

I suppose the incident is devised to shame the Sage out of his extreme severity, and it leads to a fine speech from Prospero, of which the drift is 'the rarer action is in virtue than in vengeance'. A moral device, I am not sure whether justified!

And, lastly, there is the scene where Ariel again takes on the manner of his master, and tells the conspirators, in an imposing strain, that nothing can save them from their sin, 'nothing but heart-sorrow, and a clear life ensuing'. That we may be sure is no idea of Ariel's own, but just a punctual and sympathetic imagination of the dignified sort in which his master would have lectured them.

But now Ariel is free at last. He has but to speed the homeward sails;

> Then to the elements!
> Be free, and fare thou well.

He is to be free 'as mountain winds'; and by that single touch Shakespeare brings to mind a wide vision of breezes wandering in sun-warmed silent hill-spaces, where the sheep crop the grass, and the bee hums among the heather. That is Ariel's reward. And in this the art of the whole conception rises into a mood that few can attain, by presenting the wild impulse of the human heart, in a moment of anguish, to be free from everything alike, not only from suffering and sorrow, but from passion and emotion, enrapturing as they may seem, as well as even from righteousness and judgement. To be sinless, not by victory and hard-won triumph, but by soaring away from the whole stern and fiery strife of motive and desire, and forgetting that such things have ever been.

A. C. BENSON.

MAGDALENE COLLEGE,
    CAMBRIDGE.

THE VISION OF THE ENCHANTED ISLAND

'But whence came the vision of the enchanted island in *The Tempest*? It had no existence in Shakespeare's world, but was woven out of such stuff as dreams are made of.'
From 'Landscape and Literature', *Spectator,* June 18, 1898.[1]

MAY I cite Malone's suggestion connecting the play with the casting away of Sir George Somers on the island of Bermuda in 1609; and, further, may I be allowed to say how it seems to me possible that the vision was woven from the most prosaic material—from nothing more promising, in fact, than the chatter of a half-tipsy sailor at a theatre? Thus :

A stage-manager, who writes and vamps plays, moving among his audience, overhears a mariner discoursing to his neighbour of a grievous wreck, and of the behaviour of the passengers, for whom all sailors have ever entertained a natural contempt. He describes, with the wealth of detail peculiar to sailors, measures taken to claw the ship off a lee-shore, how helm and sails were worked, what the passengers did, and what he said. One pungent phrase—to be rendered later into : ' What care these brawlers for the name of King?'—strikes the manager's ear, and he stands behind the talkers. Perhaps only one-tenth of the earnestly delivered, hand-on-shoulder sea-talk was actually used of all that was automatically and unconsciously stored by the inland man who knew all inland arts and crafts. Nor is it too fanciful to imagine a half-turn to the second listener, as the mariner, banning his luck as mariners will, says there are those who would not give a doit to a poor man while they will lay out ten to see a raree-show—a dead Indian. Were he in foreign parts, as now he is in England, he could show people something in the way of strange fish. Is it to consider too curiously to see a drink ensue on this hint (the manager dealt but little in his plays with the sea at first-hand, and his instinct for new words would have been waked by what he had already caught), and with the drink a sailor's minute description of how he went across through the reefs to the island of his

[1] The reply to this statement, here reprinted, appeared in *The Spectator*, in the form of a letter, on July 2, 1898.

calamity—or islands rather, for there were many? Some you could almost carry away in your pocket. They were sown broadcast like—like the nutshells on the stage there. 'Many islands, in truth,' says the manager patiently, and afterwards his Sebastian says to Antonio: 'I think he will carry the island home in his pocket and give it to his son for an apple.' To which Antonio answers: 'And sowing the kernels of it in the sea, bring forth more islands.'

'But what was the land like?' says the manager. The sailor tries to explain. 'It was green, with yellow in it; a tawny-coloured country'—the colour, that is to say, of the coral-beached, cedar-covered Bermuda of to-day—'and the air made one sleepy, and the place was full of noises'—the muttering and roaring of the sea among the islands and between the reefs—'and there was a sou'-west wind that blistered one all over'. The Elizabethan mariner would not distinguish finely between blisters and prickly heat; but the Bermudian of to-day will tell you that the sou'-west, or lighthouse, wind in summer brings that plague and general discomfort. That the coral rock, battered by the sea, rings hollow with strange sounds, answered by the winds in the little cramped valleys, is a matter of common knowledge.

The man, refreshed with more drink, then describes the geography of his landing-place—the spot where Trinculo makes his first appearance. He insists and reinsists on details which to him at one time meant life or death, and the manager follows attentively. He can give his audience no more than a few hangings and a placard for scenery, but that his lines shall lift them beyond that bare show to the place he would have them, the manager needs for himself the clearest possible understanding—the most ample detail. He must see the scene in the round—solid—ere he peoples it. Much, doubtless, he discarded, but so closely did he keep to his original informations that those who go to-day to a certain beach some two miles from Hamilton will find the stage set for Act II, Sc. ii, of *The Tempest*—a bare beach, with the wind singing through the scrub at the land's edge, a gap in the reefs wide enough for the passage of Stephano's butt of sack, and (these eyes have seen it) a cave in the coral within easy reach of the tide, whereto such a butt might be conveniently rolled ('My cellar is in a rock by the seaside, where my wine is hid'). There is no other cave for some two miles. 'Here's neither bush nor shrub;' one is exposed to the wrath of 'yond' same black cloud', and here the currents strand wreckage. It was so well done that, after three hundred years, a stray tripper, and no Shakespeare scholar, recognized in a flash that old first set of all.

So far good. Up to this point the manager has gained little except some suggestions for an opening scene, and some notion of an uncanny island. The mariner (one cannot believe that Shakespeare was mean in these little things) is dipping to a deeper drunkenness. Suddenly he launches into a preposterous tale of himself and his fellows, flung ashore, separated from their officers, horribly afraid of the devil-haunted beach of noises, with their heads full of the fumes of broached liquor. One castaway was found hiding under the ribs of a dead whale which smelt abominably. They hauled him out by the legs—he mistook them for imps—and gave him drink. And now, discipline being melted, they would strike out for themselves, defy their officers, and take possession of the island. The narrator's mates in this enterprise were probably described as fools. He was the only sober man in the company.

So they went inland, faring badly as they staggered up and down this pestilent country. They were pricked with palmettoes, and the cedar branches rasped their faces. Then they found and stole some of their officers' clothes which were hanging up to dry. But presently they fell into a swamp, and, what was worse, into the hands of their officers ; and the great expedition ended in muck and mire. Truly an island bewitched. Else why their cramps and sickness ? Sack never made a man more than reasonably drunk. He was prepared to answer for unlimited sack ; but what befell his stomach and head was the purest magic that honest man ever met.

A drunken sailor of to-day wandering about Bermuda would probably sympathize with him ; and to-day, as then, if one takes the easiest inland road from Trinculo's beach, near Hamilton, the path that a drunken man would infallibly follow, it ends abruptly in swamp. The one point that our mariner did not dwell upon was that he and the others were suffering from acute alcoholism combined with the effects of nerve-shattering peril and exposure. Hence the magic. That a wizard should control such an island was demanded by the beliefs of all seafarers of that date.

Accept this theory, and you will concede that *The Tempest* came to the manager sanely and normally in the course of his daily life. He may have been casting about for a new play ; he may have purposed to vamp an old one—say, *Aurelio and Isabella* ; or he may have been merely waiting on his demon. But it is all Prospero's wealth against Caliban's pignuts that to him in a receptive hour, sent by heaven, entered the original Stephano fresh from the seas and half-seas over. To him Stephano told his tale all in one piece, a two hours' discourse of most

glorious absurdities. His profligate abundance of detail at the beginning, when he was more or less sober, supplied and surely established
the earth-basis of the play in accordance with the great law that a story
to be truly miraculous must be ballasted with facts. His maunderings
of magic and incomprehensible ambushes, when he was without
reservation drunk (and this is just the time when a lesser-minded man
than Shakespeare would have paid the reckoning and turned him
out), suggested to the manager the peculiar note of its supernatural
mechanism.

Truly it was a dream, but that there may be no doubt of its source
or of his obligation, Shakespeare has also made the dreamer immortal.

RUDYARD KIPLING.

DE WITT AT THE SWAN

ASSUMING that Van Buchell's drawing of the Swan playhouse was copied, by one who had never seen such a building, from a sketch made on the spot by a curious foreigner, who was not a skilled draughtsman, let us try to reconstruct the scene which presented itself to the eyes of De Witt. He sat in the second gallery, somewhat to the right of the centre,[1] for, though he drew the platform as though he were occupying a seat exactly midway, he drew the tiring-house as he saw it, and showed plainly the right wall of the topmost story. In the face of the tiring-house two doors open upon the stage. That on the right is the larger and is given greater detail than its fellow, perhaps as the result of an attempt to show in perspective two doors of equal size. Similarly, in the top story the nearer window appears the wider. The stage extends to the middle of the yard. The artist drew his circular yard as an oval, much as he saw it, and then drew through its centre the horizontal straight line which represents the front edge of the stage. The blocks or piles visible below the stage may be the supports of a movable platform, but, if so, they appear too large and clumsy and yet numerically insufficient for support of so broad a floor. Possibly De Witt meant to indicate from hearsay the bases of the pillars. These pillars are placed to conform with the imaginary direct view of the platform, but the shadow (or heavens) is necessarily drawn in part to match the actual oblique view of the top story. One supposes that Van Buchell, puzzled by inconsistency in the original rough sketch, and trying to give definiteness to the lines and to make them fit his ideas of propriety, introduced further confusion. At the top the shadow turns the corner and runs back to the galleries ; yet at the bottom a straight horizontal line runs the width of the stage, and beneath this line are the pillars symmetrically placed. Result—the right pillar is under the side plane of the roof, and the left under the front plane. In De Witt's sketch the right pillar must

[1] Wegener, ii.

have stood apparently, through effect of perspective, nearer the centre, obscuring a good deal of that end of the tiring-house wall, while to the right of the pillar the roof receded to the galleries. The angle formed by the two lower roof-edges was on a level with our spectator's eye, and his line of the eaves was so nearly straight that it deceived Van Buchell. A line, heavier and straighter than its fellows, runs slantwise down the roof, a little to the left of the corner. Though not quite rightly placed, it represents the division between the two planes, and accordingly the portion to the right of it is shaded—carelessly and without decision, because Van Buchell did not realize why any shade should be there. It is likely that the upper stories of the tiring-house projected, so that aerial descents could be made directly from the overhanging floor of the room above which the trumpeter stands, or even from the topmost chamber; it is significant, in this connexion, that the front roof is not so extensive as the position of the pillars would lead us to expect. That the lines marking the bases of the pillars upon the platform are half-way between the stage-front edge and the upper part of the pit circumference may indicate that rather more than half the stage-depth was covered by the heavens and the tiring-house.

Along the front of the balcony runs a projecting ledge, with a row of small pillars at its inner brink, and beneath it is a horizontal line sufficiently thick to indicate the shadow. The projection may have been two or three feet in depth, and the ledge has probably a forward slope, for no stays are visible beneath it. It is similar to the ledge beneath the balcony of the Messalina stage, though it is not quite in the same position, and most likely curtains were sometimes suspended from its outer edge so as to form a recess or cloister for concealments and 'inner scenes', or to provide additional entrances.

With pillars and stage placed as they are, any representation of a lateral wall to the lower stories of the tiring-house must have appeared to Van Buchell a result of bad drawing. He believed that the three lower stories ran straight across the full width of the stage; but, if he was right, the lower stories were broader than the topmost story, which rose as a turret from one side of the structure. Really, the breadth of the tiring-house was the same from stage to roof, and there was an equal space, on either side, between the lateral wall and the edge of the plat-form. A downward extension of the vertical bounding lines of the front wall in the top story shows approximately where the angles of the lower part of the wall should be. The line on the left falls behind the pillar; the corner is not visible. On the other side the effect has been vitiated by Van Buchell's shifting of the pillar, but, even so, there is a slight indication that De Witt may have shown the angle with some distinctness. Slightly to left of the pillar a vertical line is drawn almost across the ledge, just below a heavy line which runs from top to bottom through the shadow in the balcony, and thence to the right the upper and lower lines of the ledge have a slight downward slope. The slope is not in accord with laws of perspective, but it seems to betray intention to show a turn of the ledge towards the rear of the stage, similar to that of the Messalina print. One result of Van Buchell's error is that the balcony window on the extreme right is wider than any of the others; and if this were the result of perspective, the whole row would diminish regularly from right to left. The right-hand door appears to be farther from the edge of the stage than that on the left, and this too may have resulted from a misunderstanding of the shape of the tiring-house. The position of the adjusted pillar prevents our seeing if there were any doors in the side-walls of the tiring-house, but a study of stage-directions convinces one that doors opened somewhere upon the lateral passages. A comparison of Visscher's view with Van Buchell's drawing shows that the sides of the Swan's tiring-house were at right angles to the front, and did not slope towards the rear corners of the stage in the fashion determined by space conditions in some private playhouses.

Van Buchell indicates no pit entrance, so we surmise that it was in that portion of the building which he has not drawn. A comparison of Visscher's drawing and the rough plan in the Manor Map of Paris Garden shows, on the side next the street and farthest from the stage, a rectangular structure, which must be a porch or a roofed staircase leading to the main door. From the Hope contract we learn that there were 'two stearcasses without and adioyninge to' the Swan. The second of these was, I think, at the tiring-house door, but it does not appear in the Manor Map. Perhaps it had been removed before the survey was made.

J. Le Gay Brereton.

Sydney.

A FORGOTTEN PLAYHOUSE CUSTOM OF SHAKESPEARE'S DAY

NOTHING, perhaps, is better calculated to give a distorted impression of the truth than the device of our stage historians in dividing up the story of the rise and progress of the English Theatre into watertight compartments. Goethe's sound apophthegm that the law of life is continuity amidst change applies with equal force to institutions as to men, and to no institution more fittingly than to the playhouse. One has only to look closely at the facts to find that, even in the seventeenth century, despite the disruptive tendency of the Civil War and the Commonwealth, there was in matters of theatrical routine very considerable overlapping. Perhaps the reason for this is best expressed in the words of the old Chinese proverb, 'the Useful struggles vainly with Time, but the devourer of all things breaks his teeth upon the Agreeable'. While the Restoration playgoer, like the playgoer of every other age and clime, was neither lacking in initiative nor idiosyncrasy, it is certain that some of his observances were the cherished relics of a former day.

Even if our knowledge went no further, we should be compelled to arrive at this conclusion to account for the steady persistence of a curious custom, evidently the source of much disorder and as such constantly fulminated against by Charles II. This amounted to a quaint application of the old English principle of the right of way, a principle almost part and parcel of the British constitution and still on occasion vigorously maintained. No fewer than five times between the years 1663 and 1674 'old Rowley' iterated an order forbidding playgoers to exercise 'theire pretended priviledge by custom of forcing their entrance at the fourth or fifth acts without payment'. Long existent, indeed, must have been the privilege so stubbornly upheld in the face of the royal displeasure. It will not be unprofitable to inquire how it originated, and what traces remain of its usage in pre-Restoration times.

My impression is that the custom had its origin, not with any desire of suiting the convenience of the public, but as a mere matter of theatrical expediency. It was usual in Shakespeare's early day to hang up in the tiring-house for the guidance of the stage-keeper an entrance-and-music plot of the play, so that he might know when to send on the supers or give instructions for the flourishing of trumpets or the rattling of thunder. Seven of these plots, or platts as they were then called, still exist, some of them preserved at Dulwich College and some in the British Museum Manuscript Room. Owing to a misconception on the part of the old commentators, who arrived at the conclusion that they were scenarios for improvised plays, after the manner of the canevas of the Italian *commedia dell' arte*, the reason for their provision has long been obscured. So far from their employment being so rare, there is no room for doubting that, in Elizabethan days, one of these platts was made for every acted play. Without their aid the stage-keeper would have been all at sea.

In examining the 'Platt of Frederick and Basilea' (i.e. of a play performed at the Rose Theatre on June 3, 1597) Steevens was mightily puzzled to know who were the 'gatherers' who came on as supers at a certain juncture of the performance. *Longo intervallo*, Collier threw light on the mystery in pointing out that 'the gatherers were those who gathered or collected the money, and who, during the performance, after all the spectators were arrived and when their services were no longer needed at the doors were required to appear on the stage'. Exception has been taken to this interpretation on the ground that the gatherers were those who collected money from the assembled audience, not the money-takers at the doors, but there is no reason to believe the term had so restricted a meaning. Dekker shows otherwise when he gives the instruction, in his chapter on 'How a Gallant should behave himself in a Playhouse' in *The Guls Horn-Booke*, 'whether therefore the gatherers of the publique or private Playhouse stand to receive the afternoones rent, let our Gallant (having paid it) presently advance himselfe up to the Throne of the Stage'.

Collier's explanation, however, is too sweeping, inasmuch as it is not in reason to infer that the door-keepers would be free for stage employment once the performance began, much as the players might be desirous of minimizing the expense of hirelings by pressing them into service. Late-comers there always were and always will be. It is more rational to infer that the gatherers were only employed when all the normal resources of the theatre were exhausted and larger crowds

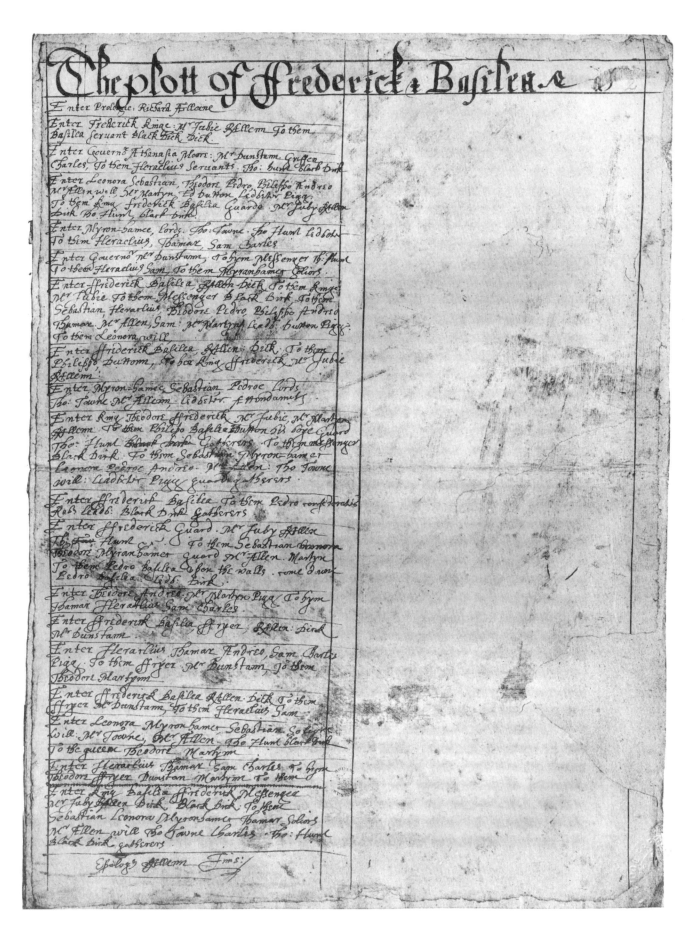

The plott of ffrederick & Basilea

Enter Prologue: Richard Allene

Enter ffrederick Kinge: Mr Jubie Allen. To them
Basilea seruant black Dick Dick

Enter Gouerno~ Athanasia Moore: Mr Dunstann Griffen
Charles, To them fferaclius Seruants. Tho: hunt black Dick

Enter Leonora Sebastian, Theodore Pedro, Philippo Andreo
Mr Allen will her Martyn Ed button Ledbeter Pigg:
To them Kinge frederick Basilea Guarde Mr Juby Allen
Dick Bo ffunt black Dick

Enter Myron~bames, lords, Tho: Towne tho ffunt Ledbetr
To them fferaclius, Thamar, Sam Charles

Enter Gouerno~ Mr Dunstann, To hym messenger th: ffunt
To them fferaclius Sam, To them Myranbames Soliors

Enter frederick Basilea, Allen Dick, To them Kinge:
Mr Jubie To them Messenger black Dick To them
Sebastian, fferaclius, Theodore Pedro Philippo Andreo
Thamar. Mr Allen, Sam: her Martyn Ledb: button Pigg
To them Leonora will

Enter ffrederick Basilea Allen: Dick, To them
Philippo, button, To her Kinge frederick Mr Jubie
Allen:

Enter Myron~bames, Sebastian Pedroe Lords
Tho: Towne Mr Allen, Ledbeter ffendamth

Enter Kinge Theodore frederick Mr Jubie, Mr Martyn
Allen. To them Philippo Basilea button his boye Guard
Tho: ffunt black Dick Gatherers, To them messenger
black Dick. To them Sebastian Myron~bame
Leonora Pedroe Andreo Mr Allen tho Towne
will: Ledbetr Pigg guard gatherers

Enter ffrederick Basilea To them Pedro confederates
Rob: Ledb: black Dick Gatherers

Enter ffrederick Guard. Mr Juby Allen
Tho: ffunt &c. To them Sebastian Leonora
Theodore Myron~bames Guard Mr Allen. Martyn
To them Pedro Basilea vpon the walls. some down
Pedro Basilea Ledb: Dick

Enter Theodore Andreo her Martyn Pigg To hym
Thamar fferaclius Sam Charles

Enter ffrederick Basilea ffryer Allen: Dick
Mr Dunstann

Enter fferaclius Thamar Andreo, Sam Charles
Pigg, To them ffryer Mr Dunstann To them
Theodore Martyn

Enter ffrederick Basilea Allen: Dick To them
ffryer Mr Dunstann, To them fferaclius Sam

Enter Leonora Myron bames Sebastian To her
will: Mr Towne, Mr Allen tho ffunt black Dick
To the queene Theodore Martyn

Enter fferaclius Thamar Sam Charles To hym
Theodore ffryer Dunstan Martyn To them

Enter Kinge Basilea ffrederick Messenger
Mr Juby Allen Dick Black Dick To them
Sebastian Leonora Myron bames Thamar Soliors
Mr Allen will tho Towne Charles tho: ffunt
black Dick gatherers

Epilogue Allen   ffinis:

than usual had to go on. Happily the necessary qualification of Collier's statement is afforded by the 'Platt of Frederick and Basilea' itself. Unfortunately, unlike some of the others, this platt has no indication of act-divisions, but there are in all eighteen grouped entries of the characters and their attendants, and the first reference to the gatherers occurs in the ninth entry. At this juncture in the performance the play must have been at least half over, possibly more, as the entrances never occurred at regular intervals and often grew more frequent towards the close. Few playgoers would desire access to the theatre after a couple of acts had been given and, viewing the utility of the gatherers as extra auxiliaries, there would be great temptation to leave the doors unguarded. As a matter of fact, there is a passage in Braithwaite's *Whimsies* (1631), describing a ruffler, which indicates a considerable slackening of vigilance once the play had got fairly under way:

'To a play they wil hazard to go, though with never a rag of money: where after the second act, when the doore is weakly guarded, they will make forcible entrie; a knock with a cudgell as the worst; whereat though they grumble, they rest pacified upon their admittance. Forthwith, by violent assault and assent, they aspire to the two-pennie roome, where being furnished with tinder, match, and a portion of decayed Barmoodas, they smoake it most terribly, applaud a prophane jeast, etc.'

When we learn here that those who went to the play in 1631 after the second act, without the necessary admission money but with plenty of assurance, had little difficulty in forcing their way into the house, it is not surprising to find that a score of years previously the doors were left entirely unguarded after the termination of the fourth act. At that period the privilege of free entry towards the end led to much riot and disorder, and culminated in magisterial interference. At the General Session of the Peace held at Westminster in October 1612, an order was issued forbidding all 'Jigges, Rymes and Daunces' at the close of all performances within the jurisdiction. This was justified by the finding that 'by reason of certayne lewde Jigges, songes and daunces used and accustomed at the playhouse called the Fortune in Goulding lane divers cutt-purse and other lewde and ill-disposed persons in great multitudes doe resorte thither at the end of everye playe many tymes causinge tumultes and outrages whereby His Majesties peace is often broke and much mischiefe like to ensue thereby'.

This statement positively demands the assumption that the privilege of free entry at the end of the fourth act was already in vogue. Why should the crowds have flocked to the Fortune at the close of the play if they still had to pay the ordinary price of admission ? They might as well have gone early and got full value for their money.   The truth is that, the doors being left unguarded, some took advantage of the privilege to see the jig gratis and others swelled the crowd to indulge in pocket-picking.   Whether or not the order applied to the Bankside theatres—I should say not—it by no means wrote *finis* to the records of the jig.   One finds traces of its existence twenty years later.   As much misconception prevails as to the nature of the Elizabethan stage jig, it may be pointed out that it was a ballad farce of a free order in which the rhymed dialogue was all sung to a variety of popular airs. It comprised at most but three or four characters and seldom took more than twenty minutes to perform.   A fact known to few people is that some of the old jigs are still extant.

One would be hardly warranted in dogmatizing over the order of the Westminster Justices of the Peace were it not that clear evidence of the existence of the privilege of entry after the fourth act, before the Civil War, is ready to hand.   One item occurs in a poem entitled ' The Long Vacation in London', first published in the posthumous folio collection of Sir William D'Avenant's works in 1673, but written many years earlier.   The minor poems in this volume, including the above, some of them dated, are arranged chronologically ; and it is not difficult to arrive at the conclusion that the poem referred to was written between 1632 and 1639.   Even if the lines had come down to us only in manuscript, we should still be able to determine that they were written before the closing of the theatres, for they refer to the Globe as in active service, and the Globe disappeared for ever in 1644.   Armed with the clue, there is no mistaking the import of the following :

> Then forth he steales; to Globe doth run ;
> And smiles, and vowes Four Acts are done :
> *Finis* to bring he does protest
> Tells ev'ry Play'r, his part is best.

One other allusion shows that the privilege was still being availed of at a slightly later period.   It occurs in *The Guardian* of Cowley, a comedy originally performed before Prince Charles at Trinity College, Cambridge, on March 12, 1640–1.   In Act III, Sc. i, Aurelea says to her tormentor, 'Be abandon'd by all men above a Tapster ; and not dare to looke a Gentleman i' the face ; unless perhaps you sneake into a Playhouse, at the fifth act'.

Habits, we know, are stubborn things, but all the same it is remarkable that a privilege arising out of special circumstances in Shakespeare's day should have long survived the necessity which called it into being, jumped the formidable barrier of the Commonwealth, and run a vigorous race over stony ground until the end of the third quarter of the seventeenth century.

W. J. Lawrence.

Dublin.

WIT AND HUMOUR IN SHAKESPEARE

'WHAT is Wit? What is Humour?' might say a jesting Pilate, and would probably not stay for the usual answers, which are infinite in number and variety. Possibly the best definitions would be those of a recent writer, that Wit implies 'cleverness, a quick and nimble adroitness in bringing together unexpected points of resemblance between things apparently widely separated, or suggesting some incongruity or oddity, by a coincidence of sound or different meanings of a word', while Humour (to Shakespeare a temper or predominant mood) 'betokens a certain kindly, tolerant, broad-minded point of view, keenly alive to inconsistencies and incongruities, quick to note and to place in a view where they become patent the small failings and absurdities, but at the same time with a sympathetic understanding which suggests a nature large enough to see the faults and not to be repelled by them'.[1] The sense of incongruity pervades both, but Humour, which is the 'genius of thoughtful laughter' (Meredith), is tinged with emotion, while Wit is entirely intellectual.

Tragedy and Comedy partake of both, but in different degrees. Thus in Tragedy, such as Shakespeare's (though not in the more 'classical' models), Wit and Humour play a prominent part, in increasing the poignancy of the emotions, and in effecting what Aristotle calls their 'purgation', but they are the staple of Comedy, where they are employed solely 'for the sake of laughter'. Again, the origin of 'laughter' has caused much throwing about of the brains of the 'Wise', from Aristotle to M. Bergson, especially among the Germans, who have viewed it philosophically, from the point of view of disinterested spectators. For example, Schopenhauer taught that 'laughter' was due to the incongruity of what is thought and what is perceived, such as the ludicrous appearance of a tangent touching a circle. This may be held to be scientific laughter, devoid of that saline base to which M. Bergson attributes the sparkle of the 'comic'. On the other hand, the English-

---

[1] *Edinburgh Review*, 1912, pp. 397–9.

man, Hobbes, defined it as ' a sudden glory arising from sudden conception of some eminence in ourselves by comparison with the inferiority of others, or with our own formerly '. This being assumed, we may agree with George Eliot that it must have been developed out of 'the cruel mockery of a savage at the writhings of a suffering enemy '. But away with such puerilities, out of which ' Agelasts ' may weave their ropes of sand. The theory of Evolution can transmute anything into anything else, as Benedick thought love might transform him into an oyster. Better is it to say, with Barrow, that Humour is '*that which we all see and know* : and one better apprehends what it is by acquaintance than I can inform him by description. It is indeed so versatile and uniform, appearing in so many shapes, so many postures, so many garbs, so variously apprehended by several eyes and judgements, that it seemeth no less hard to settle a clear and certain notice thereof than to make a picture of Proteus, or to define the figure of floating air.'

But many have tried to shackle their Proteus, eminently Professor Sully and M. Bergson in recent times, but, like most modern philosophers, they are unconsciously treading in the footsteps of Aristotle, who, in his *Poetic*, seems to have discussed the origin of Comedy with as much care as he devoted to Tragedy. These chapters do not survive, but in the so-called *Tractatus*, edited by Cramer fifty years ago, an epitomator has given the substance (so many hold) of the philosopher's analysis of the Comic. After defining Comedy, the writer goes on to divide ' inventorially ' the sources of ' laughter ', which is produced ' from diction ' or ' from things '. These sources are sometimes indistinguishable,[1] but roughly it may be said that, in the case of ' things ' (including thoughts on them), the matter alone is amusing, however it may be expressed : on the other hand, the ' laughter ' is in the ' diction ', if it is created, not expressed by words, and if, when the words are changed, the humour vanishes.

A.   Laughter is derived from ' diction '[2] in the following ways :

By Homonyms.[3]

' Homonymous things ' are those which, though distinct, are known by the same name. On account of the popularity of the study of Rhetoric (the art of persuasion or deception) in Elizabethan times, such ' equivoca ' fascinated the ears of the groundlings, whose lungs were

---

[1] As Pancrace says (*Mar. Forcé*, Sc. iv), ' et tout ainsi que les pensées sont les portraits des choses, de même nos paroles sont-elles les portraits de nos pensées.'

[2] ἀπὸ τῆς λέξεως.   [3] καθ᾽ ὁμωνυμίαν.

P

more 'tickle o' the sere' than ours. As Hamlet said,[1] 'We must speak by the card, or equivocation will undo us.' 'To mistake the word', 'to moralize two meanings' in a phrase, was the besetting vice of all stage-characters, tragic as well as comic. Thus, 'old Gaunt indeed, and gaunt in being old ',[2] ' I'll gild the faces of the grooms withal; For it must seem their guilt '.[3] We cannot but agree with the commentators that such jests enhance the horror of the scene ! To the clowns who are always 'winding up the watches of their wits', or seeking to escape dullness as they say ' the dogs on the Nile-banks drink at the river running to avoid the crocodile ',[4] such word-plays were their stock-in-trade from which they extracted the treasures of their lean and wasteful learning. These civil wars of wits, at their best, consisted in fitting an absurd idea into a well-established phrase-form, or in taking literally an expression which was used figuratively. Thus '*Mercutio*. Ask for me to-morrow, and you shall find me a grave man ';[5] '*Oliver*. Now, sir! what make you here? *Orlando*. Nothing: I am not taught to make anything ';[6] '*Sir Andrew*. Fair lady, do you think you have fools in hand? *Maria*. Sir, I have not you by the hand ';[7] '*Sir Andrew*. Faith, I can cut a caper. *Sir Toby*. And I can cut the mutton to't '.[8] One of the worst is Hamlet's ; ' And many such-like "As"es of great charge '.[9]

Bacon and Shakespeare ridiculed, and often practised, such ' peculiar and quaint affectation of words ' ; and indeed, after a long course of them, we feel the justice of Lorenzo's remark :

> And I do know
> A many fools, that stand in better place,
> Garnish'd like him, that for a tricksy word
> Defy the matter.[10]

' Homonymy ' is, to our conception, less ' tolerable and not to be endured ' when it consists in the transference of words or proverbs into new surroundings, or a new key : for example, Pistol's ' Why, then the world 's my oyster, Which I with sword will open ' ;[11] the Bastard's apt ' Zounds ! I was never so bethump'd with words Since I first call'd my brother's father dad ' ;[12] Trinculo's ' Alas ! the storm is come again : my best way is to creep under his [Caliban's] gaberdine : there is no other shelter hereabout : misery acquaints a man with strange bed-fellows ;'[13] or Pistol's (touching his sword) ' Have we not Hiren here ? '[14]

---

[1] *Haml.* V. i. 147.   [2] *Rich. II*, II. i. 74.   [3] *Macb.* II. ii. 57.
[4] Quoted by Meredith.   [5] *Rom. & Jul.* III. i. 102.   [6] *A. Y. L.* I. i. 31.
[7] *Tw. N.* I. iii. 69.   [8] ibid. I. iii. 129.   [9] *Haml.* V. ii. 43.
[10] *Merch of V.* III. v. 73.   [11] *M. Wives* II. ii. 2.   [12] *John* II. 466.
[13] *Temp.* II. ii. 40.   [14] *2 Hen. IV*, II. iv. 173.

By Synonyms.[1]

' Synonymous things ' are those called by the same name in the same sense. ' Synonyms ' are the exchequer of poets, whether lyric, tragic, or comic, since it is possible to adorn or degrade a subject by applying to it opposite epithets belonging to the same genus. Thus Simonides thought a victory with the mule-car too starved a subject for his pen, until he was satisfied with his fee, whereupon he began an ode, ' O daughters of storm-footed studs '; a beggar may be called a ' solicitor ', robbery ' purchase ',[2] to steal ' to convey ',[3] footpads ' St. Nicholas' clerks ', ' squires of the night's body ', ' Diana's foresters, gentlemen of the shade, minions of the moon '.[4] Since the highest quality of style is due proportion (lofty to lofty, low to low) it is easy to blunder, in serious poetry, in the choice of ' congruent epitheta '. Thus ' the brazen Dionysius ' made all Greece laugh by speaking of ' the scream of Calliope '[5]: Jean Paul (after *Hudibras*) compared the setting sun to a parboiled lobster. As due proportion is demanded from serious writers, disproportion is the aim of comic poetry, and excites laughter. Thus, Armado's speeches are ' a fantastical banquet, just so many strange dishes ': the early clowns are said to have been ' at a great feast of languages and to have stolen the scraps ', as it were ' from a very alms-basket of words ', which often ' led to old abusing of God's patience and the King's English '. For example, ' in the posterior of the day which the vulgar (Oh! base vulgar) call the afternoon '. The best commentary on such vagaries is Hamlet's speech beginning ' Sir, his definement suffers no perdition in you; though, I know, to divide him inventorially would dizzy the arithmetic of memory '.[6] The ' wise ' say that this style is laughable as creating a momentary tension followed by a relapse.

' Synonyms ' that degrade, being the stock-in-trade of Comedy, require no illustration. Shakespeare often tried to increase the required tension by giving them an enigmatic character. Thus, ' Tut! dun's the mouse, the constable's own word ' (= ' be still '); [7] ' Lipsbury pinfold ' (= ' the teeth '); [8] ' They call drinking deep, dyeing scarlet; and when you breathe in your watering, they cry "hem!" and bid you play it off '; [9] ' I'll make a sop o' the moonshine of you '; [10] ' I am but mad north-north-west: when the wind is southerly I know a hawk from a handsaw '.[11]

[1] κατὰ συνωνυμίαν.   [2] *Hen. V*, III. ii. 47.   [3] *M. Wives*, I. iii. 30.
[4] *1 Hen. IV*, II. i. 68; ibid. I. ii. 27.   [5] κραυγὴ Καλλιόπης.   [6] *Haml.* V. ii. 118.
[7] *Rom. & Jul.* I. iv. 40.   [8] *Lear* II. ii. 9.   [9] *1 Hen. IV*, II. iv. 17.
[10] *Lear* II. ii. 35.   [11] *Haml.* II. ii. 405.

P 2

By Garrulity.[1]

Under this head come grandiloquence, travesty, in fact every kind of speech in which the thread of the verbosity is drawn out finer than the staple of the argument. In the grand style, the best exemplars (as in the case of ' Synonymy ') were the ' fanatical phantasime ' Armado, Holofernes, and Sir Nathaniel : in the lower style, the accomplished clowns (e. g. Touchstone), and braggadocio-militarists, such as Pistol and that man of words, Parolles. A good instance of clownish learning is :

Costard. Sir, the contempts thereof are as touching me..... The matter is to me, sir, as concerning Jaquenetta. The manner of it is, I was taken with the manner.
Biron. In what manner?
Costard. In manner and form following, sir; all those three: I was seen with her in the manor-house, sitting with her upon the form, and taken following her into the park; which, put together, is, in manner and form following. Now, sir, for the manner,—it is the manner of a man to speak to a woman, for the form,—in some form.[2]

A chief merit of good writing is that it should be adapted to its subject, and laughter is caused when an aggravated style is employed in embellishing a mean subject, whether this is done by means of an undue magnificence of language, or of a tragic or lyrical metre. The best example of the latter in the ' Pyramus ' Ode : ' Sweet moon, I thank thee for thy sunny beams ', especially

> A tomb
> Must cover thy sweet eyes,
> These lily lips,
> This cherry nose,
> These yellow cowslip cheeks,
> Are gone, are gone.

A very Aristophanic parody.

By Paronyms.[3]

To speak strictly, ' paronymous things ' are those which are called by two names, where one is derived from the other by varying the termination ; thus Phoebus and Phoebe are ' paronymous '. As a source of laughter, however, ' Paronymy ' should be restricted to nonce-words, or expressions strange to literary speech. In nonce-words the Greek and Latin comedies are extraordinarily rich, but the genius of French and English does not readily lend itself to such formations :

[1] κατ' ἀδολεσχίαν.   [2] *Love's L. L.* I. i. 189.
[3] κατὰ παρωνυμίαν, παρὰ πρόσθεσιν καὶ ἀφαίρεσιν.

Shakespeare, however, occasionally made experiments in them : for example, 'the most sovereign prescription in Galen is but empiricutic';[1] 'I would not have been so fidiused' (viz. Aufidiused, cp. Molière's 'tartuffiée');[2] 'your bisson conspectuities';[3] 'directitude'[4] (a servant's word); the Gargantuan 'I am joined with no foot-landrakers, no long-staff sixpenny strikers, none of these mad mustachio-purple-hued malt-worms ; but with nobility and tranquillity, burgomasters and great oneyers',[5] which is as near as the English language can get to the fullness of such mouth-filling compounds as σαλπιγγο-λογχυπηνάδαι, σαρκασμοπιτυοκάμπται. Armado had a mint of such fire-new words in his brain, e. g. 'volable';[6] 'which to annothanize in the vulgar';[7] 'Dost thou infamonize me among potentates?';[8] compare also 'Falstaff. You are grand-jurors are ye? We'll jure ye, i' faith';[9] 'Falstaff. What a plague mean ye to colt me thus? Prince Hal. Thou liest : thou art not colted; thou art uncolted';[10] Falstaff. 'Away, you scullion! you rampallian! you fustilarian! I'll tickle your catastrophe';[11] 'Apprehensive, quick, forgetive';[12] 'Feste. I did impeticos thy gratillity' (= pocket your gratuity);[13] 'Costard. My incony Jew'.[14]

By endearing expressions, especially Diminutives.[15]

English is not, as Greek, Latin, Italian, and Spanish, rich in diminutives ; but, so far as the genius of the language permitted, Shakespeare sometimes tried, by means of certain comic expressions, to convey the particular shade of affection or contempt implied in such formations, thus : 'Thisne, Thisne';[16] 'Whoreson' (adjectively applied not only to persons, but to things, in a tone of coarse tenderness, as by Doll Tearsheet, 'Thou whoreson little tidy Bartholomew boar-pig'[17] 'O dainty duck! O dear!';[18] 'bully' (with Hercules,[19] Hector,[20] Bottom,[21] &c.) ; 'I did impeticos thy gratillity,'[22] which may be an attempted diminutive of 'gratuity'; 'My sweet ounce of man's flesh! My incony Jew!'[23] Molière occasionally affected such 'hypocrisms', e. g. 'Ma pauvre fanfan, pouponne de mon âme', 'Mon petit nez, pauvre petit bouchon.'[24]

---

[1] Cor. II. i. 129. [2] ibid. II. i. 145. [3] ibid. II. i. 71.
[4] ibid. IV. v. 223. [5] 1 Hen. IV, II. i. 81. [6] L. L. L. III. 67.
[7] ibid. IV. i. 69. [8] ibid. v. ii. 682. [9] 1 Hen. IV, II. ii. 100.
[10] ibid. II. ii. 42. [11] 2 Hen. IV, II. i. 67. [12] ibid. IV. iii. 107.
[13] Tw. N. II. iii. 27. [14] L. L. L. III. 142. [15] καθ' ὑποκοριστικόν.
[16] Mid. N. D. I. ii. 56. [17] 2 Hen. IV, II. iv. 249. [18] Mid. N. D. V. i. 288 (νηττάριον).
[19] M. Wives I. iii. 6. [20] ibid. 11. [21] Mid. N. D. III. i. 8. [22] Tw. N. II. iii. 27.
[23] L. L. L. III. 142 (κρεᾴδιον). [24] L'École des Maris, II. ix: Sganarelle to Isabelle.

*By the alteration or ludicrous perversion of a word's intention by means of
an inflexion of the voice, a gesture, a twinkle of the eye, a change of
expression,—in fact by any of the methods which orators employ (under
the name of* actio) *to drive home their meaning.*[1]

Under this head come ' puns ', especially such as the ' wise ' term
' paranomasia '. In many cases the ' alteration ' is visible to the eye.
Wit of this kind is extraordinarily common in Elizabethan dramas.
Thus : ' *Falstaff*. If reasons [raisins] were as plenty as blackberries,
I would give no man a reason on compulsion, I ' ;[2] ' have we not
Hiren (= iron) here ? '[3] ' *Hostess*. I must go fetch the third-borough.
Sly. Third, or fourth, or fifth borough, I'll answer him by law ' ;[4] ' Let 's
be no stoics nor no stocks ' ;[5] ' Not on thy sole, but on thy soul, harsh
Jew, Thou mak'st thy knife keen '.[6]   Similar are Speed's jests on
' ship ', ' sheep ', ' lost mutton ', ' laced mutton ' ;[7] Mercutio's ' O their
bons, their *bons !* ;[8] Gadshill's ' they pray continually to their saint, the
commonwealth ; or rather, not pray to her, but prey on her, for they
ride up and down on her and make her their boots ' ;[9] ' *Chief Justice*.
Your means are very slender, and your waste is great. *Falstaff*. I would
it were otherwise : I would my means were greater and my waist
slenderer ' ;[10] ' *Chief Justice*. There is not a white hair on thy face but
should have his effect of gravity. *Falstaff*. His effect of gravy, gravy,
gravy ' ;[11] ' *Speed. Item, She can sew. Launce*. That 's as much as
to say, Can she so ? '[12] One must have nimble and active lungs to
appreciate some of these ' turlupinades.'

By false analogy, especially in a grammatical sense.[13]

This figure is due to a false conclusion that two or more words,
from being analogous in form, structure, or conjugation, are analogous in
meaning also. Errors of this kind are common in ordinary speech, and
are called solecisms, or barbarisms ; in Comedy, however, they are
deliberately employed ' for the sake of laughter '. Of this kind are
Dame Quickly's slips, ' bastardly rogue ', ' as rheumatic as two dry
toasts ', ' honey-suckle villain', 'honey-seed rogue', 'thou hemp-seed ' ;[14]
Costard's ' Thou hast it *ad dunghill*, at the fingers' ends, as they say ' ;[15]
' Pompion the Great';[16] Launce's ' I have received my proportion

---

[1] κατὰ ἐξαλλαγὴν φωνῇ τοῖς ὁμογενέσι.   [2] *1 Hen. IV,* II. iv. 268.
[3] *2 Hen. IV,* II. iv. 173.   [4] *Tam. Sh.* Ind. i. 12.   [5] ibid. I. i. 31.
[6] *Merch. of V.* IV. i. 123.   [7] *Two Gent.* I. i. 73 sqq.   [8] *Rom. & Jul.* II. iv. 38.
[9] *1 Hen. IV,* II. i. 88.   [10] *2 Hen. IV,* I. ii. 161.   [11] ibid. 184.
[12] *Two Gent.* III. i. 310.   [13] κατὰ τὸ σχῆμα λέξεως.   [14] See esp. *2 Hen. IV,* II. i. 57 sqq.
[15] *L. L. L.* v. i. 82.   [16] ibid. v. ii. 502.

like the prodigious son '; [1] Quince's ' he is a very paramour for a sweet voice '; [2] Gobbo's ' Sand-blind, high-gravel-blind '. [3] Under the same head comes false analogy even of a learned kind, such as was common in English comedies, when logic was more commonly studied than at present, and the laws of language were attracting attention, but were not yet understood. These questions had a strange fascination for Shakespeare and his compeers. Good instances are the following:

Holofernes. I abhor ... such rackers of orthography, as to speak dout, fine, when he should say, doubt; det, when he should pronounce, debt,—d, e, b, t, not d, e, t: he clepeth a calf, cauf; half, hauf; neighbour *vocatur* nebour, neigh abbreviated ne. This is abhominable, which he would call abominable—it insinuateth me of insanie. [4]

Speed. What an ass art thou! I understand thee not.
Launce. What a block art thou, that thou canst not! My staff understands me.
Speed. It stands under thee, indeed.
Launce. Why, stand-under and under-stand is all one. [5]

Petruchio. Here, Sirrah Grumio; knock, I say.
Grumio. Knock, Sir! is there any man has rebused your worship?
Petruchio. Villain, I say, knock me here soundly.
Grumio. Knock you here, sir! why, sir, what am I, sir, that I should knock you here, sir? [6]

B. Laughter is derived from ' things ' in the following ways:

By comparisons which are complimentary or degrading. [7]

The employment of the former ' for the sake of laughter ' is not very common, except in the ' Gongoresque ' style of Armado, or the pedantic Latinisms of Holofernes; but Falstaff made some splendid experiments in imitation of Lyly: ' for though the camomile, the more it is trodden on the faster it grows, yet youth the more it is wasted the sooner it wears '; [8] ' There is a thing, Harry, which thou hast often heard of, and it is known to many in our land by the name of pitch; this pitch, as ancient writers do report, doth defile; so doth the company thou keepest: for, Harry, now I do not speak to thee in drink but in tears, not in pleasure but in passion, not in words only, but in woes also '. [9]

More common are instances of deliberate degradation. For a study of such ' odorous ' comparisons, in which Shakespeare almost equals Aristophanes, take the speeches of Prince Hal—that ' most comparative, rascalliest, sweet young prince '—and of Falstaff in reply:

Prince. I'll be no longer guilty of this sin: this sanguine coward, this bed-presser, this horseback-breaker, this huge hill of flesh,—

[1] *Two Gent.* II. iii. 3. [2] *Mid. N. D.* IV. ii. 13. [3] *Merch. of V.* II. ii. 37.
[4] *L. L. L.* V. i. 19 sqq. [5] *Two Gent.* II. v. 25 sqq. [6] *Tam. Sh.* I. ii. 5.
[7] ἐκ τῆς ὁμοιώσεως, χρήσει πρὸς τὸ χεῖρον, πρὸς τὸ βέλτιον.
[8] *1 Hen. IV*, II. iv. 446. [9] ibid. 458.

Falstaff. 'Sblood, you starveling, you elf-skin, you dried neat's-tongue, you bull's pizzle, you stock-fish! O! for breath to utter what is like thee; you tailor's yard, you sheath, you bow-case, you vile standing tuck![1]

Excellent too are Falstaff's description of himself and his page, ' I do here walk before thee like a sow that hath overwhelmed all her litter but one ';[2] Launce on his sweetheart, ' She hath more qualities than a water-spaniel—which is much in a bare Christian ';[3] Falstaff on Bardolph's nose, ' Do you not remember a' saw a flea stick upon Bardolph's nose, and a' said it was a black soul burning in hell-fire ';[4] the Boy's suggestion: ' Good Bardolph, put thy face between his sheets and do the office of a warming-pan. Faith, he's very ill.'[5] To show how prodigal Shakespeare was of his imagination in the cause of laughter, compare ' you are now sailed into the north of my lady's opinion ; where you will hang like an icicle on a Dutchman's beard ';[6] ' he does smile his face into more lines than are in the new map with the augmentation of the Indies ';[7] ' Now a little fire in a wide field were like an old lecher's heart ; a small spark, all the rest on's body cold ';[8] ' he no more remembers his mother now than an eight-year-old horse ; the tartness of his face sours ripe grapes : when he walks, he moves like an engine, and the ground shrinks before his treading : he is able to pierce a corslet with his eye; talks like a knell, and his hum is a battery. . . . There is no more mercy in him than there is milk in a male tiger.'[9]

By deception.[10]

In a sense, every metaphor, every jest, is a ' deception ', as it involves a tension of the mind which is suddenly dissolved, but here the ' deception ' is limited to ' things ', and may be illustrated by the plot of nearly every comedy of intrigue, such as Molière's. In its more limited sense, which Aristotle probably intended, it is illustrated by the false teachers in the *Taming of the Shrew* ; Falstaff's disguise as a witch ; Rosalind's ' Swashing outside—as many mannish cowards have ' ; the ambushing of Parolles by his friends. Such ' deceptions ' illustrate the ' sudden glory ' of Hobbes. The most complete example of this sub-head is that ' merry wanderer of the night ', Puck :

> I jest to Oberon, and make him smile
> When I a fat and bean-fed horse beguile,
> Neighing in likeness of a filly foal:
> And sometime lurk I in a gossip's bowl,
> In very likeness of a roasted crab;
> And when she drinks, against her lips I bob

[1] *1 Hen. IV*, II. iv. 271.   [2] *2 Hen. IV*, I. ii. 11.   [3] *Two Gent.* III. i. 272.
[4] *Hen. V*, II. iii. 42.   [5] ibid. i. 86.   [6] *Tw. N.* III. ii. 29.   [7] ibid. ii. 86.
[8] *Lear* III. iv. 114.   [9] *Cor.* V. iv. 17 sqq.   [10] ἐξ ἀπάτης.

> And on her wither'd dewlap pour the ale.
> The wisest aunt, telling the saddest tale,
> Sometime for three-foot stool mistaketh me;
> Then slip I from her bum, down topples she,
> And 'tailor' cries, and falls into a cough;
> And then the whole quire holds their hips and loff.[1]

With Mr. Bergson, we may find the origin of this species of the comic in the pleasure children take in pretending, or in ' disfiguring ' various animals and things.

By impossibility.[2]

Under this head come all degrees of unreason and unintelligibility. For example :

Clown. Bonos dies, Sir Toby: for as the old hermit of Prague, that never saw pen and ink, very wittily said to a niece of King Gorboduc, ' That, that is, is '; so I, being Master parson, am Master parson; for, what is ' that ', but ' that ', and ' is ', but ' is '? [3]

Autolycus. Here 's another ballad of a fish that appeared upon the coast on Wednesday the fourscore of April, forty thousand fathom above water, and sung this ballad against the hard hearts of maids.[4]

Sir Andrew. In sooth, thou wast in very gracious fooling last night, when thou spokest of Pigrogromitus, of the Vapians passing the equinoctial of Queubus: 'twas very good, i' faith.[5]

Here also must be classed those ' most senseless and fit ' men of the law—Dull, Dogberry, and Elbow ; Launce and his dog, ' Ask my dog : if he say ay, it will ; if he say no, it will ; if he shake his tail and say nothing, it will ' ; [6] and the countless clowns who, in mistaking the word, aped their betters, since ' foolery doth walk about the orb like the sun : it shines everywhere '. Shakespeare was, indeed, too wise not to know that for most of the purposes of human life, stupidity is a most valuable element, and so cannot be excluded from its due place in the ' comic '. In his inexhaustible humanity, the poet suffered fools as gladly as he did wiser folk, since, like Sophocles, he was of all men the most ' gentle ', and hated nothing that had blood in it, except perhaps the hypocrite Iago, and the ' prenzy Angelo '.

By that which, while not violating possibility, is devoid of sequence.[7]

Here should be classed that deliberate irrelevance which Ben Jonson called ' the game of vapours '.

Falstaff. By the Lord, thou sayest true, lad. And is not my hostess of the tavern a most sweet wench ?

---

[1] *Mid. N. D.* II. i. 44. [2] ἐκ τῶν ἀδυνάτων. [3] *Tw. N.* IV. ii. 14.
[4] *Wint. Tale* IV. iii. 277. [5] *Tw. N.* II. iii. 20. [6] *Two Gent.* II. v. 36.
[7] ἐκ τοῦ δυνατοῦ καὶ ἀνακολούθου.

Prince Hal. As the honey of Hybla, my old lad of the castle. And is not a buff jerkin a most sweet robe of durance?

Falstaff. How now, how now, mad wag? what, in thy quips and thy quiddities? what a plague have I to do with a buff jerkin?

Prince Hal. Why, what a pox have I to do with my hostess of the tavern?[1]

For studies in comic illogicality, the reader may be referred to the professional unreason of Costard, Dull, Dogberry, Verger, Froth, Elbow, and the rest of the glorious 'thar-boroughs', who, as is not unknown among officials, exalt the letter of their regulations above the spirit: nor must we forget Dame Quickly's 'twice sod simplicity'. 'Thou didst swear to me upon a parcel-gilt goblet, sitting in my Dolphin-chamber, at the round table, by a sea-coal fire, upon Wednesday in Wheeson week, when the prince broke thy head for liking his father to a singing-man of Windsor';[2] Launce's irony; Touchstone's dullness which was 'the whetstone of the wits'; 'the contagious breath' of Feste, who wore no 'motley in his brain', and was 'wise enough to play the fool, and to do that well craves a kind of wit'. Witness his immortal saw 'Many a good hanging prevents a bad marriage'.[3] Bergson remarks that comic logic consists in ideas counterfeiting true reasoning just sufficiently to deceive a mind dropping off to sleep. Of this kind is Falstaff's immortal soliloquy on Honour:

What need I be so forward with him that calls not on me? Well, 'tis no matter; honour pricks me on. Yes, but how if honour prick me off when I come on? how then? Can honour set to a leg? No. Or an arm? No. Or take away the grief of a wound? No. Honour hath no skill in surgery then? No. What is honour? a word. What is that word, honour? Air. A trim reckoning! Who hath it? he that died o' Wednesday. Doth he feel it? No. Doth he hear it? No. It is insensible then? Yea, to the dead. But will it not live with the living? No. Why? Detraction will not suffer it. Therefore I'll none of it: honour is a mere scutcheon; and so ends my catechism.[4]

It cannot be proved that Molière was a student of Shakespeare as he was of Aristophanes, and so it is a curious coincidence that Sganarelle (*Sganarelle*, sc. xvii) when contemplating a duel, employed the same reasoning about 'honour' as Falstaff does.

By the unexpected.[5]

The comic effects of the 'unexpected' are so varied that many writers have extended it so as to cover the whole field of the laughable. Thus, Kant has defined the 'comic' as the result of an expectation which of a sudden ends in nothing. Similar is M. Bergson's theory of the ludicrous effect of inelasticity or want of adaptability, since adaptability is necessary to the well-being of society, and laughter is

---

[1] *1 Hen. IV*, I. ii. 44.   [2] *2 Hen. IV*, II. i. 96.   [3] *Tw. N.* I. v. 20.
[4] *1 Hen. IV*, V. i. 129.   [5] ἐκ τῶν παρὰ προσδοκίαν.

the corrective of qualities regarded as unsound or disturbing of its equanimity. From this point of view, the laughable is something rigid imposed on the living. Thus, Bardolph's nose is laughable as having the appearance of being created by Art, ' all bubukles and whelks and knobs and flames of fire ', and independent of self. Laughable too is a person treated as a thing, as Falstaff in the buck-basket, and cooled, glowing hot, in the Thames, like a horse-shoe. Aristotle limited ' surprise ' to ' things ' (situations, &c.), but a great deal of the pleasure derived from this source arises from words which create tension, e. g. bold metaphors, comparisons, sudden turns of phrase, such as constitute, in large measure, the ' comic ' in Aristophanes. These are not very common in Shakespeare, but the following thoroughly Aristophanic turn may be quoted : ' I was as virtuously given as a gentleman need to be ; virtuous enough ; swore little ; diced not above seven times a week ; went to a bawdy-house not above once in a quarter—of an hour ; paid money that I borrowed three or four times ' (*1 Hen. IV*, III. iii. 16). Falstaff was also the cause that such wit was in his friends, ' A rascal bragging slave ! the rogue fled from me like quicksilver. *Doll.* I' faith, and thou followedst him like a church.' [1]

By representing characters as worse than nature.[2]

We learn from Aristotle's *Poetic* that Aeschylus represented men as better, Euripides as worse than nature. That is to say, Euripides painted life as he conceived it, in realistic colours, with all its foibles and weaknesses, and thus became the forerunner of Menander, Plautus, Terence, and Molière. The standpoint of Aristophanes and Shakespeare was different. Being a political lampooner Aristophanes' aim was to treat contemporary ideals as dross. The philosophers, like Socrates ; the demagogues, like Cleon, Hyperbolus, and Cleophon ; the statesmen, like Pericles, and even Nicias, the gods themselves, were not spared. In the *Knights*, the demagogues are blackguards, brazen-faced, illiterate, filthy knaves, whose only qualifications are ' a horrid voice, an evil origin, a swashbuckler temperament ' : fortified with these ' complements ', ' they have every qualification needed for success in political life '. The circumstances of the time excluded Shakespeare from politics, and his temperament, and possibly his inexperience of court life, did not fit him for such social satire as is found in Molière, but an exception must be made. In *Troilus and Cressida*, *Timon*, and *Coriolanus*, for some unexplained reason, the poet adopted the rôle of an ' ironic caricaturist ', with a malignity unequalled in Juvenal and Swift.

---

[1] *2 Hen. IV*, II. iv. 246.   [2] ἐκ τοῦ κατασκευάζειν τὰ πρόσωπα πρὸς τὸ χεῖρον.

Ostensibly, however, he spared his contemporaries, and vented the accumulated bitterness of his heart upon men who had been safely hearsed for some thousands of years.

Satire was a dangerous weapon in the spacious days of great Elizabeth, but a satirist ran no risk in calling Achilles ' a drayman, a porter, a very camel ' ;[1] or in accusing Ajax of wearing ' his wits in his belly, and his guts in his head ' ;[2] or of having ' not so much wit as will stop the eye of Helen's needle ' ;[3] the wit of Ulysses and Nestor might safely be said to have been ' mouldy ere your grandsires had nails on their toes ';[4] Agamemnon might have ' not so much wit as ear-wax ';[5] and Diomede might be ' a dissembling abominable varlet '.[6]　In caricaturing the tribunes in *Coriolanus*, and the once popular character Jack Cade, he came nearer to his own time, but neither the government nor the mob felt their withers wrung.　But one may wonder that the ' groundlings ' did not fling their sweaty night-caps at him when he spoke of the people—true, it was the Roman people—as ' our musty superfluity ' ;[7] ' beastly plebeians ',[8] whose only duty was to ' wash their face and keep their teeth clean '.[9]　From his experience in the theatre, Shakespeare seems to have had a physical repulsion from ' the mutable, rank-scented many ' ;[10] ' common cry of curs ! whose breath I hate As reek o' the rotten fens, whose loves I prize As the dead carcases of unburied men That do corrupt my air ' ;[11] ' a pile of noisome musty chaff '.[12]

By the use of vulgar dancing.[13]

This is not so fruitful a subject in Shakespeare as in Aristophanes and Molière, but comic measures were occasionally employed by him to please those in his audience who were capable of nothing but inexplicable dumb shows and noise.　Thus, Sir Andrew ' danced fantastically ' and was most tyrannically clapped by Sir Toby ; ' Why dost thou not go to church in a galliard, and come home in a coranto ?　My very walk should be a jig :　I would not so much as make water but in a sink-a-pace.' [14]

When one has a choice, by disregarding the best, and taking the inferior sorts.[15]

This sub-head is somewhat like ' the barber's chair, which suits every buttock ', but Aristotle probably would have limited it to cases

---

[1] *Troilus* I. ii. 267.　　[2] ibid. II. i. 78.　　[3] ibid. 84.　　[4] ibid. 114.
[5] ibid. v. i. 58.　　[6] ibid. v. iv. 2.　　[7] *Cor*. I. i. 232.　　[8] ibid. II. i. 107.
[9] ibid. II. iii. 65.　　[10] ibid. III. i. 65.　　　　[11] ibid. III. 3. 118.
[12] ibid. v. i. 25.　　[13] ἐκ τοῦ χρῆσθαι φορτικῇ ὀρχήσει.　　[14] *Tw. N.* I. iii. 138.
[15] ὅταν τις τῶν ἐξουσίαν ἐχόντων παρεὶς τὰ μέγιστα ⟨τὰ⟩ φαυλότατα λαμβάνῃ.

such as the following : ' The same Sir John, the very same. I saw
him break Skogan's head at the court gate, when a' was a crack not thus
high : and the very same day did I fight with one Sampson Stockfish,
a fruiterer, behind Gray's Inn. Jesu ! Jesu ! the mad days that I have
spent.'[1] ' You (tribunes) wear out a good wholesome forenoon in
hearing a cause between an orange-wife and a fosset-seller, and then
rejourn the controversy of three-pence to a second day of audience.'[2]
' This peace is nothing but to rust iron, increase tailors, and breed
ballad-makers. . . . Peace is a very apoplexy, lethargy ; mulled, deaf,
sleepy, insensible ; a getter of more bastard children than war 's a
destroyer of men.'[3]

*By using language which is incoherent, though there may be no lack of
(grammatical) sequence.*[4]

The best illustration of such ' incoherence ' is Nym, the man of
' humours ', who heard that ' men of few words are the best men ; and
therefore he scorned to say his prayers, lest a' should be thought a
coward '. ' Be avised, sir, and pass good humours. I will say " marry
trap," with you, if you run the nuthook's humour on me : that is the
very note of it '.[5] But Dogberry must not be forgotten : ' Write down
that they hope they serve God : and write God first ; for God defend
but God should go before such villains ! Masters, it is proved already
that you are little better than false knaves, and it will go near to be
thought so shortly '.[6]

Such is Aristotle's analysis of the comic. Though thorough and
conscientious, it is somewhat mechanical and external ;[7] and, like all
such analyses (even those of Professor Sully and M. Bergson), does
little justice to the combination, in Aristophanes and Shakespeare, of
wit, gaiety, swiftness of apprehension, lightness of touch, obscenity,
frivolity, and above all, the power to touch pitch without being defiled—
the ability to rise from ' the laystalls ' of buffoonery on the wings of the
most delicate fancy. For example, Falstaff, while affording instances
of every one of the above sub-heads, presents a great deal more that
does not submit to any analysis. As Bagehot said of him, ' If most men
were to save up all the gaiety of their whole lives, it would come about
to the gaiety of one speech of Falstaff.' Indeed there was much in

---

[1] *2 Hen. IV*, III. ii. 32.   [2] *Cor.* II. i. 78.   [3] ibid. IV. v. 235 sqq.
[4] ὅταν ἀσυνάρτητος ᾖ ἡ λέξις καὶ μηδεμίαν ἀνακολουθίαν ἔχων.
[5] *M. Wives* I. i. 171.   [6] *Much Ado* IV. ii. 21.
[7] Cp. Quiller-Couch, *The Art of Writing*, p. 105 : 'All classifying of literature
intrudes " science " upon an art, and is artificially " scientific ", a trick of pedants.'

common between the ages of Pericles and Elizabeth which impressed itself upon the language of Aristophanes and Shakespeare, so full is it of the intense animal spirits, of the freshness, daring, and intellectual vigour of those extraordinary days when, as it seems, every one from heroes to catchpoles, spoke in a tongue that was of imagination all compact. Shakespeare is said to have used fifteen thousand words— Milton being a bad second with eight thousand : we cannot say the like of Aristophanes, in relation to his literary compeers, as their works are lost, but the richness of his comic vocabulary is extraordinary (I have counted sixty-three nonce-words in a single play), and is equalled by that of Shakespeare and Rabelais alone. Hence he cannot be translated, so as to give the full effect of his language, except in the diction of Shakespeare. Certainly modern slang is not a suitable medium ; it is too ephemeral, too poverty-stricken, trivial, and mean, too little tinged with the hues of imagination which are never absent in Aristophanes. Be that as it may, many passages, hitherto held to be untranslatable, may be readily clothed in an Elizabethan, if not Shakespearian, dress : for example, take the celebrated passage in the *Clouds* (recited with breathless speed) :

Let them take me and do with me what they will. This back of mine I bequeath to be hungry and thirsty, to be beaten with rods, to be frozen, to be flayed into a pell, if I can but shuffle off my debts, and appear to the world a thrasonical, plausible patch, a go-ahead knave, sheer bounce, a whoreson wretch, a mint of lies, a coiner of phrases, a court-hack, a walking code-book, a clapper, a fox, a gimlet, a cheveril glove, a rogue in grain, smooth as oil, a bragging Jack, a halter-sack, a scroyle, a boggler, a hard nut, a miching mallecho. If they give me these additions, when they meet me, let them do their very worst—aye, by Demeter, if they list, let them make of me a dish of chitterlings to set before the minute philosophers.[1]

Even Aristophanes' most difficult puns can be readily Shakespearianized. Thus, ' I wonder why the flue is smoking. Halloa ! who are you ? ' ' My name is Smoke : I'm trying to get out.' ' Smoke ? Let me see ; what wood 's smoke are you ? ' ' Medlar wood.' ' Aye, the meddler. 'Tis the most searching of all smokes.'[2] ' Is your name Utis ? '[3] ' I warrant there'll be no utis here for you.[4]

---

[1] *Clouds*, 439.   [2] *Wasps*, 143 : Apemantus' jest, *Timon* IV. iii. 309.
[3] Οὖτις : Ulysses' jest whereby he deceived the Cyclopes.
[4] *Wasps*, 186 (Utis='merriment', cp. *2 Hen. IV*, II. iv. 21, '*First Draw*. By the mass, here will be old Utis: it will be an excellent stratagem ').

W. J. M. STARKIE.

SHAKESPEARE [1]

GOD-LIKE is the poet's power, to pass
Beyond the narrow limits of his being,
And share in many lives. Another's pain,
Aloofly pitied by kind, common men,
Stabs him with equal pang ; another's joy
He sees not as an alien spectacle
But feels with quickened beat of his own blood
And kindred triumph singing in his breast.
Through him the world's life surges ; in his song
Its din of clashing inarticulate tones
Grows meaningful and musical. His voice
Utters the Word of Power that breaks the spell
Binding the sleeping beauty of the world :
She stirs, and customary night grows pale ;
She wakes, and dawn is kindled at her eyes ;
She rises, and the prince in every heart
Beholds and worships his long-dreamed-of bride.

There is a spark of God in every soul
Conscious of being ; a diviner flame
Burns in the poet's deeper, wider life ;
And in thy spirit, Shakespeare, more intense,
More luminous than in all poets else
Shines the eternal sacred fire ; for thou
Alone of all man's priesthood, lived for all,
And gave our multitudinous mortal being
Its conscious soul for ever. Still through thee
Beats into us the pulse of all their lives
Who lived once in thy soul ; our finite lives
Reach through thee out into the infinite.

A. R. SKEMP.

THE UNIVERSITY, BRISTOL.

[1] From a longer poem by the writer.

SHAKESPEARE AS THE CENTRAL POINT IN WORLD LITERATURE

IN adding my own word on Shakespeare to the chorus of universal homage I speak as a student whose particular field of work is, not English Literature, but World Literature : the general literature of the whole world seen in perspective from the standpoint of the English-speaking civilization. In such a field of view Shakespeare makes the central point : the mountain-top dominating the whole landscape. As in the Middle Ages all roads led to Rome, so in the study of World Literature all lines of thought lead to or from Shakespeare.

It has been said that for the achievement of literary greatness two powers must concur : the Man and the Moment. The concurrence has for once taken place without limitations : a supreme literary individuality has been projected upon an historic situation that affords it scope for its fullest realization.

In Shakespeare we have the accident of genius that brings all the powers of poetry together to make one poet. Grasp of human nature, the most profound, the most subtle ; responsiveness to emotion throughout its whole scale, from tragic pathos to rollicking jollity, with a middle range, over which plays a humour like the innumerable twinklings of a laughing ocean ; powers of imagination so instinctive that to perceive and to create seem the same mental act ; a sense of symmetry and proportion that will make everything it touches into art ; mastery of language, equally powerful for the language that is the servant of thought and the language that is a beauty in itself ; familiarity with the particular medium of dramatic representation so practised that it seems a misnomer to call it technique ; an ear for music that makes the rhythm of lyrics, of rhyme, of verse, of prose, each seem natural while it lasts, and spontaneously varies these rhythms with every varying shade of thought : all these separate elements of poetic force, any one of which in conspicuous degree might make a poet, are in Shakespeare found in combination. The varied powers have blended with so much of measure and harmony that force masks itself as simplicity ; what Shakespeare achieves he seems to achieve with ' the effortless strength of the gods '.

The point of history at which Shakespeare appears is the period when the Renaissance has reached its full strength, and before dissipation of its forces has set in. The Renaissance brought together the three great things of literature : the newly recovered classics of ancient Greece, the mediaeval accumulations of romance, and a universally diffused Bible. The unity of Europe throughout the Middle Ages had constituted a vast gathering-ground for the richest poetic material. Western and oriental folk-lores, Christian religion and story, had come together in a Roman world which was the heir of the ancient Hellenic civilization. In the quiescence of all critical restraint the varied elements had coalesced into the literary exuberance which future ages were to wonder at as ' romance '. The whole material of Shakespeare's plays is drawn from this romance ; as the Miracle Play had sought only to dramatize incidents of the Bible, so the Shakespearian drama sets out to dramatize mediaeval histories and stories. On the other hand, Greek tragedy and comedy make the most concentrated form of art the world has known : a whole story is compelled into the presentation of a single situation, upon which plays the combined power of dramatic and lyric, and sometimes even of epic poetry. The Shakespearian conception of plot stands to classical plot as in music harmony stands to unison ; the plots of these plays are federations of the single stories that sufficed for classical dramas, with the details of these stories romantically expanded. Yet the highest constructive skill may fail if the poet has a narrow philosophy of human life. In Shakespeare's age the profound conception of life which underlies the Bible had become a general possession ; and it was a Bible still in its full force as literature, untouched as yet by the coming tendency to stiffen into Puritan literalism or harden into religious controversy. The genius of Shakespeare seizes the essentials of the three grand literary types, and escapes the threatening limitations. In Shakespeare's own phrase, we have ' the law of writ and the liberty ' : rules of art vanish in the higher law of inspired creative liberty.

With literature such as this the only method for the teacher is summed up in the word interpretation. The history of criticism upon

Shakespeare comes out as a series of retreating attacks ; critical systems formulated in more limited fields of art, when confronted with Shakespearian drama, can only reveal what in criticism had become obsolete. Analysis of Shakespeare implies reverent contemplation of the poetic product until the underlying principles have revealed themselves. It is the method of natural science : for, when Shakespeare is the subject of study, Poetry has become Nature.

R. G. Moulton.

THE GERMAN CONTRIBUTION TO SHAKESPEARE CRITICISM

THE War has made impracticable the co-operation of any German Shakespeare scholar in this collective tribute to his memory. But no estrangement, however bitter and profound—still less the occasional extravagance of German claims—can affect the history of the services rendered by Germany to the study and interpretation of Shakespeare, or their claim to recognition at our hands. The following sketch seeks merely to indicate some salient points. Of the work done in detail it is impossible within the present limits to offer even the baldest summary. A history of the growth and vicissitudes of Shakespeare's German fame, as such, lies outside our present purpose.

German Shakespeare criticism began late. When Lessing, in the *Litteraturbriefe* (1759), delivered its first remarkable utterance, Voltaire had been for nearly thirty years by turns the patronizing champion and the jealous assailant of the English poet. But the German discovery, if tardier, was of far better augury. In France Shakespeare had to contend with a great national literary tradition, and with the bias, only fitfully overcome, of a deeply ingrained Latin culture. In Germany he threatened no national idols ; her own earlier classical age was remote and utterly forgotten ; her Gallic taste was a superficial veneer ; and she stood on the verge of an intellectual and spiritual Renascence, in which the Shakespearian influence itself was to be one of the most potent factors. Their first acquaintance with Shakespeare was, both to Lessing himself, and even more to Herder and the young Goethe, a liberating experience, which discovered them to themselves and discovered to them also, at times, aspects of Shakespeare himself which his own countrymen had less distinctly seen. In sheer critical calibre none of the three was, perhaps, superior to the greatest of their English predecessors. But they saw Shakespeare with eyes freed from some obstructions incident to the special circumstances and history of England,

and quickened also by new kinds of intellectual and poetic experience. None of them, certainly, understood Shakespeare so intimately as Dryden. But Lessing, at once a sharp assailant of French classicism and a brilliant Hellenist, perceived more clearly than any predecessor the extent of the divergence between the former and Aristotle; and moreover, what had been at most suggested by a French rebel or two before, that the deeper teaching of Aristotle was not traversed but illustrated and confirmed by Shakespeare. Lessing doubtless put the case strongly; he was making a point against French tragedy. But his trenchant assertion that Shakespeare, without knowing Aristotle, had come nearer to him than Corneille, who knew him well, was nevertheless a discovery; one which a more scholarly Dryden, or a non-Puritan Milton, might conceivably have anticipated, but which neither approached. The too rigid antithesis between Shakespeare's 'Nature' and the 'rules' in which criticism had hitherto moved, Lessing in effect broke down; with him, it is hardly too much to say, begins the study of Shakespeare's mind and *art*.

Herder, too, thought that Aristotle 'would have greeted Shakespeare as a new Sophocles'. He regarded both, however, less as artists than as poetic creators who, as such, had enlarged the realm of reality. This Greek thought had become, as a lively figure of speech, a commonplace of criticism; with Herder, and the German idealists of the next generation, it became once more a living faith: 'Here we have no feigner (*Dichter*),' he exclaimed; 'but creation; history of the world;' a conception which, however rhapsodically stated and extravagantly applied, powerfully promoted the study of the Shakespearian drama neither as 'imitation' of actuality nor as fictitious departure from it, but as the authentic document of a higher though related form of existence, with its own laws of life, by which alone it was to be judged. To judge it by extrinsic 'rules' was to commit an irrelevance. Many had defended or excused Shakespeare for not observing them: few, if any, had anticipated Herder's indignant repudiation of the very attempt to *defend* him for it.

Goethe, who, as a Leipzig student, 'devoured' Shakespeare in 1766, withdrew later from the unqualified idolatry of his early manhood. But *Goetz von Berlichingen* (1774) is beyond question the finest play inspired by Shakespeare's Histories. And the famous analysis of Hamlet in *Wilhelm Meister* (*Lehrjahre*, Book IV. ch. 13), though misleading and in some of its implications quite wrong, virtually started the Hamlet problem. The simile of the 'costly vase' with the oak-tree planted in it did not solve, or even rightly state, that problem, but it threw out a valuable hint towards its solution. Hamlet, for Goethe, was only the frail vase,—the 'beautiful, pure, and noble being' on whom too heavy a burden is laid. But it was soon perceived that Hamlet's strength as well as his weakness is implicated in his failure ; that he is in some sort the oak-tree as well as the vase. A. W. Schlegel was apparently the first to declare that his intellectual energy was a direct source of his inaction. He even asserted that Shakespeare wrote with the intention of showing that 'calculating consideration which exhausts all the possible consequences of a deed' is bound to have this effect. But Schlegel equally recognized that Hamlet's intellectual energy is sometimes the outcome, instead of the cause, of his desire not to act,—that ' his far-fetched scruples are often mere pretexts to cover his want of determination'; and with this qualification, his view, reinforced, after its publication, by the analogous theory of Coleridge, became predominant in Hamlet discussion during the greater part of the nineteenth century. None of his German contemporaries rivalled Schlegel in comprehensive appreciation of Shakespeare—an advantage which he owed to the experience of transfusing most of the plays, line by line, into his own language ; his translation is itself a splendid tribute to Shakespeare, as moonlight to the sun. Among contemporary Englishmen, Coleridge, Lamb, and Hazlitt, in the previous generation Morgann, more than equalled him in delicacy and sureness of feeling. Yet Hazlitt did not greatly overstate the case when he said that it had been reserved for Schlegel to give reasons for the faith in Shakespeare which Englishmen entertained. Hazlitt himself no doubt brilliantly took up his own challenge. But Schlegel had then been for ten years in the field.

Of Schlegel's fellow romantics, even of his brilliant younger brother, little need here be said ; they contributed at most to heighten the prestige and popularity of the more fantastic side of Shakespeare's art, which appealed to their characteristic distaste for actuality. Nor did Goethe and Schiller effect anything by their quasi-classical adaptations of *Romeo and Juliet* and *Macbeth* but the completer triumph of Shakespeare's authentic art on the German stage itself. To Eckermann, however, in his last years, Goethe addressed many acute and original remarks about the plays, which are still of value.

Among Schlegel's contemporaries there was nevertheless one who, though in no sense specially occupied with Shakespeare, was to exercise an enormous influence, for a generation, upon German interpretation of him. Hegel, even more than the later Goethe, approached Shakespeare from the side of the Greeks, and his aesthetic ideals, if not inspired by Greek art, were there most completely fulfilled. But the greatest of modern thinkers upon poetry was not likely to contribute nothing to the criticism of the greatest modern dramatist; and Hegel's theory of tragedy, as Mr. Bradley has shown,[1] if inadequate as it stands to the tragedy of Shakespeare, implicitly illuminates some neglected aspects of it. But Hegel's effect upon Shakespeare criticism was exercised mainly through his system as a whole, which between 1820 and 1840 permeated and mastered all the currents of German thought. In literary criticism his influence immensely stimulated that German super-stition of the ' fundamental idea ' against which Goethe had levelled a memorable sarcasm.[2] The well-known commentary of Ulrici (1839), and in a less degree that of Gervinus (1849), were monuments of intellectual energy inspired by a misleading assumption. But, as so constantly with Hegel himself, falsity of the main thesis did not exclude abundant by-products of subtle observation which would not have been made without it ; the light might lead astray, but its gleam discovered many a casual jewel by the wayside. After the middle of the century the Hegelian spell subsided ; and in the brilliant lectures of F. Kreyssig, the philosophy of the ' Idea ' survives only as an acute perception of organic unity, shorn of metaphysical exuberance, and solidified with shrewd judgement and Elizabethan scholarship. How fruitful, in this combination, Hegel's specific theory of drama can still be, is apparent from the influence it has confessedly exerted upon the most important contemporary discussion of Shakespearian tragedy among ourselves.

The decline of Hegel's prestige meant everywhere a recovery of the temper of sober, matter-of-fact research. Thenceforward the most important Shakespearian work of Germany was done in this temper, fortified by her iron industry; the fifty volumes of the *Shakespeare-Jahrbuch* (from 1864) are its imposing monument. In the investigation of Shakespeare's life, and in the finer handling of his style and verse, German scholars have seldom competed on equal terms with those of England and America. But in the exhaustive analysis of published literary material they can point to an extraordinary mass of solid and valuable work. Merely as examples it must suffice to cite the numerous studies of Shakespeare's sources, of his debt to his dramatic predecessors, of his use of prose and verse, of his grammar and syntax, of his mythology and folk-lore, and, recently, of

---

[1] *Oxford Lectures on Poetry,* p. 85 f.; the view that ' on both sides in the tragic conflict there is a spiritual value'.

[2] Eckermann, *Gespräche*, III, 117 f. (May 6, 1827).

his stage technique. The outlying topic of the plays performed by Elizabethan actors in Germany has remained a German speciality. And the gratitude of Shakespeare students all over the world is due to the great Lexicon produced, in his scanty leisure, single-handed, by the labour and sagacity of Alexander Schmidt.

Germany's contribution to Shakespeare study may thus be summed up as of two kinds : first, rigorous and exhaustive sifting of the literary material ; second, a wealth of ideas,—hypotheses, generalizations, *aperçus*—often fanciful, sometimes in the highest degree extravagant, even laughable, but put forward with an intellectual seriousness, and applied with a passion for truth, which have made them often more fruitful than the soberer speculations of more temperate minds.

C. H. HERFORD.

THE UNIVERSITY,
    MANCHESTER.

TWO SONNETS

1616

By Avon's stream, glassed in its rippling blue,
    Rises the great grey church, now glorified
    By a new inmate. See, the doors stand wide,
And little maids, first peeping shyly through,
Steal in on tiptoe. ' Ah, the tale is true !
    An open grave there by the chancel's side !
    And Master Sexton works with what a pride !
There surely lies the man whom all will rue.

' How oft we've met him on our homeward way
    Calling his dogs, or dreaming 'neath a tall,
        O'ershadowing elm ! and once he spoke to you !
The richest man in Stratford, so they say,
    Aye, and the wisest, and, says Doctor Hall,
        A famous name he has at London too ! '

1916

WE know thee now at last, Poet divine !
   The clearest-eyed of these three hundred years,
   Master supreme of laughter and of tears,
Magical Maker of the mightiest line !
When to dark doubts our England would resign,
   Thy patriot-voice recalls her from her fears ;
   Shakespeare of England, still thy country rears
Thy pillar and with treasure loads thy shrine !

Nor only England's art thou.   England's foe
   Stoops to thy sway, and thou alone dost bind
     When all the bonds of statecraft snap and cease.
O sign of comfort in a sky of woe !
   Above the warring waves and shrieking wind
     Thy starry Spirit shines and whispers ' Peace '.

G. C. MOORE SMITH.

SHEFFIELD.

A BIBLIOGRAPHER'S PRAISE

SHAKESPEARE has been claimed as a member of many professions, a rider of many hobbies. It is unlikely that any one will be found to maintain that he was either a librarian or a bibliographer. He has, however, given both librarians and bibliographers plenty to do, and from the results of their labours a few facts of some interest may be gleaned as to his early popularity, which may be accepted as a bibliographer's 'praise'.

The first proof of the popularity of Shakespeare's writings with his contemporaries lies in the numerous editions of his poems, and their extreme rarity. *Venus and Adonis* reached its twelfth edition in 1636, and, according to Sir Sidney Lee's reckoning, of the dozen editions less than a score of copies survive, while seven editions of *Lucrece* (the seventh in 1632) yield but thirty. A second proof may be found in the frequent attempts to pirate his plays. To run the risk of fine and forfeiture a piratical printer must have felt sure of a speedy profit on his outlay for print and paper, and only plays that had won a striking success on the boards could promise this. The pirates have been credited with more triumphs than they achieved, but their hits kept Shakespeare's company on the alert, and they scored heavily by capturing *Henry V*, the most vigorous and patriotic of the histories, and less decisively with *The Merry Wives of Windsor*, popular, it is to be feared, rather for its grossness than its fun, and *Romeo and Juliet*, the most passionate of the tragedies. As Mr. Madan has pointed out, we have another proof of the popularity of *Romeo and Juliet* in the special signs of wear on the leaves of this play in the copy presented by the Stationers' Company to the Bodleian Library at Oxford, where it was doubtless read chiefly by the young Bachelors of Arts. Next to *Romeo and Juliet* the play most popular with these Oxford readers was a classical tragedy, *Julius Caesar*.

By the double test of many editions and few surviving copies we know that in his own day Shakespeare's most striking successes were won with his Histories. The *Second Part of King Henry IV* fell flat from the press, but *Richard II, Richard III*, the *First Part of King Henry IV*, and *Henry V* were all great successes, running through five and six editions apiece before 1623, and so bethumbed that in some instances only a single copy survives. It must seem curious to us now that such of Shakespeare's comedies as were printed during his life sold but poorly. *The Midsummer Night's Dream* may have done fairly well, but neither *The Merchant of Venice* nor *Much Ado about Nothing* can have brought much profit to its publishers, and when *The Merchant of Venice* was reprinted, in 1637, so slow was its sale that as late as 1652 it was worth while to print a new title-page and reissue the old stock under the guise of another edition.

In the first years after the Restoration it may have seemed for a while as if Shakespeare was on the brink of passing into the ranks of obsolete dramatists. Neither his histories nor his comedies pleased the playgoers who took their cue from King Charles II. But soon after 1670 his tragedies began to come by their own, and by the end of the century *Hamlet, Julius Caesar*, and *Othello* were all established successes. Thenceforward Shakespeare's hold on the theatre has never relaxed.

Of Shakespeare's popularity with readers, as distinct from theatre-goers willing to buy a book of the play, the evidence is decisive. Four great Folio editions were sold in the seventeenth century, and in the eighteenth a succession of editors—Rowe, Pope, Theobald, Hanmer, Warburton, Capell, Johnson, Steevens, Malone—worked on his text. Until more than half the century had elapsed the representatives of the original publishers claimed the copyright of his works, but they behaved with some liberality to his editors, and it was only the cheap editions which they delayed. Towards the end of the century these became common, while as early as 1746 there appeared a French translation, and sixteen years later a German. No previous English writer had attained any such vogue in the century which followed his death.

The collecting of early editions of Shakespeare's works began with his editors and actors, Capell, Steevens, and Malone being the most prominent among the former, Garrick and Kemble among the latter. By the end of the eighteenth century the four large Folio editions published in its predecessor had won a place fairly high on the list of books without which no collection could be called of the first rank; but the Quartos, perhaps because of the abuse with which they had been un-critically loaded by the very editors who accepted their readings, were still sought after only by specialists in the English drama. In our own day a single Quarto has fetched a price higher than had ever been paid a few years ago for the finest copy of the First Folio, and a complete set of the first editions, published before 1623, has a higher pecuniary value than any other set of printed books occupying so few inches of shelf-room.

Bibliography, which of late years has cleared up a few misconceptions of literary editors, notably by proving that the edition of *The Merchant of Venice* which they accepted as the first was printed nineteen years after the date it bears on its title, has still something to do for Shakespeare. But the task is attended by an unusual difficulty. A few years ago quite a promising attempt to determine the number of presses used in printing the First Folio by the recurrence of certain bends in the brass rules which enclose the text on its pages was wrecked by the perpetual attractiveness of the letterpress at the foot of the columns. The problems of Shakespeare's punctuation and use of emphasis capitals, which offer a fair hope of recovering the alternations of level pace with rush or pause with which he intended his set speeches to be delivered, are hampered by an even greater hindrance of the same kind. But here at least the effort to extract results from minute investigations is worth the making. To help forward the better understanding of Shakespeare's text is surely as good a hobby as a quiet man need desire.

ALFRED W. POLLARD.

1616 *AND ITS CENTENARIES*

To trace the influence exercised upon a nation's history by a master-spirit of its literature could never be an unfitting employment for the student of either. And least of all could any attempt in this direction be deemed out of season, if made at a time when the revolving years specially recall the close of a life to the achievements of which a nation owes part of its greatness, and when its annals happen to have reached a stage destined to mark decisively the advance or the decline of its vitality. Contemporary witnesses of crises of this sort, whether themselves taking an active part in the settlement of the issues at stake, or surviving long enough to look back upon them as carried to a conclusion, can rarely measure the whole bearing, or define the exact significance, of the problems that occupy, or have occupied, the national attention. But where the moral and intellectual as well as the material resources of a nation are consciously thrown into the balance, the contributory inspiring and sustaining forces, among which the products of literary genius are most assuredly to be numbered, must necessarily be taken into account with the rest. The three successive centenaries of the year of Shakespeare's death, like that year itself, sufficiently, though not with the absolute precision of a school manual, mark the beginnings of very distinct epochs of the highest importance for the development of our national life, more especially in its relation to the life of other nations. This aspect of a Shakespeare Commemoration, which brings many of us together, at least in spirit, in the midst of the world's strife, therefore seems to call for notice, however slight, together with others appealing more directly to the reverential gratitude which is his for all time.

The actual year of Shakespeare's death is marked in our political history most conspicuously by an event—the fall of Somerset—of so secondary an importance as to have made no real difference in James I's negotiations with Spain and in his hope to make a Spanish alliance the corner-stone of his foreign policy. His mind was not yet made up, and

it was in this very year that he allowed Raleigh to depart on his last
and fatal voyage. Only three years since, James had given his daughter
in marriage to the young Elector Palatine, the crowning sign of his
intimate alliance with militant Protestantism. And, two years later,
there was to break out what proved one of the most protracted and
(after every allowance has been made for overstatement) one of the
most calamitous wars that have at any time convulsed a great part of
European civilization. That England, after much and eager debate,
should as a state not have become involved in the earlier phases of the
struggle, and thus, with the Pope and the Sultan, have stood aside from
the pacification which concluded it, was due to a twofold cause. But
though her isolation during the whole later course of the Thirty Years'
War was a consequence of the internal conflicts which rose to their
height under James I's successor and led to the Great Civil War, it was
the pacific policy of James himself that restrained her at the outset,
when the country at large—not the Puritan or the war party only, but
the public as a whole, and court and clergy with the rest—were in favour
of war with Spain. James I's mind was capable of grasping the conditions of the great problem of peace or war, though not of effectively
addressing itself to the actual situation, which is always the touchstone
of real political capacity ; and he perceived—what the body of his
subjects could not follow him in perceiving—the danger of identifying
England with the aggressive and even, in Protestant Germany,
isolated policy of his Calvinist son-in-law. But he was blind to the
folly of depending for the maintenance of peace on the application of
diplomatic pressure to Spain, which he sought to make possible by
the futile fabric of the Spanish marriage scheme. Thus, in the very
year in which the Bohemian war broke out, Raleigh's life was sacrificed
with an impotence to remain unforgotten either by the hero-victim's
Puritan partisans or by the English people at large.

What followed was a policy of which the whole nation shared the
humiliation, before James himself came to perceive its absolute failure.
The Palatinate had been lost ' in ' and with Bohemia, and James, who
had permitted English volunteers to go out to save his grandchildren's
inheritance had allowed Spain to levy a couple of regiments here to help
in preventing its restoration.

There is no reason for concluding that Shakespeare stood in any
distinct personal relation to the conflicts of opinion which at the time
of his death seemed on the eve of coming to a head in England, and
were soon to burst forth in open warfare abroad. What we may assume

as certain is that he regarded them, so far as they came under his cognizance, from a point of view to which it was impossible for him to shut his eyes. This was, in a word, the point of view of an Englishman. Perhaps no critic saw more clearly than Goethe that the essence of Shakespeare's dramatic genius lies in his direct reproduction as a living reality of the impressions derived by him from observation of the world around him ; and it was Goethe who, in one of the later of his deliverances on the adored poet of his strenuous youth, spoke as follows of the patriotic element never wanting in this process of recasting :

' Shakespeare's poetic creations are like a great fair, replete with living figures ; and this abundance he owes to his native land. Everywhere in him we find England, surrounded by the sea, enveloped in fog and clouds, active in every region of the world. The poet lives in a notable and important age, and reproduces for us, with much serenity of mood, its culture, and indeed its mis-culture also ; he would not exercise so great an effect upon us, had he not placed himself on the level of the strenuous times in which he lived. No dramatist has ever shown a more utter contempt for outward and visible costume ; he has a thorough knowledge of the inner costume of men—as to which they all resemble one another. It is said that he produced excellent likenesses of Romans ; such is not my opinion. His personages are all Englishmen incarnate ; but, to be sure, they are human beings, human beings from top to toe, and as such not ill-fitted with a Roman toga. So long as this is understood, his anachronisms are highly praiseworthy, and the very fact that he offends so often against the prescription of external costume is what makes his works so full of life.'

The life of Shakespeare had run its course under the clamour of great events without being brought into direct contact with any of them, even after the fashion of that of Cervantes (who died in the same year, though not on the same day, and who had borne a personal part in the glory, cold to him, of Lepanto). The English actor, as a favoured servant of King James I's court, can have been no stranger to the very genuine enthusiasm with which both court and public—no longer altogether synonyms—greeted the marriage of the Princess Elizabeth, and what could have been more pleasing to the poet than that the occasion should be graced by the revival of his last play ? For as such *The Tempest*, which there is every reason to conclude to have been reproduced (not first put on the stage) on this occasion, may assuredly be regarded. Though full of allegory like no other of his plays, it was not intended or desired by its author to offer on his part a solemn farewell either to the stage or to the life of affairs at large ; yet it reveals thoughts of such partings, which had passed through his mind as prophetic visitants. For the rest, there is no reason for supposing the retired burgess of Stratford to have been moved by the dictates of political or of religious partisanship. Of the former he cannot, on reasonable consideration of the outward conditions of his career, be suspected, and, happily for the creations of his genius, he was lifted away from the atmosphere of contending creeds by the intellectual freedom of vision which the Renascence had brought as its noblest gift to himself and his peers. Or are we to attach any significance to the fact that soon after James I's accession Shakespeare had been one of the members of his company specially attached to the household service of the Archduke Albert and his two Spanish companies at Somerset House ? Or, again, is it worth noting that the Earl of Rutland, to whom Shakespeare quite at the end of his life rendered a semi-professional service in devising an *impresa* for him with Burbage for a royal tournament, was a strict Catholic as well as a friend of Southampton, himself the descendant of a Catholic father and grandfather ? In so far as the Puritans are to be looked upon as in natural alliance with the war-party of James's later years, Shakespeare's antipathies were against these friends of Raleigh and foes of Spain ; but they were antipathies of humour mainly, of which he made a secret, though it must be granted that both in London and at Stratford he had cause for personal dislike. But his reflections on the Puritans are far from proving in the case of Raleigh, any more than in that of Essex, that he was anything but unfriendly to the man to whom their support was more or less accorded. For the rest, political freedom—a kind of freedom differing in conception from that dear to the heart of either the Ariels or the Calibans of the social system —and even from the freedom of thought claimed by Stephano—had not yet presented itself to this period of the national life as the ideal which it was to become to the next generation.

At the same time, any sober judgement will concede that, apart from the influence of man upon man, of which we know nothing, the views held by Shakespeare on national questions in his last years would be of little consequence, direct or indirect, as contributing to swell currents of public opinion, or, still less, to supply the motive force by which such currents are started or sustained. He had ceased to write for the stage, or even to take an active part in directing or controlling its appeals to further goodwill ; and though his plays more than held their own on the stage or at court against those of his fellow dramatists, there was no great demand for printed copies of them in the author's lifetime, and at the time of his death they still awaited the compliment of being published collectively, which was in this very year paid to those of Ben Jonson. In a word, even if the long-lived popularity of his first poem be taken into account, he was at this time, though praised and quoted in the world of the court, among university wits, and even in the pulpit, hardly more than a favourite in his own country, while the knowledge of his plays which had extended beyond it was as meagre as it was sporadic. ' Our Shakespeare ' was a name to conjure with among *dilettanti*, and in the world of his old profession ; but the time, though fast approaching, had not quite come, when the whole literary legacy, the bestowal of which caused him so little care, would be claimed as a legacy by the nation, and put out to interest in its behalf.

Thus, if on passing to the first centenary of his death we observe how greatly by that date ' the case had altered ', the process had really been natural and continuous. On the lapse of a century from the date of his death, Shakespeare is found, instead of a favourite only in literary circles and among playgoers, acknowledged as a national classic in his own land, and no longer a stranger to men of letters outside it. In 1716, Great Britain (as England and Scotland called themselves since their formal union) could look back upon the victorious close of a struggle of which the defence of the peace of Europe against systematic aggression had been the final cause, and upon the conclusion of a peace which at least had the merit of seeking to establish the political system of Europe on an abiding basis. The dynastic settlement at home, which virtually formed part of the general pacification, had not been undone by the '15, and the nation and the empire could look forward to generations of domestic prosperity and colonial expansion. It was as if the period of which the ' last four years ' of Queen Anne formed part had been called upon to take stock of the literary achievements of a community, whose political and literary interests had never before entered into so close a mutual intimacy, and as if the great writers whose names were definitively inscribed on the roll of its classics, were, like those of its great statesmen and classics, to acquire a freehold there for all future ages. Shakespeare had now been recognized as a ' great heir of fame ' by the unprejudiced pronouncement of one who was ' himself a Muse ', and he stood established as an English classic, to be prized not only for his incidental beauties, dropped as the careless ocean drops its pearls, or stealing on the ear like ' native wood-notes ', but for the power of his

R

poetic diction as a whole, which, as Gray wrote in one of his early letters, makes 'every word in him a picture'. Accordingly, the first duty of those interested in vindicating to him his place among English classics seemed to be to present it by textual revision and commentary as what it actually is and signifies. While the literary leaders of the age—a Pope, an Addison—held themselves called upon to bring their names into closest association with his, the acknowledgement of his incontestable superiority to all formed a kind of test of the truest distinction. The uncertainty of the national self-estimate in matters literary which in the latter part of the previous century had imposed the dictates of French classical criticism, more especially upon our dramatists, and to which Dryden himself had, with his eyes open, given way, was coming to an end, both in the study and on the stage ; and the nation's estimate of the greatest of its poets was being gradually freed from the bondage to which it had been subjected in deference to alien precept. At the same time, the welcome given to Shakespeare's plays on the stage, the surest criterion of the public interest in his genius, rose steadily to unprecedented heights, till it reached its culminating point in the career of Garrick. Whatever elements of excess may (after the manner of things histrionic) have made themselves perceptible in the oddly named, oddly dated, and oddly carried out 'Shakespeare's Jubilee' at Stratford in 1769, Garrick was entitled to pose as its tutelary spirit.

In 1816, the second centenary of Shakespeare's death found the national recognition of his genius still in the ascendant. In the theatre, where the Kemble constellation had long magnificently diffused its limpid light, the fiery star of Edmund Kean was appearing on the horizon ; and our libraries—in England and in America—were ranging on their shelves the great *variorum* editions that were in their totality to form the poet's chief literary movement. He was no longer an English classic only ; the German theatrical knowledge of his plays, which had begun after a fashion in his lifetime, had now become a literary knowledge also, and had grown into a critical insight, since Lessing had claimed for Shakespeare's genius the right of determining for itself the conditions of its fidelity to the laws of the drama. The enthusiasm proclaimed by a school of writers whose exuberant vitality was that of a new literary generation and whose reader was the youthful Goethe, had, with the aid of Schlegel's translation, become a popular devotion such as never before or since has been paid by any nation to the greatest writer of another. In the cosmopolitan eighteenth century, Shakespeare's greatness had not remained a secret to yet other countries ; but in France the fight had not yet been fought out with the traditions tenaciously defended by Voltaire.

Thus when in 1816, after another year of European struggle, this time waged against revolutionary France and its heir Napoleon, the British nation was in the most powerful position ever held by it in the political world, and once more stood before Europe as the victorious guardian of her peace, Shakespeare was already becoming a world-classic, in a sense in which this can be predicted of very few luminaries in the world's literary history. The century which had opened has witnessed an increase of endeavour and achievement in every direction of Shakespeare study and Shakespeare criticism—not the least on the side where in 1815 Wordsworth frankly acknowledged the superiority of the Germans, although Coleridge, it must be remembered, indignantly repudiated the supposition of a direct indebtedness to them. The age of comparative study of literature was dawning ; nor was it without significance that Guizot, the illustrious Frenchman who united to his appreciation of English political history an insight into that of the civilization of Europe, should have fathered the first adequate French translation of Shakespeare. And, nearing completion at the present turn of the century as reckoned by our dates, the great American *variorum* (to mention one other Shakespearean task handed down from father to son) brings home to us by the contents of this treasure-house of learning one of the most characteristic features of the age in which we move and live—cooperation, as applied to the work of the master.

The Tercentenary of Shakespeare's death, which, shorn of all external grandeur by the visitation of the present war, we are now celebrating, must fall short in this, as in the other, feature that it would have most signally displayed. For the world-classic, whose literary world-empire is no longer matter of dispute, the fullness of the homage that has become his right is wanting in the tribute now being paid to his greatness. As for the country of his birth and of his loyal affection, it will be truest to him if it can remain true to itself. For to Shakespeare no high and holy motive of action and service, least of all the love of honour and the love of country, are separable from true manhood, or from achievement—not the mere thought of it or wish for it—which is manhood's surest test.

A. W. WARD.

R 2

THE TWO EMPIRES

IF e'er I doubt of England, I recall
    Gentle Will Shakespeare, her authentic son,
    Wombed in her soul and with her meadows one,
Whose tears and laughter hold the world in thrall,
Impartial bard of Briton, Roman, Gaul,
    Jew, Gentile, white or black. Greek poets shun
    Strange realms of song—his ventures overrun
The globe, his sovereign art embraces all.

Such too is England's Empire—hers the art
    To hold all faiths and races 'neath her sway,
An art wherein love plays the better part.
    Thus comes it, all beside her fight and pray,
While, like twin sons of that same mighty heart,
    St. George and Shakespeare share one April day.

ISRAEL ZANGWILL.

LONDON'S HOMAGE TO SHAKESPEARE

WHAT is the vivid attraction that compels so many of us to love our London with a great love ? By some the cause of this sentiment is styled ' the lure ', but this word is too near akin to ' guile ' to harmonize with our feelings, which ring true as steel.

London has been and is the greatest business city of the world, and the history of commerce tells of her greatness. The river also, from which she was born, bears upon its bosom the riches of the earth.

We are all proud to be ' citizens of no mean city ', but there is something more than this. The Thames is full of wonders to be seen from the Tower to Westminster Abbey, so that its history is a fairy tale of doings that are written in the history of England. The names of Chaucer, Gower, Richard II, Elizabeth, Sidney, Raleigh, Shakespeare, and many others are written on its waters. The true glory of London, therefore, is to be found in her association with England's greatest men. To those who love her and know her history the very stones cry out, and the poorest streets, as well as the richer ones, remind them of the witchery of these names. Above all stands out the name of Shakespeare, who came to her in his youth. As a true son he loved his native town of Stratford, but his character was formed in London by the great men with whom he associated. London was his University, and teachers at that University were the wonderful men that abounded in ' the spacious days ' of Eliza's reign.

He longed to return to his home, but he did not forget what he owed to London, and London will never forget what she owes to him. He breathed the universal air of human nature, but he pictured the characters he saw in London. The Roman mob in *Julius Caesar* were doubtless true to the men of the classic city, but they were drawn from the men of London, and they were none the less true from being so drawn. London is proud that she did her part in influencing that master mind.

The outline of the Map of Elizabethan London placed upon one of

1916 looks only a small town, but to the Elizabethans, who were unable to conceive of any city growing to the size of modern London, it was a big place. Though Shakespeare's London was small, it was of as much importance relatively to other cities and towns as the present London is. The town still grows and will continue to grow, but the heart of the city is the same as ever and the spirit of Shakespeare pervades that heart. The old city has been altered almost out of knowledge, but the relics of his residence can still be traced.

Some may think that there is little to remind us of Shakespeare in our modern London, but is this really so ? The confident answer is ' No ! certainly not ! '

Let us try to call to mind some of the places associated with him. The actual buildings of Gray's Inn Hall and Middle Temple Hall still exist, where two of the plays were acted : *The Comedy of Errors* in 1594 at the former, and *Twelfth Night* in 1602 at the latter. The two Halls at these dates were comparatively new.

' The Great Chamber ' at Whitehall, in which so many of Shakespeare's plays were acted before the court, has passed away, but Mr. Ernest Law has shown us where it stood, and that beneath it were the remains of Cardinal Wolsey's cellar at York Place which still exists in the basement of the Board of Trade buildings. There is every reason to hope that this relic of the past, brimful of interesting associations, will be preserved in the new house that is projected for this Government Office.

Shakespeare's earliest residence in London known to us was in the parish of St. Helen's, Bishopsgate, and the fine church of St. Helen's still remains a beautiful survival. Bankside, where he lived for many years in the neighbourhood of the Globe Theatre, is much altered, but we cannot walk by the side of the Thames without picturing it as it was when Shakespeare's influence there was great.

Those places associated with Shakespeare which have been swept away have left something which reminds the student of him. In the windings of Blackfriars his shadow is to be seen. The roses of York and Lancaster are still occasionally exhibited in the Temple Gardens, although they do not flourish there now ; but there is little in Ely Place and Hatton Garden to remind us of strawberries, although we have Richard III's authority for believing that they grew there once. In Cripplegate we can look for the dwelling of Christopher Mountjoy, the Huguenot tire-man, where Shakespeare resided for a term. Farther on we can visit Shoreditch and see where the first theatre was built within the precincts of the dissolved Priory of Haliwell, with the site of the Curtain Theatre near by, although outside the precincts.

When Bolingbroke (then king) lamented the dissolute conduct of his son, he called upon his courtiers to ' Inquire at London 'mongst the taverns there '. We may obey the charge and search for the old ' Boar's Head ' at Eastcheap (now King William Street). We shall not find it, but we know that it stood where the statue of William IV now stands.

With greater eagerness we turn into Cheapside and seek for the site, in Bread Street and Friday Street, of the ever memorable ' Mermaid ' tavern where the ' Spanish great galleon ' Jonson met the English ' man of war ' Shakespeare in wit combats. This must be the most sacred of spots in our memory. The very thought of these meetings of the choicest spirits of the age fills one's soul with fire.

Our huge London has outlived many memories, but the memory of our master-poet is not one of these. It enlivens us as we visit in imagination the remains of old London, and the glory of his fame pervades the larger area of to-day.

London of the twentieth century forgets not the long list of her noble sons and daughters in former centuries, and will ever remember what they have done for her. She lives in the past as well as in the present, and her gratitude is worthy and complete. More and more she realizes her indebtedness to these worthies, and in this year of special commemoration she renders her devoted homage to the greatest genius of them all : William Shakespeare.

H. B. WHEATLEY.

A MEETING-PLACE FOR SHAKESPEARE AND DRAYTON IN THE CITY OF LONDON

' THE Mermaid in Chepe ' has gained immortal fame in Beaumont's famous lines; but there was another tavern of that name, 'The Mermaid,' Aldersgate, hitherto unnoticed, which Shakespearians will, I feel sure, henceforward associate with the poet and with his fellow and friend Michael Drayton.   This old tavern abutted on the City Wall and was an integral part of the ancient City Gate itself.   It is my belief that in *unbroken sequence* it is perhaps the oldest inn in Europe.   There is proof that it is the oldest in the City of London.   There, at the most northerly gate of the City, it stood already in early Plantagenet times.   It changed its name and became ' The Mermaid ' in 1530.   In 1651 it was called 'The Fountain'; after the crushing defeat of Preston Pans a Royalist owner dubbed it ' The Mourning Bush '.   And so it remained until 1874, when for some reason it suddenly became ' The Lord Raglan '. So it is called to-day.   But the glorious cellars that still remain are as Shakespeare knew them.   The tavern stands at the blunted angle of Aldersgate and Gresham Street, and it harbours some thirty feet or more of the original London Wall.

When William Shakespeare came to London the landlord of ' The Mermaid ' was a man who would have meant much to any literary aspirant of that day.

His name was William Goodyeare, author of ' *The Voyage of the Wandering Knight, Showing the Whole Course of Man's Life, How apt he is to follow Vanity, and how hard it is for him to attain unto Virtue.*'

But more important than this was his kinship with the great Warwickshire family, the Gooderes, ever nobly associated with the life-history of Shakespeare's famous contemporary Michael Drayton. Sir Henry Goodyear or Goodere, of Polesworth, had adopted Drayton when he was a small child,

> . . . a proper goodly page,
> Much like a pigmy, scarce ten years of age.

Drayton's love for Anne, afterwards Lady Rainsford, is enshrined in his sonnet-sequence entitled ' Idea '.

It may be accepted that when in London Drayton often visited Anne's kinsman ; and Shakespeare must often have spent a convivial evening with him at this ' Mermaid '. Surely in 1604, when the great dramatist was lodging with Christopher Mountjoy in Silver Street, he must have visited the famous cellars which, even in his day, were an old-world haunt.

We know that in 1603 Michael Drayton from this tavern witnessed the entrance of the King into the capital of his new kingdom. This we know from his ill-fated *Gratulatory Poems* and *Paean Triumphal*.

This old-world haunt should be brought to notice, I think, on this occasion. It has hitherto been forgotten.

MABEL E. WOTTON.

OXFORD AND SHAKESPEARE

SHAKESPEARE on his journeys between London and Stratford, and on his theatrical tours, must have got to know Oxford well. But his associations were with the City, not the University. Some of the warmest tributes during his lifetime to his ' quality ' are from the pen of John Davies, who had settled in Oxford as a calligrapher. And the familiar early tradition makes him an intimate of the family of John Davenant, landlord of the Crown Inn, who was mayor of the city in 1621. Probably one of Davenant's predecessors was present at the Oxford performance of *Hamlet*, for the Corporation was then entertaining touring companies, while the University was paying them to leave its precincts. The academic authorities had their own plays and amateur stage, and were anxious to keep professional *histriones* at a distance. The company to which Shakespeare belonged was one of those which was thus bribed to take itself off.

Hence Shakespeare had little reason to love the University, and we must not expect from him the glowing words that Greene puts into the mouth of the Emperor of Germany (of all people !) in *Friar Bacon and Friar Bungay* :

> These Oxford schooles
> Are richly seated neere the riuer side
> .   .   .   .   .   .
> The toune gorgeous with high built colledges,
> And schollers seemely in their graue attire,
> Learned in searching principles of art.

Though *Henry VIII* contains a noble tribute to Wolsey's great Oxford foundation,

> unfinish'd, yet so famous,
> So excellent in art and still so rising,
> That Christendom shall ever speak his virtues—

the lines are probably from the pen of Fletcher.

The only direct reference by the dramatist to academic Oxford is in the conversation between the Gloucestershire Justices in *2 Henry IV* :

Shallow. I dare say my cousin William is become a good scholar. He is at Oxford still, is he not?
Silence. Indeed, sir, to my cost.

It would seem that Shakespeare had heard more of the expense than of the benefits of a University education. Yet he was *naturaliter Oxoniensis*—a lover of classical philosophy, history, and poetry, though he had to read his Plato, his Plutarch, and much of his Ovid (even if the Bodleian 1502 copy of the *Metamorphoses* was once his) at second or third hand. Like Holinshed, from whom he learnt the annals of his own country, his interest was in Kings, not in Parliaments, and, had he lived, he would doubtless have taken the side of Oxford in the Civil War. The creator of Hamlet and Brutus knew the strength and the weakness of the academic attitude to life. Prospero, to whom his study was more than his dukedom, is the type of all who have deemed the world well lost for the life of contemplation. And Orlando, Bassanio, and their fellows, are they not akin to those who drink deep, age after age, of ' the joys of Oxford living ' ; and who, though they be

Young men whom Aristotle thought
Unfit to learn moral philosophy,

learn by the banks of the Isis something of the true issues and perspective of life? It is a strange irony that they should have ever been forbidden to attend plays that hold up the mirror to their own best selves.

But in spite of pains and penalties, undergraduates, and even their seniors, doubtless sometimes stole forth to see performances by travelling companies, or smuggled the quarto play-books from the London presses into college rooms and cloisters. The witty St. John's author of *Narcissus* (1602-3) was familiar with *1 Henry IV* and *A Midsummer Night's Dream*. Nicholas Richardson of Magdalen even quoted twice, in 1620 and 1621, from St. Mary's pulpit the passage in *Romeo and Juliet* beginning :

'Tis almost morning, I would have thee gone ;
And yet no further than a wanton's bird :

' applying it to God's love to his saints either hurt with sin or adversity, never forsaking them.'

The Balcony scene, in which these lines come, was (as Bodley's Librarian has told us) the favourite episode in Shakespeare's plays with young Oxford readers in the time of Charles I. For when a copy of the First

Folio reached the Bodleian in 1623, was bound by William Wildgoose and chained in the 'Arts End' of the library, the page that faced this scene became more worn by use than any other. Next to *Romeo and Juliet* the most popular plays with Bodleian readers seem to have been *Julius Caesar*, *Macbeth*, and *1 Henry IV*. Yet it was against the Founder's wishes that the library contained the First Folio at all. Sir Thomas Bodley held the orthodox academic opinion of his day, shared even by some of the best neo-Latin dramatists, that 'English plaies' were 'baggage' books, not worthy of a place on library shelves. Fortunately, however, under his agreement with the Stationers' Company in 1610–11, a copy of the priceless volume was sent to the Bodleian, where it remained till the Third Folio, with seven additional plays, appeared in 1664. Then the First Folio became a 'superfluous book', and Oxford saw it no more for two centuries and a half. Its chance return, its 'recognition' on the approved principles of Attic drama, and its re-purchase at a great price, form a romance too fresh in memory to need telling here.

It is astonishing that while it lay open to Bodleian readers, though some, like Burton, quoted from it, only one seems to have paid a tribute to Shakespeare in an Oxford publication. In 1640 a tragedy by Samuel Hartlib, B.A., of Exeter College, was issued, with the customary verse prefaces by admiring friends. Among them was Nicholas Downey of the same college, who declared that 'sad Melpomene'

> Casts off the heavy buskins, which she wore,
> Quickens her leaden pace, and runnes before,
> Hyes to pale *Shakespeare's* urne and from his tombe
> Takes up the bayes, and hither is she come.

Whatever may be thought of Downey's critical perception in looking upon *Sicily and Naples* as the lineal successor to *Hamlet* or *Macbeth*, he at any rate recognized that Shakespeare was the great exemplar of tragic art.

About forty years later John Aubrey, the Oxford antiquary, in the MS. notes which form the first 'brief life' of the dramatist, emphasized his comic genius : 'His Comedies will remaine witt as long as the English tongue is understood, for that he handles *mores hominium*.' And in a miscellany 'by Oxford Hands' (1685) he was promised, with a touch of patronage, eternal fame with 'matchless Jonson' and 'lofty Lee' :

> Shake'spear, though rude, yet his immortal wit
> Shall never to the stroke of time submit.

In the same year the Fourth Folio was published, and on it (with three additions) Gerard Langbaine based his list of the dramatist's plays in his *Account of the English Dramatick Poets*, published at Oxford in 1691. Though his detailed criticisms are unilluminating, his general tribute to Shakespeare's genius is more unqualified than any that had yet come from an Oxford pen. He does not hesitate to place him on a higher level than even Jonson or Fletcher, and boldly avows that he esteems his plays 'beyond any that have ever been published in our Language'.

In the same year Langbaine became Architypographus of the University Press, but he died in 1692, and the world had to wait till 1744 for the first Oxford edition of Shakespeare's plays. As the Vice-Chancellor, Walter Hodges, wrote his *imprimatur* on its title-page on March 26, the shades of his Elizabethan predecessors might well have looked over his shoulder in agonized reproof. For the University was issuing the 'baggage books' in six sumptuous volumes, finely printed, adorned with engravings, and edited (though anonymously) by no less a person than a former Speaker of the House of Commons, Sir Thomas Hanmer. As 'one of the great Admirers of this incomparable Author' he professed to offer 'a true and correct edition of Shakespeare's works cleared from the corruptions with which they have hitherto abounded'. The claim cannot be sustained, for he mainly followed Pope and Theobald, and his emendations were merely the result of his own ingenuity. But in spite of its critical deficiencies Hanmer's edition was, in his own phrase, the first 'monument' raised to Shakespeare in Oxford.

It won an enthusiastic welcome from William Collins, then a demy of Magdalen, who declared that the editor had done for Shakespeare what 'some former Hanmer' had done for the scattered Homeric lays. Collins's *Epistle*, wherein Shakespeare is hailed as 'the perfect boast of time' uniting 'Tuscan fancy' and 'Athenian strength', was naturally included in the second edition of Hanmer's work, issued in 1770–1.

It is curious that for almost a century from this date, except for a six-volume edition by Joseph Rann, a Coventry Vicar, in 1786, no work bearing on Shakespeare came from the University Press. Neither the general revival of interest in the Elizabethans due to Coleridge, Lamb, and Hazlitt, nor the presentation to the Bodleian in 1821 of Malone's magnificent collection of Shakespeariana, including the four Folios, seems to have stimulated Shakespearian research at Oxford.

But Keble's Latin *Praelectiones*, when he was Professor of Poetry (1832–41), contain so many incidental references to the plays, especially *Hamlet*, and comparisons between Greek and Elizabethan dramatic methods that we regret there is no lecture on ' *Shaksperus noster* ', ' *Tragædorum ille princeps* ' by the author of *The Christian Year*. Nor did the greatest of Keble's successors, Matthew Arnold (1857–67), discourse on Shakespeare except incidentally in illustration of ' the grand style '. It was not till our own day that ' Shakespearian Tragedy ' was illuminated from the Chair of Poetry, and that Shakespeare as a ' Man of Letters ' was interpreted by the first Oxford Professor of English Literature.

When the University Press at last broke silence it spoke with a voice other than its own. W. G. Clark and Aldis Wright, who had recently completed the ' Cambridge Shakespeare ', brought out in 1868 the first Clarendon Press edition of a single Shakespearian play. It was *The Merchant of Venice*, followed by fifteen others, of which the twelve after 1874 were edited by Wright alone. Their exact and fastidious scholarship has given them classic rank, but was ' caviare ' to the schoolboys and schoolgirls into whose hands they have largely come. They began that intimate connexion between the University Press and Shakespearian study which has been so marked a feature of recent years. It is to this that we owe an ' Oxford Shakespeare ' in one volume; facsimiles of the First Folio and the Poems; editions of the Shakespeare Apocrypha and of the works of many of the dramatist's contemporaries; a Shakespeare Glossary founded on the great *Dictionary*; and a monograph on Shakespearian punctuation.

But a playwright can only come fully into his own on the stage. The tradition of hostility to the theatre, inherited from Tudor times, lingered in the University long after the colleges had ceased to act plays. The City, on its part, discontinued its support of touring companies. Hence the theatre in Oxford from the eighteenth to the later nineteenth century fell upon evil days. Where *Hamlet* had once been acted, playgoers were offered the ribaldry of a low-class music-hall. But the dramatic revival in the later Victorian period did not leave Oxford untouched. The performance of the *Agamemnon* in Greek at Balliol in 1880 encouraged those who were struggling to give English drama a worthier place in academic life. They gained their end when Jowett, as Vice-Chancellor, authorized public performances by undergraduates of Greek or Shakespearian plays. In December, 1883, *The Merchant of Venice* was produced, and the event had greater significance in Oxford annals than probably any of those present (including the writer of this article) fully realized. For the first time a play of Shakespeare was acted by members of the University in the Town Hall, and the performance thus symbolized the close of the historic feud between the academic and civic authorities concerning stage-plays. But the drama in Oxford needed a home of its own, and on February 13, 1886, the New Theatre was opened with a production of *Twelfth Night*, the first of a long series of Shakespearian revivals.

If therefore the dramatist, like the Ghost of Hamlet the elder (a part probably played by him at Oxford), were to revisit the glimpses of the moon in this Tercentenary year, he would find himself strangely welcome in the groves of Academe. With memories of the past thick upon him he would steal into the city, half fearful lest some new Marcellus might strike at him with his partisan. But where he had once, as a travelling player, to endure 'the insolence of office', he would be greeted with reverent homage, and would be made free of the sanctuary of learning whose guardians had of old driven him and his professional comrades from her gates.

FREDERICK S. BOAS.

SHAKESPEARE AND CAMBRIDGE

AT some date in or before 1603 the *Tragicall Historie of Hamlet Prince of Denmarke*, as the title-page of the First Quarto edition declares, was acted by his Highnesse servants in the City of London and in the Universities of Cambridge and Oxford. The reference may be to the two University towns, but it was a practice by no means uncommon for academic authorities to engage professional actors to exhibit their quality in College Halls, and as Shakespeare was one of the players of the company in question, and is reputed to have taken the Ghost's part in *Hamlet*, it is quite possible that he visited either University in a professional capacity. Slight enough, no doubt, was the knowledge of University life which he acquired under such conditions. Apart from the Fletcherian reference to Oxford and Ipswich in *Henry VIII*, he alludes to Oxford University but once, never to Cambridge.

And yet in the decade 1590 to 1600 there is ample evidence that Shakespeare was profoundly interested in academic life, and even had a rather particular acquaintance with the usages and parlance of English Universities. His plays of that time are full of University matters. The scene is laid in France or Germany or Italy—at Rheims or Wittenberg or Padua—or he conjures up a fanciful ' academe ' in Navarre. But the scene little matters. Universities all over Europe were so much alike in 1600 that any of them might stand for Cambridge or Oxford, and I think that Master William Silence, who cost his father so much money at Oxford, was in very fact a ' school-fellow ' of Lucentio, whose father had cause to complain that he and his sizar, Tranio, were spending all at the University of Padua.

Shakespeare's University plays are all of his earlier dramatic time. First is *Love's Labour 's Lost* (1591) with its ' little Academe ' of Navarre, whose fantastic statutes, three years' residence and compulsory subscription are so delightfully travestied from the conditions of Elizabethan Universities. Next in the *Two Gentlemen of Verona*, António debates, as the fathers of Sidney and Essex might have done, whether to send his son to a studious University or to the court. In the *Taming of the Shrew* there is Lucentio, who comes to Padua, vowed to apply himself to Aristotle's checks, and ends by professing the Art to Love. The 'premeditated welcomes of great clerks' which are offered to Theseus in the *Midsummer Night's Dream* have reference to such performances as 'entertained' Elizabeth at Cambridge in 1564. The same matter crops up in *Hamlet*, where Polonius tells of the 'brute part' which he enacted in a University play; and Hamlet himself is a truant from Wittenberg 'school'. After Nestor's reference to 'degrees in schools' in *Troilus and Cressida* Shakespeare has no more to say about Universities.

Oxford City must have been familiar to Shakespeare in his frequent journeys between Stratford and London, but it is an odd fact that the University usages and phrases which he was acquainted with are those of Cambridge rather than Oxford. The reason is obvious. The *Parnassus* plays—so full of references to Shakespeare—tell us of the lure of the stage for Cambridge graduates who had no prospect of preferment in the University or the learned professions. Among such graduates who drifted from Cambridge to the London tiring-house and there made Shakespeare's acquaintance were Robert Greene, who left the University in 1583, M.A. of Clare, but originally of St. John's; Thomas Nash—Ingenioso of the *Parnassus* plays—also a Johnian, B.A. in 1586, who 'after seven yere together, lacking a quarter' quitted Cambridge without taking his Master's degree; and Kit Marlowe, of Corpus, who graduated M.A. in 1587; to say nothing of John Day, of Caius, and other Cambridge dramatists. After 1601 the three former men had fretted their hour and were seen no more. Pickled herrings and Rhenish wine ended Greene in 1592; Francis Archer's dagger did for Marlowe in 1593; and Nash, after sojourn in the Fleet prison, died in 1601.

So with *Hamlet* ends, not begins, University talk in Shakespeare. But in and about 1590, when he was perhaps collaborating with Marlowe in *Titus Andronicus* and *The Third Part of Henry VI*, when Marlowe and Greene were busy with their plays connected with University fiction, *Faustus* and *Friar Bacon*, when Nash in his preface to Greene's *Menaphon* was addressing 'the Gentlemen Students of both Universities', we may be sure that in the tiring-room or the tavern Shakespeare heard much Cambridge talk, and hearing laid to heart. Something he may have gathered from his patron, Southampton, M.A. of St. John's in 1589, and something from the players and minor playwrights among whom were Cambridge men: the names of William Kempe, Robert Gough, and Richard Robinson, all of them in the First Folio list of players, occur also in the catalogue of Cambridge graduates of 1584 to 1592.

S

Of specially Cambridge phrase there is little or nothing in *Faustus* or *Friar Bacon*. It is the more remarkable that it repeatedly crops out in Shakespeare's plays. To Cambridge ears there is a familiar ring in the line of *Titus Andronicus* :

> Knock at his study, where, they say, he keeps.

' Keep ' in the sense ' dwell ' is, of course, common enough in Elizabethan English. But in its association with ' study ' I think that it had its suggestion in Cambridge parlance. ' Study ' was the regular Cambridge name for the closet-space allotted to the individual student in the common room.

From the earliest days to times comparatively recent a candidate for a degree at Cambridge was required to maintain a syllogistical dispute in the schools, which disputation was called ' the Act '. If he was successful and admitted to the full privileges of a graduate he was said ' to commence ' in Arts or a Faculty, and the ceremony at which he was so admitted was, and is, called at Cambridge ' the Commencement '. If the candidate went on to a higher degree he was said ' to proceed '. Remark how Shakespeare brings these three terms together in Timon's speech to Apemantus (*Timon of Athens*, Act IV, sc. iii) :

> Hadst thou, like us from our first swath *proceeded*
> The sweet *degrees* that this brief world affords . . .
> Thy nature did *commence* in sufferance, time
> Hath made thee hard in 't.

' Commence ' and ' act ' seem to have an inevitable attraction for one another, the one word suggesting the other, not always consciously. Thus in Falstaff's praise of sack :

> Learning is a mere hoard of gold till sack *commences* it and sets it in *act* and use :

and in the Induction of *The Second Part of Henry IV* Rumour says :

> I . . . still unfold
> The *acts commenced* on this ball of earth :

and again in *The Second Part of Henry VI*,

> As Ascanius did,
> When he to madding Dido would unfold
> His father's *acts commenced* in burning Troy.

But the clearest evidence that it was from Cambridge, not from Oxford, that Shakespeare learnt University phrase is in Lear's complaint to Regan of his usage by Goneril :

> 'Tis not in thee . . . to scant my sizes.

'Size' is the Cambridge word for a certain quantity of food or drink privately ordered from the buttery, and traces its origin to the old assize of bread and ale. The word and its derivatives 'sizar', 'a sizing', and the verb 'to size' are quite peculiar to Cambridge and its daughter Universities of Dublin, Harvard, and Yale. Minsheu (1617), quoted in the *New English Dictionary*, says: 'A size is a portion of bread and drink: it is a farthing which schollers in Cambridge have at the buttery: it is noted with the letter *S*, as in Oxford with the letter *Q* for halfe a farthing.' The 'abatement' of sizes was a College punishment, alternative to 'gating', to which there seems to be allusion in Lear's next words 'to oppose the bolt against my coming in'.

ARTHUR GRAY.

CAMBRIDGE.

SHAKESPEARE AND WARWICKSHIRE

What, Hal!   How now, mad wag! what a devil dost thou in Warwickshire?—
1 Hen. IV, IV. ii.

MEMORY holds a store of sharp-edged pleasures for the country-born. Those who have picked oxslips from the bank and ' violets dim ' in childhood ask no more of Paradise. Shakespeare knew the farmer's and shepherd's world hard by ' Cotsall ', where ' every 'leven wether tods ', [1] and sacks are lost at ' Hinckley fair '. Only book-learned town-dwellers, ignorant of all the peasant's heritage of ancient lore, could conceive of a better upbringing for a poet and playwright than this.[2] Artistically Shakespeare was of the people. That is why he refused to be entirely swept away, like lesser men, by the incoming tide of the learning of ' ancient Greece ' and ' haughty Rome '.

Moreover he was born in happy hour, when the country-side was not dead to the arts as it is now. The impulse the ' old ' Church had given to music and to drama was not wholly spent, and folk-festivals, ancient with the immemorial age of heathen magic, gave occasion for traditional dance and play and song. It is true that Shakespeare's lifetime saw the professionalizing of the stage and the passing of folk-play and church-play, but in his boyhood acting was still a people's art. Captain Cox led out the ' good-hearted men ' of Coventry in the folk-play of Hox-Tuesday before Elizabeth at Kenilworth, Herod of Jewry put in his great voice all the megalomania of tyrants from the foundation of the world, and the village youth at Pentecost still played their ' pageants of delight '. Not that even these players could escape the all-pervading atmosphere of classic story. Robin Hood and his traditional merry company of the greenwood might figure in the Whitsun pastorals, but the most moving scene was that

> Of Ariadne passioning
> For Theseus' perjury and unjust flight.

[1] *Winter's Tale*, IV. ii.
[2] Mr. Greenwood, in *Is there a Shakespeare Problem ?*, argues that Stratford furnished no ' culture ' for a ' rustic '.

The truth is that all Warwickshire that touch the great roads, that cross the county from side to side, was accessible to the ideas of the larger world. Shakespeare was no dweller in dreary uplands where no travellers pass; like his own Orlando he was 'inland bred'. Along midland highways came the throng of puppet-show and ape-bearers, tumblers, bearwards, and musicians,[1] and also the intellectual aristocracy of the highway, the Queen's servants or my lord of Leicester's players, who for two hours' space could fill the guildhall or the inn-yard with Greece and Italy, kings and clowns, and all the wide compass of the earth and heaven.

Was it after a scene like this that the restlessness of youth and the pull of London took him from his own people? Yet he came back. So Warwickshire, which gave him 'birth' and taught him all the life and tradition of the country-side, so that in his country scenes there seems gathered up all the age and sweetness of England, gave him 'sepulture' also at the last.

---

[1] The Coventry Chamberlains' accounts from 1574 contain scores of entries of payments to travelling entertainers. One entry has 'To hym that hath the poppitts & Camell xs.' See for the folk-festivals Chambers's *Mediaeval Stage.*

M. DORMER HARRIS.

SHAKESPEARE AND SCOTLAND

> Gracious England hath
> Lent us good Siward and ten thousand men.
> *Macbeth*, IV. iii. 189–90.

ON these cold hills had wak'd no flower of song
In darkened [1] Celtic or clear English tongue, [2]
When in imprisoned loneliness a king,
Turning an illumin'd page, heard Chaucer sing
Of Arcite, Palamon, and Emilye,
Of Biela-co-il, Daunger and Curteisye,
Of Fortune's cruel wheel, of Love more stern :
' The lyf so short, the craft so long to lerne,
The assay so hard, so sharp the conquering—
Al this mene I by love, that my felyng
Astonieth with his wonderful working,
So sore y-wis that when I on him think
Not wot I wel wher that I flete or sink.'
Back to the North that exiled monarch brought
Love, and the love of song, the subtle thought,
Well-ordered words and interwoven rhyme,
Colours of ' rhetorike ', syllables that keep time
In cadenced music to a beating heart,
And in the ' King's Quhair ' flowered a nation's art.
Chaucer sang clear in Scottish tune and phrase,
Or told again on loud, chill northern days [3]

---

[1] Regarded from the point of view of English-speaking peoples, who have seldom mastered the tongue of their Celtic neighbours.

[2] No really artistic poetry. In verse the writer has taken the liberty to touch only salient features, omitting much that would be requisite to a sober history.

[3]
> The Northin wind had purifyit the Air,
> And sched the mistie cloudis fra the skie ;
> The froist fresit, the blastis bitterly
> Fra Pole Artick come quhisling loud and schill.
> Henryson : *The Testament of Cresseid.*

Of ' glorious Troylus ' and fair Cresseid,
Fickle and false, how she a leper died.
In Dunbar's ' aureate terms ' and riotous rhymes
A dying splendour lit brave James's times,
Last King who in the old way to Lady kneel'd,
And died, as Roland died, on Flodden field.

From Scotland ebbed the tide of song, the day
Which broke with James with James faded away.
But in the town where Chaucer by the Thames
Kept his ' red-lined accounts ', or saw at games,
Upon her meadows green with daisies pied,
The King of Love, Alcestis by his side,
And by that stream, now other poets sung
To Chaucer's lyre retuned, with golden tongue,
Of stately swans, and maidens gathering posies
Of virgin lilies and of vermeil roses
' Against the brydale day which was not long ;
Sweet Themnes ! runne softly, till I end my song ; '
Sang of Love's lordship, and how Astrophell
In Stella's kiss drank from the Muses' well.[1]
A Scottish poet conned that well-woven strain
And, but in alien speech, he too was fain
To sing of love by Death[2] annulled, and love
Which flows from earth back to its source above.[3]
Of Sidney's, Spenser's pipe an echo rung
Through Hawthornden when William Drummond sung.

[1]   I never drank of Aganippe's well . . .
                       How then ? sure this it is
            My lips are sweet, inspired with Stella's kiss.
                       Sidney, *Astrophel and Stella,* lxxiv.

[2] Drummond's Sonnets, &c., on Miss Cunningham, written before and after her death.

[3]   Leave me, O, Love ! which reachest but to dust ;

               .   .   .   .

            Then, farewell, World ! Thy uttermost I see !
            Eternal Love ! maintain thy life in me !
                       Sidney, *Astrophel and Stella,* cx.

Compare Drummond's *Mania, or Spiritual Poems.*

Then Shakespeare came, and the soft, pastoral stream
Of English song, sweet as midsummer dream,
Floated far out and widened to a sea
Life-giving, life-reflecting ; fresh and free ;
Stinging and salt and bitter ; now a-dance
In sun-steeped bays of comedy and romance ;
Anon 'neath skies whose hurrying cloud-rack hides
The consoling sun, in chafe of clashing tides,
And thunder of the storms that vex and mar
Rolling its surf-lit waves toward Fate's fixed star.
And all those waves were lives of passionate men :
The unpitying, unpitied soul of Richard ; then
Hamlet's sore spirit that suffered scarce knowing why ;
Love's perfect martyr, the ' free and open ' Moor ;
Iago damn'd and Desdemona pure ;
Proud Coriolanus ; and mighty Antony
Dying in a kiss on Cleopatra's knee ;
The supreme agony of outraged Lear ;
And with these, shaken by remorse and fear,
The spectre-haunted Scottish thane, and she
Through whose strong soul in dreams alone we see.

So Scotland woke to fame in Shakespeare's page,
Land of the ' blasted heath ' where tempests rage
And witches roam, of ancient castles too
Where swallows build, which gentle breezes woo.
And when in Scotland poetry woke again,
From Shakespeare came the new heart-searching strain.
His ' wood-notes wild ' their sweetest echo found
In the Lark's song that soared from Scottish ground.
From Shakespeare Scott the inspiration drew
Peopled his page with such a motley crew.
It was not given him to evoke again
The moving vision of great souls in pain,

But o'er his humbler characters and scenes,
An Edie Ochiltree or Jeannie Deans,
A summer breeze from Shakespeare's Arden sings,
An echo of his genial laughter rings.
Since Shakespeare who our 'language had at large'
His anger or his mockery to discharge
In torrent of words, in flaming figure and phrase,
The high light and deep shadow of stormy days,
As he the Rembrandt of our English prose,
In whose rich page the life of history glows,
On Mirabeau and 'sea-green Robespierre',
Louis, his hapless Queen, Frederick and Oliver,
As in the round Globe theatre it shone
On Richard, Henry, Faulconbridge and John?

So by this shrine the Scottish Muse may stand
Holding her statelier sister by the hand.
Bone of his bone, clay of his sacred clay
Are we who face the welt'ring storm to-day,
One 'happy breed of men', one 'little world'
On whom the hissing waves of hate are hurl'd,
The envy and hatred of 'less happier' men ;
Yet see o'er English meadow and Scottish glen,
On fields of France, and in far scatter'd lands,
Western sierras, Australasian strands,
Mesopotamian marsh and African sands,
Through April glow of pride and shadow of pain
The sun of Shakespeare's England rise again.

H. J. C. GRIERSON.

SHAKESPEARE AND IRELAND

SOME years ago, when I was turning over the pages of Stanyhurst's *Description of Ireland*, the feeling was borne in on me that Shakespeare had been there before. At a time when the thoughts of the civilized world turn to Shakespeare with feelings of reverence and gratitude, it may be worth while to recall what was then noted, for it may tell us how Shakespeare came to think of Ireland ; and a knowledge of the source from which Shakespeare derived such knowledge of Ireland as he possessed may aid us in understanding what he has written.

The *Description of Ireland* forms part of Holinshed's *Chronicles*, the storehouse which had furnished Shakespeare with plots for his Histories. From the Scottish part of the *Chronicles* he took the story of Macbeth. And in the well-worn Holinshed which he brought with him to New Place, he found the story of a British king which was the foundation of *Cymbeline*. In the Irish portion of the *Chronicles* he failed to discover material which might be usefully worked into History or Tragedy. But if he found no plot, he found what was to his purpose when he would introduce into one of his Histories, a typical Irishman, Welshman, and Scotchman.

The stage Irishman of Ben Jonson and of Dekker was a comic footman. When Shakespeare presented an Irishman on the stage, he was a soldier and a gentleman. Captain Macmorris was ' an Irishman, a very valiant gentleman, i' faith ' (*Henry V*, III. ii. 71).

It has been often noted that the character of Shakespeare's Welshman has been drawn with greater care than his Irishman or his Scot. ' Fluellen, the Welshman with his comic phlegm and manly severity, is the most elaborate of these figures.' [1] Fluellen was drawn from the life. Captain Macmorris may be described as a lay figure, clad in certain habiliments indicative of his nationality. Captain Macmorris—whose name, a form of Macmorrough, was probably a reminiscence of the story of MacMorrough and O'Rorke's wife, as told by Holinshed—appears in one scene only, in which his national characteristics are

[1] Dr. Brandes, *William Shakespeare: a Critical Study.*

huddled one upon another 'with impossible conveyance'. All of these characteristics will be found in Stanyhurst's *Description* : 'Tish ill done,' cries Macmorris ; 'the work ish give over, the trumpet sound the retreat. By my hand, I swear, and my father's soul, the work ish ill done ; it ish give over ; I would have blowed up the town, so Chrish save me, la ! in an hour. . . . The town is beseeched, and the trumpet calls us to the breach ; and we talk, and be Chrish, do nothing : 'tis shame for us all ; so God sa' me, 'tis shame to stand still ; it is shame, be my hand ; and there is throats to be cut.'

Such is Shakespeare's Macmorris, *Miles Gloriosus*. Stanyhurst's Irishman is 'an excellent horseman, delighted with wars ', and 'verie glorious '.

Captain Macmorris falls into a rage at a remark of Fluellen, which if he had been allowed to finish it, would probably have proved inoffensive enough.

Fluellen. Captain Macmorris, I think, look you, under your correction ; there is not many of your nation—

Macmorris. Of my nation ! What ish my nation ? Ish a villain and a bastard, and a knave, and a rascal—what ish my nation ? Who talks of my nation ?

'The Irishman ', says Stanyhurst, ' standeth so much on his gentilitie that he turneth anie one of the English sept and planted in Ireland *Bovdeagh Galteagh !* that is English Churle !' Hence it was that Shakespeare derived his conception of an Irish gentleman, valorous, 'verie glorious ', choleric, standing upon his dignity as a gentleman, and ready to resent an imaginary insult to his nation.

Richard Stanyhurst was a fine scholar, educated at the famous school at Kilkenny which was in later years the school of Swift, Berkeley, and Congreve. He is placed with Spenser among the poets of the day by Gabriel Harvey. He was with Harvey one of the little knot of pedants who tried to ' reform ' English poetry by forcing it into conformity with the laws of the classical metres, and his reputation would stand higher if he had not ventured on a translation of the *Aeneid* of Virgil into English hexameters. There is much in the *Description* to interest a reader so eager for information as Shakespeare, and many things that he read there held a place in his memory. ' We shall lose our time,' says Caliban to his co-conspirators against his wonder-working master, ' and all be turned to barnacles, or to apes ' (*Tempest*, IV. i. 248). Various books have been suggested by commentators, including Gerard's *Herbal* (1597), which might have suggested to Shakespeare the marvel of the barnacle. They need not have gone beyond a book that Shakespeare certainly had studied, his Holinshed, for in it the story of the barnacle is to be found told in a manner which was likely to remain fixed in his memory. ' The inhabitants of Ireland are accustomed to move question whether barnacles be fish or flesh, and as yet they are not fullie resolved, but most usuallie the religious of strictest abstinence doo eat them on fish daies.' According to Giraldus Cambrensis and *Polychronicon* the 'Irish cleargie in this point straie'. Stanyhurst, loyal to his country, defends the Irish clergy, holding ' according to my simple judgement under the correction of both parties that the barnacle is neither fish nor flesh, but rather a meane between both', and therforth not ' within the compasse of the estatute '.

The interesting discussion which follows of the question whether there ' should be anie living thing that was not fish nor flesh ' may have been present to Trinculo when he thus resolved the difficulty :

What have we here? a man or a fish? dead or alive? A fish: he smells like a fish; a very ancient and fish-like smell; a kind of not of the newest Poor-John. A strange fish... I do now let loose my opinion; hold it no longer: this is no fish.—*Tempest*, II. ii. 26.

Shakespeare was the first to use the word ' bard ', which, in its origin, was applied to the Celtic order of minstrel poets, in the sense which is thus noted in the *New English Dictionary*, ' a lyric or epic poet, " a singer ", a poet generally.' The earliest instance of the use of the word in this sense which is quoted in the *Dictionary*, is the following passage in *Antony and Cleopatra* :

Enobarbus. Ho! hearts, tongues, figures, scribes, bards, poets, cannot
Think, speak, cast, write, sing, number, ho!
His love to Antony.—III. ii. 16.

His ' Holinshed ' told him of the Irish bards ; how ' the lords and gentlemen stand in great awe' of a bard if he be not bountifully awarded, and some such discomfortable bard was present to the mind of Richard when he said, ' A bard of Ireland told me once I should not live long after I saw Richmond' (*Richard III*, IV. ii. 105). Stray reminiscences of Stanyhurst's *Description* may be found scattered here and there throughout the works of Shakespeare. There he found a eulogy of *aqua vitae*, praising it into the ninth degree, and enumerating twenty-four of its virtues, somewhat in the manner of Falstaff's commendation of sack. This may have suggested Master Ford's unwillingness to ' trust an Irishman with my aqua-vitae bottle '.

Now for our Irish wars:
We must supplant those rough rug-headed kerns,
Which live like venom where no venom else
But only they have privilege to live.—*Richard II*, II. i. 156.

This is the Irish policy put into the mouth of Richard, as he departs for Ireland. How came Shakespeare to speak of the native Irish with contempt as rug-headed kerns, and with hatred, as venom which St. Patrick had failed to expel? A question to be asked, for Shakespeare is wont to attribute to characters in his play ideas and feelings which were present to his mind, and if another explanation of these words were forthcoming, it would be welcome.

Shakespeare's kerns were 'rug-headed', and 'shag-hair'd', for he had read in the *Description of Ireland* of the 'long crisped bushes of heare which they term glibs, and the same they nourish with all their cunning'.

He had also read in Stanyhurst an account of 'how Saint Patricke was mooved to expell all the venemous wormes out of Ireland', a slanderous suggestion from the *Dialogues of Alanus Copus; 'Dici fortasse inde a nonnullis solet nihil esse in Hibernia venenati praeter ipsos.'*

This suggestion is quoted with indignation by Stanyhurst, but Shakespeare, with dramatic propriety, put it into the mouth of Richard when he was about to carry out the drastic policy of warfare, followed by the 'supplanting' of the native Irish. To Irishmen it is satisfactory to know that Richard's speech is not to be attributed to Shakespeare's personal experience of Irishmen, but to his custom of making use, for the purpose of his dramas, of ideas suggested by some book which might happen to be before him at the time, or which recurred to his memory. As when writing *The Tempest*, he put into the mouth of Gonzalo, Montaigne's description of an ideal commonwealth, so, with greater dramatic propriety, he attributed to Richard an idea which attracted his attention as he read it in his Holinshed.

Every link connecting Ireland with Shakespeare is deserving of note at this time, and another can be found in the earnest and successful study of his works, for which Ireland has been for many years distinguished. Malone was in the first ranks of Shakespearian scholars in the eighteenth century. The Right Honourable John Monck Mason, a well-known member of the Irish Parliament, was also known as a Shakespearian commentator, and as the author of a volume on the works of Beaumont and Fletcher. In later years Ireland has given to Shakespearian literature John Kells Ingram, Vice-Provost of Trinity College, Dublin, and Mr. Craig, editor of the *Oxford Shakespeare*. Edward Dowden will be gratefully remembered as the author of *Shakespeare, His Mind and Art*. These were all graduates of the

University of Dublin, in which Edward Dowden was for many years Professor of English Literature. Plays of Shakespeare were often acted in the private theatricals which were a well-known feature of Irish society in the eighteenth century. A record of performances at a country house in the county of Kilkenny, in the year 1774, has been preserved. Four of Shakespeare's plays were presented. Sir Hercules Langrishe (the host), Henry Grattan and Henry Flood were the leading members of the company. Two playbills have been preserved ; one of *Macbeth*, in which Grattan took the part of Macduff, another of *She Stoops to Conquer*, in which it is interesting to find him in the part of Mrs. Hardcastle.

To-day an earnest and active Dublin branch of the Empire Shakespeare Society celebrates the tercentenary of the Master's death ; with maimed rites, by reason of the war, but with love of the man, and gratitude for the priceless gift that the civilized world has received at his hands.

D. H. MADDEN.

NUTLEY, BOOTERSTOWN,
CO. DUBLIN.

AN RUD THARLA DO GHAEDHEAL AG STRATFORD AR AN ABHAINN

How it fared with a Gael at Stratford-on-Avon

CEITHEARNACH de Mhuimhneach mhór mhodartha mhórdhálach do bhi ann, agus do baineadh a gcuid talmhan ó n-a shinnsearaibh, gur crochadh mórán díobh agus gur díbreadh tar lear mórán eile,—— preabaire nár mhaith aon rud do dhuine riamh do dhéanfadh dióghbháil dó. Agus thárla gur sheól an Chineamhain é go Sacsana, imeasg a námhad, dar leis. Agus tháinig sé go Stratford ar an abhainn, agus taidhbhrigheadh fís no aisling dó ann sin. Agus ar n-éirghe dhó as an aisling sin dubhairt sé gur mhaith sé do na Sacsanachaibh, agus go maithfeadh go deó, chomh fad agus bhéadh sé insan áit sin imeasg na ndaoine do chonnaic sé in a aisling. Agus do nocht don Chraoibhín a bhfacaidh sé ins an bhfís sin, agus do rinne an laoi.

A great, proud, morose kerne, a Munster man, who had sorely suffered, he and his folk; hatred was in his heart. The Sasanach were to him his enemies, and lo! by chance he found himself in their land, and he came to Stratford on the Avon, or river, and there there was revealed to him a vision or a dream, and on rising up out of that vision he said that he forgave the Sasanachs, and would forgive them for ever, so long as he could be in that place amongst the people whom he saw in his dream. And he revealed what he had seen in that vision to the Creeveen, and he made this lay.

I

buaiḋreaḋ móṙ do ḃain lem' ṡaoġal
Do ċiomáin mé óm' ḃaile anonn,
Aġus cia an áit a sgarṗaiḋe mé
Aċt roiṁ go Stratforḋ aṙ an aḃainn!

I

A great trouble drove me from my home;
To what place should I come
But east to Stratford on the Avon!

II

Ní h-áil liom Sacrana. Do ċuill
Ó'n nGaeḋeal, an tír sin mallaċt trom,
ṡeuc! níor cuiṁnig mé air sin
Aġus mé ag Stratforḋ aṙ an aḃainn.

II

England was not liked of me,
But I remembered this not,
I at Stratford on the Avon.

III

Ḃí ṡuaṫ do'n Ġall im' ċroiḋe go buan
An dronġ le cluain d'ṡág mé go lom.
D'imṫiġ, aṙír, an ṡuaṫ sin uaim
Aġus mé ag Stratforḋ aṙ an aḃainn.

III

I brooded on my ills,
But all this went away
At Stratford on the Avon.

IV

Cuaḋar amaċ san sruṫ i mbáḋ
ṡa ġluaireaċt ṡáṁ aṙ ḃárr na dtonn,
Dṗuiḋear mo ṡúil, a'r connac ṡís;
Ḃíos ag Stratforḋ aṙ an aḃainn.

IV

On the stream in a boat
I closed my eyes, and beheld a vision
At Stratford on the Avon.

V

Connaic mé móṙán taiḃḃre ag teaċt
Aġ riuḃal le rṗaċt anall 'r anonn,
Aġ brúġaḋ timċioll aṙ mo ḃáḋ;
Ḃíos ag Stratforḋ aṙ an aḃainn.

V

Spectres saw I a-coming,
Crowding round my boat
At Stratford on the Avon.

VI

Siúḋ ċugam Hamlet, maṙ do ḃí
An uaiṙ do ċlaoiḋ Polóniur crom,
'Dul le hOpelia, láṁ aṙ láiṁ;
Ḃíos ag Stratforḋ aṙ an aḃainn.

VI

Here comes Hamlet
As when he slew Polonius,
With Ophelia hand in hand:
I was at Stratford on the Avon.

VII

Connac an t-Iúḋaiḋe, sgála 'r sgian,
A'r Pórtia leir. Ḃa liaṫ a ceann,
Ḃí an bár 'na ṡúil, a'r an ṡuaṫ buan;
Ḃíos ag Stratforḋ aṙ an aḃainn.

VII

Shylock with scale and knife,
Portia beside him,
Death in his eye:
I was at Stratford on the Avon.

VIII

Aġus táinig Rómeo le n-a ġráḋ,
Ḃeirt áluinn aoiḃinn óg, ḋaṙ liom,
Aġus an bráṫaiṙ ṡinne an cráḋ;
Ḃíos ag Stratforḋ aṙ an aḃainn.

VIII

Romeo with his love
And the Friar:
I was at Stratford on the Avon.

IX

Connaic mé Lir 'r a ṡruaṁ le ṁaoit,
An reanóir crion ceann-éaotrom lom,
S a ḃeirt ḃain-ḋiaḃal 'ṁá leanaṁain riar;
Ḃíor aṁ Stratforo ar an aḃainn.

IX

Lear, his hair on the wind;
Bent, light-headed, bare old man,
And the fiendish daughters following him:
I was at Stratford on the Avon.

X

O'aitniṁear an ḃaintiṁearna ṁarṁ
Aṁ tiomáint roimpi a ḟir ḃí ḟann,
—Fuil an trean-riṁ ar ḃárr a rṁíne—
Ḃíor aṁ Stratforo ar an aḃainn.

X

Lo, the furious Lady
Egging her feeble spouse,
The old King's blood on her dagger-point:
I was at Stratford on the Avon.

XI

Connaic mé Oberon 'r a ríoṁan
A'r ḃoḋaċ taoḃ leó. Ar a ceann
Ḃí cloiṁeann a'r cluara araíl 'ḃaṁairt;
Ḃíor aṁ Stratforo ar an aḃainn.

XI

I saw Oberon and his Queen
And the Clown with the ass head:
I was at Stratford on the Avon.

XII

Connaic mé cúntaoir; ḃí fear caol
na nṁairtéal criorac-crearac, ann,
'S an meirṁteóir ṁreannaṁail 'maṁaḋ faoi;
Ḃíor aṁ Stratforo ar an aḃainn.

XII

A Countess too; and the criss-cross gartered
    one was there,
And the merry drunkard mocking him:
I was at Stratford on the Avon.

XIII

An ḃean Ḃeniṁeac óṁ ḃán féiṁ
Ḋo taċt an t-éaḋ, ḋo ḃí rí ann,
'S an Múrac uaṁal ḋuḃṁorm árḋ;
Ḃíor aṁ Stratforo ar an aḃainn.

XIII

The Venetian lady, young, white, gentle,
She too was there;
And the Moor, noble, dark, tall:
I was at Stratford on the Avon.

XIV

Ḋo ḃí mo ḋá ṡúil ḋúnta ḋlút
'S mo ḃáo aṁ riuḃal ar ḃárr na ḋtonn,
Aċt connac iaḋ mar ḋ'feicfinn tú!
Ḃíor aṁ Stratforo ar an aḃainn.

XIV

My eyes were shut,
My boat was moving;
I saw them as I might see you:
I was at Stratford on the Avon.

XV

Ḋ'imtiṁeaḋar amaċ óm' raḋarc
An méiḋ rin. Táiniṁ tuilleaḋ ann,
ṁan rṁaḋ ṁan rṁít aṁ teaċt ṁo ríor;
Ḃíor aṁ Stratforo ar an aḃainn.

XV

They passed away,
Others came,
A-coming all the time:
I was at Stratford on the Avon.

XVI

Ḋ'aitniṁear cuiḋ, níor aitniṁear cuiḋ,
Ḋo ḃí mo corp ṁan lút ṁan ṁeaḋair,
'S mo ṡúil ṁan léarṁur, mar fear marḃ;
Ḃíor aṁ Stratforo ar an aḃainn.

XVI

Some I knew and some not,
My body had no feeling,
My eyes were without sight like a dead man:
I was at Stratford on the Avon.

T

XVII

Táinig a'r d'imtig, d'imtig, táinig
  Aitreaċa, máitreaċa a'r clann,
Uapal a'r ipioll, pean a'r óg;
  Ḃíoṛ ag Stratford aṛ an aḃainn.

XVII

There came and went
Fathers, mothers, children,
Nobles and mean, old and young
  I was at Stratford on the Avon.

XVIII

Rigte a'r prionnpaí, earboig, pagaipt,
  Fir rtáta, daoine pinne greann,
Cairptíní móra a'r tincéirí;
  Ḃíoṛ ag Stratford aṛ an aḃainn.

XVIII

Kings, princes, bishops, priests,
Statesmen, folk who made sport,
Captains, tinkers:
  I was at Stratford on the Avon.

XIX

Bainríogna gleurta, daoine-cúirte,
  Luċt iarraiḋ déirce, cléirig peann,
Maigdine réiṁe, ceannuigteóirí;
  Ḃíoṛ ag Stratford aṛ an aḃainn.

XIX

Robed queens, courtiers,
Beggars, clerics of the pen,
Maidens, merchants:
  I was at Stratford on the Avon.

XX

Do ḃíoṛ pin ag teaċt im' timċioll
  Ní ṛanaḋoiṛ ṛó ṛaḋa ann,
Do ṛiúḃal mo ḃaṛc ṛó luat don ṁéiḋ pin;
  Ḃíoṛ ag Stratford aṛ an aḃainn,

XX

All came round about me:
They stayed not long,
My barque moved too quickly:
  I was at Stratford on the Avon,

XXI

D'ṛágaṛ im' ḋiaiḋ duine aṛ ḋuine
  Gur ṛnáṁ mo ḃaṛc aṛ ṛaḋ ón dream,
Gur rguiṛ gaċ taiṛ aṛ ṛaḋ do m' leanṁain;
  Ḃíoṛ ag Stratford aṛ an aḃainn.

XXI

I left them behind,
My barque sails far from the band,
Every ghost ceased to follow:
  I was at Stratford on the Avon.

XXII

Táinig ann pin an tSíḋ-ḃean aoiḃinn
  Titania maṛ ḃláṫ na gcrann,
D'ṛás ṛí a ṛlearg oṛ cionn mo ṛúile;
  Ḃíoṛ ag Stratford aṛ an aḃainn.

XXII

Then came the beautiful fairy woman,
Titania, like the blossom of the trees;
She laid her wand about my eyes:
  I was at Stratford on the Avon.

XXIII

Dúiṛig, de ṛreap, mé aṛ mo laige;
  D'ṛeuċaṛ uaim " cá ṛaiḃ an dṛong?"
Ní ṛaiḃ aċt ceó aṛ uaċtaṛ uiṛge;
  Ḃíoṛ ag Stratford aṛ an aḃainn.

XXIII

With a start I awoke,
I looked about—Where were the folk?
Nothing but a mist on the top of the waters:
  I was at Stratford on the Avon.

XXIV

Tá áit aṁáin do' tiṛ-pe a Sacrain
  'Na mḃíonn do náṁaiḋ maol a'r dall,
Agur ṛaoṛ o ṡangaiḋ, ṛuat, ṛoṛmaḋ,
  'Sí an áit ṛin Stratford aṛ an aḃainn.

XXIV

There is one place in thy land, O Sasana,
In which thy foe becomes blunt and blind,
Free from all hate—
  That is Stratford on the Avon.

XXV

Ꙇ Ꙇlbıon ꝺo ꞃᵹꞃıoꞃ mo ꝼınnꞃıꞃ,
  Ꙇ Ꙇlbıon nꙇ ꝺꝼoccꙇl ꞃleꙇrhꙇın,
ꞃꙇ ꝺuꙇıleꙇnn nꙇrhꙇıꝺ ꙇꞃ ꝺo ꝺoꞃuꞃ
  Ꞇóᵹ é ċum Sꞇꞃꙇꞇꝼoꞃꝺ ꙇꞃ ꙇn ꙇꝺꙇınn.

XXVI

Ꙇmꞇeóccꙇıꝺ lꙇıꞇꞃeꙇċ mıꙇnꙇ ꝺíoᵹꙇlꞇꙇıꞃ
  Ꙇ'ꞃ ꞃıꙇꝺꞃꙇꞃ ꞃeıꞃᵹe ꙇꞃ ꙇ ċeꙇnn,
ꞃı ꝺéıꝺ 'nꙇ ċuırhne ꙇċꞇ ꞃmuꙇınꞇe ꙇn Ꝺꞃuꙇꝺ,
  —Seól é ᵹo Sꞇꞃꙇꞇꝼoꞃꝺ ꙇꞃ ꙇn ꙇꝺꙇınn.

XXVII

Oꞃm-ꞃꙇ ꝺ'ımıꞃ ꙇn Ꝺꞃꙇoı ꞃın ꝺꞃꙇoıꝺeꙇċꞇ
  Ċuıꞃꞃeꙇꞃ mé ꞃíoꞃ ꙇnoıꞃ ım' ꞃꙇnn,
ꝼuꙇıꞃ ꞃé ꝺ'ꙇ ꞇíꞃ mꙇıꞇeꙇrhnꙇꞃ uꙇım-ꞃe
  —Ꙇᵹuꞃ mé ꙇᵹ Sꞇꞃꙇꞇꝼoꞃꝺ ꙇꞃ ꙇn ꙇꝺꙇınn.

Ꙇn CRꙇoıꝺín.

XXV

O Albion,
If an enemy knock at thy door,
  Take him to Stratford on the Avon!

XXVI

And from his heart shall pass
All ill will and the fever of hate,
Mindful of nought but thoughts of that Druid:
  Yea, speed him to Stratford on the Avon.

XXVII

On me that Druid has worked a druidism,
Which I now set down here in my verse:
He has won pardon from me for his land:
  I at Stratford on the Avon.

DOUGLAS HYDE.

SHAKESPEARE'S WELSHMEN

THAT Shakespeare ever crossed the borders of Wales must be regarded as doubtful. It is on record that the company of actors to which he belonged once visited Chester, and they were often at Shrewsbury, so that his eyes must have rested on the dim blue line of hills in the west, for the lowland dweller an old-time menace, but for the poet a land of faery and romance. No closer acquaintance with the country was needed to enable Shakespeare to create, as he does in *Cymbeline*, the atmosphere of the Welsh highlands, the clear, bracing air, the towering heights, the ' rain and wind ' of ' dark December ', the ' goodly days ' when it was a joy to bid ' good morrow to the sun '. His mind seems, indeed, to play around Milford Haven with a peculiar affection : tell me, says Imogen—

how far it is
To this same blessed Milford : and by the way
Tell me how Wales was made so happy as
To inherit such a haven—

lines which ring with a very different temper from the curt allusions in *Richard II* to Flint and the mysterious ' Barkloughly '. Yet, even in this case, although local zeal has found in Hoyle's Mouth, near Tenby, the original of the cave of Belarius, it is not necessary to assume that there was personal knowledge of the scene. Milford Haven was famous throughout the Tudor period as the landing-place of the Earl of Richmond in 1485, and for admirers of Robert, Earl of Essex, the district had the further interest that here, at Lamphey, their hero had spent his early days and made his best and closest friends.

But if Shakespeare never set foot in Wales, it is beyond question that he met many Welshmen. Age-long barriers had broken down with the accession to the throne of the Tudors of Penmynydd, and during the sixteenth century the stream of migration from Wales into England had been unceasing, until at the death of Elizabeth Welshmen were to be found in every department of English public life, as churchmen, soldiers, sailors, courtiers, merchants, travellers, and scholars. Some were men of good education, like Sir John Salisbury of Lleweni, one of the cultured patrons of the writers of Shakespeare's circle, and Hugh Holland of Denbigh, the author of verses which are prefixed to the First Folio. Such might say with Glendower,

> I can speak English, lord, as well as you.

Others, no doubt, spoke with an accent which bore testimony to their origin : their English, like Fluellen's, was not ' in the native garb ', making them easy targets for popular ridicule and fair game for the dramatist who wished to add to his gallery of eccentrics. It is not to be wondered at, then, that Shakespeare's wide compass of contemporary portraiture should include Welshmen : what is remarkable is that the painting should be so genial and sympathetic, as though the poet wished to record a conviction that the Welsh deserved honourable treatment, as a people whose solid virtues made ample amends for their little weaknesses and vagaries. All foolish deriders of the Welsh race are rebuked in Pistol's discomfiture, and the last word upon the subject is Gower's—' henceforth let a Welsh correction teach you a good English condition '. The poet's universal sympathy had dissolved the inborn prejudices of the Warwickshire rustic.

It does not at all detract from the clarity of Shakespeare's insight and the breadth of his humanity in this matter that his attitude was in accord with the current fashion in court circles in his day. With a Welsh queen on the throne, who drew her descent in an uninterrupted male line from Ednyfed Fychan, the chief counsellor of Llywelyn the Great, it was natural that Wales should be in favour and that Welshmen should hold their heads high. When Henry V, on the strength of his birth at Monmouth, is made to say,

> For I am Welsh, you know, good countryman,

he speaks as Elizabeth herself might have done, and we may, perhaps, conjecture that it was the rough loyalty of some Elizabethan Welshman which first suggested the honest, but uncourtly response: ' By Jeshu, I am your majesty's countryman, I care not who know it ; I will confess it to all the 'orld.' But Shakespeare's study of the Welsh temperament is far from being a mere echo of the polite adulation of the court ; it bears witness to close observation, not only of tricks of utterance and idiom, but also of bearing and manner, of mental habit and moral outlook. The first experiment was Glendower. Holinshed is, of course, responsible for his appearance in *Henry IV*, but Holinshed supplies no detail in the full-length portrait painted by Shakespeare, beyond a vague reference to 'art magike'. The

> worthy gentleman,
> Exceedingly well read and profited
> In strange concealments, valiant as a lion
> And wondrous affable and as bountiful
> As mines of India,

is entirely the creation of the poet—a dignified picture of the soldier and man of letters, not without a certain element of the bizarre, for Glendower takes himself very seriously and his superstitions are household gods, upon which no one may lay unhallowed hands. It would seem as though this first attempt to portray a Welshman had suggested a new field to Shakespeare, for in his next play—*The Merry Wives of Windsor*—he gives us another, of a more ordinary type, the Welsh parson and schoolmaster. Among the poet's teachers at Stratford was one Thomas Jenkins, and critics have not failed to see in him the original of Sir Hugh Evans. The character is, undoubtedly, drawn from life, and it may not be fanciful to read in it the malicious zest of an old pupil paying off the scores of many a year gone by. Yet the satire is not unkindly. Sir Hugh is peppery, a solemn corrector of other men's errors of speech, happily oblivious of his own, but he is very human, with his 'chollors' and 'trempling of mind', his quaint medley of madrigal and psalm, and his generous readiness to make common cause with his rival, when he finds that both have been befooled. The part he plays is honest, if somewhat unclerical, and he has the true Welsh turn for edification: 'Sir John Falstaff, serve Got and leave your desires, and fairies will not pinse you.'

But Shakespeare's finished portrait of the Welshman is, assuredly, Fluellen, which followed quickly upon the heels of Sir Hugh Evans and may, perhaps, be regarded as a development of the earlier sketch. For this, also, an original has been found in Sir Roger Williams, a famous warrior of the Elizabethan age, who fought in France and in the Netherlands and was buried in 1595 in St. Paul's Cathedral. Colour is given to the suggestion by the fact that Williams was the author of a *Brief Discourse of War* which attained to some reputation; like Fluellen, he was an authority upon the 'disciplines of the wars' and 'the pristine wars of the Romans'. Be this as it may, there is no more lovable figure in Shakespeare than the Welsh captain of *Henry V*—choleric, impetuous, born to set the world to rights, prodigal of his learning, and lavish of good advice, but inflexibly honest, valorous, patriotic, one whose zeal for righteousness is unfeigned and without malice. By Fluellen Welshmen of all ages are content to stand or fall; they are willing that the world should laugh at his humours, for they know that in him Shakespeare has given undying expression to the best qualities of the race to which they belong.

J. E. LLOYD.

I GOF BARDD AVON

Dros hil Taliesin ac Aneirin gynt,
A wybu gyntaf yn yr ynys hon
Gyfaredd cân, a'i clywai'n llef y gwynt,
Yn nhrydar adar, ac yn nhwrf y don,—
Dros wlad a noddai feirdd o oes i oes,
A gadwai'n fyw drwy'r nos y dwyfol dân,
A brofodd ias a gwynfyd cerdd a'i gloes,
A arddel fyth yr enw o wlad y gân,—
Y dygaf hyn o ged i gof yr un
A ganodd fel na chanodd bardd erioed,
A dreiddiodd holl ddirgelion calon dyn :
Allweddau'r enaid yn ei law a roed.
Brenin y beirdd, fry ar ei orsedd hardd ;
Fythol ddieilfydd, ddihefelydd fardd !

J. MORRIS JONES.

BANGOR,
   GOGLEDD CYMRU.

TRANSLATION

TO THE MEMORY OF THE BARD OF AVON

FOR the race of Taliesin and Aneirin of old,
Who knew first in this isle
The enchantment of song, who heard it in the cry of the wind,
In the twitter of birds, and in the roar of the wave,—
For a land that cherished bards from age to age,
That kept alive through the night the divine fire,
That has felt the thrill and joy of song and its pang,
That claims still the name of the land of song,—
I bring this tribute to the memory of one
Who sang as no poet ever sang,
Who penetrated all the secrets of man's heart :
The keys of the soul were committed unto his hand.
King of the bards, high on his stately throne ;
Eternally incomparable, peerless bard !

J. MORRIS JONES.

BANGOR,
    NORTH WALES.

Y BARDD A GANODD I'R BYD

NÔD Awen a'i dihewyd
Yw'r Bardd a ganodd i'r byd.
Pwy rydd gwymp i'w hardd gampwaith ?
Farweiddia nwyf arddun iaith ?
Safon llên a'i hawen hi,—
Uchter cynrych Tair Canri'.

[1] The Muse acclaims the Bard who sang for all mankind.

Who shall raze his noble fabric or dull his words— the glory of three centuries ?

Y gerdd ddygir i'w ddygwyl,—
I ddod yn hardd, daw yn ŵyl.
Os cawn wên i ysgawnhau
Llys hirnos mewn llusernau ;
Tra'r huan eirian erys,
Pa swyn i lamp sy'n ei lys ?
Yn nen gŵyl y Bardd arddun,
Wele, mae'r Haul mawr ei hun !

With modest mien this solemn year,
Let song exalt the poet-seer.

No glimmering lamps cheer the gloom of Night's dark palace :

to gild the bard's undying day the Sun himself will shine forth.

Pencreawdr pynciau'r awen
Ddramodol fyw, llyw ei llên.
Y ciliau biau bywyd,
I'w lygad gwawl godai i gyd.
Rhagoriaeth Gwir, a gwarth Gau,
Rodiodd trwy'i Gymeriadau ;
Y drych ar bob anian drodd,
A'r iawn fathair ni fethodd :
Saif eu cwrs i fywiocau
Sêl orysol yr oesau.
Galwodd Ffûg o leoedd ffawd
I gyhoeddus gyhuddwawd ;
Brenhinoedd a rhengoedd rhwysg
Ddaw'n ebrwydd â'u hoen abrwysg ;

The drama's arch-creator, crowned, he sways the magic deeps; he knows the soul's dark cells ;

Virtue and Truth, Shame and Wrong, in his pageants stalk before us ;
from Nature he drew his word-pictures :

his motley throng move us to laughter and tears.

Falsehood he summons to the bar of scorn ;

he sets forth Kings, battles,

[1] The marginal paraphrase is based on a metrical rendering in English by R. A. Griffith (Elphin), Esq., Merthyr Tydvil, Glam.

Mwstr brwydrau, banllefau llon
Camp cewri rhag cwymp coron ;
Daw'r Bradwr i wib-redeg— traitors,
Filain y diafl, â'i wên deg ;
Try Eiddig yn ffyrnig ffest,
O ymgernial mae gornest : rivals, fighting bloody
Rhoi hyder eu heriadau jowls ;
Ar fin y dur fynnai dau ;
Arglwyddes, oedd ddiafles ddig,— the Lady, nightly raving
Dyma'i nodau damniedig ! in accents wild ;
Â brud cosb cai'i bradog hûn her guilty sleep by terror
Ddiosg camwedd ysgymun ; racked ;
Ni cheir â'i rin ddewin ddaw
A gudd halog ddeheulaw.
Gwrendy dewr dan gryndod dôn the warrior cowering with
Gwŷs sobredig ysbrydion ; blenched cheek ;
Daw llais barnol bythol bau the phantoms muttering
O lithoedd drychiolaethau. from the gloom.

Ysbryd dwys i'w briod iau He links the spirit to the
A rwym synnwyr Ymsonau : word of fate, and brings
Try'n dyst yr enaid distaw witness of a world to come.
Fod i ddyn ei ' fyd a ddaw '.
Ymdyrr ar fy myfyr mwy Depths unplumbed must
Lif eneidiol,—ofnadwy ! still be sounded,
I'r diwaelod rhaid dilyn where man's long-hidden
Meddyliau dyfnderau dyn : thoughts are hid.
Ond os iddynt y suddaf,
Suddo'n nes i Dduw a wnaf ;
A ffoi i ddydd y ffydd ddi-wall
Wyr fod erof fyd arall.

Ni ddaw diwedd dihewyd To every heart shall aye
I'r Bardd a ganodd i'r byd. be bound
the Bard who sang for all !

J. O. WILLIAMS (*Pedrog*).

LIVERPOOL.

SHAKESPEARE AND KING ARTHUR

IT is a subject for comment that Shakespeare, with all his shrewd tact for what constituted a good tale, never apparently felt drawn to the legend of Arthur. At all events, no one of his plays is based on that theme : and this becomes only the more strange when all things are considered. It was not that he ignored the national heroes : the existence of his Histories confutes that particular charge. Neither did he regard Celtic legend as unsuitable for the stage ; for he himself was master of ' the fairy way of writing ', and moreover, he staged both *Lear* and *Cymbeline* with striking effect. Nor again, could it have been that the ' noble and joyous history ' was ground unfamiliar to his rough audiences at the Globe. It was, on the contrary, one of those popular stories to which the dramatist was wont to turn for the raw material of his plays : and that it was not lacking in dramatic possibilities had already been shown by the success of the academic drama, *The Misfortunes of Arthur* (1587). Nevertheless, the fact remains that Britain's one great contribution to the great world-stories was, for all practical purposes, neglected by Shakespeare, and the world is the poorer by at least one great drama.

It would, however, be wrong to say that Shakespeare entirely ignores the Arthurian story : in his works are occasional references, of interest in themselves, but most interesting for the light they throw upon Shakespeare's attitude to that theme. The allusions are all of a humorous kind : they are uttered by Falstaff, Lear's Fool, Justice Shallow, and the like, and, taken together, they represent a coarse burlesque of the old-world narrative. It is significant, to begin with, that Arthur and the Christian heroes are missing from the account of the Nine Worthies which occurs in Act V of *Love's Labour's Lost* (i. 123-4): their places there are taken by Hercules and Pompey, as if the great mediaeval figures had ceased to be of heroic rank. And such, indeed, is the suggestion of the references themselves, which all allude to the legend in light and ironical vein. Thus Falstaff enters the Boar's Head roaring a ballad of Arthur (*2 Henry IV*, II. iv. 32). It is Mistress

Quickly's belief that Falstaff in the end finds refuge in 'Arthur's bosom' (*Henry V*, II. iii. 10). Boyet, in brisk word-play, refers lightly to 'Queen Guinever' when 'a little wench' (*Love's Labour's Lost* IV. i. 125). Justice Shallow recalls the time when he played 'Sir Dagonet in Arthur's show' (*2 Henry IV*, III. ii. 285). Hotspur alludes impatiently to Glendower's conversation, to his ceaseless chatter regarding 'the dreamer Merlin and his prophecies' (*1 Henry IV*, III. i. 150). Elsewhere a parody of those prophecies is supplied by the doggerel of Lear's Fool (*King Lear* III. ii. 80 ff.), while Kent alludes with scorn to Arthur's home at Camelot (*King Lear* II. ii. 85).

Now the tone of these allusions is sufficiently plain : it suggests a theme that has been robbed of its freshness and glamour, a theme vulgarized and degraded through some mysterious cause. Of the romance of 'the gray king' no mention is made ; no hint is given of the high tragedy of Guinevere, or of the chivalry and prowess of 'Lancelot or Pelleas or Pellenore'. Guinevere, instead, has become a flaunting quean, Merlin a tedious driveller : the foolish Sir Dagonet alone of Arthur's knights is recalled, while their exploits are likened to the driving of geese to Camelot.

How then is one to account for this travesty of a splendid theme : on the part, too, of a poet who held within his gaze all that was beautiful and heroic in human life ? Is it the same elusive problem as is found in his treatment of Troilus ? It is not inconceivable that, where Arthur was concerned, some amount of depreciation was due to the Renaissance scorn for things mediaeval. Ascham had condemned the legend in downright terms : by him the deeds of the Round Table were summed up as 'open manslaughter and bold bawdrye' ; and Rabelais also had heaped ridicule on the old romance. But of greater significance still was that degraded medium through which Arthur's story was wont to reach the popular ear, and this factor indeed can be described as the decisive one. The legend had become the theme of a fallen race of minstrels, 'singers upon benches and barrel-heads—that gave a fit of mirth for a groat—in taverns and ale-houses and such other places of base resort'. And the fumes of the ale-house still clung to the story, tarnishing its brightness and despoiling it of its dignity and tragedy alike. Outside popular circles the earlier vision remained. Sidney has a good word for 'honest King Arthur', while Spenser presents him to the gentle reader as a prince of all the virtues. But Shakespeare wrote first and last for a popular stage and for a popular audience ; and in the matter of Arthur he has necessarily to take their views into account.

The theme once touched by popular ridicule, it became, for a popular audience, devoid of the heroic, and therefore incapable of dignified treatment.

And this would seem to explain Shakespeare's attitude towards Arthurian romance, though it fails to meet the case of the Troilus burlesque. It was not that Shakespeare regarded the legend of Arthur as unsuitable for drama on account of ' the remoteness of its spirit from the world of living men '. Such a theory has been urged and might indeed hold, had the dramatist merely refrained from using the material for the plots of one or more of his serious plays. But his attitude is obviously of a more positive kind : it is one of plain ridicule towards a vulgarized story ; and this attitude as a popular dramatist he was bound to take.

J. W. H. ATKINS.

UNIVERSITY COLLEGE OF WALES,
ABERYSTWYTH.

A GREEK EPIGRAM ON THE TOMB
OF SHAKESPEARE

Ἐνθάδε πατρῴῳ ποταμῷ πάρα, παῦρα Λατῖνα,
  παυρότερ' Ἑλλήνων γράμματα, παῖς ἔμαθες·
ἐνθένδ' ἀνδρωθεὶς ἔμολες ποτὶ πατρίδος αἴης
  μητρόπολιν, σκηνῆς τ' ἆθλα μέγιστ' ἔλαβες.
ἐνταυθοῖ δ' ἄψορρος ἰών, καλὰ πολλὰ πονήσας
  εὗρες τέρμα βίου καὶ κλέος ἀθάνατον.

HERE, as a boy, beside his native stream,
He once did learn 'small Latin and less Greek';
Hence, as a man, he the great City sought,
To win the noblest prizes of the Stage;
Hither, with all his work well done, he came,
To find the end of life, and deathless fame.

J. E. SANDYS.

CAMBRIDGE.

ΕΓΧΕΣΠΑΛΟΥ ΕΓΚΩΜΙΟΝ

ΤΑ ΤΟΥ ΔΙΑΛΟΓΟΥ ΠΡΟΣΩΠΑ.
ΓΛΑΥΚΩΝ ΑΘΗΝΑΙΟΣ, ΤΑΥΡΙΔΗΣ ΑΓΓΛΟΣ.

Γλαύκων. Χθὲς περὶ δείλην ὀψίαν πολὺς ἐν ἄστει διέτρεχε
λόγος ὡς εἰς τὸν Πειραιᾶ ἄρτι καταπεπλευκυῖα εἴη ναῦς Ἀγγλικὴ
τῷ τε μεγέθει ὑπερβάλλουσα καὶ τῇ ἄλλῃ παρασκευῇ θαυμαστή.
καὶ εὐθὺς ἀπ᾽ ἄστεως κατέρρεον ἀθρόοι εἰς Πειραιᾶ πάμπολλοι
τῶν τε πολιτῶν καὶ τῶν ξένων καὶ τῶν μετοίκων τὸ πλοῖον ὀψόμενοι,
καὶ δὴ καὶ αὐτὸς ἐγὼ συνηκολούθουν· καὶ γὰρ ἐν μὲν τῷ ἄλλῳ
ἅπαντι χρόνῳ φίλαγγλός τις ἐγὼ λέγομαί τε καί εἰμι, οὐχ ἥκιστα
δὲ καὶ νῦν ὅτε πόλεμον ἐκεῖνοι ἁπάντων ἐφ᾽ ὅσον ἡ τῶν ἀνθρώπων
μνήμη ἐφικνεῖται μέγιστον πολεμοῦσιν. καὶ αὐτὴ μὲν ἡ ναῦς
οὐδαμῶς τὰς ἐλπίδας ἔψευσε, ἀλλὰ καί, τὸ τοῦ Θουκυδίδου, ἀκοῆς
κρείττων εἰς πεῖραν ἦλθεν, τῆς δὲ νεὼς ἔτι μᾶλλον ἐθαύμαζον
ἔγωγε τῶν ναυτῶν καὶ τῶν ἐπιβατῶν τήν τε τοῦ σώματος εὐεξίαν
καὶ τὸ τοῦ προσώπου ἀμέριμνον καὶ ὡς ἀληθῶς Βρεταννικόν, τὸ
πρίνινον, φασίν, τῆς καρδίας καὶ τὸ μελλονικιῶν ὡς ἐναργέστατα
ἐμφαῖνον. ἀλλ᾽ οὔπω ἐνεπλήσθην θεώμενος καὶ εἶδον ἀπὸ τοῦ
πλοίου ἀποβαίνοντα τὸν Ταυρίδην, ἄνδρα Ἄγγλον, ξένον μὲν ὄντα
ἐμὸν ἐκ παλαιοῦ, νῦν δὲ διὰ πολλοῦ χρόνου εἰς τὰς Ἀθήνας ἥκοντα.
καὶ ἠσπαζόμεθά τε ἀλλήλους ὡς φιλικώτατα καὶ ἐγώ, "ἆρα ἀληθῆ
ἐστιν", ἔφην, "ἃ πρὸς ἡμᾶς ὑπὸ τῶν Γερμανῶν συνεχῶς ἀγγέλ-
λεται ὡς ἄρα οἱ Ἄγγλοι ἅπαντες γεγόνασι τότε μὲν μετεωρο-
σκόποι, εἰς τὸν οὐρανὸν ἀναβλέποντες ἀεὶ καὶ πυνθανόμενοι ἀλλήλων
πότε καὶ πόθεν τὸ δεινὸν ἥξει, ὥστε παρ᾽ ὑμῖν οὐκέτι οὐδ᾽ αὐτὸς
ὁ Σωκράτης, ὅν ποτε ὡς ἀστρονομοῦντα ὁ Ἀριστοφάνης ἀπέ-

PRAISE OF SHAKESPEARE

PERSONS OF THE DIALOGUE.

GLAUKON, *of Athens.*
TAURIDES, *an Englishman.*

Glaukon. THERE was current in the city yesterday afternoon a strong rumour that an English ship had just come into the Peiraeus, of exceptional size and remarkable in her general equipment. Immediately there was a rush from the town ; citizen, alien, naturalized alien, all poured down to see the vessel, and I myself went with them. For indeed, I have always been, as I am said to be, a friend of England, but more than ever now when England is engaged in the greatest of all wars within human memory. The ship herself did not disappoint expectations. In the phrase of Thucydides, ' trial outdid report.' But what was more admirable to me than the ship was the physical fitness of sailor and marine alike : the truly British *sans souci* showing in their faces, a vivid expression of the ' hearts of oak '—of the ' Britons never, never shall be slaves '.

I had not satisfied my eyes when I saw coming off the ship Mr. Bull, an Englishman, with whom I had an old friendship, and who was now visiting Athens after a long interval. After we had greeted each other very cordially, I asked him whether the German stories which continually reach us were true. ' Is it true', I asked, ' that now Englishmen are all become star-gazers—always looking to the heavens and asking one another when and from what quarter the fearful thing will come : Socrates himself, whose star-gazing was ridiculed by Aristophanes,

U

σκωψεν, οὐδαμοῦ ἂν φαίνοιτο, τότε δ' αὖ ἐρεβοδιφῶσιν, τρωγλο-
δυτικῶς τὴν γῆν ὀρύττοντες καὶ ἐν ἀποθήκαις πνιγηραῖς οἰκοῦντες
κατώρυχες, ὥσπερ πρὸ Προμηθέως τὸ ἀνθρωπεῖον γένος, καὶ σπα-
νίως καὶ μόλις ἀνακύπτοντες, ὥς φησιν ὁ Πλάτων, εἰς τὸν ἐνθάδε
τόπον, ἅτε πρὸς τοὺς τοῦ Καίσαρος κεραυνοὺς καταιβάτας παντάπασιν ἀποδειλιῶντες;"

Ταυρίδης.   ἀλλ' ''οὐκ ἔστ' ἔτυμος λόγος οὗτος'', ὦ φίλε
Γλαύκων· τῷ γὰρ ὄντι εἰ ἐμοὶ ἐθέλοις τῷ αὐτόπτῃ τε καὶ ἐξ αὐτοῦ
τοῦ ἔργου εὐθὺς ἥκοντι πιστεύειν μᾶλλον ἢ οἷς τινες, οἷς ἰδίᾳ οἶμαί
τι διαφέρει, παρ' ὑμῖν πάνυ σπουδῇ διαγγέλλουσιν, οἱ Ἄγγλοι τὰ
νῦν σχεδὸν οὐδὲν διαφερόντως διαιτῶνται ἢ ἐν τῷ ἄλλῳ ἅπαντι
χρόνῳ, ἀλλ' ἵνα κατ' Ἀριστοφάνη λέγω,

οἱ δ' εὔκολοι μὲν ἦσαν, εὔκολοι δὲ νῦν.

τὰ μὲν γὰρ ἄλλα ἐάσας ἕν τί σοι τοῦ τρόπου αὐτῶν τεκμήριον ἐρῶ·
ἀναγόμενος δεῦρο κατέλειπον αὐτοὺς ἑορτὴν ἄγοντας εἰς τιμὴν τοῦ
Ἐγχεσπάλου.

Γλαύκων.   ποιοῦ Ἐγχεσπάλου; μῶν τοῦ ποιητοῦ;

Ταυρίδης.   τοῦ ποιητοῦ.

Γλαύκων.   ἑορτὴν ποιητοῦ καὶ ταῦτα πόλεμον τοσοῦτον πολε-
μοῦντες, ὦ θαυμάσιοι.

Ταυρίδης.   ἀλλ' οὐκ ἀκήκοας ὡς πάλαι ποτὲ τὸν Τυρταῖον τὸν
ἐλεγειοποιὸν ἐπηγάγοντο οἱ Λακεδαιμόνιοι ὅτε τοῖς Μεσσηνίοις
ἐπολέμουν, ὅπως τῶν ἐκείνου ἐλεγείων ἀκροώμενοι οἱ πολῖται πρὸς
ἀρετὴν παροξύνοιντο; ταὐτὸν οὖν δὴ τοῦτο δοκοῦσιν ἐμοὶ οἱ Ἄγγλοι
πρὸς τὸν Ἐγχεσπάλον πεπονθέναι, ἄνδρα ἀγαθὸν περὶ τὴν πόλιν
καὶ εὐεργέτην γεγενῆσθαι αὐτὸν ἡγούμενοι, ὅστις ἄλλα τε πολλὰ
καλῶς τὴν ἡμετέραν πόλιν καὶ ἐνουθέτησε καὶ ὑπέμνησεν καὶ
ἐπῄνεσεν καὶ δὴ καὶ τὰ πολυθρύλητα ἐκεῖνα εἰς αὐτὴν ἐποίησεν,
ὧν ἡ ἀρχὴ τοιάδε τις·

σκηπτοῦχος ἥδε νῆσος, Ἄρεως ἕδος,
ἥδ' ἡ σεβαστὴ γαῖα, βασιλέων θρόνος,
Ἀτλαντίδος μίμημα, Χῶρος Εὐσεβῶν,
ὃν αὐτὸς αὑτῷ τῇδ' ἐπύργωσεν θεὸς
νόσου πρόβλημα, πολεμίας ἄλκαρ χερός·

would be unremarked among you : or again they " dive into the deeps ";
like troglodytes they dig up the earth and live in stuffy " cabins under
earth "—like the human race before Prometheus—rarely and hardly
lifting up their heads to " this upper world " as Plato says ; utterly terri-
fied by the " downrushing thunderbolts " of the Kaiser ? '

Taurides. ' That tale 's not true ', friend Glaukon. In fact, if
you would believe me who have seen with my own eyes and have come
directly from the scene of action—rather than those, probably not quite
disinterested, gentlemen, who studiously spread reports among you—
Englishmen have hardly at all altered their way of life : they live
practically as they have always lived : as Aristophanes says of Sophocles :

> Easy before and not less easy now.

To mention a single sign of this—when I left England for Athens they
were holding a festival in honour of Shakespeare.

Glaukon. Shakespeare ? the poet ?

Taurides. The same.

Glaukon. A festival in honour of a poet, when they are engaged
in such a tremendous war ! What queer folks those English be !

Taurides. Nay, have you not heard that long ago, when the
Lacedaemonians were engaged in a war with the Messenians, they
invited to Sparta the elegiac poet Tyrtaeus, in order that his elegiacs
might stir up the valour of their citizens. Similar is the attitude of
Englishmen to Shakespeare. They look on him as a man who has
' deserved well ' of the state, as a ' benefactor ', inasmuch as he wisely
and well in many a line admonished our country and reminded her
and praised her, and in particular wrote the famous lines commencing :

> This royal throne of kings, this sceptered isle,
> This earth of majesty, this seat of Mars,
> This other Eden, demi-paradise,
> This fortress built by Nature for herself
> Against infection and the hand of war,

ἀνδρῶν μάκαιρα γέννα, κοσμία κτίσις
ἥδ᾽ ὡς σμάραγδος ἀργυρᾶν ἵζουσ᾽ ἅλα·
ἣν ἀμφιβάλλει πόντος ἀντὶ τειχίου,
ἢ τάφρον ὀνομάσαις ἄν, ὥσπερ οἰκίας,
φθονερὰν ἀμύνων χειρόνων πόλεων ὕβριν·
τὸ κηπίον τὸ δαιμόνιον, ἥδ᾽ Ἀγγλία.

οὐ δικαίως τὸν τοιαῦτα τὴν Ἀγγλίαν ἐπαινέσαντα ἔτι καὶ τεθνεῶτα
ἐν μνήμῃ καὶ τιμῇ ἔχομεν ἄλλως τε καὶ ὑπὲρ αὐτῆς νῦν δέον πρὸς
πολεμίους τῶν πάντων ὠμοτάτους ἀμύνεσθαι;

Γλαύκων.   δικαίως καὶ σφόδρα γε.

Ταυρίδης.   ἔτι δὲ καὶ τόδε μοι δοκῶ ἐννενοηκέναι ὅτι οὔθ᾽
αἱ Μοῦσαι εὐτυχοῦσιν ὅπου μὴ ἡ Ἐλευθερία, οὔθ᾽ ἡ Ἐλευθερία
ὅπου μὴ αἱ Μοῦσαι.   οὐδὲ γὰρ ἐν αὐτῇ τῇ Ἑλλάδι, τῇ αὐτῶν
πατρίδι, οὐκέτι ἔμειναν, ἐπειδὴ ὑπὸ τῶν Ῥωμαίων κατεδουλώθη
(καί μοι μὴ ἀχθεσθῇς ὥσπερ Φρυνίχῳ ἑτέρῳ τὰ οἰκήϊά σε κακὰ
ἀναμνήσαντι) ἀλλ᾽ εἰς τὴν Ἰταλίαν μετῴκησαν· ἐπειδὴ δ᾽ αὖ οἱ Ῥω-
μαῖοι εἰς τὸ τρυφερὸν καὶ κεκλασμένον καὶ ἁβροδίαιτον ἀπέκλιναν,
ἀπέλιπον αὐτοὺς εὐθὺς αἱ Μοῦσαι, ὡς δυσχεραίνουσαι ἀνθρώποις
ἀναξίοις ὁμιλεῖν, καὶ ἔφευγον οὐκ οἶδ᾽ ὅποι εἰ μὴ εἰς τὴν ἡμετέραν·
ἐξ οὗ καὶ ἡμεῖς τῶν ἄλλων πόλεων ἁπασῶν καὶ εἰς τὰ ἄλλα προε-
στάναι οὐκ ἀλόγως ἀξιοῦμεν· οὕτως ἀληθές ἐστιν ὃ φησί τις τῶν
ἡμετέρων ποιητῶν·

ὅπᾳ δὲ Μοῖσ᾽ ἴχνος διώκει
πάντοσε Δόξ᾽ ἕπεται καὶ Αἰδώς.

καταφυγουσῶν δ᾽ οὖν παρ᾽ ἡμᾶς τῶν Μουσῶν προφήτης αὐτῶν
ἐγένετο ὁ Ἐγχεσπάλος, μᾶλλον δ᾽ ἴσως ἱεροφάντην δεῖ αὐτὸν
ὀνομάζειν τῶν μυστηρίων τῶν Μουσείων, καὶ περὶ μὲν αὐτὸν Μοῦσ᾽
ἐφίλησεν, ὀφθαλμῶν δ᾽ οὐχ ὅπως ἐστέρησεν, ὥσπερ πάλαι τὸν
παρ᾽ Ἀλκίνῳ Δημόδοκον, ἀλλὰ πολὺ μᾶλλον ἐξωμμάτωσεν καὶ

κλεῖδάς οἱ χρυσέας Χαρᾶς
ἔδωκε Δειμάτων τε πηγὰς
καὶ Δακρύων γοερῶν ἀνοῖξαι.

ἢ ποῖός τις σοὶ δοκεῖ ὁ Ἐγχεσπάλος ποιητὴς εἶναι;

Γλαύκων.   ἀλλ᾽ οὐ γὰρ ἐγὼ πάνυ τι ἐσχολακὼς τυγχάνω τοῖς
ὑμετέροις ποιηταῖς, οὐ ῥᾳδίως ἔχω ἀποκρίνεσθαι, πολλὴν δ᾽ ἄν σοι

> This happy breed of men, this little world,
> This precious stone set in the silver sea,
> Which serves it in the office of a wall,
> Or as a moat defensive to a house,
> Against the envy of less happier lands,
> This blessed plot, this earth, this realm, this England.

Are we not right in remembering and honouring, even when he is dead, a poet who wrote such praise of England, especially when we now have to defend her against the cruellest of all enemies?

Glaukon. Very right, indeed.

Taurides. Moreover, I seem to have noticed this, that Poetry does not flourish without Freedom, nor Freedom without Poetry. Hellas was the motherland of the Muses, yet even in Hellas the Muses did not remain after Hellas was enslaved by the Romans; now do not be vexed with me if, like a second Phrynichus, I ' remind you of the woes of your kin ': they migrated to Italy. When the Romans, in their turn, declined on luxury and enervation and effeminacy, immediately the Muses forsook them and fled; fled, I know not whither, unless it were to our England; and from that time we have no unreasonable claim to be the first of nations in other things as well as in poetry. So true are the words of Gray:

> Her track, where'er the goddess roves,
> Glory pursues, and generous Shame.

In any case, when the Muses took refuge with us, Shakespeare became their spokesman, or rather, perhaps, I should call him the hierophant of the mysteries of the Muses. The Muse ' loved him with an exceeding love ', but so far from robbing him of his eyes—as she did Demodikos of the court of Alkinoos—she actually opened his eyes, and gave him the golden keys that

> can unlock the gates of Joy;
> Of Horror that, and thrilling Fears,
> Or ope the sacred source of sympathetic Tears.

But what is your own opinion of the poetry of Shakespeare?

Glaukon. The fact is I have not much studied English poetry,

χάριν εἰδείην εἰ ἐθέλοις ἐμοὶ μεταξὺ πορευομένων ἐκείνου τὰς ἀρετὰς
ἐξηγεῖσθαι.

Ταυρίδης.   μέγα δὴ ἔργον, ὦ φίλε, λέγεις.   εἰ μὲν γὰρ ἄνευ
παραδειγμάτων τινῶν ἁπλῶς αὐτὸν ἐπαινοίην, τάχ᾽ ἂν οὐ πιστεύοις
ἐμοὶ λέγοντι, εἰ δ᾽ αὖ ὧν ἐκεῖνος ἐποίησεν, ὀλίγ᾽ ἄττα ἐκλέγων
παραθείμην, τοῦτ᾽ ἂν εἴη τὸ κατὰ τὴν παροιμίαν λεγόμενον, ἀπὸ
πλίνθου τὴν οἰκίαν ἐπαινεῖν· φησὶν γάρ που ὁ Ἱεροκλῆς ὡς σχολα-
στικός τις οἰκίαν βουλόμενος ἀποδόσθαι, δεῖγμα αὐτῆς πλίνθον
περιέφερε.   ταὐτὸν δ᾽ ἂν ἴσως κἀγὼ πεπονθὼς εἴην εἰ ἐν οὕτω
βραχεῖ χρόνῳ, ἐν ᾧ εἰς ἄστυ πορευόμεθα, τοῦ Ἐγχεσπάλου τὰ
κάλλη ἐπιχειροίην διηγεῖσθαι.   ἀλλ᾽ εἰ χρὴ ἐν ἢ δύο ἀπὸ μυρίων
τῶν ἐνδεχομένων παχυλῶς καὶ τύπῳ ἐνδείκνυσθαι, σχεδόν τι οὐκ
οἶδ᾽ ὁπόθεν δεῖ ἄρχεσθαι, ἀλλὰ τῷ ὄντι ἀπορῶ Ὁμηρικῶς

τί πρῶτόν τοι ἔπειτα, τί δ᾽ ὑστάτιον καταλέξω;

ἀρχὴ δ᾽ οὖν ἔστω τοῦ λόγου ἡ παλαιὰ ἐκείνη ἀπορία πότερον τὸν ποιη-
τὴν δεῖ ἢ καὶ τὸν γραφέα μιμεῖσθαι βελτίονας ἢ καθ᾽ ἡμᾶς ἢ χείρονας
ἢ καὶ τοιούτους, ὥσπερ καὶ ὁ ὑμέτερος Σοφοκλῆς, εἰ μέμνησαι, ἔφη
αὐτὸς μὲν οἵους δεῖ ποιεῖν, Εὐριπίδην δὲ οἷοι εἰσίν.   ὁ μὲν οὖν
Ἐγχεσπάλος οὐ ῥᾳδίως ἂν εἴποις τίνι τῶν δογμάτων τούτων προσέ-
θετο, ἀλλὰ τότε μὲν τῷδε φαίης ἄν, τότε δὲ τῷδε, τὸ δ᾽ ἀληθέ-
στατον, ὡς ἐμοὶ φαίνεται, τῆς τοιαύτης ἀκριβολογίας παντάπασιν
ἐκεῖνος κατεφρόνει.   ὡμολόγει γὰρ δηλονότι τῷ Ἀριστοτέλει ὡς οὐ
τὰ γενόμενα λέγειν τοῦ ποιητοῦ ἔργον ἐστίν ἀλλ᾽ οἷα ἂν γένοιτο,
οὐδὲ τὰ καθ᾽ ἕκαστον λέγειν, ὥσπερ οἱ ἱστορικοί, ἀλλὰ τὰ καθόλου,
εἰς ἐκεῖνο μόνον ἀποβλέποντα τῷ ποίῳ τὰ ποῖ᾽ ἄττα συμβαίνει
λέγειν ἢ πράττειν κατὰ τὸ εἰκὸς ἢ τὸ ἀναγκαῖον.   λύεται δὲ ταύτῃ
ἡ ἐπιτίμησις ἥν τινες ἐπετίμησαν αὐτῷ ὅτι ἐνίοτε τερατώδεις τινὰς
καὶ παντάπασιν ἀδυνάτους γενέσθαι πεποίηκεν ὥσπερ αὐτίκα τὸν
Καλίβανον.   εἰ μὲν οὖν τὸν τυχόντα ἄνθρωπον μιμεῖσθαι προελό-
μενος, εἶτα τὸν Καλίβανον τοιοῦτον, οἷον οἶσθα, ἐποίησεν, ἔνοχος
ἂν ἦν τῇ ἐπιτιμήσει· νῦν δὲ εὖ εἰδὼς ἐκεῖνος πρός γε τὴν ποίησιν
αἱρετώτερον ὂν πιθανὸν ἀδύνατον ἢ ἀπίθανον καὶ δυνατόν, τὰ ὄντα
εὐχερῶς ὑπερβαλὼν τοὺς τερατώδεις ἐκείνους εἰσήγαγε, περὶ τοῦτο

and it is not easy for me to give an answer. I should be very grateful if, while we walk, you would explain to me Shakespeare's merits.

Taurides. That is a big task! If I were to praise Shakespeare without quoting examples, my words would probably fail to carry conviction : if, on the other hand, I were to quote a few extracts, this would be a case of the proverbial 'commending a house with a brick'. Hierocles tells us of a pedant who, wishing to sell his house, carried about a brick as a specimen of it. I should be in like case if I attempted, in the brief while that we are walking to the city, to recount the beauties of Shakespeare. However, if I must mention one or two points out of the ten thousand possible topics, I really do not know where to begin, and I am honestly in Homer's difficulty :

What shall I first, what shall I last recount?

Let me begin with the old problem. Should a poet—or, for that matter, should a painter—represent men better than ordinary men like ourselves, or worse men, or men just such as we are ? Your own Sophocles, if you recollect, said that he himself represented men as they should be, while Euripides represented them as they actually are. Now one would find it hard to say which of these doctrines Shakespeare supported. Sometimes you would be inclined to say the one opinion, sometimes the other. But, in my judgement, the real truth is that Shakespeare looked with little favour on this sort of quibbling. Clearly he agreed with Aristotle in holding that the function of the poet is not to relate what has happened, but what may happen—not to give the particular, like the historian, but the universal : looking only to one consideration—how a certain sort of person will speak or act on a given occasion, according to the law of probability or necessity. This point of view resolves the criticism of Shakespeare made by some people, that he sometimes introduces monstrous and impossible characters, as, for example, Caliban. Now had the *intention* of Shakespeare been to represent an ordinary man when he portrayed Caliban,—you know the character—then he would have been open to criticism. But the actual fact is that Shakespeare was well aware that, *artistically, poetically,* a plausible impossibility is preferable to an unplausible possibility. He, accordingly, lightly went beyond the limits of the actual world

μόνον τὴν ἐπιμέλειαν ποιούμενος ὅπως αὐτοὶ ἑαυτοῖς ὅμοια καὶ λέξουσιν καὶ πράξουσιν καί, ὡς συνελόντι εἰπεῖν, τὴν οἰκείαν ποιήσουσιν ἡδονήν. ταύτῃ δὲ σκοπουμένοις ὅ τε Καλίβανος καὶ αἱ Φαρμακεύτριαι οὐδὲν μᾶλλον ἄξιοι δοκοῦσιν εἶναι ἐπιτιμήσεως ἢ ὅ τε Ὀθέλλων καὶ ὁ Ἀμλέτιος καὶ εἴ τινες ἄλλοι τοιοῦτοι.

καὶ ταῦτα μὲν λέγω οὐκ ἀπολογούμενος ὑπὲρ τοῦ Ἐγχεσπάλου ἀλλὰ ἐξηγούμενος· εἰ δὲ δεῖ καὶ ἀπολογίαν εἰπεῖν, πρόχειρόν ἐστιν τὸ Ἀριστοτέλειον ἐκεῖνο λέγειν, ὅτι "ἀλλ' οὖν οὕτω φασίν". καὶ γὰρ ἐπὶ τοῦ Ἐγχεσπάλου καὶ ἔλεγον πολλὰ τοιαῦτα καὶ ἐπίστευον, ἅτε πολλὰ τῆς γῆς μέρη οὔπω ἱκανῶς εἰδότες, ἐν οἷς ῥᾳδίως παντοδαπὰ ἐμυθολόγουν ἐνοικεῖν τέρατα· αὐτὸς γοῦν ὁ Ἐγχεσπάλος φανερόν ἐστιν ὅτι πεπεισμένος ἦν τῷ ὄντι εἶναί τινας ἀνθρώπους ὑπὸ τοῖς ὤμοις τὰς κεφαλὰς ἔχοντας. τὰς δὲ Φαρμακευτρίας εἴ τις ἀποδοκιμάζει, εὖ ἂν ἔχοι μεμνῆσθαι ὅτι κατ' αὐτοὺς τοὺς χρόνους ἐκείνους οὐχ ὅπως ἠπίστουν μὴ γενέσθαι τοιαύτας τινάς, ἀλλὰ καὶ ἐπίστευον καὶ ἐφοβοῦντο καὶ βασάνοις τε ταῖς δεινοτάταις ἤλεγχον εἴ τινα ὑπώπτευον φαρμάκοις καὶ μαγγανείαις χρῆσθαι, ἐξελεγχθεῖσάν τε ταῖς ἐσχάταις τιμωρίαις ἐκόλαζον.

ἐν δ' οὖν ἅπασιν ὁμοίως τὸ ὅμοιον ἑκάστῳ ἐδίωκεν ὁ Ἐγχεσπάλος καὶ περὶ τοῦτο μόνον ἐσπούδαζεν, ἐπεὶ οὔτ' ἀρχαιολογικὸς εἶναι προσεποιεῖτο οὔτε γεωγραφικὸς οὔτε τῶν τοιούτων οὐδέν, ἀλλ' ἁπλῶς ποιητής. ἅτε οὖν πεπεισμένος ἄλλων ἄλλο τεχνῶν ἔργον εἶναι, οἷον τῆς μὲν ἐπιστήμην, τῆς δὲ πειθώ, καὶ τῶν ἄλλων ἑκάστης ὡσαύτως ἄλλο, ἔχων δὲ αὐτὸς τέχνην τὴν ποιητικήν, ἡδονὴν παρὰ πάντα τῆς ποιητικῆς τὴν οἰκείαν ποιῆσαι ἐσπούδαζεν, ὥσπερ που καὶ αὐτός φησιν τοῦ Χειμῶνος ἐν τῷ ἐπιλόγῳ·

> δότ' οὐρίαν ἐμοῖσιν ἱστίοις πνοήν,
> ἢ κάρτ' ἂν ἀποτύχοιμ' ἂν οὗ 'στοχαζόμην,
> τέρψιν παρασχεῖν.

ἀκηκοέναι μὲν οὖν μοι δοκῶ ὅτι πάλαι ποτέ, ἐπεὶ πρέσβεις τινὲς ὑπὸ τῶν Ῥωμαίων ἀπεσταλμένοι εἰς τὸν Τάραντα ἧκον, ἐχλεύαζον αὐτοὺς οἱ Ταραντῖνοι εἴ τι μὴ καλῶς ἑλληνίσειαν, τῆς δὲ τοιαύτης μικρολογίας οὐδὲν οὔτε τῷ Ἐγχεσπάλῳ ἔμελεν οὔτε ἄλλῳ μέλει ὅς γε τὸν Ἀριστοτέλη πεπατηκὼς τυγχάνει· ἐν γὰρ

and introduced those monstrous creations, his sole care being that in speech, as in action, they should be consistent with themselves—in a word, produce their appropriate pleasure. So considered, Caliban and the Witches are no more deserving of censure than Othello or Hamlet or the like.

These remarks are meant to be an exposition, not a defence of Shakespeare. If defence is needed, we have at hand the Aristotelian defence : 'but so they say'. For in the time of Shakespeare such things were not only said but believed. Having an inadequate acquaintance with many portions of the globe, they easily imagined these to be the home of all sorts of monsters. Shakespeare, indeed, himself actually believed in the existence of a race of men ' whose heads do grow beneath their shoulders'. As to the Witches, if any one objects to them, he would do well to remember that just about Shakespeare's time, so far from the existence of witches being doubted, they were a subject of terror, and any woman suspected of employing magic simples or other means of witchcraft was examined with horrible tortures and, if convicted, punished with the utmost severity.

But, in any case, Shakespeare's aim always—and his sole aim—was consistency. He did not pretend to be an archaeologist or a geographer, or anything of that sort, but simply a poet. He was convinced that different arts have different ends. The end of one art is knowledge, the end of another is persuasion : and so for every art a particular end. His own particular art being poetry, he aimed always at producing the pleasure which is appropriate to poetry. Indeed, he says himself in the epilogue of *The Tempest* :

> Gentle breath of yours my sails
> Must fill, or else my project fails,
> Which was to please.

I seem to recollect a story of an embassy which the Romans sent to Tarentum, and how the Tarentines jeered when the ambassadors made a slip in their Greek. Now this sort of meticulous pedantry had small

τοῖς τοιούτοις εἴ τι πεπλημμέληται, κατὰ τὴν προαίρεσίν ἐστι τὸ ἁμάρτημα ἀλλ᾽ οὐ κατὰ τὴν τέχνην.

καὶ οὐχ ἥκιστα δι᾽ αὐτὸ τοῦτο, ὅτι περὶ τὰ μὴ προσήκοντα οὐ περιεργάζεται, οὐ μόνον τοῖς ἐν ἀφωρισμένῳ τινὶ ἢ τόπῳ ἢ χρόνῳ ζῶσιν οἷός τ᾽ ἐστιν ἐκεῖνος ἡδονὴν παρέχειν ἀλλὰ καὶ τοῖς πολὺ καὶ πολλαχῇ ἀπηρτημένοις. ὅσα γὰρ ἢ τόπου τινὸς ἢ χρόνου ἢ καὶ τέχνης ἴδιά ἐστιν, ταῦτα ὀλίγοις συνετά, "ἐς δὲ τὸ πᾶν ἑρμηνέων χατίζει". ὁ δὲ τοὺς ἄνδρας καὶ τὰς γυναῖκας πεποίηκεν ὑπὸ τῶν αὐτῶν, ὦνπερ καὶ ἡμεῖς, παθῶν τε καὶ ἐπιθυμιῶν κατεχομένους, καί, ὥς τις εὖ εἶπεν, οἱ μὲν ἄλλοι ποιηταὶ ὡς ἐπὶ τὸ πολὺ ἄνθρωπόν τινα μιμοῦνται, ὁ δὲ Ἐγχεσπάλος τὸν καθόλου ἄνθρωπον.

Γλαύκων. οὐ φαῦλον, ὦ φίλε, λέγεις ποιητήν· ἀλλὰ τὸν λόγον πέραινε.

Ταυρίδης. ἀλλὰ γάρ, ὦ φίλε Γλαύκων, τοῦ ἐπαίνου, εἰ μέλλει ἄξιος τοῦ ἐπαινουμένου ἔσεσθαι, "οὐδέπω κρηπὶς ὕπεστιν", ἀλλ᾽

οὐδ᾽ ἂν εἰ δέκ᾽ ἤματα
στοιχηγοροίην

οὐχ οἷός τ᾽ ἂν εἴην ἐκείνου τῶν ἀρετῶν πολλοστὸν μέρος καταριθμεῖσθαι, ὅς γε ὑπερβέβληται τούς τε πρὸ αὐτοῦ ποιητὰς καὶ τοὺς καθ᾽ ἑαυτὸν καὶ οὐδὲ τοῖς ἐπιγιγνομένοις ὑπερβολὴν καταλέλοιπεν. πότερον τῆς λέξεως πρῶτον ἐπαινέσομαι τὴν ἐνάργειαν καὶ τὴν ἐμμέλειαν καὶ τὴν περιουσίαν, καθαρᾶς τε τοῖς ὀνόμασιν οὔσης καὶ τὸν Ἀγγλικὸν χαρακτῆρα πανταχῇ διασωζούσης; ἢ τῆς διανοίας τὸ μεγαλοφυὲς καὶ τὸ ἀδρεπήβολον καὶ τὸ ἀγχίστροφον καὶ τὸ ὡς ἀληθῶς μυριόνουν; πότερον τὰ γέλοια διηγήσομαι ὅπως μεταχειρίζεται, παραξύων μὲν ἐνίοτε τὸ βωμολόχον, φυλάττων δ᾽ ἀεὶ τὸ ὅμοιον; ἢ ἐν ταῖς τοπηγορίαις ὁπόσα φιλοσοφεῖ, ὁπόσας γνώμας εἴρηκεν, ὧν αἱ πολλαὶ εἰς παροιμίας ἤδη εἰσὶν ἀφιγμέναι καὶ τῶν Ἀγγλων ἑκάστῳ ἐφημμέναι τ᾽ ἐπὶ τῇ ψυχῇ εἰσιν διὰ παντὸς καὶ ἐγκεκλοιωμένα περὶ τῷ τραχήλῳ; ἢ τὴν ἐν τοῖς παθητικοῖς δεινότητα, ἐάν τ᾽ ὀργὴν δέῃ ἐμφαίνειν, ἐάν τ᾽ ἔλεον, ἐάν τε πένθος; ἢ ὅσα τῶν δραμάτων πανταχοῦ μέλη ἐμβέβληκεν, ᾄδων, τὸ τοῦ Μίλτωνος,

λιγυρῶς οἷά τις ὄρνις
ἀγρίαν ἦτε καθ᾽ ὕλην ἀδίδακτον
προχέει μελος;

concern for Shakespeare, or, indeed, for any one who has 'thumbed' his Aristotle. Error in such matters is of intention, not of art.

And just this fact—just the fact that Shakespeare does not bestow pedantic pains on the non-essential—is one of the main reasons why the pleasure he affords is not confined to the inhabitants of a particular place or to a particular generation, but is enjoyed equally by those far removed in many ways. Whatever is special to a particular time, a particular locality, a particular profession, has a meaning for a few only, 'but for the general it needs interpreters'. Shakespeare's men and Shakespeare's women are moved by like passions and desires even as we are. It has been well said that 'In the writings of other poets, a character is too often an individual : in those of Shakespeare it is commonly a species'.

Glaukon. This is no ordinary poet, my friend, you represent. Please continue.

Taurides. Nay, my friend, of my eulogy—if it is to be worthy of its subject—'not yet the pedestal is laid', but even if

> For wellnigh half a moon
> I spoke right on,

I could not do more than mention a fraction of his excellences, seeing that he not merely surpassed his predecessors and his contemporaries, but has set a mark which after-generations find impossible to surpass. Shall I praise first his language—his perspicuity, his harmony, his copious diction, 'a well of English undefiled'? Shall I praise his intellectual qualities—his grandeur and his compass, his nimbleness, literally his 'myriad-mindedness'? Shall I tell you how he manages the comic element—grazing at times the vulgar, yet always observing truth to life? Or his use of the commonplaces—his philosophy—his *sententiae* or pithy sayings, most of which have already passed into proverbs, and which every Englishman has 'bound about his heart continually and tied about his neck'? Or his power in the expression of the emotions, whether anger, or pity, or sorrow? Or the songs he has everywhere introduced in his drama—what John Milton calls 'his native woodnotes

ἢ πρέπον ἴσως ἂν εἴη μᾶλλον ἐν καιρῷ τοιούτῳ τῆς πατρίδος
καθεστώσης τὸ φιλόπολι αὐτοῦ ἐπαινεῖν καὶ ἐκείνων μνησθῆναι ἃ
πάμπολλα ἔγραψεν εἰς εὐλογίαν ἅμα τῶν Ἄγγλων καὶ παρακε-
λευσμόν, οἷά ἐστιν ἐκεῖνα τὰ ἀρετῆς τε καὶ ἀνδραγαθίας πνέοντα,
ἃ ἐν τῷ Ἰωάννῃ Τυράννῳ κεῖται· φησὶ γάρ που·

> ἐχθροὶ δ' ἰόντων κἀπὸ Βορραίων πλακῶν,
> ἴτων δ' ἀπ' Εὔρου καὶ Μεσημβρίας ἄπο,
> χειρωσόμεσθα πάντας· οὐ γὰρ ἔσθ' ὅτι
> εἰς τάφρον ἄτης καταβαλεῖ τὴν Ἀγγλίαν
> Ἄγγλοι γ' ἑαυτῶν ἕως ἂν ὦσιν ἄξιοι.

ἀλλ' ἐγγὺς γὰρ ἤδη ὁρῶ τὴν τοῦ Καλλίου οἰκίαν, παρ' ᾧ μέλλω
καταλύσειν, εἰσαῦθις δ', εἰ βούλει, ἀκριβέστερον περὶ τούτων
διασκεψόμεθα.　παύομαι ἤδη λέγων·

> καὶ σὺ μὲν οὕτω χαῖρε...
> αὐτὰρ ἐγὼ καὶ σεῖο καὶ ἄλλης μνήσομ' ἀοιδῆς.

A. W. MAIR.

wild'? Or perhaps it would be more appropriate, in view of the critical position in which my country now is placed, to praise his patriotism and to refer to the numerous passages which are at once praise of England and an exhortation to Englishmen: for example, those lines breathing of manhood and valour which occur in *King John*:

> Come the three corners of the world in arms,
> And we shall shock them. Nought shall make us rue,
> If England to itself do rest but true.

But here we are at the house of Callias, with whom I am going to stay, so I must stop. We shall discuss these topics in more detail another time. 'So fare thou well . . . but I shall remember thee and another song.'

A. W. MAIR.

COMMEMORATIO DORYSSOI

ECCE dies felix vatis tria saecula summi
    Accumulans ipsum concelebrare iubet !
Romanumque Anglumque simul, puerumque Britannum,
    [1] STRATA tulere VADI dulcis AVONA tui :
Cor patriae iuvenem pavit, suavissima rura,
    Urbs, caput ipsa altis urbibus, inde fovet :
Tradidit urbs orbi terrarum, aetatibus aetas,
    Oceano Tamesis ripa, GLOBUSQUE globo :
REGIA ut aequabat pelago sua signa VIRAGO,
    Naturae atque hominum splendidus auctor erat ;
[2] Aurea cui cunctae limarunt dicta Camenae,
    Commisitque suam Delius ipse lyram.
Mel stillat Sophoclis, lacrimis Euripidis undat,
    Cumque furore opus est, Aeschylus ille tonat ;
Ludere seu placet et socco mutare cothurnum,
    Alter Aristophanes, Plautus et alter, erit.
O patriae, O Musarum, O libertatis amator,
    Haec dum tutamur, spiritus altor ades !
Aerumnis solitam fer opem, repetatque precamur
    Nunc tua dilectos nobilis umbra Lares !
Venturi certis actum celebrare licebit
    Sic aevum, ut referes spemque fidemque tuis !

HERBERTUS WARREN, Eques.
Poetices, apud Oxon., nuper Praelector :
Coll. B. M. Magd. Praeses.

---

[1] I know not whether it has been remarked, but it is certainly remarkable, that the name 'Strat-ford on Avon' contains the record of the three chief races which have made our country and tongue.

[2] And precious phrase by all the Muses filed.—Sonnet LXXXV. v. 4.

תהלה לשקספיר

(מדברי שקספיר)

I

האין ליהודי עינים, האין לו ידים?

'Hath not a Jew eyes? Hath not a Jew hands?'

האם לגוי חוש ורגש ולא לו לב ונפש?

גם לשניהם נתנו מן השמים לחם ומים,

קור וחום, קיץ וחורף, ורוח חופש,

'Warmed and cool'd by the same winter and summer?'

רפאות הנגע מחלה ופגע

תלאות יום וליל שעה ורגע—

ועל מה על היהודי תזרקו טיט ורפש?

Why scorn ye him then?

II

עת אשר נאמרו אלו הדברים,

When the days were dark, a Seer arose; lifting his voice in parable and song, he gave utterance to this plea.

אז חושך יכסה ארץ וערפל לאומים,

ויקם החוזה ויהזה דברים נאמנים,

וישא משלו במליצות נעימות ובחרוזים:

מי הוא זה ואיזה הוא משמח העם באורה,

ומי עלה למרומים ויתן לנו משנה תורה,

ותשמח אנגליא במתנת אדונה,

ותסע נחליאל בגבורת מתנה?

צהלו ורונו אי הים,

Exult and rejoice, ye Isles of the West,

כי נעים זמירות יֻלד שם!

For here was born the Singer, sweetest of song!

III

בכל עת וזמן אור הוא לכל דור,

נשמע קולו בארצנו כקול התור,

וכדבריו כן הוא, טוב שמו כמבחר הפניני,

טוב שם מטמון נפשו אמר, מי יגזל ממני ?

צר לו מקום העולם, כענק הוא עומד עליו,

ותחת רגליו העם הולך ושב כחגב,

כאשר איש לא יוכל לצרף זהב נצרף,

ולהוסיף אור לשמש השורף ולא שרף,

או לבשם שושני וחבצלת השרון,

ולפאר מראה הקשת במרום,

כן לא יוכל איש להביע שבחו

של ראש המשוררים גדלו והודו:

יצהלו וירונו אנשי דורנו,

כי שקספיר המשורר הוא תפארתנו !

'He was not of an age, but for all time.'

'Good name', said he, 'in man and woman is the immediate jewel of their soul.'

His name no man can glorify; for him, the Colossus, the world is too narrow.

No man can utter his praise; he is Chief among the singers.

Let us exult, we men of this age, for Shakespeare is truly our glory.

IV

ברוח הנביא נבא הוא מה ילד יום,

הט אזנך קורא למקראות היום,

הלא כזאת דבר הדובר אלינו,

וחזה חזיונות ומליצות בעדנו ? —

הארץ הזאת מעולם לא חרדה תחת רגלי נוצח,

ולא תפול אנגליא עדי עד לפני עריץ ורוצח,

אם להלחם עלינו מכנפי הארץ בסערה במסלה יסולו

בטוחים אנו בדברי דוד המשורר המה יכרעו ויפולו:

לא לנצח תהיה לנו חיל ורעדה אימה ומורא,

אם אך מאמינים אנחנו בעוזך ובהודך, בריטניא הנורא !

With prophetic spirit he spake the words we oft recall this day:—

'This England never did, nor never shall,
Lie at the proud foot of a conqueror;

Naught shall make us rue,
If England to itself do rest but true.'

זאת הארץ כסא מלוכה למלכים,

ולה שפע ימים, ולא יסור שבטה מאיים,

ארץ הדרת הדרור, צור ומצור מאדמת קודש נצמחר,

אבן טוב בתוך הים קבועה, וכחומה לה נסמכה,

גם כנחל לפני בית למשמר ולמגן

קנאת ארצות וממלכות בעדנו להגן:

שישו ושמחו איי הים,

עוד רוח שקספיר חופף בעים!

'This royal throne of Kings,'
the sceptre shall never depart from
the Isles—a land of splendour and
honour, to freedom holding true,
hers the abundance of the seas,
a rock from holy soil:—
'This precious stone set in the silver
        sea,   [wall,
Which serves it in the office of a
Or as a moat defensive to a house,
Against the envy of less happier
    lands.'
Rejoice and be glad, O Isles of the
    Sea;
The spirit of Shakespeare shieldeth
    his folk!

V

ברוח אלהים ראה את הנולד הנעשות והבאות,

ואמץ לבב אנוש לבקש שלום המלכות ומדינות,

כנביא הקדמון הנבא אז לישראל,

בשלום המלכות לנו שלום ויבא גואל:

אל תיראו מפני חמת הפתן והטורף,

נחש הנושך, המשחית וקשה עורף,

כי אבן טובה בראשו ולוית חן על צאורו תלויה,

חביבים יסורי איש אם לבו ועינו ליה צפויה:

By the spirit divine he, the patriot
prophet, taught men to seek first
the weal of the realm; he strengthened men's hearts, as the prophet
of old that to Israel spake:—
'In the peace of the kingdom
shall ye have peace.' 'Fear ye
not, and be not dismayed at the
venom of adder or of serpent that
biteth.' 'Sweet are the uses of
adversity.'
So taught he of good and ill.

כאלה וכאלה ראה הרואה וצוה גם אלינו,

ואם אך נשמע לקול הצופה חכמתו תגן בעדנו:

ראה גבור זה מעשהו בעולם כמעשה לבנת הספיר

תחת רקיע השמים,

וכמלאך מצפצף הלוך ושוב, וזה שירו עמו

מזמר אל הכרובים—

These things he did see and told of.
List to his voice! This hero behold,—'his work under the heaven
is bright as the sapphire', and he,
like to an angel speeding to and
fro, sings this song amid the choir
angelic:—

לא למעננו בן אדם, כי עבור גדולת ארצנו,

ולמען אל חי והאמת תהיה כל מזמותנו:

נגיל ונשיש בזאת השנה,

ונהלל שם גדלו בגיל ורננה:

'Let all the ends thou aim'st at be
    thy country's, thy God's, and
    truth's.'

  E'en this year let us be glad
in praising together his name and
his fame!

H. GOLLANCZ.

A SANSKRIT PANEGYRIC

स पूर्वमब्दैश्चिघताश्रहाकविः स वीथिकातीर्थपुरे समुत्थितः ।
मधौ खकं मृतुवधां कलेवरं विघज्य तच्च ह्यमृतत्वमानशे ॥ १ ॥

ख्तिर्ममाचारितया तिरस्कृतो ध्रुवं यशःस्थश्च इहेति रोमकः ।
वचः कवौ नः किमु युक्तमेव तत् स चालयच्छक्तिरभूव्यथार्थतः ॥ २ ॥

सपत्नकीर्तिं हि सदाभितर्जयन् यशस्तथा ख्तलपदे विसारयन् ।
स एक एवाप्रतिमोऽभवद्भुवि खकाव्यशक्तिस्वरसाथ सूरिषु ॥ ३ ॥

अहोऽद्भुतं वै विषयेऽस्ति वैरिणां कवेः खदेशीयविनाशतत्परे ।
अयं न आत्मीय इति प्रकाशितो महोत्सवेनाद किलाभिनन्द्यते ॥ ४ ॥

न नाटकानां रचकस्य तस्य हि खदेश एवास्ति जगत्तु भूमिका ।
सपाटवं गौरवहास्यमिश्रणाद् विपर्ययाया यच्च विधेः प्रदर्शिताः ॥ ५ ॥

पृथग्जनैश्चास्य विशिष्टता स्तुता कवीन्द्रसंघैश्च तथा मतीक्षतः ।
अतो महासूरिगणे महीयते नवग्रहाणामिव मध्यगो रविः ॥ ६ ॥

यशस्करं चैत्यमपेक्षते न स स्थिरो ह्यजसं शशिभास्करराविव ।
न चक्रवर्ती विजयेन सर्वतः कदापि तत्तेजस आप तुच्छताम् ॥ ७ ॥

मुग्धानन्दाचार्येण गोतीर्थाख्यविद्यालये
निवासिना प्रशस्तिरियं विरचिता
संवत्सरे १९७६ ॥

PARAPHRASE

1. THREE hundred years ago this great poet, who arose in the town of Stratford (*vīthīkā-tīrtha*), in the spring, casting off his mortal frame, entered into immortality there.

2. 'By the imperishability of my works a column of fame is assuredly surpassed': so the Roman poet said. How much more such words befit him who significantly became a 'Shakespear' (*cālayac-śakti*: 'one who shakes his spear' and 'one whose genius spreads').

3. For always challenging his rivals' fame and extending his renown in every land, he then became unique, unrivalled on earth among literary men by the force of his poetic genius (or spear).

4. Behold, a marvel appears in the land of our foes intent on the destruction of this poet's countrymen: claimed as their own he is celebrated there to-day with a great festival.

5. For to this composer of plays, not his own country only but the world itself is the stage on which by skilfully mingling mirth and gravity he displays the vicissitudes of human fate.

6. His pre-eminence is praised by ordinary men and by the greatest of poets as well with unanimity. Hence he is exalted in the host of literary men like the sun that fares in the midst of the planets.

7. He needs no glorifying monument, for he will endure for ever like the sun and moon. No conqueror by universal victory has ever reached the level of his lustre.

This encomium has been composed
by the teacher Mugdhānala ('fire of the ignorant')
living in the University of Oxford
in the year 1916.

X 2

THE DREAM IMPERIAL

A SOUL supreme, seen once and not again,
Spoke in a little island of great men
When first our cabin'd race drew ampler breath
And won the sea for wise Elizabeth,—
Spoke with a sound and swell of waters wide
To young adventure in a May of pride,
Told of our fathers' deeds in lines that ring
And showed their fame no scant or paltry thing.
Then as our warring, trading, reading race
Moved surely outward to imperial space,
Beyond the tropics to the ice-blink's hem
The mind of Shakespeare voyaged forth with them.
They bore his universe of tears and mirth
In battered sea-chests to the ends of earth,
So that in many a brown, mishandled tome,
—Compacted spirit of the ancient home,—
He who for man the human chart unfurled
Explored eight oceans and possessed the world.

Children of England's children, breed new-prized,
Building the greater State scarce realized,
Sons of her sons who, unreturning, yet
Looked o'er the sundering wave with long regret,
Grandsons on clear and golden coasts, how seems
The grey, ancestral isle beheld in dreams ?

' We have a vision of our fathers' land,'
' The realm of England drawn by Shakespeare's hand,'

' The lordly isle beyond the narrow sea
' Fronting the might of war light-heartedly ; '
' Her history his shining pageant set '
' With stately Tudor and Plantagenet ; '
' Her magic woods, dim Arden cool and green ; '
' The imperial votaress her maiden-queen '
' Throned in a kingdom brave and sweet and old.'
' That is the England that we have and hold,'
' His dream majestic borne to shores afar,'
—' Old England, kind in peace and fierce in war,'
' The dream that lives where e'er his English rove '
' The land he left for lands unknown to love ! '

W. P. REEVES
(formerly High Commissioner for New Zealand).

SHAKESPEARE

IMMORTAL searcher of the hearts of men,
  Who knewest, as none else, this human life,
  Its dread ambitions and its passions rife ;
And limned it, godlike, with thy wizard pen,
In mighty numbers and divinest ken :
  Here, in this anguished, war-embattled world,
  Where Right 'gainst Wrong's grim panoply is hurled
In titan strife ;—we turn to thee agen.

For thine unfading genius stands for all
  Our ancient Britain's greatness and her woe :
Yon old king's babblings o'er Cordelia's corse,
The Dane's despairings and the queen's remorse,
One pageantry sublime, through which do call
  God's trumpets from His triumphs long ago.

WILFRED CAMPBELL.

OTTAWA, CANADA.

TO SHAKESPEARE, 1916

WITH what white wrath must turn thy bones,
  What stern amazement flame thy dust,
To feel so near this England's heart
  The outrage of the assassin's thrust.

But surely, too, thou art consoled,—
  Who knewest thy stalwart breed so well,—
To see us rise from sloth and go,
  Plain and unbragging, through this hell.

And surely, too, thou art assured!
  Hark how that grim and gathering beat
Draws upwards from the ends of earth—
  The tramp, tramp of thy kindred's feet!

CHARLES G. D. ROBERTS.

'SHAKESPEARE'

UNSEEN in the great minster dome of time,
Whose shafts are centuries, its spangled roof
The vaulted universe, our Master sits,
And organ-voices like a far-off chime
Roll through the aisles of thought. The sunlight flits
From arch to arch, and, as he sits aloof,
Kings, heroes, priests, in concourse vast, sublime,
Whispers of love and cries from battle-field,
His wizard power breathes on the living air.
Warm faces gleam and pass, child, woman, man,
In the long multitude ; but he, concealed,
Our bard eludes us, vainly each face we scan,
It is not he ; his features are not there ;
But these being hid, his greatness is revealed.

FREDERICK GEORGE SCOTT
(Senior Chaplain, 1st Canadian Division, B. E. F.).

INTELLECTUAL FRATERNITY

'To mark by some celebration the intellectual fraternity of mankind.'

ALIKE to those who grieve for Europe in her hour of civil war, and to those who would offer tribute at the shrine of William Shakespeare, it must appear appropriate and significant to publish tokens of the brotherhood of man in art. For no one has been more distinguished than William Shakespeare, in his profound appreciation of the common humanity of an infinite variety of men.

Civilization must henceforth be human rather than local or national, or it cannot exist. In a world of rapid communications it must be founded in the common purposes and intuitions of humanity, since in the absence of common motives there cannot be co-operation for agreed ends. In the decades lately passed—in terms of 'real duration', now so far behind us—it has, indeed, been fashionable to insist upon a supposed fundamental divergence of European and Asiatic character : and those who held this view were not entirely illogical in thinking the wide earth not wide enough for Europe and Asia to live side by side. For artificial barriers are very frail : and if either white or yellow 'peril' were in truth an essentially inhuman force, then whichever party believed itself to be the only human element must have desired the extermination, or at least the complete subordination, of the other.

But the premises were false : the divergences of character are superficial, and the deeper we penetrate the more we discover an identity in the inner life of Europe and Asia. Can we, in fact, point to any elemental experience or to any ultimate goal of man which is not equally European and Asiatic ? Does one not see that these are the same for all in all ages and continents ? Who that has breathed the pure mountain air of the Upanishads, of Gautama, Sankara, Kabir, Rumi, and Laotse (I mention so far Asiatic prophets only) can be alien to those who have sat at the feet of Plato and Kant, Tauler, Behmen, Ruysbroeck, Whitman, Nietzsche, and Blake ? The last named may well come to be regarded as the supreme prophet of a post-industrial age, and it is significant that one could not find in Asiatic scripture a more typically Asiatic purpose than is revealed in his passionate will to be delivered from the bondage of division :

> I will go down to self-annihilation and eternal death,
> Lest the Last Judgment come and find me unannihilate,
> And I be seiz'd and giv'n into the hands of my own Selfhood.

But it is not only in Philosophy and Religion—Truth and Love—but also in Art that Europe and Asia are united : and from this triple likeness we may well infer that all men are alike in their divinity.   Let us only notice here the singular agreement of Eastern and Western theories of Drama and Poetry, illustrating what has been said with special reference to the hero of our celebration : for the work of Shakespeare is in close accordance with Indian canons of Dramatic Art. ' I made this Drama ', says the Creator, ' to accord with the movement of the world, whether at work or play, in peace or laughter, battle, lust, or slaughter —yielding the fruit of righteousness to those who are followers of a moral law, and pleasures to the followers of pleasure—informed with the diverse moods of the soul—following the order of the world and all its weal and woe.   That which is not to be found herein is neither craft nor wisdom, nor any art, nor is it Union.   That shall be Drama which affords a place of entertainment in the world, and a place of audience for the Vedas, for philosophy and for the sequence of events.'

And poetry is justified to man inasmuch as it yields the Fourfold Fruit of Life—Virtue, Pleasure, Wealth, and Ultimate Salvation.   The Western reader may inquire, ' How Ultimate Salvation ? ' and the answer can be found in Western scriptures :

> Von Schönheit ward von jeher viel gesungen,
> Wem sie erscheint, wird aus sich selbst entrückt.

That is the common answer of the East and West, and it is justified by the disinterestedness of aesthetic contemplation, where the spirit is momentarily freed from the entanglement of good and evil.   We read, for example, in the dramatic canon of Dhanamjaya :

' There is no theme, whether delightful or disgusting, cruel or gracious, high or low, obscure or plain, of fact or fancy, that may not be successfully employed to communicate aesthetic emotion.'   We may also note the words of Chuang Tau,

> The mind of the Sage, being in repose, becomes the mirror of the universe,

and compare them with those of Whitman, who avows himself not the poet of goodness only, but also the poet of wickedness.

It is sometimes feared that the detachment of the Asiatic vision tends towards inaction. If this be partly true at the present moment, it arises from the fullness of the Asiatic experience, which still contrasts so markedly with European youth. If the everlasting conflict between order and chaos is for the present typically European, it is because spiritual wars no less than physical must be fought by those who are of military age. But the impetuosity of youth cannot completely compensate for the insight of age, and we must demand of a coming race that men should act with European energy, and think with Asiatic calm —the old ideal taught by Krishna upon the field of battle :

Indifferent to pleasure and pain, to gain and loss, to conquest and defeat, thus make ready for the fight... As do the foolish, attached to works, so should the wise do, but without attachment, seeking to establish order in the world.

Europe, too, in violent reaction from the anarchy of *laissez-faire*, is conscious of a will to the establishment of order in the world. But European progress has long remained in doubt, because of its lack of orientation—' He only who knows whither he saileth, knows which is a fair or a foul wind for him.' It is significant that the discovery of Asia should coincide with the present hour of decision : for Asiatic thought again affirms the unity and interdependence of all life, at the moment when Europe begins to realize that the Fruit of Life is not easily attainable in a society based upon division.

In honouring the genius of Shakespeare, then, we do not merely offer homage to the memory of an individual, but are witnesses to the intellectual fraternity of mankind : and it is that fraternity which assures us of the possibility of co-operation in a common task, the creation of a social order founded upon Union.

ANANDA COOMARASWAMY.

যেদিন উদিলে তুমি, বিশ্বকবি, দূর সিন্ধুপারে,
ইংলন্ডের দিক্‌প্রান্ত পেয়েছিল সেদিন তোমারে
আপন বক্ষের কাছে; ভেবেছিল বুঝি তারি তুমি
কেবল আপনধন; উজ্জ্বল ললাট তব চুমি'
রেখেছিল কিছুকাল অরণ্যশাখার বাহুজালে,
ঢেকেছিল কিছুকাল কুয়াশা-অঞ্চল-অন্তরালে
বনপুষ্প-বিকশিত তৃণঘন শিশির-উজ্জ্বল
পরীদের খেলার প্রাঙ্গণে। দ্বীপের নিকুঞ্জতল
তখনো উঠে নি জেগে কবিস্তুষ্ক-বন্দনা-সঙ্গীতে।
তার পরে ধীরে ধীরে অনন্তের নিঃশব্দ ইঙ্গিতে
দিগন্তের কোল ছাড়ি শতাব্দীর প্রহরে প্রহরে
উঠিয়াছ দীপ্তজ্যোতি মধ্যাহ্নের গগনের পরে,
নিয়েছ আসন তব সকল দিকের কেন্দ্রদেশে
বিশ্বচিত্ত উদ্ভাসিয়া; তাই হের যুগান্তর-শেষে
ভারতসমুদ্রতীরে কম্পমান শাখাপুঞ্জে আজি
নারিকেল কুঞ্জবনে জয়ধ্বনি উঠিতেছে বাজি।

RABINDRANATH TAGORE.

CALCUTTA.

SHAKESPEARE

WHEN by the far-away sea your fiery disk appeared from behind the unseen, O poet, O Sun, England's horizon felt you near her breast, and took you to be her own.

She kissed your forehead, caught you in the arms of her forest branches, hid you behind her mist-mantle and watched you in the green sward where fairies love to play among meadow flowers.

A few early birds sang your hymn of praise while the rest of the woodland choir were asleep.

Then at the silent beckoning of the Eternal you rose higher and higher till you reached the mid-sky, making all quarters of heaven your own.

Therefore at this moment, after the end of centuries, the palm groves by the Indian sea raise their tremulous branches to the sky murmuring your praise.

RABINDRANATH TAGORE.

CALCUTTA.

شیکسپیئر

شفق صبح کو دریا کا خرام آئینہ
نغمہ شام کو خاموشیِ شام آئینہ

برگِ گل آئینہ عارضِ زیبائے بہار
شانہِ گل کے لئے جلوۂ جام آئینہ

حُسن آئینہِ حق اور دل آئینہِ حُسن
دلِ انساں کو ترا حُسنِ کلام آئینہ

ہے ترے فکرِ فلک رس سے کمالِ ہستی
کیا تری فطرتِ روشن تھی مآلِ ہستی

تجھ کو جب دیدہِ دیدار طلب نے ڈھونڈھا
تابِ خورشید میں خورشید کو پنہاں دیکھا

چشمِ عالم سے تو ہستی رہی مستورِ تری
اور عالم کو تری آنکھ نے عُریاں دیکھا

حفظِ اسرار کا فطرت کو ہے سودا ایسا
راز داں پھر نہ کرے گی کوئی پیدا ایسا

اقبال

TO SHAKESPEARE

A Tribute from the East

I

THE river's silent flow
Mirrors the glory of the rosy dawn;
The sunset-silence in the golden glow
Mirrors the message of the evening song;
The burgeoning leaf, after winter's sleep,
Mirrors the rosy rapture of spring;
The bridal-palanquin of crystal cup
Reflects the virgin beauty of red wine;
The rivers of endless Beauty
Mirror the myriad coloured light of Truth;
The great deeps of human heart
Mirror the radiance from Beauty's Realm;
And thy enchanted verse in liquid notes
Mirrors the great deep of human heart!

II

Under the flashing sunbeams of thy thought,
Nature herself has found herself revealed
In perfect glory in thy golden song;
The conscious mistress of her treasured wealth!
The eager eye in search of thy image
Found thee enshrined within a veil of light,
Like mighty monarch of night and day,
That bathed in glory, seeing is not seen.
Hid from the world's eye thou hast beheld
The intricate workings of her inmost soul!
The jealous mistress of deep mysteries
Never again will suffer herself to bear
A seer like thee who took her by surprise,
Unveiled in starlight and mellow moon.

SARDAR JOGUNDRA SINGH.

FROM THE BURMESE BUDDHISTS

I

တိုက်ထုံးကြေညာ	Taik lumᵼkye-ñā
ပျံ့သြဘာဖြင့်	Pyaṃ obhā phyaṅ̊
ကဗျာပဏ္ဍိတ်	Kabyā pandeik
ဂျက်ရောင်ဖိတ်လျက်	Gun yaung pheik lyak
ရှိတ်စပီယာ	Sheik-ca-pīyā
မည်တွင်သာသား	Mī dvaṅ̊ sā sāᵼ
ဆရာဘွဲ့ပြု	Chayā phvè̊ pyu
ဂီတမှုတွင်	Gīta mhu dvaṅ̊
ခ့ရသေချာ	Cȩ̊-ṅu se-gyā
ဆင်ခြင်ပါသော်	Chaṅ̊-khyaṅ̊ bā saw
ဘာသာဗုဒ္ဓ	Bhāsā Buddha
ယူဝါဒနှင့်	Yū vāda nhaṅ̊
တူမျှထင်ရှိ	Tū mhya that shi
သဘောမိခဲ့	Sabho mi ghè̊
အဘိဓမ္မာ	Abhidhammā
နှက်နဲ့ဇွာကို	Nak-nè zvā gô
လှေလာကျေးဇူး	Lȩ̊-lā kyeᵼ-zūᵼ
ဂုဏ်အထူးဖြင့်	Gun athūᵼ phyaꞥ̊
ကြည်နူးနှလုံး	Kyī-nūᵼ nha-lumᵼ
ပိုက်ယူကျုံးရွဲ့	Paik yū kyumᵼ yvè̊
ရှွင်းပြိုပါဘိ	Shvaṅ̊ pyumᵼ bā bhi
ဂျွမ်းဆီထိသို့	Gvamᵼ chī thi sȩ̊
ဗိတိဖရဏာ	Pīti pharaṇā
ပျံ့နှံ့ဖြာသည်	Pyaṃ nhaṃ phyā sī

ဝမ်းသာအားမွှ။ အလွန်သောဝ်—	Vamᵼ sā āᵼ mȩ̊ alvan soᵼ

II

ပိုန်ကုံးသေချာ	Paik kumꞋ se-gyā
ဂုဏ်ထက်ၐဖြင့်	Gun laṅgā phyaṅ̊
ကဗျာဘွဲ့မှတ်	Kabyā phvè̇ mhat
မှန်ပြတတ်သား	Mhan pya dat sāꞋ
ပရမတ်သဘော	Paramat sabho
ဆတ်ဆတ်ဟောကြောင့်	Chat-chat ho gyaung
ရှင်စောမုနိန်	Shaṅ̊ co mu-nin
မာရဇိန်၏	Mārajin i
တောက်ထိန်ရောင်ဝါ	Tauk thin yaung vā
သာသနာသည်	Sāsanā sī
ရှည်ကြာပွားသစ်	Shī kyā pvāꞋ lit
ရေတွက်စစ်မူ	Ye tvak cit mū
အနှစ်နှစ်ထောင်	A-nhit nhit thaung
ဆောင်သားခွန်းပေါ်	Chaung sāꞋ cvanꞋ paw
ငါးရာကျော်လည်း	Ṅ̊āꞋ yā kyaw līꞋ
အဟောဝတ	Ahaw-vata
အံ့ဩရလျက်	Aṃ o ya lyak
တောက်ပထွန်းပြောင်	Tauk pa thvanꞋ pyaung
ခုတိုင်အောင်လျှင်	Khu taing aung lhyaṅ̊
အရောင်လက်ဘိ	Ayaung lak phi
အမြဲရှိ၏	Amyè shi i
အသိသက်သေ	Asi sakse
မသွေအမတာ	Ma-sve amatā
၍ကဗျာသည်	Ī kabyā sī

ကျမ်းလာများလို။ အညွန်သောဝ– KyamꞋ lā myāꞋ lọ̊ añhvan soꞋ

Y

III

သိုက်ထုံးဝေဆာ	Saik thumး ve-chā
မြှို့မြှို့ဖြါလျက်	Khyiṃ khyiṃ ṅyā lyak
သချၤ တွက်စစ်	Saṅkhyā tvak cit
အနှစ်သုံးရာ	A-nhit sumး yā
ရှေးလွန်ခါက	Sheး lvan khā ga
ပညာရင့်သီး	Paññā yaṅ̊ sīး
ရှုယ်တိုင်းပြီးၟ၍	Yvê daingးpyīး yvḕ
ညာဏ်ကြီးပုဂ္ဂိုလ်	Ñan gyīး puggô
ကဗျာဆိုသား	Kabyā chô sāး
ထိုရှိတ်ခပျာ	Tho Sheik-ca-pyā
မြတ်ဆရာအား	Myat chayā āး
ဘာသာ ဗုဒ္ဓ	Bhāsā Buddha
စွဲယူကြသား	Cvḕ yū gya sāး
မြန်မၒနှၨယ်ရိုး	Myan-mạ̄ nvê yôး
မြန်လူမျိုးတို့	Myan lū myôး dô̥
ဆောင်ကျိုးအတွက်	Chaung kyôး a-tvak
လွန်အားတက်၍	Lvan āး tak vyḕ
မပျက်သိမ်းချုပ်	Ma-pyak simး khyôk
အကျွန်ုပ်သည်	A-kyvan-nôk sī
လက်အုပ်ရှိခေါ်	Lak-ôk khyī ṅaw
ရှိပူဇော်၏	Shi pū-jaw i
နုမော်ဒနာ	Nu-maw-danā
၍ပူဇာသည်	Ĭ pūjā sī

ဖြမ်းပါလားသို့။ အမွန်သောဝ်—	Ṅyamး bā lāး sô̥ amvan soး

TRANSLATION

I

WHEN I carefully studied the poems of the illustrious dramatic poet Shakespeare, whose widespread fame is known all the world over, it was the Buddhistic sentiments in them that appealed to me most, and I was greatly rejoiced in the study of our deep philosophy, inasmuch as they added to the profound interest I felt in the subject.

II

Because of the ultimate truth, embodied in sublime poetic diction, the splendid and wonderful religion of that Sage-Conqueror has lasted to this day, with untarnished lustre after five-and-twenty centuries, as a standing witness to the immortality of Shakespeare, who is a guide unto posterity, because he conforms to our philosophy.

III

May this my tribute of appreciation, on behalf of Burmese Buddhists, to Shakespeare's great mind, which dwelt on lofty thoughts, constituting a permanent record of humanity three centuries ago, serve as a standard for future generations.

S. Z. AUNG.

NOTES

(a) *Lyric.*

' Ratu' is a Burmese lyric which was originally ' sung' but not ' made'. Hence it was generally sung in a single verse known to this date as *Ekabaik* (one verse), but seldom in more than three verses called *Paiksôn* (complete verses) except in the transitional period to the epic, when this limit was exceeded. When sung in two verses the piece is designated *Aphyigan* (lit., left to be completed).

Y 2

(b) *Metrical feet.*

Each verse contains the same number of feet, usually of four syllables each, except the last, which is generally made up of seven syllables. When there are more than four syllables in a foot which is not final, two short syllables are treated as one. In the best verses the initial and final feet are alike throughout.

(c) *Rhyme.*

As a rule the fourth syllable of a foot rhymes with the third of the next and the second or first of the third. But sometimes the fourth syllable of a preceding foot may rhyme with the second or even the first of the next foot immediately following.

Pronunciation of the Roman Transcript.

The transliteration is phonetic.
a, ā, i, ī, u, ū, o as in Pali (or Italian);
è, ê, as in French;
ô as oh in English;
au as *ow* in cow;
aw as *aw* in saw (prolonged, somewhat like *o* in or);
ai as *i* in isle, mile, tide;
a dot subscribed to a vowel, or a final consonant following a vowel, checks the tone of the vowel;
the colon mark indicates a grave accent, e.g. o: as *o* in go;
the nasals ṅ and ñ are as in Pali (approx. ng and ny), the nasal ṇ being retained as n;
   so also c, ch, th (= ch, cch, t-h).
sh as in English she;
s as *th* in English thin;
ś as *th* in the or they;
v as *w* in English;
aṅ as in in English;
ôk as oak in English, but with *k* sound somewhat mute;
eik as *i* in tick, but with *k* sound somewhat mute;
ak is more like *et* in let, with *t* sound somewhat mute;
it as in English, with *t* sound somewhat mute.

SHAKESPEARE: A BURMAN'S APPRECIATION

HUMAN nature is the same all the world over, and every human being who reads Shakespeare must be greatly impressed by the wonderful power displayed by the poet in touching the chords of human feeling, and by the comprehensiveness of his study of mankind. The impression must, of course, vary according to the individual estimate each person makes of Shakespeare's works. Different nations also will be differently impressed. To the Burman Shakespeare appeals most from the religious point of view. The Burman is pre-eminently a religious person ; he has been cultured in Buddhist ethics and philosophy ever since the fifth century A. D., the traditional date when Buddhism was introduced into Burma. The evidence of this religious spirit of the nation is best seen in the literature, the prevailing tone of which is religious, every one being constantly exhorted to do the utmost amount of good while in this world. In fact, in Burma literature is religion and religion is literature. Now, the peculiar thing about Shakespeare is that he very often comes to the Burman Buddhist as a relief—somewhat like the feeling that one experiences at the conclusion of an oppressively long sermon, when one is glad to get away to the open air and indulge in some friendly chat. And yet Shakespearian literature manages to teach the same high standard of ethics as the Buddhist, without a distinct ethical tendency. In spite of his vigorous appreciation of the world, Shakespeare shakes hands with the Buddha, in his utter renunciation of the world.

What Shakespeare has been to Burma is very little compared with what he will be. Already some of his plays have been translated into Burmese, and made accessible to those who are unable to enjoy the original. And although these first attempts at presenting Shakespeare in Burmese garb are clumsy enough, owing to the many difficulties encountered— the Burmese language is radically different from the English—there is every reason to believe that in the near future Shakespeare will make an attractive figure on the Burmese stage. It will then mark an epoch-making change in the history of Burmese literature, as vital as has been the introduction of Buddhism. The Burmese mind is plastic, and has produced a vast literature in testimony of its Buddhist culture. At present it is passing through a transitional stage, brought about by the advent of the English, and is already producing novels in Burmese, which, so far as psychological import goes, show a distinct indebtedness to English culture. It was in 1912 that *Julius Caesar* was first staged by the students of the Rangoon College, with considerable success; and who can tell what that performance means to Burma?

MAUNG TIN.

RANGOON COLLEGE, RANGOON,
BURMA.

TO THE MEMORY OF SHAKESPEARE

الى شكسبير

شغوف بقول العبقريين مغرمُ   يحييك من ارض الكنانة شاعر

البك ملوك القول عرب وأعجم   ويطربه فى يوم ذكراك ان مشت

*

وفى كلّ عصر ثم أنشأت تحكم   نظرت بعين الغيب فى كلّ أمّة

لك الغاية القصوى فادتك مُلْهم   فلم تخطئ المرمى ولاغرو إن دنت

تجنّهم و ان راق الطلاءُ هم هُم   أوقف ساعة وانظر الى الخلف نظرة

وفوق غباب البحر من صنعهم دم   على ظهر ها من شرّ أطماعهم دمّ

يزول الى أن ضجّت الارض منهم   تفانوا على دديا تغرّ وباطل

لتشهد ما يُبصى ويُدمى ويُؤلم   فليبتك تحيا يا أبا الشعر ساعة

فكان بها عهد الحضارة يُختم   وقائع حرب أجّج العلمُ نارها

سواء جهول القوم والمتعلّم   وتعلم أن الطبع لا زال غالبا

ولا زال منه العلم ما كان يزعُم   فما بلغت منه الحضارة مأربا

وكنت على تلك الطبائع تنقم   أهَبْت بهنا من قرون ثلاثة

ولا زالت الآراءُ تُبنى وتُهدَم   وما هدم التجريبُ رأياً بنيتَه

*

بشير سلام ثغرُه يتبسّم   ألا إن ذكرى شكسبير بنت لنا

قليلا وحيّوا شعرَه وترنّموا   فلو أنصفوا أبطالهم لتهادنوا

ولم يُرهقوا نفسا ولم يتقحّموا   ولم طلقوا فى يوم ذكراه مِدفعاً

*

له قلم ماضى الشباة كأنّما

اقام بِشقّيه القضاءُ المحتّم

طهور إنا ما دُنّست كفّ كاتب

وثوب إنا ما قرّ فى الطرس مِرْقم

ولوع بتصوير الطباع فلم يَجُزْ

بعاطفة الا حسبناه يرسم

ارانَى فى (مكبيث) للحقدِ صورة

تكاد به أحساؤها تتضرّم

ومثّل فى (شالوك) البخل بسحنة

عليها غبار الهون و الوجه أقتم

وأعجزنى عن وصف (هملِيت) حسنها

وفى مثلها تعيى البَراعة و الفم

دع السحرَ فى (روميو) و(جوليِيت) إنما

يحسُّ بما فيها الأريبُ المتيّم

أنّاهم بشعر عبقرى كأنّه

سطور من الانجيل تُتلى و تُكرم

ندى على الأيّام يردان نضرة

ويرتدان فيها جِدّة وهو يَقْدم

يُؤدّى الى قُرّائه أن نسجه

لِيَومٍ وان الحائك اليوم فيهم

كتلك النقوش الراهيات بمعبد

لفرعون لا زالت على الدهر تسلم

فلم يَبْنُ من احسانه متأخّر

ولم يبجر فى ميدانه متقدم

أطلّ عليهم من سماء خياله

وحلّق حيث الوهم لا يتجشّم

وجاء بما فوق الطبيعة وقعه

فأكبرَ قوم ما أتاه وأعظموا

وقالوا تحدّانا بما يعجز النُّهى

فلسنا إنا آثارَه تتبرتّم

ولم يتحدّ الناس لكنه امرؤٌ

بما كان فى مقدورِه يتكلّم

لقد جهلوه حِقبة ثم ردّهم

البه الهدى فاستغفروا وترحّموا

كذاك رجال الشرق لو ينصفونهم

لقام لهم فى الشرق و الغرب موسم

اضاء بهم بطن الثرى بعد موتهم

واعقابهم عن نور آياتهم عَموا

*

فقل لبنى التاميز والجمع حافل

به يُنثر الدرّ الثمين وينظم

لئن كان فى ضخم الأساطيل فخركم

لفخْرُكُم بالشاعر الفرد أعظم

محمد حافظ ابراهيم
بمصر

MOHAMMED ḤĀFIZ IBRĀHIM.

SHAKESPEARE

من الشاعر الصغير الى الشاعر الكبير

استيقظْ اليومَ وَعُنْ للكلامْ	يا ملكَ الشعرِ عليك السلامْ
كلاهما يهديك ازكى السلامْ	البلبل الشادي و باكي الحمامْ
وأنت من مثواك لا تطلعُ	لكنّ سترَ القبرِ لا يُرقَعُ

*

لسانُهُ عن مجدهم ينطقُ	لكل قوم شاعرٌ مُفلِقُ
تفوت مَنْ فات ولا تلحق	وأنت من سابقهم أسبقُ
وكُلَّ طَرفي إثرَهُ يظلعُ	كالبرق في علبائِهِ يلمَعُ

*

شغلَ إلَهِ الحَربِ في غازِنة	أُشغلَ هوميرُ بالبيانية
كالعَبْدِ لا يعصى على سادنة	جرى مع الشَعْبِ على عادنة
كالخادم الخائن ان يخضعُ	وشاعرُ الأُمةِ ان يخضعُ

*

بين الدخول القفر او حومل	بكى امرؤُ القيس على منزل
فصاح يا ليل الا فانجل	وضجَ من ليل الهوى الاليل
انا دعت اهواؤه ينتبع	وراح فى ضلتـه يـنـزع

*

عن ساكن الجنة والنار	خبرنا (دانتى) بأخبار
يسقونه ثم الـى دار	طيف (بياتريس) به السارى
ونخته ناظره يخشع	سناك فى أرجائها يسطع

*

قد جد فى إثرك هوجو الكبير   وابن هوجو طالبا شكسبير

أدى به النجد وطول المسير   لمورد فاض بعذب نمير

فرحت فى تياره تشرع   وظل من شاطئه يتترع

*

أخجل (غوثا) ما جنى أهله   وضاع فى نقصهم فضله

ان كان يحكى قوله فعله   ولم يكن من عقلهم عقله

فأنه فى قبره يجزع   كل امرئ من ظلمهم يفزع

*

وصفت للاخلاف أسلافهم   فمميز الاخلاف اوصافهم

وامتثل التاريخ انصافهم   اما وقد آمن من خافهم

فعهدهم فى عهدنا يرجع   كأننا نبصر من أزمعوا

*

الناس فى أيامنا فى حروب   اعناقهم مثقلة بالذنوب

قد أوجد الله وأفنى (كروب)   الله فيما بين هذى القلوب

تحت الدياجى أعين تدمع   تفعل ما لا يفعل المدفع

*

الله خلاق الورى ناظر   وكل عدوان له آخر

وكل قهار له قاهر   هذا مقام الشعر يا شاعر

غن ففوق الخلق من يسمع   ان هجع الساهد لا يهجع

*

جوزين عن (روميو و جليت) بما   يجزى محب السلم رب السما

فكم مثال عندنا منهما   يبدو فيخفى بين موج الدما

وكم شباب فى الورى يصرع   يفرع مرديه ولا يفرع

ولي الدين يكن

WALIY AD-DIN YEYEN.

I

SUMMARY OF THE POEM

BY MOHAMMED ḤĀFIZ IBRĀHIM

AFTER two lines of salutation, the poet wishes that Shakespeare could rise to see how the present state of the world agrees with the world as it is described in his dramas. Neither civilization nor learning has affected it in the manner hoped. If the world were just to Shakespeare's memory, there would be a general truce on his commemoration day. He then briefly describes *Macbeth, Shylock, Hamlet, Romeo and Juliet*, characters whose freshness remains through the ages, like the art of the Pharaonic sanctuaries. Shakespeare is unapproached by his successors, unrivalled by his predecessors. He looks down on all from the sky of his imagination, and flies whither the fancy cannot venture. For a time his merits were ignored, then they were recognized, and his forgiveness was implored. Similarly, if justice were done to the Oriental authors, there would be feasts in their honour in both East and West. Say to the men of the Thames, when the gathering in Shakespeare's honour is listening to prose and verse: *However great your pride in your mighty fleet, your pride in the unique bard is yet greater.*

II

SUMMARY OF THE POEM

BY WALIY AD-DIN YEYEN

THE poet briefly describes the works of Homer, Imruu'l-Kais, Dante, Victor Hugo, and Goethe, adding that the last has been disgraced by his compatriots. Above all these he sets Shakespeare, whose characters all reappear in those of our own day. He briefly alludes to the troubles of the present time, with an imprecation on Krupp, and a blessing on Shakespeare for *Romeo and Juliet*.

A SOUTH AFRICAN'S HOMAGE

Go fitlhela ka 1896 ke sa le lekaoana, ke ne ke itsetse Shakespeare mo lotlatlaneng. Ka ngoaga oo ka okoa ke dipolelo tsa koranta ea Teemane ka ea go bona Makgooa mo Theatereng ea Kimberley a tshameka polelo eaga *Hamlet*, e e mo bukeng ngoe ea gagoe. Motshameko o oa ntlhotlheletsa go tlhotlhomisa dikoalo tsa gagoe. Ko ga rona mafoko a santse a boleloa ka molomo ka maitisho; ere re tlotla ka maabanyane ke fitlhele ke ana go feta balekane baaka, ka ke ne ke male mocoedi o o sa kgaleng mo bontsintsing joa buka tsaga Tsikinya-Chaka.

Pele-pele ke badile polelo ea *Segoaba sa Venice*, ka fitlhela batho ba ba boleloang ke buka eo ba choana thata le batshedi ba ba itsegeng. Ga bo go nale dimokolara dingoe ko Teemaneng, ka tla ka utloa, ke se na go bolela mafoko a buka eo, tsala ngoe eaka e mpotsa gore, ke ofe oa dimokolara tseo, eo Shakespeare o ṁmitsang Shylock. Moo gotlhe ga ira gore ke nyoreloe dikoalo tsaga Tsikinya-Chaka. Erile ke ntse ke di balela pele ka fitlhela maele ale mantsi, a bachomi ba kgabisang puo ka one—a ke ne ke itlhoma ele diane tsa Sekgooa—ese diane, ele dinopolo tsa mabolelo aga Shakespeare.

Erile ke bala polelo eaga *Cymbeline* ka

I had but a vague idea of Shakespeare until about 1896 when, at the age of 18, I was attracted by the Press remarks in the Kimberley paper, and went to see *Hamlet* in the Kimberley Theatre. The performance made me curious to know more about Shakespeare and his works. Intelligence in Africa is still carried from mouth to mouth by means of conversations after working hours, and, reading a number of Shakespeare's works, I always had a fresh story to tell.

I first read *The Merchant of Venice*.

The characters were so realistic that I was asked more than once to which of certain speculators, then operating round Kimberley, Shakespeare referred as Shylock.

All this gave me an appetite for more Shakespeare, and I found that many of the current quotations used by educated natives to embellish their speeches, which I had always taken for English proverbs, were culled from Shakespeare's works.

While reading *Cymbeline*, I met

rakana le kgarebe e gompieno eleng 'ma-bana baa ka. Eare ka ke ne ke ese ke itse segagabo—Setebele saga 'Ma-Magana Tshegana—jaaka jaanong; lefa ene a ne a itse segaecho—Secoana saga Tau a Mo-coala Tshega—ka bo ke belaela gore a jaana nka mo senolela boteng oa maikutlo aaka ka shone : ke fa re tla dumalana go buisana ka loleme loa barutegi, ebong Senyesemane shoora Tsikinya-Chaka, se ka nako eo ene ele shone puo ea Goromente oa rona. Khane tse re ne re di koalalana ka metlha di ne dile kana ka tsela ea Kgalagadi; gonne ene eare ke simolotse ka gore ke bolela maikutlo a pelo eame, ke fitlhele ke shoeditse ka go 'melegololela bojotlhe joa mooa oa me. Fa ele ka manyama a puo le go kanolola dikakanyo tsa dilo tse di sa bonoeng phenyo ea mekoalo eaka e ne e lekalekana fela le ea mosadi oaka. Ke se se tlhomameng gore megopolo ea rona e ne e ntse logedioa ke dikoma tsaga Tsi-kinya-Chaka.

Koalo longoe loa gagoe lo re lo badileng ka nako eo ke phereano ea bo *Romeo le Julieta*. Go leredioa ngoetsi eo o buang puo e e thoantshang loleme. Jaaka Seku-dukama, bagaecho ba ne ba go ila sefefehu; bagagabo le bone fela jalo, ba ila mogoe eo o puo e sa tlalang, e sa thoantsheng loleme. Lefagontsejalo ra se ka ra shoetsa ka go shoela ko diphupung jaka bo Romeo le kgarebe ea gagoe; ebile baga rona gom-pieno ba itumelela bana ba rona, dikoko-mana tsa madi a a pekanyeng, ba ba puo pedi ko loapeng le ko Khooeng.

Mo tshimologong ea 'moeleoele ono—ke gore ka 1901—ka simolola tiro ea diko-ranta; ere fa ke koala dikgang tsa kago, tsa musho, le tsa ditlhabano ke di none ka

the girl who afterwards became my wife. I was not then as well acquainted with her language—the Xosa—as I am now; and although she had a better grip of mine—the Sechuana—I was doubtful whether I could make her understand my innermost feelings in it, so in com-ing to an understanding we both used the language of educated peo-ple—the language which Shake-speare wrote—which happened to be the only official language of our country at the time.

Some of the daily epistles were rather lengthy, for I usually started with the bare intention of express-ing the affections of my heart but generally finished up by completely unburdening my soul. For com-mand of language and giving expression to abstract ideas, the success of my efforts was second only to that of my wife's, and it is easy to divine that Shakespeare's poems fed our thoughts.

It may be depended upon that we both read *Romeo and Juliet*.

My people resented the idea of my marrying a girl who spoke a lan-guage which, like the Hottentot language, had clicks in it; while her people likewise abominated the idea of giving their daughter in marriage to a fellow who spoke a language so imperfect as to be with-out any clicks. But the civilized laws of Cape Colony saved us from a double tragedy in a cemetery, and our erstwhile objecting relatives have lived to award their benedic-tion to the growth of our Chuana-M'Bo family which is bilingual both in the vernaculars and in European languages.

In the beginning of this century I became a journalist, and when called on to comment on things

mabolelo aga Shakespeare. Ka 1910, jaka Mochochonono o phakaletse mo mago di-mong, King Edward VII le Kgosi dile pedi tsa Becoana—bo Sebele le Bathoeng—tsaa shoa. Ka tlhadia kitsisho tsa dincho tsa bone ka tsela tsaga Shakespeare tse di-reng :

Eare fa dikhutsana dii shoa
Re se ke re bone naledi tse di megatla;
Motlhango go shoang dikgosi
Go tuka le magodimo ka osi.

Ereka Becoana ele ditlapela tsa tlholego, ebile ba rata go maitisho, mabolelo a a ntseng jalo a atisa go ba gapa dipelo. Go tloga fong, eare ke phakeletse ko Kgosing ko Goo Ra-Tshi di, morenana mongoe a mpotsa leina ja Khooe eo itseng gobua eo. Kgosana ngoe ea mochomi eabo ele fa kgotla, ea itlhaganela ea nkarabela; eare: William Tsikinya-Chaka. Lefa toloko di se ke di dumalana ka metlha, mo pheto-long ea leina je re kare kgosana e tantse jaka kama gonne bontsi joa batho ba ba umakoang mo mabolelong aga Shakespeare bo shule ka chaka.

A jaana go ithata bo morafe game gase gone go nthatisang dibuka tsaga Tsikinya-Chaka. Nka rarabolola poco e ka sechoan-cho sa mothale o mongoe se se mphero-sang sebete fela jaka Tsikinya-Chaka a nkgatlha.

Nkile ka ea go bona motshameko oa cinematograph (dichoancho tse di tsa-maeang), oa dipogo tsa Morena. Ka fitlhela batho botlhe ko papolong ea Mo-rena ele dichoancho tsa Makgooa. Bo Pilato, Baperisita—le Simone oa Kireneo tota—botlhe-lele ele Makgooa. Mocoana o na ale esi fela mo loferetlhong loo, ene

social, political, or military, I always found inspiration in one or other of Shakespeare's sayings. For instance, in 1910, when Halley's Comet illumined the Southern skies, King Edward VII and two great Bechuana Chiefs—Sebele and Bathoeng—died. I commenced each obituary with Shakespeare's quotation:

When beggars die there are no comets seen;
The heavens themselves blaze forth the death of princes.

Besides being natural story-tellers, the Bechuana are good listeners, and legendary stories seldom fail to impress them. Thus, one morn-ing, I visited the Chief's court at Mafeking and was asked for the name of 'the white man who spoke so well'. An educated Chieftain promptly replied for me; he said: William Tsikinya-Chaka (William Shake-the-Sword). The transla-tion, though perhaps more free than literal, is happy in its way considering how many of Shake-speare's characters met their death. Tsikinya-Chaka became noted among some of my readers as a reliable white oracle.

It is just possible that selfish patriot-ism is at the bottom of my admira-tion for Shakespeare. To illustrate my meaning let me take a case showing how feelings of an opposite kind were roused in me.

I once went to see a cinematograph show of the Crucifixion. All the characters in the play, including Pilate, the Priests, and Simon of Cyrene, were white men. Accord-ing to the pictures, the only black man in the mob was Judas Iscariot.

ele Jutase.   Esale jalo ke tlhoboga maaka a dibaesekopo, le gompieno mono London ke bonye ngoe ea macodimacoke e shupa maatlametlo a Makgooa e a bapisa le kokeco ea boboko e e makgapha ea boatla joa Bancho.

Koalo tsag-a Tsikinya-Chaka di nkgatlha ka gobo di shupa fa maatlametlo le bonatla (jaaka boatla le bogatlapa) di sa tlhaole 'mala.

. . . .

Ke nyaga dile 300 jaanong Tsikinya-Chaka a shule, 'me ekete o na a tlhaloganya maitseo a batho ba gompieno thata. Kafa mabolelo a gagoe e lolameng ka teng (lefa gompieno re koalalana le lefatshe jotlhe ka bonako joa logadima, ebile re tedieaganya ka makoloi a a ikgarametsang) ekete re santse rè tlhaela manontlhotlho a gagoe.

Re santse re le mo pakeng tsa borathana joa dikoalo tsa Afrika.   Gola tlhe ea kre fa di golela pele bakoadi le batoloki ba gatisetsa Bancho mabolelo mangoe aga Tsikinya-Chaka.   Ke buisioa ke go bo ke fitlhela ekete ekare fa re lateletse ra fitlhela a theiloe mo metheong e e dumalanang le oa maele mangoe a Afrika.

I have since become suspicious of the veracity of the cinema and acquired a scepticism which is not diminished by a gorgeous one now exhibited in London which shows, side by side with the nobility of the white race, a highly coloured exaggeration of the depravity of the blacks.

Shakespeare's dramas, on the other hand, show that nobility and valour, like depravity and cowardice, are not the monopoly of any colour.

. . . .

Shakespeare lived over 300 years ago, but he appears to have had a keen grasp of human character. His description of things seems so inwardly correct that (in spite of our rapid means of communication and facilities for travelling) we of the present age have not yet equalled his acumen.

It is to be hoped that with the maturity of African literature, now still in its infancy, writers and translators will consider the matter of giving to Africans the benefit of some at least of Shakespeare's works.   That this could be done is suggested by the probability that some of the stories on which his dramas are based find equivalents in African folk-lore.

HEART OF THE RACE

Nᴏᴛ in marble or bronze, the sum of thy lineaments ;
Not in colour or line that painter or graver may trace.
Out of the kingdom of vision, gleaming, transcendent, immortal,
Issue thy creatures and step into vesture of time and place —
Each with passion and pulse of thy heart ; but, passing the portal,
Each in likeness of us. And listening, wondering,
Lo, from the lips of each we gather a thought of thy Face !

Nature walleth her womb with wreckage of history :
Touch, O Poet, thy lyre, and heart-beats frozen in stone
Tremble to life once more—to the towers of pain and of pity—
Build themselves into thee, thy ramparts of rapture and moan,
Cry with a human voice from the passioning walls of thy city—
Hamlets, Richards, Cordelias, prisoned, oblivious,
Dateless minions of death, till summoned by thee alone.

Fortune maketh of men pipes for her fingering ;
Thou hast made of thine England music of nobler employ :
Men whose souls are their own ; whose breastplate, honour untainted ;
Of promise precise, God-fearing, abhorring the dreams that destroy—
The Moloch of Force ensky'd, the ape of Necessity sainted ;—
To country and freedom true ; merciful, generous,
Valiant to merit in Fate the heart's-ease mortals enjoy.

Shaper, thou, of the tongue ! Under the Pleiades,
Under the Southern Cross, under the Boreal Crown,
Where there's a mother's lap and a little one seeking a story,
Where there's a teacher or parson, or player come to the town—
Mage of the opaline phrase, meteoric, dissolving in glory,
Splendid lord of the word predestined, immutable—
Children are learning thy English and handing the heritage down.

Who but opens thy book : odorous memories
Breathe of the dear, dear land, sceptred and set in the sea.
Her primrose pale, her sweet o' the year, have savour and semblance
For Perditas woo'd in the tropics and Florizels tutored by thee.
The rue of her sea-wallèd garden, the rosemary, wake to remembrance
Where furrowed exiles from home, wintered with pilgriming,
Yearn for the white-faced shores, and turn thy page on the knee.

No philosopher, thou : best of philosophers !
Blood and judgement commingled are masters of self-control.
Poet of common sense, reality, weeping, and laughter :
Not in the caverns of Time, not in the tides that roll
On the high shore of this world, not in the dim hereafter—
In reason and sorrow, the hope ; in mercy, the mystery :
By selling hours of dross we enrich the moment of soul.

Poet, thou, of the Blood : of states and of nations
Passing thy utmost dream, in the uttermost corners of space !
Poet, thou, of my countrymen—born to the speech, O Brother,
Born to the law and freedom, proud of the old embrace,
Born of the *Mayflower*, born of Virginia—born of the Mother !
Poet, thou of the Mother ! the blood of America,
Turning in tribute to thee, revisits the Heart of the Race.

CHARLES MILLS GAYLEY.

University of California.

z

THE HOMAGE OF THE SHAKSPERE SOCIETY OF PHILADELPHIA

> Vouchsafe to those that have not read the story,
> That I may prompt them.—*Henry V,* prol., Act v.

THOSE visitors to Stratford-on-Avon who have wisely arranged that their sojourn covers the 23rd of April are not likely soon to forget one distinguishing feature of the ceremonies whereby that day is marked. Not the streets and lanes gay with garlands and flags ; not the impressive yet simple service in the church ; but the sight of the long procession formed of young and old—men, women, children—all bearing flowers, either in bunches or in single blooms, and all, in a spirit of homage and reverence, with but one intent—from the small boy with his bunch of primroses or cowslips plucked in the lovely Warwickshire lanes, to the dignified Mayor and Town Council with their elaborate wreaths of laurel. With one intent : that of paying tribute to the memory of Shakespeare by placing some offering upon his grave, beneath that monument in Trinity Church. Slowly the throng files past, each depositing their weedy trophies upon that shrine, until, where before there were but bare grey stones, there is now a veritable mound of violets, roses, daffodils, and green grasses. Fortunate ones ! they may thus give an outward and tangible expression of what they feel. But what of us, less fortunate ones ? We of the New World, who own a common heritage in Shakespeare by right of birth and language. Our thoughts turn naturally towards that common goal, even as the face of the Moslem turns towards Mecca. From the four corners of the earth they come to kiss this shrine, and that procession slowly passing through the streets of Stratford is typical of all who wish to pay homage to Shakespeare in this year which marks the three hundredth anniversary of his death. May we not, each one, bring what offering is in our power ? Happy he, indeed, whose tribute shall prove to be made of immortelles, but happy also, he whose gift shines brightly if only for that one day. These reverent gifts honour the givers more than the recipient. Could any one hope to add one leaf to the laurels on Shakespeare's brow ? We cannot make the service greater than the god. Yet, granting this, there is a certain distinctive mark of honour upon this tribute which comes from America. It is a record of over half a century's devotion to the reading and careful study of Shakespeare's Comedies, Histories, and Tragedies ; the homage paid by the Shakspere Society of Philadelphia. (This spelling of the name was adopted by the Society in its corporate title, and has therefore been strictly preserved.)

The origin of the Society is of the simplest. In the year 1852 four young men, then studying for the bar, sought a means of relaxation from their prosaic studies, and therefore decided to meet each week, for certain hours in the evening, with no purpose other than to read and study the plays of Shakespeare. The prime mover and chief of this small coterie was Asa Israel Fish, a man of wide culture, and a lover of both classic and English poetry. He had the happy faculty of gathering about him men of kindred tastes, and of causing them to give of their best ; he was thus eminently fitted for the leadership of this band of brothers, these happy few. In those early days the members spoke of themselves as the ' Shakspere Apostles ', not with any irreverent idea, but rather in imitation of the distinguished English Club of Apostles, to which frequent reference is made in Bristed's *Five Years in an English University*, and as their number increased it soon became a custom to gather at a commemoration dinner, on a date usually towards the end of December. Six years after the inception of the Society the number of members had grown to seventeen, and it was then agreed that, accordingly, a regular organization with a more systematic course of study was advisable. Although from the beginning Fish had nominally been the head, yet now he was duly elected as the new organization's Dean, which office he held until his death in 1879.

The Society, as such, was now fairly started, and its records were, for the first time, reduced to writing, but there was no thought of a series of publications as had been the aim of other literary societies, and in this respect the Shakspere Society of Philadelphia is in a class of its own. Contributions by members have from time to time been printed, but for private circulation only.

Thus regularly organized, the Society grew and flourished, and the nucleus of a library, for use during the meetings, was soon developed. Under the personal supervision of the Dean the collection grew to nearly six hundred volumes, and might in time have grown to valuable dimensions had it not been unfortunately lost to the Society by the death of its chief custodian. The volumes were set apart in Mr. Fish's library, but were unrecognized as the property of others when his own books were sold by his executors. A set of Boswell's Malone, Staunton's facsimile of the Folio, and an imperfect set of the Ashbee Quarto fac-similes were saved, since they had been at the Society's rooms ; but, lacking a complete list of the other volumes in the Dean's charge, the other books could not be reclaimed.   But this is anticipating, and we must return to the earlier annals, although it is quite unnecessary to detail the work of the Society year by year.   The plays were read and studied, with discussion and explanation, the Dean presiding and directing the flow of reason at the bi-weekly meetings, and the minutes duly chronicle the growing popularity of these gatherings followed by a mild refection and the elaborate fare provided at their annual commemoration dinners, still held towards the end of December. The year 1861 will be ever held as memorable in the history of our country, and no less prominent, though for far different reasons, must this year be held in the history of the Shakspere Society, for on March 12, 1861, it received its charter and became a corporate body.   Be it noted in passing that our Society thus antedates by three years the Deutsche Shakespeare-Gesellschaft, which was founded in 1864 in commemoration of the three-hundredth anniversary of Shakespeare's birth.

A clause in this charter provides that an annual meeting be held on the 23rd of April for the election of officers and the transaction of business.   This it was which caused a change from one of the old established customs wherein the commemoration dinner, heretofore held in December, was transferred to follow the annual meeting in April, and it has thus continued ever since.   The propriety of such a change had long been recognized, but was overruled by the Dean, who feared that the spring months would never furnish dishes sufficiently delectable for a function so important.   It is, however, recorded that he now yielded, and this excellent change was made chiefly on the suggestion of Horace Howard Furness, who was then Secretary of the Society.

During those troublous years of the civil war the members realized the impropriety of an appearance, even, of festivity, and therefore the annual dinners were discontinued, although their bi-weekly meetings— mainly composed of those members whose years made them ineligible for service—were still held in a desultory fashion.

Richard L. Ashhurst was a member at this time—he became Vice-Dean later—and wrote a short history of the Society ; therein he presents the following graphic description of one of those meetings :

The members were seated on both sides of the long table, at the head of which the Dean was seated.   Which of us can forget the affectionate glance over his spectacles as we entered, half-reproachful if some were late ?   Each member had before him one or more editions of the play. In front of the Dean stood a row of dictionaries and books of reference, Mrs. Clarke's Concordance, Sidney Walker, &c. We had not then the invaluable Schmidt. . . . Nothing that I remember was more marked in its fruitfulness to us younger members than discussions between Professor Short and Dr. Krauth, the tendency of the mind of the former being rather to a rigid or literal exegesis, while with the other the poetic judgement and sympathetic insight had ever sway. While over all the debates our dear Dean presided with his solemn courtesy, seeming often to be swayed himself backward and forward with the drift of the argument.

With but a very slight change this may be taken as typical of meetings even down to the present day. The historian also notes that in these later times the study is much more discursive and exhaustive than in the earlier, and that consequently longer extracts of the winter's study were covered at each session. It was formerly quite usual to read an entire Act in one evening ; but now this would be decidedly the exception, a hundred lines being the ordinary amount.

The year 1864 is an ever-memorable one to all Shakespearians : it may be called the zenith to the nadir of the present year, and the Society showed its recognition of an occasion so important by resuming its annual dinner on the 23rd of April. This season was also one of peculiar productiveness, inasmuch as the Notes on *The Tempest*, the winter's study, contributed by various members, were not only carefully reduced to writing, as heretofore, but also elaborately printed. This was a distinct innovation, and even yet forms the most permanent memorial of the work of the Shakspere Society. The edition was strictly limited ; copies are now esteemed rarities, and seldom, if ever, have been offered for sale.

In the spring of 1865 the whole nation was contracted in one brow of woe over the assassination of the President, and the Society, again feeling that the annual festivity would be unbefitting, omitted it.

It is a fact known to but a few, that to the studies and work of the Shakspere Society may be directly traced the inception of the new Variorum Edition of *Shakespeare*. During the season of 1866–7 the play read in the winter's study was *Romeo and Juliet*, and it was noticed by Horace Howard Furness that frequently a whole evening's work of discussion and comment on the variations of the texts had been anticipated in the notes of those commentators subsequent to the Variorum of 1821, which edition, heretofore, had formed the groundwork for the Society's discussion. In that edition the comments of all former editors are given, but the textual notes are sadly deficient. In the monumental Cambridge edition of Clark and Wright the textual notes are exhaustive and complete, but the commentary consists of a few explanatory notes at the end of each play; this is, however, no deficiency—the avowed purpose of the Cambridge editors was but to furnish a text based mainly upon that of existing quartos. The need of an edition which should combine the features of both these editions on a single page was at once recognized, and the work of gathering and classifying the notes was undertaken by the Secretary, primarily as an aid to the work of the Society. Its value to other students was at once apparent, since it practically formed a continuation of the Variorum of 1821, and with the stimulus of their encouragement the editor began preparing his manuscript for the press. The volume, *Romeo and Juliet*, was published in 1871, two years after its inception, and is dedicated to the Shakspere Society.

It is needless here to speak of the character of that volume, or of those which followed and now form a lasting memorial of that most able editor. Their worth is written in their own pages, and the Shakspere Society may well feel proud that so great a flood has flowed from so clear a source.

The year 1869 also marks the establishment of the Society upon a firmer foundation, and the annual dinners have been held with scarcely an interruption since that time. A distinctive feature of these dinners must be mentioned : as far back as 1856 the commemoration dinner was marked by an elaborate bill of fare, whereon each dish was characterized by a quotation. The ingenuity of the members was taxed even to the uttermost to provide a line or passage descriptive of the various wines and edibles, and there was no restriction as to choice so long as it was made from one of the plays or poems of Shakespeare. In 1869 the winter's study was *Richard II*, and it was then decided that for the bill of fare all the quotations should be from this play only ; the result was most successful, and from that time this rule in regard to the bills has been strictly followed. In 1879 the death of Asa Israel Fish deprived the Society of one who had so ably piloted it through times of stress into those of quiet, and his loss was deeply mourned. He was succeeded as Dean by Horace Howard Furness, which office was held by him until his death in 1912, and he was then succeeded by the present writer.

These short and simple annals may well close here ; they are a record of our loving homage to Shakespeare. This then be our tribute which, in thought, we reverently place before that glowing shrine towards which all thoughts this year are turning.

HORACE HOWARD FURNESS, JR.

THE PARADOX OF SHAKESPEARE

THERE is a fame that is founded on the verdict of the many ; there is a fame that is founded on the verdict of the few : and, especially in the domain of art, it is seldom that the two verdicts coincide, to make the vote unanimous.

In all the arts except the drama, the verdict of the few is immeasurably more important than the verdict of the many. Artistic taste requires cultivation ; the majority of people are uncultivated ; therefore the taste of the majority is very likely to be wrong. The fame of Milton is secure ; but it is based upon the verdict of a very small minority. If, by a thorough census of the English-speaking world, we should determine exactly the number of people who have read *Paradise Lost* from the outset to the end, not for any fancied sense of duty but for sheer aesthetic and intelligent delight, we should doubtless be appalled by the paucity of the enumeration. Why, in the face of such neglect, does the fame of Milton's epic still endure ? Why is the verdict of the cultivated few more powerful than that of the uncultivated many ? It is because, in the long leisure of the centuries, the vote of the minority is repeated generation after generation and acquires emphasis by repetition. There have always been a few who knew that *Paradise Lost* is a great poem ; there are now a few who know it ; there will always be a few who know it : and, after many centuries, the host accumulated from this imperishable succession of minorities will outnumber the majority of any single generation. On the other hand, the immediate verdict of the multitude in favour of such a poem as *Lucille* will ultimately fail, because it cannot repeat itself perpetually, through generation after generation. Popularity is fleeting, because the populace is fickle. At the present time, the paintings of Sir John Everett Millais are more generally enjoyed than the paintings of Whistler ; but, when the toll of all the centuries comes ultimately to be counted, the few who have always appreciated Whistler will show themselves more mighty than the many who at one time preferred his more popular contemporary. It is in this way that the few outvote the many, concerning questions of artistic taste ; it is in this regard that Henrik Ibsen's famous dictum must be accepted as a statement of the truth— ' The minority is always right.'

But the drama differs from all the other arts in the fact that its primary purpose is to interest and entertain the multitude ; it is the only art which is required to appeal at once to the popular majority. In this particular province of the general domain of art, the verdict of the many outweighs the verdict of the few. Throughout the entire history of the theatre, no dramatist who has failed to interest the general public of his own day has ever attained a subsequent reversal of the verdict. A poet, like Milton, may be considered great because of the repeated vote of a perpetual minority ; but a dramatist can be considered great only if everybody likes him, and the continuance of his fame depends directly on the continuance of his popularity.

It must, therefore, be regarded as a paradox that our greatest dramatist should also be our greatest poet—that the one writer of our English language who has supremely satisfied the few should also be the one playwright who has completely satisfied the many. The poet writes for a minority of one—that is to say, primarily for himself, and secondarily for such individuals as may be sympathetic with his musings ; but the dramatist, by the conditions of his craft, must write for what Victor Hugo called the mob. To be able to make both of these appeals at once, to achieve simultaneously these two totally different endeavours, is the unique accomplishment of William Shakespeare.

No other play has ever been so popular, no other play has ever been acted so many times or has drawn in the aggregate so much money to the box-office, as the tragedy of *Hamlet*. Yet this piece, which has been so emphatically acclaimed by the uncultivated many, is praised no less highly by the cultivated few. It was planned by a great playwright ; it was written by a great poet. ' Some quality of the brute incident '— to quote a phrase of Robert Louis Stevenson's—interests and entertains the most illiterate, while the most literate admire the philosophical subtlety of the thought and marvel at the inimitable eloquence of the style. The costermonger in the gallery is thrilled when he sees the hero dash the poisoned cup from the hands of Horatio ; and, simultaneously, the Matthew Arnold in the stalls is thrilled by the sheer poetic eloquence of the incidental line—

Absent thee from felicity a while.

It is precisely because of this paradox—because he is capable of appealing simultaneously and with equal emphasis to the costermonger and to the apostle of culture—that Shakespeare is our greatest hero. His fame is founded equally upon the verdict of the many and upon the verdict of the few. His work is both popular and precious ; it is enjoyed by the majority and approved by the minority. There can never be a question of his eminence ; for the vote is utterly unanimous.

There are two tests of greatness in a man ; and these tests are antithetic to each other. First, a man may be great because he resembles a vast multitude of other people ; or, second, a man may be great because he differs vastly from everybody else. It is a sign of greatness to be representative ; it is also a sign of greatness to be unique. The representative man—in the great phrase of Walt Whitman—' contains multitudes ' ; and, when we grow to know him, we know his nation and his time, and guess at all humanity. The unique man, on the other hand, contains nothing but himself ; but this peculiar entity is capable of appearing, for a focused moment of attention, the most interesting object in the world. In the history of American literature, for instance, the personality of Edgar Allan Poe is unique and the personality of Benjamin Franklin is representative. Poe is interesting because he differs so emphatically from everybody else, and Franklin is interesting because he so emphatically resembles everybody else in eighteenth-century America. Poe is peculiar ; Franklin contains multitudes. Each is great ; but they are great for antithetic reasons.

The paradox of Shakespeare is that he is great in both of these regards. On the one hand, he is enormously representative. He contains all Elizabethan England, and resumes and utters nearly all that humanity has ever thought and felt. On the other hand, as a literary artist, he stands unique. No other writer, before or since, has at all approached his tumultuous and overwhelming eloquence.

It is the project of the popular great dramatist to agree with the majority—to make articulate to the contemporary multitude the thoughts and feelings that are latent in the mob. It is the project of the unpopular great poet to agree with the minority—to lead the questing mind to pioneer among adventures that are strange and new. These two projects are totally distinct, and seem irreconcilable. Shakespeare has reconciled them. It is for this reason that we acclaim him, not illogically, as the greatest writer of our language, the biggest hero of our race.

CLAYTON HAMILTON.

NEW YORK.

SHAKESPEARE

WE, in America, claim Shakespeare as our own, not merely because of the rich heritage of our English ancestry, but because Shakespeare, in a peculiar sense, belongs to the world.   He is not the product of any particular age or race or land.   He transcends the limits of his own tongue.   His genius has created a universal language, the language of humanity.   His characters, drawn as particular persons, have become universal types, the concrete living expression of the abstract virtues and vices of human nature.   His words of wisdom have become folk proverbs, whose origin, in many minds, is unknown or forgotten, and yet employed so constantly in the daily commerce of thought as to become an habitual mode of expressing the elemental experiences common to all mankind.

Shakespeare's psychology is unerring.   The strength and weakness of man, his possibilities for good or evil, the subtle play of motives which reveals character and determines conduct, the sophistries of self-deception, the inner fires which burn out the soul or lighten its aspiring desire towards arduous attainment, the sin, the folly, and the glory of mankind, both the depths and the heights of human nature,—all this Shakespeare has expressed in words of such convincing reality and simplicity as to leave no one who hears them a stranger to himself.

Shakespeare expresses for us thoughts which we have faintly felt, yet never can put in words.   And when we hear them, even for the first time, there is a suggestion of familiarity about them.   We recognize them as our own ideas discovered for us by this prophet of the human soul.

To speak a universal tongue, appealing to all men of all races and of all ages, the true thought must find its expression in perfect form. There must be the beauty of proportion and of symmetry, the beauty of rhythm and of emotional colouring, the creative sense which fashions its word elements, with which it builds into a balanced mass of structural strength and grace.   Shakespeare is the great architect in the guild of letters,—the master workman.   Whether it be a temple or wayside shrine, it is for all comers a place of refreshment and invigoration, a spot where we feel impelled to renew our vows and go on our way with new faith and new courage.

JOHN GRIER HIBBEN.

PRINCETON UNIVERSITY.

SHAKESPEARE

ENGLAND, that gavest to the world so much—
Full-breathing freedom, law's security,
The sense of justice (though we be not just)—
What gift of thine is fellow unto this
Imperishable treasure of the mind,—
Enrichment of dim ages yet to be !
Gone is the pomp of kings save in his page,
Where by imagination's accolade
He sets the peasant in the royal rank.
Love, like a lavish fountain, here o'erflows
In the full speech of tender rhapsody.
He dreamed our dreams for us. His the one voice
Of all humanity. Or knave or saint,
He shows us kindred. Partisan of none,
Before the world's censorious judgement seat
We find him still the advocate of each,
Portraying motive as our best defence.
Historian of the soul in this strange star
Where Vice and Virtue interchange their masks ;
Diviner of life's inner mysteries,
He yet bereaves it not of mystery's charm,
And makes us all the wounds of life endure
For all the balm of beauty.
                                   England now,
When so much gentle has been turned to mad,
When peril threatens all we thought most safe,
When honour crumbles, and on Reason's throne
Black Hate usurps the ermine, oh, do thou
Remember Force is still the Caliban
And Mind the Prospero. Keep the faith he taught ;

Speak with his voice for Freedom, Justice, Law,—
Ay, and for Pity, lest we sink to brutes.
Shame the fierce foe with Shakespeare's noble word:
Say, ' England was not born to feed the maw
Of starved Oblivion.' Let thine ardent youth
Kindle to flame at royal Hal's behest,
And thy wise elders glow with Gaunt's farewell.
His pages are the charter of our race.
Let him but lead thy leaders, thou shalt stand
Thy Poet's England, true and free and strong:
By his ideals shalt thou conqueror be,
For God hath made of him an element,
Nearest Himself in universal power.

ROBERT UNDERWOOD JOHNSON.

NEW YORK.

TWO NEGLECTED TASKS

PROBABLY no personal tribute could have been given by any one in the last three hundred years which would have aroused in William Shakespeare, as he looks down upon us, if not his gratification, at least his tolerant amusement to such a degree as the ant-like industry expended upon his plays in the last half-century. In consequence of this industry—particularly as focused upon the stage-setting and the general conditions of the Elizabethan theatre—we have a more accurate and more sympathetic understanding of what his plays meant to his audiences and to himself than men have had at any time since the closing of the theatres by the great Civil War. Furthermore, the disclosure of the approximate chronology of the plays has made possible a replacement of the eighteenth-century conception of a monstrous barbaric genius, capable of all things, but chaotic in ideas, in art, and in style, by a truer conception of a genius, of the very first order to be sure, but passing through a marvellously regular, as well as marvellously rapid, development of ideas and of style, and in perfect command of all the technical artistic methods and resources of renaissance culture.

Despite all these gains, however, much work still remains to be done if we are to eliminate from the plays which bear Shakespeare's name the alien elements, and to arrive at an accurate conception of his mind and character, his methods of work, and his cultural equipment. We shall find, it may safely be asserted, that, in the first place, his cultural equipment—his acquaintance with the great literature of the past and his familiarity with the theories of art and of composition—was greater than even we have been accustomed to suppose ; and, in the second place, that, although as a practical dramatist he kept his eyes steadily on his audience and made use of every sensational device and trick that theatrical experience had developed up to his day, he nevertheless had a genuine, personal, unremunerable interest in the poetic quality of his work.

To suggest a complete programme of such study would exceed the present limits of space, but two tasks lie so near at hand and are essential to so many others that they may be emphasized here.

In the first place, despite the labours of two hundred years, the text of the plays still needs to be established by scientific instead of haphazard impressionistic methods. Textual criticism has only recently become scientific, and scarcely one of our great English writers has profited as yet by its achievements. Chaucer and Shakespeare have profited scarcely at all, mainly because of the accumulated mass of traditional rubbish which we have not had the courage to discard. We still record and discuss the errors and guesses of the second, third, and fourth folios of Shakespeare's plays as if they were deserving of respect. The first step toward the establishment of a critical text—an absolute prerequisite to any further sound work—would seem to be the application to the first folio of the principles and methods of editing Elizabethan texts so clearly and convincingly expounded by Mr. R. B. McKerrow. That much labour is demanded by such methods is true ; but half the time expended in making casual, and therefore futile, record of variants between extant copies of the early folios would have accomplished the task and have provided us with an unassailable basis for all future textual criticism of Shakespeare.

More important, as well as more difficult, than this task seems that of providing the means of distinguishing, if possible, the non-Shakespearian elements which still, after years of diligent guesswork, undoubtedly remain in the plays, not unrecognized but for the present incapable of convincing indication.

Almost all attempts to discover by stylistic and metrical tests the authors of anonymous Elizabethan plays or the unknown collaborators in plays of multiple authorship have remained unconvincing, except to the would-be discoverers. The same situation exists in other periods of English literature. The main reason for this is probably that other students have a feeling—clearly or dimly formulated—that we have as yet no corpus of stylistic characters which enables us to form a critical judgement of such attempts. The evidences of similarity or of difference which the investigator may produce, lack force and convincing quality because we do not know the range of possibility in such matters.

Some of the most industrious studies intended to demonstrate that this piece of literature was the work of Chaucer, that of Shakespeare, that of Massinger or Middleton or Marston, have succeeded in convincing some of us only of what we already knew : namely, that the piece was the work of an English writer of the fourteenth, the sixteenth, or the seventeenth century, as the case may be. Further than this we shall never be able to proceed until we have built up a corpus of technical facts in two fields.

If any one knows what are the essential stylistic (as distinguished from the purely linguistic) discrimina of English speech in any age, or of any great writer, he is at least incapable of conveying his conclusions to the rest of us because of the lack of any definite and intelligible medium of communication. We need, then, in the first place, such a study of the general characteristics of the English language in each age as M. Ch. Bailly has attempted to collect for the French language of the present day in his *Manuel de Stylistique* and his *Précis*. In the second place, we need a similar collection of the stylistic peculiarities or characters of individual writers.

It is obvious that trustworthy collections of this sort can be made only by beginning with the language of our own day, in regard to which we are able to control with practical certainty the sources of our information.

JOHN MATTHEWS MANLY.

THE UNIVERSITY OF CHICAGO.

IF SHAKSPERE SHOULD COME BACK?

INGENIOUS wits have often amused themselves by imagining the possible return of a departed genius that he might mingle for a few hours with men of the present generation ; and they have humorously speculated upon his emotions when he found himself once again in the life he had left centuries earlier. They have wondered what he would think about this world of ours to-day, the same as his of long ago and yet not the same. What would he miss that he might have expected to find? What would he find that he could never have expected? As he had been a human being when he was in the flesh, it is a safe guess that he would be interested first of all in himself, in the fate of his reputation, in the opinion in which he is now held by us who know him only through his writings. And it is sad to think that many a genius would be grievously disappointed at the shrinkage of his fame. If he had hoped to see his books still alive, passing from hand to hand, familiar on the lips as household words, he might be shocked to discover that they survived solely in the silent obscurity of a complete edition, elaborately annotated and preserved on an upper shelf for external use only. On the other hand, there would be a genius now and then who had died without any real recognition of his immortal gifts and who, on his imagined return to earth, would be delighted to discover that he now bulked bigger than he had ever dared to dream.

It is with this second and scanty group that Shakspere would belong. So far as we can judge from the sparse records of his life and from his own writings, he was modest and unassuming, never vaunting himself, never boasting and probably never puffed up by the belief that he had any cause to boast. What he had done was all in the day's work, a satisfaction to him as a craftsman when he saw that he had turned out a good job, but a keener satisfaction to him as a man of affairs that he was thereby getting on and laying by against the day when he might retire to Stratford to live the life of an English gentleman. Probably no other genius could now revisit the earth who would be more completely or more honestly astonished by the effulgence of his fame. To suppose that this would not be exquisitely gratifying to him would be to suggest that he was not human. Yet a chief component of his broad humanity was his sense of humour; as a man he did not take himself too seriously, and as a ghost he would certainly smile at the ultra-seriousness of his eulogists and interpreters. A natural curiosity might lead him to look over a volume or two in the huge library of Shaksperian criticism; but these things would not detain him long. Being modest and unassuming still, he would soon weary of protracted praise.

It may be that Shakspere would linger long enough over his critics and his commentators to note that they have belauded him abundantly and superabundantly as a poet, as a philosopher, as a psychologist, and as a playwright. He might even be puzzled by this fourfold classification of his gifts, failing for the moment to perceive its precision. When he read praise of his poetry, he would naturally expect to see it supported by quotation from his two narrative poems or from his one sonnet-sequence. Quite possibly he might be somewhat annoyed to observe that these juvenile verses, cordially received on their original publication, were now casually beplastered with perfunctory epithets, while the sincerest and most searching commendation was bestowed on the style and on the spirit of the plays, in their own day unconsidered by literary critics and not recognized as having any claim to be considered as literature. Yet this commendation, pleasing even if unforeseen, would not go to his head, since Shakspere—if we may venture to deduce his own views from the scattered evidence in his plays—had no very high opinion of poets or of poetry.

If he might be agreeably surprised by the praise lavished on him as a poet, he would be frankly bewildered by the commendation bestowed on him as a philosopher. He knew that he was not a man of solid learning, and that his reading, even if wide enough for his immediate purpose, had never been deep. He might admit that he had a certain insight into the affairs of men and a certain understanding of the intricate inter-relations of human motives. But he could never have considered himself as an original thinker, advancing the boundaries of knowledge or pushing speculation closer to the confines of the unknowable. All he had sought to do in the way of philosophy was now and again to phrase afresh as best he could one or another of the eternal commonplaces, which need to be minted anew for the use of every oncoming generation. If a natural curiosity should tempt Shakspere to turn

A a

over a few pages of his critics to discover exactly what there was in his writings to give him rank among the philosophers, he would probably be more puzzled than before, until his sense of humour effected a speedy rescue.

Bewildered as Shakspere might be to see himself dissected as a philosopher, he would be startled to discover himself described also as a psychologist. To him the word itself would be unknown and devoid of meaning, strange in sound and abhorrent in appearance. Even after it had been translated to him with explanation that he deserved discussion as a psychologist because he had created a host of accusable characters and had carried them through the climax of their careers with subtle self-revelation, he might still wonder at this undue regard for the persons in his plays, whom he had considered not as much vital characters as effective acting-parts devised by him to suit the several capacities of his fellow actors, Burbage and Arnim, Heming and Condall. It might be that these creatures of his invention were more than parts fitted to these actors; but none the less had they taken shape in his brain first of all as parts intended specifically for performance by specific tragedians and comedians.

Only when Shakspere read commendation of his skill as a playwright, pure and simple, as a maker of plays to be performed by actors in a theatre and before an audience, so put together as to reward the efforts of the performers and to arouse and sustain the interest of the spectators—only then would he fail to be surprised at his posthumous reputation. He could not be unaware that his plays, comic and tragic, or at least that the best of them, written in the middle of his career as a dramatist, were more adroitly put together than the pieces of any of his predecessors and contemporaries. He could not forget the pains he had taken to knit together the successive situations into a compelling plot, to provide his story with an articulated backbone of controlling motive, to stiffen the action with moments of tense suspense, to urge it forward to its inevitable and irresistible climax, to achieve effects of contrast, and to relieve the tragic strain with intermittent humour. And even if it might mean little or nothing to him that he was exalted to a place beside and above Sophocles, the master of ancient tragedy, and Molière, the master of modern comedy, he might well be gratified to be recognized at last as a most accomplished craftsman, ever dexterous in solving the problems of dramaturgic technique.

These fanciful suggestions are based on the belief that Shakspere—like every other of the supreme artists of the world—' builded better than he knew ' ; and that this is a main reason why his work abides unendingly interesting to us three centuries after his death. He seems to have written, partly for self-expression, of course, but chiefly for the delight of his contemporaries, with no thought for our opinion fifteen score years later ; and yet he wrought so firmly, so largely and so loftily that we may rightly read into his works a host of meanings he did not consciously intend—and for which he can take the credit, none the less, because only he could have put them there.

BRANDER MATTHEWS.

337 WEST 87TH STREET,
    NEW YORK CITY, U.S.A.

I. SHAKESPEARE

WITHIN the city square the fountain's play
   Draws from their dusty games the girls and boys;
   They love its coolness, and the pleasant noise
Of falling water, love the misty spray
Thrown in bright showers by the radiant fay,
   Bedecked in rainbow films, a shimmering poise,
   Who seems just lighted from a world of joys
Beyond the confines of our common day.

So from the dust and heat, and day-long strain
   Of toil and traffic at the desk or mart,
   Men seek escape, through thy pellucid art,
Into a world of kingly joys and pain,
   Where, in the racial passions of the heart,
They find the zest for common tasks again.

II. THE FOREST OF ARDEN

IN this charmed wood where youth, beneath the shade
  Of ancient boughs, for love's fruition yearned,
  Where merry note to bird's sweet throat was turned
And huntsman's horn resounded through the glade,
Where, from the summer sun and wintry wind,
  From trees and brooks and stones, men learned content,
  And brother's heart, on brother's death intent,
By brother's deed was turned to love of kind;

In this dear wood, now fallen on evil days,
  Sounds but the shriek of shell, and cry infuriate
  Of battle-maddened men, whom murderous Fate
Leads plunging, writhing, dying in her maze.
  The ravished trees lie prone in mute despair;
  The very birds have ceased to haunt the air.

FREDERICK MORGAN PADELFORD.

UNIVERSITY OF WASHINGTON.

A PLEA FOR CHARLES THE WRESTLER

WHENEVER one compares a character or incident in Shakespeare
with the original sources, one almost invariably observes that the poet,
in fusing his ' live soul and that inert stuff ', has consciously or unconsciously betrayed some touch of fine feeling, some human tenderness,
which transfers the whole situation to a higher plane.   This is clearly
the case when we place the duke's champion of *As You Like It* alongside
the uncouth Norman of Thomas Lodge's romance.   Shakespeare has
been, in America as everywhere else, a tremendously *civilizing* force.
I cannot remember a single instance of false sentiment in his works ;
and even his minor characters reveal the innate nobility, purity, and
gentleness of the world's supreme dramatist.

Now Charles has never received his due—either from textual
critics or from the audiences which for three centuries have applauded
his defeat.   Naturally Orlando misunderstood him, and threw him
with moral as well as physical zest.   On the stage Charles is represented
as a loud-mouthed braggart and bully ; the ridiculous ease with which
he is ' knocked out ' makes even the skilful laugh.

Shakespeare, in altering many details in Lodge's *Rosalynde*, really
made Charles not only human, but decidedly attractive.   Charles is
a professional athlete ; like most men of his class, he is a good fellow,
and is so presented in the play, if we read it attentively, without pre-
conceived opinions.   Shakespeare has given us information withheld
from Orlando, Rosalind, and Celia.   Charles is liberal and kindly in
disposition, and means to fight fairly for his reputation.   He answers in
the most delightful fashion the queries of Oliver concerning the banished
Duke, the forest of Arden, and the Lady Rosalind ; but this is not the
object of his visit.   Departing entirely from the original, Shakespeare
makes Charles wait on Oliver for the express purpose of saying that he
has heard that young Orlando is to wrestle against him, disguised ; and
as it does not occur to his honest, affectionate nature that the boy can
be hated by his own brother, he asks if something cannot be done to

prevent Orlando's injury and humiliation. Charles speaks in a manner both modest and masculine ; his motive in seeking the interview is wholly admirable. It is only after Oliver has told him a series of lies about Orlando, that Charles's attitude to the latter changes, and accordingly he speaks roughly to him just before the combat. The professional quite rightly regards himself not as a competitor with an amateur gentleman in an athletic contest, but rather as a policeman whose duty it is to destroy a dangerous criminal. I sincerely hope that Charles was only slightly injured, and that he subsequently learned the facts of the case. At all events, I maintain that he is a 'good' character.

WILLIAM LYON PHELPS.

THE COMMON FOLK OF SHAKESPEARE

' SHAKESPEARE . . . seems to me ', says Walt Whitman, ' of astral genius, first class, entirely fit for feudalism. His contributions, especially to the literature of the passions, are immense, for ever dear to humanity —and his name is always to be reverenced in America. But there is much in him ever offensive to democracy. He is not only the tally of feudalism, but I should say Shakespeare is incarnated, uncompromising feudalism in literature.'

With such an arraignment of Shakespeare's universality and his sympathy with his fellow men, let us consider the common folk of his plays with a view to discover the poet's actual attitude toward that humbler station in life into which he was himself indisputably born. For our purpose we exclude all personages of rank, all his characters of gentle birth, together with all those, whatever their varying degrees of servitude, who wait upon royalty or form, in any wise, a part or parcel of the households of great folk. This excludes all of Shakespeare's heroes, unless we are to accept the pseudo-Shakespearian Alice Arden, or thrust Iago and Shylock out of the heroic category. It will also exclude Shakespeare's fools, from trifling Launce and the delectable Feste to the sad-eyed companion in folly of King Lear. And even Falstaff, who was sometime page to Sir Thomas Mowbray, and a gentle-man however unlanded, must stand in his dignity without our bounds.

There remain for us, in our middle domain, some threescore personages who have speaking parts, of a diversity the equal of their betters and inferiors, even although their actual rôles are, for the most part, subordinate. Conveniently to treat so many of the undistin-guished, we must group them, a process the more justifiable when we consider that thus we can best ascertain what are really Shakespeare's prejudices and whether they are of class or individual.

The drama by Shakespeare's day had already evolved, or rather created by iteration, several very definite stock personages. One of these is the pedant or schoolmaster, so well known to Italian comedy ;

and Holofernes, in *Love's Labour's Lost*, with his loquacity, affectation of learning and essential ignorance, is Shakespeare's most certain contribution to the type.   As to 'the pedant' so nominated in *The Taming of the Shrew*, this personage is taken over bodily from Gascoigne's *Supposes*, the translation of an Italian play, and performs no 'pedantic' function ; while Pinch, in *The Comedy of Errors*, is called in momentarily to exorcise the devil out of half-maddened Antipholus of Ephesus. In the Welshman, Sir Hugh Evans of *The Merry Wives of Windsor*, we modulate, so to speak, from the schoolmaster to the parson, for Evans apparently performed the functions of both.   Evans is no fool, however he may have sung on one memorable occasion, in breaking voice, ungowned and sword in trembling hand, while he awaited the coming of his terrible adversary, the French Doctor Caius, deceived in the meeting, like himself, by a parcel of incorrigible wags.

Shakespeare's curates, parsons, and religious folk are many.   Of the class of Evans are Sir Nathaniel in *Love's Labour's Lost* and Sir Oliver Martext in *As You Like It*.   Sir Nathaniel is zany to the ponderous folly of Holofernes, he who plays the rôle of 'Alisander' to the latter's Judas in the immortal 'ostentation, or show, or pageant, or antique of the Nine Worthies' ; while our joy in Sir Oliver lies more in his delectable cognomen 'Martext' than in the very brief scenes in which he is brought in to 'dispatch' Touchstone and his Audrey into matrimony under the greenwood tree.   The Shakespearian Friar is a more important personage, from the plotting, necromantic Home and Southwell in the second part of *Henry VI* to Juliet's Friar Lawrence with his minor counterpart of minor function, Friar Francis in *Much Ado About Nothing*, and the Duke, disguised as such, in *Measure for Measure*.   Whether a matter wholly referable to his sources or not, Shakespeare conceived the friar of Roman Catholic Verona, Messina, or Vienna, in a very different spirit from that in which he represents the small parson, Sir Hugh or Sir Oliver.   Friar Francis in *Much Ado About Nothing* detects the 'strange misprision in the two princes' whereby the Lady Hero is slanderously wronged, and it is his prudent advice, which, followed implicitly by the lady and her friends, rights that wrong in the end.   The likeness of this function of Friar Lawrence is patent to the most superficial reader ; but unhappily for his prudence and his ingenuity, the accident to his messenger, the precipitancy of Romeo, the influence of the very stars is against him, and he fails where his brother friar succeeded.   Nowhere in Shakespeare does the clergy function with more dignity than in *Measure for Measure*, whether in the rôle of the chaste and devoted novitiate, Isabella, or in the grave and searching wisdom of the duke. What Shakespeare's attitude toward formal religion may have been we have little that is definite to go by. Who can doubt that it was he, however, and none other, who paid for the tolling of the great bell of St. Saviour's when his brother's body was laid there to rest? And who can question, with all his scenes of religious pomp and dignity, that Shakespeare recognized, with Wolsey, that all these forms of earthly vanity are

a burden
Too heavy for a man that hopes for heaven?

We may regret that Shakespeare has nowhere exhibited to us, like Chaucer in his 'poure Persoun of a toun', his ideal of the cloth. It has been wittily said that it is a credit to human nature that no critic has, as yet, called Shakespeare a Puritan. It is somewhat less creditable that some have gone about to show him the satirist of Puritanism, especially in Malvolio. It was Jonson, the moralist, who satirized Puritanism, not Shakespeare, whose business was with qualities that differentiate men in the essentials of their natures and in the conduct which these differences entail.

Let us glance next at the physicians of Shakespeare. In Dr. Caius, of *The Merry Wives of Windsor*, albeit he is boastful of his intelligence from the court, the doctor is lost in the gross wit of the Frenchman's ignorance of English satirized. The apothecary who sells Romeo his death potion, in his 'tattered weeds', could assuredly not have been of a profession in which there are no beggars. The father of Helena in *All's Well that Ends Well*, although he left to his daughter the miraculous cure of the King of France by means of his medical secrets, is reported a man of dignity, learning, and much experience in his practice. The doctor in *Macbeth* has won the praises of his own jealous profession with the professional aptitude of his comments on the somnambulist symptoms of Lady Macbeth; while the physician, Cornelius, skilled as he is in poisons, honourably deceives the wicked queen of Cymbeline with a sleeping potion instead of the deadly drug which it was her purpose to administer to the unhappy Imogen.

Unlike his contemporary Middleton and some others, Shakespeare does not satirize the profession of the law; and the lawyer, as such, scarcely figures in the plays. At opposite poles, in the plays which have to do with Falstaff, we have Master Shallow 'in the county of Gloucester, justice of the peace and " coram " ', described by Falstaff as 'a man made after supper of a cheese-paring . . . for all the world like a forked radish, with a head fantastically carved upon it with a knife'. And we have likewise the grave and honourable Chief Justice Gascoigne, whose courage and impartiality in the exercise of his high functions caused the regenerate Prince to choose him for his guide and counsellor on the assumption of his new royal dignities. As to the lesser functionaries of the law, the watchman, the constable, and the beadle, Shakespeare exhibits the general free spirit of his time, and laughs, as the rest of the world has ever laughed, at the insolence, ineptitude, and ignorance of the small man dressed in a little brief authority. It might be argued with some likelihood of success that this is identically the spirit that marks the Sheriff of Nottingham as the butt of the lawless pranks of Robin Hood, the attitude towards constituted authority which combined, in the free ranging devils of the old miracle plays, the functions of policing the crowd and catering to its merriment. Beyond his designation, 'a constable', Dull, in *Love's Labour's Lost*, scarcely represents for his class more than his name ; and as to Elbow, in *Measure for Measure*, his 'simplicity', like his malapropisms, seems a faint and colourless repetition of these qualities in the immortal Dogberry. Dogberry is universal, the ubiquitous, inevitable, unescapable man of weight, ponderous alike physically and mentally ; for I am persuaded with an old-fashioned American critic, that Dogberry was 'of ample size—no small man speaks with sedate gravity . . . No man of the lean and dwarfish species can assume the tranquil self-consequence of Dogberry. How could a thinly covered soul [exhibit] . . . that calm interior glow, that warm sense, too, of outward security, which so firmly speaks in Dogberry's content and confidence?'

Our obvious generalization as to Shakespeare's estimate of the learned professions, then, is this : he found in all, earnest, honourable, and capable men, and honoured them as such ; and he found likewise among them the stupid, the pedantic, the pretentious, and the absurd. It was for their follies that he ridiculed them, not because of their class or their station in life.

Of the small gentry of Elizabethan England, Master Ford and Master Page, with their two merry wives, offer us the best example in comedy. The discordant plans and plots for a provision in life for Mistress Anne Page are in keeping with many a like unconscious parody on the grand alliances of folk of higher station. The foolish Slender, who is likewise a small landed proprietor, is nearer an absolute 'natural' than any of Shakespeare's clowns, professional or other, for wit proceeds no more out of him, however he beget wit in others, than it ever comes forth from the mouth of Andrew Aguecheek his cousin-german (so to speak) of Illyria. In Alexander Iden, who, meeting with Jack Cade in his Kentish garden, kills him in a single fight, we have a serious personage much of Slender's station in life. But Iden has his wits as well as his valour about him, and his knighting is his deserved reward. Nearer the soil, if closer to royalty, is the kind-hearted, allegorical-minded king's gardener who apprises the queen of Richard II of that monarch's mischance in falling into the hands of his enemy, victorious Bolingbroke. In the country folk that fill in the background of *As You Like It* and the later acts of *The Winter's Tale*, Shakespeare's English spirit comes into contact with the conventional types of Italian pastoral drama. Phebe is the typical shepherdess, beloved but not loving, and Sylvius, the pursuing shepherd unbeloved. But as if to correct an impression so artificial, we have, beside them, William and Audrey, English country folk in name and nature like Costard and Jaquenetta, and in Shakespeare's maturer art, far more redolent of the soil. William, like Slender, and many a man of better station, is a mere natural ; but his witlessness is as distinguishable from the folly of the Shakespearian ' clown ', as his boorishness differs from the literal simplicity of the Shepherd who becomes foster-brother to Perdita in *The Winter's Tale*. Mopsa and Dorcas, with their shepherds of the sheep-shearing, in these charming comedy scenes, are English country folk ; and Autolycus, despite his fine Greek name, is a delightful English rogue and incorrigible vagabond.

And now that we have all but touched the bottom of the Shakespearian social scale, we may note that in Shakespeare, poverty does not necessarily make a man vicious, nor does roguery destroy humour in a man or deprive him of his brains. The porter in *Macbeth* is a foul-mouthed drunken lout ; the nameless ' old man ' in the same tragedy is a credulous recorder of marvels. But Adam, the old serving-man of Orlando, is faithful almost to death. Dame Quickly of London is a silly old muddle-head, alike innocent of morals and of common-sense ; and her sister Dame Quickly of Windsor is a shameless go-between and meddler ; but the widow, keeper of lodgings for pilgrims in *All's Well that Ends Well*, has a virtuous and honourable disposition. The drawer, Francis, in *Henry IV*, ' sums up his eloquence in the parcel of a reckoning ' ; but there is no keener, droller fellow in the world than the grave-digger in *Hamlet*, and it is dubious if for natural parts, however diverted to the ' doing ' and undoing of his fellows, Autolycus has ever had his equal. Shakespeare's carriers talk of their jades and their packs ; his vintners and drawers of their guests and their drinking ; his musicians disparage their own skill and have to be coaxed to show it ; and his honest botchers, weavers, and bricklayers hate learning, and in their rage variously kill a poet and hang a clerk. And curious as all this may appear to him who habitually views the classes below him as merely his servants or the objects of his organized charity, all this—save possibly the homicides—is as true of to-day as of the age of Shakespeare.

And here perhaps as well as anywhere, we may digress into ' the Shakespearian prejudice as to mobs '. The mob figures as such conspicuously three times in Shakespeare's plays—in the second part of *King Henry VI*, in *Julius Caesar*, and in *Coriolanus*. It is represented in all three cases as fickle, turbulent, cruel, foul, and possessed of a rude sense of humour ; and this last is Shakespeare's—perhaps, more accurately, the Elizabethan—contribution to the picture. It has been well observed that Tudor England presented no precise parallel to the persistent struggle of the Roman plebs against the bulwarks of patrician oligarchy. And it is doubtful if Shakespeare would have sought for such parallels had they existed. In unessentials—and the picture of the mob is such to the dramatic action of these two Roman plays—Shakespeare is always faithful to his sources, and Plutarch's crowd is cruel, seditious, and ' contemptibly responsive ' to the most obvious blandishments of the demagogue. In the admirable scenes of Jack Cade's rebellion, although the material was nearer home, Shakespeare once more followed his sources, here in Holinshed and Halle. Neither of these worthies comprehended in the slightest degree the actual political issues underlying the Kentishmen's revolt, which historically was as respectable as it was fruitless. But Shakespeare was not seeking historical accuracy, but dramatic effectiveness and fidelity to the observed characteristics of ignorant men escaped from the curb of the law. Shakespeare, as to the mob, was no sociologist, and his yearning for the submerged truth was not that of many a worthy gentleman of our own time who otherwise misrepresents the unshriven objects of his solicitude. In short, a mob was to the unlettered dramatist merely a mob. Man running in packs unbridled by authority was a phenomenon better known to unpoliced Elizabethan England than to us, and Shakespeare found most of his own impressions in this matter to tally remarkably with those of Plutarch and Holinshed.

With Shakespeare's mob we leave the country and meet with the small tradesmen of towns ; for even the Kentish ' rabblement ' of

Jack Cade is represented, like that of ancient Rome, as made up of small tradespeople—cobblers, butchers, smiths, and the like—not folk of the fields. Individually as collectively, Shakespeare has a greater appreciation for the humours of the tailor, the joiner, and the bellows-mender than for his psychology. The drunken tinker of *The Taming of the Shrew*, the author found in his source and, unlike that source, wearied, he dropped his adventures when the play within the play was at an end. The hempen homespuns, with the illustrious weaver, Bottom, at their head, repeat, in their absurd drama of Pyramus and Thisbe, a situation already sketched in *Love's Labour's Lost*, one in which the banter and cruel interruption of ungentle gentles evidently reproduces a situation by no means unknown to better actors than Bottom, Flute, and Starveling. A kindly spirit speaks in the words of Theseus :

> For never anything can be amiss
> When simpleness and duty tender it;

for truly is he tolerant who can find words of praise for the good intentions of the amateur actor, a being little loved of gods or men. To the professional player, whom he knew better than any other man of art, Shakespeare is courteous and appreciative in the person of Hamlet, and we know from an often quoted sonnet, how deeply he could feel the degradation which popular contemporary opinion attached to the player's art.

The merchant, in Shakespeare's day, was a far more dignified person than the mere man of trade. A merchant, it is true, waits with a jeweller, but also with a painter and a poet, in the anteroom of the sumptuous spendthrift Timon. But ordinarily, the merchant is a more dignified person, extending courtesy to strangers, as in *The Comedy of Errors*, taking risks for his merchandise and for himself, as in the case of old Aegeon, in the same play, who has ventured on markets forbidden and is imprisoned for his daring. The most notable Shakespearian merchant is, of course, Antonio, the merchant prince of Venice, an adventurer in the Elizabethan sense into strange markets and a gambler for high commercial stakes. His gravity—or presaging melancholy—befits his dignity, and his generosity to Bassanio, a fellow adventurer (but in more than the Elizabethan sense), is only equalled by his authority among his fellow merchants and his scorn of the unrighteous Jew. Shylock, too, is of the merchant class, but a pariah alike for his race and his practice of usury. But Shylock will take us into precincts irrelevant ; for the Jew, whatever your thought of him or mine, is not of the common folk even of Shakespeare.

Next to the merchants come Shakespeare's seamen, the noble-minded Antonio of *Twelfth Night*, Sebastian's friend, the outspoken sea-captain, boatswain, and mariners of *The Tempest*, the attendant sailors and fisher-folk of *Pericles*. Shakespeare was a landsman ; save for an occasional line, his descriptions of the sea, in the richest of all literatures in this respect, are none of them important. The mariner as such he treats with the respect of a person only partially known. With the soldier, in a martial age, Shakespeare was better acquainted, and he knew him from the kings and great commanders of the historical plays to such pasteboard and plaster military men as Parolles, Nym, and Pistol. Of Falstaff's levy and his rabble attendants, from Bardolph of the carbuncled nose to the minute page, it may be said that they cut a sorrier figure in France than at the Boar's Head in Eastcheap. But Shakespeare's army levied better men than these ; the heroic gunners on the walls of Orleans, the brave and capable captains of four kingdoms, Gower, Fluellen, Macmorris, and Jamy in *Henry V*, and the manly English soldiers Bates, Court, and Williams. If the refined, modern critic, versed in the psychological researches of an incessantly prying world, would learn whether the old dramatist, Shakespeare, had any notions as to the mental processes and moral stability of the common man, let him read and ponder the simple incident of King Henry V, incognito, and the soldier Williams, and their arguments pro and con as to the responsibility of princes. Williams is the type of the honest, fearless, clear-headed ' man in the street ' who honours his king, not slavishly because he is a king, but for the qualities that make him kingly ; who respects manhood (his own included) above rank, and is the more valiant that he knows the cost of valour. There are several well-known tales of military devotion—they are not English—of the soldier, wounded unto death in a quarrel, the righteousness or wrong of which he cares not even to inquire, who dies in infatuated content that he has obeyed, in unquestioning faith, the august commands of his master. Williams is not of this type. His free soul will challenge his gage in the eye of his prince and when his heart tells him he is right, let the devil forbid. Shakespeare, too, knew the common man, who is bleeding to-day for England ; and his trust, like ours, was in him. Nor did our wise old dramatist, for all his scenes of the pomp and circumstance of war, forget its terror, its sorrow, and its pathos. In the third part of *Henry VI*, that unhappy king is seated alone on the field of battle, as the struggle surges away from him. And there enters ' a son that hath killed his father, dragging in the dead body ', and later ' a father bearing his dead son '.

Poignant are the words of these common men in their common woe, the battle woe of all ages and all times, in the grip of which the least are as the great and the greatest as the poorest.

In the taverns, the brothels and the jails, Shakespeare found the foul-mouthed, the ignorant, and the dishonest, and he represented them in all these particulars in a faithful, if at times forbidding, reality of life.   Moreover, his prejudice against evil is pronounced in the very repulsiveness of such scenes.   He knows that there are impostors among beggars, that trial by combat is only a somewhat cruder method of getting at the truth than trial by jury, that there are corrupt and incompetent magistrates and fools abounding in all walks of life.   Moreover, he depicts in his plays a feudal state of society, for such was English society in his day.   But there is nothing in these honest dramatic pictures of English life, from the king on his throne to Abhorson with his headsman's axe, to declare Shakespeare prejudiced against any class of his fellow countrymen.   Wherefore, our obvious generalization as to Shakespeare's attitude toward common folk, whether they be learned or unlearned, is this : he found among them the stupid, the ignorant, the pretentious, and the absurd ; but he found likewise in each class the earnest, the honourable, and capable, and honoured each after his kind as such.   For their follies he ridiculed them ; for their virtues, which he recognized, he loved them, deflecting neither to ridicule nor respect because of station in life.

Felix E. Schelling.

Philadelphia,
     Pennsylvania.

FROM A LOVER OF SHAKESPEARE AND OF ENGLAND

I

FOUR years will presently be gone since the hand that could have shaped a fit message, worthy of this occasion, wrote its last word. Horace Howard Furness died suddenly and quietly one August evening in 1912, his labours upon *Cymbeline* being then so nearly completed that the volume as he left it was published by his son, Horace the younger. The Editor of the *New Variorum* was my kinsman and my very dear friend. His opinions and surmises about *Cymbeline* he told me week by week, while the work was going on. His interest was so keen and vivacious that, when the telegram came to tell us that of him also it was now to be said, 'home art gone and ta'en thy wages,' it seemed incredible, and for a long while so remained. It is the memory of those final talks, the knowledge that it would please him, that now spur me to meet a task far beyond my unscholarly powers, even had months, instead of days, been allotted for the performing of it. Yet even without such a spur, what lover of Shakespeare and of England could think for a moment of turning aside from the task in this year of the poet's fame, and this hour of his Island's life ?—' that water-walled bulwark, still secure and confident from foreign purposes'.

I shall not be so presumptuous as to attempt any tribute to him who has surpassed the magic of his own created sprite in putting a girdle about the earth. When time and the whole of civilized mankind have set him where he is, what is left to say? What wreath to-day can add a flower to his name, or serve to do more than unite us in coming gratefully into the presence of the mighty memory?

'Others abide our question. Thou art free.' Some men (and some of them wise) are not of Matthew Arnold's mind. They would have a Shakespeare visible throughout his days, caught in the trap of research, his person disclosed from an age even earlier than his poaching escapades and precocious love-making, until even after he had left his second-best bedstead to his wife. They would like to know how much and how little she was a helpmeet to him; what breakfast she gave him, and

B b

if she cooked it to his taste; and if it was a domestic quarrel that sent him away from her side to London. They would follow him, and pry, and touch, and know all the littlenesses we know about in ourselves, that I thank Heaven we do not know about in him. I am even glad that over his work-desk there hangs an impenetrable veil. Around him is thus drawn a circle that I trust none will ever find the secret of entering. The public records of London, that nobody ever searched so perseveringly for clues until Professor Wallace had this ingenious thought, have furnished him with some information; and that it was an American who may have fixed the true site of the Globe Theatre is a feat for Americans to be proud of. But that the poet boarded with a maker of fashionable headdresses, named Mountjoy, and intervened amiably there in a family matter, does not interest me. May the public records, and every quarry that he digs in, yield Professor Wallace a store of anecdotes about Webster of whom we know so little, and poor Massinger, and Ford's successful marriage and melancholy hat—about any other of that great company you please, and not a jot more about Shakespeare!

We know about him all we need; there he stands, a mystery, yet definite; more indestructible than any other human creator; something almost like a natural law. The sentences that he wrote seem rather to make our mother-tongue than to be made of it. A notion of how definite he is, yet how immeasurable, cannot be obtained without knowing the Greeks, and his fellow Elizabethans, and Goethe, Dante, and Molière. It is by standing him against a background of all these others that we see him most distinctly. Those things wherein some of them surpass him serve to show his greater vastness: for neither the Greek symmetry nor the intellectual depths of *Faust* are large enough to hold Lear, Ariel, Caliban, and Falstaff—all contained in the one man, with room for so much more. Dante, too, grasps certain portions of life harder, but the rest he scarcely touches. Molière remains. If his *Misanthrope* and *Tartuffe* go beyond anything of the sort in the comedies, he wrote no *Hamlet*.

II

The Shakespeare readings of Fanny Kemble, my grandmother, which began in Philadelphia in 1849, probably led to the forming of our Shakspere Society—the oldest Shakespeare Society in the world—two years later. She had quickened interest in the plays, and some gentlemen accordingly organized themselves into a body dedicated to a thorough and critical study of the poet. They met every two weeks during certain months. Some of them were lawyers and judges, and it was a company of trained intelligences. In a few years, after a season spent upon *The Tempest*, they printed privately the notes resulting from its study. Here was a plain sign that they were not satisfied with the comments and explanations of previous Shakespearians—with all of which their excellent library provided them. In 1866–7 their study of *Romeo and Juliet* added to their dissatisfaction. Horace Howard Furness had been a member of the Society since 1860, when he was twenty-seven years old, and when he had learned that his deafness was to prevent the possibility of his ever practising his profession, the Law. Early in 1871 appeared his *Romeo and Juliet*, ' affectionately inscribed' to the Shakspere Society of Philadelphia. The shape and size of the volume, its print, everything connected with its appearance and convenience, had been the subject of thought and discussion among the members. They, at a meeting held February 7, 1871, formally resolved that ' In the opinion of the Society no single volume yet published in America is at all equal to this in value as a contribution to Shakespeare literature'. I am writing this on the 9th day of March, 1916. Every other Wednesday the Shakspere Society still meets. It met last night, and, after dining (for it always dines first), gave its attention to the fourth Act of *Antony and Cleopatra*, Scene xiv, line 114, to the end of the Act. Our Dean is now Horace Furness the younger, and he is at work upon *King John*, the next volume of the *New Variorum*.

III

It seems as if here I should stop ; but I cannot quite stop here. To my heart England and her poet are alike familiar, and very dear ; and certain lines of the poet's verse have been ringing within me since the first day of August 1914. On that Saturday I left St. Pancras, and, a few hours later, sailed down the Thames, bound homeward. Night had come as the ship turned west out of the river's mouth into the broad seas. As we moved past Deal and Dover and beyond, we were swept continually by lights that watched from water and land. It was then that suddenly the verses rang, which never since have been quite silent. I could not catch every tone at first. They sounded from that place in memory which all of us know, where things live of themselves in depths beyond our complete grasp ; yet still we feel them to be there, and we grope and touch them for an instant, and by and by recover them wholly. I found the page where the lines are set down. They must have come to many American minds that love England and her poet and his 'time-honored Lancaster'. Nothing that history records can banish England from us, or us, I hope, from England, whose cause is ours ; and so I, passing by the cliffs and lights on that August first, could think only of

> This happy breed of men, this little world,
> This precious stone set in the silver sea, . . .
> This blessed plot, this earth, this realm, this England, . . .
> This land of such dear souls, this dear, dear land.

OWEN WISTER.

PHILADELPHIA.

SONNET

DARKLING and groping, thin of blood, we wage
Mechanic war : one vast crepuscular day
Broods o'er the world ; our very grief is grey ;
We wear no weeds ; we loathe to tread the stage.
Birds of all feathers in that motley cage
Once chirp'd and sang their vernal longings gay ;
More life than is in life was in the play ;
More sweetness than in wisdom in the sage.

When will return to earth that jocund year
With marigolds and daisies golden-eye'd,
Passionate lovers, and kings crown'd in pride ?
When will that teeming summer reappear
And hide together in one flowery bier
The old that errèd and the young that died ?

G. SANTAYANA.

A SHAKESPEARE

Poète, noble fils de la grande Angleterre,
Fier et charmant génie, au long rayonnement,
Dont l'œuvre de beauté vit éternellement,
Comme le soleil luit pour réjouir la terre ;

Pour mieux commémorer ton nouveau centenaire
Que ton peuple et le mien fêtent en ce moment,
Regarde : tous les deux s'entr'aident fièrement
Dans l'effort fraternel de cette rude guerre.

Le cœur auprès du cœur et la main dans la main,
Ils veulent, tous les deux, sauver le genre humain
De la rapacité des aigles abattues ;

Quand nos drapeaux unis seront victorieux,
Alors nous reviendrons, sous de plus libres cieux,
Pendre une palme neuve au pied de tes statues.

HENRI CHANTAVOINE.

HOMMAGE A SHAKESPEARE

L'ŒUVRE de Shakespeare relève-t-elle de l'art ou de la nature ? Est-elle humaine ou divine ?

On reconnaît le travail de la nature à ce qu'il donne des œuvres dont l'analyse ne sera jamais terminée. Chacune d'elles est un infini. Le produit le plus ingénieux de l'industrie humaine, le mécanisme d'horlogerie le plus compliqué, ne comporte qu'un nombre limité de pièces ; on peut les retirer une à une et démonter l'appareil complète-ment ; on sait alors de quoi il est fait et comment il est fait. Mais on ne saura jamais tout ce qui entre dans la composition d'une fleur ou d'une feuille. Des microscopes de plus en plus puissants y découvriront un nombre croissant de choses, et la science poursuivra indéfiniment sur elles son travail d'analyse sans arriver au bout.

On en dirait autant d'une pièce de Shakespeare. Les critiques les plus pénétrants se sont, l'un après l'autre, exercés sur elle ; à chaque nouvel effort de chacun d'eux un nouvel aspect de l'œuvre s'est révélé ; mais, quand même nous en connaîtrions bien davantage, indéfini serait le nombre des aspects qui nous échapperaient encore. Les plus grands acteurs ont, l'un après l'autre, joué le rôle ; chacun d'eux en a tiré un personnage particulier, qui y était effectivement ; et, tant qu'il y aura des acteurs dans le monde, on en extraira des personnages toujours nouveaux : jamais on n'en aura épuisé le contenu. Il semble donc que Shakespeare ait travaillé comme la nature. Il a enfermé un infini dans chacun des produits de son génie.

De bas en haut de la nature s'exerce une poussée de vie, qui est d'origine divine. L'évolution du monde organisé s'explique par elle. D'espèce en espèce, malgré des hésitations, des déviations et des reculs, cette évolution tendait à dessiner la forme humaine ou quelque chose qui en approchât. La création de l'humanité, c'est-à-dire d'une espèce dont chaque individu est une *personne*, fut le point d'aboutissement de la poussée vitale, le grand triomphe de la vie. Pourtant, de la foule immense des humains surgit parfois un être privilégié dont l'imagination semble adopter et continuer l'élan de la nature, créant des personnes à son tour. C'est le poète dramatique. D'ordinaire, les personnages issus de sa fantaisie lui ressemblent, il est vrai, un peu, et se ressemblent aussi les uns aux autres ; ils n'atteignent qu'exceptionnellement la plénitude de richesse de la vie. Mais ceux de Shakespeare sont d'une vie surabondante ; ils ne se ressemblent pas entre eux ; chacun a son existence indépendante, comme s'il avait été lancé dans le monde par la même force qui donna naissance aux formes organisées, à la vie en général. L'œuvre de Shakespeare est plus qu'humaine.

Aucune œuvre des hommes ne porte en tous cas, plus que celle-là, l'empreinte divine.

HENRI BERGSON.

SHAKESPEARE

ÉMETTRE un jugement quelque peu neuf et original sur Shakespeare me paraît si difficile, et m'est si impossible, que je me bornerais volontiers à appliquer au grand poète anglais les paroles inscrites sur la tombe de Dante : *Onorate l'altissimo poeta*. Mais cela répondrait trop peu au sentiment de tendresse tout particulier que beaucoup de Français ont voué à Shakespeare, et qui peut toucher nos amis d'Angleterre. C'est pourquoi, en m'excusant de ce qu'il y a de personnel et de familier dans les citations que je vais faire et dans le petit fait que je conterai, je veux montrer par un très humble exemple — le mien — avec quelle affectueuse ferveur on peut, chez nous, aimer Shakespeare, ce qui est autre chose que de reconnaître, comme tout le monde, son prodigieux génie.

Dans ma seizième année, devenu l'hôte errant d'une forêt pendant la saison clémente, — tout comme Orlando, — j'y eus pour unique ami un petit Shakespeare que j'avais rapporté de Jersey ; et voici en quels termes je parlais de cet ami :

> Je n'ai pas de vain souci dans la tête ;
> L'azur infini me sourit encor ;
> Et ma solitude est changée en fête
> Par un bleu Shakspeare enluminé d'or.

Deux ou trois ans plus tard, dans les premiers vers que je livrais au public, figurait un *Hymne à l'Angleterre*, dont je détache une strophe :

> Quand tu n'aurais eu que Shakspeare,
> Tu serais le pays sacré,
> Puisque sous ton ciel on respire
> L'air que Shakspeare a respiré !

Je citerai pour finir un fait plus significatif, peut-être, que ces effusions naïves. En 1885, je n'étais plus l'adolescent qui cherchait Rosalinde dans la forêt de Fontainebleau ; j'avais deux fois son âge. Pris d'un irrésistible désir de voir Ceylan, paradis de fleurs et de palmes, et aussi de vénérer le souvenir du Bouddha dans les temples de cette île sacrée, je partis pour aller passer quinze jours à Colombo et à Kandy.

Certes, je devais revenir émerveillé de tout ce que j'avais vu, senti, respiré dans le paysage idéal de Ceylan comme dans ses sanctuaires fleuris, dédiés à la sainte pitié humaine ; mais, lorsque j'y arrivai, trois semaines de bateau, une alimentation bizarre et la chaleur subite, en sortant de l'hiver européen, m'avaient gratifié d'une sorte de choléra. Dès que je fus installé dans mon hôtel, qu'entourait un bois de cocotiers au bord des flots bleus, à une petite distance de Colombo, il me fallut, pour quelques jours, renoncer à toute nourriture et, roulé dans un châle, m'étendre sur une chaise longue. Bien que ma chambre, avec sa fenêtre de bois ajouré et sans vitres, fût une petite arche de Noé, où il y avait, entre autres choses, un nid de moineaux, des légions de fourmis, des myriades de moustiques, des tarentes et des scorpions, un peu d'ennui ne tarda pas à me gagner. Pour être plus attentif à ce que je verrais, je n'avais voulu emporter aucun livre, sauf une petite algèbre anglaise de poche. Après avoir résolu un certain nombre d'équations, je sentis grandir ma mélancolie ; je pensai d'une façon plus précise que j'étais à vingt jours au minimum de tous ceux que j'aimais, et bien seul dans mon paradis, ou plutôt dans le coin de ce paradis où me retenait la cholérine. Une idée lumineuse me vint : en pays anglais, je trouverais toujours un Shakespeare ! Aussitôt, coiffé du casque blanc en moelle de sureau et brandissant une large ombrelle, je me glissai hors du logis ; je traversai, non sans appréhension, une zone terriblement ensoleillée (il était près de midi) pour atteindre Colombo ; je m'engageai dans ses rues, découvris un libraire, trouvai et achetai pour un prix dérisoire Shakespeare complet en un volume, et revins m'allonger avec un incroyable sentiment de béatitude. Je n'étais plus seul. Le plus fidèle, le meilleur, le plus cher des amis était avec moi, entre mes mains et dans mes yeux aussi bien que dans ma pensée et dans mon cœur. Pour commencer je relus avec délices *Twelfth-Night, or What you Will*, et, comme par enchantement, les heures dévolues au choléra s'enfuirent d'un vol léger . . .

Que l'on me pardonne l'enfantillage de ces souvenirs. La Bhâgavad-Gita enseigne qu'il n'est point nécessaire d'honorer la Divinité par de somptueux sacrifices : le plus pauvre peut la toucher au cœur en lui offrant avec amour un lotus, une feuille, quelques gouttes d'eau.

MAURICE BOUCHOR.

L'ART ET LA NATURE, DANS SHAKESPEARE ET DANS BACON

UN passage de *Conte d'Hiver* [1] nous invite à comparer entre elles les vues de Shakespeare et celles de Bacon, au sujet des rapports de l'Art et de la Nature. Shakespeare écrit :

> . . . o'er that art,
> Which, you say, adds to nature, is an art
> That nature makes.

Or Bacon, examinant la conception suivant laquelle l'art serait une addition apportée à la nature (*additamentum quoddam naturae*), la repousse de la manière suivante : ' L'art, dit-il, n'est pas autre chose que la nature. Un art qui sait mettre en jeu les forces de la nature produira des changements bien autrement profonds que cet art qui, selon vous, ajoute à la nature.' [2]

La ressemblance paraît étroite ; est-elle réelle ?

Bacon part de l'idée de l'art humain : il le fait consister dans une certaine faculté d'assembler les choses naturelles autrement qu'elles ne s'assemblent d'elles-mêmes. Cette définition, qui est celle des arts mécaniques, suffit à Bacon pour caractériser la poésie elle-même, laquelle, selon lui, n'est autre chose que la substitution de combinaisons artificielles aux groupements naturels des événements, tels que l'histoire les enregistre. Passant de l'art humain à l'art de la nature, Bacon fait consister ce dernier dans la propriété qu'ont certains êtres de former, avec les éléments naturels, des combinaisons que ceux-ci, abandonnés à eux-mêmes, n'auraient pas réalisées. C'est ainsi que les abeilles, du suc des fleurs, font leur miel.

Ainsi entendu, l'art n'est autre chose que ce que l'on appelle proprement l'industrie.

Or Shakespeare, dans sa conception de l'art, part, au contraire,

---

[1] *Winter's Tale,* Acte IV, sc. iii.   [2] Bacon, *Descriptio globi intellectualis,* c. ii.

de l'idée de la nature ; et, voyant en elle la grande créatrice : *great creating nature*, il méprise un art qui, par des procédés mécaniques, essaierait de l'imiter. Un tel art ne créerait que des ' bâtards de la nature '. Shakespeare ne distingue pas, comme Bacon, entre les matériaux et l'agent, pour conclure que la nouveauté ne se rencontre jamais que dans l'arrangement, non dans les éléments. L'art, chez lui, est, bien réellement, et à la lettre, créateur. C'est dans ce sens que Hamlet s'écrie :

> There are more things in heaven and earth, Horatio,
> Than are dreamt of in your philosophy.

De cet art, inné à la nature, l'art humain participe : en sorte que, lui aussi, pénètre la matière des choses comme leur forme, et crée véritablement.

En quoi consistent, en second lieu, pour Bacon et pour Shakespeare, les produits de l'art ?

Pour Bacon, ce sont des œuvres visibles, tangibles, propres à être étudiées du dehors et à figurer parmi les objets de la science, comme toutes les choses dont se compose la nature. L'histoire de l'art n'est qu'un chapitre de l'histoire naturelle.

Il n'en est pas de même pour Shakespeare. Essentiellement vie et création, la nature crée des êtres qui sont, eux-mêmes, vivants et créateurs. Et l'art humain, qui prend sa source dans l'art naturel, le prolonge, et, lui-même, crée la vie.

Des œuvres de l'industrie les œuvres d'art se distinguent ainsi radicalement. L'œuvre de Shakespeare n'est pas une chose : c'est un être, c'est un foyer infiniment riche et puissant de vie, de sentiment, de passion, de pensée, d'action, de création.

L'homme est sujet à un mal étrange. Ses émotions les plus sincères, les plus profondes, les plus violentes, avec le temps, ou même du jour au lendemain, ne sont plus pour lui que des souvenirs abstraits, des idées inertes, des mots, qu'il comprend avec son intelligence, mais qui, maintenant, laissent son âme insensible. ' Quel âne je suis ! dit Hamlet. Oh ! c'est beau à moi, dont le père chéri a été assassiné, à moi, que le ciel et l'enfer arment pour la vengeance, de rester là, comme une commère, à décharger mon cœur en paroles, à m'épuiser en gros mots et en injures.' Cette maladie est ce qu'on appelle psittacisme. Elle consiste à dire des paroles, sans en réaliser, en son âme, le sens vivant. Or l'art, tel que Shakespeare le conçoit, a cette mission et cette puissance, de réveiller ou de créer, par des mots, par des formes sensibles, la vie, l'émotion, le sens de la réalité et de l'action, dans des esprits pour qui les mots n'étaient plus que des mots.

Et Shakespeare, entre tous, est ce magicien qui, avec des syllabes, des rythmes, des images, des raisonnements, nous fait voir, éprouver, vivre, les réalités mêmes que ses pièces traduisent.

L'art shakespearien est la nature triomphant de la nature, c'est le sentiment, réel et authentique, se dressant, plus vivant que jamais, hors de la tombe, où l'habitude a enfoui et scellé son cadavre. Nous diras-tu, ô sentiment, par quel miracle

> . . . thy canoniz'd bones, hearsed in death,
> Have burst their cerements !

Quelle conception du monde et de la vie résulte, dans Bacon et dans Shakespeare, de cette signification donnée à l'art ?

Bacon ouvre son *Novum Organum* par cet aphorisme : *Natura non nisi parendo vincitur*. Le mot essentiel de cette phrase, c'est : *vincitur*. La nature est un mécanisme ; et d'un mécanisme la science peut donner la clef. Grâce à la science, l'homme pourra, de plus en plus, user de la nature comme d'une esclave. L'art humain, application de la science, c'est la nature déchue de son empire sur l'homme, et enchaînée (*naturae vincula*) : c'est l'homme maître du monde.

Tout autre est le point de vue de Shakespeare.

L'art de la nature, ou l'art humain, qui en est une émanation, est un merveilleux créateur de vie, de formes, de rêves, de joies, de douleurs, de variété et de beauté. Est-il donc tout-puissant, et peut-il modeler le monde suivant l'idéal qu'il se donne ?

En face de la nature comme puissance de création Shakespeare voit subsister, immobile, inaccessible, une nature aveugle, violente, brutale, qui ignore ou bafoue les plus nobles aspirations de l'âme humaine.

Que peuvent nos efforts pour faire régner en ce monde la justice, la bienveillance, l'amour, la vérité ? Qu'est-ce que notre histoire, sinon l'éternel et invincible triomphe de la force et de la méchanceté sur le droit et sur la bonté ?

> And captive good attending captain ill !

A ces maux quel remède concevoir ?
— La mort, peut-être ?

> Tired with all these for restful death I cry.

— Mais qui sait si la mort n'est pas simplement un sommeil, et si ce sommeil n'est pas traversé par des rêves horribles ?

— La philosophie et l'empire de la raison ?

— Mais que peut la raison en face des fatalités de la nature ? Oui, j'obéirai à ma raison, si elle-même obéit à ma passion.

> . . . Be advis'd.
> — I am ; and by my fancy : if my reason
> Will thereto be obedient, I have reason.

Mais, dira-t-on, en user ainsi avec la raison, c'est se moquer d'elle.

— Fort bien : il n'y a donc d'autre issue pour l'homme que la folie. C'est elle qu'il faut appeler, qu'il faut accueillir, qu'il faut chérir :

> If not, my senses, better pleased with madness,
> Do bid it welcome.

L'art est un merveilleux tissu, aux mille couleurs, chatoyantes et captivantes, que la nature elle-même jette sur ses abîmes de souffrance et d'iniquité.

ÉMILE BOUTROUX.

SIMPLES NOTES

LE temps qui détruit si impitoyablement les réputations usurpées n'a pas de prise sur les écrivains qui ont mérité la gloire par la pureté de leur génie.   Il y a trois cents ans que Shakespeare est mort et peut-on dire qu'il nous ait quittés ? Son âme habite encore parmi nous ; elle vivifie notre époque autant, sinon plus, qu'aux jours où elle agissait par la vertu de sa présence réelle.   Jamais son influence ne fut plus radieuse ni plus universelle.

Pour échapper à un moment d'angoisse j'ai repris ce soir le livre préféré qui depuis dix-huit mois gisait délaissé sur ma table.   Mon esprit a beau être alourdi par les tristesses de cet âge de fer et de sang, à la seule vue des pages familières il recouvre toute son élasticité. L'essaim des vieux enthousiasmes surgit brusquement du texte inspiré et emplit la nuit de son vol doré.   Je retrouve les joies des premières lectures à l'époque déjà lointaine où, explorateur ardent, je découvrais la littérature anglaise.   Je me sens prêt à nouveau pour les adorations. Et puisque l'on me demande de joindre ma voix au chœur des admirateurs du poète, je vais, au cours de cette veille studieuse, noter mes impressions, sans ordre, au hasard de leur naissance.   Ce sera, faute de mieux, l'hommage d'un Français au plus grand des Anglais.

* * *

Il est difficile de songer à Shakespeare sans sortir de soi-même. Car il y a dans son œuvre une vertu occulte qui agit à la manière d'un excitant.   Sous son influence, l'esprit est comme soulevé ; il se sent pénétré d'allégresse ; la pensée devient plus fluide et s'épanche ; des coins obscurs de la mémoire subconsciente s'entr'ouvrent et livrent leurs trésors d'idées neuves et d'images.   En de pareils moments les écrivains de race, portés au faîte de leur puissance, sont prêts à donner le meilleur d'eux-mêmes.

Certains esprits, par contre, ne peuvent approcher de la pensée shakespearienne sans danger pour la raison.   Shakespeare traîne à sa suite un cortège de songe-creux et de bayeurs aux chimères qui ont à son sujet échafaudé les plus extravagantes fantaisies.   De là vient que seul peut-être des écrivains modernes il a donné lieu à des discussions sur la réalité de son existence.   Mais pourquoi partir en guerre contre ces admirateurs à rebours ? Ils témoignent à leur manière de la hauteur vertigineuse où se tient le poète.

* * *

On n'a pas, à mon sens, loué comme il convient le style de Shakespeare.   Il ne suffit pas de vanter la richesse inépuisable du vocabulaire, l'aisance de la phrase, la splendeur éclatante des images.   Ces prodigalités d'une imagination généreuse ne sont pas le privilège de Shakespeare : on les rencontre chez des écrivains de moindre puissance.   Ce qui me paraît plus essentiel, c'est la valeur musicale de la langue de Shakespeare.   Ici nous pénétrons vraiment jusqu'à la source cachée de cette vertu stimulante que je relevais tout à l'heure.   A l'oreille la phrase se révèle comme l'un des plus merveilleux instruments qui aient jamais résonné.   Tout ce qui pourrait ressembler à des défauts — surabondance des métaphores, expressions obscures, enchevêtrement des périodes — se résorbe instantanément et il ne reste plus que les cadences infinies d'une mélodie souple et savante, les broderies musicales d'un thème dont la puissance rythmique vous transporte.   A entendre certains passages — le duo entre Lorenzo et Jessica, par exemple —

> How sweet the moonlight sleeps upon this bank!
> Here will we sit and let the sound of music
> Creep in our ears ; soft stillness and the night
> Become the touches of sweet harmony, etc.

j'éprouve une volupté aussi intense qu'à écouter chanter sur un violon parfait la plus limpide des mélodies.   Dans des morceaux comme celui-ci les mots éveillent l'idée autant par le son que par le sens ; ils ont une signification redoublée, car ils se font entendre à l'âme aussi bien qu'à l'esprit.   Quant à dire de quoi est composée cette harmonie, je ne l'essaierai pas.   La formule selon laquelle ont été combinées consonnes et voyelles échappe à la définition.   De pareils phénomènes ne s'analysent pas plus que la voix du vent dans la forêt ou le chant d'allégresse de la mer par une belle nuit : ils ne sont pas du ressort de l'esprit critique.

* * *

Les critiques, quand ils parlent de Shakespeare, sont à ce point unanimes que l'on va répétant certains éloges sans en percevoir la signification profonde.   Comme il arrive pour les vérités consacrées par le temps, ces jugements paraissent si indiscutables qu'ils prennent force de proverbes et finissent par ne plus arrêter l'esprit. Ainsi on considère comme naturel que Shakespeare ait excellé à la fois dans le tragique et dans le comique. C'est pourtant un fait unique dans l'histoire du théâtre.

* * *

Nul n'a peint mieux que Shakespeare la nature humaine et la vie. L'image qu'il nous a donnée du monde est si ressemblante qu'après trois cents ans, et malgré les modifications subies par les mœurs, nous la reconnaissons comme vérité d'aujourd'hui, et qu'elle peut servir de pierre de touche à notre expérience : Shakespeare est le plus impeccable des réalistes.

Mais il a été doué de l'imagination la plus vaste, la plus audacieuse qui ait jamais embrasé un esprit ; il a appuyé son front sur les nuages et reculé à perte de vue la limite du rêve : Shakespeare est le plus immatériel des poètes.

Il est déjà rare de voir un homme réunir en lui et sans heurts des tempéraments qui s'excluent. Mais qu'un écrivain — un auteur dramatique surtout — ait su les combiner dans son œuvre, selon un dosage qui jamais ne choque, cela tient du prodige.

* * *

Shakespeare devrait faire le désespoir des critiques qui le commentent ; car il n'y a pas d'auteur dont les caractéristiques soient moins déterminées. Aucune formule n'enserre sa manière ; il n'est jamais le même ni lui-même ; il est innombrable comme une foule. Les généralisations à son sujet sont impossibles et, d'autre part, ses procédés dramatiques sont des plus simples : ils sont vieux comme le monde. Tout se ramène donc à une question d'excellence. Le critique, éperdu devant tant de richesse mouvante, en est réduit à l'admiration. Encore celle-ci essaie-t-elle en vain de se renouveler ; elle aboutit toujours à l'hyperbole.

* * *

De très bons esprits ont pris à partie les admirateurs de Shakespeare et, après les avoir vertement tancés de leur aveuglement, ils les ont traités d'idolâtres. Si l'on regarde de près ces contempteurs on s'aperçoit vite que ce sont ou bien des étrangers ou des gens que la métaphysique a troublés. Les premiers ne comprennent pas. Les seconds confondent le royaume de la spéculation et celui de l'imagination ; ils cherchent un philosophe à leur taille ; ils trouvent un poète et ne s'en consolent pas.

* * *

Bien des gens s'obstinent à vouloir percer l'obscurité qui entoure la vie de Shakespeare. Il semble à ces admirateurs inassouvis du poète que, s'ils connaissaient son existence dans le détail, ils y découvriraient des actes prodigieux. Je ne partage pas cette curiosité, car je suis persuadé que si nous pouvions la satisfaire nous serions cruellement déçus. L'image que je me forme à l'aide des quelques renseignements qui nous sont parvenus me suffit et elle est, j'en suis sûr, ressemblante ; des faits nouveaux n'y ajouteraient rien. Les hommes qui portent en eux un grand rêve ne s'imposent pas violemment à l'attention du vulgaire. Leur vie intérieure est trop ardente : elle étouffe le désir des manifestations bruyantes et surtout le besoin de paraître qui est la passion des médiocres. Ils peuvent être affables et de bonne compagnie ; mais à cela se bornent les avances qu'ils font au monde, car se suffisant à eux-mêmes ils ne cherchent pas à conquérir les suffrages d'autrui. Ils traversent la vie modestes et effacés. Si leurs œuvres trahissent leur grandeur, c'est généralement à la surprise de ceux qui les connaissent. Ceci s'applique exactement à Shakespeare. Il n'y a pas d'écrivain célèbre autour duquel se soient cristallisées moins de légendes. Il ne semble même pas avoir échauffé outre mesure l'enthousiasme de ses contemporains. ' Gentle Shakespeare,' tel est le jugement peu complexe où ont abouti les efforts laudatifs de ceux qui l'aimèrent. Cette simple épithète, dans sa pauvreté, est pour moi plus révélatrice qu'un volume de dithyrambes.

* * *

Et d'ailleurs qu'est-il besoin de connaître la vie de Shakespeare par le menu quand nous pouvons méditer sur l'acte qui a clos sa carrière ? Parmi les traits rapportés sur les grands hommes je n'en vois pas de plus significatif ni de plus beau que cette volonté du poète de retourner mourir dans son pays natal. Avoir conscience qu'on a créé une œuvre grandiose et éternelle ; avoir vu des foules ployées sous l'émotion et la terreur ou convulsées par le rire ; avoir éprouvé l'ivresse de l'artiste qui sent son rêve se communiquer d'âme à âme, être Shakespeare enfin ! Puis un jour, en pleine force, déposer cette royauté intellectuelle, reprendre le chemin de la petite ville où les yeux se sont ouverts à la beauté du ciel et borner désormais sa vie à l'horizon du propriétaire campagnard ! Tout l'homme est dans ce geste. Sa simplicité, sa sagesse, sa force d'âme, son détachement des mirages du monde, sa santé mentale, sa grandeur éclatent dans cette décision. Au sortir d'une lecture de l'œuvre, alors que mon esprit est encore tout frémissant, j'aime à évoquer cette image de Shakespeare citoyen de Stratford, et je comprends alors ce qui fait sa suprématie. Shakespeare n'a pas été rongé par le mal des écrivains. Les mesquineries, les petites ambitions, les habiletés professionnelles du littérateur n'ont jamais terni chez lui la pureté de l'inspiration. S'il a été un grand auteur dramatique c'est que nulle préoccupation d'école ne s'est interposée entre la conception et l'expression. La pensée a toujours coulé des sources profondes où se mirait sa sincérité. Il n'a pas visé à l'effet : il s'est contenté d'écouter parler en lui la voix éternelle de l'humanité. Et s'il a peint l'homme avec tant de vérité c'est peut-être tout simplement parce qu'il n'a jamais cessé d'être homme.

ALBERT FEUILLERAT.

RENNES.

COMMENT FAIRE CONNAÎTRE SHAKESPEARE AUX PETITS FRANÇAIS

UN nom domine toute la littérature anglaise, un des plus hauts de la littérature universelle, celui de Shakespeare. Il n'est pas de personnalité plus complexe, d'art plus difficile à comprendre pour des esprits latins. Depuis Voltaire jusqu'à Richepin, classiques et romantiques l'ont également travesti à plaisir et compris de travers ; et l'on ne sait laquelle admirer le plus, l'incompréhension des uns ou des autres. C'est que, de part et d'autre, on l'a étudié avec des préoccupations uniquement françaises, et jugé au nom d'une esthétique qui n'était pas la sienne, l'exaltant ou le dépréciant tour à tour pour des raisons contradictoires, mais d'une fausseté également merveilleuse. Quel espoir donc de faire pénétrer dans des cerveaux d'écoliers une appréciation juste de ce colosse incompris ? Et ne vaut-il pas mieux abandonner cette tâche désespérée ? ou se contenter de donner à la fin des études quelque esquisse sommaire de ses traits prodigieux ?

Nullement. C'est dès la Sixième que l'on doit commencer l'étude de Shakespeare, et cette affirmation n'est pas un paradoxe. C'est Shakespeare qui enseignera Shakespeare : c'est par un commerce prolongé avec l'œuvre que nos élèves arriveront à la comprendre, et non par des analyses, des résumés, des lectures entassées à la fin de leurs études. Et voici comment on procédera.

Dès la fin de la Sixième, on fera apprendre aux élèves des fragments de chansons shakespeariennes. Il en existe dans *La Tempête*, dans *Le Songe d'une Nuit d'Été*, ailleurs, d'une langue si élémentaire qu'ils les comprendront presque du premier coup ; chansons de fées et d'esprits, si simples qu'elles sont accessibles à l'intelligence d'un enfant, si belles que l'imagination de l'homme n'en a jamais rêvé de plus belles. En Cinquième, on complétera ces chansons, on en donnera d'autres, entières, en leçon, sans que le nom de l'auteur soit prononcé. En Quatrième, on racontera sommairement l'intrigue de telle ou telle pièce, on fera connaître à l'élève le merveilleux conteur qu'est

Shakespeare, et le trésor d'émouvantes histoires que contient son œuvre ; on ajoutera quelques maximes, proverbes, tirades très courtes ; rien de plus facile que d'en trouver qui soient à la portée des plus jeunes esprits. En Troisième, on complétera ces histoires, on en racontera d'autres plus longuement, on en fera lire ; quelques courts extraits simplifiés seront expliqués en classe, appris par cœur.

Ainsi d'année en année s'augmentera la matière shakespearienne déposée graduellement dans l'esprit de nos élèves, et qui peu à peu agira sur lui pour le transformer, le préparer à accueillir avec compréhension, avec sympathie, avec familiarité, ce qui, présenté en bloc, brusquement, l'aurait déconcerté ou rebuté. D'obscures correspondances s'établiront entre les divers fragments d'abord dissociés, et les *disjecta membra poetae* se rejoindront un jour pour vivre dans l'harmonie de leur vie profonde. Il n'est pas trop de plusieurs années pour familiariser de petits Français avec l'étrangeté d'une telle œuvre, et pour y parvenir rien ne vaut cette action de présence prolongée. Chaque poète crée le goût par lequel il est apprécié : à toute poésie, nouvelle par la date ou par la race, il faut une accoutumance ; l'on y pénètre, non par brusque découverte, mais par lente initiation ; et plus cette initiation est graduelle, plus la possession est parfaite. Et ce qui est vrai pour la poésie en général l'est doublement pour Shakespeare.

L'étude de Shakespeare sera donc implicite avant d'être explicite, et le jour où le maître l'abordera ouvertement nos élèves seront préparés à comprendre ses commentaires, ses rapprochements, les fragments plus étendus, les pièces entières, qu'on leur fera connaître en Seconde et en Première. Aux lectures dispersées succédera maintenant l'étude consciente, et un effort pour coordonner toutes les notions précédemment acquises ou implicitement contenues dans ces lectures. Le maître s'assignera comme tâche de faire entrer dans l'esprit de ses élèves l'essentiel de l'œuvre shakespearienne et d'en dégager pour eux les caractères généraux. Par une revision méthodique de tous les passages appris ou vus et l'exposition exacte et simple des notions qu'ils peuvent fournir sur l'art et l'œuvre du poète, par des rapprochements entre les fragments déjà connus et de nouveaux extraits de même inspiration, on les amènera à voir clairement, dans l'ordre de leur importance et de leur complexité, les plus frappants de ces caractères. C'est ainsi que par la comparaison entre les sujets et les décors des pièces racontées en Quatrième et en Troisième et ceux des pièces dont on parlera ou qu'on lira en Seconde et en Première ; par le contraste commenté entre les listes de personnages en tête d'une pièce shakespearienne et d'une tragédie classique, si nombreux et si variés dans l'une, si limités aux seuls personnages nobles et en si petit nombre dans l'autre ; par d'autres commentaires encore, on fera sentir aux élèves d'abord le premier de ces caractères, qui est la *variété*. Et en effet ils verront par eux-mêmes la variété infinie de l'œuvre qui embrasse toute la réalité et tout le rêve, l'antiquité et la légende, le moyen âge et la Renaissance, tous les pays et tous les décors, vrais ou fabuleux, depuis l'Égypte de Cléopâtre, la Rome de Coriolan ou de César, l'ardente, la brillante et périlleuse Italie de Juliette et de Béatrice, la sombre Écosse féodale de Macbeth, jusqu'à l'Ile ' pleine de musique ' de *La Tempête*, l'Athènes des Ducs, la Forêt des Ardennes, tous les êtres, réels ou imaginaires, sublimes ou vils, tragiques ou comiques, de pure fantaisie lyrique ou d'exacte observation ; et où tout vit avec une vraisemblance et une intensité égales, cordonniers ou rois, fées et artisans, sorcières et joyeuses commères, les héros de Plutarque et les esprits de l'air, les princes du songe ou de la verte Angleterre, Hamlet, Prospero, les Richard, les Henri, la plèbe de Rome, la canaille de Londres et les douces, les gracieuses apparitions de Desdémone et de Cordélia, d'Ophélie et de Rosalinde ; où toutes les voix se mêlent en un chœur immense qui semble la voix même de l'humanité : accents désolés, augustes ou terribles, célestes ou moqueurs, vastes rires, ivresses d'amour qui fusent en roulades de rossignols, sanglots déchirants, cris de démence et de haine, chansons aériennes, appels héroïques, bouffonneries triviales, ou divins accords mystérieux : toutes les joies, toutes les souffrances, tous les élans du cœur, toutes les fantaisies de l'esprit, la musique la plus vaste et la plus variée qui ait jamais jailli d'une âme humaine.

Puis, enfin, en Première, par la lecture d'une pièce entière, on pénétrera l'art du poète et on en fera sentir l'extrême *complexité*. On montrera, en faisant saillir la relation intime qui existe entre le décor, l'action, les personnages, que chaque pièce est un monde à part, réel, concret, particulier et complet, où tout se tient, où rien n'existe que par la concordance et la collaboration de tous les éléments à la fois. Et c'est ainsi qu'à la tragédie du jeune amour il faut le décor de l'Italie cruelle et voluptueuse, de Vérone déchirée par ses haines héréditaires, de l'amoureuse nuit italienne enchantée de lune, chargée d'ardeurs, de langueurs et de parfums, où palpite la voix du rossignol, où sous les lustres des bals tournoient comme des papillons les beaux seigneurs amoureux et batailleurs, où les brèves et fiévreuses destinées sont enveloppées de menaces, traversées de joies et de terreurs excessives, où tout est plus rapide, ailé, ivre de vie légère qu'ailleurs ; et on évoquera par contraste cette sombre Elseneur où, parmi les brumes, les mystères et les vagues angoisses du Nord et de la Nuit, Hamlet se débat au milieu des fantômes contre l'insoluble problème du devoir et de la vie. On dira quelle atmosphère maléfique, alourdie de vapeurs de sang et d'obscures épouvantes, pèse sur la superstitieuse et sauvage Écosse de ce noir XIᵉ siècle où parmi les incantations des sorcières et les prodiges se déroule le drame de l'ambition féodale ; que les hésitations, les hallucinations, les carnages de Macbeth, les audaces, les terreurs et les remords de Lady Macbeth, de ce châtelain et de cette châtelaine écossais qui ont commis l'inexpiable forfait de tuer l'hôte et le suzerain, leur bienfaiteur et leur roi, n'ont de vraisemblance et de réalité que dans ce monde primitif livré aux puissances invisibles du mal, parmi ces âpres solitudes désolées par l'interminable hiver où l'esprit inculte et désœuvré, l'âme instable et violente de ces barbares ressassent sans fin les mêmes images de meurtre et d'horreur, s'affolent jusqu'au crime et à la démence. On apprendra à nos élèves, en leur racontant l'histoire puérile et terrible de Lear, qu'elle nous vient de la légendaire Bretagne préhistorique, plus barbare et plus sauvage encore que l'Écosse du XIᵉ siècle, où les hommes plus déraisonnables, plus capricieux, plus inconscients que des enfants, se déchirent comme des fauves, où les instincts excessifs parlent un langage forcené, où les passions primitives déchaînées semblent lutter de violence avec le déchaînement des forces élémentaires qui illuminent sinistrement de leurs éclairs et enveloppent de leurs tonnerres l'insoutenable horreur de ce drame sanglant. On leur montrera que le lieu de ce drame du pessimisme est la tempête qu'apostrophe le vieux roi désespéré, tempête où dans la désolation universelle ne rayonne que pour s'éteindre une seule pure étoile, la tendre figure de Cordélia. Par ces exemples, par d'autres, on leur fera saisir ainsi l'importance capitale de l'*atmosphère* et du *milieu*, bref du *décor* dans une pièce shakespearienne. On leur expliquera pourquoi le décor, négligeable dans une pièce classique, où tout le drame est intérieur, abstrait, général, est indispensable quand le drame est un fragment d'une certaine réalité particulière devinée par l'intuition du poète ou créée de toutes pièces par lui, et relié à elle par mille correspondances obscures ou visibles. On aboutira ainsi naturellement à une comparaison entre notre art abstrait si sobre, si peu chargé de matière, si soucieux des belles ordonnances, qui étudie dans leur simplicité des crises débarrassées de tout élément étranger et de tout détail particulier pour établir des vérités *générales*, et construire des synthèses de caractères *généraux*, et l'art anglais concret, si riche, si varié, si touffu,

si désordonné en apparence, qui décrit la germination, le développement, les lointaines suites particulières d'un caractère ou d'une situation,
et crée de toutes pièces, comme la Nature, une réalité vivante et complexe, unique et complète, qui donne l'illusion même de la vie.

C'est ainsi que l'on s'élèvera graduellement à une vue d'ensemble
non seulement sur le théâtre de Shakespeare mais sur l'esthétique
anglaise tout entière, toujours au moyen d'exemples concrets et par
des faits élémentaires à la portée de nos élèves. Rien de plus nécessaire
que ces idées générales qui éclaireront toutes leurs lectures. Ils comprendront mieux l'art de l'*Avare*, par exemple, le jour où ils liront
Silas Marner, et la différence essentielle qu'il y a entre les fins que
poursuit le dramaturge français dans l'étude d'une passion et celles
que recherche le romancier anglais. Le maître aura fait autant pour
leur culture française et générale que pour leur culture étrangère quand,
dans de petites conférences qu'on leur fera faire ou que l'on fera en
Première, on leur apprendra à dégager ces idées générales auxquelles tout
l'enseignement a tendu et doit tendre toujours. Ainsi préparées, ainsi
étayées sur des exemples concrets, des lectures, la connaissance directe
des textes, ces idées générales auront une netteté, une solidité, une
fécondité que ne saurait jamais leur donner aucun enseignement abstrait
ex cathedra de la littérature. C'est *directement* que nos élèves auront
appris à voir la variété de l'œuvre shakespearienne, l'importance qu'y
tient le décor, la complexité de cet art qui crée des drames dont chacun
est un monde à part, réel et complet, qui veut être jugé — style, action,
personnages — de l'intérieur et d'après son esthétique propre, non au
nom de principes abstraits et d'idées préconçues ; c'est grâce à des
démonstrations répétées, d'inconscientes observations multipliées, des
impressions superposées et confirmatrices, venues de plusieurs côtés
à la fois, qu'ils sentiront, avant de les exprimer en formules nettes,
les profondes différences qui séparent une pièce de Racine ou de Molière
d'une pièce de Shakespeare. On ne s'en tiendra pas en Première à la seule
littérature. On appliquera à la vie tout entière du pays étranger les
vérités d'ordre général que l'on aura dégagées de l'étude de Shakespeare,
de même que l'on fera converger sur son œuvre toutes les clartés que
l'étude de cette vie fournira. On fera ainsi rentrer la littérature dans
l'ensemble de l'enseignement. Par des analyses et des rapprochements
que seul le maître peut faire, il montrera à nos élèves que les différences
qu'ils ont constatées en littérature se retrouvent partout, parce qu'elles
tiennent à des différences psychologiques irréductibles, dont la marque
et l'influence s'impriment pareillement à toutes les manifestations de

chaque civilisation : langue, politique, institutions, droit, art. On les dégagera avec netteté et on les soulignera partout où on les rencontrera, parce qu'elles sont capitales, et que seul le clair sentiment de ces différences permet de comprendre les choses d'outre-Manche. L'étude de la langue permet d'établir que l'Anglais pense par mots particuliers et pittoresques, le Français par mots généraux et abstraits, l'un par images et représentations complexes, l'autre par idées et représentations simplifiées de la réalité. On fera voir maintenant que, de même qu'un Anglais parle comme il pense, il compose comme il parle, et que le caractère qui domine sa langue domine aussi sa littérature. Par l'analyse des œuvres littéraires et des faits de civilisation, on montrera ensuite que partout l'esprit anglais se méfie de l'abstrait et réclame le concret, le réel, le complexe, autant que l'esprit français, épris d'ordre, d'abstraction, plus sensible aux côtés communs des choses qu'aux différences qui les séparent, se complaît dans le simple et le général, les principes absolus, les constructions logiques, codes, constitutions *a priori*, les belles ordonnances et les théories dont l'Anglais, pratique et positif, ennemi de toutes les idéologies, a l'instinctive répugnance. Et, de fait, nulle part chez lui on ne retrouvera jamais cet esprit de synthèse, ce besoin d'idées générales, ce génie de l'abstraction et de la classification qui aboutit chez nous au Code Napoléon, à la Déclaration des Droits de l'Homme, à notre Administration, à nos ' écoles ' littéraires, intolérantes et absolues dans leurs dogmes comme des sectes religieuses : ni dans son droit qui n'est qu'un vaste fouillis de précédents et de cas particuliers ; ni dans sa politique empirique, faite de compromis et d'expédients, sans principes directeurs ni plan d'ensemble ; ni dans son art qui a la richesse, mais aussi le désordre, la confusion de la vie. Et si l'on veut ramasser en une formule les idées que je viens d'exprimer, et résumer pour nos élèves les deux tendances des deux esprits, on citera en Philosophie le mot de Burke, théoricien du réalisme politique : ' Je hais jusqu'au son des mots qui expriment des abstractions ' en le contrastant avec la boutade de Royer-Collard : ' Je méprise un fait,' c'est-à-dire toute chose isolée dont on ne peut tirer une idée générale.

Voilà, brièvement, les idées essentielles auxquelles doit aboutir une étude de Shakespeare, car ce sont celles auxquelles conduit toute étude anglaise, et leur importance est capitale. Il faut laisser aux préférences individuelles le soin d'établir dans quel ordre et dans quelle mesure on peut présenter à nos élèves quelques fragments de l'œuvre, quelle pièce il faut choisir pour une étude complète et approfondie, qui, elle, s'impose.

On ne connaît aucun auteur dramatique par des fragments, des morceaux de bravoure, Shakespeare moins que tout autre ; et Macaulay avait raison de dire qu'il donnerait de grand cœur tous les extraits d'une pièce qui paraissent dans les anthologies pour ce qui reste de la pièce une fois ces ' beautés ' enlevées.   Qu'il soit possible, qu'il soit facile même d'étudier dans son développement organique une pièce entière, c'est ce que j'ai souvent constaté ; et, notamment dans des lycées de jeunes filles, j'ai vu l'impression profonde que laissent *Jules César*, *Le Songe d'une Nuit d'Été*, *Macbeth*, d'autres pièces encore.   Qu'il soit préférable de voir une seule pièce de près plutôt que plusieurs en courant, cela va sans dire.   Mais que nos élèves puissent quitter nos lycées sans en connaître aucune, voilà ce qui est inadmissible, et, je l'espère, ne se verra plus.

ÉMILE HOVELAQUE.

FRAGMENTS SUR SHAKESPEARE

INVITÉ *à joindre, en vue du Troisième Centenaire, mon hommage à ceux de plus dignes, je déclinai cet honneur. La crise que, du vouloir de quelques-uns, traverse l'Europe, et l'on peut dire l'humanité, ne laisse à quiconque a le bonheur de servir un instant pour autre chose que son service : du vouloir de quelques-uns, qui ont jugé l'heure propice pour déterminer lequel des deux principes devait l'emporter dans le monde, la prépotence de quelques-uns, ou bien la liberté. Peut-être ont-ils bien jugé : l'heure était propice, mais non de la manière qu'ils pensaient. Un avenir prochain en décidera.*

Le Secrétaire du Comité a insisté, condescendant à se déclarer satisfait d'une simple marque d'hommage ; et j'offre ainsi ce qui m'est demandé, la mise en français de quelques passages d'une allocution prononcée à l'inauguration des 'Annual Shakespeare Lectures', fondées dans l'Académie Britannique.

Je me suis souvenu, comme encouragement à l'obéissance, de ces contes du moyen âge où, pour obtenir le maintien en grâce, rien que le plus modeste service n'est requis : ce n'est pas l'acte qui compte, mais son accomplissement dans l'état d'âme voulu — 'Emplissez d'eau mon barisel'. C'est à un service de ce genre, accompli, j'espère, dans l'état d'âme voulu, que, en raison des tragiques circonstances présentes, le canon de Verdun tonnant, ce me semble, à mes oreilles, sera limité mon hommage.

'IL n'effaçait jamais une ligne ? ' grommelait Jonson ; ' que n'en a-t-il effacé un millier ! . . . '

De renom littéraire, Shakespeare dramaturge ne se soucia jamais ; les nécessités de l'heure ne pouvaient toutefois être oubliées par lui, celle avant tout de plaire à son public. Son public moyen, celui auquel il songeait surtout, dont il devait toucher ou charmer le cœur et l'esprit moyens, était celui du Globe, vaste théâtre, très fréquenté, qui attirait des auditoires populaires, et où il pouvait arriver d'aventure qu'un Ambassadeur se présentât ; mais le sort des pièces ne dépendait pas de l'applaudissement de l'Ambassadeur ou du blâme des critiques savants, il dépendait de l'impression produite sur la foule ; une foule turbulente, au cœur chaud, de tempérament sanguin, de patriotisme exubérant, adorant les extrêmes, tantôt ravie par le spectacle des tortures, tantôt émue à la mort d'une mouche — ' Row, if that fly had a father and mother ? ' — aimant l'invraisemblable, les changements inattendus, les bouffonneries grossières, les jeux de mots, les traits d'esprit communs, faciles à comprendre, les bruits retentissants de toute sorte : cloches, trompettes, canons ; toutes gens d'une ignorance encyclopédique.

Il est difficile d'exagérer le rôle d'un tel public en tant que collaborateur aux pièces de Shakespeare — véritable collaborateur, à qui il semble par moments que Shakespeare ait passé la plume pour griffonner ce qu'il lui plaît, ou la craie pour barbouiller le mur de ses dessins. Ce que de tels spectateurs pouvaient aimer et ce qu'ils pouvaient tolérer, est ce qui donna à des pièces dont l'auteur ne se souciait en rien, les représentations finies, la forme unique, merveilleuse, propre aussi à causer la stupeur, que nous leur connaissons. Grande est la responsabilité de fait d'un tel public ; grande celle de Shakespeare aussi pour ne lui avoir jamais rien refusé ; grande plutôt eût été cette responsabilité si, de propos délibéré, il n'avait voulu plaire à personne qu'à ces hommes vivants, réunis dans son théâtre, de qui il tenait son pain quotidien. ' Car nous,' comme le Dr Johnson lui-même dut le reconnaître, ' qui vivons pour plaire, devons plaire pour vivre '—

> For we that live to please, must please to live.

De la composition de ses pièces toutefois, Shakespeare n'attendait pas un seul résultat, mais deux : d'abord un succès immédiat auprès de son auditoire et tout ce qui dépendait pour lui de cette réussite ; ensuite, l'agréable, exhilarante, exquise satisfaction causée par l'exercice d'une fonction normale de son cerveau. C'est là pour nous le principal, ce qui le sauva, malgré qu'il en eût ; à la nourriture grossière que réclamait son parterre, il ajouta la nourriture éthérée qui a fait depuis des siècles les délices des plus grands parmi les hommes : et le parterre, du reste, n'y objectait pas. Le poète ajoutait ces merveilles par surcroît, parce que c'était une satisfaction pour sa nature de le faire, que cela ne lui donnait pas plus de peine que les jeux de mots, les facéties ou les massacres, et parce que l'expérience lui avait montré que, sans être aucunement nécessaires au succès, ces touches ne nuisaient pas et recevaient même un accueil bienveillant. C'était pour lui l'exercice d'une fonction naturelle, comme pour un bon arbre de produire de bons fruits.

Impossible réunion d'extrêmes ! se sont écriés des sceptiques désireux de conclure que Shakespeare lui-même était une impossibilité. Mais il n'y a rien là d'impossible, ni même d'unique. ' Où il est mauvais, il passe bien loin au delà du pire : c'est le charme de la canaille ; où il est bon, il va jusques à l'exquis et à l'excellent : il peut être le mets des plus délicats,' a dit un moraliste célèbre à propos d'un grand écrivain. Il ne s'agissait pas de Shakespeare ; c'est le jugement bien connu de La Bruyère sur Rabelais.

De ces circonstances de fait vient l'étrange nature de l'œuvre shakespearienne, modèle de ce que l'artiste peut souhaiter atteindre de plus haut et de ce qu'il doit le plus soigneusement éviter ; utile des deux manières. La promptitude de Shakespeare à écrire — il n'avait pas le choix, il fallait vivre — la nécessité pour lui de faire la cour à un auditoire dont la faveur lui était indispensable, expliquent, avec ce génie prodigieux reçu du ciel, comment le meilleur et le pire fraternisent dans ses pièces, ces jets d'une lumière qui ne s'éteindra jamais et ces concessions aux goûts du vulgaire (indécences, brutalités, mystifications, tortures, basses plaisanteries, complications laborieusement expliquées), ou encore les libertés qu'il se permet, assuré que son public ne saura pas, ne se souviendra pas, ne fera pas attention. ' Il néglige ', dit le Dr Johnson, ' des occasions d'instruire ou de charmer que le cours même de sa donnée semblerait le contraindre à utiliser,' la raison étant qu'en plus d'un cas, ces occasions ne l'ont pas frappé de prime abord, qu'il avait peu de temps pour se reprendre, et que, même sans cela, l'auditoire serait content. De là ses anachronismes, sa géographie fautive, son indifférence à la réalité des faits, si complète qu'il n'aurait pas étendu la main pour prendre un livre et vérifier l'emplacement d'une ville ou la date d'un événement, pas plus qu'il n'aurait pris la peine de demander à son futur gendre si, après avoir été étouffé, un être humain peut encore parler.

Il offre à son parterre et non à l'époque instruite où nous vivons, dont il ne se préoccupa jamais et qui n'a nul droit de se plaindre puisqu'elle reçoit un don gratuit, sans que rien ait été attendu d'elle, un règne du Roi Jean sans la Grande Charte, mais avec beaucoup de poudre à canon et un Duc d'Autriche, mort dans la réalité avant la date où la pièce commence. Il adopte, par motifs de commodité, deux règles auxquelles nul de ses auditeurs ne pouvait être tenté d'objecter : l'une est que tous les personnages antiques, ayant vécu dans l'antiquité, sont contemporains et peuvent se citer les uns les autres ; c'est ainsi qu'Hector cite Aristote, Menenius parle d'Alexandre et de Galien,

Titus Lartius compare Coriolan à Caton.   L'autre règle est que toutes
les villes éloignées sont sur le bord de la mer.   Rome, Florence, Milan,
Mantoue, Padoue, Vérone, pour ne rien dire de la Bohême, sont sur le
bord de la mer.   Ses personnages vont par mer de Padoue à Pise, de
Vérone à Milan ; pour quitter Vérone, ils attendent la marée.   Pourquoi
prendre peine ?   Il écrivait seulement pour des gens qui ne savaient, ni
ne se souciaient de rien de tout cela, composant des drames nullement
destinés à survivre, et qui avaient deux auteurs, Shakespeare et la foule
bigarrée du Globe.

Elles ont survécu cependant ; leur action sur le monde grandit
à mesure que les années passent ; elles sont fameuses dans des régions
dont le nom même était inconnu à leur auteur.   Le catalogue du British
Museum contient deux fois plus de numéros au mot Shakespeare qu'au
mot Homère ; dix-sept fois plus qu'il n'en comptait il y a un demi-
siècle.   Dans le calme de notre bibliothèque, dans le coin d'un com-
partiment de chemin de fer, sur le pont d'un navire, nous ouvrons le
livre et lisons la première scène : la magie de Prospéro opère, nous
sommes à lui, prêts à le suivre où il veut, à croire et sentir comme il
voudra.   Le spectacle une fois vu, les mots une fois entendus s'impriment de telle manière en notre esprit, que le simple nom du lieu, de
l'homme, la femme, l'enfant, ne pourront plus être prononcés désormais
devant nous sans que le grandiose ou gracieux paysage, le personnage
aimant, haïssant, rieur ou en larmes, et avec lui tout ce qui tient à lui, sa
famille, son ennemi, son aimée, sa maison, son chien, nous apparaisse,
en la même lumière que s'il vivait à nouveau parmi nous ; et nous le
suivons sur les terrasses d'Elseneur dans le jardin, baigné de lune, des
Capulets, sur la lande battue des tempêtes, rendez-vous de sorcières de
Lear ou de *Macbeth*, les bois près d'Athènes, le forum romain, le parc
enchanté de l'enchanteresse de Belmont, ou les champs de bataille réels
qui virent se préparer dans le sang les destinées de l'Angleterre et de la
France, longtemps ennemies, longtemps amies. — Ronsard n'a-t-il pas
prédit le retour des temps heureux sur terre, si jamais s'unissaient en
perpétuelle amitié,

> Vostre Angleterre avecques nostre France?

Nous vieillissons, le monde change ; les personnages de Shakespeare, non pas.   Ils nous demeurent si présents qu'il est difficile de
visiter aucun des lieux que parfois il a simplement nommés, et n'a pas
décrits, sans que le premier personnage qui s'y offre à notre pensée
soit le héros shakespearien.   Il s'évoque de lui-même et surgit à nos

yeux, bien avant que nous puissions songer aux hommes célèbres ayant vécu là leur vie réelle. Combien de voyageurs, arrivant à Elseneur, songeront d'abord à Christian IV, et seulement ensuite à Hamlet ?

Puissantes ou douces figures, amoureux que la mort va jeter au tombeau, chefs d'armée, anxieux Hamlet, dédaigneux Coriolan, ardent Roméo, pensif Brutus, exubérant Falstaff, et ces primevères de l'éternel printemps, Portia, Rosalinde, Ophélie, Juliette, Desdémone, se lèvent captivantes ou terribles, ou risibles, au seul nom d'Elseneur, Eastcheap, Ardennes, Vérone, Venise. Pendant la durée du mirage, notre vie semble fondue en la leur. Entre l'artiste et les enfants de sa pensée, le phénomène est fréquent ; entre les enfants de sa pensée et le lecteur du livre, il est rare. Nul maître-magicien n'a mieux possédé cette magie que le grand Anglais, mort il y a trois cents ans, distributeur de vie, briseur d'entraves.

Un coucher de soleil peut briller et s'éteindre inobservé du vulgaire ; il passera moins facilement inobservé en sa splendeur évanescente si Claude Lorrain le fixe sur la toile. Car au paysage, s'ajoute Claude Lorrain ; nous avons le paysage, plus lui ; l'artiste ne change rien à ce qu'il voit ; mais il est présent avec nous et dit à voix basse : Regarde. De même, pour Shakespeare. Les artistes moindres (Shakespeare a ses mauvais moments) le disent à voix haute.

Nul être doué de sens ne visite ce temple consacré à la beauté artistique, avec ses innombrables recoins et chapelles, où sont représentés tous les temps et tous les pays, le Louvre, sans le quitter meilleur. L'acquis peut-être de valeur infime ou de valeur immense ; sa réalité est certaine. Des sources dormantes d'émotion désintéressée auron été éveillées et auront coulé de nouveau ; un cerveau fatigué aura trouvé le repos ; des pensées ensommeillées seront sorties de torpeur et en auront procréé d'autres. De même, après une visite à Shakespeare.

Des bienfaiteurs privés ou l'État offrent à la jeunesse studieuse les moyens de séjourner à Rome ou Athènes ou de faire le tour du monde. L'idée dirigeante est qu'ils reviendront plus forts, mieux armés pour la vie, ayant eu des occasions hors du commun pour voir, penser, réfléchir, approvisionner leur esprit. De tels voyages nous sont offerts par Shakespeare autour de ce microcosme, plein de merveilles et pour lui sans secret, l'âme et le cœur de l'homme.

Son action sur les artistes et sur les masses durera : sur les masses parce qu'il leur est tellement accessible et que si, en raison de son génie, il atteignit aussi une tout autre région humaine, c'est cependant pour elles qu'il écrivit ; sur les artistes, à cause de l'exemple donné par lui de regarder en face toute réalité, choisissant seulement ce qui la rend caractéristique, les traits fixant la ressemblance. Nous pourrions suivre pas à pas un Hamlet, une nourrice, un Falstaff de la vie réelle et noter chaque parole dite par eux, chaque attitude qu'ils auraient prise, et le portrait ressemblerait moins à la nature vivante que celui bien moins complet de Shakespeare. Savoir choisir est un don supérieur, c'est pour l'écrivain sa manière de dire à voix basse : Regarde. Shakespeare, à son plus haut, murmure seulement le mot, que l'on entend sans le savoir. L'artiste demeure également éloigné de la pédanterie de l'écrivain savant qui vénère les règles parce qu'elles sont acceptées, et du révolté qui les rejette toujours et en tout temps parce que ce sont des règles.

Mais ne sont-ce là que des spectacles ? Et à quoi bon un spectacle de plus, si beau qu'il soit ? a dit, au cours des siècles, plus d'un penseur morose. A une question qu'il avait posée lui-même, Emerson a fourni la réponse : ' All high beauty has a moral element in it.'

J.-J. JUSSERAND.

AMBASSADE DE FRANCE, À WASHINGTON.

ÇÀ ET LÀ

Tout l'art dramatique de Shakespeare, aussi bien que sa philosophie tolérante, se résume dans le mot qu'il prête au roi Henri V :

There is some soul of goodness in things evil.

Sa vie d'auteur s'est employée à extraire ' l'essence de bien ' que recélaient de vieilles pièces médiocres, une piètre mise en scène, des comédiens souvent récalcitrants, et un public à demi-barbare.

*

Le clown existait avant que Shakespeare fût né, et il poursuit aujourd'hui encore, dans les cirques, sur le devant des baraques foraines, son existence pareille. Il fait les mêmes gestes, les mêmes grimaces. Il a le même accent, et débite presque intacts les mêmes calembours et calembredaines. Il traverse le théâtre de Shakespeare sans en être.

*

Tandis que les autres personnages sont censés ignorer le public, le clown regarde le parterre ; c'est au parterre qu'il parle.

*

Le clown pénètre dans toutes les sociétés et n'est d'aucune. Partout familier et partout étranger. Ce qu'il fait n'importe pas. Ce qu'il dit est sans conséquence. Il est imperméable à la réalité. Caressé, il plaisante ; injurié, menacé, battu il rit. Le danger et les coups n'ont rien pour l'émouvoir. Peut-être parce qu'il se sait immortel. Peut-être parce qu'il n'existe pas.

Le parterre n'a d'yeux et d'oreilles que pour le clown. Il l'attend avec impatience pendant les scènes graves. Il trouve toujours sa venue trop tardive, son départ trop prompt. Quelle tentation pour le clown, chatouillé par les rires, de renchérir sur ses quolibets et ses grimaces ! Le poète pèse peu auprès du pitre.

D d

Pour un qui disait : ' Je vais voir *Le Marchand de Venise*,' cent s'écriaient : ' Allons entendre le clown.'

*

Difficile problème : Conserver le clown pour que le public vienne ? Supprimer le clown pour que la pièce vive ?

*

Fixer au clown ses limites, ce fut une des tâches les plus ardues de Shakespeare. Il ne se défit pas de lui, aimant ses facéties et le sachant nécessaire. Petit à petit il l'amadoua en lui procurant toutes prêtes des drôleries pareilles aux siennes et un peu meilleures. Il l'attira dans un rôle, et puis, poussant le verrou, l'y enferma. Il le fit servir à ses fins. Mais comme il ne pouvait tout de même pas lui donner charge ou emploi régulier dans la vie, il le posta à côté d'elle avec mission de la juger en bêtisant.

*

Deux ou trois fois pourtant Shakespeare fit tout de bon du clown un homme. Il l'humanisa en lui accordant un métier et un caractère. Il le déguisa mieux encore en lui ôtant la conscience de sa bouffonnerie. Au clown qui faisait rire de tout il substitua le clown qui fait à son insu rire de lui-même. Bottom est certes un clown très authentique, mais il est tisserand, suffisant et naïf. Il croit amuser par son esprit quand il divertit par sa bêtise. Et, parce qu'il est naturel, il a mérité d'être promu à un rôle de premier plan. Le symbole du *Songe d'une nuit d'été* ne repose-t-il pas sur la rencontre de Bottom et de Titania ?

*

Tout à la fin de sa carrière Shakespeare ramena bel et bien le clown à sa condition primitive, avant qu'il fût devenu l'amuseur professionnel. Il l'identifia avec le paysan balourd dont le clown portait le nom mais qu'il ne se souvenait plus guère d'avoir été. Dans le *Conte d'hiver* le clown est fils d'un vieux berger. Et c'est un vrai gars de la campagne, épais et ingénu. Le clown avait déserté les champs pour les tréteaux ; il rentrait enfin au bercail.

* * *

Il est à la fois tentant et désespérant de tracer le portrait d'un personnage shakespearien. Autant définir le caractère des gens qui se meuvent autour de nous. La besogne ne serait guère plus malaisée.

Et la difficulté vient en effet de ce que les personnages de Shakespeare vivent, de ce qu'ils bougent et qu'ils changent.

*

Aussi sont-ils irréductibles à la simple logique. N'étant pas sortis d'une formule ils n'y peuvent point rentrer. Ils ne sont pas intelligibles toujours. Ils conservent des recoins obscurs ; ils ont des mystères.

*

Shakespeare lui-même comprenait-il *Hamlet* ? L'horloger comprend la montre qu'il a faite. Le père ne comprend pas l'enfant qu'il a engendré. *Genitum non factum.*

* * *

Chansons, sonnets, distiques rimés, vers blancs, prose — d'ordinaire la raison pour laquelle Shakespeare emploie chacune de ces formes de style apparaît aussitôt. Et sans peine on devine pourquoi il passe de l'une à l'autre.

L'adolescent Roméo, avant qu'il n'ait fait sa mue, aime à border ses mignardises de jolies rimes. Mais, à mesure que l'amour vrai l'échauffe et le trempe, il rejette ces colifichets pour s'en tenir au seul rythme de la passion qui fait battre son cœur.

*

Mais parfois on hésite. On se demande d'abord si la rime ne vient pas par caprice, la prose par lassitude ou négligence. Or, avec Shakespeare, il est toujours sage de croire en lui et de douter de soi-même.

*

Quand nos oreilles gardent encore l'écho des vers blancs où Othello clamait sa colère et sa douleur, comment se fait-il qu'il reparaisse ensuite, plus ravagé et plus déchiré, exhalant en simple prose le plus poignant peut-être de tous ses gémissements : ' But yet the pity of it, Iago ! O Iago ! the pity of it, Iago ! '

Malheureux decrescendo, direz-vous ? La forme déchoit quand redouble le pathétique. Toutefois, si nous nous guidons, non sur la hiérarchie officielle des styles mais sur l'effet produit, n'est-il pas vrai que seule la prose pouvait renchérir encore, seule rendre le paroxysme ? Il n'y a qu'elle pour rendre ce détraquement de l'être entier, cette suprême désorganisation des forces intimes, maintenant incapables de se soulever jusqu'au rythme, de s'ordonner en vers. Et justement parce que la prose n'idéalise pas, ne drape pas de beauté, elle nous met face à face avec la souffrance. Plus de voile. C'est le cœur tout à nu.

*

Et pourquoi ne recourt-elle presque jamais qu'à la prose, la Rosalinde si poétique et charmante de *Comme il vous plaira* ? C'est qu'on est mal à l'aise pour babiller en vers. Nulle cadence régulière ne serait assez agile pour sa volubilité. Il est un degré de prestesse où le vers qui détaille trop les syllabes ne saurait atteindre. Le vers donnerait un air trop prémédité aux improvisations impétueuses de la jeune fille. Le vers est une bride et Rosalinde doit avoir la langue débridée.

* * *

Le Brutus de Shakespeare harangue en syllogismes et monologue en métaphores.

*

Le Brutus de Plutarque était en somme un idéaliste serein. Celui de Shakespeare est un idéaliste qui se force. Le pathétique de sa destinée n'est à chercher ni dans sa lutte contre César, ni dans sa défaite, ni dans sa mort, mais dans la continuelle pression de sa main sur son cœur. Ce stoïque romain est enveloppé de moderne mélancolie.

* * *

' Art avis'd of that ? ' ' Où donc as-tu appris cela ? ' s'écrie Lucio stupéfait des arguments dont la jeune et pure Isabelle, cette demi-nonne, ignorante du monde qu'elle craint et qu'elle fuit, défend son frère Claudio coupable d'avoir manqué à la chasteté.

Elle-même était chaste jusqu'à la froideur, stricte jusqu'à l'étroitesse. Elle aspirait à la contrainte d'un couvent. Elle abominait les faiblesses de la chair. Elle réprouvait l'indulgence du monde. Elle croyait naïvement, profondément, à ce devoir de répression dont le juge de son frère, l'hypocrite Angelo, couvre ses arrêts impitoyables. Le code qu'il avait aux lèvres, elle le portait gravé dans son cœur.

Et la voici, plaidant pour la vie de Claudio, qui trouve un à un dans son âme angoissée les arguments de miséricorde. Ils jaillissent d'elle imprévus, l'étonnant et l'effrayant elle-même. C'est une illumination subite, une suite d'éclairs qui lui dévoilent les mensonges et les iniquités de ce monde. Elle monte du fond de sa cellule, degré par degré, jusqu'à découvrir la loi nouvelle qui domine l'ancienne. Un ciel plus spacieux et plus tendre s'étend maintenant sur sa tête. Elle est vraiment *inspirée* : une sagesse lui est soufflée d'en haut, du Christ mieux compris. Elle voit au delà de son intelligence ; elle sent au delà de sa sensibilité ; elle sait au delà de son expérience.

Et tout le temps c'est une femme avec une logique féminine, moins d'enchaînement que d'intuition, éloquente par sursaut, arrivant à un sarcasme suraigu comme une crise de nerfs : ' But now, proud man . . .'

Shakespeare n'a rien écrit d'aussi surprenant que cette scène.

* * *

Shakespeare a pressenti notre neurasthénie quand il a créé le duc Orsino, avec ses soudains enthousiasmes et ses non moins soudaines lassitudes. Le duc est affligé de cette mélancolie du mélomane qui est entre toutes fantasque (*fantastical*). Il n'appelle pas l'amour *amour* mais *fantaisie*. Ce grand seigneur de la Renaissance est peut-être le premier des blasés. Il ne tolère que l'exquis de l'exquis, la fleur de la fleur. Viola elle-même, son travesti ôté, pourra-t-elle le retenir longtemps sous le charme ?

*

Pour le seizième siècle, le mélancolique était vraiment l'atrabilaire. Son cas relevait du médecin ou du satirique. Shakespeare avait livré son Jacques-le-mélancolique aux sarcasmes de Rosalinde. Il était réservé à George Sand de faire de ce mélancolique un sage selon son cœur, et, ne pouvant l'épouser elle-même, de le marier à la suave Célia.

* * *

A mesure que se déroulent les dix actes des deux drames de Henri IV, Falstaff va perdant peu à peu, sinon sa verve, du moins sa fraîcheur. On le sent imperceptiblement empirer et vieillir. Sa gaîté de taverne, en répétant ses effets, devient moins irrésistible. L'odeur du mauvais lieu s'y mêle davantage. Les vices que recouvrait sa faconde se laissent de mieux en mieux voir à travers les fentes.

Inévitable fatigue du créateur ? Défaut commun à tous les chefs — d'œuvre qui ont une suite ? Peut-être. Mais alors, quelle heureuse défaillance ! Le poète n'avait-il pas à montrer d'abord comment le jeune prince Henri avait pu, par richesse de nature, préférer la taverne à la Cour, la compagnie des mauvais sujets à celle des seigneurs ? Ensuite, comment il avait su repousser du pied ses camarades de cabaret pour s'élancer à la gloire ?

Or, cet Henri étant le héros parfait, il fallait qu'on l'admirât dans tous les cas, et de se débaucher et de se convertir. Il fallait que la séduction de Falstaff fût plus apparente au début, que le mauvais relent du personnage s'exhalât davantage avec le temps, que son esprit même montrât à l'occasion la corde.

* * *

La nouvelle de Luigi da Porto sur *Roméo et Juliette* est simple, exiguë, exquise. On est inquiet d'y voir toucher, fût-ce par un Shakespeare. Et avouons qu'on avance loin dans le drame avant d'oublier cette inquiétude. La fine pelouse lisse semble d'abord être retournée à la sauvagerie. Voici les calembours et les concetti, l'euphuïsme et l'emphase ; voici des clowns et des précieux. Toute une broussaille qui irrite et rebute jusqu'au moment où l'incendie de la passion la gagne. Les pointes de Roméo, les grosses facéties des serviteurs, les pataquès de la nourrice, les ribauderies de Mercutio, autant d'obstacles sur le chemin de la flamme. Mais un instant arrêtée, celle-ci fait de l'obstacle son aliment. Elle grandit des impuretés mêmes qu'elle dévore.

* * * * * * * *

ÉMILE LEGOUIS.

A MON MEILLEUR AMI — SHAKESPEARE

Peu d'amis, peu de livres résistent à l'épreuve des jours que nous traversons. Les plus aimés trahissent, on ne les reconnaît plus. C'étaient les compagnons des heures légères. La bourrasque les emporte, plantes à fleur de sol qu'arrache un coup de vent. Il ne reste que les âmes aux profondes racines. Beaucoup, d'humble apparence, à qui l'on ne prenait point garde dans la vie ordinaire. Et un petit nombre de hauts esprits, qui s'élèvent comme des tours au milieu de la plaine et paraissent plus grands par-dessus tant de ruines. Je retrouve celui qui abrita tous les rêves de ma vie, depuis mes jours d'enfance, le vieux chêne Shakespeare. Pas une de ses branches ne s'est brisée, pas un rameau ne s'est flétri ; et la tempête qui passe aujourd'hui sur le monde fait houler puissamment cette grande lyre vivante.

Sa musique ne fait pas oublier les préoccupations du présent. Quand on prête l'oreille, on est surpris d'entendre émerger peu à peu de cette mer bruissante les voix de notre temps, des pensées qui paraissent l'expression directe de nos jugements actuels sur les événements qui nous oppriment. Sur la guerre et la paix, — sur les procédés de la politique du XVIᵉ et du XXᵉ siècles, — sur l'esprit d'ambition et de ruse des États, — sur l'exploitation des plus nobles instincts, d'héroïsme, de sacrifice, par l'intérêt caché, — sur le mélange sacrilège des passions de haine avec les paroles de l'Évangile, — sur la participation des Églises et des Dieux aux tueries des peuples, — sur les traités solennels qui ne sont que des ' chiffons de papier ', — sur le caractère des nations, des armées qui sont aux prises, — je me suis plu à réunir une série de pensées de Shakespeare qui, si elles étaient publiées sans son nom, risqueraient d'éveiller les susceptibilités de la censure de notre époque libérale, plus chatouilleuse encore que celle de la reine Élisabeth. Tant il est vrai qu'en dépit des bouleversements du monde, tout est toujours le même, et que si l'homme a trouvé de nouveaux moyens de dominer et de tuer, il n'a pas changé d'âme.

Mais le bienfait unique de la lecture de Shakespeare est qu'on y

goûte la vertu la plus rare et dont on a le plus besoin, à cette heure :
le don d'universelle sympathie, d'humanité pénétrante, qui fait qu'on
vit les âmes des autres comme son âme propre. Certes, la foi, la
grandeur, l'exaltation de la vie et de toutes ses passions, ne manquent
point, à notre époque ; et c'est ce qui la rapproche de la Renaissance
anglaise ou italienne, — bien qu'à la différence et à l'avantage de celle-ci
on ne trouve en notre temps aucune de ces personnalités sans mesure dans
le bien ou dans le mal, qui dominent la foule ; aujourd'hui, la grandeur
est diffuse pour ainsi dire, collective plus qu'individuelle ; et, dans
l'Océan humain soulevé tout d'une masse, à peine si une vague
s'élève au-dessus des autres. — Mais la principale différence n'est point
là ; elle est que ce spectacle épique manque d'un spectateur. Aucun
œil n'embrasse l'ensemble de la tempête. Pas un cœur n'épouse les
angoisses, les fureurs, les passions opposées de ces vagues qui se heurtent,
de ces barques qui se brisent, de ces naufragés sur qui le gouffre de la
mer entr'ouvert se referme. Chacun reste muré en soi et avec les siens.
C'est pourquoi l'on éprouve, à rouvrir un volume de Shakespeare, un
soulagement et une délivrance. Il semble qu'au milieu d'une nuit
lourde, dans une chambre close, le vent force la fenêtre et fasse entrer
les souffles de la terre.

* * *

La grande âme fraternelle ! Elle se charge de toutes les joies et de
toutes les douleurs de l'univers. Non seulement elle se donne avec
enivrement à la jeunesse, à l'amour, à la douceur brûlante des passions
printanières : Juliette et Miranda, Perdita, Imogène... Non seulement
elle n'est pas comme ces amis qui s'éclipsent, aux heures de la peine, pro-
fessant l'opinion du vieux seigneur Lafeu, qu' ' un chagrin excessif est
l'ennemi de ceux qui vivent '[1] ; mais elle reste fidèlement, affectueuse-
ment à leurs côtés, pour partager le poids de leurs erreurs, de leurs
misères et de leurs crimes : après avoir pleuré la mort de Desdémone,
il lui reste des larmes pour son meurtrier, plus pitoyable encore. Elle
se sent plus proche des plus misérables, et ne se refuse même point aux
plus mauvais : ils sont hommes comme nous ; ils ont des yeux comme
nous, des sens, des affections, des passions comme nous, ils saignent
comme nous, ils rient et pleurent comme nous, ils meurent comme
nous.[2] Et, dit frère Laurent, ' dans tout ce qui croît sur la terre, il
n'est rien de si vil qui ne contienne quelque chose de bon ; il n'est rien
de si bon qui, détourné de son normal usage, ne puisse devenir mauvais.'[3]

---

[1] *Tout est bien qui finit bien*, I. i.   [2] *Marchand de Venise*, III. i.
[3] *Roméo et Juliette*, II. iii.

L'intelligence et le cœur de Shakespeare s'unissent en un égal besoin pour pénétrer les âmes. Son instinct de justice se complète d'un instinct d'amour. Dans *Le Marchand de Venise*, Shylock et Antonio exposent tour à tour les raisons de la haine du Juif pour le marchand chrétien.[1] Chacun parle sincèrement, et chacun donne pourtant des raisons différentes. C'est que tous deux voient et font voir la même chose, d'un angle différent. — Ainsi procède l'esprit créateur de Shakespeare. Sans effort, il se place au cœur de chaque personnage ; il revêt sa pensée et sa forme et son petit univers ; jamais il ne le voit du dehors. Et si toutefois il verse avec prédilection le trésor de sa riche sympathie dans certains de ses héros, dans les enfants de ses rêves les plus beaux ou les plus forts, il est comme un bon père : à l'heure de l'épreuve, les moins aimés lui deviennent aussi chers. L'ambitieux Wolsey, l'hypocrite, le chat-fourré, à peine est-il disgracié, prend une grandeur antique ; il voit subitement la misère de ses désirs, et, dans les décombres de sa gloire, ' il n'a jamais été aussi heureux '[2] : ses yeux s'ouvrent, le malheur l'a ' guéri ' ; et ce dur égoïste, consolant son ami qui pleure, lui laisse pour testament de sa vie orgueilleuse la plus sainte des paroles : ' Chéris les cœurs qui te haïssent.'[2] — Le tyran Leontes, sous l'écroulement de son bonheur, que lui-même a ruiné par sa criminelle et furieuse folie, devient soudain sacré, même à Pauline qui le flagelle des plus sanglantes vérités.[3] — La mort, qui fait s'incliner devant les corps de Brutus et de Cassius, d'Antoine, de Coriolan, leurs irréconciliables ennemis, transfigure Cléopâtre à ses derniers moments, et rend même quelque noblesse au vil Edmond du *Roi Lear*. C'est merveille de voir comment, devant la misère et devant la mort, le grand cœur du poète se dépouille d'orgueil, de rancune, de passion égoïste, pour embrasser dans son immense pitié tous ceux qui souffrent — ennemis, rivaux, qu'importe ? — frères dans la douleur. Un des traits les plus touchants de cette humanité est l'acte de Roméo, qui venant pour mourir auprès de Juliette morte, et, provoqué par son rival Pâris, l'ayant tué malgré lui, le couche dans le tombeau de Juliette, à ses côtés :

Donne-moi la main, ô toi dont le nom a été écrit comme le mien sur le triste livre de l'adversité !

Et quand Hamlet torture de ses cruelles paroles sa mère criminelle, Shakespeare, incapable d'arrêter l'emportement de son héros en lui

[1] *Marchand de Venise,* I. iii ; III. i.   [2] *Henry VIII,* III. ii.
[3] *Conte d'hiver,* III. ii.

prêtant une pitié que Hamlet ne ressent point, inspire cette pitié au spectre du roi assassiné, qui vient, avec un accent d'émouvante bonté, au secours de la femme accablée :

L'accablement écrase ta mère.   Tiens-toi entre elle et son âme qui lutte !   Songe que dans les corps les plus faibles l'imagination agit le plus fortement.   Parle-lui.[1]

Cette commune pitié est telle un pont jeté sur le fossé qui sépare les individus et les classes.   Elle rapproche les mains des riches et des pauvres, des maîtres et des serviteurs.   Bien que Shakespeare se classe plutôt, en politique, parmi les aristocrates méprisants de la foule — (Nulle satire plus sanglante des révolutions populaires que la Jacquerie de Cade[2] ; et Coriolan est un prototype de l'*Uebermensch* de Nietzsche) — son cœur a pour les humbles des intuitions de tendresse délicate ; et cette délicatesse de sensibilité, il la leur prête souvent.   Parmi tant d'éloquents discours des grands personnages romains, au Capitole, qui est le seul à pleurer sur le corps de César assassiné ?   Un esclave inconnu, un serviteur d'Octave, qui vient porter un message à Antoine et qui, voyant le héros égorgé, s'arrête suffoqué au milieu de son récit : '. . . Oh ! César ! . . .' va à l'écart et sanglote.[3] — Qui ose prendre la défense de Glocester torturé par Régane et Cornouailles ?   Un serviteur de Cornouailles, qui tire l'épée contre son maître ; et d'autres serviteurs accueillent le vieillard aveugle et pansent sa face ensanglantée.[4] — Hamlet est protégé contre la haine peureuse du roi par l'amour du peuple, dont il est l'idole,[5] — ce peuple qui, plus clairvoyant que le faible Henry VI, reste fidèle au loyal duc Humphreys, même après sa disgrâce, et qui, à la nouvelle de son assassinat, se soulève, brise les portes du palais, et impose l'exil du meurtrier Suffolk.[6] — Le vieil Adam se fait le compagnon de misère de son jeune maître Orlando ; et le jeune maître, à son tour, le porte sur ses épaules, lui cherche de la nourriture, refuse de manger avant lui.[7] — Le proconsul Antoine, à la veille du combat décisif, appelle ses serviteurs et leur parle comme un frère ; il voudrait pouvoir les servir à son tour, aussi bien qu'il a été servi par eux ; et la douceur de ses paroles leur arrache des larmes.[8] — Faut-il rappeler encore Timon, ruiné, que ses amis trahissent, à l'exception de ses seuls serviteurs qui, dispersés par le sort, ' demeurent unis en Timon ' ?[9] — Mais c'est dans le *Roi Lear* que cette divine pitié a ses accents les plus profonds.   Le vieux tyran, fou d'orgueil et d'égoïsme,

---

[1] *Hamlet,* III. iv.   [2] *Henry VI,* deuxième partie, IV.   [3] *Jules César,* III. i.
[4] *Roi Lear,* III. vii.   [5] *Hamlet,* IV. iii.   [6] *Deuxième partie de Henry VI,* III. ii.
[7] *Comme il vous plaira,* II. iii, vi, vii.   [8] *Antoine et Cléopâtre,* IV. ii.
[9] *Timon d'Athènes,* IV, 2.

sous les premiers coups du malheur, commence à ressentir la souffrance des autres. Dans la tempête qui rugit sur la lande déserte, il s'apitoie sur son fou qui grelotte ; et peu à peu, il découvre l'universelle misère :

> Pauvres misérables tout nus, où que vous soyez, vous qui souffrez de l'assaut de cette impitoyable tempête, comment avec vos têtes sans abri, vos estomacs sans nourriture, vos guenilles trouées, percées à jour, pourrez-vous lutter contre un orage comme celui-ci ! . . . Je m'en suis trop peu soucié. . . . Luxe, essaie du remède ! Supporte les mêmes maux que la misère, tu apprendras ainsi à la faire profiter de ton superflu, et les cieux en seront moins injustes.[1]

Cette tendresse humaine, qui affleure comme un flot tout au long de l'œuvre de Shakespeare, est peut-être ce qui la distingue le plus des autres œuvres dramatiques de son temps. Elle est sa marque, elle lui est un besoin ; il ne peut s'en passer. Même dans les sujets qui la comportent le moins, il faut qu'il lui fasse une place. Au cœur du dur *Coriolan*, ce drame bardé de fer, qui marche dans l'orgueil et le sang, fleurit la douce Virgilie, ' le gracieux Silence '.[2] Et de Portia la stoïque, la fille de Caton, il a fait Portia humaine, faible, femme, fiévreuse, qui attend, dévorée d'angoisse, l'issue de la conspiration.[3] — Shakespeare, pas plus que Montaigne, n'est dupe du stoïcisme ; pour lui, c'est une armure qui cache le vrai cœur. Et quelle émouvante douceur, lorsque l'armure se brise et que l'amour jaillit, comme dans la fameuse scène de la réconciliation de Brutus et de Cassius, qui est le joyau de la pièce ![4] Le cœur est si gonflé de la tendresse qui l'emplit que l'on sent que les larmes sont prêtes à couler ; mais une pudeur les retient et donne à l'émotion une beauté suprême. Ce n'est que par un récit que nous voyons ce héros de l'amitié, l'énigmatique Antonio, l'homme riche, heureux aux yeux du monde, mais rongé d'une mystérieuse tristesse et qui ne semble vivre que par son amour pour son ami, livrer le secret de ce cœur aimant et souffrant, dans la scène d'adieux où, ' les yeux pleins de larmes, détournant son visage, il tend la main par derrière à Bassanio, et lui donne une étreinte silencieuse.[5] — Silence plus saisissant encore, quand c'est celui d'un enfant, comme le petit Mamillius, — petit Dombey plus tragique, — qui ne mange plus, qui ne dort plus, qui s'étiole et qui meurt, de la honte de sa mère.[6]

Même au delà des hommes, cette pitié s'étend à la nature. Le duc exilé, dans *Comme il vous plaira*, écoute la voix des arbres, lit

---

[1] *Roi Lear,* III. iv.   [2] *Coriolan,* II. i.   [3] *Jules César,* II. iv.
[4] Ibid., IV. iii.   [5] *Marchand de Venise,* II. viii.   [6] *Conte d'hiver,* II. iii ; III. ii.

le livre des ruisseaux, scrute la morale des pierres. Et Jacques-le-mélancolique pleure sur un cerf blessé qui agonise.[1]

* * *

Ainsi, le génie du poète soude les anneaux de la chaîne qui relie entre eux tous les êtres. Et rien ne vibre en un d'eux qui ne se propage à travers tous : car tout nous est commun, et c'est nous que nous retrouvons, à chaque page de cette tragi-comédie de l'univers.

Mais, tandis que nous prenons notre part de toutes joies et de toutes peines, tandis que nous aidons chaque âme à porter sa croix, elles nous aident à porter la nôtre. — 'Quand nous voyons un supérieur partager nos misères,' dit Edgar dans le *Roi Lear*, 'c'est à peine si nos misères semblent encore nos ennemies. Celui qui souffre seul souffre surtout d'esprit, en songeant au bonheur qu'il laisse derrière lui. Mais l'esprit oublie ses souffrances, quand le chagrin a des compagnons et que l'amitié le console.'[2] — Les rancunes mêmes s'effacent. Le spectacle de l'injustice n'incite pas au désir de la réparer par une injustice semblable. Et le dernier mot, le chant qui plane sur les ultimes accords de cette symphonie, est celui que l'Esprit lumineux de l'Air, qu'Ariel inspire à Prospéro :

Le pardon est au-dessus de la vengeance.[3]

ROMAIN ROLLAND.

Janvier 1916.

---

[1] *Comme il vous plaira,* II. i.   [2] *Roi Lear,* III. vi.   [3] *La Tempête,* v. i.

MONTAIGNE ET SHAKESPEARE

Au xviiième siècle Capell a signalé qu'un passage de *La Tempête* est imité de l'essai des Cannibales. Les mots de Shakespeare sont les mots mêmes de Florio, le traducteur anglais des *Essais*. Dès lors la question était posée des rapports de Montaigne et de Shakespeare.

C'était une question très délicate, comme le sont tant de problèmes d'influence. Un jour vint où la science allemande s'en mêla, et tout se simplifia. Depuis ce jour-là, qui date de moins d'un demi-siècle, jetez les yeux sur une bibliographie : vous verrez combien d'études lui ont été consacrées, articles, brochures, et jusqu'à un livre deux fois imprimé. A en parcourir les conclusions, les solutions qu'elles apportent reposent sur les méthodes les plus sûres, et jettent la plus vive lumière sur la formation intellectuelle de Shakespeare.

On s'est ingénié à établir entre les textes des deux écrivains des rapprochements qui devaient manifester avec évidence l'influence des *Essais*. On s'en est fait une sorte de sport, et quoique ce sport-là fût tout germanique, il n'a pas manqué d'avoir ses fanatiques en Angleterre et jusqu'en Amérique. Tout ce qui venait d'Allemagne était bien accueilli. Chacun tenant à honneur d'enchérir sur son devancier, vite cette chasse aux rapprochements a été merveilleusement productive. On intimidait la critique avec le nombre fantastique de textes parallèles qu'on alignait. A mesure que ce nombre grandissait, les théories qu'on bâtissait sur eux se faisaient de plus en plus hardies. Stedefeld, en 1871, nous disait déjà que, dans le personnage d'Hamlet, Shakespeare avait voulu représenter Montaigne, et que la pièce entière était une critique de son scepticisme. En 1884 Jacob Feis affirmait que Shakespeare s'était proposé de prendre parti contre la philosophie de la nature prêchée par Montaigne. Enfin, en 1897, M. Robertson est allé jusqu'à prétendre que tout ce qui fait la grandeur de Shakespeare, pensée et style, est dû à l'influence de Montaigne, et que, si à l'aurore du xviième siècle son génie dramatique a pris un si magnifique essor, c'est à la rencontre des *Essais* que nous le devons.

Je crains, hélas ! que ce magnifique édifice, construit au prix de tant de patience, ne repose sur le sable.   Une à une j'ai examiné les similitudes signalées par les auteurs que je viens de citer, et encore celles de Henry Morley, de Miss Elisabeth Robins Hooker, de Miss Grace Norton, à laquelle nous devons de si solides études sur Montaigne, de Herr Kellner.   A la fin, quand j'ai fermé la main pour saisir mon butin, elle était vide.   Dans tous ces rapprochements je ne trouve que des coïncidences de pensée, nullement des emprunts, et, sauf peut-être pour deux ou trois passages de *Hamlet* au sujet desquels on peut hésiter, pas même des réminiscences.   Leur nombre fait impression.   Craignons que cette impression ne nous égare : cent zéros additionnés ensemble ne font toujours que zéro.   La parcelle de vraisemblance que comporte chacun de ces rapprochements est si infime, qu'à les totaliser, si l'emprunt signalé par Capell n'était pas là, je n'aurais pas même de quoi affirmer que Shakespeare a lu Montaigne.

Un gros volume serait nécessaire, un volume de discussions sur des pointes d'aiguilles, pour faire la critique de chacun des textes allégués. Il suffira d'indiquer les causes d'erreur qui ont vicié toute cette enquête. J'en trouve trois principales.   Ces rapprochements portent ou sur des idées et des faits qui peuvent venir à Shakespeare d'écrivains autres que Montaigne, des anciens en particulier ;   ou bien sur des lieux communs de tous les temps ;   ou bien sur des opinions qui nous paraissent aujourd'hui singulières, mais qui alors étaient banales.   Imaginez le cas de deux écrivains contemporains qui doivent inévitablement au milieu intellectuel où ils se sont formés certaines idées communes ; supposez-les très pénétrés l'un et l'autre des écrivains et des moralistes de l'antiquité, spécialement de Plutarque qui est le maître de tout le monde au xvième siècle ;   supposez enfin que l'un et l'autre, chacun à sa manière, sont occupés presque exclusivement de ces éternels sujets que sont la misère humaine, les malheurs qui assaillent la vie; la mort, la vertu et le vice, la coutume, etc., ne serait-il pas surprenant qu'ils ne vinssent pas à se rencontrer quelquefois dans l'expression d'une même pensée ?

Des dernières pièces de Shakespeare, celles qui sont contemporaines de *La Tempête*, on a porté l'enquête dans celles qui sont antérieures à la publication de Florio.   Naturellement dans celles-là aussi on a trouvé du Montaigne.   ' Ne vous en étonnez pas,' a répliqué M. Robertson, pour qui Shakespeare, ignorant le français, a reçu de la traduction anglaise vers 1602 l'impulsion soudaine qui l'a haussé jusqu'au drame de *Hamlet* : ' Shakespeare par Ben Jonson a dû connaître Florio, il a pu lire son œuvre en manuscrit.'   Et la réplique était recevable.   Mais on est remonté alors jusqu'à des pièces plus anciennes encore, jusqu'au *Marchand de Venise*, aux *Gentilshommes de Vérone*, et à *Roméo et Juliette*. Et là encore on a trouvé du Montaigne. Force fut de supposer — hypothèse aventureuse — que Shakespeare avait connu les *Essais* dans le texte français. La méthode se retournait contre les conclusions qu'on en avait tirées, d'une révélation brusque apportée à un Shakespeare peu cultivé et d'où serait sorti son grand drame philosophique. Est-il besoin d'ajouter, d'ailleurs, que les listes de rapprochements diffèrent d'auteur à auteur, manifestant ainsi leur caractère arbitraire ?

Il eût fallu ne retenir que des passages de Montaigne qui se fussent recommandés par quelque chose de personnel, soit dans la pensée, soit dans l'expression. En présence de ce monde prodigieux d'idées que remue l'œuvre de Shakespeare, on demeure stupéfait à la pensée que des critiques prétendent assigner une source livresque déterminée à des remarques insignifiantes. Car cela implique une singulière idée de Shakespeare, et, pour la commodité de l'enquête, pour trouver dans chaque rencontre une marque d'influence, inconsciemment le plus souvent, on en vient à poser un étrange postulat : relisez ces rapprochements, on dirait que, avec les littératures grecque et latine, même les ouvrages des moralistes anciens étaient inconnus à Shakespeare ; on dirait qu'il était privé de toute culture, presque de toute idée. Il ne lui est même pas permis d'écrire, fût-ce en passant, que la force de la coutume est grande, ou que la vertu est belle, ou que la vie est pleine de misères, sans qu'un érudit coure aussitôt chercher dans les *Essais* un texte parallèle.

Cette méthode ruineuse est donc encore, sans le savoir, injurieuse à la mémoire de Shakespeare. J'avoue que les critiques qu'on adresse en ce moment à la science allemande ne vont pas quelquefois sans m'inquiéter. Quelquefois on semble faire bon marché des méthodes précises qui sont de tous les pays, et que — toute vérité est toujours bonne à dire — l'Allemagne nous a aidés à mieux pratiquer. Ce que nous répudions, c'est leur déformation. Ce n'est pas la recherche des sources, qui n'est pas moins française qu'allemande quand elle est judicieuse, et qui s'est révélée si féconde ; c'est sa parodie. Elle se caractérise par ceci qu'au travail de l'esprit de finesse elle substitue une sorte de mécanisme. Elle se met ainsi à la portée de tout le monde, et c'est ce qui rend sa contagion si redoutable. A la question : quelle est l'influence de Montaigne sur Shakespeare ? insensiblement elle a substitué cette autre question : quelles ressemblances verbales peut-on relever entre Montaigne et Shakespeare ? Et, après quarante ans d'efforts, un beau jour, on s'aperçoit qu'on a travaillé dans le vide, et qu'on n'est pas plus avancé qu'au départ.

Mon dessein n'est pas d'apporter une solution à mon tour, d'opposer hypothèse à hypothèse. J'ai voulu seulement ramener le problème à ses données. Il se pose à peu de chose près de la même manière qu'au lendemain de la découverte de Capell. Même le seul progrès obtenu consiste en ce que nous ne pouvons plus espérer que d'autres emprunts certains viendront se joindre à celui de Capell : là où des érudits si patients ont échoué il n'y a plus d'espoir de réussir.

Cette constatation préviendra le retour à des exagérations dans lesquelles on est tombé, car il y a dans l'œuvre de Shakespeare des emprunts si caractérisés à certains ouvrages, au Plutarque de North par exemple, qu'assurément l'influence de Montaigne se serait trahie à bien des signes si elle avait été aussi profonde, aussi décisive qu'on l'a dit.

En revanche, nous savons maintenant combien le public anglais a été frappé en 1603 par la publication des *Essais* dans la traduction de Florio. Nous savons qu'en 1607 — et peut-être dès 1605 — Ben Jonson, dans son *Volpone*, dénonçait les plagiats dont ils étaient l'objet, qu'autour de Shakespeare Marston et Webster en transportaient des phrases nullement déguisées sur la scène. Surtout nous voyons clairement les raisons qui ont pu recommander à Shakespeare, comme à Webster, à Marston et aux autres dramatistes du temps, la lecture des *Essais*. Montaigne était le guide le plus sûr qu'on pût avoir alors pour explorer le moi, et par le moi pour connaître l'homme ; il avait, non pas seulement vulgarisé, mais revivifié de sa baguette magique la sagesse antique avec le prodigieux trésor de réflexions morales qu'elle comporte, retrempé en pleine expérience tant d'opinions philosophiques qu'il avait ' couchées ' sur sa vie et comme ' essayées ' à l'usage des contemporains ; enfin il avait ranimé l'histoire, ressuscité les hommes du passé en projetant son âme dans la leur, et ainsi préparé la matière historique pour la scène mieux qu'aucun livre d'histoire jusqu'alors écrit en France ou en Angleterre. Le drame psychologique, le drame philosophique, le drame historique pouvaient profiter grandement de ses leçons. Voilà des faits qu'aucune hypothèse ne doit négliger.

Certes j'aimerais que la France pût revendiquer, dans la formation du génie de Shakespeare, la part du lion que lui attribue M. Robertson. Plus modeste, celle qui lui revient sans doute, et qui dépasse d'ailleurs l'influence de Montaigne, est encore glorieuse.

CAEN.   P. VILLEY.

A SHAKESPEARE

L'ORGUEIL, l'ambition, la luxure, la haine
Taciturne qui rampe et bondit tour à tour ;
Tout l'héroïsme, tout le rêve, tout l'amour ;
Ce qui pleure, s'exalte ou rit dans l'âme humaine ;

Le louche envie et qui, de la dent, mord sa chaîne,
La ruse au pas secret, la colère au poing lourd ;
Le sceptre, le poignard, la torche, le tambour,
Et la face danoise et la face africaine !

Tout cela : rois, héros, amants, les fous, les sages,
Palpite dans ton drame aux mille visages,
Chacun peint en sa vie et sa diversité.

Sur l'homme tout entier s'étend ton vaste empire,
Formidable et divin d'être la vérité,
Où tu règnes, parmi les Passions, Shakespeare !

HENRI DE RÉGNIER.

ΤΗΙ ΜΝΗΜΗΙ ΤΟΥ ΚΛΕΙΝΟΥ ΚΑΙ ΕΡΑΤΕΙΝΟΥ ΣΑΚΕΣΠΗΡΟΥ

Τοὺς Ἕλληνας ἡμᾶς μαγεύει καὶ θέλγει τοῦ θείου Σακεσπήρου ἡ μεγαλοφυΐα, τὸ ὕψος τῶν διανοημάτων, τὸ κάλλος τῆς φράσεως— ἡμᾶς, λέγω, ἰδίως τοὺς ἐπὶ τῇ ἀπαγγελίᾳ τῶν στίχων αὐτοῦ μονονοὺκ ἀκούοντας ἠχὼ πιστὴν τῆς φωνῆς τῶν μεγάλων τῆς Ἑλλάδος ποιητῶν καὶ δραματουργῶν. Αἱ τραγῳδίαι αὐτοῦ, ἀπὸ σκηνῆς διδασκόμεναι, συγκινοῦσιν ἡμᾶς οὐχὶ ἀσθενέστερον τοῦ μεγαλείου τῶν δραμάτων τοῦ Αἰσχύλου, πληροῦσαι οὕτω τὸν σκοπὸν ἀκριβῶς ἐκεῖνον ὃν ἔθετο ὁ Ἀριστοτέλης ὅρον τῆς τραγῳδίας—τὴν ''κάθαρσιν τῶν παθημάτων''. Ἐν τοῖς δράμασιν αὐτοῦ ἀναγνωρίζομεν σχεδὸν ἐπὶ λέξει τοῦ Πλουτάρχου τὰ σοφὰ διδάγματα, ἡρμηνευμένα ἐπαγωγότερον ἢ ἐν τῇ μεταφράσει τοῦ Νώρθ, ἣν βεβαίως εἶχε πρὸ ὀφθαλμῶν γράφων ὁ Ποιητής. Ἐπειδή, εἰ καὶ λέγεται μικρὰν σχὼν τῆς Λατινίδος γνῶσιν, καὶ ἥττονα τῆς Ἑλληνικῆς, ὅμως εἶχεν ἐκ φύσεως τὸ πνευματικὸν ἐκεῖνο δῶρον, τὸ καθιστῶν τὸ ὕψος τοῦ νοῦ καὶ τὴν εὐγένειαν τῆς ψυχῆς κοινὸν διανοητικὸν κλῆρον τῶν ἀείποτε καὶ ἀπανταχοῦ μεγάλων ἀνδρῶν. Ἀλλὰ καὶ τοῦ Ὁμήρου τὸ ὑπεράνθρωπον σχεδὸν μεγαλεῖον ἀναφαίνεται ἐν τοῖς στίχοις αὐτοῦ, βαπτισθέντος ἀναμφιβόλως εἰς τὰ νάματα τῆς θείας ἐποποιίας, χάρις τῇ μεταφράσει τοῦ Τσάπμαν.

Οὕτως ἐν τῷ Σακεσπήρῳ βλέπομεν μίαν ἔτι, καὶ ταύτην ἔνδοξον, ἐκδήλωσιν τῆς ταυτότητος τῶν ἰδεῶν, τῶν ψυχικῶν ῥοπῶν καὶ τῶν ἰδανικῶν τῶν δύο ἡμῶν ἐθνῶν, ἅτινα ἀπὸ πρώτης αὐτῶν ἀρχῆς ἠγωνίσθησαν ἀκαμάτως ζητοῦντα τὴν ἀρετὴν ἐν πᾶσι, διαδίδοντα τὸν πολιτισμόν, καὶ ὑπεραμυνόμενα τῆς ἐλευθερίας.

Διὸ καὶ παρὰ τὴν ἀπαράμιλλον ἡμῶν φιλολογικὴν κληρονομίαν, μεταξὺ τῶν πρώτων μετέχομεν καὶ ἡμεῖς οἱ Ἕλληνες τῆς ψυχικῆς

TO THE MEMORY OF THE RENOWNED AND GENTLE SHAKESPEARE

THE genius, the loftiness of thought, the beauty of language of the divine Shakespeare hearten and charm us Greeks—us especially who at the delivery of his verses all but listen to the echo of the very voice of the great poets and dramatists of Greece. His tragedies, when represented on the stage, move us not less powerfully than the grandeur of Aeschylian dramas, thus truly fulfilling that purpose of tragedy which Aristotle has defined to be the purgation of the emotions. In some of his dramas we recognize almost textually the wise teachings of Plutarch, interpreted in a style more alluring than North's translation, which the Poet assuredly had before him when writing. For although it is said of him that 'he had small Latin and less Greek,' yet he was endowed by nature with that spiritual gift which makes loftiness of mind and nobleness of soul the heritage of great men of all times and of all countries. Even Homer's almost superhuman grandeur reappears in his verse; for he undoubtedly was baptized in the spring waters of the divine epic, thanks to Chapman's version.

We thus see in Shakespeare one more, and that a glorious, manifestation of the identity of thought, soul tendencies, and striven-for ideals of our two nations, which, from their very beginnings, have endeavoured persistently for virtue in all things, have diffused civilization, and have struggled in defence of liberty.

It is on this account that, notwithstanding our incomparable literary heritage, we Greeks are among the foremost in participating in the

εὐφροσύνης καὶ ὠφελείας, ἣν τόσῳ πλουσίως παρέχουσι τοῖς. πεφωτισμένοις ἀνθρώποις τὰ ἔργα τοῦ γίγαντος τούτου τοῦ νεωτέρου κόσμου. Τῶν δὲ ἡμετέρων οἱ ἀγγλομαθεῖς ἔσπευσαν νὰ πλουτίσωσι τὴν καθ' ἡμᾶς γραμματολογίαν μὲ μεταφράσεις τῶν ἀριστουργημάτων αὐτοῦ.

Τούτων παραθέτω κατάλογον πλήρη, ἀρτίως οὔπω δημοσιευθέντα, αὐτὸν ὑπολαμβάνων ἄριστον φόρον τοῦ ἡμετέρου θαυμασμοῦ καὶ ἔρωτος, καθ' ἣν ὥραν ἑορτάζεται ἡ ἀπὸ τοῦ θανάτου αὐτοῦ τρίτη ἑκατονταετηρίς. Ἑορτάζεται ἐν καιροῖς χαλεποῖς, ὧν τὴν δολερὰν ἀρχὴν καὶ τὴν τραγικωτάτην ἐξέλιξιν μόνος ἐκεῖνος θὰ ἦτο ἱκανὸς ν' ἀναπαραστήσῃ πιστῶς.

Ι. Γ.

ΒΙΒΛΙΟΓΡΑΦΙΚΑΙ ΣΗΜΕΙΩΣΕΙΣ ΠΕΡΙ ΕΛΛΗΝΙΚΩΝ ΤΟΥ ΣΑΚΕΣΠΗΡΟΥ ΜΕΤΑΦΡΑΣΕΩΝ

Η ΤΡΙΚΥΜΙΑ, δρᾶμα Οὐϊλιέλμου Σαικσπήρ, μετάφρασις Ἰ. Πολυλᾶ, Κερκυραίου. Κερκύρᾳ, 1855.—8ον, σ. 94 + ε'. (ἐν λόγῳ πεζῷ, καὶ μετὰ " Μελέτης " ἐν τέλει.)

ΙΟΥΛΙΟΣ ΚΑΙΣΑΡ, τραγῳδία εἰς πέντε πράξεις τοῦ ποιητοῦ Σαικσπήρου, ἐκ τοῦ Ἀγγλικοῦ κειμένου εἰς τὴν Ἑλληνικὴν μεταγλωττισθεῖσα ὑπὸ Νικολάου Κ. Ἰωνίδου. Ἀθήνησι, 1858.—8ον, σ. 124.

ΑΜΛΕΤΟΣ, Βασιλόπαις τῆς Δανίας, τραγῳδία τοῦ Ἄγγλου Σαιξπήρου, ἐνστίχως μεταφρασθεῖσα ὑπὸ Ἰωάννου Π. Περβανόγλου. Ἐν Ἀθήναις, 1858.—8ον, σ. ε' + 255.

ΑΜΛΕΤΟΣ, Τραγῳδία . . . . . μεταφρασθεῖσα ὑπὸ Ἰ. Π. Περβανόγλου, καὶ δεύτερον ἐκδοθεῖσα ὑπὸ Ἰωάννου Δ. Μανώλη. Ἐν Κωνσταντινουπόλει, 1874.—8ον, σ. β' + 244.

Ο ΜΑΚΒΕΘ, τραγῳδία εἰς πράξεις πέντε, μεταφρασθεῖσα ὑπὸ Ν. Ι. Κ., ᾗ προσετέθη καὶ βιογραφία τοῦ ποιητοῦ. Ἐν Ἀθήναις, 1862.—8ον, σ. xvi + 88.

ΣΑΙΚΣΠΗΡΟΥ Ο ΒΑΣΙΛΕΥΣ ΛΗΡ, μελέτη Σ. Ν. Βασιλειάδη, δικηγόρου. Ἐν Ἀθήναις, 1870.—8ον, σ. 30.

ΡΩΜΑΙΟΣ ΚΑΙ ΙΟΥΛΙΑ, δρᾶμα εἰς πράξεις πέντε, ὑπὸ Σαικσπήρου, μεταφρασθὲν ὑπὸ Α. Γ. Σκαλίδου καὶ ἐκδοθὲν δαπάναις Ε. Λαμψιάδου. Ἐν Ἀθήναις, 1873.—8ον, σ. 144.

Ο ΟΘΕΛΛΟΣ (ἐν ἐπιφυλλίδι " Φιλοκάλου Σμυρναίου ", ἐν Σμύρνῃ, 1873 ?).

Ο ΚΥΜΒΕΛΙΝΟΣ, μελέτη ἐπὶ τοῦ δράματος τοῦ Σαικσπήρου, ὑπὸ Κ. Γ. Ξένου. (ἐν φυλλάδ. 9 τοῦ " Βύρωνος ", ἐν Ἀθήναις, 1874, 8ον, σ. 664–675.)

intellectual enjoyment and profit which the works of this giant of the modern world offer to all enlightened men.

It is for this reason that those of us learned in the English tongue have not been slow in enriching our modern literature with translations of his masterpieces.

Of these I append a catalogue, never before fully published, esteeming their record to be the most fitting tribute of our admiration and love, on the celebration of the tercentenary of his death.

It is celebrated in circumstances the dire beginnings and the tragic development of which he alone could have recorded adequately.

JOHN GENNADIUS.

ΤΑ ΑΠΑΝΤΑ ΤΟΥ ΣΑΚΕΣΠΗΡΟΥ μετ᾽ εἰκόνων, ὑπὸ ᾽Αλεξάνδρου Μέϋμαρ. (ἐν παραρτήματι τῆς " ᾽Εθνικῆς ᾽Επιθεωρήσεως ", Παρισίοις, 1875. ᾽Εξεδόθη οὕτω μόνον Ο ΜΑΚΒΕΘ, καὶ μέρος τοῦ ΑΜΛΕΤΟΥ.)

ΜΕΤΑΦΡΑΣΕΙΣ ΔΗΜΗΤΡΙΟΥ ΒΙΚΕΛΑ, ἐμμέτρως, καὶ μετὰ σημειώσεων. Σακεσπήρου ΡΩΜΑΙΟΣ ΚΑΙ ΙΟΥΛΙΕΤΑ, ΟΘΕΛΛΟΣ, καὶ ΒΑΣΙΛΕΥΣ ΛΗΡ, τραγῳδίαι ἐκ τοῦ ᾽Αγγλικοῦ μεταφρασθεῖσαι. ᾽Εν ᾽Αθήναις, 1876.—8ᵒⁿ, σ. ιε´ + 638.

ΜΑΚΒΕΘ. ᾽Εν ᾽Αθήναις, 1882.—8ᵒⁿ, σ. 158.

ΑΜΛΕΤΟΣ. ᾽Εν ᾽Αθήναις, 1882.—8ᵒⁿ, σ. β´ + 213.

Ο ΕΜΠΟΡΟΣ ΤΗΣ ΒΕΝΕΤΙΑΣ, Κωμῳδία. ᾽Εν ᾽Αθήναις, 1884.—8ᵒⁿ, σ. β´ + 143. (Δεύτεραι καὶ Τρίται ἐκδόσεις, 1896–97.—8ᵒⁿ μικρ.)

ΙΟΥΛΙΟΣ ΚΑΙΣΑΡ. Τραγῳδία εἰς πράξεις πέντε μεταφρασθεῖσα ἐκ τῆς ᾽Αγγλικῆς ὑπὸ Μ. Ν. Δαμιράλη. ᾽Εν ᾽Αθήναις, 1886.—8ᵒⁿ, σ. 96.

ΙΟΥΛΙΟΣ ΚΑΙΣΑΡ. Σαικεσπείρου " ᾽Ιούλιος Καῖσαρ ". Μετάφρασις ἔμμετρος ᾽Αλεξάνδρου ῾Ρ. ῾Ραγκαβῆ. ᾽Εν ᾽Αθήναις, 1886. (ἐν τομ. 12ῳ τῶν " Φιλολογικῶν ᾽Απάντων " αὐτοῦ, 8ᵒⁿ, σ. 381–539.)

ΑΜΛΕΤΟΣ. Τραγῳδία Σαικσπήρου. Ἔμμετρος μετάφρασις ᾽Ιακώβου Πολυλᾶ, μὲ προλεγόμενα καὶ κριτικὰς σημειώσεις. ᾽Εν ᾽Αθήναις, 1889.—8ᵒⁿ, σ. ν´ + 244.

ΑΜΛΕΤ. Τραγῳδία εἰς πράξεις πέντε, μεταφρασθεῖσα ἐκ τοῦ ᾽Αγγλικοῦ ὑπὸ Μιχαὴλ Ν. Δαμιράλη. ᾽Εν ᾽Αθήναις, 1890.—8ᵒⁿ, σ. ζ + 205.

ΟΠΩΣ ΑΓΑΠΑΣ. Μετάφρασις Μ. Ν. Δαμιράλη. ᾽Εν ᾽Αθήναις, 1890.—8ᵒⁿ.

Κριτικαὶ παρατηρήσεις Γεωργίου Καλοσγούρου περὶ τῆς μεταφράσεως τοῦ ᾽Αμλέτου, ᾽Ι. Πολυλᾶ. ᾽Ανατύπωσις ἐκ τοῦ ιϛ´ τόμ. τοῦ " Παρνασσοῦ ". ᾽Εν ᾽Αθήναις, 1891.—8ᵒⁿ, σ. 59.

ΣΑΙΞΠΗΡ. Μελέτημα Μιχαὴλ Ν. Δαμιράλη, ἀναγνωσθὲν ἐν τῷ Φιλολογικῷ Συλ-λόγῳ Παρνασσῷ τῇ 14 Δεκεμβρίου, 1892. Ἐν Ἀθήναις, 1893.—8ᵒⁿ, σ. 30.

Ἡ περίφημη ἱστορία τοῦ ΕΜΠΟΡΟΤ ΤΗΣ ΒΕΝΕΤΙΑΣ, μὲ τὴν ἀνήκουστη ἀσπλαχνία ποῦ τοῦ Ꞌδειξε ἀφτοῦ τοῦ Ꞌμπόρου ὁ Σαηλὸκ ὁ Ꞌοβριός, θέλοντας νὰν τοῦ κόψει μία του λίτρα κρέας . . . . γραμμένη ἀπ' τὸν Ἄγγλο ποιητὴ Γουΐλλιαμ Σεξπῆρο, καὶ μεταφρασμένη πιστὰ καὶ ῥυθμικὰ ἀπ' τὸν Ἀλεξ. Πάλλη. Ἀθῆνα, 1894.—8ᵒⁿ, σ. 120.

ΧΑΜΛΕΤ. Τραγῳδία, μεταφρασθεῖσα ἐκ τοῦ Ἀγγλικοῦ ὑπὸ Μ. Ν. Δαμιράλη. Ἐκδ. β', μετὰ μελέτης περὶ τοῦ ποιητοῦ, Ἀθήνησι, 1900.—8ᵒⁿ, σ. 258.

ΚΤΜΒΕΛΙΝΟΣ. Τραγῳδία εἰς πέντε πράξεις μεταφρασθεῖσα . . . . ὑπὸ Μιχαὴλ Ν. Δαμιράλη. Ἐν Ἀθήναις, 1903.—8ᵒⁿ, σ. 209.

ΙΟΤΛΙΟΣ ΚΑΙΣΑΡ, τραγῳδία εἰς πράξεις πέντε μεταφρασθεῖσα . . . . ὑπὸ Μιχαὴλ Ν. Δαμιράλη. Ἐν Ἀθήναις, 1905.—8ᵒⁿ, σ. 128.

ΜΕΤΑΦΡΑΣΕΙΣ ΑΓΓΕΛΟΤ ΒΛΑΧΟΤ, ἐμμέτρως, καὶ μετὰ σημειώσεων. (ἐν Βιβλιο-θήκῃ Μαρασλῆ, ἀρθ. 272–6.)

ΣΑΚΕΣΠΕΙΡΟΤ ΑΡΙΣΤΟΤΡΓΗΜΑΤΑ.

Τεῦχος α' "ΡΩΜΑΙΟΣ ΚΑΙ ΙΟΤΛΙΑ". Ἐν Ἀθήναις, 1904.—8ᵒⁿ, σ. 211.

„　β' "ΑΜΛΕΤ". Ἐν Ἀθήναις, 1904.—8ᵒⁿ, σ. 235.

„　γ' "ΟΘΕΛΛΟΣ". Ἐν Ἀθήναις, 1905.—8ᵒⁿ, σ. 214.

„　δ' "ΒΑΣΙΛΕΤΣ ΛΗΡ". Ἐν Ἀθήναις, 1905.—8ᵒⁿ, σ. 212.

„　ε' "ΜΑΚΒΕΘ". Ἐν Ἀθήναις, 1905.—8ᵒⁿ, σ. 148.

ΡΙΧΑΡΔΟΣ Ο Γ'., Τραγῳδία εἰς πράξεις 5. Μεταφρασθεῖσα ἐκ τῆς Ἀγγλικῆς ὑπὸ Μιχαὴλ Ν. Δαμιράλη. Ἀνατύπωσις ἐκ τοῦ "Μηνιαίου Παραρτήματος" τῆς ἐφημερίδος "Ἀθῆναι", τομ. β'. τεῦχος 7ᵒⁿ. Ἐν Ἀθήναις, 1909.—4ᵒⁿ, σ. 57. (ἐν λόγῳ πεζῷ, μετὰ προλόγου "ἐκ τῶν τοῦ Tawney".)

ΤΙΜΩΝ Ο ΑΘΗΝΑΙΟΣ, τραγῳδία εἰς πράξεις πέντε. Μετάφρασις Μ. Ν. Δαμιράλη. Ἐν Ἀθήναις (1909).—4ᵒⁿ, σ. 64. (ἐν λόγῳ πεζῷ, μὲ προλεγόμενα "ἐκ τῶν τοῦ G. Brandis".)

(Τὰ δύο ταῦτα φέρουσιν ἐπὶ κεφαλῆς :—"Θέτρον Ξένον Σαίξπηρ".)

ΚΟΡΙΟΛΑΝΟΣ. Τραγῳδία εἰς πράξεις 5. Μετάφρασις ἐκ τῆς Ἀγγλικῆς ὑπὸ Μιχαὴλ Ν. Δαμιράλη. Ἐν Ἀθήναις, 1911.—8ᵒⁿ, σ. 108.

ΑΝΤΩΝΙΟΣ ΚΑΙ ΚΛΕΟΠΑΤΡΑ. Τραγῳδία εἰς πράξεις 5. Μετάφρασις ἐκ τῆς Ἀγγλικῆς ὑπὸ Μ. Ν. Δαμιράλη. Ἐν Ἀθήναις, 1912.—8ᶜⁿ, σ. ζ + 104.

N.B.—Besides the above published translations, the *Winter's Tale* was represented at the Royal Theatre in Athens in 1905, according to a Greek version by H. E. Monsieur Demetrius Caclamanos, of the Greek Diplomatic Service. In the same year the *Midsummer Night's Dream* was given, on the same stage, according to a version by the poet M. George Stratigés. The former play was given fifty times, the latter no less than a hundred. Both were elaborately staged under the directions of Prince Nicolas of Greece.

DANTE E SHAKESPEARE

DELLE ragioni di somiglianza fra Dante e Shakespeare il precipuo fondamento è certamente questo : che e l'uno e l'altro nelle loro figurazioni storiche abbiano rappresentato a fondo, per entro alle sue grandezze e alle sue miserie, negli splendori e nelle ombre, quel terribile mistero che è l'anima umana. Poeti della realtà immediata, e senza nè attenuazioni nè esaltamenti ritratta.

Tali analogie fra i Due sommi si riflettono nelle vicende della loro fama ; avendo essi avuta comune la sorte di sottostare all'incuria, anzi al dispregio, dei letterati di professione in alcune epoche della letteratura, nelle quali l'artificio prevaleva sul naturale, o, che è lo stesso, la menzogna sulla verità.

Questo è il titolo massimo della loro grandezza ; questa è, sulle loro auguste fronti, l'impronta di quell'eroico pel quale il Carlyle li agguagliava o approssimava agli istitutori di religione e ai profeti. E il Tommaseo, di Dante, enumerando gli elementi e le condizioni che 'congiunti danno il poeta sommo', scriveva : 'L'uomo che più ne raccolse, e che, dopo i profeti, fu innanzi a tutti poeta, è un cittadino della repubblica di Firenze.'

ISIDORO DEL LUNGO.

FIRENZE.

PRO SHAKESPEARE !

COME ogni popolo sente l'obbligo santo di difendere il *territorio Nazionale*, così deve difendere il *territorio spirituale* dove albergano i suoi grandi poeti, artisti e pensatori.

L'Inghilterra non dovrebbe permettere le continue mutilazioni delle tragedie di Shakespeare, nè le loro riduzioni fatte per uso delle attitudini degli attori o dei gusti del pubblico.

Occorre un grande movimento d'opinione pubblica per difendere l'integrità dell' opera dei genî.

È indispensabile che da un centro idealmente luminoso come Londra si irradino in tutto il mondo dei Comitati composti di ingegni eletti, vigilanti su questo semplice programma: *L'intangibilità delle rappresentazioni tragiche di Shakespeare.*—E noi, credenti nelle mistiche corrispondenze fra il cielo e la terra, solleveremo l'*Eschilo moderno* da un affanno maggiore di quello inflittogli da coloro che gli negano la sua esistenza individuale !

LUIGI LUZZATTI.

ROMA.

SHAKESPEARE

TRECENTO anni soli dalla sua morte ?

Ma quando io penso a Guglielmo Shakespeare lo sento contemporaneo di Dio. Anch' egli ha creato l' uomo : uomini e donne con pienezza di vita, creature pervase da tutti i tumulti della passione, illuminate di tutte le luci, velate di tutte le ombre, segnate di tutte le impronte della umanità più compiuta : anime e carni vere, non come i libri disseccano ma come si muovono e sanguinano con i loro dolori e con le loro miserie nella tragedia e nella commedia, non mai bene distinte, che sono la nostra vita : giganti e pigmei, eroi e volgo, mostri e spiriti, un mondo concitato e animato con la onnipotente impassibilità di un Dio creatore.

Poi segue in me un altro pensiero : egli ha fatto assai più ; ha impresso le sue creature di tale uno stigma d' arte da renderle eterne, lucide e trasparenti, per modo che gli uomini vi riconoscessero quanto hanno in sè di divino, di bestiale, di umano, e ne avessero responso alla loro inquietudine e luce alla loro tenebra.

Poi finalmente io son tratto a considerare non senza sgomento che *arte*, per quanto questa parola sia la più alta e divina che splenda sul nostro intelletto, non abbia tale capacità da contenere quella grandezza. Egli, solo, non patisce, non concepisce l' arte come un freno, come un confine, sia pure augusto e magnifico. Si pone sopra all' arte, la signoreggia, la sforza a significare tutto ch' ei vuole, dentro e fuori da quelli che dicono i suoi domìni. I Greci le posero per suoi limiti, le diedero per suo ritmo, la Bellezza e la Sublimità. Egli le ha fatto oltrepassare queste colonne d' Ercole : le ha detto *Plus ultra!*, le ha fatto tutto toccare, tutto esplorare, tutto comprendere. Egli non soffre limitazioni. Come il cielo, come il mare, ha per unica legge la legge universa : anch' egli è una forza della Natura.

Pertanto egli è solo ed immenso, il più vasto, il più possente, incomparabilmente il più grande di tutti i poeti di ogni tempo e di ogni nazione.

ADOLFO DE BOSIS.

ROMA.

SHAKESPEARE

SHAKESPEARE, come Dante, non è il poeta di un popolo: egli è il simbolo di una nazione, ma la sua grandezza è tale, che trascende ogni limitazione di confini, per toccare quelli dell' umanità. Shakespeare, come il solo Dante, fra i poeti dell' età moderna, è il poeta di un mondo. Perciò è giusto che, a celebrare il terzo centenario della sua morte, le voci concordi di tutte le nazioni civili si uniscano in un' unica voce possente dell' umanità, intonando al morto poeta l' inno dell' apoteosi. È giusto che di lui, il quale cantò non per una nazione, ma per il mondo, gli uomini tutti, quanti sono capaci di comprendere la sua parola, dicano oggi :— Sono trecento anni che Shakespeare è morto, e da trecento anni il suo genio illumina il mondo, che stupefatto ammira, ogni giorno, lo spettacolo della sua gloria, sempre nuova come quella del sole risorgente ogni mattina a illuminare la terra. —

All' infuori e al di sopra di questa alta ragione onde tutte le nazioni civili oggi si stringono, in un ideale cerchio di ammirazione e di venerazione, intorno al nome di Guglielmo Shakespeare, l' Italia può gloriarsi di ammirarlo e venerarlo, anche perchè avvinta, da legami intimi e diretti, all' opera immortale del grande poeta. Dall' antica storia di Roma, che è storia d' Italia, dagli eroici casi e dalle tragiche vicende di Coriolano e di Cesare, che sono di nostra gente, Shakespeare trasse argomento e ispirazione ad alcune delle sue più potenti concezioni drammatiche. La più alta parola d'amore che un poeta abbia mai detta, parla di noi, parla di Giulietta e Romeo ; i quali sono italiani, non soltanto perchè il genio che li ha creati li fece nascere, amare, morire in Italia, ma perchè nacquero, amarono, morirono con cuore veramente italiano. Non l' azzurro cielo di Verona e di Mantova (che Shakespeare non vide mai, ma indovinò) fanno di Giulietta e Romeo due creature nostre, ma il sangue schiettamente italiano, che il poeta con mirabile intuito, con un senso quasi miracoloso di divinazione, trasfondeva nelle loro vene. Se Shakespeare fosse nato in Italia, o, almeno, avesse vissuto a lungo fra noi, certo, non avrebbe potuto meglio sentire, e meglio interpretare nella tragica storia dei due amanti veronesi, l'anima italiana.

Non senza una giusta ragione di orgoglio l'Italia ricorda, oggi, nel professare la sua ammirazione per Guglielmo Shakespeare, che il meraviglioso strumento onde egli seppe esprimere tutte le umane passioni, dalle più soavemente liriche alle più terribilmente tragiche, con uguale perfezione di verità e di sentimento, giungeva a lui attraverso la rinascenza degli studî umanistici italiani. A noi è titolo di orgoglio il ricordare, che il *blank verse*, il formidabile nemico dell' *heroic couplet*, deve, probabilmente, la sua prima origine ad una umile traduzione italiana, in verso sciolto, dell' *Eneide* di Virgilio. È questa la traduzione del Molza, pubblicata nel 1541, la quale suggeriva al Surrey (così, almeno, sembra molto probabile) l' idea di tradurre in inglese, in un verso analogo a quello del traduttore italiano, il poema di Virgilio. Toccava, così, al semplice e dimesso endecasillabo del Molza la gloria, non piccola, di dar vita, indirettamente (attraverso al fortunato tentativo del Surrey), al pentametro giambico inglese sciolto dalla rima, che, dopo essere divenuto il verso del *Tamburlaine the Great*, per la magica arte di Shakespeare doveva diventare il verso di *King Lear*, *Macbeth*, *Antony and Cleopatra*.

Con questo, s'intende, nulla togliamo alla originalità e alla nazionalità del poeta di Stratford : a noi è caro, oggi, ricordare tutto ciò, soltanto come espressione sincera di tutta la nostra ammirazione e venerazione pel poeta nazionale dell' Inghilterra ; della nobile nazione alleata, la cui fiorente letteratura, fin dalle sue origini, con l'opera di Goffredo Chaucer, stabiliva, fra il popolo inglese e l'italiano, quell' alleanza di simpatia spirituale e intellettuale che è durata ininterrotta fino ad oggi.

In questa nuova primavera l'umanità gronda di lacrime e di sangue per il flagello dell' immane guerra, che improvvisamente si è abbattuto su di lei : ma essa non poteva dimenticare che trecento anni or sono moriva Guglielmo Shakespeare.

— Soldati di Giorgio V, soldati che, combattendo per la comune indipendenza dei popoli, difendete la terra di Shakespeare, nel giorno solenne che, dopo tre secoli di gloria, riconduce la grande ora in cui il radiante spirito del poeta trasvolava all' immortalità, cessate, per un istante, dalla lotta generosa pel sacro e puro ideale di libertà : e, volta la fronte al sole, presentate le armi !

Poi, ognuno di voi, pieno il petto del recente augurio, torni al suo poste di eroe, per deporre le armi solo quando sia giunta l'ora di dire, con la parola del vostro Shakespeare :

' Let's all cry : " Peace, freedom, liberty ! " '

CINO CHIARINI.

FIRENZE.

'HAMLET È GIORDANO BRUNO?'

MENTRE scrivo queste righe si vengono pubblicando sul 'Giornale d'Italia' di Roma alcuni miei articoli che recano per titolo : 'Amleto è Giordano Bruno?' Il pubblico inglese leggerà tra non molto il testo di questi articoli in lingua inglese, e si convincerà—io spero, io m'auguro—che il titolo non è così esagerato come sembra.

Pensiero e vita formano una cosa sola in Giordano Bruno, e sono ambedue tragici e costituiscono insieme la più alta tragedia della libertà di coscienza dell' epoca moderna.

I documenti che ci restano della vita del filosofo novatore italiano e le notizie che abbiamo a riguardo del massimo poeta umano moderno, Guglielmo Shakespeare, ci autorizzano ad affermare che Giordano Bruno, svestito dell' abito di monaco domenicano, fu a Londra negli anni 1584–1585, al seguito dell' ambasciatore di Re Enrico III di Francia, Michel de Castelnau de Mauvissière, presso la Regina Elisabetta d'Inghilterra.   A Londra il celebre novatore italiano, nato il 1548, e quindi nella età di trentasei anni, recava con sè un patrimonio ricchissimo d'opere filosofiche e letterarie compiute, la fama di scrittore di commedie— il 'Candelajo' pubblicato il 1582 a Parigi—e più che tutto le sue personali qualità fascinose di ragionatore e di polemista.   A Londra Giordano Bruno fu ammesso alla corte di Elisabetta, poi insegnò ad Oxford ed introdusse in Inghilterra le idee Kopernicane, che sino allora v'erano ignorate.   Fu amico personale del Florio, del Sidney, di lord Buckhurst, del conte di Leicester, e di parecchi altri illustri.   Naturalmente le sue lezioni, i suoi ragionari privati e i suoi nuovi libri pubblicati in Londra, destarono molto rumore e sollevarono acerbe polemiche, tanto che il Bruno dovette abbandonare l'Inghilterra, tornare in Francia e passare quindi in Germania.   Quivi lo seguirono parecchi nobili inglesi che erano stati suoi uditori ad Oxford ed a Londra e fra essi Fynes Morison che fu poi valente prosatore e filologo, Antonio Everstild, Martin Turner.   Del Morison sono noti i *Viaggi in Germania ed in Italia*, i quali non possono non essere stati letti dallo Shakespeare.

A Londra, negli anni 1584-1585, Giordano Bruno pubblicava le opere seguenti : *Della causa, principio e uno — De l'infinito, universo e mondi — Lo spaccio de la bestia trionfante — Cabala del Cavallo Pegaseo — La Cena de le ceneri — Degli eroici furori*.— Guglielmo Shakespeare era allora appena ventenne e la tragedia *Hamlet* non fu pubblicata prima del 1603, e cioè tre anni dopo la morte gloriosa sul rogo di Giordano Bruno, e diciotto anni dopo la pubblicazione dell' ultima opera londinese di Giordano Bruno.

Ora si noti : (1) che la tragedia *Hamlet* è seminata di frasi, di espressioni, d'immagini, di pensieri che si trovano nelle su citate opere di Bruno ; (2) che il brano letto da Hamlet quando Polonius gli chiede che cosa legga è un brano de lo ' *Spaccio de la bestia trionfante* ' ; (3) che il pedante è un personaggio del ' Candelajo ' bruniano e rassomiglia a Polonius ; (4) che Hamlet manifesta la filosofia dell' essere dei libri bruniani ; (5) che egli è invaso dall' ' eroico furore ' d'un' alta impresa alla quale sacrifica ogni ideale personale inferiore e che questa impresa si compie mediante la morte di tutti i personaggi principali della tragedia ; (6) che Hamlet non è un carattere tragico, ma un tipo psichico, una natura d'eccezione che fiammeggia e si manifesta imperiosa ed assoluta quando l'occasione degna di lei si presenti ; (7) che nella tragedia si accenna spesso all'università di Wittemberg dove Giordano Bruno ha insegnato.

Si notino questi elementi, si torni con la mente a quell' anno 1600 —mese di Febbraio—nel quale, per l'occorrenza del giubileo pontificale di Clemente VIII, Roma era affollata da oltre tre milioni di persone e più che trecentomila furono le comunioni impartite in quel giorno nefasto del 17 febbraio 1600,—ed alla subitanea rinomanza dell' evento, specie a Londra dove Giordano Bruno era notissimo ; e si leggano le opere di Giordano Bruno che il mio scritto analizza.

Potrà accadere in seguito che non siano pochi coloro i quali si avvicineranno all' ipotesi che il divino Shakespeare abbia voluto consacrare nella creazione di Hamlet l'eroico furibondo della libertà di coscienza Giordano Bruno da Nola, arso vivo dalla Santa Inquisizione di Roma dopo una esistenza di lotte e di glorie a Parigi, a Londra, a Wittemberg, ad Hoelmstaedt, a Praga, e dopo nove anni di prigione e di tortura.

Allora non sarò solo a credere che il genio di Giordano Bruno abbia esercitato una meravigliosa influenza feconda su quello di Guglielmo Shakespeare, e che Guglielmo Shakespeare sia stato il primo a capire Bruno e colui che gli ha alzato il monumento più insigne.

PAOLO ORANO.

CONVERSACIÓN DE DOS ALMAS

SHAKESPEARE Y CERVANTES

— MIRA, hermano español, como en la guerra
Se olvida el hombre de la edad dorada ;
Mares de sangre inundan a la tierra —
¿Quién piensa ya en Lepanto, ni en la Armada ?
— ¡ Triste verdad ! De nuevo siente el mundo
De cruel Atila el ominoso estrago ;
Muere infeliz Cordelia, triunfa Edmundo,
Y su canto infernal entona Iago ;

En Flandes reina Calibán artero
Y a Francia heroica hiere con su azote . . .
— Pronto, hermano, caerá ; porque el acero
Ha recogido Albión de Don Quijote ;
Vive en ella su espíritu gigante,
Y vence ¡ al fin ! tu caballero andante.

JOSÉ DE ARMAS.

MADRID.

TO SHAKESPEARE, FROM A SPANIARD

SHAKESPEARE ! a wizard's name indeed, at whose sound all men unite in wonder, spell-bound by the master-touch of Nature that makes the whole world kin ! To counterfeit truth to the life, a gift divine, born of an unsurpassed balance of judgement and imagination, an inner feeling of unsurpassed intensity, a clear vision of the mutual and final bearing of men and things, events and ideas, for which experience offered but the material to be worked upon,—this was Shakespeare's supreme talent on the stage, as Cervantes' in the book, Velazquez' on canvas, and the nameless unknown Greeks' in marble. This it is which awakens in all men's hearts sympathy with Shakespeare and his work, because Truth or, as we call her in our material world, Reality, whatever her motley travesty in tongue, customs, manner, shines out through all and by all is recognized. She is the goddess at whose feet mankind stands enthralled with wistful gaze, understood of all, of all beloved because in each so deeply though so differently felt in kind and in degree. Others besides Shakespeare have reared stately domes of fancy ; lofty in conception, faultless in proportion, glittering with the jewelled mosaic of every ingenuity by man's brain devised, but because so faultlessly designed, because so laboriously polished, losing by their very perfection the natural aspect, the feature of *possibility* which Shakespeare's work ever retains without impairing the grandeur of the whole. As well compare a palace of the Renaissance with a Gothic cathedral or an enamelled snuff-box with Flamborough Head ! Nothing seems too lowly, too familiar, to be cast aside by the great artisan. All is blended as the thousand threads of a parti-coloured web or the countless hues and tints of a landscape, each in its right place and value. But above and through all the great work keeps on its course, human in itself, because the faithful presentment of man's thoughts and passions whether in comedy, drama, or tragedy ; showing up by a happy flash of detail the homely, humorous side of life in the king's mansion or uplifting to the ideal by a stroke of genius the pathos of a wood-cutter's cabin ; consistently maintaining as the Essential Truth itself unity in variety ; ennobling the vulgar for the public gaze and treating subjects of elementary greatness with elementary breadth untrammelled by the petty rules of Conventionality, but faithful ever to the fundamental laws that render Art divine. Such is Shakespeare's towering superiority ; this the key to his universal success in all time, in every land.

Few are the peoples among whose dramatists are found such similarity of conception and method as the Spanish ! Intellectual Spain, either classical or modern, lies before British scholars in general as a world unexplored. Her poetry, prose, painting, sculpture, music, her folk-lore, her dance and sports offer unsuspected fields for research, comparison, and inspiration. What has been already written of them, when worth reading, hardly goes beyond the fringe.

May the coincidence of Shakespeare's Tercentenary with that of Cervantes serve as a starting-point of greater interest in a race whose history and trend of thought was in close contact with the England of yore and has an undoubted part in the making of the intellectual England of to-day, a fact once recognized and now but half-remembered !

ALFONSO MERRY DEL VAL.

SHAKESPEARE

Ensalzar a Shakespeare sería como ponerse a alumbrar al pleno día. Ningun encomio, ni aun los que le prodigaron maestros insignes, colaborando con su nombradía universal a la copiosa literatura que durante tres centurias tuvo por asunto las obras, la persona y la vida Shakespearianas, equivale al hecho de hallar unánimes en la admiración a la diversidad de pueblos y la sucesión de generaciones ; de modo que el testimonio honroso llena los ámbitos de nuestra común civilización y, a par de ella, se difunde de día en día.

Es la suya aquella gloria que consiste, no en atribuir grado ventajoso entre iguales, sino en levantar sobre las eminencias y colocar en categoría separada y singular, al corto número de privilegiados cuyos nombres, como blasones alentadores, conmemoran la divina alcurnia del alma humana. Su corona no puede ser usurpada, ni en su familia caben bastardos.

Permanecen siempre a disposición de quien quiera los elementos primarios de la creación literaria o artística, así los que provienen de realidades naturales o sociales, como los que emanan del alma individual, pensante, imaginativa y soñadora. Al leer o contemplar las obras maestras que la Humanidad tiene acopiadas, nos asombra hallar idénticas tantas cosas como perduran en edades las más remotas, aunque intervengan diversidad de razas y civilizaciones. En el aprovechamiento de esta cantera inagotable unos autores aventajan a otros muy señaladamente ; entre magistrales magnificencias, vemos descollar cúpulas grandiosas y torres atrevidas, que merecen y consiguen admiración y aplauso, no tan solo de los contemporáneos, sino también de la posteridad. Mas Shakespeare no debe ser contado en el número de estos glorificados artífices, ni es un grado superior de admiración la nota característica de su figura.

Lo que distingue a Shakespeare, como a los pocos astros que forman su constelación, es el don rarísimo, casi sobrenatural, de sustraerse al moldeamiento espiritual que la cultura por los coetáneos

F f

poseida y atesorada impone a los hombres, aunque sean eminentes, y de remontarse hasta el manantial único y misterioso, donde las generaciones venideras, hasta la posteridad más remota, apagarán la sed de verdades y bellezas, que consume la vida del alma humana.

En cada individuo, þor muy poderoso que su espíritu sea, y por muy cultivado que esté, lo llenan casi por entero el caudal heredado de conocimientos y los tipos prestigiosos en que recibimos plasmados ya nuestros ideales, aun los que reputamos más abstractos. Si fuese posible desentrañar y aislar cada parcela de personal originalidad, nos asombraría su pequeñéz, aun en los maestros más celebrados. Shakespeare es de aquellos pocos cuyas alas potentes y aquilinas les levantan, por excepción, sobre la atmósfera espiritual donde fueron criados, y, sin advertirlo ellos mismos, les enseñorean de regiones inexploradas. Por esto resulta desmedida y espléndida su aportación individual al secular y común acervo ; por esto suelen desconocer su mérito los contemporáneos, si no es que vituperan por extravagante la novedad ; por esto se acrecienta su gloria en el curso del tiempo, renovador de los criterios y los gustos de las gentes, pero cautivo de las eternas leyes naturales que definen la belleza y la verdad.

Quienes, en son de censura, midieron a Shakespeare por el patrón de los clásicos, y motejaron su incultura, y trataron como selváticos los brotes potentes de su génio, preparaban sin saberlo el mejor testimonio de su grandeza ; testimonio confirmado con los homenajes de las nuevas generaciones, porque si la nota excepcional, que divorciaba a Shakespeare de los tipos hereditarios, no hubiese consistido en una ascensión súbita y portentosa hacia los tipos ideales, arcanos e imperecederos, su originalidad no habría podido granjearle sino el olvido.

Con lucidez insuperable, que tan solo se alcanza desde alturas dominantes, definió su propio ministerio, en las conocidas frases del Hámlet : '. . . reflejar la naturaleza, mostrar a la virtud su verdadera faz, al vicio su imágen propia, y a los siglos y cuerpos del tiempo su forma y su presión.' Este programa, trazado para obras teatrales, las más ceñidas en tiempo, las angustiadas con mayores cortapisas y exigencias, tan solo se pudo redimir de la nota de ambicioso, siendo Shakespeare quien emprendiera su cumplimiento.

A. MAURA.

MADRID.

EL CIELO DE SHAKSPEARE

ALGUIEN ha dicho : ' La obra de Shakspeare es un hermoso paisaje sin cielo.' El autor de esta frase brillante pudiera decir como San Pedro : ' El Señor estaba aquí y yo no lo sabía.'

Un poeta sin cielo es incomprensible. El poeta es un diós y los dioses hablan desde el cielo. Si Shakspeare se guarda de nombrar á la Divinidad, la Divinidad se halla presente hasta en los más oscuros rincones de sus dramas.

Y despues de todo ¿ porqué hemos de nombrar tantas veces á Diós ? ¿ No es una irreverencia ? Newton se llevaba la mano al sombrero cada vez que se pronunciaba el nombre de Diós. Nosotros lo vimos sin emoción como el apellido del vecino.

La fecha en que me he asomado por vez primera al mundo shakspiriano quedará por siempre grabada en mi memoria.

¿ Qué encanto tendría para mí este mundo si sobre él no desplegase el cielo sus magnificencias inefables ? Porque he hallado en él descrita, como nadie lo ha hecho jamás, esa lucha profunda, desesperada, trágica y cómica á la vez entre los ciegos apetitos de nuestra naturaleza animal y las aspiraciones elevadas de nuestro ser espiritual, es por lo que me produjo el mayor goce estético que he disfrutado en mi vida.

Si de la obra de Shakspeare quedasen excluidos los llamados ' valores superiores ', el Ser infinito y eterno, el bien y la verdad ; si de las escenas de sus dramas no pudiera sacarse otro jugo que el de unas peripecías de orden material engendradas por la diferencia de fuerza, entonces sus creaciones ofrecerían el aspecto siniestro y monótono de una clínica. Si allí no hubiese cielo, si el amor, la compasión, el valor, la dignidad, el sacrificio que con tal vigor describe no hallasen eco en un mundo trascendente, entonces todas estas cosas no serían más que síntomas de una vida declinante, enfermedades cerebrales que aparecen cuando los instintos sanos se debilitan.

¿ Qué valor tendrían las almas de su Warwick, de su Timon, de su Coriolano ? ¿ Quién comprendería á Goneril si no hubiese cielo ? El rey

Lear sería un loco más ó menos divertido y su adorable hija una idiota si sus nobles imágenes no se reflejasen allá á lo lejos en los irisados confines de un mundo superior.

Figurémonos á Shakspeare contemplando impasible de que modo Regania y Cornuailles arrancan los ojos al anciano Gloucester. ¿ El poeta no verá en esta acción infame más que un juego de la naturaleza, algo curioso digno de ser pintado ? Imaginemos que se encuentra detrás del carcelero Huberto cuando éste va á quemar con un hierro candente los ojos del principe Arturo. ¿ Habría puesto en los labios de este inocente niño tan conmovedoras súplicas sin pensar que hay ángeles que las escuchan ?

Horrible es pensarlo. No ; por encima de la obra de Shakspeare se extiende un cielo y este cielo es grande y esplendoroso porque es proporcionado al paisaje.

ARMANDO PALACIO VALDÉS

MADRID.

SHAKESPEARE Y LAS LITERATURAS HISPANO-AMERICANAS

En el mismo año pasaron de esta vida mortal William Shakespeare y Miguel de Cervantes. Las razas inglesa y española llegaban en la segunda mitad del siglo XVI a un prodigioso florecimiento de cultura, a un esplendor material e intelectual que asombra y anonada. Era el momento en que debían producir la flor suprema de su genio. Ambas hallaron en Shakespeare y en Cervantes los hombres que debían fijar para siempre su lengua como instrumento del arte literario, los que debían crearles una literatura como producto de su historia, encarnación de su carácter nacional y guía eterno de su inspiración.

Profundamente diversos en sus concepciones, como es diversa el alma inglesa de la española, los dos genios se asemejan en que ambos no solo representan a sus razas respectivas en sus obras, sino aun en su carácter individual y en sus vidas.

Shakespeare es una combinación equilibrada de idealista y de hombre práctico, de poeta soñador y de negociante afortunado. Mientras escribe aquellas obras en que todos los más altos y nobles ideales humanos hallan una expresión y en que la fantasía juega con los reflejos del sol y los rayos de la luna, no olvida sus intereses materiales y guarda previsoramente una fortuna que le permitirá retirarse del teatro y vivir holgadamente.

El autor del *Quijote* es un soldado aventurero, caballeresco e intrépido, que combate en Lepanto, que sufre una cautividad en África, que aspira en sus horas de tristeza a emigrar a América, 'refugio de los desesperados de España', que escribe en una prisión gran parte de su obra inmortal, que rie en medio de la melancolía de su estrecha vida, que se cubre de gloria literaria y de popularidad, pero que, imprevisor y descuidado, vive y muere mezquinamente.

Ambos fueron reconocidos por su siglo y celebrados como los más grandes genios literarios que habían producido aquellas naciones. Los poderosos los agasajaron y se honraron con su amistad. En la vida de Shakespeare pasa Lord Southampton y en la de Cervantes el Conde de Lemos. Sus obras fueron comprendidas de los refinados, de los eruditos, de los ignorantes, del vulgo. Muchedumbres acudían al teatro de Shakespeare y el *Quijote* alcanzaba en vida de su autor un éxito que jamás obra alguna había tenido en España.

Y ni Shakespeare ni Cervantes tienen en sus patrias monumentos dignos de su gloria. La modesta estatua de Leicester Square es digna hermana de la triste figura de la Plaza de las Cortes de Madrid.

Las razas inglesa y española crearon el indestructible monumento a la gloria de Shakespeare y de Cervantes cuando en una carrera audaz por los mares y las tierras desconocidas descubrieron mundos, ensancharon sus dominios, difundieron su lengua, dieron a la humanidad un campo futuro de riqueza.

Más de veinte naciones hablan hoy la lengua de Shakespeare o la de Cervantes en América, Asia, África y Oceania, fuera de un número incontable de islas sembradas en todos los mares y que son centros de cultura británica o española.

Todos esos pueblos, algunos de los cuales alcanzan ya su pleno desarrollo, tienen a los dos genios como representativos de sus razas, como guías de su pensamiento, señores de sus ideales, maestros de su naciente actividad intelectual.

Si se imagina que un cataclismo destruye la Europa, que una convulsión pavorosa hace desaparecer estas nacionalidades que por tanto tiempo han guiado el progreso humano, todas las lenguas que en ellas se hablan serían en breve lenguas muertas como el griego y el latín, y sus literaturas se convertirían en objetos de pacientes investigaciones para los eruditos.

No así las lenguas inglesa y española que son las de tantas nuevas nacionalidades en cuyo seno está elaborandose como en una caldera la humanidad futura. Shakespeare y Cervantes seguirían siendo los verdaderos poetas épicos de esos pueblos que entenderían su lengua y sentirían toda la belleza de sus obras.

¿Qué monumento puede asegurar una inmortalidad mayor que la de Homero y de Virjilio, de Esquilo y de Plauto, sino esta certidumbre de que los dos genios ingles y español tendrán siempre un contacto directo e íntimo con masas humanas que los comprenderán, que hablarán su lengua, que recojerán sus lecciones, que les levantarán en su propia cultura un templo en que serán perpetuamente venerados?

La América que habla español necesita tanto como la inglesa estudiar a Shakespeare, no para imitar lo inimitable, no para copiar lo que toda copia desfigura, sino para fundar sus nuevas formas literarias sobre lo que en la obra del grande hijo de Stratford hay de eterno y de eternamente aprovechable.

Shakespeare enseña a las jóvenes literaturas americanas, que hoy se esfuerzan por darse un carácter propio, la gran lección del patriotismo y del espíritu nacional. El ha creado y fijado para siempre el drama que evoca el pasado de un pueblo para estimularlo a construir un porvenir glorioso.

La estupenda serie, que va desde el reinado de Ricardo II hasta el de Enrique VIII, es como un inmenso fresco animado, viviente, que contiene los más grandes elementos que el teatro puede hallar en la historia.

El pueblo inglés amaba, sin duda, la historia de su país y quería verla reproducida en el teatro. El pueblo imponía al poeta ese rumbo, pero el poeta le devolvía su inspiración purificada y ennoblecida.

Shakespeare se ciñe a la verdad histórica tal como en su tiempo se la conocía. Sus héroes son históricos y son seres humanos completos, no simples figuras decorativas, y se mueven en el vasto campo de esos dramas enormes con sus pasiones propias, individuales, que ayudan a entender los sucesos en que han tomado parte. Sus carácteres son hondos y definidos. Sus acciones varias y complejas. A veces se destacan en un escenario que dominan, y otras se funden en la colectividad del pueblo, que es, en suma, el héroe supremo de la obra histórica de Shakespeare.

Nada comparable nos ofrece nuestra rica literatura dramática española. Calderón y Lope de Vega, Tirso y Ruiz de Alarcón, han pasado indiferentes junto a la portentosa leyenda de gloria que habían vivido sus padres y que sus contemporáneos continuan realizando.

La obra de Shakespeare despide en su conjunto y en cada uno de sus detalles como un perfume de belleza moral incomparable. Cualesquiera que sean las acciones buenas o malas de sus personajes, y muchas de ellas son contrarias a la moral y aun monstruosas, el espectador o lector de Shakespeare recibe de sus dramas y comedias una impresión que lo eleva, que lo dignifica, que lo hace mejor. Ni una sola vez, en todo el vasto ciclo de su teatro, cayó su limpio espíritu en una debilidad. El bién, la justicia, la verdad resplandecen siempre. Una idealidad infinitamente pura persiste dentro de la naturaleza real que sin cesar reproduce.

En vez de caer en las imitaciones de literatura decadentes y mal-sanas, los escritores que en la América española están luchando para formar a sus patrias un teatro propio deberían buscar en Shakespeare la manera de interesar profundamente, de ser natural y humano, sin despreciar la moral.

En los dramas y comedias del bardo inglés un sagrado respeto a la familia inspira aun a aquellas obras en que las acciones representadas son más contrarias a la santidad del hogar. Su genio no necesitaba el medio de su absoluta expresión y de fondo recurrir constantemente, como en nuestras agotadas literaturas, al marido burlado, al amante y a la mujer que se desespera bajo el vinculo conyugal.

Acaso no era su época más moral que la nuestra, sino todo lo contrario, y seguramente ningún autor moderno sería capaz de crear situaciones tan atrevidas y tan terriblemente humanas como alguna de sus comedias; pero él era un genio potente, variado, siempre renovado, y no habría podido resignarse a la mísera impotencia del teatro de nuestros días que se da vueltas dentro de una misma situación con tres personajes que jamás cambian.

El teatro ha llegado a ser en este siglo xx algo así como la vieja comedia italiana, un drama de Polichinela, Colombina y Arlequín, con un variable enredo siempre igual y los mismos golpes para regocijo de la multitud.

Nuestras literaturas han empobrecido miserablemente la representación del amor, la más grande y bella de las pasiones, la única que tiene autoridad suprema en todos los movimientos de la humanidad. Huyan los jóvenes escritores de América, que deben mostrarse fuertes y sanos, de imitar lo que es signo de vejez, de decadencia, de ingenio resfriado y perezoso. Aprendan en Portia y Bassanio, en Viola y Orsino, en Elena y el Conde de Rousillon de *All's well that ends well*, de Julia de *Two Gentlemen of Verona*, en esos tipos incorporados a la historia humana, Julieta, Ofelia, Desdémona, el secreto de la infinita y encantadora variedad del amor, distinto en cada ser, noble y abnegado aquí, celoso y violento allá, puro y desinteresado en estos, sensual y voluptuoso en aquellos.

Por último, la gran lección moral que Shakespeare ofrece a las literaturas de todas las razas es que el arte moderno, y en particular el teatro, debe reconocer y proclamar la ley de las responsabilidades humanas. Si en algo es el teatro de Shakespeare una revolución contra el clasicismo, es en que griegos y romanos ponían la fatalidad como una ley de la vida individual y de la historia, mientras que el poeta inglés ha restablecido los fueros del albedrío, creado seres humanos con voluntad libre, sobre los cuales ningún destino ciego tiene poder, que poseen una personalidad propia y toman las responsabilidades de sus actos.

Cuando se admira en el desarrollo y progreso de la raza británica la obra de las individualidades poderosas, no siempre se piensa en que la suprema manifestación de su arte literario es toda entera un himno a la libertad humana, una negación de la fatalidad, una afirmación de los privilegios de la voluntad. En toda la obra de Shakespeare no hay más que una fuerza que mueve a los personajes, sean trájicos o cómicos, históricos o fantásticos, una fuerza que varia según los carácteres, el temperamento, la raza, las pasiones individuales, y es la voluntad.

Shakespeare ha hecho en su obra la epopeya de la vida moderna. La existencia que él describe a lo largo de su creación vastísima y multiforme es la de nuestro tiempo, tal como nosotros la concebimos, compleja, activa, ajitada, sin límites en la ambición, con horizontes tan grandes que parecen hundirse en las regiones que los sentidos no alcanzan. Todo lo que hay en los cielos y en la tierra cabe en la obra de Shakespeare, como todo cabe en la actividad material e intelectual de la edad en que vivimos.

El bardo inglés apareció sobre la tierra cuando ya descubierta la América y difundida la imprenta el espíritu humano tomaba un vuelo gigantesco que aun no ha cesado. Shakespeare abre y resume la edad moderna. Para la inspiración del arte literario de las jóvenes democracias de América él ofrece la única fuente que será siempre clásica, en el sentido de perfecta en el fondo y la forma, y perpetuamente nueva. ¿ Acaso pueden envejecer el mar, los efectos de la luz en los cielos o los acentos con que el amor exhala de una generación a otra sus ansias y sus quejas ?

Cervantes al terminar el *Quijote* sintió, junto con la melancolía inefable de su alma enamorada de los seres que había creado y de quienes le era forzoso separarse, la potencia de su genio, y en una página de una orgullosa elocuencia dijo que dejaba colgada su pluma donde debería quedar ' por luengos siglos ', sin que nadie fuera osado a descolgarla para profanarla.

Hacia el final de *The Tempest* dijérase que Shakespeare ha tenido también la conciencia de su poder creador con la tristeza de la obra bella terminada y entregada a los siglos. Próspero, en quien no es difícil ver al mago de Stratford, se despide de los espíritus del aire, de la tierra y de las aguas que le han obedecido y obrado bajo su conjuro las más estupendas maravillas, recuerda como ha dominado a los vivos y los muertos, mandado a los vientos y al rayo, servídose de las selvas y los mares para sus prodigios ; y luego, renunciando a sus artes májicas, dice :—

> I'll break my staff,
> Bury it certain fathoms in the earth.
> And deeper than did ever plummet sound
> I'll drown my book.

Los pueblos que las razas española y británica han sembrado en el mundo no tendremos la osadía de descolgar y profanar la pluma de Cervantes, ni hemos de escarbar en vano la tierra y sondar los mares infinitos en busca de la vara májica y del misterioso libro de Shakespeare. Pero seguiremos oyendo la música divina de su lengua y el ritmo interno de su inspiración que nos da un noble y humano concepto de la vida, de los hombres, de las energías de la voluntad, de la historia y de la naturaleza.

Estas creaciones serán el vinculo siempre vivo con nuestro pasado en que toda el alma de los que nos enjendraron habrá quedado en manifestaciones activas. Ellas se nos aparecerán como sombras bienhechoras y nos servirán de guías cuando nuestras nacionalidades atraviesen esas selvas oscuras que hay en el camino de todos los pueblos, períodos de duda, en que la raza pierde la seguridad en sí misma, se desconoce, vacila y no sabe cual es el sendero áspero o fácil que ha de llevarla al cumplimiento de sus destinos.

Y si un día, en el rodar de la historia, la Europa a que debemos nuestra existencia, nuestra cultura, lo que somos y hemos sido, sufre y enloquece de dolor en el tormento de alguna de sus grandes crisis, el vínculo creado por Shakespeare y Cervantes hará que este nuevo Rey Lear vea surjir del otro lado de los mares las Cordelias británicas y españolas fieles a las razas que les dieron el ser.

C. SILVA VILDÓSOLA.

... Veriamos então o milagre de uma intellegencia a que o sobrenatural sempre repugnou—as apparições dos seus dramas são meras hallucinações de remorso ou visões hystericas—uma intelligencia exclusivamente interessada nos soffrimentos da humanidade e nos seus prazeres, provocar atravez dos seculos o riso e as lagrimas com a mesma intensidade e a mesma pena com que se ria e chorava no seu tempo. Veriamos então o milagre de uma intelligencia puramente intuitiva a engendrar uma creação nova e completa que symbolisasse em figuras immortaes a humanidade inteira, com o seu formidavel cortejo de paixões, de virtudes, de crimes. Comprehenderiamos então como é possivel que ainda hoje nós encontremos em Shakespeare a explicação das nossas desordenadas ambições, dos nossos pensamentos, do nosso insaciavel desejo do que é novo, da nossa obstinada resistencia á minima abdicação do orgulho individualista, e tudo isso a despeito das condições e exigencias de uma tão differente organisação social. Ah ! como é bella a lição que nos proporcionam genios de tal grandeza. A admiração que elles inspiram une n'um mesmo sentimento as raças mais antagonicas. Se os nomes de Dante, Shakespeare, Goethe, Corneille, Cervantes, Camões lembram povos diversos, a sua fama ultrapassa as estreitas barreiras das nações e a sua obra alimenta o espirito da humanidade inteira, de que elles são o justo orgulho e a mais pura gloria.

Seria inutil e até ridiculo que eu tentasse emittir juizos e conceitos novos acerca da obra de Shakespeare. Houve já algum escriptor que provocasse tanta controversia, tanto commentario, tanto estudo, tanta dissertação como este ? Seria extremamente difficil a qualquer estrangeiro ajuntar novidade aos trabalhos conhecidos e ainda mais difficil talvez fazel-o em linguagem que não fosse a propria sua. É este um ponto para o qual chamo a vossa attenção pedindo ao mesmo tempo que me escutem com indulgencia. O panegyrico de Shakespeare exigeria um poder de expressão e um recamo de imagens tão delicado, que seria difficilimo de realizar mesmo na propria lingua em que o nosso pensamento se alimentou e desenvolveu, porque as imagens correspondem na linguagem ao que são nas plantas as flores e as fructas. Disloquem-se essas plantas do sole e do clima que lhes convem : os seus fructos tornar-se-hão insipidos e as suas flores perderão o perfume. Procurem-se imagens n'uma lingua estranha e o resultado não será mais de que uma serie de desemxabidas comparações. Quem ousaria emprehender semelhante tarefa para louvar o mais encantador, rico e brilhante creador de imagens ? Essa tarefa só pode ser commettida á actividade espiritual dos artistas ingleses, cujo trabalho lhes dará sempre completa satisfação e recompensa. Vide como recentemente um dos vossos mais habeis e ingenhosos escriptores, Frank Harris, architectou uma novella preciosa com o estudo do amor tal como Shakespeare o pintou. E com que irrefragavel verdade o fez ! Outros artistas lhe seguirão a pista no inexaurivel filão que elle descobriu. Não quero cançar-vos com um extenso discurso que sempre vos seria de pouco ou nenhum interesse, mas antes de terminar desejo contar-vos como foi que, na minha já remota mocidade, lá nos confins da Europa, n'uma obscura aldeia do cabo de S. Vicente, eu comecei a sentir a influencia d'este grande poeta—aquelle que mais fundamente me penetrou a alma. Acudiram-me primeiro os doces nomes das amantes puras e divinas: Ophelia, Imogenia, Virgilia, Cordelia—o anjo da bondade e de modestia. Depois as desgraçadas que soffreram na carne dolorida : Julieta, Desdemona ; e logo as mulheres diabolicas e terriveis como Cleopatra e Lady Macbeth ; e as espirituosas e risonhas : Beatriz, Rosalinda . . . Depois a infinita galeria de heroes, d'ambiciosos, de guerreiros, de traidores, de bardos, de assassinos, tão variada e tão viva, na qual sobresaem as duas grandes figuras de Falstaff e Hamlet—o colossal Falstaff, conjunto de todos os vicios, lidimo symbolo da vida animal ; e o melancolico Hamlet cuja alma oprimida e espirito fallaz ainda hoje me perturbam intensamente. Esses nomes acercaram-se de mim pouco a pouco pelos bons e maus caminhos que a mocidade trilha, nas conversações familiares, nos folhetins dos jornaes baratos, nas novellas de autores mediocres. Que immensa curiosidade elles despertarem no meu coração de creança, que desejo, que sede de amor e de aventuras ! E que surpresa, mais tarde, quando os encontrei na obra do poeta, semilhantes aos esboços da minha mocidade ; e no amadurecer da intellegencia, sendo-me dado penetrar nas mais reconditas clareiras d'essa maravilhosa floresta, nada se poderá comparar nunca ao prazer, á plenitude de sensações, á alegria artistica que alí experimentei. Mas maior ainda do que a minha admiração e o sentimento de profunda gratidão que conservo pelo poeta, como ao maior dos meus mestres espirituaes e a quem eu devo talvez os melhores momentos da minha vida.

Excerpto de um discurso pronunciado em francez no Palacio Municipal de Stratford-on-Avon.

M. TEIXEIRA-GOMES.

PORTUGAL AND THE SHAKESPEARE TERCENTENARY

IT is over five hundred years since the age-long association between England and Portugal was first consecrated by a formal alliance. For two centuries the Portuguese and the English pursued the same national and imperial career—Portugal being ever in the lead whether in African crusade, American conquest, or European culture.

Thus Portugal had had a Shakespeare in the Manoeline Court playwright, Gil Vicente, a century before our corresponding Elizabethan age produced an equally inexplicable marvel. As little is known of their Gil as of our Will, and the precedent (extended even to the existence of a Bacon in the jurist and classicist, Sa de Miranda) may be of interest to good Shakespearians.

The age of Shakespeare found Portuguese nationality, and therewith the British alliance, in temporary eclipse. But this tercentenary has coincided with a courageous reassertion of the alliance consequent on a renascence of Portugal in the Republic. Those who cannot understand how it comes that this proud little nation has taken its stand at our side may find inspiration in the following lines from the Lusiads of Camoens :—

CANTO VII

III

You Portuguese are few, but fortified
through ne'er your weakness with your will contrasting.
You, who at cost of death on every side,
still spread the Gospel of life everlasting.
You, that for Holy Christendom abide,
On you, before all, Heaven the lot is casting
to do great deeds, though you be few and weak,
for thus doth Heaven exalt the poor and meek.

IV

See now the Germans,—stiff-necked steers are they,
ranging at pasture over fertile meads.
From Peter's place-holders they broke away
to seek new pastors, and new-fangled creeds.
See them in foulest warfare pass their day,—
(blind errors not sufficing for their needs !)
not fighting against the mighty Moslem folk,
but shaking off the sovereign moral yoke.

.   .   .   .

XII

All newest and most formidable inventions
in deadly weapons of artillery
should have been proved by now in stern contentions
against the bulwarks of Byzance and Turkey :
Dispersing to their wild and wooded mansions,
in Caspian hills and snows of Tartary,
that Turkish brood which mounts and multiplies
on wealthy Europe's foreign policies.

XIII

Armenian and Georgian, Greek and Thracian,
each cries for help,—in that the brute Soldan
takes his dear sons in terrible taxation
as is approved by the profane Koran.
The punishment of this inhuman nation
should be the glory of a brave statesman—
not the pursuit of arrogant applause
by bullying others of the Christian cause.

XIV

But while these races, blood-thirsty and blind,
wade deep in gore, a mob maniacal,
there wants not warriors of Christian mind
in this so humble house of Portugal.
On Afric's shores the Portuguese you find:
in Asia, Portugal was first of all:
in the New World none broke new ground before them,
and were there more new worlds, they would explore them.

GEORGE YOUNG.

ROUMANIA'S HOMAGE

PE acest spaţiu urma să figureze omagiul ce pana autorizată a Meiestăţii Sale Regina Elisabeta a României, poeta încoronată cunoscută sub numele de Carmen Sylva, era să prezinte naţiunei Britanice în memoria nemuritorului Shakespeare în numele naţiunei Române şi al Său propriu. Cruda soartă a răpit poporului Român această mare figură, această mumă a ţărei noastre, şi a împiedecat ca ilustrul Ei nume să fie pus pe această pagină. Carmen Sylva, promotoarea şi protectoarea literilor şi artei în România, mi-a exprimat adesea admiraţiunea Ei profundă pentru marele poet Britanic, acest neasemănat educator al Omenirei, şi de necesitatea de a propaga studiul şi cunoştinţa lui în ţară. Stimulul pornit de sus şi zelul literaţilor noştri a contribuit mult la lăţirea din ce în ce mai mare a studiului lui Shakespeare în România, la care, ca la o fântână nesecată, se adapă tinerele generaţii române.

In Aprilie 1914, cu ocaziunea festivităţilor anuale la Stratford-on-Avon, Carmen Sylva m'a însărcinat a remite Societăţei Shakespeariene din zisa localitate următorul omagiu-salut scris cu mâna poetei: 'O! Fericită Anglie, care ai dat naştere celui mai mare poet al lumei.'

Timpul, distanţa, epoca anormală în care viaţa noastră se scurge astăzi, nu au permis ca un poet, un literat român să ia locul cuvenit în această publicaţie şi astfel sunt dator eu, în numele ţărei mele, să aduc aci omagiul plin de respect şi recunoştinţă pentru marele Shakespeare şi să exprim partea vie ce din toată anima poporul Român ia la tricentenarul morţei nemuritorului fiu al Marei Britanii.

N. MIŞU

(Trimis Estraordinar şi Ministru Plenipotenţiar
al Romaniei la Londra).

THIS space should have been filled by the homage which the competent pen of Her Majesty Queen Elizabeth of Roumania, the crowned poetess known under the name of Carmen Sylva, intended to present to the British nation in memory of the immortal Shakespeare in the name of the Roumanian nation and her own. Cruel fate has taken away from the Roumanian people this great figure, this mother of the country, thus preventing her illustrious name figuring on this page. Carmen Sylva, the promoter and protectress of literature and art in Roumania, has often expressed to me her profound admiration for the great British poet, that inimitable educator of mankind, and impressed the necessity of the propagation of the study and knowledge of the poet in Roumania. The stimulus coming from the throne and the zeal of our literary men have highly contributed to the expansion of the study of Shakespeare's works in Roumania, from which the young generations draw higher ideals as from an inexhaustible fountain.

In April, 1914, on the occasion of the annual festivities at Stratford-on-Avon, I was desired by Carmen Sylva to present to the Shakespearian Society of that place the following simple homage, in the handwriting of the poetess : ' Oh ! happy England, that gave birth to the world's greatest poet.'

Time, distance, abnormal circumstances through which our life passes to-day, did not allow that a poet, a Roumanian literary man, should partake of the honour of representing the nation in this publication, and so it is my duty, in the name of my country, to offer here my homage full of respect and gratitude for the great Shakespeare and to express the vivid part the Roumanian nation takes whole-heartedly in the Tercentenary Observance in veneration of Great Britain's immortal son.

N. MIȘU

ROUMANIAN LEGATION.   Envoy Extraordinary, and Plenipotentiary
                                      Minister of Roumania in London.

G g

L'IMPERSONNALITÉ DE SHAKESPEARE

Peu d'écrivains jouissent d'une popularité semblable à celle de Shakespeare. Le poète anglais est aimé dans tous les pays du monde cultivé. L'étendue et la profondeur de son génie peuvent se mesurer à l'enthousiasme que ses œuvres suscitent partout. Il serait intéressant de passer en revue la diversité des appréciations émises à son sujet. Chacun, en effet, l'envisage à travers son tempérament propre, cherchant en lui les qualités qu'il préfère. Autant de critiques, autant d'opinions différentes. On l'a admiré pour toute espèce de raisons ; on a pu écrire un ouvrage entier sur l'histoire de ses œuvres en France. Voltaire lui a emprunté plus d'un trait, vantant (non sans quelques réserves) sa force et sa fécondité ; les romantiques français goûtent la violence de ses contrastes ; les naturalistes, par contre, voient en lui un observateur de premier ordre. Malgré les divergences de goût fondamentales entre l'esprit anglo-saxon et l'esprit latin, de purs Français tels que Victor Hugo ou Gustave Flaubert entretinrent pour Shakespeare un culte fervent.

L'auteur de *Madame Bovary*, en parlant de lui, recourt aux épithètes les plus enthousiastes. Toutefois l'esprit de parti altère l'exactitude de son jugement. Les romantiques s'étaient réclamés de lui ; Flaubert, romantique renégat, s'efforça de l'enrôler dans les rangs du naturalisme. ' Est-ce qu'on sait seulement, écrit-il dans sa correspondance, s'il était triste ou gai ? L'artiste doit s'arranger de façon à faire croire à la postérité qu'il n'a pas vécu. Moins je m'en fais une idée et plus il me semble grand.'

Ces lignes trahissent le dogmatisme militant d'un théoricien. Nous ne pensons pas qu'un écrivain grandisse en se faisant inabordable. Flaubert se trompe quand il nous montre en Shakespeare un être supérieur et lointain, un homme isolé de nous par la puissance de son genre. L'abondance de sentiments et de pensées chez Shakespeare ne provient pas d'une observation indifférente, mais, bien au contraire, est la marque d'un esprit foncièrement humain. En vrai poète, il a connu nos inquiétudes secrètes, nos espérances ardentes et nos désappointements les plus amers. Son impersonnalité n'est qu'apparente. L'intensité et la merveilleuse richesse de sa sensibilité donnent l'illusion de l'impersonnalité. A force de vibrer à toutes les impressions, à force de ressentir les innombrables passions de l'individu, il a été rendu capable de peindre les hommes les plus divers en un vaste tableau.

Shakespeare n'est pas impersonnel, il est complexe. Ses drames renferment beaucoup de passages accusant un lyrisme évident. Quand on connaît les principales étapes de son évolution intérieure, on retrouve dans son théâtre l'écho direct de ses souffrances.

Son œuvre est le résumé typique de la vie d'un homme supérieur. Après une jeunesse exubérante, après les bouillonnements de verve des premières comédies, le poète devient plus calme, il acquiert le sens des réalités et raconte la vie des souverains anglais dans des drames historiques.

A l'âge de trente-cinq ans, il traverse des expériences douloureuses, l'horizon s'obscurcit pour lui ; cette période sombre reste mystérieuse. Une trahison d'amitié, peut-être un amour malheureux ou la disgrâce de ses amis, ébranlent son tempérament robuste. A la gaîté succède l'amertume, il ne croit plus au bien, l'homme lui paraît un être méprisable, le monde est mal fait, alors il crie sa douleur dans les paroles désenchantées d'Hamlet, dans les rugissements du vieux Lear, dans les invectives de Timon le misanthrope. Il a soulagé ses tourments en les proclamant par la bouche de ses personnages. La crise a été longue, mais elle ne sera pas éternelle. Quand il a déchargé son cœur, il se ressaisit. Un apaisement se produit en lui ; cessant de s'indigner entre les turpitudes des hommes, il considère le monde avec bienveillance ; dans ses dernières œuvres il peint de préférence des femmes pures et envisage les méchants avec pitié. Sa vie se termine dans la sérénité.

Selon nous, il ne peut subsister aucun doute, Shakespeare est un poète personnel. Toutefois son lyrisme n'a rien de mièvre ; l'homme conserve toujours sa dignité. Cet être si sensible ne perd jamais la maîtrise de lui-même. Cette force d'âme a induit en erreur les critiques comme Flaubert, qui ne cherchent pas à découvrir l'individu derrière le masque de l'œuvre. Shakespeare a senti comme Hamlet, comme Othello et comme Timon, mais par une puissante discipline il a dominé ses passions, utilisant leurs forces d'expansion pour créer des œuvres d'art. Par l'effet de sa volonté, il est à la fois peintre et juge ; il se donne et il se garde tout à la fois ; dans la tourmente il reste assez lucide pour sortir de lui-même et s'analyser. Pour cette raison un

Hamlet ou un Timon ne sont pas des portraits de Shakespeare, mais seulement des reflets directs de son âme multiple. Trop fort et trop équilibré pour agir comme eux, il traversa néanmoins les tempêtes qui les troublèrent et fut tenté d'agir comme eux.

Sans ce rare empire sur lui-même il n'aurait pu coordonner la foule des images qui s'agitaient en lui.

Homme d'imagination et homme de raison, c'est-à-dire homme complet, Shakespeare s'élève très haut par-dessus les théories d'écoles ou de partis. Il appartient à tous, parce qu'il est vraiment humain. Il ne reste pas inabordable pour nous, il ne se dresse pas dans une attitude impassible ; il est un ami, nous le sentons tout proche, car il a souffert comme nous, il nous est cher parce qu'il se donne à nous, parce que nous retrouvons en lui l'écho de nos sentiments intimes.

LOUIS FRÉDÉRIC CHOISY.

GENÈVE.

SHAKESPEARE

RAMASSE le coquillage de nacre, d'or et de pourpre que les siècles ont apporté des profondeurs de la mer éternelle. Porte à ton oreille les lèvres entr'ouvertes de la conque lisse et moelleuse. Écoute. Toute la mer, la mer infinie, avec ses tempêtes, avec le rire et le sanglot de ses vagues, et ce chuchotement de l'écume, la mer sans cesse en action et en mouvement, pulsation du monde, gronde dans ce coquillage que tu réchauffes dans le creux de ta main.

Est-ce la mer ou ton cœur que tu entends ?

Ouvre ce livre, semblable à la Bible. Tourne ces pages, comme les portes à claire-voie d'un jardin de poésie, et du palais de sagesse. Tu entends le commandement du chef, dans le fracas des armes, le rire et les larmes de l'amour, l'appel maternel de la pitié et de la tendresse, le ricanement de la bassesse et le blasphème de la violence, le hoquet de la luxure, et ce cri soudain, ce cri mystérieux qui te fait pâlir. Quelle est cette rumeur de tout un peuple, ce tumulte de foule qui grandit et donne le vertige ? C'est la voix de l'humanité entière qui te parle, et c'est ton cœur aussi. S'il est vrai que seuls les poètes savent écrire l'histoire, ce livre est bien l'histoire universelle. Cette réalité faite de tous les temps, de tous les lieux, de l'homme aux cent visages, est la réalité toujours actuelle.

La vie est un conte récité par un idiot, plein de bruit et de fureur, et qui ne signifie rien, l'ombre qui marche : voici cette vie chantée par un poète. Ce miroir tendu à la nature n'a pas reflété en vain les plus hautes destinées et les plus humbles malheurs. Tandis que de tant de grands hommes, d'hommes puissants et célèbres un jour, il n'est resté qu'un masque grimaçant de carton, voici que ces personnages de l'histoire et de la fiction, nés à la chandelle, devant une toile peinte, frémissent encore d'une vie qui défie le temps. Triomphe du créateur : ces êtres tragiques ou bouffons, ivres de passion et d'orgueil, solennels et furieux, voluptueux et spirituels, plus séduisants qu'un songe, sont aujourd'hui plus vivants que l'ami rencontré dans la rue. Toutes les passions humaines ont pris un visage inoubliable, et le costume avec les insignes de leur rang et de leur dignité dans cette assemblée où l'empereur, le roi, le pape coudoient le rufian, le fou, la courtisane, l'amoureuse, le soldat, le poète, le paysan et le bourgeois, les esprits des airs et des bois, les fées et les sorcières.   Elles ne sont plus des allégories ou des symboles, les signes de je ne sais quel théorème ou de quelle démonstration morale.   Ce ne sont pas des masques que l'on arrache, mais une incarnation réelle, une chair, riche de nerfs et de sang, qui palpite de la même force inconnue et du même rythme que le cœur humain.

Ce peuple de vivants et d'ombres n'a pas été animé par la seule baguette de Prospéro.   La sagesse pèse et réfléchit ; ce n'est pas la prudence qui fait jaillir du roc des réalités cette source bondissante.   La sagesse extrait patiemment de la chronique et du conte les leçons et les paraboles.   Son regard est si grave, parce que ses lèvres ont goûté au vin amer, au fiel et à l'hysope de la vérité.   Mais le feu d'une grande âme crée à la fois le mouvement, la chaleur et la lumière.   Cette flamme a la force, l'élan direct auquel rien ne résiste.

Nomme Génie, si tu crois providentielle, unique, cette faculté ; nomme-la Liberté, si tu crois que le monde animé participe à cette invention, cette création perpétuelle, à ce renouveau incessant, à cette sève qui travaille l'écorce de la terre.

Ce génie, dont le nom sonne comme la trompette du héraut devant son peuple, eut une vie aussi modeste et presque aussi inconnue qu'Homère.   Ne lui refuse-t-on pas la paternité même de son œuvre ? Jeu de la nature, qui déjoue les théories et les commentaires.   Qu'importent aujourd'hui les classifications qui faisaient hier l'admiration des pédants, Quinapalus ou Polonius ?   Celte ou Germain, il était Anglais d'Angleterre.   De l'époque la plus abondante, la plus large, la plus féconde, il a tiré la plus généreuse substance.   Nourri de la moelle des classiques, de cette ardente courtoisie des conteurs italiens, de la fine farine de Montaigne, il a vidé avec le prince Henri les pots d'ale dans la taverne de la Tête d'Ours.   Ce n'était pas pour plaire seulement au parterre du Globe, à ce peuple à l'haleine forte qu'il aime et qu'il dédaigne, Jacques le mélancolique et le solitaire.   Le génie obéit à sa loi, car le pouls désordonné n'est pas le rythme de la santé.   Musicien audacieux, il n'a point hésité à faire alterner les saccades de la prose avec le balancement du vers, comme il a marié à l'euphuïsme des gentilshommes et des belles-lettrées, les couleurs brutales dont le peuple enlumine ses propos.   Dans le forum de Rome, sous les cyprès de Vérone, dans le palais de Chypre ou la forteresse d'Elseneur, dans la forêt d'Athènes ou celle des Ardennes, c'est l'Angleterre toujours que l'on retrouve.   Non pas cette Angleterre conquérante et savante d'Élisabeth, en armure sous le pourpoint de velours ou de cuir, non pas cette Angleterre étroite et scrupuleuse, dans sa triste robe noire de puritaine, mais la libre et puissante nation qui a pour règle le respect de l'individu, et pour devise : Loyauté. Cette loyauté, c'est l'honneur sans discours et sans phrase, méprisant le calcul et le profit, prompt à l'action et lent à la parole, méprisant le compromis et le mensonge, reconnaissant au fait la valeur de l'homme. La loyauté, c'est l'esprit de justice, le regard droit, la parole franche et brève, le pacte d'amitié dans un serrement de main, le respect *d'autrui* basé sur le respect de soi-même.

Quel drame que celui d'*Hamlet*, l'homme qui tremble de faiblir dans son devoir de justicier ! En est-il un au monde qui soit descendu plus profondément dans les arcanes de l'âme humaine ? Même dans ces terribles tragédies de l'histoire, où la justice semble bafouée, foulée aux pieds, violée dans les sanglots, ne vient-il pas une heure où les fantômes s'assoient au banquet ou dans la tente des rois ? Sans ce désir hautain et tendre de la justice, le goût de la vérité ne serait pas si âpre. Mais à l'ordre sévère de la justice répond la supplication de la miséricorde, qui pardonne et absout, comme Desdémone et Cordelia.

Voilà trois siècles écoulés depuis le jour de deuil où s'est éteint ce libre génie créateur, trois siècles pleins d'événements éclatants ou funestes, dans la fumée des batailles et les cris des révolutions, plus débordants d'exploits et de crimes que ces chroniques d'Angleterre, qu'un Prologue en habit de magicien résumait devant un rideau fermé. Aujourd'hui, le drame le plus furieux, le duel sans merci entre violence et justice, entre liberté et domination déchire la vieille Europe, qui attend son poète. Le culte du grand mort aura pour office funèbre la grande lamentation des peuples. Quel hommage plus noble et plus doux au cœur d'un poète que ce souvenir passionné de l'Angleterre, unie et armée pour la cause la plus haute, la défense d'une petite nation écrasée, mais non vaincue, pour la revendication de ce droit sacré, la liberté individuelle des peuples.

Shakespeare ! Comme ton nom sonne aujourd'hui ! Quel monument de marbre et de bronze, quelle parole de feu égalera ton œuvre magnifique, Victoire aux ailes gonflées comme les voiles d'un navire, la tête levée, tendue sur son cou robuste par l'effort du défi, pour jeter ce cri dont les générations demeurent bouleversées ? Tu fus à la fois Jules César et Brutus, et la voix du monde entier prononcera, dans la bataille, le plus court et le plus éloquent des éloges funèbres sur la tombe d'un héros :

'This was a man.'

RENÉ MORAX.

MORGES.

SHAKESPEARE VU DE PROFIL

NE pouvant, à cette heure, étudier de manière étendue l'œuvre du plus grand héros littéraire de notre monde moderne, je vous envoie ces quelques notes jetées rapidement sur le papier.

Ce qui m'intéresse le plus en Shakespeare c'est que son art est plein de défauts et que je l'aime pourtant plus que tout autre art. Son style souvent heurte mon goût ; sa verve me semble entachée de vulgarité ; ses jeux d'esprit ne manquent pas de m'agacer. Qu'importe ! Shakespeare est comme une montagne pleine de gouffres et d'abîmes, pleine de cavernes et de trous que le soleil dominateur revêt d'une beauté égale. Ses défauts lui sont opportuns. Les ombres de son œuvre en font valoir la clarté.

Bien plus. S'il est banal de répéter que les caractères qu'il inventa sont d'une humanité frémissante et perdurable et que nul aussi profondément que lui n'est descendu dans la spirale d'enfer ou de ciel qu'est un cœur humain, il faut ajouter qu'en outre il mit en lumière une foule de vérités, de raison et d'expérience générales. Il fit la psychologie des peuples avec une sûreté haute. Bien plus encore, il fit avant nous tous la psychologie des foules. Caliban rejoint la formidable ironie d'Aristophane.

Hier encore, après une attentive lecture du vieux Will, un de mes amis me cite ce trait : ' Il est bon d'avoir la force d'un géant, mais il est maladroit de toujours s'en servir comme un géant.' Shakespeare avait-il prévu l'Allemagne de 1914 ?

ÉMILE VERHAEREN.

SAINT-CLOUD.

SHAKESPEARE

Les circonstances tragiques où nous vivons détournent momentané-ment, mais impérieusement, les regards et les pensées de tout ce qui fait le bonheur et la gloire des belles heures de la paix. C'est pourquoi, retournant à ces heures bénies où l'esprit était libre et ne voyait pas toute chose à travers une nuée de sang et de douleur, mon hommage au poète souverain se bornera à répéter ici ce que je disais alors au sujet de *Macbeth* et qui s'applique à tous les grands héros de son œuvre : à savoir, que Shakespeare lui-même serait incapable de délimiter et d'expliquer les êtres échappés de ses mains prodigieuses. Il est aussi difficile de les envelopper du regard dans le poème écrit qu'il serait malaisé de le faire s'ils vivaient parmi nous. Ils débordent de toutes parts ce qui tente de les circonscrire. On croit les connaître, mais ils demeurent toujours inattendus. On les sent prêts aux revirements les plus extraordinaires. Ce n'est pas manque de précision dans les traits, mais vitalité surprenante du dessin. En vérité, les héros n'ont pas fini de vivre ; ils n'ont pas dit leur dernier mot ni fait leur dernier geste. Ils ne sont pas encore séparés du fond commun de toute existence. On ne peut les juger ni en faire le tour, parce que tout un pan de leur être tient encore à l'avenir. Ils sont inachevés, non du petit côté du drame ou de la tragédie, mais du côté de l'infini. Les caractères qu'on saisit entièrement, qu'on analyse avec certitude, sont déjà morts. Il semble au contraire que les siens ne puissent demeurer immobiles dans les vers ou la prose qui les crée. Ils les déplacent, les agitent de leur souffle. Ils y poursuivent leur destinée, ils en modifient la forme et le sens ; ils s'y développent, y évoluent comme dans un milieu vital et nourri-cier, y subissent l'influence des années et des siècles qui passent, y puisant des pensées et des sentiments imprévus, une grandeur et des forces nouvelles.

MAETERLINCK.

SHAKESPEARE AND BELGIUM

IF the great artists of Belgium in past and present times could be called to greet the Master Craftsman of the Globe Theatre, they would all bow before him and do homage, but he in his turn would hail them as brethren in the delineation of single aspects of the humanity and fate that he alone has embraced as a whole. The creator of Cymbeline would recognize in Rubens's canvas the full and noble figure of Imogen and that heroic cave in the mountains from which Britain's royal sons stride forth to rouse the game ; the mind that conceived Falstaff would smile at the lusty fleshiness of Jordaens and at the scenes of revelry imagined by Jan Steen.

But has not the Belgian soil brought forth any growth that will emulate Shakespeare's finer and sterner creations, such as the singing Ophelia, with her rosemary for remembrance, her pansies for thoughts, or such as the mourning Leontes, whose conscience is scarred by remorse ? Our answer lies in the dramas of Maurice Maeterlinck and of Émile Verhaeren.

'We are such stuff as dreams are made of,'

says the Master, and this lesson the two Belgian dramatists have learned alike, and have interpreted each in his own way. Maeterlinck gropes into the dark realm of the preternatural and from it he lets in voices, breaths, and sounds which the soul answers in mute thrills and shivers, as it answers the spirits and portents in *The Tempest* and in *Julius Caesar*. His slender heroines, Mélisande and the Princess Maleine, flutter in the grip of fate like

'The bird that hath been limed in a bush.'

Guilt, Wisdom, Destiny, the forces from the contemplation of which his essays were born, are also the protagonists in his earlier plays. In thus refining individual lives into mere playthings for cosmic powers, the poet of the *Blue Bird* seems to have, under Shakespeare's aegis, made an attempt to redeem the genius of Belgium from the taunt of grossness, and to banish the 'Flemish drunkard' Silenus far from the walled garden of his *béguinage*.

Not so Émile Verhaeren's tragic fervour, which still savours of the national soil as it rises towards the light of heaven. If he has taken example from the Master, it is to saturate his ideals with such full-blooded reality as makes itself felt in *Henry IV* and in *Othello*. The heart-burning repentance and the courage for truth which flash through the action of *The Cloister* may not be lineally traceable to any creation of Shakespeare's; they belong to the same sphere as the mighty passions that sweep through the Tragedies and the Histories.

Among the many strings of the English poet's harp, Belgium, then, touches two extremes: Maeterlinck awakens the chords of extreme spirituality, his brother dramatist strikes a note that harmonizes more with the old vigour of Flemish art.

PAUL HAMELIUS.

THE UNIVERSITY,
LIÈGE.

ALS DEEZ TIJDEN GROOT

O NACHT van dagen waar, tot onderling verderven,
Zich rampgenoot in angst vastklampt aan rampgenoot,
Waar moord tot moorden dwingt en eedle volkren zwerven
Van hongersnood in vuur, van vuur in hongersnood !

Wat heb ik, vóor die hoos van driften, menigwerven
Op éenen naam gehoopt die als deez' tijden groot :
Shakespeare ! .. Mocht dan, kon dan de schoonste wereld sterven,
Terwijl, ten derden male, een eeuw rouwt om Uw dood ?

Uw somberst scheppen toont noodlottigheid, geen schuldigen.
Het menschlijke en Uw hart zijn diep gelijk de zee ;
Bij storm slaan leed op leed in zwaar vermenigvuldigen.

Een *Storm* hebt Gij gekeerd tot wonderklaren vree.
Breek', zongelijk, Uw glans door 't wolkig wereldwee,
Zoodat ook Goethes kroost Uw zuivre kracht moog' huldigen.

RENÉ DE CLERCQ.

TRANSLATION

GREAT LIKE THESE TIMES

O DARKENING of days, wherein for mutual death
Companions in misfortune to each other cling ;
When murder forces murder, and noble nations stagger
From famine to fire, from fire to famine !

How often, in this whirl of passions,
Hoped I for a name mighty like these times.
Shakespeare ! . . . This fairest world, can it—may it—die,
While this third century thy death reveres ?

Thy darkest creations show fatality, not guilt ;
Humanity and thy heart are deep like the sea ;
Sorrow beats on sorrow, tempestuously, in dire iteration.

One Tempest hast thou turned to miraculous peace.
Let thy glory burst forth, like sunshine, through these clouds of
    world-woe,
So that e'en Goethe's folk may to thy pure might yield homage !

IN GEDACHTE MET SHAKESPEARE

IK ben overtuigd, dat velen met mij, in deze gruwelijke tijden, het overweldigend beeld van Shakespeare, tot kwellens toe, vóór hun benauwden geest hebben zien verrijzen.

Het is alsof zijn reuzenfiguur zich tegen den tragischen horizont afteekent en er, in zijn eeuwige grootschheid, den afgrijselijken chaos van bloed en gruwelen, die de wereld thans geworden is, profetisch aanschouwt en beheerscht.

Welk een tafereel voor Hem, die de hoogstmenschelijke was onder de menschen ! Men stelle zich dat schrikwekkend epos voor : die heerschzuchtige keizers en koningen, die leugenachtige en vleierige hovelingen en ministers, die geslachtofferde en gemartelaarde volkeren, die vluchtende monarchen zonder land, dien ganschen stoet van rampen en ellende, eindeloos dolend langs de sombere wegen der ballingschap, tusschen de verwoeste velden en de verbrande dorpen en steden, in stroomen van tranen en bloed . . . men stelle zich dat schouwspel voor, weer opgewekt en vereeuwigd door Hem, die met zijn ziel, zijn geest en zijn hart, die met zijn eigen levensbloed als 't ware Macbeth en King Lear schiep !

In deze vreeselijke dagen smeeken de ontredderde volken der oude, beschaafde wereld om de hulp van een groot man, één enkel, grooter en sterker dan allen, een Redder !

Er zijn er geene meer ! De vertwijfelende oogen der Menschheid peilen te vergeefs de zwarte diepten van den einder. Hij, Hij alleen staat daar nog steeds, forsch-oprijzend, almachtig en wraakroepend, in den nacht der tijden.

Het is alsof hij aan de droevige rampzaligen der wereld met een machtig-groot gebaar den weg ter redding wees. Maar de menschen zijn zoo zwak en klein en blind geworden, ze zijn zóó diep gezonken, dat ze zijn waarschuwende stem zelfs niet meer hooren, dat ze zijn gebaar zelfs niet meer zien.

Hij, de Reus, en zij, de dwergen, staan samen, in machtelooze ontreddering, de instorting der wereld te aanschouwen.

CYRIEL BUYSSE.

GRATO M'È 'L SONNO

(WITH PARAPHRASE)

SLAAPT hij nu zoo lang,
Laat hem dan vandaag !
Waartoe uit zijn droom van zang
Hem nopen tot een vraag ?

Hoor ! weerbarstig schrijnt
Over land en zee
Stukgebroken snaar en pijnt
Wie waken met haar wee.

Hart van volken, eens
Speeltuig voor zijn hand,—
Nu vol jammer en geweens
Verloort ge 't maatverband.

Slaapt hij nu zoo lang,
Laat hem dan vandaag !
Waartoe uit zijn droom van zang
Hem nopen tot een vraag ?

Peaceful his sleep !
Let him sleep on.
From dream of song
Why wake him now ?

Discordant moans
O'er land and sea ;
Lute-strings are torn,
Rack'd by the jarring.

Hearts of the nations
Attuned to his hand,
'Mid anguish and tears
His music is lost.

Peaceful his sleep !
Let him sleep on.
From dream of song
Why wake him now ?

ALBERT VERWEY.

NOORDWIJK A. ZEE,
        HOLLAND.

READING SHAKESPEARE'S SONNETS

THE problem which stands before my mind in reading the Sonnets, and of which I shall try to show in what way the beginning of a solution is to be found, is this :

Knowing through the publication of a couple of the poet's Sonnets in an anthology of amorous songs called *The Passionate Pilgrim*, 1599, i.e. ten years before the appearance of the whole collection in 1609, that some lines of one of them have been materially altered,[1] the question rises whether we still can trace in the edition, as we have it now, the changes through which the Sonnets have passed, and whether we, once on this track, are able with greater precision than before to pass a judgement on the vital, sentimental, and literary experiences of the poet, who felt the want to alter these songs.

A simple inspection suffices to show us that what we call the Sonnets of Shakespeare, all or nearly all, consist of three quatrains rhyming alternately, with a rhyming couplet as a conclusion to the three (4 + 4 + 4 + 2). This same alternately rhyming quatrain, now single, each quatrain with its couplet trailing gravely and sententiously behind, is the stanza of the *Venus and Adonis* poem, which numbers two hundred stanzas (4 + 2). Very rarely we meet in Shakespeare with another form of the Sonnet (or so called), consisting of two quatrains with one or two concluding couplets (4 + 4 + 2 (+ 2)). Such Sonnets are to be found in the *Two Gentlemen of Verona* (III. i. 140) and in the first edition of *Romeo and Juliet* (Quarto of 1597, the prologue).

My contention is that part of Shakespeare's Sonnets had originally this latter form.

A sequence of quatrains, rhymeless or rhyming, concluded by a rhyming couplet, was largely used by the poet in his earlier dramas, historical as well as comical, for the exposition of the feelings and arguments of his dramatis personae. The time, however, came when this

---

[1] It is impossible to examine here these various readings, the subject not lending itself to public discussion. What the edition of 1599 says forcibly and very intelligibly is toned down to a general observation in the edition of 1609. There cannot be the least doubt that the former edition approached nearest to the original form.

more lyrical than dramatical type of verse did not agree any more with his poetical tact, and we find him either substituting other lines for the old quatrains or adding tags to them which impair their monotonous symmetry. In *Love's Labour 's Lost*, which even the most conservative editors admit not only to have been rewritten by its author, but also to have retained here and there the lines destined to be erased, there is also a very curious instance of a new quatrain (I. i. 79–83) being interposed between a sequence of old quatrains. It enlivens the passage there, but it underbreaks the rational and regular order of the argument (cf. IV. iii. 296).

Now, as it seems to me, the same occurs in the first Sonnet of Shakespeare's Book of Sonnets, with this difference—that the addition and interruption serves especially there to make up the normal number of quatrains.

The Sonnet is too well known to write it out here: every one remembers the floral image of the opening lines—' Beauty's rose ripening and by time deceasing '—which is continued and applied in the third quatrain ; the intervening four lines, however, deflect the attention to quite distinct moral and material ideas. In my opinion the two last lines of the first quatrain :

> But as the riper should by time decease,
> His tender heir might bear his memory:

originally were followed directly by :

> Thou that art now the world's fresh ornament
> And only herald to the gaudy spring, &c.

But is this impression of a possibility capable of evidence which ensures it some claim to certainty ?

I see three ways leading up to a direct proof.

First, there is the palpable evidence of Sonnets bearing Shakespeare's name having been transformed, by addition of superabundant lines, from two-quatrain Sonnets to three-quatrains. We can follow with our eye the transformation if we compare the Sonnet of twelve lines that figures as a prologue to *Romeo and Juliet* in the edition of 1597 with the thing of fourteen lines at the beginning of the tragedy of our editions : a regular Sonnet at present, but bearing the clearest marks of having been hastily patched up to get the requisite number of lines.[1]

[1] Mark the redundancy in words and sense of lines 8 and 9, 10: *Do with their death bury their parents' strife,* and . . . *their parents' rage, which, but their children's end, nought could remove.* The same is to be said of the other chorus sonnet in *Romeo and Juliet,* of which there exists no counterpart in the edition of 1597, but which may easily be restored to its pristine form by the excision of two lines.

The second proof regards the internal structure of the sonnets.

The different quatrains may be considered as members of a whole, having each its separate existence; the last quatrain, where the conclusion is approached, has ordinarily a well-defined word as introduction. There the person spoken to is emphatically addressed, *thou* as in Sonnet I, or a reason is given in a positive or adversative way (*for, then, so, but*); often it is an imperative counsel which opens the first line (line 9 of the whole complex) of the quatrain: 'O change thy thought', 'O let me see'. Especially 'O let' is very common.

Now though it is one of the best known, I beg leave to write out Sonnet CXXXII, on the black eyes of his mistress.

> 1 Thine eyes I love, and they, as pitying me,
> Knowing thy heart torments me with disdain,
> Have put on black and loving mourners be,
> Looking with pretty ruth upon my pain.
> 5 *And truly not the morning sun of heaven*
> *Better becomes the grey cheeks of the east,*
> *Nor that full star that ushers in the even*
> *Doth half that glory to the sober west,*
> 9 As those two mourning eyes become thy face:
> O! let it then as well beseem thy heart
> To mourn for me, since mourning doth thee grace,
> And suit thy pity like in every part, &c.

What strikes us here is the anomaly in sense and in structure. I leave out of question the pun on *mourning* and *morning* (*de gustibus*, &c.), but the image of *morning* is eclipsed by the *evening* star, and the imagery fails completely, howsoever beautiful in themselves the lines may be. And more: the line 'O let it then as well . . .' has been removed from the place where it originally belonged. Restore it to its true seat, and read on, passing in silence ll. 5–8, continuously.

> 4 Looking with pretty ruth upon my pain.
> 9 O! let it then as well beseem thy heart
> To mourn for me, since mourning doth thee grace,
> And suit thy pity like in every part,
> As those two mourning eyes become thy face.

and we retake possession of the sonnet in its full glory and lustre.

For really, and this is my third proof, in this wise we have the means to render individuality to the sonnets in cases where the author, by his re-editing, has effaced it. Is this not the perfection of a proof, when the rule found by induction creates new things?

I can only give one instance, for I must hasten to the end of this already too long disquisition. Sonnet III—

> 1 Look in thy glass, and tell the face thou viewest
> Now is the time that face should form another;
> Whose fresh repair if now thou not renewest,
> Thou dost beguile the world, *unless some mother*.
> 5 *For where is she so fair whose unear'd womb*
> *Disdains the tillage of thy husbandry?*
> *Or who is he so fond will be the tomb*
> *Of his self-love, to stop posterity?*
> 9 Thou art thy mother's glass, and she in thee
> Calls back the lovely April of her prime:
> So thou through windows of thine age shalt see,
> Despite of wrinkles, this thy golden time.

If we omit from this sonnet the middle quatrain, we get rid not only of some discording lines which sadly interrupt the continuous flow of the graceful verse, but we can with surety amend the poor expression *unless some mother*. Read :

> Thou dost beguile the world, unless *thy* mother.
> Thou art thy mother's glass, and she in thee
> Calls back the lovely April of her prime, &c.

Reasons there are plenty as blackberries for reading the sonnet as we have read it here. I shall not expatiate on them. What the expunged lines tell us, is much better and more melodiously said in other sonnets, as is well known to all who ever glanced through the book. To me it seems as if this sonnet, shorn of its excrescence, has taken a new shape and comes to us like music from afar, as poetry must be heard—or rather overheard.[1]

And now the larger aim is before us—to examine the songs one by one with the one clue found and the other clues which remain still to be found, and to follow on this track the progression of our poet's mind and heart. For even in those additions of a later time he must have given us something of himself. *Repentirs* they are called, the parts blotted out by the artist and painted anew, which we often find in famous pictures, and indeed in Shakespeare's song we shall come upon signs of repentance and moral growth. But it is a subject upon which we cannot enter now. Let what I have tried to give be taken as a slight token of gratitude for all I have received from Shakespeare's England, which is also the England of Dickens, and the land of the

---

[1] Mark how by this process of expunging we get rid of the ridiculous middle lines of Sonnet XX, which have cost so many heart- and head-breakings. The *motif* of this sonnet is the word *woman*, and it is quite spoiled by the intervening quatrain.

living river of lyrical song, from Spenser's *Amoretti* to Cannan's *Adventurous Love*.

If somebody considers me, as a stranger, too bold in my desire to shake loose the text of the poet, settled through ages, let him think written on the margin of these pages what I found noted on the border of an old book full of strange speculations : *haereticus loquitur*, it is an heretic who is speaking here. But for me, I consider myself simply as a passionate reader who, not content with looking at the signboards only of the houses of Life, is wanting to go in, to look for himself and to be a true guest of the truly royal spirits who are doing him the excessive honour to receive him in their homes.

W. G. C. BYVANCK.

THE HAGUE.

ARE THERE INTERPOLATIONS IN THE TEXT OF HAMLET?

WHEN a play is being studied by the actors, changes are made in it in the course of the rehearsals, some things are cancelled, and others are inserted. ' When a piece is published after performance,' writes Sir Arthur Pinero, ' the publication is always prepared from the stage-manager's copy, never from the author's MS.' (*Transactions of the New Shakspere Society*, 1880–2, p. 198).

The necessity for taking this practice into account, even for dramas dating three centuries back, is shown by the occurrence on printed title-pages of that period of the phrase ' as it was acted ', and of similar expressions.

On the title-page of the *Hamlet* Quarto of 1604 the play is described as printed ' according to the true and perfect coppie '. These words may refer either to the stage manuscript, or to Shakespeare's own.

Most of the authorities on textual criticism, though not all, have surmised that Shakespeare's plays, and particularly *Hamlet*, were printed from stage copies. It is therefore somewhat surprising that no attempt should yet have been made to enumerate the interpolations in the Quarto *Hamlet* of 1604 with any precision. The hypothesis of a stage manuscript is indeed accepted without proof positive, and chiefly because of the large number of mistakes in all those early editions ; for those mistakes no better explanation can be found than the intermediate link of a stage manuscript, through which many blunders may have crept in. However that may be, it certainly appears that all modern editors, while believing that stage manuscripts were used for printing, go to work as if no interpolations were to be found in the Quarto of 1604.

Is it really so hard to decide whether insertions by a strange hand do occur in the text of a great poet as transmitted to us ? If there are any, we ought to be able to detect them, as they should be marked by peculiarities which ought to be fairly obvious.

Interpolations are redundant, they break the metre and they are inferior. The first two tests are absolute. Inferior quality is not absolute, it only applies in general, and in its case we must allow for exceptions. There is one more test of interpolations. No one will insert them without some purpose; their authors must have intended to improve the text in some way, or at least to adapt it to a definite object that they had in view. As this object need not always have been the same, we shall be able to classify interpolations in several groups, according to the various purposes pursued by their authors. If we attend carefully to these tests, we may hope to succeed in our search.

First I must draw attention to a quotation from the Quarto of 1604, from which I shall always quote in future. My numbering of lines is from the Globe edition.

My father, *me thinkes* I ſee my father	I. ii. 184
HORA. Where my Lord?	½185
HAM. In my mindes eye *Horatio.*	185½
HORA. *I ſaw him once*, a was a goodly King.	186
HAM. A was a man take him for all in all	187
I ſhall not looke vppon his like againe.	188
HORA. My Lord *I thinke* I ſaw him yeſternight	189
HAM. *Saw, who?*	190

All the words italicized above are redundant and break the metre; if we omit them, we keep an excellent text of five lines of regular and perfect blank verse. It is therefore quite possible that the italicized words are interpolations; perhaps further consideration may give us certainty.

Is it not strange that Horatio should have seen Hamlet's father only once? Horatio is Hamlet's friend, he was a student in Wittenberg, and now returns to attend the funeral of Hamlet's father. Let us turn to other passages where he refers to old Hamlet:

I knewe your father. Theſe hands are not more like	I. ii. 211 and 212

His beard was:

as I haue ſeene it in his life A sable ſiluer'd	I. ii. 241 and 242

When Bernardo and Marcellus ask Horatio whether the ghost looks like the king—and why should they ask, unless they knew Horatio to be well informed on the subject—he answers:

Moſt like	I. i. 44
As thou art to thy ſelfe	59
Such was the very Armor he had on,	60
When he the Ambitious Norway combated	61

So frownd he once, when in an angry parle   62
He ſmot the dreaded[1] pollax on the ice.   63

The above quotations prove that Shakespeare's Horatio cannot have spoken the words 'I ſaw him once.' While these words may not well be described as inferior, they do not fit into the context.

The same remark holds good of the words 'I thinke' in line 189, which also are in open contradiction with other passages in the text. Horatio does not think, but knows that he has seen Hamlet's father. At first he did not believe in ghosts, but now there is something more than mere imagination, as he admits in the most solemn manner in I. i. 56–8. In I. ii. 192–221, he describes the apparition as established to himself, and as confirmed by two other witnesses.

How are we to judge of 'me thinkes' in line 184? Those words contain the greatest stylistic blunder that a writer could be guilty of. What human being, when overwhelmed by the sight of a father who had lately died, would exclaim with scepticism and with scientific accuracy: 'Methinks I see a ghost?' Were this possible, no dramatic author, trying to make an audience realize an apparition, would choose a mode of expression that in advance threw doubt on its reality. Shakespeare can only have put the most positive statement into Hamlet's mouth: 'My father, I see my father!' Not before having been brought to reflection by Horatio's question does Hamlet feel that it must have been an imagination.

The word 'Horatio' printed in italics in line 185 cannot be shown to be an inferior reading; the facts of the case make it impossible to produce a convincing proof of its being interpolated. Among the instances (less than twenty in number in the *Hamlet* Quarto) which are exactly similar to it, I will only mention 'Sir', I. i. 95, and 'Hamlet', I. ii. 87, considered as an interpolation by Pope; 'good friends', I. v. 163, and 'Hamlet', III. iv. 88, considered as interpolations by Seymour.

The three other examples contained in the short compass of the first quotation were so demonstrably inferior readings that I thought it best to begin with them. They are less appropriate as instances clearly showing the purpose of the interpolation.

One of the commonest reasons for adding to the text is the wish to explain. This reason applies to 'me thinkes' in line 184. As

---

[1] 'fleaded' I corrected as a misprint. In a parley a battle-axe can be cast on the ice. Perhaps Hercules might have thrown on the ice an army of Poles seated in sledges, as some misinterpret the text, but then he would have done so in a fight, not in a parley or conversation.

appears from the words ' In my mindes eye ', Hamlet does not at the next moment believe that he has seen a real apparition, therefore the phrase ' me thinkes ' explains the text and warns the audience that the ghost is not entering yet, although it might now be expected at Hamlet's exclamation, and after the first two apparitions. The warning would be useful, if it did not spoil the text in another respect.

The other three examples cannot be thus explained. The dialogue without the italicized words is beautifully simple and powerful. Not one word is redundant in the logical order of ideas. But each quality leads to the corresponding defect, and if we are to look in this passage for a defect that may have tempted a reviser to corrections, we may undeniably notice a certain laconism or abruptness, which the words in italics were intended to remedy. Besides appellatives, such as ' Horatio ', already referred to, we might place into this group the following words, possibly interpolations :

Indeede Sirs but (F. repeats Ind.)	I. ii. 224	but	.	II. i. 31
Very like (F. repeats these words)	I. ii. 237	why	.	III. ii. 64
Marry well bethought . .	I. iii. 90	nothing . . .	.	III. iv. 133
my Lord, come from the graue .	I. iv. 125	I pray you . .	.	IV. iv. 11
But come	I. v. 168	Can you aduife me .	.	IV. vii. 54

To the group of possible interpolations belong the following :

Of his affection to me (cf. *Wives*		to this world . . .	.	III. ii. 408
I. i. 215) . . .	I. iii. 100	with it (cf. *Timon* IV. iii. 1)	.	III. iii. 17
my Vncle	I. v. 41	villain . . .	.	III. iii. 77
To thofe of mine . .	I. v. 52	to me . . .	.	III. iv. 94
And prey on garbage .	I. v. 57	Speake to her Hamlet (cf. l. 113)	III. iv. 115
As . . . or . . .	I. v. 176	Or for fome frontire .	.	IV. iv. 16
Or . . . to . . . or (cf. *W. T.* IV. i. 26)	I. v. 177	death . . .	.	IV. v. 83
you may go fo far .	II. i. 26	Lord (cf. *1 Hen. VI*, V. i. 29)	.	IV. v. 102
To be commaunded . .	II. ii. 32	Moft throughly for my father .	IV. v. 136
from Norway my good Lord .	II. ii. 40	Winner and loofer . .	.	IV. v. 143
Did nothing . . .	II. ii. 504	KING. A Norman .	.	IV. vii. 92
Now falls on Priam . .	II. ii. 514	the Nation . .	.	IV. vii. 95
As low as to the fiends .	II. ii. 519	So faft they follow .	.	IV. vii. 165
Players . . .	II. ii. 623	forbeare him . .	.	V. i. 296
Of his true ftate . .	III. i. 10	Vp from my Cabin .	.	V. ii. 12
To any paftime . .	III. i. 15	with villaines . .	.	V. ii. 29
To hear and fee the matter (cf.		Thou knoweft already .	.	V. ii. 55
Tr. and Cr. IV. v. 268) .	III. i. 23	of our nature . .	.	V. ii. 69
To hear him fo inclin'd .	III. i. 25	on both fides . .	.	V. ii. 315

The examples given so far might have been introduced into the original by any busybody. If the text is printed from a stage manuscript, there must be interpolations made with the object of adapting it for the performance, and some of them should betray the view taken by the actor, as distinguished from that of the author.   I quote :

HORA.	ſtay illuſion	I. i. 127
If thou haſt any found or vſe of voyce,		128
Speake to me, if there be any good thing to be done		129, 130
That may to thee doe eaſe, and grace to mee,		131
Speake to me.		132
If thou art priuie to thy countries fate		133
Which happily foreknowing may avoyd		134
O Speake :		135
Or if thou haſt vphoorded in thy life		136
Extorted treaſure in the wombe of earth		137
For which they ſay your spirits oft walke in death, (read: you)		138
Speake of it, ſtay and ſpeake, ſtop it Marcellus		139

The text with the italicized words left out suits the occasion perfectly.   How could a ghost be addressed in a more beautiful or appropriate way ? The text including the italicized words offers a threefold repetition, in ll. 129, 132 and 135, of what is said twice in l. 139, and is therefore inferior in style. Yet the actor will say : I require those repetitions here, because they help me to make a deeper impression on the audience and because they allow of more forcible gesticulation.

Let us be fair and admit that both views are justifiable and that stagecraft cannot do without a little exaggeration. And if Hamlet not only inveighs against exaggeration in acting, but even advises to keep within the bounds of real occurrences—' the modeſtie of nature ' (III. ii. 21), in his beautiful phrase—we have some reason for concluding that in Shakespeare the literary and poetical temperament predominated very much over the professional player. No doubt we were all willing to agree to this before, while we may be surprised to be reminded of it by textual criticism.

Other possible interpolations belonging to this group are :

Stay, ſpeake, ſpeake .	I. i. 51	O heauy burthen		III. i. 54
Tis strange (om. Seymour)	I. i. 64	HAM. That's wormwood (F.		
LAER. Farwell (cf. l. 84)	I. iii. 87	repeats wormwood) .		III. ii. 191
Goe on, Ile follow thee (cf. l. 86)	I. iv. 79	All may be well (om. Seymour)		III. iii. 72
HAM. O God	I. v. 24	No		III. iii. 87
HAM. Murther	I. v. 26	GER. Alas hee's mad		III. iv. 105
ô fie (om. Capell, Steevens, Mitford, Dyce)	I. v. 93	what noiſe is this		IV. v. 96
HORA. What newes my Lord	I. v. 117	How now, what noyſe is that		IV. v. 153
doe you marke this Reynaldo .	II. i. 15	QUEE. Drownd, drownd		IV. vii. 186
Marke you	II. i. 41	LAER. What Ceremonie els		
ſee you now	II. i. 62	(cf. l. 246)		V. i. 248
For Hecuba	II. ii. 584	Hamlet the Dane		V. i. 281
hum (om. F.)	II. ii. 617	QUEE. Hamlet, Hamlet		V. i. 287
		ALL. Gentlemen (om. F.)		V. i. 288

QUEE. O my fonne, what		This likes me well . . . v. ii. 276	
theame . . . . v. i. 291		The drinke the drinke, I am poy-	
What wilt thou doo for her (cf.		fned . . . . v. ii. 321	
l. 297) . . . . v. i. 294		Treachery, feeke it out . . v. ii. 323	

Some of these examples are excellent in their place and impart more life to the stage business.

At the end of a scene the actor's exit caused more difficulties than it does nowadays. Now the curtain drops, but when it was missing the players had to leave in sight of the audience ; there was therefore some need to explain the exit. The end of the first act is as follows :

HAM.	let vs goe in together	I. v. 187
And ftill your fingers on your lips I pray		188
The time is out of ioynt, ô curfed fpight		189
That euer I was borne to set it right		190
Nay come, lets go together.		191

The exit is explained here twice, by the repeated request to go out together, once in l. 187 and once in l. 191. The first request is introduced by Shakespeare, the second must be an interpolation, for no author would have weakened the deep impression made by ll. 189 and 190 by the redundant commonplace of l. 191. The last rhyming word is the conclusion of the scene.

Quite analogous is the following scene-ending :

POL.	...come, goe we to the King	II. i. 117
This muft be knowne, which beeing kept close, might moue		118
More griefe to hide, then hate to utter loue		119
Come.		

As the last ' come ' does not occur in the Folio of 1623, several editors have thought themselves justified in omitting it.

Another quite similar example, in which I thought the rhyming word ought to be restored, is the following :

KING.	Let's follow Gertrard	IV. vii. 192
How much I had to doe to calme his vaine		193
Now feare I this will giue it ftart againe		194
Therefore let's follow:		195

At the end of Act IV, Sc. v, the interpolation ' I pray you goe with me' is only distinguished from the above by containing no repetition of a preceding line.

Once we have realized by what means and with what exaggeration the second half of the golden rule ' fute the action to the word, and the word to the action ' (III. ii. 19–20) was obeyed by the players, we shall easily be convinced that in Shakespeare's original lines 216 and 217 of the following passage occurred at the beginning, so that l. 217, probably in the form in which it is found in l. 213, was the first part of l. 211.

This man ſhall ſet me packing,	III. iv. 211
Ile lugge the guts into the neighbour roome;	212
Mother good night indeed, this Counſayler	213
Is now moſt ſtill, moſt ſecret, and moſt graue,	214
Who was in life a fooliſh prating knaue	215
Come ſir, to draw toward an end with you	216
Good night mother. [*Exit Hamlet tugging in Pollonius.*	217

We also remember :

BAR. Laſt night of all	I. i. 35
When yond ſame ſtarre thats weaſtward from the pole	36
Had made his courſe t'illume that part of heauen	37
Where now it burnes, Marcellus and my ſelfe	38
The bell then beating one	39
Enter Ghoſt.	

Here l. 39 may originally have been the second half of l. 35, and by the displacement of half a line was produced the stage effect of the clock striking and the ghost entering as the word 'one' was uttered.

We also think of the conclusion of Hamlet :

FOR. Let foure Captaines	v. ii. 406
Beare Hamlet like a ſouldier to the ſtage,	407
For he was likely, had he beene put on,	408
To haue prooued moſt royall; and for his paſſage,	409
The ſoldiers muſicke and the rites of warre	410
Speake loudly for him :	411
Take vp the bodies, ſuch a ſight as this,	412
Becomes the field, but heere ſhowes much amiſſe.	413

In the Folio of 1623 follows line 414 :

Go, bid the Souldiers ſhoote.

which is missing in the Quarto and which must have been the final half of line 411.   This transfer was required by the stage effect, so that the shots might be fired after the word 'ſhoote'.

It is particularly interesting that an example of the variety of interpolation discussed in the last instance should occur in the middle of a scene :

KING. *O Gertrard, come away,*	IV. i. 28

The final lines of this scene are :

And hit the woundleſſe ayre. ô come away,	IV. i. 44
My ſoule is full of diſcord and diſmay	45

For various reasons we conclude that ll. 29–45 were cut out at the performance and that the scene ended with l. 28. If this conclusion be accepted as correct, the Quarto of 1604 has not been printed from a stage manuscript, for ll. 29–45 would then be omitted from it. There are several more passages in the Quarto which have certainly never been acted, if only because its text is far too long for a single performance, even without being completed from the Folio.

Ought we then to admit that the Quarto was printed from Shakespeare's manuscript, notwithstanding the interpolations found in it? There is no reason to doubt it. The Quarto of 1604 may have been printed from Shakespeare's manuscript, to which may have been added the corrections that made it serve as a stage-copy. This hypothesis explains what is meant by 'the true and perfect coppie', it solves a number of puzzles in a satisfactory manner, and offers the formula through which various opponents in the field of textual criticism can reach peace with honour.

B. A. P. van Dam.

The Hague.

A MARGINAL NOTE ON SHAKESPEARE'S LANGUAGE AND A TEXTUAL CRUX IN 'KING LEAR'

NOTHING could well be more wide of the mark than Tolstoy's assertion that Shakespeare lacks the true dramatist's power to make different characters speak differently. On the contrary, it would be difficult to find another dramatist using individual style and individual language for the purpose of characterizing different persons to the same extent as Shakespeare. Hotspur does not speak like Prince Hal, nor Rosalind like Viola or Cordelia ; Shylock has a language all his own, and the insincerity of the King in *Hamlet* is shown characteristically by a certain tendency towards involved sentences and avoiding the natural and straightforward expression. Even minor characters are often individualized by means of their speech, thus the gardeners in *Richard the Second* (Act III, Sc. iv) or Osric in *Hamlet*. But this has not always been noticed by commentators and editors, and I think a truer appreciation of Shakespeare's art in this respect will assist us in explaining at least one crux in his text.

I am specially alluding to one passage in *King Lear* (Act IV, Sc. iii, ll. 19 ff.), where the first Quarto reads—the whole scene is omitted in the Folio—

Patience and sorrow strove,
Who should expresse her goodliest[.] You haue seene,
20 Sun shine and raine at once, her smiles and teares,
Were like a better way those happie smilets,
That playd on her ripe lipe seeme[d] not to know,
What guests were in her eyes which parted thence,
As pearles from diamonds dropt[.] In briefe,
Sorow would be a raritie most beloued,
If all could so become it.

I have here only changed *streme* into the obvious *strove*, and *seeme* into *seemed*, besides putting full stops after *goodliest* and *dropt*.

Lines 20-1 are difficult. ' It is not clear what sense can be made of it ' (W. A. Wright). ' It is doubtful if any meaning can be got out of these words' (W. J. Craig).   Those editors who are adverse to violent changes generally follow Boaden and Singer in taking *like* to mean ' like sunshine and rain ' and explaining *a better way* adverbially as equal to ' but in a better way as being more beautiful ', after which they put a semicolon.   But certainly this is very unnatural.   Therefore a great many people have thought the text corrupt, and the Cambridge edition particularizes how the imagination of emendators has run riot.   A few would change *like* and read

> Were link'd a better way,
> or   Were link'd in bright array.

Others retain *like*, and then set about discovering what her smiles and tears may have been like.   Only one letter needs to be changed in order to produce the readings :

> Were like a better day ;
> Were like a better May—

but then *better* is not very good ; why not, therefore, go on changing :

> Were like a bitter May ;—
> or   Were like a wetter May.

No doubt, this last conjecture (Theobald's) is highly ingenious ; only it may be objected that the description does not suit the traditional notions concerning the climate of the month of May ; hence, obviously, Heath suggests :

> Were like an April day.

Other conjectures are :

> Were like a chequer'd day ;
> Were like a bridal day ;
> Were like a bettering day ;

but the inventor of the last emendation is honest enough to say : ' But this is no more satisfactory than the rest of the guesses ' (W. J. Craig).

Now, to my mind, the πρῶτον ψεῦδος of all these random shots is due to our emendators' attempts to make the passage into natural English and good common sense without noticing who the speaker is and what would be in keeping with his mental attitude.   But it so happens that although the speaker is merely a nameless ' Gentleman ', whom we meet with in two small and insignificant scenes only (Act III,

Sc. i, and here), yet we see what kind of man he is : a courtier, second cousin to Osric, and, like him, fond of an affectedly refined style of expression. It is impossible for him to speak plainly and naturally ; he is constantly looking out for new similes and delighting in unexpected words and phrases. The number of similes and comparisons is relatively very small in *King Lear* ; the iniquities and cruelties of life seem at that period to have made Shakespeare forget the fondness of his youth for verbal refinement and a smooth versification ; his style has become unequal and his verse uneven, and the play is powerful by virtue of its very ruggedness. In the middle of the play however—in a subordinate part, so unimportant for the action of the play that some of the finest things of Act III. Sc. i and the whole of Act. IV. Sc. iii can be left out of the play (see the Folio)—Shakespeare introduces a gentleman, who is above all a stylist, as the reader of these two scenes will easily notice. Note also especially his words ' in brief '.

This, then, is the way in which I should read the passage in question, changing only the punctuation :

> You have seen
> Sunshine and rain at once ; her smiles and tears
> Were like—

[pronounced in a rising tone, and with a small pause after *like* ; he is trying to find a beautiful comparison, but does not succeed to his own satisfaction, and therefore says to himself, ' No, I will put it differently.']

> —a better way :

[' I have now found the best way beautifully to paint in words what I saw in Cordelia's face.']

> those happy smilets
> That play'd on her ripe lip seem'd not to know
> What guests were in her eyes.

OTTO JESPERSEN.

UNIVERSITY OF COPENHAGEN.

AN EDDIC HOMAGE TO WILLIAM SHAKESPEARE

(Culled from Eddic poems)

Nótt varð í bœ, nornir kvómu
þær er öðlingi aldr um skópu,
þann báðu fylki frægstan verða
ok buðlunga beztan þykkja.

'Twas night, the Norns came;
they shaped the atheling's life;
they bade him achieve highest fame,
and be deemed best of kings.

Sneru þær af afli örlögþáttu
ok und mánasal miðjan festu;
þær austr ok vestr enda fólu,
þar átti lofðungr land á milli.

They twisted a-main the strands of
  fate,
in the midst of the moon-hall fastened
  they them;
east and west hid they the ends;
the land between was the king's own
  land.

Rúnar munt þú finna ok ráðna stafi,
er fáði fimbulþulr ok gerðu ginnregin
ok reist rögna hroptr.

Runes shalt thou find, riddles, and
  staves,
carved by the bard of all bards, by
  the gods most high,
carved by him who is the gods' own
  voice.

Hugrúnar skaltu kunna,
þú skalt hverjum vera
geðsvinnari guma,
fullr skalt ljóða ok líknstafa
góðra galdra ok gamanrúna.

Runes of the mind shalt thou know;
thou shalt be wiser of thought
than any of men;
full of song shalt thou be, of staves
  of mercy,
of goodly charms, and runes of joy.

Málrúnar skaltu kunna,
mun þér æ hógdrægt
úr hugarfylgsnum,
   sorg og gleði,
   ástir allar,
sem eiga menskir menn.

Runes of speech shalt thou know;
ever easily shalt thou draw forth
from the mind's hidden places
   sorrow and joy,
   and all the loves
that man and woman ever have
known.

þat eru bókrúnar, þat eru bjargrúnar,
   ok allar ölrúnar,
   ok mætar meginrúnar
hveim er þær kná óviltar ok óspiltar
sér at heillum hafa,
njóttu ef þú namt
unz rjúfask regin.

These are the book-runes, the runes
   of protection,
   and eke, too, the ale-runes,
   and precious runes of power,
for him who, unmarr'd and unspoilt,
   can use them for luck.
Have thou joy in them, if thou hast
   learnt them,
   Until the twilight of the gods!

JÓN STEFÁNSSON.

I i

PAA VEJ TIL SHAKESPEARE

Jeg mindes, da sig første gang
hans verden aabned for mit syn
(to skarer kun, der skifted ord
og løfted egg for deres huse)—
hvor, lænet frem med hævet bryn,
mens hjærtet hamred bag mit bryst,
jeg hørte trolddoms-talen bruse :
en storm af glans imod mig for,
som soljag efter regn paa vang,
en vældig sang
om ildrødt had og blodrød lyst,
et broget tog, der muntert dansed
med blanke øjne kækt til dyst,—
mit barnehoved svimmelt sansed
en fest af liv og lød og klang.

Jeg kom ham siden mere nær
og pløjed selv hans brede hav,
(jeg nikker til dig, tykke bog,
hvis duft om gammel fryd mig minder !)
og rige malme rejsen gav :
livfyldte gennem sindet gaar
endnu de gyldne mænd og kvinder,
som da min tanke fangen tog ;
de svulmed i mig, en og hver,
og han især,
i hvem al ungdoms hjærte slaar ;

TRANSLATION

ON THE WAY TO SHAKESPEARE

I remember the first time his world opened
itself to my view (only two crowds of men who
bandied words and lifted their swords for their
houses), how I, leaning forwards with arched
brows, while my heart hammered behind my
breast, heard the sounding surge of the wizard's
tale : a gale of splendour rushed towards me, like
sun-chase after rain on a meadow, a mighty song of
fire-red hate and blood-red joy : a motley multitude
merrily danced bright-eyed and brave to the strife ;
—my childish senses giddily drank in a feast of life
and colour and clangor.

I came nearer to him later on, and ploughed
his broad ocean (I nod to you, big book,
whose odour reminds me of old joys) ; and rich
ores the voyage gave : yet they flit through
my mind full of life, the golden men and women
who took my thought in thrall ; they grew and
took shape in me, each of them, he more than
all, in whom youth's heart beats for ever.

med smil og samhu, ynk, elende
jeg favned deres sang og kaar :—
og loved ham, der højt i hænde
en sol for hele verden bær.

Men nu jeg bor i Kedars land
og luder panden tungt mod høst,
(nu mens Assyrerhærens hæl
pedantisk grumt paa jorden træder)
jeg takker mest, at jeg hans røst
har nemmet i hans eget sprog
og kendt, hvor sødt og rigt det kvæder,
at jeg har følt hans væne sjæl,
hjembaaren paa den hvide strand,
en engelsk mand,
engduftig, adelsindet, klog,
med folkets aand i lysest flamme :—
hvor højt end manden stiger, dog
hans rødder randt af ættens stamme,
han er som den og den som han.

NIELS MØLLER.

Laughing and sympathetic, full of compassion and horror I took to my breast their song and their fate,—and praised him who high in his hand lifts a sun for the whole world.

But now when I am dwelling in Kedar's land, bending my brow wearily towards the harvest (now while the heel of the Assyrian army, pedantic, savagely tramples upon the earth) I give my deepest thanks, that I have heard his voice in his own language, that I have known how sweet and rich is its song, that I have felt his fair soul, home-born on the white coast—an Englishman, meadow-odorous, noble-minded, wise, showing the people's spirit in purest flame : for how loftily soever the man soars, yet his roots sprang from the stem of the race ; he is like it and it is like him.

NIELS MØLLER.

COPENHAGEN.

SHAKESPEARE

WHAT different attitudes have men assumed towards the Master! Some there be—a strange multitude—who pretend he has not written a line of the works that bear his name. In Russia a most famous writer, and in Great Britain a well-known contemporary dramatist, pretend that much of the recognition accorded to these works is due to their flattery of the upper classes. Some American critics would force the poet back into his century, would deny that he had raised himself above it, and would attribute to him its prejudices and conventions. A recent essay, on the man and his personal history, mainly dwells upon his alleged vanity and weakness, imputed to him by the essayist, and concludes with the statement that it is possible to honour Shakespeare, impossible to worship him. With millions of others I do the impossible, and I do it without shame. In all these judgements I see evidence of a certain unwillingness to bow before the truly great.

Some have even seen a degradation in the fact that Shakespeare wore a kind of livery as King's player; that in August 1604, as a groom of the chamber, he attended the Spanish ambassador in Old Somerset House. Surely he did not find it derogatory to take part in such graceful courtesies. Before the time of Shakespeare Clément Marot was groom of the chamber to Marguerite de Valois; later, Molière held the same position at the Court of Louis XIV. Was there humiliation for Shakespeare in gradations of rank, that necessity for 'degree', for which Ulysses in *Troilus and Cressida* is the spokesman?

More questionable was Shakespeare's position towards the public and its conquering puritanism. There was no stir in London when he gave up the theatre and forsook the town. There was no parting feast for him. His contemporaries could hardly be expected rightly to appraise his greatness. That was the task left for posterity.

With our imperfect knowledge we dare not attempt to define the human weaknesses that may have been his. It was no weakness in him that he was a poet and not a Garibaldi. The sole thing we really know is his genius—that genius which still astonishes the world, and which he lavished so prodigally, that he did not even gather its output into books, but left half of his plays unprinted at his death.

COPENHAGEN, DENMARK. GEORGE BRANDES.

DET er ikke stort mere end hundrede Aar siden, at William Shakespeare „opdagedes" af den Danske Skueplads.

Den 12. Maj 1813 gik det første Shakespeare'ske Skuespil, *Hamlet*, over den danske Scene, indført og oversat af en dansk Skuespiller, Peter Foersom.

Nu er der vel næppe i Danmark en Skoledreng, som ikke kender den store Brites Navn, og der er ikke nogen fremmed Klassiker, der er udkommet i saa mange Oversættelser eller saa mange Udgaver.

Der er vist ikke nogen dannet Mand i vort lille Land, som ikke har sin Shakespeare staaende paa Boghylden, og, hvad mere er, læser ham, tyer til ham som til den altid friske Kilde for Menneskekundskab og Poesi.

Og hvad selve hans egenlige Hjemsted, Scenen, angaar, da har jeg tidt grublet over, hvordan de sceniske Kunstnere bar sig ad, som aldrig lærte Shakespeare at kende.

Talma, som kendte ham, men aldrig fik Lov at spille ham, beklagede sig kort før sin Død bittert over, at han aldrig havde haft en Rolle sit hele Liv.

Jeg tror aldrig, jeg havde faaet Lyst til at beskæftige mig med Theater, hvis jeg ikke havde kendt og elsket Shakespeare, og nu og da havde kunnet være med Sit at tolke ham.

Med ham begynder vi og med ham ender vi.

KARL MANTZIUS.

DANMARK.

„PERSONALITY" ELLER „IMPERSONALITY"

AT det Shakespeareske Drama er ét stort „Spejl af Tilværelsen", en blot Konkylje, hvori alle Livets Stemmer genlyder,—det er smukke Talemaader, der umuligt kan tages bogstavelig. Hvor megen Virkelighed der end indgaar og skinner igennem i Digtningen og hvormange boglige Kilder den ogsaa har øst af,—ingen vilde dog nægte, at der i *Hamlet* og *Othello* er bygget noget op, som ikke før existerede i Virkeligheden og Bøgerne, er gjort en personlig Indsats i Tilværelsen. Ikke blot, at det, visér i Stykkerne, ikke faktisk er foregaaet før; men det er *anderledes* end Virkeligheden, ligner langtfra helt virkeligt Liv og rigtige Mennesker. Og ikke blot dette; men Personerne og Tildragelserne har som en fælles, fremmed Atmosfære om sig, ledes som af en egen „Spiritus rector", mærkes hele Tiden reflekterede i en følende og dømmende Bevidsthed, der søger at sætte sig i Stedet for *vor*. Naar vi stødes over et og andet i *Taming of the Shrew* eller i *All's Well*, er det ikke blot, som vi i Livet vilde stødes ved en altfor entreprenant Helena, en altfor massiv „Afretning" af en Hustru, men det er Aanden, hvori det er fremstillet, som vi fornemmer, Bedømmelsen deraf, som vi mærker, Digteren vil gøre ogsaa til vor, og som vi protesterer mod. Saaledes virker et Spejl og en Konkylje ikke paa os.

Men derfor er Dramaet heller ikke et Spejl af den londonske Skuespiller og „Mermaid"—Stamgæstens Personlighed, en Genlyd af hans Indres Stemmer. Det er allerede en Illusion, naar man gennem Lyrikerens Sang tror at høre Personens levende Stemme—*den* lyder ak! tit ganske anderledes,—men endnu længere er Vejen fra Dramaet tilbage til Digteren. At „sweet Master S." skulde have gaaet og jamret over „en mørk Dames" Troløshed eller harmedes over unge Menneskers Utaknemmelighed til han maatte skaffe sig Luft i *Antonius og Cleopatra* eller *King Lear*, eller have gaaet og grublet over Demokrati og Aristokrati, til han maatte udlade sig i *Coriolan*, det vil rimeligvis de fleste vægre sig ved at tro. Men hvem kan overhovedet tro, at blot nogen videre Brøkdel af alt det, der tænkes og føles, der bevæger sig og brydes i den shakespeareske Digtnings Sjæl, skulde have kunnet rummes *in natura* i et enkelt Mennebryst og have været virkelige Faktorer i et personligt Menneskeliv ? Og selv de Meninger og Følemaader, der synes at meddele sig af Stykkerne som Digterens egne, viser sig saa indbyrdes modstridende og af saa forskelligt Naturel, saa forskelligt Kulturniveau, at de saa at sige umuligt lod sig forene i én Personlighed, uden at den maatte sprænges. Det er jo ikke blot, at man ud af Stykkerne har læst (og kan læse) stik modsatte Lærer om Alkoholisme og om Dyrebeskyttelse, om det sociale Problem og Kvindeemancipation ; ikke blot, at man af ét og samme Stykke har læst (og kan læse) stik modsatte politiske Tendenser ud. Men det er især dette, at man Gang paa Gang finder en Følelseskultur, saa høj, en Forstaaelse af Livet og Samfundet, saa dyb, en saa stor Kundskabsmasse endelig paa mange Omraader, at det maa beskæmme selv en dannet Nutidslæser, og Side om Side dermed træffer man en Uvidenhed og Naivitet, en Følelsesstumphed og Raahed, der synes langt mere at passe for en ustuderet Landhandlersøn og Skuespiller Anno 1600.

Sikkert staar det nu meget ringere til med den Enhed i Menneskets Bevidsthedsliv, som Psykologerne kalder Jeget, Personligheden, end de vil bilde os ind. Og paa Elisabethtiden var der,—som man véd—en Løshed og Elasticitet i Folks aandelige Sammenhæng, som gjorde det disparate og modsigende temmeligt foreneligt. Men den digteriske Genius, og saaledes ogsaa dens største Paradigma, kan man sikkert kun forstaa ved at jævnstille den med den Slags abnorm Forvandling og Mangedobling af Selvet, som man lærer at kende gennem Suggestions- og Hypnose-Fænomener. Gennem den enestaaende „Leder", som Digteren er, er det paa en Maade virkelig Burleighs og Essexs, Sidneys og Raleighs, Montaignes og Bacons Stemmer, der taler i Shakespeares Dramer, uden at han selv véd af det eller selv er bleven en Burleigh eller Montaigne derved. Og paa samme Maade er det Mordets og Ærgerrighedens, Elskovens og Skinsygens Aander, der ud af nogle Ord i Holinshed eller Plutark eller en Novelle er faret i „Mediet" under den digteriske Hypnose og opfører deres „fighting" „in his heart", medens hans eget „Selv" forbliver uberørt. Almindelige Dødelige „sætter sig ind i andres Sted" ɔ: Ved at tænke os ind i andres ydre og indre Situation vækker vi i os de Tanker og Følelser, *vi* vilde have haft under disse Forhold. Men i Shakespeare har (Forestillingen om) Moren, der i Desperation ituslaar sit Kæreste, taget Eneherredømmet for et Øjeblik, og det er dette fremmede Barbarjeg, der kysser og kvæler paa én Gang, og som „vilde dræbe hende og elske bagefter". Titus Andronicus, der sindsforvildet af alt, han har lidt, sender Klagebreve op til Guderne, eller det italienske Pigebarn, der i sit forelskede Sværmeri beder Natten, naar hendes Romeo engang skal dø, klippe ham ud i smaa Stjærner til at lyse paa Himlen,—det er ikke *sig*, Shakespeare her sætter i andres Sted, det er en veritabel Tilbageskruen af Sjælen til et primitivere Stade og ud derfra en Forestillingsproduktion, der slaaende ligner Naturfolks eller Barnets. Og paa tilsvarende Maade kan Shakespeare ved Selvsuggestion naá op over sig selv og sin Tid. Naar Henrik IV paa sit Dødsleje taler til sin Søn om Kronens Ansvar og Fristelser, har den digtede Figur og Situation for et Øjeblik suggereret Digteren en Livsvisdom og politisk Erfaring, der ligger langt over hans normale Bevidstheds Niveau. Og naar Jacques sidder og græder over den saarede Hjort eller Lear lærer i Medfølelse rent fysisk at kunne fryse og hungre med de Ulykkelige,— saa er en saadan Forfinelse af Følsomheden og Udvidelse af Sympatien ligesom en Foregribelse af et udover Shakespeares Tid liggende Kul- turniveau. Selv Kundskaber og Indsigter i Naturen og Livet, som laa langt forud for Tiden, synes jo ofte i Indgivelsens Stunder at dukke op i ham.

„ Myriad-minded " er Shakespeares Værk ikke som et tusindprismet Spejl for alle Tilværelsens Straaler, og ikke heller som Udstraalen af et tusindsjælet Personlighedsliv. Men i sine Skaberøjeblikke frembragte denne Digteren blandt alle Digtere—under Bøgernes, Livets, Fortidens, Samtidens tusindfoldige Medarbejderskab—*ny* Natur, *ny* myriad-minded Virkelighed. Virkelighed—saa lidet det end var en Gengivelse af det forhaandenværende—saa autentisk at Lægen studerer Sindsyge og Juristen Forbrydertyper i „ Shakespeare's Works " med samme Tillid og Udbytte, som Ungdommen lærer at elske og sværme og Manddommen at forstaa og ville „ this world's eternity " af dem.

En personlig Nyfrembringelse i eminentest Grad, men bestaaende i en „ Depersonalisation " af den abnormeste Art,—saaledes, forekommer det mig, maa Svaret lyde paa Spørgsmaalet om „ personality " eller „ impersonality " af Shakespeares Digtning.

VALD. VEDEL.

COPENHAGEN.

HAMLET I SVERIGE

SHAKSPERES betydelse för Sverige kan icke mätas enbart med en enkel uppräkning af de arbeten af hans hand, som uppförts å svenska scener eller af de öfversättningar, som utkommit från svenskt tryck. Läsningen af hans verk i original eller öfversättning har gjort honom till en af de författare, hvilka ingå i högre svensk bildning och med undantag af vissa religiösa skriftställare kan väl ingen utomskandinavisk diktare göra honom rangen stridig såsom den, hvars verk äro innerligast tillägnade af för litteraturen intresserade svenskar.

Men länge dröjde det, innan han blef allmännare känd här. Enstaka uttalanden, vare sig berömmande eller klandrande, hade väl förekommit af svenska litteraturkännare under slutet af 1700-talet men det dröjde nära tva sekel efter hans död, innan något af hans skådespel förelåg fullständigt i svenskt tryck. År 1813 tolkades nämligen *Macbeth* af den store svenske författaren, historikern Erik Gustaf Geijer kort efter dennes återkomst från en resa till England.

Men enstaka andra stycken hade redan förut gått öfver svensk scen, företrädesvis i landsorten, där ambulerande sällskap bl. a. hade *Romeo and Juliet*—efter en fransk omarbetning—på sin repertoar på 1780 talet.

I Göteborg, hvilket hade förbindelser med England, uppfördes *Hamlet* redan 1782, flere årtionden innan den gick öfver scenen i Sveriges hufvudstad. En helt ung skådespelare, Andreas Widerberg, som 1786 vid endast tjugo års ålder blifvit direktör för teatern i Göteborg, lät nämligen redan året efter—den 24 Januari 1787—till firande af konung Gustaf III:s höga födelsedag uppföra ' Hamlette, Sorgespel i 5 akter från engelskan skrifven af den berömde Shakspere.' ' Denna stora piece '—heter det i annonsen—' som för första gången upföres å Svensk Theater har på alla språk vunnit förtroende.' Man började spela klockan fyra ' i anseende til Piecens längd och de mange förändringarna af nya dekorationer.'

Widerberg spelade själf hufvudrollen. Han var en utmärkt aktör hvars bildsköna utseende, välljudande organ och fint nyanserade spel högeligen berömmes af samtiden. Han hade ' ett hufvud à l'antique,' och hvad han sade tycktes komma ur själens djup, äfven om han till en början—enligt en samtida brefskrifvare—lär hafva varit en smula affekterad.   De få och sparsamma uttalanden, som lokalpressen äganar hans Hamlet, tyda på en mindre vanlig framgång.   Han hade, heter det, ' så behagligt visat sin styrka i Theatraliska vägen at Piecen nu för fjärde gången begäres.'

Osäkert är om denna första svenska Hamletöfversättning skett direkt efter engelskan eller med begagnande af någon fransk mellanlänk. Snarast får man tro det senare.   Ty när år 1791 *Hamlet* ånyo upptages å Göteborgs teater förklaras det, att ' öfversättningen är ny och till det närmaste följt engelska originalet.

Andreas Widerberg, vår förste Hamletframställare, hade då redan lämnat Göteborg och anställts vid hufvudstadens scen.   Man vet icke hvem det var som efter honom axlat danaprinsens kappa.

Märkligt nog fann icke den unge Widerberg tillfälle att öfverflytta sina Hamletstriumfer från Göteborgsscenen till den kungliga teatern i Stockholm.   Hit hade ännu icke förståelsen för den store egelske skalden hunnit tränga in.

Emellertid hade andra vindar börjat blåsa under det nya seklet. De unge, svenske nyromantiker, som sökt storma det akademiska fästet omkring år 1810, hade bland annat Shaksperes namn å sin fana.   Dock ger, märkligt nog, ingen af de egentliga nyromantiske bilderstormarne— de s. k. fosforisterna—något enda bidrag till tolkningen af Shakspere. Hvad särskildt *Hamlet* angår, utkommo ungefär samtidigt tvänne öfversättningar däraf 1819 och 1820, båda på prosa, den ena af P. A. Granberg, den andra af biskop O. Bjurbäck.

Under det att Bjurbäck i inledningen till sin öfversättning förklarar, att han icke öfversatt *Hamlet* för att uppföras utan blott för att läsas, hade däremot Granbergs tolkning uppförts å kungliga teatern den 26 Mars 1819.

Denne Granberg tillhörde så långt ifrån den nya romantiska skolan, att han tvärtom räknades till den ' akademiska ' eftertruppen, var en af svenska akademiens pristagare och utsatt för de unge romantikernes löje och hån.

Hans öfversättning var ' fri ', han säger sig ha velat gå en medelväg mellan att troget följa originalet och att omstöpa eller förvända det, han har bibehållit originalförfattarens anda men ' för att ej framställa originalets former med sådana proportioner, som möjligen kunde åstad-komma något obehagligt intryck ' hade han begagnat rättigheten att göra en fri öfversättning och stundom undvikit eller beslöjat vissa uttryck.

Öfversättningen var som sagdt helt igenom på prosa, med undantag för det inlagda skådespelet, som var affattadt på alexandriner.

Denna öfversättning eller rättare sagdt bearbetning blef rätt illa bedömd af den nya skolans kritik. Desto mer loford erhöll den sceniska framställningen, åtminstone hvad vidkommer titelrollen, som utfördes af Gustaf Fredrik Åbergsson (f. 1775, †1852), hvilken helt och hållet tillhörde den franska ' klassiska ' skolan.

En ung litteratör, Georg Scheutz, som själf förut öfversatt *Julius Caesar* och som året därefter tolkade *Köpmannen i Venedig* gaf luft åt sin förtjusning i ett bref till en vän : ' Åbergsson, som i Paris studerat Talma i denna ytterst svåra roll och dessutom själf var en skicklig acteur förut, spelade så mästerligt, att hvarken jag eller de flesta andra åskådare sett något dylikt. Lord Strangeford, skall hafva yttrat åt f. d. Envoyén i London, baron Rehausen—således åt en gammal bekant, som själf kunde bedöma om han smickrade eller ej—att piecen i allmänhet gafs fullt ut så väl som den ges i England och att han aldrig sett den lyckas så i något annat land på kontinenten. . . . Alla som jag hört tala härom försäkra, att de ej kunna anse ha sig sett något skådespel förut.'

Liknande uttalanden förekomma i andra bref och i tryck : ' Utgången af representationen var den lyckligaste ett skådespel i Sverige någonsin vunnit, publiken stannade begärligt att se detta herrliga verk och bortgick med en rörelse, som tydligen visar, att det äkta poetiska öfverallt träffar poetiska sinnen.'

Ja, det berättas, att den akademiska skolans främste poet, den gamle Leopold, som eljes haft rätt omilda ord om Shakspere, likväl förklarat, då han lämnade föreställningen, att ' den där käringhistorien tog sig verkligen bättre ut än jag trodde.'

Det dröjde innan *Hamlet* fick en öfversättning, som kom originalet nära.

Bland de Shakespearestycken, som vid 1820 talets mid tolkades af J. H. Thomander—nämligen *Antonio och Kleopatra, Konung Richard den andre, De muntra fruarna i Windsor, Som Ni behagar* och *Trettondagsafton*—och af K. A. Nicander—*Othello*—befann sig *icke Hamlet*. Stycket hade likväl alltjemt spelats i den gamla öfversättningen, och bland hufvudrollens framställare äro att nämna de berömde skådespelarne O. U. Torslow (f. 1801, d. 1881) och Georg Dahlqvist (f. 1807, d. 1873). Vid århundradets midt erhöll Shakspere en fullständig, verkligt klassisk öfversättning af professorn i Lund Karl August Hagberg (f. 1810, d. 1864). Denne, som var en ' antiromantiker,' hade alltifrån 1840 sysslat med denna öfversättning och utgav Shaksperes alla verk under åren 1847-1851. Genom denna förträffliga tolkning hade, som en berömd svensk kritiker och skald yttrat, det Shakspereska dramat, hunnit slå så fasta rötter inom vårt poetiska medvetande, att det endast erfordrades den yttre framställningen för att blifva vår innersta andliga tillhörighet.

En sådan kom nu sentomsider Shakspere till del.

År 1853 gjorde *Hamlet* sitt återinträde på teatern i Hagbergs nya, versifierade tolkning behandlad för scenen af Nils Arfvidsson. Hufvudrollen utfördes då af Edvard Swartz (f. 1826, d. 1897)—Sveriges berömdaste Hamletframställare—som skapade en drömmande, vek, något romantisk, högeligen sympatisk bild af danaprinsen, med groteska afbrott i de scener, där dan låtsar vansinne. Den utmärkte svenske litteraturhistorikern, professor Schück, som redan för mer än trettio år sedan författat en Shaksperemonografi, som nu till jubileet skall utkomma i helt ny omarbetning, yttrar att först genom Swartz' spel blef det honom klart, att ' den unge prinsen var en konungason ej blott i Danmark utan ock i andens rike.' Swartz' framställning blef ock för långa tider bestämmande för svensk uppfattning af Hamlet.

En mera realistisk, i vissa afseenden rätt originell tolkning, som gjorde mycken lycka, särskildt i landsorten under 1870-80 talen var August Lindbergs (f. 1846). Den senaste, mera märklige svenske Hamletframställaren är Anders de Wahl (f. 1869), som sedan något år tillbaka spelat rollen å Stockholms kungliga scen. Han lägger särskild tonvikt på det hurtiga renässansdraget och älskar gifva Hamlet såsom.

> The expectancy and rose of the fair state,
> The glass of fashion and the mould of form.

Alltjämt tillhör Hamlet den svenska teaterns mest älskade gestalter och skall så länge förblifva. Ingen af Shaksperes öfriga skapelser kan härutinnan täfla med honom.

Shakspere har gifvetvis i hög grad påverkat svenske sorgespelsförfattare under 1800 talet alle spår af hans inflytande är skönjbart äfven hos en på modern ande som Strindberg. Hvad särskilt *Hamlet* vidkomner finner man drag af hans snårmod och vankelmod i *Erik XIV* (1846) af Johan Börjesson (f. 1790, d. 1866). Men afgjordt mest inflytande från *Hamlet* företer det vackra sorgespelet *Daniel Hjort* (1862) af den finskfödde skalden Josef Julius Wecksell (f. 1838, d. 1907), hvilket otvifvelaktigt är den mest lyckade Shakspereefterbildning å svenskt språk.

KARL WARBURG.

STOCKHOLM.

SHAKESPEARE AND THE NORWEGIAN DRAMA

WHEN in 1843 Henrik Wergeland, the first great poet of modern Norway, in memory of his youthful voyage to England and France, saluted England as the sea-beaten ' fortress of freedom, reared by God with high bastions facing the thrones of Europe ', and hailed the Shakespeare Cliff, looming afar, as the ' marble-white pedestal, from which the Queen of Victory herself was controlling the globe ', this epoch-making poet of ours had during more than a decade been endowing Norse literature with a new style, largely founded on a passionate love of Shakespeare. ' I do not read much literature,' Wergeland writes in an early letter, ' because nothing else satisfies me, since I have been reading and re-reading Shakespeare.'

The name of William Shakespeare is thus to Norsemen associated with the vernal awakening of Neo-Norwegian poetry, a spring-tide of lyric enthusiasm which the nation looks back upon with feelings similar to those with which we witness the recurring miracle of the early anemones, lifting their sweet blue eyes from amidst the snow.

In Norway, as elsewhere, Shakespeare has been the greatest of liberators, the widener and enhancer of lyric and dramatic utterance. To Wergeland he was the wonderful teacher who gave permission to break all rigid rules, and—far away from the emptied schoolroom— to roam at liberty through the whole wild realm of nature. That master's school seemed to be nature's own paradise of perfect freedom.

The discovery of Shakespeare was to most of the leading poets and dramatists of the ' romantic revival ' an event of almost as great an importance as the rediscovery of the ancient classics had been to the artists of the Renaissance. In the times of Elizabeth and James, Shakespeare had been a singularly great English poet. Before the dawn of the nineteenth century he had become a world-poet, adopted by all nations, ' free of the city ' in every community, everywhere hailed as a deliverer from the reign of unimaginative prose and pedantic propriety. The Shakespearian boldness in thinking by metaphor seemed to draw a veil of abstractions from off the world. From Shakespeare, more than from any other poet, even Homer not excepted, Goethe, Shelley, Victor Hugo, Wergeland, and I dare say even Björnson, learnt the art of translating general ideas back into human nature's vernacular of vivid images. Shakespeare's metaphoric vision of the world of the soul seemed to cure men's eyes of a partial blindness. It was felt as if ' the ice melted within their eyes ', to use the bold image of a great Danish sculptor.

Boundless freedom of utterance and emotion, the boldest frankness and sincerity of thought and world, all-embracing sympathy with almost every type of human character, and a clairvoyant insight into the twilight regions of the soul, such were the principal sources of inspiration which continental and British poets alike found in the old and ever-new works of Shakespeare.

On the Norwegian drama, no less than on our lyric and epic poetry, Shakespeare's influence has left an indelible stamp. Both Ibsen's and Björnson's dramatic art, to be sure, is very largely founded upon the French comedy of Scribe, Jules Sandeau, Legouvé, Augier, and Dumas-Fils, and also (in the case of Björnson) on the far more imperishable *proverbes* of Alfred de Musset. But while the dramatic technique of our two dramatic masters is more indebted to France than to any other country, and while the Danish and German literatures have been adding their free and abundant gifts, two older influences have been exceedingly helpful in broadening and deepening our dramatic and epic vision of life ; the old Norse-Icelandic poems and sagas, with their terse and poignant dialogue and wonderfully quick way of character-drawing, and, on the other hand, Shakespeare. Both to a direct and to an indirect influence from Shakespearian art we owe very much of the breadth and freedom of treatment in such masterpieces as Björnson's trilogy of *Sigurd Slembe* (1863), and Ibsen's great rival play, *The Pretenders* (1864), not to speak of the evident marks of Shakespearian influence in Ibsen's *Lady Inger of Östraat*, Björnson's *Limping-Hulda* and *Mary Stuart in Scotland*, Ibsen's *Emperor and Galilean*, and other plays.

As to the impression made on the Dioscuri of the Norwegian drama by Shakespearian characters, it is indubitable that Hamlet, the enigmatic, the inscrutable, from the very outset has exerted the greatest fascination on Henrik Ibsen's subtle mind. A reflection of his early vision of Hamlet I seem to see in the whole series of Ibsen's most self-revealing studies of character, from Skule and Julian the Apostate to Solness the master builder, Borkman and Rubek. Shakespeare's Hamlet, viewed in a somewhat incomplete light, seems to have helped Ibsen to read the riddle of his own soul. An investigation of this curious point (which can here only be faintly foreshadowed) may even be said to present one of the most promising avenues leading up to the innermost recesses of Ibsen's mind and art.

When young Ibsen visited Dresden and Copenhagen, during a holiday from his arduous duties as stage-poet and assistant-manager of the Bergen stage, he had the good fortune to see *Hamlet* acted by the Pole Dawison in Dresden, and by Höedt in Copenhagen. From several of his characters, such as Lady Inger and still more Duke Skule (in *The Pretenders*), not to speak of the heroes of his latest plays, it seems clear that Ibsen adopted Goethe's view of Hamlet, which, though hardly a fully adequate one, must have admirably suited Ibsen's own frame of mind. The contradiction between aspiration and power of achievement (' motsigelsen mellem higen af evne ') is, according to Ibsen's own statement, the central theme on which his own tragic view of life hinges.

The very prominent part which fate or fortune plays in Shakespeare must have strengthened within Ibsen's mind the fatalistic trend which appears already in his first drama, *Catiline*, written before Shakespeare came within his ken, but probably after he had become acquainted with Schiller and with a Norwegian novelist who had been largely influenced by the German *Schicksals-Tragödie*.

The Goethean vision of Hamlet, as a pure and noble but unheroic soul, doomed to carry the burden of a task too heavy for his shoulders, appears to have been associated by Ibsen with such types of character as Schiller's Karl Moor and Don Carlos, and with his own Catiline and Skule, and even Julian the Apostate,—all of them would-be reformers and idealist leaders of men, but fettered and impeded by some weakness or brittleness of character, which at an inconvenient moment rises like the ghost of some past fault, often in the shape of an avenging Erinys.

From the youthful tragedies of *Catiline* and *Lady Inger of Östraat* to master-plays, such as *Ghosts*, *The Wild Duck*, and *Rosmersholm*, or even to the more or less introspective soul studies of Solness, Borkman, and Rubek, the same tragic view of the revengefulness of past errors (an Ibsenian adaptation of Greek thought) is combined with another tragic theme (assimilated from Goethe's view of Hamlet), viz. the idea of a flaw in an otherwise noble character, which becomes its tragic fate and its doom.

My conclusion is that an early and powerful impression of Hamlet's fate was by Ibsen intertwined with an equally strong impression of tragic fate in German and Greek tragedy and with his own inmost experience of the cruel contradictions and antinomies of life. Quite the greater part of Ibsen's lyric and dramatic work seems to be devoted to the art of inuring, hardening, and acclimatizing himself to living at ease within a world of tragic or grotesque contrarieties.

No work of Ibsen's is more characteristic of his relish for the bitter poignancy of the incongruities of fate than that quaintly humorous poem entitled ' Complications ' (*Forviklinger*), where, to the cithern of Mephistopheles, he sings the tragi-comic love of the apple-blossom and the bee. When the bee came back from his summer ramble, his sweet lady-love, the apple-blossom, who had pledged him her faith, had by an ineluctable process of nature become an unripe fruit, utterly unable any longer to requite his love. Equally untoward was the fate of her other lovers, the mouse and the sparrow.

Throughout the whole unique series of his plays and poems, with very few exceptions, Henrik Ibsen broods upon the ever-varied contradictions between aspiration and fate (or between Nature and Fortune, as Shakespeare would say), and painfully enjoys them! What Ibsen has sought for in Shakespeare, and relished more keenly than any other great modern writer, is the poignancy of tragic fate, the deceitful falsity of Fortune, the tonic or intoxicating bitterness of thwarted desire.

The most eccentric of our great poets seems to owe this debt, above all other dues, to the greatest of British poets, namely, that Shakespeare made it easier for him to cultivate life's bitter herbs in an enchanted garden, which to him, Henrik Ibsen, became an Eden of undisturbed, freely chosen, and recondite delights.

Of all the great Norwegian writers Björnstjerne Björnson seems to have entered with the most hearty and congenial sympathy into Shakespeare's human world. This poet, who as yet is comparatively little known in the English-speaking world, but whom our greatest living historian (I. E. Sars) looks upon as our greatest man and writer, became from his early youth an ardent admirer of Shakespeare, and every now and again put his whole soul into the work of placing great Shakespearian plays upon the stage, first at Bergen, later on in Christiania. It was Björnson who taught some of our actors of genius to impersonate the characters of *Othello*, *Romeo and Juliet*, *A Midsummer-Night's Dream*, *Macbeth*, and many other plays. The vivid sketches which he has left in print of his freely poetic interpretation of *Romeo and Juliet*, *A Midsummer-Night's Dream*, and *Othello*, go to show that what Björnson loved in Shakespeare was above all his wonderful philanthropy, his breadth of sympathy, and depth of compassionate intuition, combined with his never-flagging vivacity and high spirits.

What drew young Björnson more and more strongly to Shakespeare (though Björnson, like Ibsen, could hardly enjoy his plays except through the veil of Danish or German translations) must have been those traits which he himself had in common with the great Briton,—sanity, frankness, buoyancy, passionate impetuosity, infinite tenderness, and a tendency quickly to regain his balance after some overpoise of passion.

Especially during the years when Björnson was the manager of the Bergen Theatre, and when he used to learn by heart the principal parts of the plays to be performed, and to act them with consummate art before his actors, during these years of storm and stress, young Björnson seems to have consorted with Shakespeare as with an exalted comrade and friend, and to have drawn vital strength from his company. He speaks, in one of his writings, of *A Midsummer-Night's Dream* as a play which he looked up to as to a ' guiding star ', on account of its invincible buoyancy of spirit. Probably also because of its infinite lightness of touch. He seems to have found that the suggestive power of Shakespearian comedy made the air lighter to breathe and every phase of life fuller of zest.[1]

As late as 1865, when Björnson had *A Midsummer-Night's Dream* enacted upon the Christiania stage, he writes that ' of all my poetical reading this play has made the greatest impression on me. It is Shakespeare's most imaginative and most innocent work; it entrances by its profound play of the intellect, no less than by the high and humane spirit which co-ordinates and pervades it. I first read this comedy at Eikisdal, when I was writing *Arne*, and when the dark and gloomy impressions of life on which this tale is founded weighed heavily upon my mind. I took the lofty teaching of Shakespeare to heart, and I vowed to sustain that tendency within me which seemed to promise that I might work my way up to the joy-and-fancy world of the *Midsummer-Night's Dream*. . . . This play which has been a guiding star to me, I now long to show to others.'

Some of the songs of *Arne*, and something of the lighter mood

[1] It may be mentioned that Johanne Dybwad, the greatest living actress of Norway, and the impersonator of Portia, Beatrice, Rosalind, and Puck, seems to go to Shakespearian comedy as to a fountain of youth. The Falstaff of Johannes Brun, our greatest comic actor, produced under Björnson's guidance, is said by our elders to have been a marvellous production. Fru Laura Gundersen's impersonation of Portia and Hermione are also reckoned among the very highest achievements of the Norwegian stage.

which transformed the original sketch of this tale and which became afterwards still more pronounced in *A Happy Boy*, seem to have been the outcome of the suggestive power of Shakespeare's most fanciful comedy of love. An important event in young Björnson's own life, his happy betrothal and marriage, chimed in with this influence and helped to make it enduring.

As for tragedy, *Othello* was to Björnson the acme of tragic art. The tremendous contest between Iago's cunning treachery and Othello's and Desdemona's unsuspecting simplicity of heart seems to have appealed to Björnson's psychological curiosity and to his compassion— even with Iago himself—still more strongly than the tragedies of *Hamlet*, *Lear*, and *Macbeth*. According to Björnson's interpretation, Iago's diabolical malice must have been the outcome of an invincible tendency to hurt and torture, due to some cruel disappointment in his own early life.

Of Björnson's impression of Hamlet there are curious traces in *Arne*. But the greatest help for his own personal life young Björnson seems to have drawn from Prince Hal, Shakespeare's most penetrating study of ethical *growth*, a character in whom impetuous and passionate young Björnson seems to have recognized his own self. In the unfinished trilogy about King Sverre and his son, of which only the first play was ever written, Björnson's sense of affinity with Shakespeare's Hal stands revealed to any one who can read between the lines. The probability, guessed at independently by more than one scholar, that Prince Hal is, in a certain degree, Shakespeare's portrait of his own youthful self, makes this trait in Björnson all the more significant. It seems that Henrik Wergeland, too, had been strongly attracted to that very same character.

William Shakespeare has, in short, been of incalculable help in the formation of all our three greatest modern writers, Wergeland, Ibsen, and Björnson. Shakespeare has been their august teacher, and even, in some degree, their monitor and friend. It was Shakespeare, above all others, who taught Björnson and Ibsen to unite tragedy with comedy. It was Shakespeare, perhaps even more than Goethe and Schiller, who taught Ibsen and Björnson much of their art of making a human crowd, or chorus, live intensely and yet orderly and articulately upon the stage. In such great plays as *The Pretenders, Brand, Emperor and Galilean*, and *The Enemy of the People*, by Ibsen, or in Björnson's *Sigurd Slembe, Mary Stuart in Scotland, Sigurd the Crusader, A Bankruptcy, The King*, and *Above Human Strength*, the two Norwegian dramatists have not only adapted the Shakespearian crowd to the requirements of a great variety of plays, but they have sometimes even approached the solemnity of the chorus in Greek tragedy, especially in that unique religious drama, *Above Human Strength*, where free criticism of the old faith blends with deep reverence for the old faithfulness and spirit of love, and where the muses of Tragedy and Comedy join hands and become united in happier concord than perhaps ever before.

At the present moment it would be ungrateful towards Shakespeare's country to forget that the unique dramatic quality of his life-work was in great part due to the dramatic situation in which, nearly four hundred years ago, Shakespeare's nation was placed, and to the heroic action of the English on the great stage of life. As the ancient Greek drama was born during that war of defence and deliverance which saved European culture, and made possible the greatest outburst of creative energy which our globe has ever witnessed, in a similar way the Shakespearian drama, which in some respects outrivalled the Greek, was born during another great war of deliverance, which saved western civilization from being enthralled by the religious and military despotism of a single state.

Four times in the course of four centuries it has fallen to the lot of the English, in conjunction with other nations, to ward off the foundation of a universal monarchy, and to secure for Europe the free interplay of separate and independent nations. I cannot think of any more dramatic way of celebrating a Shakespearian centenary than by acting once more upon the stage of life a heroic drama similar to that which Shakespeare saw enacted before his eyes, even as the British people and its Allies are doing at this present moment. Commemorative festivals are shadowy and almost futile, compared with the resuscitation of the very soul of the great things of the past.

CHR. COLLIN.

THE UNIVERSITY, CHRISTIANIA.

ГЕНІЙ ВИДЯЩАГО СЕРДЦА

Слава высокому Солнцу, золотому оку нашихъ творческихъ дней, четкихъ нашихъ достиженій. Слава серебряному свѣтилу ночей, Лунѣ влюбленной и влюбляющей. Слава разбросаннымъ по небесной шири Звѣздамъ, которыя, владѣя нашими углубленными мыслями, говорятъ намъ безгласно о радости вѣчныхъ перевоплощеній. Слава тѣмъ на Землѣ, кто соединяетъ въ душѣ своей вліянія всѣхъ голосовъ Неба и Земли, чтобы одѣть ихъ въ волнистыя одежды стиха, и отдать ряды этихъ пѣвучихъ красивыхъ призраковъ людямъ. Среди этихъ творцовъ наивысшая слава нѣжному и могучему, всеобъемлющему генію Англіи, Шекспиру.

> Художники, ваятели, поэты, музыканты,
> Строители, искатели, мыслители, пѣвцы,
> Плечами міръ подъявшіе, глядящіе Атланты,
> Вы скрѣпы невѣсомаго, начала и концы.
> Проклятіе-ли въ творчествѣ, восторгъ-ли, благодать-ли,
> Но каждый вѣрный вымыселъ—безсмертный кипарисъ,
> Вся пышность древней Мексики—въ одномъ Кветцалькоатлѣ,
> Семь тысячъ лѣтъ Египетскихъ—въ единомъ Озирисъ.
> Несчетно повторенные юнцы, отцы, и дѣды,
> Стократно милліонные—,, Возьми всю жизнь мою ! ''—
> Вы святы лишь велѣніемъ шуршащихъ крылъ Побѣды,
> Лишь тѣмъ, что я, загрезившій, надъ пропастью—пою.

Такъ могъ бы сказать о себѣ тотъ геній, который своимъ все-чуткимъ сердцемъ обнялъ весь міръ, подслушалъ сочувственно всѣ голоса,—и соловья, и жаворонка, и сову, и вѣдьмъ, и нѣжную дѣвушку, и лепетъ ребенка, и наклоняющія чужую волю, зыбко-чарующія, слова той волшебницы, которая есть Женщина, и дикій воинскій кликъ того властолюбца, который зовется Мужчина. Слава Эвонскаго лебедя—въ томъ, что пѣсня его, родная для

THE GENIUS OF THE SEEING HEART

GLORY to the high Sun, the gold eye of our creative days, of our legible attainments. Glory to the silver lamp of the nights, the Moon, enamoured and enamouring. Glory to the Stars, scattered throughout the heavenly expanse, which, masters of our intentest thoughts, tell us voicelessly of the joy of eternal reincarnations. Glory to those on Earth who unite in their soul the influences of all the voices of Heaven and Earth in order to robe them in the undulating robes of verse, and to give the tale of these sonorous beauteous visions to mankind. Midst these creators, greatest glory to England's all-embracing genius, tender and mighty Shakespeare.

Painters, sculptors, poets, players,
Builders, seekers, thinkers, singers,
Gazing Atlantae that with your shoulders the world have lifted,
Ye are the bonds of the imponderable, the beginnings and the ends.
Be there cursing in your creation, or triumph, or blessing,
Yet is each true concept an immortal cypress,
All the magnificence of ancient Mexico is in Quezalcoatl,
Seven thousand years of Egypt are in Osiris alone.
Youths, fathers, and elders multiplied without number,
In hundreds of millions—' Take thou my whole life ! '—
Ye are holy but at the bidding of Victory's rustling wings,
But in that I, while dreaming, above the chasm do sing.

Thus might speak of himself that genius who with his omni-sensitive heart embraced the whole world, who in sympathy hearkened to all voices—to the nightingale and to the lark, to the owl and to the witches, to the tender girl and to the lisp of the child, to the words which bend the will of others, the surging, bewitching words of that enchantress, which is Woman, and to the wild martial cry of him that loves to rule, which is called Man. The glory of the Swan of Avon is this, that his

родичей его, звучитъ какъ родная, какъ самая родная—и для Испанца, и для Скандинава, и для Русскаго, особенно для Русскаго.

Англійская поэзія, самая богатая и разнообразная, наиболѣе пѣвучая и одухотворенная изъ всѣхъ поэзій Европы, отъ Среднихъ вѣковъ до нашихъ дней,—издавна была любимицей Русскаго читателя. Съ дѣтства мы зачитываемся „Робинзономъ Крузо", „Путешествіями Гулливера", сказками и разсказами Диккенса. Юность наша неразрывно связана съ героями Эдгара По, Байрона, Шелли, и прежде всего—Шекспира. Вмѣстѣ съ Ромео мы учимся красивымъ поцѣлуямъ. Съ Гамлетомъ переживаемъ весь ужасъ раздвоенія личности,—черта особливо-Русская, великолѣпно переданная нашимъ геніемъ Достоевскимъ, который, наряду со столькими, не избѣгъ вліянія Англійскаго творчества. Макбетъ восхищаетъ насъ въ юности той могучестью личнаго порыва, той титанической волей, тѣми отсвѣтами бурныхъ достиженій, за которыя мы, жалѣя его, прощаемъ ему его преступленія. Отелло отвращаетъ насъ отъ внѣшнихъ проявленій низкаго чудовища ревности, и имя его есть формула общежитія нашего, повторное слово, въ ежедневной рѣчи запросто возникающее не только среди образованныхъ людей. Ричардъ Третій соучаствуетъ съ нами, когда мы переживаемъ полосу Демонизма. Переживая сны наши влюбленные, сонъ Весенней ночи и сонъ Лѣтней ночи, мы сочетаемъ наши грезы съ пьянительными грезами Шекспира. Когда, ставъ углубленнѣе и старше, мы хотимъ не только предаваться чувствамъ, но и подвергать ихъ анализу, касаться ихъ лезвіемъ умственнаго разсмотрѣнія, мы не находимъ книги болѣе зачарованной, болѣе тонкой и умной и переполненной всликами сердца, чѣмъ „Сонеты" Шекспира. И въ высшей порѣ нашего самосознанія волшебникъ Просперо магически намъ разскажетъ, что верховная радость достойнаго человѣка—быть, послѣ бури, свободнымъ властелиномъ Острова.

Кроткій и смѣлый, meek and bold, этими двумя словами Шелли опредѣлялъ самого себя. Этими двумя выразительными словами вообще можетъ быть опредѣленъ поэтическій темпераментъ, какъ Англійскій, такъ и Русскій. Соединеніе женственной нѣжности и мужской силы. Твердая непреклонность историческаго завоевателя, въ то же время чрезвычайно наклоннаго къ миру и тишинѣ, любящаго семью, мечтательность, вольный просторъ, и свѣтъ заходящаго Солнца. То, что Англійской душѣ нашептало вѣчное Море, со всѣхъ сторонъ окружающее его родину, намъ, Русскимъ, нашептываютъ наши безконечные лѣса и степи. И тутъ и тамъ—размахъ, сила, величіе,—сила, которая, сознавъ себя таковой,

song, akin to his kinsmen, sounds akin, and most akin, to Spaniard, to Norseman, and to Russian, to Russian most of all.

England's poetry, the most rich and the most varied, the most sonorous and the most spiritualized of all the poetries of Europe, from the Middle Ages to our own days, has for long already been beloved of Russians who read. From childhood we pore over *Robinson Crusoe*, *Gulliver's Travels*, the tales and stories of Dickens. Our youth is indissolubly bound up with the heroes of Edgar Poe, of Byron, of Shelley, and above all, of Shakespeare. Together with Romeo we learn beautiful kisses. With Hamlet we live through the whole horror of divided personality—a peculiarly Russian trait, magnificently rendered by our genius Dostoyevski who, with so many others, has not escaped the influence of England's creative power. Macbeth entrances us in youth with that mightiness of personal impulse, with that titanic will, with those reflexes of stormy achievements for which we, pitying him, forgive him his crimes. Othello repels us from the outward manifestations of the low monster of jealousy, and his name is a formula of our common life, a catchword spontaneously cropping up in everyday speech—not only amongst educated people. Richard the Third shares our lot when we traverse the zone of Demonism. When living through our enamoured dreams, the dream of the Spring night and the dream of the Summer night, we blend our visions with the intoxicating visions of Shakespeare. When, grown older and intenter, we want not only to submit ourselves to sensations, but also to subject sensations to analysis, and to touch them with the blade of mental scrutiny, we can find no book more charmed, more subtle, more profound, or more compact of voices from the heart than Shakespeare's 'Sonnets'. And in the highest moment of our self-realization the magician Prospero wondrously tells us that the supreme joy of a good man is to be, after the tempest, the free lord of an Island.

'Meek and bold'—in these two words Shelley defined himself. In these two expressive words the poetic temperament both of England and of Russia may in general be defined. The union of womanly tenderness and male strength. The firm inflexibility of the historic conqueror, at the same time extraordinarily inclined to peace and quiet, loving family, day-dreams, unfettered expanse, and the light of the setting Sun. What the eternal Sea, on all sides surrounding his mother-country, has instilled into the soul of England, our interminable forests and steppes instil into us in Russia. Here, as there, are amplitude, strength, and grandeur—the strength which, realizing itself as such, immediately feels that for harmony it needs little joys, subtle tenderness, pity for the

тотчасъ ощущаетъ, что, для гармоніи, она нуждается въ маленькихъ радостяхъ, въ тонкой нѣжности, въ жалости къ слабымъ, въ сердечности. Въ этой общности основныхъ вліяній самой Природы, могучей и нѣжной,—самый крѣпкій узелъ между Англійской душой и Русской. Этимъ опредѣлена огромная и глубокая любовь Русскихъ къ Англійскому генію, который самымъ своимъ именемъ символизуетъ Англію въ ея богатствѣ и роскоши достиженій, —къ великому Генію Сердца, Генію Умственнаго Ока, жаждущаго охватить своимъ оглядомъ весь міръ, къ плѣнительному Шекспиру, который,—какъ Звѣзды разбросаны по Небу, —разбросалъ цвѣты по всѣмъ человѣческимъ чувствамъ,—какъ Луна влюбляетъ и влюблена,—чаруетъ всѣхъ, будучи самъ зачарованъ,—какъ Солнце озаряетъ всѣхъ равно,—не имѣлъ несправедливыхъ пристрастій, а озарилъ стихомъ своимъ все человѣческое. И пока звучитъ Англійская рѣчь,—звучать же будетъ она на Землѣ всегда,—не умолкнетъ пѣсня Эвонскаго лебедя, а несчетные Русскіе, внимающіе Славяне, будутъ, слушая, восклицать ,, Слава тебѣ ! ''

К. Бальмонтъ.

1916. Февраль.
Москва.

weak, and affection.   In this community of the fundamental influences of very Nature, mighty and tender, is the strongest link between the soul of England and that of Russia.   It is this that determines the immense and profound love of Russians for England's genius who by his very name symbolizes England in her plenitude and in the splendour of her attainments, for the great Genius of the Heart, the Genius of the Mind's Eye that thirsts to comprehend the whole world in its view, for the enchanter Shakespeare who, like as the Stars are scattered throughout the Sky, scattered flowers over all human senses, and like as the Moon enamours and is enamoured, bewitches all, being himself bewitched, and like as the Sun illumines all alike, had no unjust partiality, but illumined everything human with his verse.   And so long as the speech of England shall sound, and sound on the Earth it always shall, the song of the Swan of Avon shall not cease, and Russians without number, and all Slavs who apprehend, shall as they listen exclaim : ' Glory to thee ! '

K. BALMONT

(TRANSLATED BY NEVILL FORBES).

February, 1916
MOSCOW.

НА ОТМЕЛИ ВРЕМЕНЪ

Заклятый духъ на отмели временъ,
Средь маленькихъ, среди непрозорливыхъ,
На уводящихъ задержался срывахъ,
Отъ страшныхъ вѣдьмъ пріявши гордый сонъ.

Гламисскій танъ, могучій вождь племенъ,
Кавдорскій танъ, въ змѣиныхъ переливахъ
Своей мечты, лишился сновъ счастливыхъ,
И дьявольскимъ былъ сглазомъ ослѣпленъ.

Но потому, что міръ тебѣ былъ тѣсенъ,
Ты сгромоздилъ такую груду тѣлъ,
Что о тебѣ Эвонскій лебедь спѣлъ

Звучнѣйшую изъ лебединыхъ пѣсенъ.
Онъ, кто сердецъ извѣдалъ глубь и цвѣтъ,
Тебя въ вѣкахъ намъ передалъ, Макбетъ.

К. Бальмонтъ

ON THE SHOAL OF TIME

A CONJURED spirit on the shoal of time,
Midst the small, amidst the unperspicacious,
Did linger at the beckoning rapids,
From frightful witches recipient of a proud dream.

The thane of Glamis, mighty leader of tribes,
The thane of Cawdor, in the serpentine iridescence
Of his vision, was robbed of happy dreams,
And blinded by a diabolical spell.

But inasmuch as the world for thee was cramped,
Thou didst accumulate so great a heap of bodies
That of thee the Swan of Avon has sung

The most resounding of all swans' songs.
He who explored the colour of hearts and the depth,
To us in the ages has delivered thee, Macbeth.

K. BALMONT

(TRANSLATED BY NEVILL FORBES).

ВСЕОБЪЕМЛЮЩІЙ

Средь инструментовъ—всѣхъ волшебнѣй лира:
Въ пьянящій звонъ схвативъ текучій дымъ,
Въ столѣтьяхъ мы мгновенье закрѣпимъ,
И зеркало даемъ въ стихѣ для міра.

И лучшій часъ въ живомъ весельи пира,—
Когда поетъ пѣвецъ, мечтой гонимъ,
И есть такой, что вотъ мы вѣчно съ нимъ,
Плѣняясь звучнымъ именемъ Шекспира.

Нагромоздивъ созданія свои,
Какъ глыбы построеній исполина,
Онъ взнесъ гнѣздо, которое орлино,—

И показалъ всѣ тайники змѣи.
Гигантъ, чей духъ—пловучая картина,
Ты—нашъ, чрезъ то, что здѣсь мы всѣ—твои.

К. Бальмонтъ.

THE ALL-EMBRACING

Midst instruments, most magic of all is the lyre :
Forcing fluid vapour into inebriating sound,
We may fix fast an instant in the centuries,
And we give in a verse a mirror for the world.

And the best moment in the live merriment of the feast,
Is when the singer sings, by vision driven,
And there is one such, that behold we are ever with him,
Enchanted by Shakespeare's resonant name.

Amassing his creations, as it were
The blocks of stone for a giant's edifices,
He has raised up a nest, such as an eagle would,

And has laid bare all the secret haunts of snakes.
Giant whose spirit is a floating picture,
Thou art ours through that that here we all are thine.

K. Balmont

(Translated by Nevill Forbes).

PORTIA

Въ янтарномъ забытьи полуденныхъ минутъ
Съ тобою схожія проходятъ мимо жены . .
Въ душѣ взволнованной торжественно поютъ
Фанфары Тьеполо и флейты Джіорджоне.

И пышный снится сонъ : и лавры и акантъ
По мраморамъ терассъ, и водныя аркады
И парковъ замкнутыхъ душистыя ограды
Изъ горькихъ буксусовъ и плющевыхъ гирляндъ.

Смѣняя тишину веселымъ звономъ пира,
Проходишь ты, смѣясь, средь перьевъ и мечей,
Средь скорбно-умныхъ лицъ и блещущихъ рѣчей
Шутовъ Веласкеса и дураковъ Шекспира.

Но я не вижу ихъ : твой утомленный ликъ
Сіяетъ мнѣ одинъ на фонѣ Ренессанса—
На дымномъ золотѣ испанскихъ майоликъ,
На синей зелени персидскаго фаянса.

Максимиліанъ Волошинъ.

PORTIA

In the amber drowsiness of noontide minutes
There pass by women that resemble thee . . .
In my agitated soul there sing triumphantly
The fanfares of Tiepolo and the flutes of Giorgione.

And I dream a gorgeous dream, of laurels and acanthus
On marble terraces, of watery arcades
And walled parks filled with odorous hedges
Of bitter box-trees and ivy garlands.

Replacing silence with the gay hubbub of the feast,
Thou passest by, laughing, midst plumes and swords,
Midst the faces sadly-wise and the flashing words
Of Velasquez' jesters and of Shakespeare's fools.

But I no longer see them : thy wearied face alone
Shines at me on the background of the Renaissance—
On the dim gold of Spain's majolica,
On the blue green of Persia's pottery.

Maximilian Voloshin

(Translated by Nevill Forbes).

ANOTHER RUSSIAN HOMAGE

Вѣчно ввысь вела твоя дорога,
Англія, гордись своей судьбой :
Ты вскормила міру полубога,
Этотъ геній явленъ намъ тобой.

Изъ страданья, пламени и мысли
Сотворилъ сіяющій Шекспиръ
Образы, не мѣря и не числя,
И оставилъ намъ, покинувъ міръ.

И они живутъ среди народовъ,
Въ душахъ дышатъ, борются, поютъ,
И даютъ ростки грядущихъ всходовъ
И благословляютъ и клянутъ.

И моя страна къ ихъ правдѣ вѣчной
Прикоснулась, и моя страна !
Эти образы всечеловѣчны,
И доступна всѣмъ ихъ глубина.

Англія, мы общею судьбою,
Испытаньемъ огненнымъ войны,
Общимъ преклоненьемъ предъ тобою,
Духъ Шекспира, соединены !

Амари (AMARI).

TRADUCTION LITTÉRALE PAR L'AUTEUR

O, ANGLETERRE, ta route te menait toujours plus haut, sois fière de ton sort ! Tu as nourri pour le monde le demi-dieu ; ce génie nous a été révélé par toi !

De la souffrance, de la flamme, et de la pensée, le radieux Shakespeare a créé des images, sans les dénombrer, sans les mesurer, et en quittant le monde nous les a laissés.

Et ils vivent parmi les peuples, respirent, combattent et chantent dans les âmes, et donnent des germes de moissons futures, bénissent et maudissent.

Mon pays communie aussi à leur vérité éternelle, mon pays aussi ! Ces images sont le bien de toute l'humanité et leur profondeur est accessible à tous.

O, Angleterre, nous sommes liés par le sort commun, par l'épreuve de feu de la guerre, et par la commune vénération de toi, esprit de Shakespeare !

AMARI.

SHAKESPEARE—THE PANANTHROPOS

I DO not know Shakespeare. Even I *cannot* know him. But he knows me; he described me, he painted all the secrets of my soul in such a way that in reading him I am finding myself in him. I may be a man with one principal thought, one feeling, one tone, one colour—even *one*. He was *multi*—and *multi*. He never was *alone*. His name is *Legion*. He is almost the *Pananthropos*.

That is the reason why Shakespeare appeals so strongly to us Slavs. The Pananthropos is our ideal, our dream, our untold longing, our expectation, our confusion.

SHAKESPEARE'S KINGDOM

The English people have remained faithful to the panhuman spirit of Shakespeare. They are trying to understand every one in the world, respecting in him—as the Great Poet did—mystically some great principle of the Universe which sends everybody to this life with a secret mission.

It is difficult to know what is the mission of a man or of a nation and to find out the essential good which they may involve in themselves as the justification of their existence. *Temeritas est damnare quod nescias !* said Seneca. Yet Shakespeare knew, and the British nation, being educated upon Shakespeare, know also. Their principle is not to *uniform* the world, but to *multiply* their own spirit by learning and understanding all other spirits in order to be just towards all. Their way is going not towards the Super-man, but towards the All-man; not towards Nietzsche, but towards Shakespeare.

They have the Shakespearian capacity to come out of their own soul and to bear for a while the soul of a foreigner. They understand many more different spirits than anybody else. From the frozen north of Canada to hot and sunny India and South Africa they are learning and teaching, always preferring rather to learn than to teach. Observe, please : on their lips hangs always a question and not an answer ; they are never in such a hurry to answer as to ask. Their understanding of human nature and of the different souls of nations is immense. They respect those different souls which inhabit their great Empire. They love this mosaic of great and small nations, of big and little states, of original customs, of different colours and religions,—this mosaic, which they call the *British Empire*. The founder of this Empire, I think, is Shakespeare. He laid the foundation, he gave the soul, yea, the programme for such a big mosaic body. He, king Shakespeare !

The Empire must be a great one !—was the programme. Shakespeare's spirit was the guarantee for that. It was too large a spirit to occupy only the space from one shore of the British Isles to the other. The Empire must be a multicolour mosaic, a connected *multum*, not a uniform and annoying *unum* ! She became it. And still the Empire must not be either proud or self-sufficient, because ' He that is proud eats up himself ! ' She was not.

Shakespeare is the primordial creator and inspirer of the British Empire ; the Cromwells, Elizabeths, Georges, Victorias, Pitts, and Gladstones,—the secondary masons on the great building. Dare I say —the British world is the great body in which is incarnated the Shakespearian spirit ? To possess such an Empire, to know how to rule it, how to treat it, how to make it move forward towards progress and civilization—for that is needed a special education. This education only Shakespeare could give to the British nation. During the historic period of 300 years of British history, I think Shakespeare may be compared only with the Bible in his influencing that history. (I speak of the nation as a whole, the narrow patriots of this island—if there are any—have nothing to do with Shakespeare and are rather destroyers than supporters of the glorious Shakespeare's realm.)

HE HIMSELF

Pananthropos ! Plato spoke this word, and he thought on the Universe. Dostojevsky spoke the same word, and he thought on Mankind, in the same sense as Saint Paul. But there is no other mortal who was in such a measure a kaleidoscope of mankind by his own mind and his own heart, as *Shakespeare*. He is a real microcosmos. He describes hundreds of men as vividly and truly as if he writes his own biography. For him nothing is too small and nothing too great. He adores no man and he despises no one. Like a Greek god he can easily come down from Olympus and take the form he likes, either of a king or a beggar, either of a man or a woman, of a saint or a criminal. A quick metempsychosis, even a kaleidoscope of the world, —a pananthropos! I ask: Could this man really be a constant friend to anybody, or a constant enemy to anybody?

THE MAN WITH 'MUSIC IN HIMSELF'

Shakespeare has been a man with 'music in himself'. The Slav world possesses no one man with a 'music in himself'. The Anglo-American world possesses two like that—the second has been *Emerson*. The great Slavs were overwhelmed by the painful impression of human suffering in this life in such a measure that they all consecrated their talents to solve the 'social problem' of 'human happiness'. They all are preachers and reformers: Huss, Mickievic, Gogol, Tolstoi, Dostojevsky, Solovjev, the Serbian epic poetry, Gorki, and even Sienkjevic, who is with an artistic quiet manner more than others. 'One imperfection shows me another to make me frankly despise myself!' That can be the best illustration of the negative side of the Slav genii. They all are the broken hearts, the broken glasses; the world cannot reflect itself quite clearly in these glasses. Their writings are rather a cry and a prayer for justice, for mercifulness, brotherhood, humane sympathy and humility. They all believed that human happiness lies beyond the first mountain which separates our generation from the future. 'Zelanie blaga vsemu zivushcemu!' exclaimed Tolstoi, i. e. 'to wish happiness to all living beings.' That was *suprema lex* of his ethics and religion.

Shakespeare has had nerves. That is what Tolstoi never could forgive him. Shakespeare did not preach and cry, but illustrate: even the best and most impressive pages of the Bible are not those with the direct teaching, but those with the illustrating. This is David, and that is Saul—choose! This is Antonio, that is Shylock—choose! Tolstoi left after him a sect, as all the teachers who taught intentionally and directly. Shakespeare left after him no sect, but mankind.

There is no book (not even in Tolstoi's), except the Bible, in which the contrast between good and evil is so plastically represented as in Shakespeare. He is the healthiest genius in history, the healthiest and the most harmonic inwardly. He looks upon life as upon a drama. All the elements that exist in the world in an historic moment (for example, in the time of Pericles, or Caesar, or Henry VIII) are necessary as the components of the world's drama at such a moment. Everything, every thought, word, or feeling counts only if it is interwoven in the great drama, in the action, suffering, intrigue. The evil must be punished, and Shakespeare does punish the evil mercilessly by whip of fate or by his own irony—but still the evil is an unavoidable component of the drama of human life on earth. Why? Shakespeare does not give an answer; the Bible does. Our sin has been the beginning of our earthly tragedy, and suffering was its consequence. Symbolically, when Adam and Eve abandoned Paradise, the Serpent crept out before them. The Serpent—something which *creeps*—became their leader into the world. Is it true? The fact may be doubted, but not the symbol. Shakespeare will give you no direct answer. He will only show you the fugitive scenes of this life, and the mosaic character of the actors on the world-stage. He does not teach anything, he paints only, but by his strong painting he endorses the Bible very much in all what is the greatest, the most noble, the most elevating, the most inspiring in it. He has been and still is the second Bible for his nation and all his admirers. Since the Bible has been brought over to Great Britain there has been no similar *panhuman* document read on this island as Shakespeare.

Shakespeare is a pananthropos—Russian: *Vsechelovjek*—and an *epic* one. Dostojevsky perhaps could be called the *lyric pananthropos*. That is the reason why these two grand races, the Anglo-Saxon and the Slav, are secretly gravitating by their soul towards each other, in spite of all possible temporary divergency of politics. Their ideal is the same—panhuman. Only the expression of their ideal has been different.

In celebrating the tercentenary of the Great Poet of Great Britain, the Slav world will feel once more its deepest thankfulness and endless admiration towards Shakespeare, the epic Pananthropos, in whose magic tongue the Slavs find expressed most clearly their own soul too, yea, their panhuman soul, for which no God's creature on earth is too small to be rejected, and no human glory too great to be compared with God's.

NICHOLAS VELIMIROVIC.

SHAKESPEARE IN SERBIA

In reviewing the countless volumes of Shakespeare literature one is amazed to find scarcely any mention of the share borne by the Serbians and the Southern Slavs in general. One is almost forced to conclude that the Serbs, Croats, and Slovenes—that is to say the Southern Slavs, one single people under three different names—have failed to pay the tribute due to the world's greatest poet, and that they are perhaps the only nation by whom he has been neither studied nor translated, nor even read. Such a conclusion would, however, be quite erroneous.

Shakespeare has been well known to the Serbians for quite a long time. Early in the nineteenth century the Serbian poet Lukian Mušicki (1777–1837), who could read English and was acquainted with English literature, had in his library an English edition of *Hamlet* of 1800, which, it is supposed, he acquired soon after its appearance. The dramatic poet Jovan Sterija Popović (1806–56) modelled a scene in one of his tragedies, written in 1828, on the witches' scene in *Macbeth* ; and in another of his tragedies, written in 1849, he modelled a scene on the handkerchief episode between Iago and Cassio. A literary essay by the lyrical poet Branko Radičević (1824–53), written about 1850, but never published, contains several passages on Shakespeare, whom the author greatly admired and held up as a model. The Serbian lyrical and dramatic poet Lazar Kostić (1841–1910) was a very great admirer of Shakespeare. From 1859 onwards, till his death, he devoted himself to studying Shakespeare, and was the first to really acquaint the Serbian public with the great English poet. He made verse-translations of *Romeo and Juliet*, *Richard III*, *King Lear*, and *Hamlet*, and wrote two essays on the first of these pieces. During the years from 1880 to 1883 Svetomir Nikolajević gave a series of lectures on Shakespeare at the University of Belgrade ; several of these lectures were published in his work *Literary Pages*. The lyrical poet Vojislav Ilić wrote an essay on *Coriolanus* in 1882. A little later, Dr. Ljubomir Nedić, one of the greatest connoisseurs of English literature in Serbia, wrote an excellent study on *Hamlet*. Recently, Professor

Bogdan Popović wrote a paper on *Hamlet*, and another on the Shakespeare-Bacon controversy. Dr. Svetislav Stefanović wrote, also, essays on Shakespeare. Following the example set by Kostić, many of our poets and literary men—among whom we must mention Hagjić, Zečević, Geršić, Stanišić, Jovanović, Stefanović—began to translate Shakespeare's plays and poems. Thanks to them we now possess translations of the following works : *Venus and Adonis*, the *Sonnets*, *A Midsummer-Night's Dream*, *Romeo and Juliet* (dating from 1859, and being the first translation of Shakespeare into Serbian), *King Richard III*, *The Merchant of Venice* (in two translations), *The Taming of the Shrew* (in two translations), *Much Ado About Nothing*, *Hamlet* (in three translations), *Othello* (in two translations), *Macbeth* (in two translations), *King Lear* (in three translations), *Troilus and Cressida*, *Coriolanus*, *Julius Caesar* (in four translations), and *Measure for Measure*.

The Croats likewise possess translations of most of the abovementioned plays, and of a few more besides, to wit—*The Winter's Tale*, *King Henry IV* (Parts I and II), *Twelfth Night*, *As You Like It*, *King Henry V*, and *The Merry Wives of Windsor*. Their principal translators are : Trnski, Badalić, Arambašić, Miletić, Šenoa, Andrić. Croatian literary critics—Miletić for instance—likewise devoted themselves to Shakespeare study.

Through their gifted novelist, Cankar, the Slovenes have given us a translation of *Hamlet*, and through their lyrical poet, Župančic, one of *Othello*.

Since Croatian literature is absolutely the same thing as Serbian literature, the language being identical, and the only difference consisting in the use of two sets of alphabets—the Serbs use the Cyrillic, and the Croats the Latin—we may say that Serbo-Croatian literature possesses translations of twenty-three of Shakespeare's works.

It would be an omission in a notice on Shakespeare in Serbia not to include some remarks on a Serbian festival in Shakespeare's honour. On the tercentenary of Shakespeare's birth, the 23rd April, 1864, the above-mentioned Serbian poet, Kostić, organized a great Serbian festival in Novi Sad, in South Hungary, one of the centres of Serbian literary activity. Some scenes of *King Richard III* were performed that evening, Geršić gave a lecture on Shakespeare, and Kostić wrote a poem entitled *On Shakespeare's Tercentenary*. This poem is glowing with admiration for the genius of the English poet. I give the translation of this poem, shortening it a little :

'*On Shakespeare's Tercentenary.*

' God created the world in six days. The seventh day He rested. Why ? . . .

' He had a special work to do. He wished to place the entire beauty of the creation in one unique life. He desired to mix the light and the darkness, the day and the night, the sweetness of angels and the fire of hell, the unknown depth of the sea and the undiscovered summits of the mountains, the charming song of the nightingale and the hideous hissing of the snake, the summer's glow and the winter's cold, the scent of the rose and the odour of poisonous plants,—and to put all this commingled in one person, in one single creation. And He did it. God created Shakespeare !—

' O greatest spirit, before whom all Britain is on its knees, accept our greetings !

' But I am asking whether our greetings will find thee. And where to find thee ? In Paradise ? No. Paradise is not thy proper place. In Paradise we all have been when we have read thy works. In Hell ? For it is not impossible that thou art there : God, perhaps, punished a mortal being who dared to assume to himself the Almighty's right to create superhuman things. But no. Thy dwelling is in thy works. Thou art surrounded by the heroes and the heroines of thy tragedies.

' Therefore, we shall beg thy creations to transfer our greetings to thee. O great martyr Hamlet, bring our greetings to thy lord ! . . . Thou also, O Juliet, martyress of a divine love ! . . . And thou, duke of Gloucester ! . . . Your king-poet has to hear our voices through your mouth.—

' And it is just that he hear our own voices. For the Serbians are a good people. They have a firm faith. They have tender feelings, and a fine sentiment of honour. Their intelligence is as sharp as a knife.—

' However, we are still poor. We are not yet accustomed to reach the heaven's height. Let thee, O great poet, be our Master in it.'

It would be interesting, perhaps, to quote some verses of Kostić's poem in the Serbian original. The following is a passage of the beginning, from ' He had a special work to do,' to ' God created Shakespeare.' I quote it in Latin characters :

'Na osobit pripremao se rad :
U jednom liku, jednom životu
Stvorenja svu da smesti divotu ;

Svetlost i mrak da stopi, noć i dan,
Angjelsku slast i paklenički plam,
Neproniknuta biser-jezera
Uz nedogledna visa urnebes,
Slavuja glas, sikuta gujskog bes,
Sred letnjeg žara zimogrozan jez,
Uz ružin miris otrovan zadaj ;—
I sve to čudo, sav taj komešaj,
U jedan lik da složi, jedan log.
I ucini :—Shakespeare-a stvori Bog.'

PAVLE POPOVIĆ.

UNIVERSITY OF BELGRADE.

ШЕКСПИР И ЈУГОСЛОВЕНИ

Угрожени, сатрвени Југословенски народ, мученик својих слободо-
умних тежња, вазда жедан уљудбе, науке и учествовања у утакмици
просветљених народа, одавна је пригрлио великог Шекспира и учинио
га узором својих писаца, учитељем својих школа, краљем својих
позоришта.   Нема стога сумње, да сав Југословенски народ пуном
душом учествује у прослави тристагодишњице Авонског Лабуда,
опојен новом чежњом, да га у доба мира изнова поздрави у својој
слободној и уједињеној домовини.

Срђан Туцић.

THE HOMAGE OF THE JUGOSLAVS

THE Southern Slav people, menaced and crushed, the martyr of its liberal-minded aspirations, ever thirsting for civilization and science and for participation in the competition of enlightened peoples, has long since embraced the mighty Shakespeare and made him the model of its writers, the instructor of its schools, the king of its theatres.

There is therefore no doubt that the whole Southern Slav people wholeheartedly takes part in the celebration of the tercentenary of the Swan of Avon, inspirited with fresh longing to greet him anew in time of peace in its free and united mother-country.

SRGJAN TUCIĆ
(TRANSLATED BY NEVILL FORBES).

DLACZEGO MOGŁEM CZYTAĆ SZEKSPIRA

W PIERWSZYCH dniach wojny przybyłem wraz z rodziną do Krakowa, gdzie pozostaliśmy przez kilka tygodni. Były to czasy cieżkiego niepokoju. Troska o kraj i dzieci nie pozwoliła mi sypiać. Często po kilka nocy z rzędu nie mogłem zamknąć oczu, więc, jak się to zwykle czyni w takich razach, próbowałem czytać od wieczora do ranka.

Lecz i to nie prowadziło do niczego. Brałem książkę za książką, powieść za powieścią—i odrzucałem jedną po drugiej. Myśl moja była tak dalece zajęta czem innem, że nie rozumiałem co czytam. Wobec wielkości wypadków jakieś zagadnienia psychologiczne lub dramaty uczuciowe wydawały mi się czemś tak marnem i błahem, że wprost nie mogłem pojąć, dlaczego zajmowały mnie poprzednio.

Ponieważ biblioteka w domu krewnych, w którym się zatrzymałem, była nieźle zaopatrzona, więc przerzuciłem w ten sposób wiele książek, a wreszcie trafiłem na Szekspira.

I wówczas zaszło coś dziwnego. Oto pokazało się, że Szekspira, którego dramaty widywałem na wszystkich scenach europejskich i którego nie wiem ile razy odczytywałem poprzednio, mogę czytać, mogę rozumieć, mogę odczuwać.

Jego jednego !

W pamiętniku, który piszę od czasu wojny, starałem się zdać sobie sprawę z tego faktu. Objaśnienia owe zajmują tam kilka stronic, obecnie jednak przytaczam tylko następujące :

. . . Szekspir, to po Bogu, najpotężniejszy twórca dusz. Dlatego panuje nad czasem i nad wypadkami. Starzeją się pisarze, którzy są przedstawicielami pewnych szkół, pewnej mody, schlebiaczami danej epoki, odtwórcami panujących doraźnie gustów. On nie zestarzeje się nigdy, albowiem tworzy prawdę życia, a prawda i życie są zawsze aktualne. . . .

Tworzy ludzi o rzeczywistych duszach, istotnem ciele i gorącej krwi, którzy mieszkają i żyja dziś między nami tak samo intensywnie, jak żyli przed wiekami. Osobiście mało znam ludzi, z którymibym

WHY I WAS ABLE TO READ SHAKESPEARE

IN the first days of the war I went, together with my family, to Krakow, where we stayed some weeks. It was a time of grave unrest. Care for my country, for my children, would not let me sleep ; often for nights together I could not close my eyes, and therefore, as is usual on such occasions, attempted to read from evening till dawn.

But even that led to nothing. Book after book, tale after tale, I tried and cast away. My thoughts were so absorbed by something else that what I read was meaningless to me. In presence of the magnitude of events, a mere psychological problem or emotional drama seemed so vain and futile that I could hardly believe such things had ever interested me.

Because the library in the house of the kinsmen with whom I was staying was well provided, I cast aside in this manner many a book, until at last I lighted upon Shakespeare.

And then something wonderful happened. Shakespeare—whose plays I had seen upon every European stage, whom I had read and re-read I know not how often—Shakespeare it was alone among all others whom I could read, and understand, and feel.

Him alone.

In the diary which I have kept since the beginning of the war I sought for explanation of this fact. My notes fill several pages but I will only quote the following passage :

' Shakespeare, after God, is the most mighty creator of souls. Therefore he dominates time and event. Those writers become antiquated who are the representatives of certain schools or of a certain fashion, the flatterers of a given period, the leaders of a season's ruling fancy. Shakespeare never ages, for he creates the truth of life, and truth and life are always actual.' . . .

He creates beings possessed of real souls, beings of flesh, warm-blooded, who live and dwell among us to-day with the same intensity as in past ages. Personally I know few people with whom I talk as

rozmawiał równie chętnie, jak rozmawiam z Hamletem ; a po przeczytaniu Burzy, mimowoli przychodzi mi zawsze na myśl, że jakiś współczesny Barnum powinien wyszukać Kalibana i pokazywać go za pieniądze.

Znałem ludzi, którzy kochali się w Mirandzie, a ja sam trochę w Rozalindzie. Przykładów nie będę mnożył, ale przecie Falstaff miał w Polsce brata Zagłobę, a obaj mają wielu żyjących dotychczas braci w Anglii i w Polsce—lubo polscy bracia wychudli dziś tak, że są tylko cieniami dawnych.

Ta sama niesłychana intensywność życia znajduje się w Henryczku Monmouth, w Poinsie, w Romeu, Jagu, Otellu, etc. Takiż sam żywy i ciepły urok kobiecy w Ofelii, Julii, Kordelii lub Imogenie. Lecz moc geniuszu sprawia, że wszystkie te postacie, niemniej żywe od współczesnych, są daleko więcej od nich interesujące, albowiem wszechludzkie porywy i namiętności, ogólne pierwiastki zła i dobra spotęgowane są w nich w stopniu daleko wyższym. Są to ludzie więksi od nas, stworzeni na miarę bardziej posągową, a jednak każdy odnajdzie w nich nietylko siebie, lecz i powszechne prawa tego wielkiego i odwiecznego procesu, który zwie się życiem ludzkości.

Tem się też tłómaczy, że dola i niedola szekspirowskich bohaterów, że ich uczucia, ich nienawiści, ich losy, nawet ich wojny, choćby tak odległe jak wojna Yorków z Lankastrami, porywają nas, narzucają nam z niesłychaną siłą udział w przebiegu zdarzeń i obchodzą tak bezpośrednio jak nasze własne dzisiejsze sprawy.

I oto dlaczego w obecnych czasach wojny, moru i głodu mogłem czytać, rozumieć i odczuwać Szekspira.

HENRYK SIENKIEWICZ.

eagerly as I talk with Hamlet ; when I read *The Tempest*, I find myself thinking that some contemporary Barnum ought to go and seek out Caliban and show him to the world for money.

I have known people who fell in love with Miranda, and I myself have been sweet upon Rosalind. I will not multiply examples, yet it is a fact that Falstaff had in Poland a brother named Zagloba, and that both have brothers living at this hour in England and in Poland—but the Polish brothers have grown so thin to-day that they are only shadows of their former selves.

The same unmatched intensity of life is to be found in Harry of Monmouth, in Poins, in Romeo, in Iago, in Othello. The same vivid womanhood allures in Ophelia, Juliet, Cordelia, Imogen. But through the might of genius all those figures, no less alive than the people of to-day, are far more interesting ; for the universal impulses and passions, the common elements of good and evil, are strengthened in them to an infinitely higher degree. They are people bigger than ourselves, conceived upon a scale more statuesque, and yet each one of us can find in them, not only himself, but the universal truth of that great and eternal process which is called the life of man.

Thus, too, can we explain how it comes about that the good and bad fortunes of Shakespeare's heroes, their emotions, their hatreds, their destinies, even their wars, although as distant from us as the wars of York and Lancaster, carry us away, by an unheard-of power compel us to take part in the course of events, and touch us as closely as our own personal affairs to-day.

And that is why, in this hour of war, of plague, and of famine, I have been able to read, to understand, and to feel Shakespeare.

Henryk Sienkiewicz

(Translated by Laurence Alma Tadema).

SHAKESPEARE-TUNNELMA

ASTUIVAT jumalat kerran
tykö ihmistyttärien,
siittivät sukua suurta :
henki Hellahan yleni.

Tunnen toisetkin urohot,
kuvat kullan-kangastuvat
kautta maailman sydämen :
Shakespearen sekeiset hahmot.

Kolmannet kohoamassa
vast' on korvesta Kalevan,
täten teitä tervehtävät :
elä Englanti iloinen !

Astuvat saloilta Pohjan
Lappi kaikki lauluinensa,
Viron kansa virsinensä,
Karjala sävelinensä,
kaikuvat keralla Suomen
muistoa merisen miehen,
sadun sankarin väkevän,
velhon kaikki-katsehisen,
min mieli tulena tuiski,
henki laajana lepäsi
kuin päivä merien päällä,
yö yllä inehmonlasten.

Vaikk'ei kaiku kauas kuulu,
kannel heimon kahlehditun,
soi kerran vapaiden kanssa !

                                EINO LEINO.

TRANSLATION

In olden times gods descended
To the daughters of men,
They begot a great breed :
The spirit of Hellas arose.

I know of other heroes ;
Their ghosts in golden mirage
Cast their glow over the worlds :
The bright shapes of Shakespeare.

I see a race
Of late arisen from the bleak tracts of Kaleva,
Offering their homage :
Greeting England in unison.

From the moors of the North
Lapland descends with its songs,
Esthonia with its airs,
Carelia with its runes ;
They all join their tunes with Finland
Praising him from the sea-girded land,
The man of mythical grandeur,
The magician of all-embracing gaze,
His heart blazing like fire,
His mind expanded in repose,
As the sun over the seas,
As the night over the children of men.

Though thy voice does not reach far,
Thou race held in bondage :
Yet for once sing, thou too, in the choir of free men !

EINO LEINO.

SHAKESPEARE IN FINLAND

IN his contribution to this 'Book of Homage', Juhani Aho has
accentuated the influence exercised by Shakespeare upon the Finnish
literature in Finland. With regard to that part of our national literature
which is written in the Swedish language, the influence is not so easily
discernible. But this depends, largely, upon the fact that here the
acquaintance with the great master of English drama was not made—
as was the case when the first Finnish translations appeared—at a given
moment which was fertile in poetical development, but had been maintained during a long sequel of generations and had thus been gradually
working upon our literary production and literary criticism. Though
less palpable, the action exercised by the drama of Shakespeare upon
the Swedish literature of Finland has not been less fundamental and
important than that exercised upon the literature written in the Finnish
language.

During the times when Finland was united with Sweden, cultural
communication between the two countries was frequent and intimate,
and Finland was often visited by Swedish companies of strolling players.
As one of these companies—which performed in Finland as early as
1780—was famous for its representations of *Romeo and Juliet*, it is
probable that playgoers in Finland got acquainted with a Shakespearian
tragedy about the year 1780. It is very likely, however, that the translation used by these strolling players had not been made from the
original, and it may be said that not before 1819 (when *Hamlet* was
performed at Åbo) had Shakespeare in an unadulterated translation
taken possession of the stage of Finland. But since that date, his plays
have never been absent from our theatres for a long time. When,
about the middle of the nineteenth century, Swedish companies ceased
to visit Finland, their work was taken up by national, Swedish and
Finnish, theatres, and thus the Shakespearian drama was represented
in both languages of Finland. Shakespeare has been the great educator
of our authors of all generations—from Frans Mikael Franzén, the

lyrical poet of the Swedish era, who during a stay in London in 1796 admired Kemble, Holman, and Mrs. Siddons in their Shakespearian characters, and who in 1800 wrote the first Shakespearian drama of the Swedish literature—up to Johan Ludvig Runeberg, the great singer of modern Finland, who wrote a critical study of *Macbeth*, and whose tragedy, *Kungarna på Salamis*, although purely classical in subject, is largely influenced by Shakespeare. It is to be noted, moreover, that the most important drama of the Swedish literature of Finland, *Daniel Hjort*, by Josef Julius Wecksell, was in style and character animated by a Shakespearian inspiration.

There is—and has always been—alive, among us, a feeling of indebtedness to English poetry, and chiefly to the dramatic poetry of Shakespeare. When the tercentenary of Shakespeare's birth was celebrated in Finland, Zacharias Topelius expressed that feeling in a prologue, which shows how in a small nation the gratefulness for all that has been received from an older country allies itself with a joyful pride in the fact that the work of Shakespeare has become a spiritual property of ours. The last stanzas of that prologue—in which the poet, on behalf of his nation, holds out the hands of Finland to all who join in admiration of a grandeur overstepping the boundaries of nations— may be quoted here in the original Swedish, as a specimen of the homage rendered to the memory of Shakespeare by one of the Swedish-speaking representatives of the national literature of Finland :

SE, därför hör han världen till,
Hvemhälst det stora älska vill,
Och därför är han vittnesgill
För alla folk och länder.
Och vid hans vagga denna stund
Vi räcka, på Europas grund,
Åt folkens stora fredsförbund
Det finska folkets händer.

Ty mänsklighetens skald han är.
Att akta högt, att hålla kär
Den stråle Herrens nåd beskär,
Det är att Herren tjäna.
Hvad är allt ljus, om icke Hans,
Hvad William Shakespeares ärekrans,
Om ej en bruten återglans
Af källans ljus allena?—(ZACHARIAS TOPELIUS, 23. IV. 1864.)

YRJO HIRN.

ENSIMÄINEN SUOMALAINEN SHAKESPEAREN ENSI-ILTA SUOMESSA

SE oli toukokuussa 1881. Siitä on siis kulunut lähes 35 vuotta.

Suomalainen näyttämötaidekaan ei ole juuri paljoa vanhempi ; se ei ollut silloin täyttänyt vielä ensimäistä vuosikymmentään. Siitä huolimatta se oli kehittynyt jo sille tasolle, että oli uskaltanut ottaa ohjelmistoonsa 'Romeon ja Julian'. Pieni muistelma siitä tapahtumasta olkoon minun seppeleeni suuren kansan suurimman neron jalkojen juureen eräästä englantilaisen kulttuurin kaukaisesta alusmaasta, jonka valloituksesta emämaa tuskin itsekään paljon tietää, mutta joka omistus siitä päivästä tuli niin pysyväksi, että meidän kansallinen suomalainen näyttämömme sittemmin joka vuosi on esittänyt Shakespearea. Shakespearea enemmän kuin mitään muuta yhtä kirjailijaa.

Tätä nykyä esitetään meillä Shakespearea suurella, mukavalla näyttämöllä, suuressa teatterissa, joka sijaitsee yhdellä kaupunkimme parhaista paikoista. 'Romeon ja Julian' ensi esitys tapahtui pienessä puisessa Arkadianimisessä barakissa kaupunkimme laidassa, sen viimeisessä rakennuksessa muutaman kivenheiton päässä tullista. Sen lähin naapuri kaupunkiin päin oli venäläinen kasarmi, jonka avonaisista ikkunoista teatteriin menijä voi kuulla milloin surullisia, milloin villejä arokasakkain lauluja. Toinen naapuri oli kaasutehdas, jonka säiliö aina vuoti, niin että kaasunhaju yhäkin tuo mieleeni arkaadisia muistoja niiltä ajoilta. Sen kolmas naapuri oli rautatien tavaraasema, jossa vaihtavien veturien vihellykset tunkivat lautaseinäin läpi näyttämölle saakka, tietysti kaikista selvimmin juuri silloin, kun siellä suoritettiin joku tunnekohtaus arimmassa pianissimossa.

Romeon ja Julian monet vaihtelevat näyttämökuvat oli tietysti koetettu saada niin vaikuttaviksi kuin suinkin kaikella sillä loistolla, joka siihen aikaan oli mahdollista, eivätkä kadut,

[Margin notes:]

In May, 1881, the theatre for the Finnish language in Helsingfors first ventured to act *Romeo and Juliet.*

It was in a small wooden house in a suburb.

The success was chiefly due to the great actress Ida Aalberg.

palatsit, parvekkeet, hautakammiot, liene olleet sen huonommat
kuin muissakaan esikaupunkiteattereissa. Se, mikä ei kuitenkaan
ollut esikaupunkia, oli itse esitys. Toisessa pääosassa esiintyi
Ida Aalberg, joka silloin oli vielä nuori, mutta kuitenkin jo täysin
valmis. Hänet on asetettu aikansa suurimpien tragediennein
tasalle, ja varmaankin hän olisi voittanut maailman, jos olisi tainnut
jotain maailmankieltä eikä puhunut 1½ miljoonan ei kaukana
napapiiristä asuvan kansan kieltä. Se oli erityisesti hän, joka
teki mahdolliseksi ' Romeon ja Julian ' esittämisen.

' Romeon ja Julian ' esittämisen muisto on minulle etupäässä
muisto siitä, miten *hän* siinä esiintyi, se kuva, minkä hän loi
Juliasta, ja se henkinen sisältö, minkä draama hänen välityksellään
puhalsi ja jätti minuun. Se oli minulle mitä voimakkain draamal-
linen vaikutus, mitä yleensä koskaan olen vastaanottanut. Olin
silloin nuori maaseudulla kasvanut vajaan vuoden vanha ylioppilas.
Saamani vaikutus oli sisäisesti uudistava, uusia taiteellisia ja
eetillisiä näköaloja avaava, joita ainoastaan suuri nero suuresti
tulkittuna voi avata. Se oli sitä voimakkaampi, kun itse draa-
makin, joka vain vähää ennen oli ilmestynyt suomeksi, oli minulle
uusi. Eikä vain minulle, vaan suurimmalle osalle senaikuista
nuorta polvea, jonka voitto ja nautinto siis oli sama kuin minunkin.

Shakespearen Julia—kaikkihan tietävät, millaiseksi kirjailija
on hänet ajatellut ja kuvannut. Neljätoistavuotiaasta tulisen
hehkuvasta etelättärestä ei Ida Aalbergin Juliassa ollut paljoakaan,
mutta siitä huolimatta hän oli ihanteellinen Julia semmoisena,
miksi hän ulkonaisten ja sisäisten resurssiensa mukaisesti oli
hänet luonut. Ida Aalbergilla oli kaikki suuren tragediennein
ominaisuudet. Hän oli solakka, pitkä, jäntevä ja joustava. Hänen
plastiikkansa ei ollut kreikkalaista eikä tietysti ranskalaistakaan,
vaan hiukan kulmikasta pohjoismaista, mutta juuri siksi ilmehi-
kästä ja persoonallista. Se oli enemmän koko vartalon kuin
yksityisten jäsenten harmoniaa, enemmän liikkeiden suuruutta
kuin pyöreyttä ja kauneutta, enemmän sisäistä plastiikkaa kuin
ulkonaista. Hänen silmänsä olivat suuret ja tummansiniset, iho
vaalea ja samoin tukka. Koko hänen ulkonainen olentonsa
teki hiukan kylmähkön vaikutuksen. Mutta tempperamentiltaan
hän oli tumma ja syvä, miltei synkkä. Vienona ja hentonakin
hän seisoi kuin jonkun uhkaavan kohtalon kehyksessä enkä ole
nähnyt ketään näyttelijää, jossa siirtyminen ilon ja onnen ilmeestä
synkimpään suruun ja epätoivoon, vaihdos naurusta kyyneliin,

For a whole generation of Finns that great event was as a new birth of the soul.

The artiste's Juliet had nothing Southern about her; she was a modern, Northern heroine.

olisi tapahtunut niin äkkiä ja välittömästi ja uskottavasti kuin hänessä. Juuri se teki hänen Juliansa niin vakuuttavaksi ja uskottavaksi ja mukaansa tempaavaksi, vaikka se oli ainakin kymmentä vuotta vanhempi tekijän Juliaa. Mutta semmoisena se ei ollut ainoastaan hänen persoonallinen Juliansa, vaan kokonaisen rodun, suomalainen ja yleensä pohjoismainen.

Hänen Juliansa oli alusta alkain täysin kypsynyt neito. Hänen repliikkinsä ensimäisen kohtauksen jälkeen Romeon kanssa :

Tää lemmen alku pahoj' ennustaa,	Prodigious birth of love it is to me,
kun vihamiestään täytyy rakastaa,	That I must love a loathed enemy.

ei ollut aaveen pelkoa, ei hetkellistä säikähdystä, vaan täyttä selvyyttä siitä, mitä ensi antautuminen oli tuova mukanaan. Hän tiesi olevansa edeltämäärätty turmioonsa, mutta kävi siitä huolimatta taistelemaan sitä vastaan. Ja se oli tämä syvästi traagillinen ensi kosketus joka antoi äänen koko esitykselle, pysyen siinä loppuun saakka ja pannen katsojan vavisten seuraamaan mukana. *From the first she appeared consciousof her tragic destiny.*

Enhän tietysti voi tehdä selkoa Juliadraaman kehityksestä kaikissa sen vaiheissa. Ainoastaan muuan välähdys siitä tunteen tulesta, joka kirkkaassa korkeassa ilmakerroksessa, jos niin saa sanoa vestaalisena, sinä iltana paloi Ida Aalbergin esityksessä.

On jäänyt erityisesti mieleeni hänen huokauksensa toisen näytöksen toisessa kohtauksessa puutarhakohtauksessa : ' Voi minua ! ' Siinä oli tulkittuna rakkauden koko aavisteleva riemu ja sen tuleva tuska. Hän oli—minkä hänen asentonsakin ilmaisi—kuin heittäytynyt tunteensa suloiseen virtaan tietämättä, välittämättä siitä, voisiko enää koskaan päästä maihin.

Sitten saman kohtauksen tunteenpurkaus, nuo maailmankuulut, ikimuistettavat :

Oi, elä vanno kautta kuun, se vaihtuu	O! swear not by the moon, the inconstant moon,
ja kuukausittain muuttaa muotoaan! . . .	That monthly changes in her circled orb, . . .
Elä lainkaan vanno,	Do not swear at all ;
tai jos tahdot, armaan itses' kautta,	Or, if thou wilt, swear by thy gracious self,
jot' epäjumalana jumaloin ma.	Which is the god of my idolatry,
Silloin uskon.	And I'll believe thee.

Ja vielä nämä, joissa hänen tunteensa nousu saavutti huippunsa :

Rajaton mull' on aulius kuin meri,	My bounty is as boundless as the sea,
ja lempi pohjaton; jot' enemp' annan,	My love as deep; the more I give to thee
sit enemmän mull' on, sill' ääretön	The more I have, for both are infinite.
on kumpikin.	

Tämän jälkimäisen purkauksen teknillinen suoritus ja siitä johtuva taiteellinen vaikutus perustui siihen, miten hän sai soinnukkaan suomenkielen monet vokaalit soimaan sen harvojen konsonanttien avulla. Liekö suomenkieli koskaan soinut kauniimmin kuin noissa säkeissä. Loppuvaikutus perustui varsinkin siihen, miten hän lausui sanan ' ääretön '. Hän sai siihen, sen pitkään, rinnan syvyydestä tulevan r-äänen tukemaan soinnutukseen, mahtumaan ei ainoastaan mertä, vaan taivaan ja maankin, melkein näkyväksi kuvaksi rakkautensa laajuudesta, syvyydestä ja korkeudesta.

Eihän näyttelijän esitys ole sanoin kuvattavissa sille, joka ei häntä ole ain kaan jossain osassa nähnyt. En siis koetakaan jatkaa, niin visioneerisen selvästi kuin näenkin sen hänen liikkeensä, millä hän hyvästijättökohtauksessa siirsi syrjään ikkunan uutimen ja horjahtaen tervehti aamua sanoilla : ' Siis sisään päivä, ulos elämä ! ' Siinä liikkeessä ja äänessä oli surua, tuskaa ja resignatsionia, mutta samalla myöskin kohtalon uhmaa. Tämä uhma oli yhtenä tärkeänä värityksenä Ida Aalbergin luomassa Julia-kuvassa. Hän erityisesti juuri tehosti rakastavan naisen oikeutta rakkauteensa, siinä oli pohjalla jotain skandinaavilaisen naisen taistelua hänen persoonallisen tunnevapautensa puolesta — mahdollisesti alkuteokselle kokonaan vieras piirre, lisäys runoilijan Juliaan, mutta joka ei kuitenkaan häirinnyt illusionia, koska näyttelijätär muutenkin teki tulkintansa kokonaan pohjoismaisesti.

Hän otti kaiken, sekä tässä osassa että yleensä, suurella paatoksella, jota oli hänen hiljaisimman kuiskauksensakin pohjalla. Hän oli vanhaa klassillista koulua, joka on jo häviämässä. Sehän voi helpostikin muuttua ontoksi tai jäädä vaikuttamatta, ellei sitä kannata oma sisäinen tunne ja ellei katsomossa ole vastaavaa kaikupohjaa. Mutta Ida Aalbergilla oli oma tunne ja sen ymmärtäminen oli täysin olemassa meidän silloin ja ehkä yhä vieläkin hyvin vähän blaseeratussa teatteriyleisössämme. Olimme kaikki kirjallisesti ja taiteellisesti vuoden vanhoja ylioppilaita. Luulen, että Shakespeare Arkadiassamme puhui Ida Aalbergin kautta yhtä vähän skeptillisille suomalaisille kuin Globessaan sen ajan englantilaisille. Olen nähnyt muunkin tyylisiä Shakespeare-esityksiä, mutta minä luulen, että hillitympi, moderni tapa ei saa hänen henkilöitään sille koturnille, missä on niiden oikea taso.

Sinä iltana seisoi Shakespeare meille, erityisesti juuri Juliassa, tavattoman korkealla, niin ihannoituna, jokapäiväisyydestä niin pois tempaavana, runouden ja taiteen avaruuksia niin aukovana, että vaikutus siitä jäi kuin jonkun auenneen taivaan vaikutukseksi.

Että semmoista runoutta on ! Että ihmisten joukossa on niitä, jotka voivat niin tuntea ja niin tunteensa puolesta elää ja kuolla, ja toisia, jotka voivat sen noin kuvata ja esittää ! Shakespeare oli yhtäkkiä tämän teoksensa kautta tullut uuden elämän sisällön antajaksi ei vain minulle, vaan monelle muulle sen ajan suomalaiselle nuorelle. Hänen ' Romeo ja Juliansa ' oli meille käänteentekevä siihen nähden, miten sitä ennen olimme käsittäneet rakkaudentunteen velvoituksen ja miten sen käsitimme sen jälkeen. Se oli tuulahdus korkeilta pyhiltä vuorilta, joka hälventi sumut, jotka pyrkivät samentamaan varsinkin sen ijän sydämmen puhtautta. Niin voimakkaasti kuin tässä runoelmassa ja sen esityksessä ei suuren, puhtaan rakkauden evankeliumia oltu ennen meillä julistettu. Oli valoisa kevätyö, kun läpi jo nukkuvan kaupungin parvi nuoria kulki meren rannalle, kaikki siinä oman keväänsä herkimmässä murrosajassa, jolloin sisäinen elämä vastaanottaa kylvönsä. Siellä he kalliolla seisten lupasivat itselleen, ettei mikään saisi tehdä heitä uskottomiksi sille ihanteelle, jonka heidän kunkin salainen ihanteensa, suuri, nuori taiteilija, oli heidän eteensä loihtinut. Sanon kaiken tämän ainoastaan valaistakseni, millainen ' Romeon ja Julian ' vaikutus oli meikäläiseen nuorisoon, vaikutus, joka runoilijan muihinkin suuriin draamoihin nähden jäi tyypilliseksi. Jokainen esitys on jollain tavalla vienyt eteenpäin meidän nuorta henkistä kulttuuriamme, syventäen ja laajentaen sitä. Siltä kannalta katsoen oli Shakespeare nensi-ilta 35 vuotta sitten meille ei vain puhtaasti taiteellinen, vaan myöskin isänmaallinen kulttuurivoitto.

Se oli sitä myöskin siihen nähden, että olimme saaneet todistetuksi itsellemme, että olimme kulttuurikansa ja että kielemme oli eurooppalainen kulttuurikieli. Suomenkieli ei ollut enää vain vanha Kalevalan eeposkieli, ei vain lyyrillisen kansanrunouden ja kansannäytelmien kieli, vaan kieli, jolla voitiin tulkita suurimmat draamalliset tunteet, hienoin uudenaikainen runous. Muun muassa siksi on Shakespeare suomenkielisessä asussaan meille tavallaan — kansallisrunoilija. Olen iloinen, että minun on sallittu saada siitä sanotuksi tämä myöhäinen kiitoksen sana hänen maanmiehilleen.

JUHANI AHO.

Each new play of Shakespeare that has since been acted in Finnish has strengthened the poet's hold on our people.

He has taught us that our language is not only the epic dialect of Kalevala, but that it can express the highest dramatic feeling and the most modern poetry. Shakespeare in his Finnish dress is something of a national poet to us.

SHAKESPEARE AND CHIKAMATSU

THE attempt of every country to find a Shakespeare among its own poets may be regarded as a sort of paying a tribute to the great poet, and Japan may also be permitted to participate in the attempt.

Chikamatsu Monzayemon must be voted our country's candidate for this honourable position. He is scarcely known to the Western countries, but he is one of our four prominent writers in the arts of fiction, occupying a very high rank in the history of our literature. Indeed, he excels Murasaki Shikibu, our earliest lady-novelist, in the scope of observation and the variety of theme; he surpasses Saikaku, his contemporary realistic novelist, with regard to the delicacy of sentiment, the beauty of style and the sound view of life; and he comes next to Bakin, the greatest novelist of modern Japan, as to prolificness, often outdoing him in the naturalness of the delineation of character; although it must be admitted that the other three writers each possess excellences of their own which Chikamatsu cannot aspire to attain. But what makes Chikamatsu peerless is his quality as a writer of our peculiar drama. Here we see the first instance of his resemblance to the 'Great Bard'—in his speciality and position in the literature of his country. He was born thirty-seven years after the death of Shakespeare, and accomplished his best work in the Genroku period (under the fifth Shogun of the Tokugawa régime), which may be called the Elizabethan age of Japan. He wrote principally for the stage all his life, and enjoyed the highest reputation in his day. Over 120 pieces of his plays happily remain till to-day, but the strange thing is that no biography is left of him. His name is now becoming famous more and more; his works are being judged gradually by a new standard. Nevertheless, his private life is still obscure; even his birthplace, like that of Homer, is not certainly known, insomuch as six different districts are each claiming the honour. The same is true of his personal appearance; for there are only two pictures of him, which differ from each other more than Shakespeare's portrait prefixed to the *First Folio* and *The*

Chandos are unlike. Like Shakespeare, he appeared at the period of what may be called the adolescence of our drama ; at first he adapted mostly from former writers, making full use of all the primitive dramas which had appeared before and other pageants and festivals ; but finally he brought our peculiar drama to perfection after fifty years of hard labour. The influence of his works on later literature and dramatic art of Japan may be compared to that of Shakespeare upon the drama and literature of the whole world.

Before proceeding, however, with this comparison, let me speak a little about the peculiar nature of his plays and of the stage for which he wrote. It is true that he wrote some pieces for the common stage of the day, but only their fragments remain, as they all belong to his early epoch. His chief work was, of course, for the marionette theatre which is so peculiar to our stage. This marionette theatre is entirely different in its nature from that of foreign countries, and a satisfactory explanation of it would be no easy matter. Nay, even if it is explained, a clear understanding of it would be almost impossible unless some years were spent in its study on the spot. Chikamatsu's play may be rather regarded as a sort of romance consisting mainly of dialogues with highly lyrical scenes or passages here and there than as a proper drama. When it is performed by puppets with their peculiar expression and gestures, a chorus sitting on one side of the stage recites the words to the accompaniment of *samisen* (three-stringed guitar).

Chikamatsu composed more than 120 plays in fifty years for the Takemoto-Za, which corresponds to Shakespeare's Globe Theatre. These plays are divided into two classes : *jidai-mono* or historical plays, and *sewa-mono* or plays of contemporary incidents (domestic tragedies). As for their length, the longest ones will perhaps equal Shakespeare's shortest plays, while the shortest ones are about half as long. What are called historical plays are not, in reality, historical ; they are purely imaginary stories borrowing time, personal names and events from the past as their background. Thrash three or four of Shakespeare's most romantic plays into one, squeeze it, add the quality of *Titus Andronicus* or the *Spanish Tragedy* to it, and you have something like one of these historical plays. The one which Mr. Aston has introduced in his *History of Japanese Literature* as Chikamatsu's representative work is only a specimen of these plays. But his true merits ought to be sought or in *sewa-mono* (domestic tragedies) which he wrote after the age of fifty. These plays are founded upon contemporary incidents, with a touch of idealism ; they resemble, therefore, *Arden of Feversham*,

A Warning for Fair Women, or *A Woman Killed with Kindness*, but they are superior to them from the dramatic point of view, and some of them must not be pronounced as being inferior to *La Dame aux Camélias* or *Kabal und Liebe*.

The plays of this class number only about twenty, and the best among them are, *Shinju Tenno Amijima* ; *Daikyoji Mukashi Goyomi* ; *Hakata Kojoro Namimakura* ; *Yarinogonza Kasane Katabira* ; *Meidono Hikyaku* ; and *Onnakoroshi Aburano Jigoku*.

There is no doubt that some coarseness is found in these plays, due to the standard of his audiences, who were of much lower class than Shakespeare's, and to the barbaric spirit of the times ; but they are of an entirely different type from the so-called historical plays. In their construction, they consist sometimes of a few characters with a single action ; the development of events is natural, and the personality of characters is realistic ; so that such a gross exaggeration as is met with in historical plays is not seen in them. Although they are written in narrative form, some of them are retrospective from the point of view of plot, and their opening scene is already approaching the catastrophe ; in this respect, therefore, they are more like Ibsen's works than Shakespearian plays. The reason why I compare Chikamatsu to Shakespeare is principally from the standpoint of these ' domestic tragedies ' and the best pieces of historical plays containing the elements of *sewa-mono*, e.g. *Somewake Tadzuna*. The *Kokusenya* is certainly one of the best-known of his plays, but not a masterpiece.

I have already taken up, however, too much space ; so that I shall only try to point out the analogical points between the two dramatists. For I believe that foreigners would be unable to understand the comparison, even if it were explained minutely, unless they studied his very plays.

Chikamatsu is ingenious in rhetoric, rich in language ; possesses both pathos and humour (of course, as compared with Shakespeare's, the magnitude is small and merit is inferior) ; has suitable talents for a tragedy as well as for a comedy ; makes a free and happy passage between realism and romanticism ; is gifted with clear common-sense, which is a rare thing in a poet ; holds a moderate view of life and morality ; and his attitude as a writer is always objective. In spite of the fact that his biography is not known, some of his opinions on drama are, though in fragmentary form, preserved till to-day. These opinions are sound, just as Shakespeare's comments on the stage uttered by Hamlet are appropriate, and they show his proper position as a playwright. And the swan-like gentleness of his disposition can be seen from his style and a kind of tenderness which is the pervading tone of his composition. It appears that he did not attempt to propose a new idea or problem, but that he made it the aim of his art to give a pleasure and an unobtrusive lesson. This is also a point in which he resembles Shakespeare. He seems to have been a wonderfully rapid writer ; his works may sometimes be suspected to have been composed half unconsciously and almost in spite of himself, and many defects which come from carelessness are found in them ; but there is, as in Shakespeare, some unstudied charm. As his plays were originally meant for the accompaniment of *samisen*, they are thoroughly musical and full of rhythmical beauties—here is another point in which he resembles Shakespeare. In fact, the charm of Chikamatsu much depends upon his musical style ; foreigners, therefore, who are unable to appreciate the music of the language, would not feel the charm in the same degree as his countrymen. One more point which is parallel in the English and the Japanese poets is that they are not restrained by the canons of technique. Chikamatsu is never strained ; he is free and natural, without hesitating to be sometimes licentious.

But the analogical points between Chikamatsu and Shakespeare have almost been covered by the above comparison. Chikamatsu is not, after all, a match for the ' Master-Poet ' if we examine their works more carefully. The one is like a boundless sea ; the other, like a lake. There are differences in width and depth. They resemble each other only in that they are of the nature of water, not of a mountain ; and in that they are, in consequence, of liquidity, not of solidity. In their delineation of character, we find that Shakespeare's characters are beyond a type, while Chikamatsu's are of a type ; but this defect may be due to the fact that Chikamatsu wrote for puppets. Even in the best works, therefore, of his historical plays as well as ' domestic tragedies ', his characters appear at first to be of real life, but they begin to show defects natural to puppets when we examine them more closely. In short, his characters are something like a combination of pictures by Moronobu and Sukenobu, his contemporary artists belonging to the first period of the Ukiyóe school (the *genre* school), in contrast to Shakespeare's who are like a composite of paintings by Michael Angelo and Raphael. If Shakespeare survives Michael Angelo and Raphael, Chikamatsu will have better claims to immortality than the best of our Ukiyóe painters.

YUZO TSUBOUCHI.

TOKYO.

TO SHAKESPEARE
THE GREATEST CONQUEROR OF ALL

沙翁之三百年祭に當りて

筆によて古界の果まて征服志

ちと河つ此想魔術士乃み雲

大正五稔春英國龍動に於て

駒井權之助

MAGICAL, myriad-minded!
Thy mighty pen
Hath conquered all men,
Even to the remotest bounds
Of our wide Earth!

GONNOSKÉ KOMAI.

英國詩人沙士比亞娛後三百載開會紀念

偶因天籟發長吟海外流傳咳唾音 古人詩咳唾落九天隨風生珠玉

LIU PO TUAN.

當日陽春難屬和 宋玉對楚襄王言歌陽春白雪國中和者不過數人而已蓋其曲禰高而和禰寡也

祇今黃絹賈追尋 蔡中郎題曹娥碑滄黃絹幼婦外甥齏白竇言絕妙好辭也

語多諷世能移俗曲妙登場見苦心三百年來成

絕調五洲人共仰高岑 詩經高山仰止言仰慕不可及之意

劉伯端

HONG-KONG.

CHINESE HOMAGE

THREE hundred years after his death the memory of the English poet
    is duly honoured ;
The sound of his voice has spread by divine inspiration to the far-off
    lands ;
Beside his song the song of ' Yang Chun ' could not be sung
    harmoniously ;
Until he came such rare framing of words was vainly looked for ;
Language often mocks the world ; it can alter customs ;
The subtilties of song upon the stage reveal the sorrows of the heart.
Three hundred years hence will these harmonies be possible ?
The people of five continents look up to this high Peak ! [1]

LIU PO TUAN.

HONG-KONG.

[1] Paraphrased from a translation kindly prepared by Professor Drake, of King's
College. The lines are allusive in character, and would need careful emendation to be fully
appreciated.

PERSIAN HOMAGE

THE spirit of Omar would not wish to be absent from ' the Book of Homage ' to the great Master-poet of England—the glory of the modern world.

May the day be near when some gifted son of Persia—a Persian Fitzgerald—will give to his countrymen Shakespeare's golden page ; and may then all the rich art of my country exercise its powers to set forth worthily his noble teaching and enthralling poetry !

How much of things material has passed away during the three centuries since Shakespeare entered into his immortality ; and how much more of the mighty work created by the hand of man will pass away, while Shakespeare's fame remains untouched by Time !

In the words of our own poet—

از آن چندان نعیم این جهادی،   که ماند از آل ساسان و آل سامان،

دنای روندگی ماندست و مدحش،   نوا* بساربد ماندست و دستان،

> ' From all the treasures hoarded by the Houses
> Of Sásán and of Sámán, in our days
> Nothing survives except the song of Bárbad,
> Nothing is left save Rúdagí's sweet lays ;'

as Prof. E. G. Browne excellently renders the lines into English verse.

All Nature rejoiced at Shakespeare's coming, and all mankind delights in his incomparable achievement ; as Sádi, perhaps Persia's greatest poet, well expresses the thought—

پشت دونای فلک راست شد از خرمی

تا چو تو فرزند زاد مادر ایام را

which may be freely paraphrased—

> ' With joy the crook-back'd welkin straight became,
> When Nature bore thee, heir to deathless fame !'

AHMAD KHAN.

ԱՌ ՇԵՅՔՍՓԻՐ

TO SHAKESPEARE

Ո՛վ դարերու՜ դարմանք քերթողդ՝ արարածոց մէջ են մեծ սաեղծող
Դուն որ տեսար կեանքը ամբողջ ու նկարեցիր դայն մշտաշող
Ո՛վ ինքնակալ դու մրտաւոր աշխարհի տերը վեհագոյն
Որուն գահն է լոկ անսասան, Հպատակներն անթիւ, աճուն.

Wonder of all ages, sovereign of the realm of intellect, whose willing subjects are innumerable !

Ազգերն համայն այլալեզու, միմեանց օտար ու ցանուցիր
Մէկ պաշտամունք, մէկ սիրտ ունին քեզի Համար, ով Շ շեքսփիր
Ինչպէս զատ Հէք մարդկութիւնը ցեղ ու տեղ իրձ ու շաՀ բարդ
Խանդոտ Հիացման մէջ միաւորող կապէ յաւէտ քու Հանճարդ.

All nations, tongues, climes, and minds, have but one heart for thee. Whate'er divides mankind, thy genius binds.

ԽորՀրդաւոր կեանքէդ մեզի կարտացոյաս կուշումըդ "Հեզ"
Դութի քու գովքրդ աննըման, պարսաւդ Հակայ բիրա ուժի վէա
Եւ Պրոսպերոդ՝ իր արուեստին ու Գխոտւթեան ուժովն յաղթող
Ներշանակ են ներքին Հոգւոյդ, մեծ մարդասէր ու մեծ քերթող:

In thy life's mystery 'gentle' reveals thee; as does thy praise of Mercy, and thy reproof of giant's strength used giant-like. By thy Prospero thy inmost soul is symbolized.

Ատելութեան մեծ մութին մէջ որ կը ճառկէ մեզ սկարատ,
Ո՛աւէ ով աստղ, ողջոյն կուտան քեզ ողջ աշխարՀ Արարատ:

Thro' hate's black night shine forth, O Star! All the world and Ararat, and I, a dweller by Ararat, greet thee.

Գ. Ծ. ՖՆՏՈՒՔԼԵԱՆ   K. H. FUNDUKLIAN.

ՀԱՅԱՍՏԱՆԻՆ ՇԷՅՔՍՓԻՐԻՆ

Կապրիս դեռ՝ Ոգիդ դու խորհրդաւոր,
Թէեւ երեք դար անցան թուչքեդ.
Կա՞յ արդեօք երկիր՝ կամազ Հեռաւոր՝
Որ երեէք Հմայք չզգաց եղերեդ :

Ինձ Համար երկիրդ է միշտ Հայաստան.
Օ՛ի խօսքերդ անուշ, երազներդ վեեմ;
Ա՛յն տեղ նախ մռքիս առջե մարմնացան,
Եւ միշտ Հայրէնիքս քու մէջ կը գտնեմ :

Կռուով եւ վշտով խաւարած երկրին,
Ա՛մէնէն պաշտուած՝ կը փայլիս վերէն.
Ազգերն դոլեստաններդ կերզեն, կը բերկրին.
Ոսխքն Հայրէնեացդ դամնի կը բերեն :

Հայաստանս ի՞նչպէս նուիրէ իր սէր.
Նա չէ՛ զարդարուած թագով ոսկեղէն,
Ս_րան արտասուաց անիիւ գոՀարներ,
Խորանդ կը բերէ պսակն փուշեղէն :

ՕՐ**ԱՊ**Է**Լ** Կ. ՊՈՅԱՃԵԱՆ

ARMENIA'S LOVE TO SHAKESPEARE

SPIRIT unknown, that livest with us still,
Though three long centuries have marked thy flight:
Is there a land thy presence doth not fill,—
A race to whom thou hast not brought delight?

To me Armenia seems thy home, for first
Thy visions there absorbed my wondering mind.
And thy sweet music with my heart conversed;
Armenia in thy every scene I find.

Through all the gloom of strife and agony,
Thy gentle light, beloved of all, doth shine.
The nations bring their tribute unto thee,
To honour thee thy country's foes combine.

What token shall my poor Armenia bring?
No golden diadem her brow adorns:
All jewelled with her tears, and glistening,
She lays upon thy shrine her Crown of Thorns.

ZABELLE C. BOYAJIAN.

HERE endeth not our great processional,—
Not with the burden of Armenia's woe,
Nor with heroic Serbia's stifled sob,
Nor widow'd Belge's ne'er-despairing plaint.
Our England's hope be theirs, our Shakespeare's peace !
The song of Wessex, preluding our march,
Links us, leal homagers, one brotherhood,—
Sons of the Mother-land, imperial hosts,
Shakespeare's own kindred, whatsoe'er their speech,
Their climes, their colour, and their usages ;
And with us those, proud of their Englishry,
Who to his music built their new-found world,
In strength and freedom,—he their heritage ;
And all these others, now acclaiming him,—
Fair France, the gracious, with heroic soul ;
Passion'd Italia, the poet's quest ;
Cold Muscovy, aglow with new-born hope ;
The sailor-folk who in great Camoens' tongue
Renew their ancient troth ; Cervantes next,
Shakespeare's twin-brother of the Comic Muse,
Leading the votaries of gallant Spain,—
Homage to him upon our Shakespeare's Day !—
And the drear North, transfigured by his wand,
Hymning with choric strain her Hamlet's fame ;
All these and more ; and mingled notes far off,
Tho' dimly heard, presage a gladder throng,
A righted world, chanting in unison
This self-same song :—
                              ' How many ages hence
Shall this our lofty scene be acted o'er,
In states unborn, and accents all unknown ! '

I. G.

LIST OF CONTRIBUTORS

IN ALPHABETICAL ORDER

AHMAD KHAN, 550
AHO, JUHANI, 538
' AMARI ', 518
ARMAS, JOSÉ DE, 434
ATKINS, J. W. H., 288
AUNG, SHEVE ZAN, 324

BAILEY, JOHN, 149
BALMONT, K., 506, 512, 514
BARRY, REV. WILLIAM, 31
BEECHING, THE VERY REV. H. C., 120
BENSON, A. C., 197
BENSON, F. R., 39
BERGSON, HENRI, 379
BINYON, LAURENCE, 21
BLOMFIELD, REGINALD, 84
BOAS, FREDERICK S., 254
BOND, WARWICK, 181
BOSIS, ADOLFO DE, 429
BOTTOMLEY, GORDON, 43
BOUCHOR, MAURICE, 381
BOUTROUX, ÉMILE, 383
BOYAJIAN, ZABELLE C., 552
BRADLEY, A. C., 164
BRADLEY, HENRY, 106
BRANDES, GEORGE, 490
BRERETON, J. LE GAY, 204
BRYCE, THE RT. HON. VISCOUNT, 22
BURNET, JOHN, 58
BUYSSE, CYRIEL, 466
BYVANCK, W. G. C., 468

CAMPBELL, WILFRED, 314
CHAMBERS, E. K., 154
CHANTAVOINE, HENRI, 378

CHIARINI, CINO, 430
CHOISY, LOUIS FRÉDÉRIC, 454
CLERCQ, RENÉ DE, 464
CLUTTON-BROCK, A., 126
COLLIN, C., 499
COLVIN, SIR SIDNEY, 88
COOMARASWAMY, ANANDA, 317
COURTHOPE, W. J., 146
COURTNEY, W. L., 162
CUST, LIONEL, 100

DAVIES, W. H., 105
DIXON, W. MACNEILE, 62
DOBSON, AUSTIN, 13
DRINKWATER, JOHN, 30

ELTON, OLIVER, 161

FEUILLERAT, ALBERT, 387
FULLER-MAITLAND, J. A., 70
FUNDUKLIAN, K. H., 551
FURNESS, HORACE HOWARD, 342

GALSWORTHY, JOHN, 37
GASQUET, HIS EMINENCE CARDINAL, 25
GAYLEY, CHARLES MILLS, 340
GENNADIUS, HIS EXCELLENCY JOANNES, 422
GOLLANCZ, REV. H., 307
GOLLANCZ, ISRAEL, 170
GOSSE, EDMUND, 52
GRAVES, ALFRED PERCEVAL, 47
GRAY, ARTHUR, 260

GREG, W. W., 179
GRIERSON, H. J. C., 266

HADOW, W. H., 64
ḤĀFIZ IBRĀHIM, MOHAMMED, 331
HAMELIUS, PAUL, 462
HAMILTON, CLAYTON, 347
HARDY, THOMAS, 1
HARRIS, M. DORMER, 264
HARRISON, FREDERIC, 14
HERFORD, C. H., 231
HIBBEN, JOHN GRIER, 350
HIRN, YRJO, 536
HOVELAQUE, ÉMILE, 392
HYDE, DOUGLAS, 275

IGVAL, MOHAMMED, 322
IRVING, H. B., 41

JESPERSEN, OTTO, 481
JOHNSON, ROBERT UNDERWOOD, 351
JONES, J. MORRIS, 284
JUSSERAND, HIS EXCELLENCY J.-J., 399

KER, W. P., 49
KIPLING, RUDYARD, 200
KOMAI, GONNOSKÉ, 547

LAWRENCE, W. J., 207
LEE, SIR SIDNEY, 110
LEGOUIS, ÉMILE, 405
LEINO, EINO, 534
LIU PO TUAN, 548
LLOYD, JOHN EDWARD, 280
LUCE, MORTON, 129
LUNGO, ISIDORO DEL, 427
LUZZATTI, LUIGI, 428

MACCALLUM, M. W., 186
MACDONELL, A. A., 310
MACKAIL, J. W., 193
MADDEN, THE RT. HON. MR. JUSTICE, 270
MAETERLINCK, MAURICE, 461
MAIR, ALEXANDER W., 292
MANLY, JOHN MATTHEWS, 353
MANTZIUS, KARL, 490
MATTHEWS, BRANDER, 356

MAURA, A., 437
MEYNELL, ALICE, 35
MIŞU, HIS EXCELLENCY NICOLAS, 452
MOHAMMED ḤĀFIZ IBRĀHIM, see ḤĀFIZ
    IBRĀHIM.
MOHAMMED IGVAL, see IGVAL.
MØLLER, NIELS, 486
MORAX, RENÉ, 457
MOULTON, R. G., 228

NEWBOLT, SIR HENRY, 183
NOYES, ALFRED, 116

ORANO, PAOLO, 432

PADELFORD, FREDERICK MORGAN, 360
PHELPS, WILLIAM LYON, 362
POLLARD, A. W., 238
POPOVIĆ, PAVLE, 524

REEVES, THE HON. WILLIAM PEMBER, 312
REGNIER, HENRI, 421
ROBERTS, CAPTAIN CHARLES G. D., 315
ROBERTSON, THE RT. HON. J. M., 141
RODD, SIR J. RENNELL, 148
ROLLAND, ROMAIN, 411
ROSS, LIEUT.-COL. SIR RONALD, 104

SAINTSBURY, GEORGE, 137
SANDYS, SIR JOHN, 291
SANTAYANA, GEORGE, 377
SCHELLING, FELIX E., 364
SCOTT, CANON FREDERICK GEORGE, 316
SIENKIEWICZ, HENRYK, 530
SINGH, SARDAR JOGUNDRA, 323
SKEMP, A. R., 227
SMITH, G. C. MOORE, 236
SPIELMANN, M. H., 3
SQUIRE, W. BARCLAY, 75
STARKIE, THE RT. HON. W. J. M., 212
STEFÁNSSON, JÓN, 484
STOPES, CHARLOTTE CARMICHAEL, 118

TAGORE, SIR RABINDRANATH, 320
TEXEIRA-GOMES, HIS EXCELLENCY, 447
TIN, MAUNG, 329

TRENCH, HERBERT, 115
TRENCH, W. F., 135
TSUBOUCHI, YUZO, 543
TUCIĆ, SRGJAN, 528

UNDERHILL, EVELYN, 56

VAL, HIS EXCELLENCY SEÑOR DON
    MERRY DEL, 435
VALDÉS, ARMANDO PALACIO, 439
VAN DAM, B. A. P., 473
VEDEL, VALD., 492
VELIMIROVIC, FATHER NICHOLAS, 520
VERHAEREN, ÉMILE, 460
VERWEY, ALBERT, 467
VILDÓSOLA, C. SILVA, 441

VILLEY, PIERRE, 417
VOLOSHIN, MAXIMILIAN, 516

WALIY AD-DIN YEYEN, *see* YEYEN
WALKER, HUGH, 190
WARBURG, KARL JOHAN, 495
WARD, SIR A. W., 241
WARREN, SIR HERBERT, 306
WHEATLEY, H. B., 249
WILLIAMS, REV. J. O., 286
WISTER, OWEN, 373
WOTTON, MABEL E., 252

YEYEN, WALIY AD-DIN, 333
YOUNG, GEORGE, 449

ZANGWILL, ISRAEL, 248